DATE DUE
DATE DE RETOUR

All We Knew Was to Farm

All We Knew Was to Farm

Rural Women in the
Upcountry South, 1919–1941

Melissa Walker

THE JOHNS HOPKINS UNIVERSITY PRESS
Baltimore & London

The Johns Hopkins University Press
2715 North Charles Street
Baltimore, Maryland 21218-4363
www.press.jhu.edu

Library of Congress Cataloging-in-Publication Data will be found at the end
of this book.
A catalog record for this book is available from the British Library.

ISBN 0-8018-6318-x

Earlier versions of some of these chapters appeared previously in other publications and are used here with permission: portions of chapter two in *Journal of
East Tennessee History*, Spring 1997; portions of chapter four in *Southern Historian*, 1994; portions of chapter four in *Agricultural History*, Summer 1996; portions of chapter five in *Agricultural History*, Spring 1998; and portions of chapter
seven in *Tennessee Historical Quarterly*, Summer 1998;

For my parents

and

for Chuck

Contents

Figures

Tables

Acknowledgments

In many ways this book is a tribute to my roots in a rural upcountry community. One of the things I learned from that upbringing was that no one achieves anything without help. Just as mutual aid networks helped farm women endure the unpredictability of rural life, mutual aid networks have sustained me through more than six years of work on this project, first as a dissertation, then as a book. This work is a product of help from dozens of friends, family members, and even strangers. Moreover, like any intellectual endeavor, the book builds on the things I have learned from hundreds of scholars, many of whom are credited in the bibliographical essay.

As all scholars know, the dreary quest for research dollars claims too much time and energy that could be used in the actual research. I've been blessed with financial support for this work. Clark University provided funding in the dissertation stage; the Rockefeller Archives Center, with a generous travel to collections grant, which enabled me to complete an important chunk of research for this project; and Converse College and its Faculty Development Committee, with a trustee summer research grant that made the final research and revisions possible. I am most grateful for all of this support.

Of course, this project could not have been completed without assistance from countless librarians and archivists at collections around the country. Staff members at the National Archives in Washington, D.C., the University of Tennessee Special Collections Library, the University of Tennessee Hodges Memorial Library, Blount County Public Library, Loudon County Public Library, the Schlesinger Library of Women's History at Radcliffe College, the South Caroliniana Library, the University of South Carolina Library, Greenville County Public Library, Sevier County Public Library, Clemson University Library, Dacus Library at Winthrop University, and the Archives of Appalachia at East Tennessee State University referred me to countless resources, both archival and human. Michael Rogers and Mary Ann Bailey at the National Archives and Records Center, Southeast Region, in Atlanta directed me to TVA files that I would not even have considered checking. Erwin LeVold and the staff at the Rockefeller Archives Center in Tarrytown, New York, helped me find treasures buried in the papers of the General Education Board. Pete Daniel and Smitta Duta of the National Museum of American History made some wonderful oral histories available to me after LuAnn Jones alerted me to their existence. Ed Best helped me locate several obscure documents in the TVA Technical Library in Knoxville. Steve Cottam and the staff of the McClung Collection at the Lawson McGhee Library in Knoxville do a superb job making an outstanding local history collection available to researchers, and I appreciate their help. Martha Dickens in the Kennedy Local History Room at the Spartanburg County Public Library acquainted me with countless resources on upstate South Carolina.

Reference librarians at my successive home institutions made this task much easier. Clark University reference librarians Edward J. McDermott, Mary Hartman, Cynthia Shenette, and Irene Walch helped me track down the most obscure sources via interlibrary loan, saving me countless dollars in travel costs. At Converse College, Becky Dalton has also cheerfully filled a whole range of strange interlibrary loan requests, and Mark Collier has assisted me in tracking down citations.

Many friends and family members referred me to oral history subjects and other local sources of information. Thanks to Guy and Rachel Walker, Sarah McNeill, William Brown, Korola Lee, and Margaret Proffitt for their help in this regard. I owe a special debt to Ann Ross Bright for going beyond anything I would ever have asked by arranging eight interviews, guiding me to the interviewees' homes, feeding me, and showing me endless hospitality. In the process, I gained a friend. Margaret Ripley Wolfe and Ruby Nell Jeter referred me to other sources. My aunt, Laura Tate, spent several hours in East Tennessee libraries tracking down last-minute sources, enabling me to finish the dissertation on time. Edna Spencer provided me with considerable insight into race relations in Depression-era East Tennessee. Mike Corbin introduced me to upstate South Carolina peach farming with his superb photography, pointed me to several important oral history sources, and generously shared transcripts of his own interviews. I owe much to the named and anonymous oral history sources who brought their worlds to life for me.

Several people have assisted me in locating photographs. Sally R. Polhemus at the McClung Historical Collection helped me locate one especially appropriate image as did James Edward Cross in the Special Collections at Clemson University Library. Sanford N. Smith generously shared family photos as well as family stories. Fred Daab turned my rough sketches into clear and useful maps.

Tim Sullivan shared graduate school woes with me and gave encouragement when I was at my lowest. For his boundless help and support, I can never offer enough thanks. Rebecca Tulloch-Bowman, Dennis Bowman, and Lori and Rob Love provided not only supportive friendship but also hospitality and housing during my research trips. Mary Lee, Joe Thomas, Linda Durant, Mike Deotte, Kevin Shirley, Mary Alice Conlon, and Elaine Catlow gave me friendship and support during the hard times and the good ones as well as welcome distractions when I was too involved in my work. My colleagues at Bryant College, who were unfailingly supportive, will never know how important that was. I thank my colleagues and students at Converse College for the warm welcome they have given me, for their interest in this project, and for their spoken and unspoken encouragement. They have made my life as a teacher and scholar everything I had hoped it would be.

My graduate school colleagues also provided endless support and were perhaps the people who best understood what I was going through. John Potter, John Murnane, Marty Green, Lisa Hauptman, Barbara Shulman, Angela Bowen, Paul Lambert, and Alan Demarjian all listened to various pieces of this work, gave constructive suggestions, and asked probing questions. They also injected a dose of sanity and humor into graduate school. Lydia Savage and Michelle Reidel were my strongest supporters, always available to read a chapter or listen when things weren't going well. I am sure I could not have persevered without them.

My advisor, Sarah Deutsch, pushed me to be a far better scholar than

I ever thought I could be. She insisted from the beginning that I was writing a book, not a dissertation, and as a result, she never stopped urging me to polish my writing and my thinking. Her support, encouragement, and challenges to think more analytically were crucial to this project. She never let me settle for less than the possible. Janette Thomas Greenwood and Douglas Little, my other committee members, provided support and constructive criticism. Janette, in particular, shared the insights of her own rural childhood and challenged me when I tended to accept other historians' interpretations that did not ring true. Her work on black and white class formation in post-Reconstruction Charlotte helped me refine my own conceptions about rural class structure.

This book has been improved immeasurably by critical readings of portions or all of the manuscript by various scholars including Jeanette Keith, Pete Daniel, Anita Gustafson, Madelyn Young, and anonymous reviewers at historical journals. Comments on conference papers by Jeanette Keith, Mary Neth, Rebecca Sharpless, and Jess Gilbert proved invaluable. A conversation with Carroll Van West on the nature and diversity of southern agriculture helped me clarify my own thinking on the distinctions between the plantation and upcountry South. Mary Neth's detailed and insightful comments helped me to revise the dissertation into a more focused—and, I hope, stronger—book. Chuck Reback read the final draft and saved me from several embarrassing errors. Any factual or analytical errors that remain are my own.

Bob Brugger and the staff at Johns Hopkins University Press have been most helpful in the preparation of the manuscript. Elizabeth Yoder's superb copyediting improved my prose.

My family not only allowed me to talk endlessly about this project but also provided unending support: Bill and Evelyn Lewellyn, Michelle and Steve Kennedy, Laura Tate, Walt Lewellyn, Bob Lewellyn, Spence Walker, and all my cousins. I am grieved that my grandmother, Maude Walker, did not live to see the completion of this book. Rob Kennedy was always a reminder to me that his foremothers' stories should be told.

I met Chuck Reback in the middle of writing the dissertation, and the project became a constant presence in his life for four years. He has tolerated my ceaseless distraction and occasional hysteria, dried countless tears, and continually "bucked me up" to tackle the project yet again. He has listened to me talk through various analytical questions, read the manuscript, offered cogent suggestions, and often restored my sanity by taking me away from the work. He has truly been my best friend. For the peace and love he has added to my life, I give him gratitude and much love.

Finally I must thank my parents, Guy and Rachel Walker. Without them, a farm girl from the hills of East Tennessee would never have had the audacity to think she could earn a doctorate, much less write a book. Their lifetime of love, support, and encouragement has enabled me to travel down several paths that were rather unorthodox for a girl from my hometown. They never thought there was anything I couldn't accomplish, and they never tried to hold me back—even when they had no idea where I got my ideas. They have spent countless hours worrying about me, praying for me, listening to me, and loving me. They have given me many precious gifts, especially the proverbial roots and wings. I have been able to do whatever I have done because I knew that whatever happened, I could go home.

"All We Knew Was to Farm"

In her 1929 novel, *Homeplace,* Maristan Chapman describes the impending modernization of the fictional mountain village of Glen Hazard, Tennessee, through the eyes of young Bess Howard. Logging companies have moved on, leaving Glen Hazard's always unstable economy in decline. Subsistence hill farmers eke out a living the best way they can. As the novel opens, the village is being overrun by road builders scrambling to construct a new highway that will bring tourists and trade to the mountains. Local citizens are divided on the issue of the road. Some farmers refuse to sell right-of-way land, while others rush to make profits working on the road or supplying the construction crews. Change is coming to Glen Hazard whether people are ready for it or not.[1]

Bess Howard, the daughter of a poor mountain landowner, is on the brink of marriage to a poor mountain boy. In Bess's world, folks survive on mutual aid and exchange: giving cloth for her trousseau, caring for the disabled, passing vegetable garden cuttings from one neighbor to another, and nursing the sick during an influenza epidemic. This practice of sharing resources not only enables the rural folk of Glen Hazard to outlast lean times but also reduces the social isolation of living in remote mountain communities.

Like her neighbors, Bess Howard is ambivalent about the choices facing her. On the one hand, she anticipates life as a traditional farm wife. She plans her wedding and still tries to guarantee herself some financial stability by refusing to marry her fiancé until "he gets him a homeplace," a farm of his own. To Bess, landholding is not only a prerequisite for independence from her natal family but also the key to the economic security she craves. When her betrothed, through a series of lucky accidents, finally succeeds in acquiring a homeplace, she proceeds with equipping her "hope chest," the collection of household goods every young married woman needs. Yet even as she plans her future as a farm wife, Bess is restless. Via the road builders, she has glimpsed possibilities in the world beyond Glen Hazard, and she wonders if she is settling too easily for the endless round of hard work and hard times that make up the life of a Glen Hazard woman. One afternoon, in frustration, she flares out at her fiancé: "Maybe you fail of knowen how a woman wants out. You never figured the times I just stand looking at that stretch of road that runs up to Sunview and beyond to the outside, and hate it for going away 'n' leaving me here. I hate the trains that cry out in the night carrying folks up and down the land, and me forgot on this little old downgone farmplace."[2] The world beyond Glen Hazard offers alternatives—the possibility of a different and perhaps easier life—and Bess briefly considers pursuing these alternatives.

Of course, *Homeplace* was a novel of its time. Bess might question her lot in life, but only the occasional young *man* of Glen Hazard went "wandering," and he always returned when he got his fill of the evil and harsh world beyond the mountains. Predictably, Bess comes to her senses and chooses to stay in Glen Hazard where she belongs. On her wedding day, she reflects on her connections to her mountain community and on the meaning of home and place: "A homeplace is like that. Hit wraps a person around; hit's where things happen to a person."[3] In the end, for Bess it is a clear choice between the warmth and familiarity of life in her rural community and the ugly uncertainty of life outside, between the support of her neighbors and the dubious material opportunities beyond the mountains.

For the real Bess Howards, however, the choices were not so clear cut or so easily controlled in the 1920s and 30s. Growing up in the hills of East Tennessee, I spent many hours listening to the stories of women like Bess. My grandmothers, their relatives and friends, my elderly public school and Sunday school teachers, all rural women, often regaled me with tales about the lean years "back before the War" and the shortages and excitement "during the War." I was fascinated with their stories of survival—of hard times outlasted and obstacles overcome. These were the stories of women who found their identities in their work, in their central role in preserving their families, and in the mutual support networks of their communities. Yet for them the choices were not as clear as they were for Bess Howard. They did not necessarily believe that life on the farm was superior to life in town; in fact, many of them were ambivalent about the rewards of country life. Moreover, the life choices they described had often been complicated by competing personal desires, family demands, and the restraints of economics.

For the women of the upcountry South, the years between the end of World War I and the end of World War II marked a liminal moment in their struggles to shape their own lives—a point at which the modern industrial world and the intervening hand of big government intruded on their once-insular communities, forcing new choices and redefinition of their roles as women. Upcountry women faced multiple transforming agents; the complex interactions of race, economic class, government policy, industrial opportunities, and personal and family considerations shaped different strategies for different women. Indeed, for many the constraints of race and class limited their options in ways that left them to choose the best from a bad set of options. But race and class alone do not explain the myriad choices made by the women I knew. This book tells their story.

Regional labels are useful shorthand for scholars of American life. A certain level of regional distinctiveness is well established, and labels evoke particular images of that distinctiveness. When referring to rural history, "Midwest" evokes images of prosperous family grain farms; whereas "the South" generates pictures of black slaves and, later, sharecroppers tending miles of cotton fields. The mental models created by regional labels are nonetheless problematic. Labels have a way of masking complexities and tempting us to engage in a one-dimensional analysis of a region's past and present.

The internal diversity of the region we call the South has been long recognized and little studied. Indeed, in a landmark Depression-era study of the economic conditions of the southeastern states, the sociologist Howard Odum found remarkable homogeneity among the population, but at the same time, he found enough intraregional difference to divide the states into thirty-seven subregions. The areas included in this study—the eastern counties of Tennessee, the northwestern counties of South Carolina, and the southwestern counties of West Virginia—all lie within the states that the Census Bureau classifies as "the Southeast." Their rural past, however, differs from that of the rest of the South in significant ways.[4]

By the same token, the label "Appalachian" is misleading. At various times East Tennessee, upstate South Carolina, and southwestern West Virginia have all been classified as part of Appalachia. Most of East Tennessee and upstate South Carolina, and all of southwestern West Virginia are now part of the quasi-federal regional development agency known as the Appalachian Regional Commission. That designation summons up images of mean mountain cabins, poor garden patches, and grinding poverty. Most scholars now contend that while "Appalachia" describes a physical landscape, the term derives its meaning from a social construct created by local color writers, missionaries, and settlement workers in the late nineteenth century. For some observers, rural Appalachians shared a violent and primitive culture that needed modernizing and civilizing. Others believed that the mountain people were a romantic remnant of a purer past before modernization spoiled America and that their culture was worthy of preservation. In both cases, simplistic and often inaccurate perceptions of the mountain people bore little relationship to the complex realities of their lives. The editors of one recent collection of essays on rural Appalachia contend that the regional patterns labeled "Appalachian" are not necessarily unique to the Appalachians or general to the entire mountain region. The area known as "Appalachia" is as varied as the area known as "the South."[5]

Labels are nonetheless helpful devices for the prose writer and reader, eliminating the necessity for repeating unnecessarily unwieldy geographic descriptions. Thus I have tried to come up with an accurate descriptive label that is not laden with as much mental baggage as the terms "southern" and "Appalachian." I have chosen to use the term "up-country South" to describe the areas examined in this study. First and foremost, this area is southern. All the counties except those in southwestern West Virginia were part of the Confederacy, and slavery existed in all three areas until the Civil War. The entire area shared southern segregation patterns and racial attitudes. But it is also high country—an area of foothills and mountains. The label "upcountry South" recognizes the commonalities that the region shared in the interwar years—commonalities explored in Chapter 1—but it perhaps discourages us from overgeneralizing about the people who lived there.

The upcountry South is an appropriate location in which to explore the interaction of multiple transforming agents within a regional economy and to assess their impact on farm women. Steep terrain and poor soil made agriculture a marginal activity in many upcountry counties, a tendency exacerbated by the post–World War I agricultural depression. This fact, combined with the upcountry's relatively small black population and its relatively high tenancy rate, made for a large population of cheap white industrial workers that, along with ample natural resources, attracted outside investors. The upcountry was the first area of the South to experience large-scale invasion by outside capitalists even as it faced transformations in the agricultural economy and in federal agricultural policy.

In the years after World War I, change pummeled upcountry folk. The postwar plunge in farm prices stretched into a twenty-year agricultural depression for the people of the upcountry South. As the region's farm men inched further and further into the farm commodities market in search of elusive cash, most of the burden for family survival fell on the region's farm women. Upcountry farm women at first tried to deal with the rapid change by intensifying their traditional coping efforts based on subsistence production and mutual aid networks. It was the women who stretched resources, juggled family purchasing, and "made do." Many women, already active in the marketplace, expanded their own cash-producing activities in order to contribute to the family income. For them, hard times provided a way to maintain a central place in the family economy even as the family became more embedded in a cash economy.

As the economic downturn continued in the region, twentieth-century change marched in. New industries popped up around the upcountry, providing off-farm job opportunities for both men and women. Massive government projects, such as Tennessee Valley Authority dams, military installations, and the Great Smoky Mountains National Park, displaced thousands of rural people even as they provided them with new economic opportunities. The gendered nature of government and industrial policies often meant that these changes had strikingly different effects on men than on women. Men and women had different employment opportunities, with women's options being more limited. The transition to a wage-based economy often undermined women's centrality to the family economy thereby altering power relations within the family.

Class and race also mediated women's options for coping with all this change. Although class was hardly deterministic, the options of upcountry farm women depended on class more than on any other single factor. Throughout the period, wives of prosperous white landowners had more options than poorer women of both races; a persistent racial caste system left black women with few opportunities to take advantage of the changes.

This study shows that, due to the transformation of farming from a way of life to a business and the accompanying change in farm women's work, the meaning of class itself changed. Traditional urban definitions of class, based on occupational categories and wealth, did not fit the lives of country people in the years before the industrialization of agriculture. In the upcountry South, social status was based on rural, communal values—a complex and dynamic mix of economic and cultural factors. Resources alone did not determine where one fell in the social hierarchy. While political power and ambition, which rural folk often referred to as "pride," could raise the status of farm families with limited wealth, farm families with plentiful resources could lose status if they were perceived to be lazy, immoral, or lacking in social responsibility.

As the rural agricultural culture of the upcountry South became industrial, these class definitions shifted, and class stratification increased. Now shifts in occupational categories and wealth had more impact on social status than before, and the class fluidity that had marked social relations during the earlier period disappeared. More rigid class boundaries and a more overt class consciousness developed among rural people. These developments further circumscribed the options of the upcountry's rural women. This book explores how this transformation of the meaning of class took place and how it affected farm women, demonstrating that the formation of class consciousness was not restricted to the urban industrial North.

Neither prosperity nor poverty fully determined rural women's choices; race and class alone do not explain the wide variety of women's responses to change. Many women used the changes to exercise their own preferences: to leave the land, to move to town, to become partners in commercial farming operations, to take off-farm jobs, to model themselves after middle-class housewives, or to expand home-based businesses. For rural upcountry women, as for the fictional Bess Howard, modernization opened up a whole new world of bewildering yet enticing opportunities, and many women eagerly seized these opportunities to shape different lives.

It is important to remember that sociocultural change is a protracted process that evolves slowly over time, and nowhere more haltingly than in the rural upcountry. Periods of rapid change were followed by periods of backlash and attempts to return to the old ways. Country folk made selective choices about which elements of modern life they would adopt. For many women, life in 1939 was not very different than life in 1920. For others, things had changed dramatically. Yet virtually all women in the region had seen their traditional way of life threatened during those turbulent decades. Although the transformation to a mixed economy of industry and capitalist agriculture was never complete and some distinctively rural values still persist today among many upcountry people with rural roots, the seeds of the transformation were sown in the years between 1920 and 1945.

In the 1920s and 1930s, the upcountry's rural women largely coped with, and benefited from, the changes that were overtaking rural America. But often material improvement came after years of struggling to find a niche in the new order or after sacrifice of a way of life that many would have preferred to keep. As one of the region's women put it, "All we knew was to farm."[6] Yet most upcountry farm women learned to do things besides farm in the last half of the twentieth century. This is the story of those women.

One

Rural Life in the Upcountry South

The Scene in 1920

To say that geography is destiny is perhaps to oversimplify; nonetheless, geography has undeniably shaped human history. Climate, topographical features, and the availability of natural resources influence the development of the economy, the culture, and the politics of a region. So it has been in the upcountry South. Life in East Tennessee, southwestern West Virginia, and upstate South Carolina has been determined in part by such environmental factors as average rainfall, elevation and terrain, the abundance of particular mineral deposits, and numerous other factors. To understand events in the upcountry, we must begin with the ways the land shaped the lives of its people.

Geography and Settlement

In Tennessee, natural boundaries from the Appalachian crest to the Mississippi River produced a state with three distinct physical subregions, and the people of these subregions proclaimed different identities. Historian Wilma Dykeman has observed:

Tennesseans . . . seldom identify their home state by its name alone. Their usual response: "I live in West Tennessee," or "My home is in Middle Tennessee," or "I'm from East Tennessee."

This is no . . . exercise in petty provincialism. It is a statement of geography, a reminder of sociology, a hint of cultural variety shaped by geographical fact.

With widely varying settlement, agricultural, and transportation patterns, the geographic divisions also profoundly affected the economy, politics, and culture of the state. West Tennessee is flat river delta land, well suited to growing cotton. Middle Tennessee, bounded on the west by the Tennessee River and on the east by the Cumberland Mountains, is made up of gently rolling hills, ideal for livestock and crop farming. Both regions were well suited for slaveholding plantations in the antebellum period. This fact meant that Middle and West Tennessee also had significantly larger black populations than did the eastern portion of the state.[1]

East Tennessee's Great Valley runs from northeast to southwest across the region bounded by the Cumberland Mountains on one side and the Great Smokies on the other. The Tennessee River and its tributaries dominate the Great Valley, an area about 200 miles long and 55 miles wide at the northern end (fig. 1). The best land was rapidly snapped up in the settlement process, leaving latecomers and poorer families to settle on the mountain slopes. This settlement pattern created a region of small farms with marginal soil on upland slopes and in wooded mountain valleys surrounding larger farms in rich river valleys. Mountainous terrain may have been ill suited for farming, but it was full of coal and timber, resources that attracted outside and local investors beginning in the late nineteenth century.[2]

Southwestern West Virginia was also shaped by its geography. A series of mountain peaks known as the Allegheny Front divides the state into two subregions along a line running southwest from the Maryland border to the Virginia border. West of this line, a combination of plateaus and hilly terrain is broken by swift rivers. On its southern and western edges, the Big Sandy and Tug Fork Rivers divide the state from Kentucky and Virginia (fig. 2). Southwestern West Virginia's rocky mountain slopes made for difficult crop farming, yet these same heights contained rich coal and iron deposits and plentiful stands of hardwood. As in East Tennessee, these natural resources attracted entrepreneurs who would exploit the local landscape, often taking the profits with them.[3]

As in West Virginia and East Tennessee, the presence of mountains

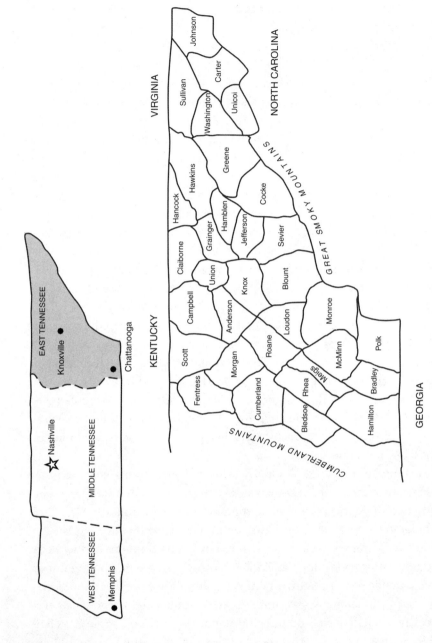

Fig. 1. State of Tennessee, Regional Divisions and Major Cities; Counties of East Tennessee

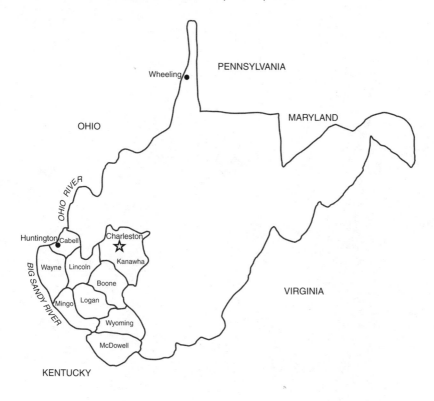

FIG. 2. Counties of Southwestern West Virginia

and hills gave shape to upstate South Carolina. The northern part of the region includes 450 square miles of the Blue Ridge Mountain range (fig. 3). The rest of the region boasts smaller mountain masses separated from the Blue Ridge by mountain foothills, fertile river valleys, and, at its southern edge, the beginnings of the piedmont's gently rolling hills. The upstate drains southeast through the extensive Savannah and Santee River systems. Its hot, humid summers with long growing seasons and mild winters were a particular attraction to settlers.[4]

The first white settlement of all three areas began in the mid to late eighteenth century when migrants from Pennsylvania, Virginia, and North Carolina began moving west and south in search of cheaper and more abundant land. Most of the migrants were of Scots-Irish or German origins. Upstate South Carolina also attracted small but significant clus-

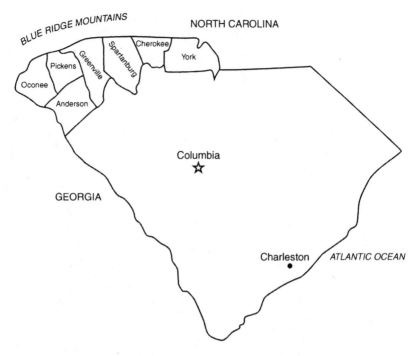

FIG. 3. Counties of Upstate South Carolina

ters of French Huguenots and English. After the Revolution, South Caro-linians poured into East Tennessee. The upcountry's early settlers cre-ated a yeoman culture rooted in Calvinist religion. They sought a certain amount of self-sufficiency with regard to their food supply even as they engaged in limited market agriculture, producing livestock and selling surplus foodstuffs in marketplaces reached on foot and by river. As a result, farming developed rapidly in the upcountry. Small sawmills, flour mills, and, in South Carolina and West Virginia, iron works sprang up to serve the local farmers. By the time of the Civil War, all three regions were well settled.[5]

Civil War and Change

The Civil War brought wrenching changes to the upcountry. For the inhabitants of the western counties of Virginia, the war served as a catalyst for statehood, bringing intrastate political and cultural rivalries to a crisis that resulted in the "secession" of the western counties. Every county in the western region had slaves (albeit few), but slavery was not really the heart of the controversy. Plantation oligarchs in the eastern part of the state had long dominated state politics, and the formation of West Virginia was less about opposition to slavery than about western elites' attempts to expand local autonomy, something statehood allowed them to do.[6]

The area now known as West Virginia had long been a target for land speculators, and after the end of hostilities, a group of capitalists began to develop railroads that would provide access to the rich seams of coal and dense stands of virgin hardwoods in the southwestern part of the state. Timbering and mining would change the socioeconomic structure of southwestern West Virginia, transforming a rural agrarian society to a class-based society of landless wage earners, managers, and a wealthy and politically influential industrial elite. Timber and mining leases shut off access to mountain rangelands that were vital for the livestock grazing on which many farmers depended for cash. Partible inheritance practices steadily diminished the size of landowners' holdings, forcing them to supplement their incomes with off-farm work. Thus West Virginia's small farmers were lured into the cash economy. Counting on wages, many landowning farmers became indebted and lost their land when economic downturns resulted in the loss of mining and timbering jobs. In the years before World War I, many descended into tenancy or moved permanently to company towns. Still, the drift from agriculture was gradual. Tens of thousands of folks in southwestern West Virginia were still farming at the outbreak of World War I.[7]

The industrialists who took control of West Virginia's early twentieth-century economy also fashioned its politics. Political party affiliation was of scant importance in West Virginia. First Democrats, then Republicans would take control of the state's affairs in the years around the nineteenth century's turn, but the party in power made little difference in how the state was run. Both parties were dominated by the industrialists who controlled the state's railroads, coal mines, and logging operations. These businessmen cum politicians manipulated state government for the benefit of their own firms, ignoring national party platforms and, often, the needs of the state's citizens.[8]

Like the folks in the southwestern counties of West Virginia, East Tennesseans had owned few slaves in the antebellum years. Only a few landowners in valley counties engaged in plantation agriculture. Bradley County had the region's largest number of slaves in 1860, yet they made up only 10 percent of the county's population. These slaves would be the ancestors of the region's small postbellum black population. Almost none of the upland farmers owned slaves because small, steep upland farms did not lend themselves to the large-scale commercial production that could profitably utilize slave labor. Here, too, war wrought profound changes. Much fighting took place in East Tennessee, and some families were split apart, with relatives fighting on both sides. Unionist sentiment prevailed in most of the region. As a result, East Tennessee has remained a bastion of the Republican Party down to the present.[9]

A Republican stronghold in a state dominated by the Democratic Party faces special challenges, and East Tennessee was no exception. One observer described Tennessee politics before World War II as "two one-party systems." As a result of Democratic control of the state legislature, East Tennessee became what historian David D. Lee has called "the neglected stepchild of Tennessee politics." Until the 1940s, Democrats funneled the majority of state projects and spending to the needs of Middle and West Tennessee, an act particularly devastating for the underdeveloped upland counties with their tiny tax bases. Schools and roads throughout the region remained poor. Except in Knoxville and Chattanooga, most counties had few paved roads until 1940.[10]

Just as East Tennessee's post–Civil War political history resembled West Virginia's, so did its economic history. Industrialists also found East Tennessee an attractive prospect in the years after the Civil War. Several counties in the heart of the northern half of the region were home to rich coal reserves, and mines were established in the last quarter of the nineteenth century. Railroads constructed just before and after the war provided ready access to eastern markets both for the region's coal and for the timber being cut in the Great Smoky Mountains. As in West Virginia, some of East Tennessee's rural folk found themselves drawn into a wage-earning economy, but farmers were more prosperous here. Fewer sank into tenancy for several reasons: slightly better quality soil on most farms, terrain that was more suited to cropping than West Virginia's livestock herding, and larger farms. Tens of thousands remained on the land.[11]

As was the case in Tennessee and West Virginia, war changed life in South Carolina. Upstate South Carolina was home to more slaves than either West Virginia or East Tennessee, and open Unionist sympathizers were few. In spite of the fact that the region was home to some of the South's most rabid secessionists, the upstate suffered less from the ravages of war than the rest of the state because little fighting occurred there. Nonetheless, war and emancipation transformed the economy. Many landowners lost their cash investments in the collapse of the Confederate economy, and with the emancipation of their slaves, they lost property valued at tens of thousands of dollars.

The sharp rise in cotton prices after hostilities ceased led many upstate yeomen to abandon self-sufficient general farming and commit most of their resources to raising cotton. Many freed slaves went to work for local landholders as day laborers and, increasingly over time, as sharecroppers in expanding cotton fields. The construction of railroads throughout the upstate provided easy access to cotton markets. Between 1860 and 1880, five of the upstate counties (Oconee, Pickens, Anderson, Greenville, and Spartanburg) quintupled their cotton production. However, the shift to cotton farming left small farmers at the mercy of furnishing merchants and locked them into a cycle of overproduction, declining cotton prices, and continual indebtedness. One upstate furnishing merchant testified that the price he and his colleagues charged for goods furnished to sharecroppers under the crop-lien system was 20 percent more than that charged farmers who purchased goods with cash. By the early twentieth century, thousands of poor whites joined their fellow black farmers as tenants.[12]

For many, hope for a better life appeared in the form of the new textile mills springing up throughout the region. The railroads that linked the cotton fields to world markets also provided convenient transportation for the products of local textile firms, and disappointed farming folk furnished cheap labor for the factory floors. In South Carolina the number of textile mill workers grew from 891 in 1860 to 54,629 in 1920. Most of these mills and this employment was clustered in the upstate. Spartanburg County alone had 104 mills. By 1920 South Carolina mills were manufacturing one-fourth of the nation's output of cotton yarn and cloth.[13]

Just as the war transformed South Carolina's economy, it also affected the state's politics. Rejecting the Republican Party as the party of the freedmen, South Carolina's whites formed what was essentially a one-party state. After a turbulent Reconstruction, an oligarchy of conservative Democrats, most of them from the old planter aristocracy, controlled the state's politics for about fifteen years. They promoted a policy of white supremacy with racial moderation.

After 1880 a fall in cotton prices, increasing problems with soil erosion and fertility, and the spread of the crop-lien system created considerable discontent among the state's white farmers, a discontent that led to political upheaval. Led by a demagogic young politician, "Pitchfork" Ben Tillman, a Farmer's Association accused the conservatives of incompetence, of allying themselves with the railroads who were charging farmers exorbitant shipping rates, and of doing nothing for farming folk. Tillman appealed to upstate resentment of the low country's control of state politics, a rivalry dating back to the colonial period. A hard-liner on racial issues, Tillman also accused the conservatives of waffling on white supremacy. The Tillmanites managed to seize control of the Democratic Party and elected "Pitchfork" Ben governor in 1890. His racist rhetoric created a climate of racial hostility that led to an increase in lynchings and violence against blacks after his election. Tillman was also the architect of the disfranchisement of African Americans in the 1895 constitution. Although the Tillmanites made some reforms, especially in the area of state-supported higher education, their era is most notable for the way segregation and white supremacy became entrenched in South Carolina politics and society.

Although political factions came and went in early twentieth-century South Carolina, race baiting had come to stay. The agrarian Tillmanites were in turn pushed out in 1910 by another race-baiting demagogue, Coleman Blease, who succeeded in creating a powerful voting bloc among poor white mill workers.

Varieties of Agriculture

The diversity of the agriculture and rural populations of the three areas considered here belies the similarity in their geography and history. By many measures East Tennessee's small farmers, with their diversified livestock and grain farms, were somewhat prosperous. Though the ma-

FIG. 4. Rural housing in the upcountry ranged from very fine to distressingly poor. The farmhouse of Sherman Stiner in Union County, Tennessee, was an example of one of the better houses. The photographer called Stiner "a prosperous and progressive farmer." Most of his 1,500-acre farm was later flooded by the Norris Dam reservoir, a Tennessee Valley Authority project. (Lewis W. Hine photograph, 1933. NWDNS-142-H-108. Courtesy of Still Picture Branch, National Archives at College Park.)

jority of farmers in the fertile Great Valley as well as in the mountains were general and subsistence farmers, better transportation and accessible markets encouraged the development of large commercial operations in some of the valley counties. Burley tobacco gained popularity as a cash crop during the first quarter of the twentieth century and was generally more profitable than the cotton grown in Middle and West Tennessee. Farmers in the fertile valley areas also raised corn, wheat, and hay as cash crops. Some counties in the southern part of the region raised large quantities of truck crops for the Chattanooga and Knoxville markets.[14]

The average 1920 farm size of 98 acres, an indicator of farm prosperity, was considerably higher than the state average of 83.82 acres. About two-thirds of East Tennessee's farmers owned their land as compared to a state average of 58.8 percent. More than half of the region's farm tenants were relatively prosperous cash renters or cash tenants rather than sharecroppers. Renters paid a fixed rate for the use of farmland, bought their own seed and fertilizer, and usually owned their own tools and work stock, an indicator of some measure of capital resources. Cash tenants usually received a house, a large garden plot, and cash wages in exchange for work on the landlord's farm. Often they kept poultry and sold garden surplus to earn additional cash. Cash renters and cash tenants had more opportunity to turn a profit each season and considerably more independence in dictating terms with a landlord. By contrast, sharecroppers were forced to depend on a landlord to supply tools, work stock, seed, and even household provisions. They offered only their labor on the landlord's crops, and he kept a proportion of the crops, usually one-half to two-thirds. As a result of their utter dependence on the landlord for basic necessities, sharecroppers were more vulnerable to abuse and exploitation and had fewer choices in farming situations.[15]

The region's small population of black farm owners and tenants (4 percent of all farmers as compared to 15 percent in the rest of the state) were also more prosperous than black farmers elsewhere in Tennessee, but still significantly less well off than white farmers. Nearly two-thirds of all East Tennessee blacks owned their farms compared to less than one-third elsewhere in the state. Black farmers generally worked approximately 59 acres in the eastern region, again higher than the state average of 39.9 acres for blacks but considerably less than the white average of 98 acres.[16]

In neighboring upstate South Carolina, farm conditions were not as prosperous as those in East Tennessee. Here the average farm size ranged from as large as 64 acres in Oconee County to only 44.4 acres in Anderson County. This was barely enough land to support a family through subsistence production and hardly adequate for the commercial cotton production that dominated in the upstate. The area's high tenancy rate reflected the hardships wrought by inadequately sized farms: Anderson County also had the highest rate in upstate, 72.6 percent. Only 137 (or 2 percent) of the county's 6,475 tenants were cash renters; the rest were poorer sharecroppers. This was considerably higher than the state's abysmal

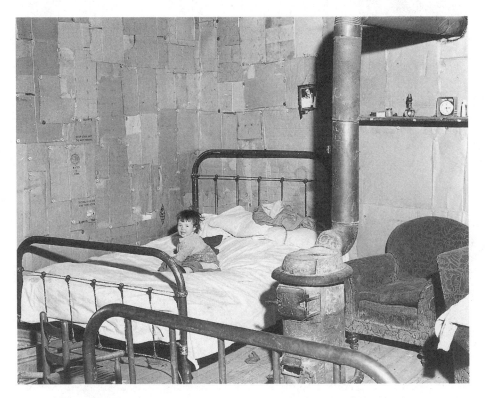

Fɪɢ. 5. The desperate poverty of this South Carolina tenant farm family is clear from the interior of their home. (Jack Delano photograph, ca. 1940. LC-USF34, 43520. Library of Congress.)

average tenancy rate of 64.5 percent. Upstate South Carolina tenants were likely to be farming significantly smaller plots of land than farm owners. The average Anderson County farm owner held 70.6 acres of land, while the average tenant farmed only 34.7 acres.[17]

The upstate counties were the whitest in the state, with black populations hovering at or below 25 percent. African Americans made up about one-third of upstate South Carolina's farmers, and nearly half of the region's tenants were black. Ironically, Greenville County's black tenants were more likely to be cash renters or cash tenants, while white tenants were more likely to be sharecroppers, suggesting that African Americans resisted the total dependence of sharecropping. Cash renters and tenants also had more control over the labor of their family members than did sharecroppers, another reason black farmers probably preferred this arrangement. Nonetheless, black tenants and farm owners were poorer than their white neighbors, indicating that racial discrimination limited their economic mobility. For example, although blacks made up 42.5 percent of Anderson County's farm population, they farmed an average of only 35 acres of land compared to their white counterparts' 51.5 acres.[18]

It is harder to determine the role race played in the lives of southwestern West Virginia farmers because there were so few African American farmers in the region. The 1920 agricultural census found only 18 blacks among the 2,952 farmers in Kanawha County and only one black farmer in Logan County. African Americans never made up more than 2 percent of the population of any southwestern West Virginia county, and the agricultural census often did not break down tenancy figures in West Virginia by race.[19]

Nor was tenancy as pronounced in most of southwestern West Virginia as in upstate South Carolina. Tenancy rates ranged from 19.5 percent in Kanawha County to 41 percent in Wyoming County. Only in McDowell County were tenants a majority, with about 46 percent of its farmers owning their own land. Even here, farm size was small: 71.1 acres in Kanawha County, a figure much lower than the state average of 110 acres and hardly enough to support a large family or to engage in significant commercial production.[20]

The farming practiced by West Virginia landowners and tenants was shaped by the area's topography. Steep and rocky terrain limited the amount of cropping a family could do. Most raised large garden patches and a little grain for family use, corn for livestock feed, and perhaps a small plot of tobacco for personal use or sale. Livestock was the major source of cash income, and most farmers herded on mountain slopes owned by absentee landlords as well as on their own land. Grazing land became increasingly scarce as timbering and mining interests encroached. This also diminished the supply of the game that provided families with additional meat. Another cash crop for many landowners was timber, which they periodically cut and sold from their own land.[21]

Daily Rural Life and the Gendered Division of Labor

In spite of their considerable agricultural diversity, patterns of daily rural life varied little among the three regions. The seasonal rhythms of work, the mix of market and subsistence production, the gendered division of labor, and even the organization of rural society was similar. When listening to farm families describe life in the interwar years, one is struck by the commonalities in their stories. Daily life on a West Virginia apple farm was really little different from that on a South Carolina cotton farm or an East Tennessee general farm, particularly for women, whose lives were dominated by ceaseless labor.

The lives of three upcountry women illustrate the similarities of rural life and the gendered division of labor in the three regions. Mobile Moss Brown, the wife of an African American cash tenant in Blount County, Tennessee, gave birth to twelve children between 1934 and 1954. She and her husband and their children raised tobacco, soybeans, and truck crops for cash sale as well as working their landlord's crops for daily wages. Mobile worked alongside her family in the fields. This farm labor was just one more task among her daily burdens of child care, sewing, cooking, preserving food, washing, and cleaning. She also milked the family cows and cared for a poultry flock. Like many of East Tennessee's black farm families, even tenants, the Browns enjoyed reasonably good living conditions. One daughter reported that the family had had running water and electricity as far back as she could remember. No doubt these amenities helped Mobile cope with her tremendous workload, but they did not prevent endless days of hard work.[22]

Ryan Page's description of his mother's experiences as the wife of a Spartanburg County, South Carolina, sharecropper bears marked similarities to Brown's life, though her living conditions were not as good. Sally Turner Page struggled to raise her nine children in substandard housing that varied little during the family's twenty moves between 1907 and 1945. The family's homes usually lacked foundations, allowing cold drafts and dirt to blow through cracks in the floor into the house. A lack of indoor plumbing made cleaning an endless battle. One of Sally's finest moments was in the late 1920s when her husband bought a sink that drained outside. Although she still had to carry fresh water, she no longer had to lug buckets of waste water back outside. Page reported that "Mama was prouder of that sink than anyone else." In addition to producing and preserving almost all the family's food, she processed milk from the family's cows for home consumption and for sale. The sink would certainly have eased the endless burden of cleaning up the milk processing equipment. When her children were too small to do much work, Sally Page joined her husband in the fields, picking cotton, hoeing corn, and helping tend their large truck patch. As her children grew old enough to carry part of the workload, she withdrew to the house and barnyard, where younger children, the garden and cows, and household responsibilities consumed her days. The family sold milk, surplus vegetables, and cotton on the market.[23]

Mrs. Lessie Shiveley and her husband farmed on Tupper's Creek in Kanawha County, West Virginia. Married in the early 1920s, they purchased a small farm where they raised corn and oats to feed their livestock and sold milk, butter, and truck crops for cash. Lessie gardened and preserved her produce for their consumption. The couple had only one child, who died shortly after birth. Although their lack of children meant fewer mouths to feed, the Shiveleys also had fewer hands to share the work, so Lessie Shively not only milked and processed dairy products for sale but also did field work. She recalled that "pretty near every woman . . . done a man's work. I've done everything but plowing. I've worked in hay, I've binded oats, I've cut corn, I've shucked corn. Done everything in the world that a man could do but plow."[24]

As the lives of these women suggest, the quality of life on the region's farms varied widely. Yet women, regardless of where they lived, their landholding status, or their level of prosperity, focused on family subsistence. As farmers began to make the transition from subsistence to commercial farming, the gendered division of labor often shifted. In the upcountry, farmers had begun the protracted transition from subsistence to participation in the market economy in the mid-nineteenth century, and by 1920 most upcountry farm families were largely focused on market production. As men engaged in more market-oriented activities and reinvested most of the proceeds from these activities in the farm, farm women gradually took on more of the burden of the family's maintenance. While men were responsible for field work and large-scale livestock production for the market, women managed most of the farm's subsistence activities. Men now spent most of their time producing crops and livestock for the market and less time growing food for the family, hunting to supplement the meat supply, or similar subsistence activities.

For women, this shift was not marked by a radical change in responsibilities but rather by a shift in emphasis. Men may have plowed the gardens, but women usually tended them and harvested and preserved the family's annual food supply during the long summer season. Men and women may have shared the barnyard responsibilities, but women were most often responsible for the daily care and feeding of cows and chickens that provided the family's milk, meat, and eggs. Women were also almost exclusively responsible for the household tasks of cleaning, sewing, and caring for the family's clothing, and for tending children and the sick. In some cases, men assisted women with household tasks by chopping wood or carrying water, but in times of heavy field labor, these burdens invariably fell to farm women. Men rarely assisted with tasks more clearly labeled "women's work," such as laundry and cooking, but farm women often assisted their husbands with field work, reflecting the high priority that commercial agricultural activities received.[25]

Black families used a similar gendered division of labor. Black farm women raised most or all of the family's food. They also devoted as much of their time as possible to child care, and they assumed responsibility for food preparation and clothing production. Like white women, black women also supplemented the family income whenever possible by selling vegetables, eggs, and butter. Many earned additional income by taking in laundry or ironing. Unlike their white counterparts, who were often free to withdraw from field work except in the busiest times, black farm women regularly worked in the fields, whether for themselves or for a farm owner. Black farm women in East Tennessee, upstate South Carolina, and southwestern West Virginia were also far more likely than white women to leave the farm and home to work for wages. They might work in a white woman's kitchen or as a day laborer on a nearby farm.

Upcountry blacks and whites viewed women's wage work differently. Whites, even poor whites, objected to the idea of their women working outside the home under the control of other men. Such a situation violated patriarchal notions of the male household head's right to control the labor (and behavior) of his women. Nonetheless, whites believed that black women *should* work outside the home—indeed that they were obligated to work for whites. They used every power available to them to force black women to take wage-earning jobs. Sharecropping contracts often included requirements that *each* family member do field work or that black women also do domestic day labor for the white landowner's wife. The issue of control of black women's work was highly contested terrain between sharecropping families and landowners. Whites' insistence that black women should perform wage work was reflected in later New Deal policies that discharged black women from WPA jobs if whites complained of a shortage of domestic workers.

African Americans, however, viewed things differently. Black families shared white families' belief that farm women should not perform wage work off the farm if such a situation could possibly be avoided. Nonetheless, the fact that black men usually earned far less than white men in comparable jobs often pushed black women into the labor market. We can see this by comparing counties where black and white farm families had roughly the same economic status to counties where whites were significantly better off than blacks. In the former, the proportion of black and white women taking off-farm jobs was roughly equal; while in counties where whites were better off, a much higher percentage of black women worked outside the home. Whenever economically possible, black women avoided working off the farm. As some historians have argued, rural blacks of both sexes were generally reluctant to participate heavily in the market economy because of the exposure it gave them to white control.[26]

Race and Class in the Upcountry

The South's distinctive racial caste structure shaped life for African Americans in the upcountry, although the extent of racial barriers varied across the region. Predictably, upstate South Carolina was the most restrictive area for blacks. Disfranchisement laws had been enacted in 1895, and blacks were legally prohibited from sharing most public accommodations with whites, including schools, theaters, hotels, and hospitals. De facto segregation existed in town neighborhoods, and discrimination kept most African Americans out of all but the least desirable and lowest-paying jobs. Lynching and Klan activity surfaced periodically. There were eight lynchings in the upstate counties between 1900 and 1931. As late as 1940, the *Spartanburg Journal and Carolina Spartan* reported on the beating of several African Americans by white men wearing hoods. As in the rest of the South, unwritten codes of behavior served to regulate relations between blacks and whites.[27]

Life for African Americans was somewhat less restrictive in neighboring East Tennessee. De facto and de jure segregation existed throughout the region and was most explicit in the cities. Although Tennessee never formally disfranchised black voters, the poll tax, actions by partisan registrars, intimidation, and violence had discouraged political participation since the 1890s. As in most of the state, few blacks voted or otherwise participated in electoral politics in the eastern counties, except in the cities of Chattanooga and Knoxville. Little data exists on black voting in rural counties. Five blacks had been lynched in the eastern counties between 1900 and 1931, four of them in rural communities. A race riot in Knoxville in 1919 and Klan activity there and in rural counties throughout the early decades of the century served to remind local blacks of the costs of attempting to exercise their constitutional rights. Apparently most blacks heeded the warning, turning inward to their own communities in order to survive.[28]

West Virginia boasted the least oppressive atmosphere for African Americans. As in East Tennessee, blacks were never disfranchised here, though a climate of fear discouraged most rural blacks from voting. Schools were segregated, but most other public accommodations were not. Towns, especially company-owned mining towns, engaged in residential segregation, but a strong commitment to interracial organizing by the United Mine Workers undermined mine owners' efforts to divide workers by race by defining the worst jobs as "black jobs." This is not to say that blacks enjoyed the same opportunities as whites, but rather that in the interests of worker solidarity, the union periodically attempted to address some issues of discrimination against blacks.[29]

In rural areas of all three states, race relations were highly individual. There was no residential segregation in the countryside; blacks and whites were often neighbors, though African Americans were generally relegated to the poorest land. Even segregated rural social institutions, such as churches, were often in close proximity. One Jefferson County, Tennessee, woman recalled that the black and white churches in her childhood community faced each other across a road. Black and white children played together until the age of puberty, and although unwritten etiquette demanded that adult whites not eat with blacks, children often ate in the homes of families of the other race. East Tennessean Lucille Thornburgh recalled, "If we happened to be in a black family's home at lunch time, we ate with them. And if the black kids were over playing with us, they ate with us."[30]

Race remained a powerful part of status definition in the upcountry. Rural Southerners were a class-conscious lot, yet traditional urban-based definitions of class do not fit country people. Neither is it useful to envision rural folk as belonging to only one class—all poor or all middling farmers. Class was a complex and dynamic concept, complicated by race. For this reason, this study tries to define social status as did the farm people themselves.[31]

White farm folk in the three regions defined themselves and their neighbors according to a three-tiered class hierarchy that was a complex mixture of economic factors, power, and perceptions of personal industriousness. Elite farm families topped the hierarchy. Although these families were always landholders and sometimes supplemented their farm incomes with off-farm businesses, they were not always extremely wealthy. White families of moderate means could achieve elite status in the upcountry because of their leadership or longevity in the community or because they were related to the community's founding families. Rural elites assumed positions alongside town leaders in county politics and local civic organizations. Elites headed local farm organizations, groups that came to have considerable influence over local, and later national, farm policy.

Elites claimed to respect the middling white farm families who were the majority in East Tennessee and southwestern West Virginia and a large minority in upstate South Carolina. The primary reason elites respected middling whites was that they conducted themselves in a respectable and respectful manner. Middling farmers were usually landowners, but a few tenants and sharecroppers were seen as middling if they were perceived by elites and other middling folk to be ambitious, law-abiding, and hardworking. The major distinction between middling farmers and elites was not wealth but the fact that middling farmers did not hold positions of power within the community. Although middling white folks might privately express some resentment of the power held by elites, they nonetheless cultivated elite favor and many aspired to elite status.

Poverty was the distinguishing factor for whites at the bottom of the class hierarchy. Elite and middling families attributed this poverty to a lack of industriousness. White trash, as these families were called, were perceived as lazy, shiftless, and lacking in ambition—all grievous faults to a rural people who placed so much emphasis on work. Although most of the whites in this category were tenant farmers and sharecroppers, many poorer landholders were also seen in this category. Elite and middling whites not only believed that lower-class whites lacked ambition but also that they engaged in behaviors beyond the pale of acceptability, such as drinking and sexual misconduct. Often elite and middling whites dismissed poor whites as being "no better than blacks." Historian Joel Williamson notes that many of the South's whites feared these "men with black hearts under white skins" as much as they feared African Americans. For their part, poor whites disdained white farmers who grew wealthy from the labor of others, and they resented the middling folk who looked down on them. Poor whites often recognized structural economic and social factors that denied them the same opportunities as middling and elite whites, and their rough behavior was sometimes an open rejection of white bourgeois values.[32]

All three classes of rural white people defined themselves in large part by the fact that they were not black. Historians have noted that notions of blackness and whiteness developed in relation to one another. For lower class whites, whiteness was especially significant. Whiteness was a sort of property—a possession that conferred certain privileges: access to better jobs, entrée to the best public accommodations, full civic participation, and access to the cheap labor of African Americans. The value that whites placed on whiteness was demonstrated by the lengths to which southern legal codes went to punish African Americans who attempted to "pass" as white. But more than material privilege, whites derived what W. E. B. DuBois termed a "psychological wage" from the fact that they were not black. They were given public deference by blacks simply because they were white. Southern segregation constantly reminded them of their superior status to blacks because they enjoyed access to all public accommodations on equal status with middling and elite whites, while blacks were denied these privileges.

Rural white farm folk generally defined black families as fitting into one of two categories, based more on blacks' adherence to white standards of appropriate behavior than on economic factors. The upper tier of black citizens, often referred to as "high class blacks" or as "one of the better sorts of black families" or simply "Negroes," were often land-holders but were also sometimes tenants, sharecroppers, or laborers. These families were characterized as ambitious, hard-working, and clean. They often worked hard to educate their children. But most of all, they were deferential to whites. The lower sort of blacks, usually called "nig-gers," were perceived by whites to share many of the same characteristics as poor whites. They were believed to be shiftless, lazy, and dirty. They were also seen as immoral and insolent to whites.

Blacks recognized class differences among themselves, but they did not always attribute the same values to each class as whites did. Certainly most better-class blacks adopted middling white values and sought a level of upward mobility for themselves and their children. They often expressed fears that working-class blacks were damaging the reputation of the entire race, and they cultivated the patronage and protection of influential whites. For their part, working-class blacks accused better-class blacks of being pretentious and snobbish or of "selling out" the race to whites, and they almost universally disdained poor whites. Working-class blacks' rejection of white values and restrictions was demonstrated in their drinking, dancing, and gathering at juke joints and cock fights. The leisure world of working-class blacks was not only a means of escap-ing the harsh realities of their daily lives but also part of a conscious exer-cise of free will—of defining themselves in opposition to white values.

Race and class intertwined in complex ways. Whiteness brought with it a presumption of respectability. Until your behavior proved otherwise, middling status and white skin were assumed to be synonymous. On the other hand, blacks were forced to prove their respectability. They were assumed to be of the lowest class of blacks until a certain level of defer-ence, diligence, and adherence to white middling standards of respect-ability proved them to be part of the black "better class."

Gender also figured in class definitions. White women did not gener-ally hold a class status on their own; rather their status was determined by their relationship to a husband or father. A woman married to an elite man enjoyed the privileges of elite life, but an elite woman who married a poor man would lose status and privileges. A woman's own respectabil-ity was not enough to buy her middling or elite status. A decent, hard-working white woman married to a poor, shiftless man might be pitied, she might even become the object of charity from her social betters, but she would never enjoy higher status. By the same token, women could move up the class ladder by marrying a man of higher status. The daughter of a middling farmer might improve her life by marrying an elite man. Not only was a woman's status dependent on her relationship to a man, but her behavior could also bolster a man's status. Wives of middling and elite farmers were expected to maintain family ties to mutual aid networks and to perform acts of charity for the poorer members of the community. These actions helped cement a man's social status. For elites, a wife's engagement in certain types of conspicuous consumption could also be badges of social standing.

Among blacks, too, class and gender intertwined. The hard-working, church-going, and upright behavior associated with "better class" status was most often associated with black women. Unlike white women, however, a black woman's status did not necessarily depend on her husband or father. She might obtain some level of better class status in the eyes of blacks and whites alike even if her husband or father caroused or engaged in petty crime. By the same token, a black woman who rejected middling standards of respectability was consciously rejecting white notions of gender propriety.

World War I and the Upcountry Economy

World War I had a profound impact on the agricultural economy of the region and the South generally. A number of government programs encouraged farmers to increase production dramatically in order to alleviate Europe's food shortages. One of the most far-reaching effects was the easing of farm credit strictures, which enabled farmers to borrow large amounts of money to buy more land, livestock, and modern equipment. The federal government also increased funding for agricultural extension agents whose job it was to advise farmers on how to increase farm yields. Increased production and high wartime prices helped upcountry farmers realize some of their most profitable years ever. At the same time, wartime inflation drove up the cost of living and the price of agricultural inputs such as seed and fertilizer.

When the war ended, prosperity continued into the first half of 1920. Then the demand for farm products plummeted, followed by farm prices.

The summer of 1920 saw the beginning of the agricultural depression that gripped U.S. farmers until the outbreak of World War II. The total value of crops sold or traded in Tennessee fell from $318,285,307 in 1919 to $171,878,708 in 1924. The decline in values continued into the next decade with the value of Tennessee's crops totaling $90,414,617 in 1929 and $57,284,587 in 1939. Corn prices fell from $1.51 a bushel in 1919 to 62 cents in 1920. Tobacco fell from 31.2 cents per pound to 17.3 cents in the same period. Cotton plunged from 40 cents a pound in the spring of 1920 to 13.5 cents in December of the same year. A slight recovery began in 1922 precipitating cotton's climb to 28 cents, but prices never regained their wartime levels and fell yet again in 1930 in the wake of the stock market crash. Wholesale farm prices fell an additional 21 percent between August 1929 and August 1930, and a severe drought exacerbated the farm crisis.[33]

The fall in farm income had a ripple effect in rural communities. Farmers who had taken on mortgages to modernize their operations during the war found themselves unable to meet their payments. During the prosperous 1910s, citizens in many of upcountry's rural counties had responded to Progressive and Country Life Movement calls to improve schools and roads in rural communities by raising property taxes. In the face of an agricultural depression, other rural counties increased property taxes to try to meet revenue shortfalls, creating a greater burden for already strapped "land poor" farmers. Farm property taxes in Tennessee increased 175 percent in absolute dollars between 1913 and 1922. As more and more farmers were unable to meet their obligations, tax sales and mortgage foreclosures grew more common.[34]

This agricultural depression exacted a terrible price from many of the upcountry's farm families. During the 1910s they had faced a hopeful future, and many dreamed of improving their standard of living and participating in the national consumer economy. The postwar depression dashed these hopes. Real incomes declined because although consumer prices fell, they did not fall as much as commodity prices, and many key agricultural inputs actually increased in price. In 1919 the sale of a bushel of corn would yield enough to buy five gallons of gas; by the end of 1921, a farmer needed to sell two bushels of corn to buy a single gallon of gas. Farmers were also more dependent on the market than they had been before the war. Many farmers had purchased expensive equipment such as tractors. Other families had purchased automobiles. They had reduced the volume of home food production in order to produce more crops for the market, requiring them to buy more of the family's diet. Some had purchased labor-saving appliances and electrified homes. All these products and services required cash that was increasingly difficult to earn in the early 1920s. Many farm families who had bought into the USDA's vision of mechanized commercial farming or who aspired to a middle-class lifestyle now found themselves unable to make ends meet.

A farm family encumbered by a heavy mortgage, high taxes, and other debt could not significantly reduce costs by reducing output; farmers simply stretched to produce more. The USDA's 1922 *Annual Report* noted, "Certainly no other industry could have taken the losses agriculture has taken and maintain production, and we have no evidence to show that any other group of workers would have taken the reduction in wages in the spirit in which farmers have taken their reduction." Unfortunately, farmers' increased production only added to the commodities surplus, which in turn further reduced prices.[35]

Farm families unable to survive the economic crisis sold off part of their acreage, migrated to cities and towns in search of jobs, or moved down the agricultural ladder. Between 1910 and 1920 the average farm in Blount County, Tennessee, had increased from 93.2 acres to 106.4 acres. By 1925 the average Blount County farm was only 74.4 acres, suggesting that some families were selling off acreage in order to pay bills, a strategy that further reduced their ability to make a living by farming. Many counties saw considerable out-migration. A Works Progress Administration study found that most East Tennessee counties lost between 15 and 30 percent of their populations through migration in the years between 1920 and 1930. Another study found that, while the rural population of East Tennessee increased 14.7 percent in the first three decades of the century (considerably less than the natural rate of population increase), the population of the region's urban areas increased 243.6 percent. Upcountry cities and towns were swelled by rural migrants in search of opportunity.[36]

This, then, was the world confronted by rural upcountry women in 1920. The post–World War I crisis in the agricultural economy was undermining farm families' ability to survive with the old combinations of subsistence and market farming supplemented by wage labor. The racial caste system, more violent in upstate South Carolina than in the other two regions, limited black women's coping strategies. The political structures of each state were extremely conservative and were dedicated to preserving the status quo, leaving little hope of economic development assistance from the state.

For the women of these regions, the pace of change begun in the first decades of the century would escalate in the 1920s and 1930s. Farm families would face a dizzying array of choices in their quest for economic survival and success. By 1945 the upcountry South would join the ranks of what historian Jack Temple Kirby has called "rural worlds lost."[37] The old rural world with its economic system would be virtually gone by the end of World War II, and the characteristic rural way of life that dominated the lives of most rural upcountry folk would be transformed.

Women like Lessie Shiveley, Sally Page, and Mobile Moss Brown found their choices constrained by race and class and by the economic opportunities in the counties in which they lived. Nonetheless, they seized on the opportunities created by government intervention, expanding industry, and structural changes in the agricultural economy to reshape their lives.

Two

Making Do and Doing Without

Farm Women Cope with the Economic Crisis,

1920–1941

When the 1933 *Yearbook of Agriculture*, USDA's published annual report, announced that "Readjustments in Family Living Are as Drastic as Those Effected in Farming," the agency was simply recognizing what farm people had long known: that "tightening the belt" and survival on the farm required men and women to make new decisions about resource allocation and market involvement. The authors, two home economists, outlined the hardships the Depression had visited upon farm families across America and the coping strategies farm wives had adopted to deal with the crisis. These strategies included producing more of the family's necessities at home, doing without unnecessary items, making more use of community facilities such as free clinics and libraries, better planning to facilitate the wise use of farm resources, and contributing to the family's cash income.[1]

Implicit in the title of this *Yearbook of Agriculture* article and the authors' presumption that farm women were responsible for family readjustments while men handled farm work was the USDA's assumption that the household economy was separate from the farm economy. On most farms in the upcountry South, however, the two economies were inextricably intertwined, making the situation more complicated. All members of the family contributed to a greater or lesser extent both to the family's subsistence and to the commercial farming operation. For this reason, women's contributions to the family economy remained central not only to the survival of the family but also to the survival of the farm. In fact, the division of labor on upcountry farms meant that most of the burden for surviving the economic downturn fell on the region's farm women. By producing more of the family's needs at home and by "making do" with fewer consumer products that required cash outlays, farm women ensured not only that their families had enough to eat but also that more cash resources were available to invest in the maintenance and improvement of the farm. At the same time, farm men responded to the crisis in two ways. First, many intensified their commercial farming activities in an attempt to earn sufficient cash for farm and family needs: they tried to produce more acres of cash crops or to increase yields on existing acreage. Second, many tried to supplement their incomes with off-farm jobs. Even with both partners struggling to make the farm pay, however, many upcountry families found it impossible to stay on the land in the 1920s.

Farm women's economic crisis had not begun with the stock market crash in 1929 and the subsequent Depression but with the collapse in farm prices after World War I. In order to cope with the economic downturn, upcountry farm women adapted traditional coping strategies like those outlined in the USDA's annual report, strategies that were simply more intense versions of farm women's traditional roles. Although all farm women shouldered the responsibility for seeing families through the economic crisis, not all women had the same range of resources on which to draw. Their options were mediated by class and, to a lesser degree, by race. Poor white women and black women always had the smallest number of alternatives.

In these crisis years, women's responsibilities did not end with their own families, however. Women were primarily responsible for the complex, reciprocal support that had formed the basis of rural "social services" for generations. In order to cope with the downturn, farm women relied on the same kin, friends, and neighbors as always. They intensified organized efforts to provide community relief. In short, as was the case with urban and suburban women, when economic crisis struck, it was up to farm women to stretch scarce resources so that farm families could survive. Yet even as most of the burden for family and community survival fell on women, men's commercial farming activities continued to be seen as the highest priority because farm families believed that commercial agriculture was the key to a more secure future on the land.

Agricultural Depression in a Mixed Economy

The drastic fall in farm prices after World War I ravaged the upcountry South's small farmers. A look at farms in individual East Tennessee counties tells the desperate story. In mountainous Sevier County, the value of crops sold or traded fell from $1,700,830 in 1924 to only $419,686 in 1929. Values climbed slightly to $438,519 in 1939, but the number of farmers selling crops had increased 31 percent. This meant that the average farmer selling crops had revenues of $231 in 1929 but only $183 in 1939. In the same ten-year period, the total number of farmers in Sevier County decreased by 14 percent. In other words, the number of farmers actually selling crops on the market increased even as the total number of farmers fell, indicating that more subsistence farmers were entering the market economy in spite of, or perhaps because of, the economic crisis. Similar patterns were prevalent elsewhere in the three regions.[2]

The surprising increase in farmers' market activity in spite of worsening farm prices in the early 1930s was due in part to the mixed economy. While the agricultural downturn of the 1920s had been difficult for upcountry farm families, the stock market crash and the resulting industrial decline was a disaster. Historians of the Great Depression era have assumed that the Depression was hardest for farm families who were entirely dependent on commercial agriculture, but few have recognized that in mixed economies, such as those in the upcountry South, families faced a double burden. Although the falling prices of the 1920s had wiped out whatever profits farmers had realized from their commercial farm products, many were initially able to cope because they turned to part-time employment in the region's manufacturing and extractive industries. Farm men and women supplemented the farm's subsistence with money earned in the coal fields, lumber camps, and textile mills of the upcountry. Works Progress Administration (WPA) sociologists found that half of all East Tennessee families surveyed reported having had some source of nonfarm cash income *before* the Great Depression. Even tenant farmers, particularly African Americans, were likely to work off the farm part of the time. This income enabled them to continue their commercial farming operations, albeit sometimes at a loss. Some were even able to use this cash income to expand their farms or to mechanize.[3]

Unfortunately, after 1929 rural industrial employers gradually scaled back or closed down their operations, leaving farmers who were also industrial workers under- or unemployed. The cash incomes that had sustained families in spite of the crash in farm prices disappeared, leaving some farm families desperate indeed. Many farmers who had formerly used the land only for subsistence operations tried to enter the market arena in order to replace the cash incomes formerly provided by wage labor. The situation was particularly devastating for farmers who were still heavily indebted after their World War I era expansion or for those who had been able to continue expanding farm operations in the twenties because of their nonfarm cash incomes.

Data on relief applications reveals the significance of the loss of off-farm jobs. A 1934 Federal Emergency Relief Agency (FERA) report found that fully 30 percent of relief recipients in rural Bledsoe County, Tennessee, applied for assistance because a member of the household lost supplementary employment. Similarly, a 1935 WPA survey of rural areas with high relief rates found that in the Appalachian-Ozark region, which included the mountainous counties of northeast Tennessee, the main reason rural families gave for seeking relief was the loss of off-farm employment. In counties with little industrial development, families' lack of dependence on wage work translated to a lower rate of relief applications. For example, another 1934 FERA report found that only 12 percent of the families in Grainger County, Tennessee, were on the relief rolls. In contrast to Bledsoe County, which had some industrial development, Grainger County contained no incorporated town and few opportunities for off-farm work. The implication is that families engaged in subsistence farming may have fared somewhat better during the 1930s than families who had entered the wage economy part-time and had developed some dependence on a steady source of cash with which to buy goods and meet debts.[4]

Farm Women Cope With Crisis: Four Case Studies

Although the hardships faced by farm women varied depending on their race, class, and place in the life cycle, most farm women faced the same basic challenges: feeding and clothing a family with a sharply reduced cash income. An examination of the lives of four women illuminates the variety of strategies women used and the ways in which class and race shaped those strategies.

Carrie Jerome Anderson grew up on a prosperous cotton farm in York County, South Carolina. Her father worked his land with the help of two tenant farm families who lived on the place. He also owned a local drugstore and served as mayor of the town of Rock Hill during some of the depression years. Carrie Anderson recalled a comfortable childhood in a modern house complete with an indoor toilet. Her mother's burdens were eased with the help of a cook, a houseman who waited on them at the table and worked around the house, and a yard man who maintained their lawn and tended the stables. The family's laundry was even sent out to a local black woman. Even this prosperity did not mean that Mrs. Jerome was a woman of leisure. With the assistance of the yard man, she worked the family's vegetable garden, and she preserved all its produce with the help of the cook. She also made and mended much of the family's wardrobe, did much of the housecleaning, and cared for sick children and servants alike. As a white woman, Jerome benefited from access to cheap African American labor to help maintain her household and her husband's farm. The cash income from her husband's off-farm work, although reduced during the depression years, provided a modern house, money to send her children to school and later to college, and salaries for household help; but it did not relieve her from all the work of ensuring her family's survival.[5]

Delilah Woodruff's life was perhaps less comfortable, but her family used the mixed economy to great advantage. She raised four children in the hills and lumber camps of Sevier and Blount County, Tennessee, where her husband worked as a foreman building railroads for Little River Lumber Company. Except for periods when the family resided in lumber camps, they lived in a small, well-constructed cabin on their 20-acre farm outside the village of Pigeon Forge. Although there were periodic layoffs, Johnson's husband worked fairly steadily through the 1920s, managing to pay off their farm. Like most of the white women whose families eked out a living on farms and lumber camps, Woodruff learned to survive by growing or making most of the things her family needed. In this way she minimized cash expenditures, freeing up more of her husband's wages for investment in the farm. By the time of the stock market crash in 1929, Woodruff's children were grown and she was helping to raise her grandchildren.[6]

The onset of the Great Depression was a blow to the family. Delilah Woodruff and her husband lost all of their savings in the bank failures of the early 1930s. For some families, bank closures led to disastrous losses, but because the Woodruffs had no debts, the loss was not as tragic as it might have been for a poorer family. Nonetheless, the bank failure had a profound psychological impact. After that, the Woodruffs never trusted banks again, but they didn't stop saving money. The couple used every opportunity to earn a little extra, and they quickly recovered from the setback, partly because Delilah Woodruff often brought in extra income by keeping four or five boarders who worked in the lumber camps. Whenever she could earn some extra cash, she stashed it under her straw tick mattresses; and by 1938 the couple had accumulated enough cash to pay off their granddaughter's farm mortgage when the younger woman's husband lost his lumbering job.

In the meantime, Delilah Woodruff continued to care for her family in the same ways she always had: she grew and made nearly everything. She bartered eggs and butter for sugar, salt, and coffee. An avid gardener, she grew all of the family's vegetables as well as herbs that she used in her own home remedies. She preserved the year's fruits and vegetables by drying everything because glass jars were not yet available in the mountains. At hog killing time, she smoked hams and preserved sausage in corn shucks to provide her family with meat for the rest of the year. Her granddaughter joked that "she could use everything about a hog except its squeal." Delilah Woodruff could produce so much of the family's food precisely because she and her husband owned their land. Ownership meant that they made decisions about the allocation of resources for various products rather than being told by a landlord what to plant.

Land ownership was also key to Woodruff's ability to clothe her family and to engage in creative endeavors. Land provided space needed to graze sheep and cattle. She made all of the family's clothes, knitting their socks out of wool from her own sheep. At holiday time, she saw to it that her grandchildren received small gifts. Somehow she still found the time to make needlecraft heirlooms, many of them crocheted from string she had saved from feed sacks.[7]

Delilah Woodruff was not unusual. She coped with the hardships of the Great Depression by using the same strategies that had allowed the Woodruffs to save money and pay off debts during the 1920s: she minimized the need for cash by producing as much of the family's food, clothing, and supplies at home as possible and seized opportunities to earn extra cash at home. But Woodruff had several distinct advantages over many of her counterparts. First of all, by the time the Depression took hold, her children were grown. The availability of well-paying off-farm jobs for men, the types of jobs reserved for whites in the upcountry, enabled the Woodruffs to subsidize the farm with wage work. This in turn meant that she and her husband had been able to pay off their debts, an accomplishment that allowed them to subsist with limited cash through the worst of the hard times. Finally, land ownership provided them with the means to produce the things they needed.

Debt-free landowning also provided black women with the ability to survive the economic downturn. Nonetheless, racism created hardships that made a family's economic position more tenuous. Edna Spencer's great-grandparents raised three generations of their family in a solid, four-room frame house on the small farm they owned near Oak Ridge, Tennessee. Spencer's great-grandfather was a subsistence farmer who had been injured when a white co-worker on an electrical line crew, angry at the black man's independence, deliberately dropped a wrench on his head. The wound left him unable to do most wage work for many years. Since heavy labor was practically the only work available to blacks at the time, his ability to earn cash was seriously impaired.

Like the white women in the upcountry, Spencer's great-grandmother, known as "Mama" to the whole family, raised and preserved all of the family's food and made their clothing. In fact, Spencer saw an old iron kettle that sat in Mama's yard as symbolic of her great-grandmother's contributions to the family's support. Spencer recalled that Mama did everything in that kettle. She made soap in it and later used that soap to boil the family's laundry in the kettle. She also cooked hominy, a popular food made of corn processed in lye and preserved for the winter. At butchering time in the fall, she cooked sausage and rendered lard in that same kettle.

Not only did Mama provide a bountiful diet for her extended family, but she also took on the central role of providing them with psychological support. Edna Spencer believed that this was her great-grandmother's most important contribution because it provided her children and grandchildren with the self-esteem to resist white domination. Spencer remembered her great-grandmother as someone who would "take a stand against anyone who bothered her children or grandchildren." She indoctrinated young family members with the importance of education and made sure that all of the children attended school.

As was the case with many white families, Spencer's family adopted collective coping strategies. After raising their children, the couple raised grandchildren and great-grandchildren whose parents had died or moved North for better opportunities. Spencer herself spent her first six years in the care of her great-grandparents after her father's death sent her mother to live with relatives and enter domestic service in Worcester, Massachusetts.

Mama also functioned as the family money manager. The family did not put its savings in the bank, probably because they feared bank crashes or because there were no black-owned banks in East Tennessee. Instead, Mama secreted cash in a corner of her trunk—cash earned when she took in laundry, sold eggs, or picked strawberries for a local farmer, or cash earned by her husband or son in occasional off-farm jobs. Spencer recalled that there was always money for shoes each fall when the children returned to school. Furthermore, there was always cash for emergencies.[8]

Spencer recalled relatively little harassment of her land-owning great-grandparents because of their race. Overt action against black farm families was infrequent in the mountains as compared to the rest of the state. Except when they worked side by side with whites, as was the case of her great-grandfather on the electrical crew, there was little white violence against rural blacks. This may have been because there was less need for a class of dependent black farm laborers in East Tennessee, a region of subsistence farms best supported by maximizing "free" family labor. Nonetheless, race was a factor in creating Spencer's great-grandparents' depression-era hardships. Because of the racially motivated attack on her great-grandfather, he was unable to take off-farm jobs to supplement their farm production. The types of off-farm jobs available to southern black men and women were menial and paid little. Unlike many white families, they were unable to supplement their farm income with industrial wage labor because few factory jobs were available to blacks in East Tennessee.

The Spencers were able to maintain an adequate level of subsistence because they owned the land necessary to raise a garden and livestock. The case of Sena Lewellyn, a white woman from Sevier County, Tennessee, illustrates the difficulties created by losing land. Married in 1920 at the age of 15, Lewellyn settled on a hardscrabble mountain farm with her twenty-one-year-old husband, a farmer and occasional road construction worker. Unlike the small, sound house occupied by the Woodruffs, the Lewellyns lived in a ramshackle two-room cabin without weather sealing. Lewellyn recalled finding snow in the kitchen on the morning her oldest son was born in 1921. Like Delilah Woodruff, Sena Lewellyn also raised and preserved the family's food, made its clothing and household linens, and generally tried to get by without any cash. But things were much more difficult for a young family just starting out. For a couple with small children or no children, the labor demands of a small farm often outstripped the energies of a husband and wife.

The Lewellyns had no savings and no accumulation in the way of household or farm equipment. They needed more cash, which Winford Lewellyn attempted to earn through moonshining, a common strategy for many mountaineers in all three regions. Moonshining provided a more profitable means of disposing of a corn crop than hauling the grain over the mountains to market.[9] When revenue agents arrested him, Winford mortgaged his farm to pay his legal bills, and when he was convicted, the young family lost the land. The loss of the farm deprived Sena of both her home and the resources necessary to support herself and her son. Nor were there many job opportunities for a young mother with a baby to care for in isolated Sevier County. As a result, Sena Lewellyn spent a year living in the jail with her son and her husband, cooking for other prisoners in order to earn the little family's room and board.

After his release from jail, Winford Lewellyn had little choice but to seek an industrial job. In the mid-1920s, the young family moved to Blount County so that Winford Lewellyn could work for the Aluminum Company of America (ALCOA). In town, the family enjoyed low but

Fig. 6. Landless white and black women like this Chesnee, South Carolina, tenant farm wife had the smallest range of options for surviving the Great Depression on the land. (Dorothea Lange photograph. LC-USF34, 18130. Library of Congress.)

steady wages and better housing. Sena Lewellyn continued to raise a garden and preserve food, but the presence of a cash income made her life somewhat easier.

This stability was short-lived, however. Soon Winford was exhibiting the first symptoms of tuberculosis, symptoms exacerbated by working conditions at ALCOA. So he moved his family several miles from the small town of Maryville to a rented farm in southern Blount County. Here he and his brother tried to scrape out a living on marginal land, growing corn and tobacco. Sena Lewellyn again tried to provide all of her family's needs from the farm products. In the end, with Winford unable to work because of the disease, the family returned to the outskirts of Maryville. Here they lived with Sena's parents until Winford died in 1929.

Now Sena herself was forced to enter the job market to try to provide for two small sons. Fortunately, as a white woman, she had a broader range of options than Edna Spencer's great-grandmother would have had. First she worked in a hosiery mill in nearby Maryville; then the promise of better wages lured her to Standard Knitting Mills in Knoxville, fifteen miles away. She left the boys in the care of her parents and lived with a relative in Knoxville during the week, visiting her sons on weekends. The onset of the Depression ended her working days at Standard when the knitting mill cut its work force, leaving Sena little choice but to return home to her parents' subsistence farm.

Remarriage to a construction worker in 1931 did not immediately ease Sena's hardships, because her new husband also suffered periodic unemployment. Not only did Sena join her mother in subsistence production to support the large extended family, but she was also forced to turn to the government for help. She signed up for government commodity food distribution at the county courthouse. For Sena Lewellyn and her family, as for many families throughout the South, life did not really improve until World War II made new industrial opportunities available to them both inside and outside of the state.[10]

Sena Lewellyn's life illustrates the difficulties the economic downturn caused for young women facing the heavy burdens of supporting a new family. To deal with the crisis, Lewellyn adopted several common coping strategies. For young widows and other single mothers, one of these was taking industrial jobs, leaving their children in the care of other family members. (This coping strategy, however, was not available to black women, who were excluded from industrial jobs.) As was the case in other areas of the South hit hard by industrial unemployment, it was also common for East Tennessee families who lost their town jobs to return to family farms during the Depression. The farm offered a roof over one's head and some measure of subsistence. This practice resulted in overcrowding in farm homes and strains on already thinly stretched resources, particularly the overworking of worn-out soil. But for some families, it was the only viable option.

The work of each of these women was essential in helping her family through the depression years. USDA studies corroborate the importance of women's subsistence activities in reducing the need for cash outlays on upcountry farms. For example, in a 1926 study of 861 white farm families in Tennessee, Kentucky, and Texas, USDA economists found that the average family provided over 60 percent of its own food, saving more than $400 a year that would otherwise have been spent on groceries.

A family's ability to provide its own food increased in proportion to its economic resources, particularly possession of land and the accompanying control over decisions about how to use that land. Owner families, who consumed goods valued at $1,635 (household average), furnished 66 percent of their own food; while sharecropper families, who consumed goods valued at only $946, furnished only 47 percent of their own food. In other words, families with the resources to buy garden seed, livestock, and fertilizer were able to save more cash by producing more of their own needs on the farm. Prosperous families would have been able to buy a greater variety of products with what cash they did have available because they were producing more of their basic needs themselves.[11]

Ironically, farm owners not only produced more of their own needs, but they also had more children than tenant families. One study in Tennessee and West Virginia found that about one third of rural women, particularly educated women, made some attempt to limit their family size, usually for medical and economic reasons. Condoms and douching were the most common methods of birth control. Most family farms, however, depended on the free labor of family members in order to expand and prosper. As a result, new babies were not simply additional mouths to feed but were also important resources. Young families without children old enough to assist with farm work, like Sena Lewellyn and her husband, found it difficult to accumulate capital and land or even to survive. Tennessee Valley Authority (TVA) relocation workers often found families with eight or more living children. In 1925 the average upcountry farm family contained 4.64 people. Middle-aged parents had more children left at home than young or elderly parents. African Americans did not have significantly more children than whites: the average upcountry black family had 4.8 members, while the average white family had 4.6 members. Farm owners, however, had more children than tenants, averaging 5.5 and 4.5 family members respectively. This suggests that the additional labor provided by an additional child may have helped the family accumulate capital in the form of land.[12]

Divisions of Labor as a Coping Strategy

All these children created an almost overwhelming burden of child care for farm women on top of an endless round of hard physical labor. Following the example of previous generations of farm women, upcountry farm wives coped with the tremendous workloads by devising various divisions of household labor. Mothers put their older children to work early on. East Tennessean Eva Finchum recalled standing on a chair at around the age of six in order to reach the counter so that she could bake bread while her mother worked in the fields. Even at this young age, Finchum took the loaves in and out of the hot wood stove herself. West Virginian Maude Chadwick recalled that her mother stayed busy with cooking, child care, and household tasks, leaving the garden and field work to her husband, four sons, and five daughters. Maude Walker was the oldest daughter among ten children in a very prosperous East Tennessee farm family. Prosperity did not, however, lighten her workload. From the time she was twelve years old, she cooked breakfast for the entire family, including farmhands, and then got the younger children and herself off to school. When asked why she took on so much responsibility, she replied that her mother was "always having another baby." Similarly, Wilma Williamson recalled that her grandmother had provided most of her care while her mother was having babies and that Wilma herself was involved in helping to care for the younger siblings.[13]

Grown female children also continued to provide essential help for the family. East Tennessean Korola Lee recalled that her parents did not ask her and her younger sister to contribute their schoolteaching salaries to help out at home. Instead, "we used our legs and arms [to help]." They worked in the fields as well as in the house. She and her sister got their college degrees in summer school at an East Tennessee University, alternating summers so that one of them would always be home to help out.[14]

An innovative division of labor seemed to be especially helpful in households where the presence of more than one adult woman threatened to create tensions over territory. TVA relocation records and oral histories often note the presence of several grown women in a household and the resulting division of responsibilities. Laverne Farmer's parents and grandparents ran a commercial dairy operation in Townsend, Tennessee. They processed milk and butter from their own cows and sold it

Fɪɢ. 7. Women performed a full range of tasks on upcountry farms. Here the women of the Stooksberry family boil sorghum into molasses on their Anderson County, Tennessee, farm. (Lewis W. Hine photograph, October 1933. NWDNS-142-H-22. Courtesy of Still Picture Branch, National Archives at College Park.)

in Townsend and Maryville. For many years, Laverne's parents lived in her grandparents' house. Her mother did the housework and cooking for the family and the hired help, while her grandmother processed milk. In this way, the work got done without creating any competition between mother-in-law and daughter-in-law. A similar situation existed in Jessie Felknor's household because her husband's sister lived with them. The two women worked out a division of labor in which the sister-in-law cooked breakfast while Jessie and her husband milked each morning. The two women took weekly turns at cooking the family's other meals. The Walker sisters of Little Greenbrier Cove in Sevier County, Tennessee, used a similar strategy to divide the work in their household. The five unmarried sisters lived alone in their cabin after their father's death in 1921. Margaret, the oldest sister, served as the "final decision maker," according to the sisters' account. Each sister was responsible for specific chores. Nancy, who was asthmatic, did most of the housework, while the others spent most of their time in the fields and gardens. Martha did domestic work for nearby families and sometimes stayed with families for short periods to care for sick people. In this way, she brought some cash income to the household. This division of labor took advantage of each sister's special needs, skills, and preferences in order to prevent conflict within the household.[15]

Women in the Fields

As the lives of these women indicate, many farm women were actively involved in farm work as well as housework. The gendered division of labor was negotiated differently on each farm, depending on the disposition of both the husband and wife, the power dynamics of the household, and demands for labor. Some women rejected field and farmyard work outright. West Virginian America Jarrell preferred to stick to housework. She told an interviewer, "Before I was married I said [to my husband], 'I'm going to ask you one thing. . . . You are going to stay out of my kitchen. . . . You keep your horses at the barn and I'll never go about them. . . . My place is in here, that is your place out there with the horses.'" Other women performed tasks usually designated as men's work out of necessity. Hettie Lawson was forced to take over field work and care of the livestock on their upland Tennessee farm whenever her husband was employed off the farm in "public" jobs, such as stints with the Civilian Conservation Corps (CCC) and ALCOA. Wanda Brummitt recalled that her grandmother would take a team of mules into the woods where she would cut a tree and saw it up for firewood. She also did field work, even heavy plowing, while Brummitt's grandfather worked in the coal mines of upper East Tennessee. Gladys Trentham Russell recalled that her mother regularly worked in the family cornfields on their Tennessee mountain farm.[16]

Not all women did field work out of necessity. Some women preferred the field work to housework, contrary to the gendered division of labor being promoted by USDA officials and farm magazines at the time. TVA relocation workers sometimes commented that the farm women they interviewed stated a preference for outdoor work. East Tennessean Della Sarten remembered that she had enjoyed milking and working in tobacco. She would often get up early and put food on to cook for the day before going to the fields. Eva Finchum recalled that her mother was delighted when her children became old enough to look after themselves and do the housework. "I think she enjoyed outside work more," Finchum explained.[17]

Although farm women often engaged in field work out of necessity or choice, farming folk had very definite ideas about the types of outdoor work appropriate for women. Alice Hardin's mother hoed and picked cotton on their South Carolina sharecropping plot. Hardin recalled that local folk considered hoeing and picking "women's work," while the heavier task of plowing was "men's work." For many families the ability to spare women from some types of field work was a source of pride, symbolic of a certain level of prosperity. White sharecroppers Marshall and Edna Webb of Spartanburg County, South Carolina, had seven daughters and three sons, a gender balance that left them dependent on the labor of their daughters as well as their sons in their cotton fields. Nonetheless, their daughters reported that Marshall and Edna Webb strictly limited the types of work the girls would do. They could hoe or pick cotton but never plow. Plowing with a mule was the hardest of field chores, requiring considerable physical strength. It was a task associated with white men or with African Americans of either sex, and it was a point of pride with this white sharecropper that he could spare his women from that kind of labor. He was able to do so largely because his brother sharecropped on an adjacent farm, and the two exchanged labor. By the time the oldest Hardin girls could remember details of family life, their mother did not do field work of any type. She spent her time on housework, child care, and an enormous amount of home food production. Her daughters reported that she put up between 500 and 1,000 quarts of blackberries a season, in addition to other foods. Other mothers sought to protect their daughters from the burdens of farm work. Missionary John C. Campbell recalled a mountain woman who told him, "I don't aim to learn my girls how to milk. If they learn how, they'll have hit to do."[18]

Just as white farm folk had distinct ideas about the field work appropriate for women, they were clear that men should not do housework. The flexibility in the gendered division of labor found on many farms rarely extended to males. West Virginian J. C. Kessell recalled that while the girls and women in his family were sometimes expected to do farm

work, the "boys never was required to do any housework such as washing dishes or washing clothes or anything like that." Still, this prohibition
on men doing "women's" work was not a hard-and-fast rule. In one
Tennessee family, a son became a proficient and artistic quilter, while his
sisters preferred outdoor work, something no one in the family seemed to
think particularly alarming.[19]

Belying our mental picture of farm wives as willing helpers to their
farmer husbands, some farm women carried the major part of the farm
work load because their husbands were unwilling or unable to farm.
Evelyn Lewellyn recalled that her "Aunt Babe did the farming while
Uncle Moss watched." Lewellyn characterized her uncle as a man who
disliked manual labor. Similarly, Lizzie Broyles recalled that her husband
John "didn't know nothin' about farming. . . . I had to do it all." She raised
tobacco and wheat crops on their Limestone, Tennessee, farm. For these
women the fact that the family owned farmland made farming a logical
choice, but their husbands' inability or unwillingness to perform farm
labor left them responsible for the farm operation.[20]

Not only did upcountry farm women engage in tasks traditionally
considered men's work, but often they were also asked to take on tasks
that were part of their husbands' paid jobs, indicating that earning cash
was considered to be a priority for the entire family. Effie Temple kept the
books for the milling company her husband managed in Sevier County,
Tennessee. He would often leave her in charge at the mill while he
worked on the family farm. Arthur Tipton's father was the head dairy-
man on the farm of a state senator in Loudon County during the early
1930s. In return for his $60 salary each month, Tipton and his sons were
expected to work on the farm, and his wife and daughters were expected
to assist the senator's wife with housework. Jessie Felknor's mother
cooked lunch daily for patrons of her husband's grist mill. Edwin Best's
mother worked at his father's rural general store during the busy Christmas shopping season.[21]

Some of these shifts in the gendered division of labor for rural families grew out of the changes in the agricultural economy. Men and
women alike recognized and appreciated the fact that farm women's
subsistence labor was essential to the family economy even as rising taxes
and increasing indebtedness forced members of both sexes to seek new
ways to earn cash. Without consciously devaluing women's traditional

housekeeping and reproductive work, men and women alike believed that men should focus more on market activities. Rural people saw the transformation to commercial agriculture looming on the horizon and recognized that capital was the key to participating in the new rural economic order. For this reason, women shouldered much of the burden for subsistence deliberately, in order to free men to engage in market activities. While for the poorest farm women taking on field work was often a matter of necessity, many more prosperous women used the shifts in the economy to carve out new roles for themselves, roles that appealed to their own preferences.

When Hard Work Was Not Enough

For many rural women, flexibility in the gendered assignment of tasks and redoubled coping efforts were enough to insure that their families survived the economic downturns of the 1920s and 1930s. But for other women, poverty, the loss of a farm or a mate, or a husband's inability to find work multiplied the economic hardships almost beyond tolerance. Everett Hobbs's father died when he was only a baby. His mother survived by renting most of the East Tennessee farm to another farmer and by raising the family's own food. She managed to keep her three children in school until they graduated from high school. Fay Ball's mother continued to run the family's Culloden, West Virginia, farm after Fay's father's death. She and the five children still living at home managed a subsistence living on their hilly parcel of land.[22]

Nor was widowhood the only way in which farm women lost their mates. In 1939 Mrs. Bonnie Faulkner of Washington County, Tennessee, appealed to Eleanor Roosevelt for assistance in obtaining a WPA job after her husband deserted her and their three children. Similarly, Wilma Fisher recalled that her maternal grandmother, a resident of Meigs County, Tennessee, had a particularly difficult time. The mother of four children, she was periodically abandoned by Fisher's grandfather, who, in despair over his inability to find a job, rode the rails as a hobo and gambled, leaving his wife to get by as well as she could. It was a very hard life for the young family. At one point in the 1930s, Fisher's grandmother nearly died from a tubal pregnancy, but a kind neighbor took her to the hospital and paid for her surgery. The neighbor allowed her and the children to work on his farm in order to repay him. Later she got a job forty miles away in Sweetwater at a laundry where she earned five cents an hour. Boarding with her sister during the week, she caught a ride home on the mail truck each weekend, carrying a week's supply of groceries with her. The oldest daughter, who was not yet a teenager, was left in charge of the children while their mother was away. Often the daughter took the baby to school with her. It was the mid-1930s before Fisher's grandfather finally got a WPA job and began to stay home and, in Fisher's words, "help out."[23]

Although the poorest women had the most difficult time during the depression years, more prosperous farm families also faced hardships and adjustments. Often these hardships caused shifts in household power relations as was the case in 1931 when, due to investment losses, Minnie Delozier's father-in-law lost the Loudon County, Tennessee, farm that had been in the Delozier family for four generations. Minnie and her husband managed to scrape together a down payment and obtain a mortgage so that they could hang on to the ancestral home. Doing so required them to avoid spending money on home improvements for a number of years as they tried to raise a family and pay for the farm. But the belt-tightening experienced by the younger woman would have been much less devastating than the older woman's feeling of dependency on her son and daughter-in-law. When the young couple bought the farm, the parents clearly became dependent on them for housing and support. This apparently distressed the elders, because years later Minnie's husband recalled that his wife had tried to reassure her father-in-law, "This will be home for as long as you want it to be." The elder Deloziers lived in the family home until their deaths in the 1940s and 1950s. They had expected midlife to be a time of relative financial security, but instead they found themselves dependent on their children. This situation undermined their authority in their own household, which must have been devastating to them.[24]

For some city families with farming backgrounds, the farm proved to be a refuge from the economic downturn. As Sena Lewellyn had done, families often returned to the farm, where at least food was plentiful, when it became too difficult to make ends meet in town. When the Depression struck, other families, disillusioned by the lack of security offered by wage labor, used savings accumulated during more prosperous years to return to the land. Georgia Thomas recalled that when her father was laid off from the Southern Railway in the early 1930s, her parents used their savings to buy a farm near Sweetwater, Tennessee. The family was able to raise their children in a comfortable farmhouse there for nine years until the father was called back to his job with the railroad. "My mother always considered being on the farm a blessing with four small boys and three daughters to keep up with," Thomas says of the experience.[25]

The adjustment to country life was not so smooth for other former city dwellers. On two separate occasions in the 1930s, Evelyn Lewellyn's father was unable to pay the rent on the family apartment in Knoxville because he earned too little in his work as a musical evangelist. As a result, he moved the family back to his ancestral home in Anderson County, Tennessee. The farmhouse was a tiny, dilapidated log cabin with no electricity or indoor plumbing, amenities that Lewellyn's city-born mother had never done without. Lewellyn recalled that the chinking in the logs was so badly cracked that daylight shone between the logs into the cabin and that snakes often crawled into the house. To compound the hardship, her father returned to work in the city during the week, leaving her mother on the isolated farm with the children.[26]

Mutual Aid Strategies

As the lives of these women reveal, although various factors determined the severity of the depression years for East Tennessee farm women, their individual survival strategies were remarkably similar. To cope with the economic downturn, upcountry women learned to stretch already scarce household resources, shifted the divisions of household and farm labor, and shared resources with extended family members. The region's rural women also drew on traditional strategies of mutual aid for survival, strategies that were an extension of earlier community-based social welfare efforts. From the time of white settlement, the small communities of the rural South had always "looked after their own" informally, rejecting the aid of government agencies. A gospel of hard work meant that community members who were perceived as idle were scorned, yet industrious workers who fell on hard times were eagerly assisted. Rural people depended on kin and neighbors for many of the necessities of daily life. Although some of these rural social relationships were organized through formal social institutions such as schools and churches, the most significant social networks were informal relationships of reciprocity. Women were the backbone of these informal support networks.

For rural women, who rarely controlled land or other economic resources, mutual aid networks were an important source of power. By developing reciprocal relationships with neighbors and kin, women could gain access to other resources that helped offset their lack of legal control of family resources. Women organized gender-integrated formal rituals such as Christmas pageants and revivals, based in community institutions such as the school and church, as well as seasonal labor exchanges and informal visiting networks to create larger communities that shared resources of labor and goods. These exchanges also helped balance economic inequalities between the prosperous and the poorer families in communities. By pooling labor at harvest time, or food in case of economic crisis, communities shared their resources and aided poorer families in survival.[27]

Labor exchanges were the most common mutual aid strategies. West Virginian Fay Ball recalled that at threshing time local men helped each other with the harvest while "us women would all go to the other women's houses and help 'um cook for the thrashing machine men." She noted that on one occasion men from neighboring farms were away working on temporary jobs in a natural gas field, so the women took their places at harvest time. Ruby Booth's Lincoln County, West Virginia, neighbors assisted with cornhusking, barn building, and hog killing. Sylvia Sowards' neighbors also gathered to share women's work at quilting bees and apple peeling parties, preparing large quantities of apples for use in apple butter.[28]

Labor exchanges were not the only basis of ties among women and families. Naomi Banks Bridges recalled that when her father inherited his parents' South Carolina farm and set up his own farming operation, a neighbor gave him ten or fifteen chickens with which to begin the family's flock. She noted that "it was a generous neighborhood. . . . People down there had more . . . generosity than they had money." She added that when a new family moved in, "they was so glad to get more people into the neighborhood that they had housewarmings" complete with gifts. In later years when new people moved into the neighborhood, her own family carried on the tradition by giving them pigs or chickens. Similarly, social and visiting networks often provided social welfare services. East Tennessee schoolteacher Korola Lee recalled that the social events she organized to raise funds for her two-room school were popular not only with the parents of her pupils but also among the people of the community. Visiting was a favorite rural pastime that helped cement mutual aid networks. Laverne Farmer recalled that neighbors passing by her family's home on the way to the store or church would often stop in to visit. Visiting after supper was also common. People played checkers and listened to battery-powered radios to pass the time.[29]

These informal social events, usually organized by the women of the community, served to maintain the ties among neighbors that translated into mutual aid in times of crisis. East Tennessean Laverne Farmer and West Virginian Sylvia Sowards both recalled that if a family was having a tough time due to an illness or a death in the family, neighbors pitched in to do housework and fieldwork, to provide food, or to prepare for a funeral. Farmer explained: "If there was serious sickness or deaths or needs in the community, the neighbors would . . . just go, no matter how much work they had to do. You know, it was just kindly an extended family. If people around needed things, why, they'd help each other out. But back then I don't recall anybody being much poorer than anybody else. They just shared what they had."[30]

Informal mutual aid networks such as the one in Farmer's community provided families with a social circle in good times and a "safety net" in times of need. As Farmer suggested, among families who shared a similar social status, these networks served to minimize the differences among families created by varying levels of economic prosperity.

The support of mutual aid networks went beyond food, labor, and household goods to the sharing of financial resources when necessary. Some families who nearly lost their farms found that it was the generosity of neighbors and family members that saved them from certain disaster. A 1924 *Maryville Times* story called for community contributions to aid East Tennessean Mrs. Clyde Poe and her baby after her husband was shot to death by an intruder in their home. A follow-up story reported on the outpouring of support. Similarly, Ethel Davis recalled that she and her husband were on the verge of losing their dairy farm to creditors in the late 1930s when a neighbor got wind of their predicament and loaned them the money to pay off their mortgage.[31]

Although these examples suggest that mutual aid networks minimized class boundaries, this was not always the case. Rural women often helped those who were less fortunate, but the amounts and types of aid they could offer were determined by how much they had to share. Resources were in turn shaped by class and racial factors. Prosperous rural white women had more to share than poor black and white women, and their aid was sometimes undertaken as charity rather than as mutual assistance.

During the depression years, many rural East Tennessee women aided downtrodden strangers. Unlike hardworking but unlucky neighbors, who would return some favor in a future exchange, these objects of rural charity were often seen, at best, as unfortunate victims, and at worst, as shiftless folk in need of care from their social betters. Rural women often fed the hoboes that were ubiquitous features of the Great Depression. French Clark lived near a railroad stop, and hoboes came to her door looking for food almost daily. "They'd get off them trains and come out to the house to get something to eat," she recounted. "I grabbed what I had. If it wasn't nothing but bread, I'd grab it and give it to them. I know one day one came out there and wanted something to eat, and I put something in a poke [a paper bag] and give it to him and looked out and they was five in a boxcar with their heads sticking out you know. He took it out there and divided it with them." Clark recalled that on another occasion a hobo came to her door before dawn, scaring her. She gave him her children's breakfast. West Virginian Lucy White shared similar memories. "Lots of people didn't have any work," she recalled. "They was beggars. I never turned anybody away from the door." These women, wives of struggling but middling white rural men, saw this sharing as charity rather than mutual aid.[32]

These charitable actions often reflected the legacy of Southern paternalism, a belief that social "betters" had some responsibility to aid the poor and downtrodden and that in return the poor and downtrodden would show appropriate respect and deference to their benefactors. The wife of a prosperous white Blount County, Tennessee, farm owner would buy fabric and make dresses and shirts for the children of white tenants on the family farm. She would cut their hair and get them "cleaned up" to start school each year. Unfortunately, the children often disappointed her by dropping out after the first week, failing to live up to their benefactor's expectations by succeeding in school.[33]

Like the children this farm wife assisted, some poor women found that neighbors' well-meaning kindness was accompanied by attempts to impose the values of middling rural folk on their poorer neighbors. Gladys Trentham Russell recalled her mother's efforts to befriend a homeless woman who made the rounds of mountain cabins in the Great Smoky Mountains looking for assistance:

> One "lady tramp" made a habit of stopping by our house two or three times a year. She had illegitimate children and was a genuine early twentieth-century hippie of smelly rank. We always opened up a canvas army cot and put the wagon tarpaulin on it for her bed, which was better than what she had at home. It was apparent Ma had lost all patience with her as she combed the woman's natty hair one morning. Ma lectured her on the merits of cleanliness and of trying to be somebody. As soon as Ma finished the rough treatment, the woman jerked up her little son Jessie by the arm and headed down the road.[34]

For women like this "lady tramp," independence may have been more important than falling under the influence of well-meaning neighbors in exchange for material comfort, while for women like Trentham's mother, such interference was a way of reinforcing her position as a virtuous middling farm wife.

Middling rural families saw their ability to give to others as a mark of their status. East Tennessean John West recalled assisting a young father who came to his door during the Depression, begging for food for three small children. West explained why he gave the man food: "I didn't really need it; I had a little backlog coming in all the time, you know, out of my chickens and cream and stuff. . . . I don't think you lose anything by being good to people." In West's eyes, simple charity was an act of human decency, but the act also symbolized his own success and prosperity.[35]

Elite and middling attitudes toward charity often extended to their poorly-paid domestic and agricultural laborers. Many elite white women implicitly recognized their own exploitation of household help by tolerating petty theft. Carrie Jerome Anderson noted that her mother ignored it when her black household servants smuggled out loads of wood and farm produce underneath the family's laundry. She chuckled, "They always had other things under there. They considered that they was just dividing things up a little bit." Her mother's decision to ignore the theft was a tacit acknowledgment of the poverty of her employees and also probably an excuse for continuing to pay low wages.[36]

Not only did women use informal mutual aid relationships to delineate and reinforce class hierarchies in rural communities, but they also attempted to strengthen racial lines through these interactions. A look at the relationships between rural midwives and the women they assisted offers insight into the tensions inherent in rural race relations. Sometimes racial boundaries proved impermeable, but more often the dependency of a childbearing woman led women to cross racial boundaries, if only temporarily.

Childbearing and child rearing were especially perilous pursuits for women on isolated farms far from medical care. The work load of farm women also made it difficult to take proper care of themselves during pregnancy and after childbirth. East Tennessean Eva Finchum recalled that when she was pregnant, "I worked right on, just like I always did." By the 1920s, some rural women had access to doctors whom their husbands fetched from town or called from the home of the nearest neighbor with a phone. Other women used midwives either because midwives were the only care providers available, because they were cheaper, or because they preferred midwives. Finchum noted that she used a doctor with her first baby but preferred a midwife with the other two because the doctor "tried to take [my son] with forceps" and bruised his head. The doctor was in a hurry, according to Finchum, "because it was night, and he was wanting to get back to bed." Midwives were noted for taking their time and letting birth occur naturally.[37]

Midwives were the primary childbirth attendants in the isolated and poor upland counties. Many attended hundreds of women. White midwife Etta Grigsby Nichols delivered 1,026 babies in the mountain coves around Del Rio, Tennessee. Midwives usually charged less, and they often stayed on several days to provide care to the mother and the newborn. West Virginian Bertha Mae Asbury noted that the midwife who delivered two of her babies stayed about three days after the birth, assist-

ing her with cooking and caring for the baby. Midwives taught uneducated women about sanitary conditions needed to keep a baby healthy.
Lizzie Broyles, another white midwife, recalled that she often had to give
clothing, towels, and washcloths to the poor women she delivered. She
stayed a few days after the birth, doing the family's washing, cooking,
and cleaning. A black Carter County, Tennessee, midwife who delivered
over a thousand babies, mostly for poor white families, recalled that she
often had to make women clean up their homes in the weeks before they
gave birth.[38]

The Carter County midwife's experience also sheds light on the complexities of race relations within rural women's mutual support networks. Although most women and most midwives were white, black
midwives served poor white women who had no other options, and
white midwives served black women upon occasion. This study found
no evidence that midwives charged differential fees based on race or that
they ever refused to attend a childbirth for a woman because of racial
differences. Likewise, caring for ill community members also sometimes
transcended racial lines. East Tennessean Edna Spencer recalled that her
great-grandmother took turns with white neighbors sitting up with a
white woman who was sick. Later the illness of a black woman led some
white women to return the favor by taking their turns sitting with her.
The closeness of the community led blacks and whites to deal with each
other as individuals instead of as representatives of a racial group, at least
in times of crisis. As Spencer put it, "Outsiders would have some difficulty with this. It's best understood when you realize that there were
good people in that Valley, and they came in more than one color." When
it came to childbearing and illness, women of both races reluctantly recognized some limited sisterhood.[39]

Nonetheless, subtle racial resentments often entered into these interactions. White women, in particular, resented their dependence on a
black midwife and were incensed when a black woman gave them orders. The Carter County midwife recalled with amusement that her insistence on cleanliness often infuriated white mothers-to-be. She overheard
one woman say, "She's the most independent black woman I ever seen.
She thinks she's something because she's a midwife and a nurse." Her
patient resented taking orders from a black woman she considered to be

her inferior, believing that her position as midwife allowed her to step "out of her place." Midwifery not only gave women a powerful sense of providing a needed service to other women, but it could give black women a sense of power denied them in most other arenas.[40]

In spite of the tensions inherent in interracial midwife-mother relationships, for rural women of both races, midwives provided medical help that was not accessible or that they could not otherwise afford. Most rural counties had very few doctors, and those they did have were concentrated in towns. Particularly in the upland counties, doctors were often too far away to attend deliveries, even when they were willing. "Folks was just so glad to have me; it was just impossible to get a doctor from Newport," recalled Cocke County, Tennessee, midwife Mrs. Arthur Smith. Midwives were also cheaper than doctors and often accepted farm commodities as payment. Some, such as Lizzie Broyles, even delivered babies at no charge. Etta Grigsby Nichols charged only $3 for deliveries throughout most of the 1930s.[41]

As these fees demonstrate, midwives were not primarily motivated by money. In some counties doctors refused to attend rural women, but in others physicians resented midwives for undercutting their business. An unidentified midwife who practiced somewhere in northeastern Tennessee told an oral history interviewer: "The doctors was hard down on midwives because these midwives, some of 'em would go for nothing; some would go for 50 cents or a dollar, whatever they could get. Well, I went the same way; if anybody didn't have nothing to pay me, I went anyway. It didn't make no difference." Many midwives were motivated by a desire to assist other women as well as by the opportunity to earn some income. Their services were an extension of a long tradition of mutual aid among rural women.[42]

Churches and Rural Women

Rural women not only constructed informal mutual aid networks through social circles, labor exchanges, and even midwifery, but they also offered assistance to their neighbors through formal organizations such as schools and churches. Although churches have traditionally been seen as social centers for rural communities, in many rural neighborhoods and towns barriers based on racial, class, and gender distinctions appeared in sharp relief within the churches.

The Depression took a great toll on southern churches. Declining attendance and division had plagued white churches for much of the twentieth century, and poverty and unemployment exacerbated the problem. Upcountry congregations found it difficult to pay ministers, and services were often infrequent. Largely due to a lack of resources and to class divisions among denominations, white churches played negligible roles in local relief efforts. As was the case throughout the South, most of the churches in the upcountry were racially segregated. Although black churches suffered greater poverty and hardship than white churches, under the leadership of black women, black churches organized the bulk of local relief efforts to the black community.[43]

Varying styles and standards in some denominations worked to discourage white church attendance. Evangelical denominations, such as Methodists and Baptists, had dominated Southern life since the early nineteenth century, but they began to lose their evangelical fervor by the early twentieth century as church hierarchies became established. Theological historians have pointed out that southern evangelicals tended to see the conversion experience as the end of the church's responsibility to the individual, and this translated into an emphasis on developing the church as a local institution and into somewhat limited mission work in the home community. Cabell County, West Virginia, resident Alice Hall noted that her church did not assist families during the Great Depression. Instead, "if our neighbors needed anything, why, the neighbors all pitched in and done for 'um."[44]

By the early twentieth century, many local churches were dominated by prosperous elite members, especially in rural towns. These class divisions became more pronounced with the onset of economic crisis. Bill Lewellyn recalled that his mother was a Baptist but that she stopped going to church during the 1930s. Although Sena Lewellyn Fagg sent her children to the Baptist Sunday school regularly, "she didn't attend church because her and Frank [her second husband] didn't have good enough clothes to wear, you know." Like informal mutual aid networks, churches could help define and reinforce class boundaries. This seemed especially true of Baptist, Methodist, and Presbyterian churches in small towns such as Alcoa, where Lewellyn's family lived. In this Baptist church, fashionable clothing was symbolic of social status, and those who were not able to dress as fashionably as the elite church leaders did not feel welcome or comfortable.[45]

Sena Lewellyn Fagg had a very different experience a few years later when she switched denominations. As her son recalled, "She finally started going to the Church of God. Her clothes were good enough to go there, I reckon." The Pentecostal Church of God, founded in East Tennessee's Monroe County in 1886, provided a place where Lewellyn felt that her contributions were welcomed in spite of her poverty. The Pentecostal movement began as an interracial revival meeting among poor and powerless Los Angeles workers in 1906. This democratic denomination, with its emphasis on religious spirit and a personal experience with God rather than on doctrinal purity, spread rapidly among disenfranchised people all over the country. Although the denomination became racially segregated as it entered the American South, Pentecostals preached a gospel of spiritual equality regardless of economic status. They promised that God was going to give the rich and poor their just rewards and that rich and poor, black and white, men and women were all the same before God. The Church of God was highly critical of mainstream denominations, which they accused of accommodating degenerate urban industrial mores.[46]

For Sena Lewellyn Fagg and many other poor women, Pentecostal churches offered a sense of power and hope in a powerless and hopeless time. These new denominations became the center of social and mutual aid activities. Pentecostalism appealed largely to women, who became the primary carriers of the new faith. Women used the Pentecostal idea of a personal blessing from God, signified by speaking in tongues and other physical manifestations of the Holy Spirit, to justify their assumption of leadership roles in the local church. Sena Lewellyn Fagg took an active role in organizing the new church and helped raise funds for the construction of a church building by selling her handmade quilts. In this denomination, poor women were able to take an active role in building a community. Their worth as community members was determined, not by symbolic criteria such as clothing, but by their own labor and their piety.

Among Pentecostals, many of East Tennessee's most deprived families found a sense of belonging.[47]

Class and race were not the only divisive force in rural southern churches during the 1920s and 1930s. Church teachings sometimes divided communities along gender lines. In the mining and farming communities near the Tennessee-Kentucky border, conservative ministers were often highly critical of the hard-living miner/farmers of the area. Herbert Douglas recalled that the churches in the Jellico community were very strict, especially in forbidding drinking and dancing. As a result, "mostly the women and kids went to church while the men got drunk." In this community and many others, the values espoused by the church were "women's values," and church work was "women's work." Masculinity was defined by behaviors that ran counter to church teachings, such as drinking and carousing. Tensions between women and men, tensions that may have originated in economic hardships and power relationships within the family, were played out in their conflicts over church attendance.[48]

In spite of class and gender divisions within the churches, they remained a significant social center for many women. Revivals and camp meetings were popular events. The only organized activities in which the Walker sisters of Greenbrier Cove, Tennessee, participated were church-related. They attended services at Little Greenbrier Primitive Baptist Church and also enjoyed shaped-note singing, a mountain tradition that uses shaped notes to allow people who cannot read music to follow the melody.* Church provided the opportunity for the sisters to leave their isolated home once a year when they attended a church conference in another East Tennessee town. West Virginian Alice Hall recalled that weekly church services were an important social event in her community. She and her siblings would attend the Methodist Sunday school on Sunday morning and the Baptist one in the afternoon. The two churches held worship services on alternate Sunday evenings so people could attend at both churches.[49]

---

*A triangular-shaped note, for example, told the singer to hit a particular location on the musical scale, while a square note denoted a different location on the scale. Shaped-note singing was popular among rural evangelists because it was easy to teach musically untrained audiences to read shaped-note scores.

Intensified Mutual Aid Efforts

The onset of the Depression created new needs and new efforts by rural women. The number of organized mutual aid projects increased in the early 1930s as did coverage of these efforts in local newspapers. In 1931 in Blount County, Tennessee, the town-based Red Cross chapter formed a committee of twelve middling and elite women from the town and the outlying rural areas to raise funds for drought relief and to find jobs for the unemployed. Subsequent newspaper stories indicated that the women had some limited success in obtaining donations but little luck in locating jobs. In Spartanburg County, South Carolina, two farmers' wives, Mrs. Fred Brown of Pacolet and Mrs. Sam Irby of Woodruff, spearheaded the Red Cross's winter fund drive for unemployment relief in their respective rural communities.[50]

During the early 1930s, the Hoover administration launched a campaign to enlist all rural people in the relief campaign. Farm women were urged to donate surplus food for relief efforts. In December 1931, the President's Organization on Unemployment Relief and the Committee on the Mobilization of Relief Resources placed an ad in the *Farm Journal*. The copy asked farm women to build on long traditions of rural relief to help those devastated by the economic downturn. Using the patriotic language of a righteous war, the administration called on rural women to do their duty for their country:

CERTAINLY WE WILL LEND A HAND

Grandmother never waited! When a neighbor's wife was having a baby and the doctor couldn't get there, grandmother put on her bonnet and shawl!

Mother never waited! When the neighbor's house burned down in the night, mother opened her door. She said, "Come right in."

The instinct to help is *in your blood.*

A few valleys away may be folks who need your helping hand now.

By giving generously you will have your share in a great common achievement. America is marshaling her forces to deal a death blow to depression. She is setting an example to the world. She is laying the firm foundation for better days for all.

The ad went on to ask farm women to donate canned goods and clothing to local relief agencies. The illustration that accompanied the ad depicted a homemaker in a matronly dress surveying ceiling-high pantry shelves lined with glass jars of farm produce. The agency was calling on a long rural tradition of neighbors helping one another to encourage farm women to assist their cause. Articles in farm magazines, extension service records, and even the USDA annual reports noted the extensive efforts of farm women who were donating canned goods to schools, to relief organizations, and to neighbors.[51]

Women not only joined forces to aid the needy but also united informally in efforts to improve community life. Women often spearheaded efforts to upgrade the local schools. In 1929 East Tennessee's *Maryville Times* reported that "the women who made up the PTA at one county (rural) school* opposed local government spending for a new municipal power plant until local schools were improved." Similarly, Mary Evelyn Lane recalled that women in one Blount County community joined together to organize a hot lunch program in their rural elementary school. The local farm women assembled periodically to can surplus garden produce for the school's use. The school also received government commodity foods for the lunchroom. A hired cook provided hot meals for students each day. German-American cooks in the Cumberland Mountain community of Allardt, Tennessee, started a similar program but did it without any government funding. The Allardt women did not receive any county dollars to hire a cook, so they took turns doing the cooking themselves. In 1935 the Spartanburg County, South Carolina, Council of Farm Women donated 48,000 cans of surplus vegetables for school lunches.[52]

Farm magazines encouraged farm women to engage in these community projects with articles praising the mutual aid efforts of rural women all over the country. A 1933 article in *Progressive Farmer* profiled Mrs. Ben Anthony, president of the Texas State Home Demonstration Association. According to the article, Mrs. Anthony became involved in home demonstration work to combat the loneliness of farm life. She had

---

*In Tennessee, city and county school districts were separate. City school districts controlled all the schools within the city limits, while the county school district controlled the rest of the schools, generally rural schools. In Blount County, there were three school districts: Blount County, Maryville, and Alcoa.

channeled her efforts into projects which benefited the entire community. Similarly, a 1934 *Farm Journal* article called "Rural Club Women Lead," outlined the efforts of various women's organizations all over the South. The author reported that in 38,000 local clubs enrolling 760,000 farm women nationwide, rural women were "helping individually and collectively in an effort to increase and conserve farm incomes and to build a better community life." One example the article described was the work of women in the Red Cross clubs in Roanoke County, Virginia, who established a lunchroom that raised funds for indigent hospital patients.[53]

In spite of farm magazines' emphasis on the work of farm women's organizations, few of the women interviewed for this study reported participating in such clubs. Even elite and middling farm women cited a lack of time and transportation as the key reasons they did not regularly join these formal organizations. They preferred to organize specific projects, such as the Blount County, Tennessee, school lunchroom, rather than to serve on the long-term, ongoing basis described by farm magazines.

Help From Uncle Sam

Rural upcountry women's mutual aid networks were crucial to the ability of many families to survive the economic crisis of the 1920s and 1930s. All of these collective efforts, however, were not always enough to fill the needs of every family. Sometimes women were forced to seek help from the state or federal government, a last-ditch measure that cost dearly in terms of a fierce rural pride that did not accept handouts from outside the community. Rural people believed it far preferable to accept assistance from neighbors because you might someday be able to reciprocate. Government assistance was charity, evidence for all that the family was unable to care for its own. Bill Lewellyn recalled his embarrassment when, after his stepfather had been injured and was unable to work, his mother sent him to the courthouse to pick up government commodity foods that were given away to the poorest citizens:

It embarrassed me to go over there and haul that stuff—we had to go to the courthouse and get it. And I remember the flour had a shock of wheat on it. And I took me a tow sack along, you know. I had a little old red wagon somebody had given me. I fixed it up and painted it, and anyway, to keep people from seeing that flour, I'd cover it up, you know. But I guess they knew what it was. [laughter] I had some pride even back then. But anyway, we had a rough time then. I don't remember, seem to me like there was beans, pinto beans, and mackerel and bacon. . . But that helped.

Like Bill Lewellyn's mother, the most desperate rural families saw little alternative except to apply for government relief in spite of the cost to their pride. A 1934 FERA report on rural Bledsoe County, Tennessee, reported that 40 percent of the county's population was receiving relief payments that year. A survey of these 589 families revealed that 77 percent of the heads of household were farmers, nearly 30 percent of them farm owners.[54]

Although government charity was anathema to farm families, federally funded jobs programs were preferable to outright relief payments or commodities distribution because participants had a sense of having earned their benefits. Upcountry folk often derided the WPA as "make work," claiming that the agency's initials stood for "we piddle around" or "woodpecker's army." Nonetheless, as one West Virginia man noted, "Lots of people give it a black eye, but it helped many a poor man out. . . . On the WPA, you had to work if you got paid." For rural folk, work was honorable, and working for the WPA was not as humiliating as accepting charity. Many rural upcountry folk survived the Depression thanks to jobs in New Deal programs. Hettie Lawson's husband took a job as a supervisor at a CCC camp in the Great Smoky Mountains. This income allowed the family to continue to pay property taxes on their farmland and keep their oldest children in school. A WPA nursing job sustained black South Carolinian Bessie Reed for a year until she was able to find a job as a cook outside the New Deal program. Lessie Shiveley of Kanawaha County, West Virginia, explained that the $4 a week her husband earned on a WPA job and the milk, butter, eggs, and garden vegetables that she provided enabled them to weather the worst years of the Depression.[55]

Officials determined that many farm families were not eligible for jobs programs or other forms of relief because government regulations defined farmers as constantly employed regardless of whether their crops could earn enough cash to pay the family's bills. By the same reasoning, local officials often reduced the number of people on WPA rolls by cutting off benefits to people classified as farmers. The Depression often hit poor landowners hardest. For farmers without capital, there was no money with which to farm either. The Cabell County, West Virginia, agricultural agent noted that "these folks who are completely down and out, no cash, no credit and no property . . . really have a better chance in many cases than another class in Cabell County. The County Court is making a special effort to help these people [the landless]. The other class is the ones that have no cash and no credit . . . but have a little home and possibly some stock. . . . The poor fund does not fit this class."[56]

Upcountry farm women sometimes appealed directly to President or Mrs. Roosevelt in their despair. In December 1938, Tennessee widow Mrs. Minnie Adcock wrote to Franklin Roosevelt about her inability to find a farm or home to rent in her rural community: "I can't find a vacant house no where. They all say, 'No; don't need no body. the acreage is cut.' Well tell me what i am to do what is the poor old tenant going to do i am so worried i cant sleep you had all this done to help the farmer well it shure has got us in a mess i have no home no place to live. . . if you dont help me i will haft to live with the dogs." Minnie Adcock's pleas reflect not only her desperation in finding a home and a plot on which to raise a subsistence, but also her awareness that New Deal programs were responsible for displacing her from the farm where she had lived for years. In many upcountry counties, as in counties throughout the South, landowners found it more profitable to take land formerly farmed by tenants out of production in order to receive Agricultural Adjustment Administration (AAA) crop reduction payments. Although AAA regulations required landowners to share AAA payments with tenants, this provision was rarely enforced. The practice left tenants like Mrs. Adcock with literally no place to go. In response to her desperate pleas, President Roosevelt's office forwarded her letter to the Farm Security Administration, which instructed her to contact a local Resettlement Administration official for assistance. No further follow-up on her case appears in the files.[57]

The lack of options forced some families to take drastic and heartbreaking measures. Mary Evelyn Lane recalled a family in her neighborhood who could no longer care for their elderly grandmother, so they sent her to live at the Blount County Poor Farm. In a rural society that valued taking care of its own, this was a desperate measure that left the family feeling guilty for its inability to care for the elderly woman and humiliated in the eyes of the larger community.[58]

As the lives of upcountry farm women indicate, rural women shouldered most of the burden for surviving the agricultural depression of the 1920s and 1930s. Not only did they adopt many individual and collective strategies to survive the economic crisis, strategies mediated by class and race, but they also made shifts in their own labor and production patterns in order to maximize the family's ability to earn and accumulate cash. Because their driving commitment was to the future of their families, and because they believed that a successful transition to commercial agriculture would help assure that future, women took on the responsibility for family subsistence so that men could devote more attention to earning cash. They also sought to earn cash themselves. In the process, by adopting the values of the marketplace instead of those of communal subsistence, they ultimately started down a path that marginalized women's non-cash-earning activities.

Three

"Grandma Would Find Some Way to Make Some Money"

Farm Women's Cash Incomes

Bill Lewellyn remembered the life of his grandmother, Alta Henry Scarbrough: "My poor old Grandma, she kind of held the family together, you know. She'd make some money some way with her cows and this and that and the other. . . . Grandma made the living when my granddad had slack times."

In 1920 Alta Scarbrough was thirty-nine years old. She had eight living children ranging in age from two to twenty-two, and she would give birth to two more children in the decade. The family lived on the edge of the growing commercial center of Maryville, Tennessee, where Scarbrough's husband farmed and sold scrap metal and firewood. As the agricultural depression of the 1920s worsened, life for the Scarbrough family became harder and harder. To supplement her husband's meager income, Scarbrough began to keep boarders, mostly young women who worked at the local hosiery mill. When a large, run-down mansion with some acreage came up for rent nearby, Scarbrough moved her family there and expanded her boardinghouse operation. The pasture land also allowed her to expand her herd of cows and increase her production of milk and butter for the market. To supplement the income from the boardinghouse and dairy, she and her husband grew truck crops, which they sold in the nearby town. By 1931 there were at least twelve family members and several boarders living in the big house because Scarbrough's grown daughter, unemployed son-in-law, and two small grandsons had moved in. As her grandson recalled, it was Scarbrough who provided most of the family's subsistence and cash support during those years. Using a combination of strategies to enter the market economy and earn cash, she ensured her family's survival.[1]

In sharp contrast to the experience of Alta Scarbrough, who provided most of her family's earnings during the agricultural depression of the 1920s and 1930s, Jessie Felknor was married to a prosperous, landowning commercial farmer. Like most middling farm families of the period, the Felknors had to tighten their belts during the lean interwar years, but their economic straits were never as dire as the Scarbroughs' were. Nonetheless, Jessie Felknor entered the marketplace, raising a large flock of chickens, turkey, geese, peafowl, ducks, and guineas, and selling her meat and eggs to local merchants. Since Felknor was obviously not motivated by economic necessity in her entry into the marketplace, we must look more closely at when, how, and why farm women engaged in cash-earning activities.[2]

Oral histories, letters, TVA records, and other sources reveal that women like Alta Scarbrough and Jessie Felknor were the rule rather the exception in the upcountry South during the years between the two world wars. They not only adopted numerous strategies to feed their families and stretch resources that grew more scarce with each passing year, but they actively entered the marketplace, making significant contributions to the family income. They often provided cash that proved critical in allowing some families to remain on the land.

Farm women's entrance into the marketplace was about more than financial expediency, however. Upcountry farm women engaged in these cash-producing activities in the context of a rapidly changing agricultural economy. Not only was rural industrialization producing a mixed economy that provided new off-farm jobs for both men and women, but the collapse of the agricultural economy and government interventions to aid victims of that collapse were restructuring the region's agricultural system, pushing subsistence farmers into commercial agriculture or off the land. In an earlier era, when farm families earned their living primarily through subsistence activities, farm women's small-scale home production was essential to the family's economic well-being. As the region's rural economy became more cash-based, however, farm families, men and women alike, came to view women's subsistence production as necessary but less critical than income-producing activities. For this reason, women sought to retain a central place in the family economy by contributing to the family's cash income. The changing economy provided women with a wedge that they used to expand their own sphere of activities. Both the need for cash and the satisfaction of controlling their own incomes motivated many farm women to seek new or expanded opportunities to earn cash incomes.

Regardless of their motivations for earning cash, upcountry farm women found that the changing economy of the interwar South restructured their income-producing opportunities, expanding options in some areas while reducing options in others, opening doors for some women and closing them for others. The economy and labor markets of the upcountry were segmented by gender, and within these gender categories, by race and class. Petty production and sale of poultry and dairy products had long been the province of farm women. Yet the region's elaborate racial structuring of the economy gave white women access to markets for their produce, while limiting black women's access to markets. The most prosperous women had the resources to invest in a broad range of activities and the potential for greater profit than poorer women.

At the same time, new opportunities for women in developing industries were also structured by gender, class, and race. The few women employed by the extractive industries or heavy manufacturers in the region were restricted to clerical and service jobs; higher paying manufacturing jobs were seen as too physically demanding and too highly skilled for women. Poorer white women were hired for low-skilled operator's jobs in the expanding textile and canning industries, but middling women who took such jobs risked their respectability because this work would place them under control of, and in contact with, unrelated males. At the same time, black women were excluded from even these lowest level factory jobs, thus forcing those who needed off-farm jobs to work as agricultural laborers or domestics. The limits to opportunities for African American women in turn benefited upcountry whites by providing a ready pool of cheap labor for their farms and homes.

Women's Income-Producing Work in the Farm Press

The subtleties of opportunities and limits were largely obscured in the farm press's coverage of women's income-producing work. Farm magazines had long recognized that farm women contributed to the family's cash income through their productive activities, and farm leaders frequently used this forum to promote farm women's commercial production. Nonetheless, male and female editors maintained a narrow view of the appropriate means and goals for women's cash earning. In 1926, *Woman's Home Companion,* a popular women's magazine that counted thousands of middling rural women among its subscribers, published an article by home economists Florence E. Ward and Katherine Glover entitled "The Farm Woman Goes Into Business and Successfully Reconciles a Home and a Career." The authors characterized the farm woman as a dedicated, self-sacrificing wife and mother, whom they compared favorably to city women:

> While the woman in the city has been puzzling over how to reconcile a home and a career, the farm woman has quietly and successfully solved the problem.
>
> There is this fundamental difference between the way in which the farm woman has gone about her new independence and that of many of her sisters in the city, and it may have something to do with the results: the woman in the country has sought her new field of activity chiefly through a desire to give back the increase into the family treasury rather than to win laurels for herself.

The authors went on to outline the money-making efforts of farm women all over the country, singing the praises of rural mothers who used their profits for home improvements and children's college funds. Ward and Glover's implicit critique of city women served to define the limits of appropriate cash-earning activities for farm women. In the minds of the home economists, farm women's participation in the market was laudable precisely because it allowed them to remain focused on the needs of their families.[3]

Farm magazine advertisements and articles often focused on specific ways farm women earned cash. These stories indirectly legitimized wom-

en's productive activities even as they tried to establish specific boundaries for women's activities. For example, ads for poultry feed and equipment often featured illustrations of white women working in the poultry
house. One ad even featured a female poultry expert. Touting a new
poultry feed mix, the headline proclaimed "Bessie Carswell, the Poultry
Woman" shares "My Amazing Discovery That Doubles Your Egg Profits." A photo of Carswell holding a hen accompanied the ad copy. Advice
articles on poultry raising also recognized women as the primary poultry
farmers. In a 1926 *Farm Journal* article entitled "The Woman in Poultry
Culture," the author noted, "Time and again it has been proved that
women are more adapted to the care of poultry than is the average man.
They put love into their work. A woman works carefully; she gets down to
a system." The male author saw poultry production as a logical task for
women because of stereotypical notions about women's attention to detail and their careful nurturing of living creatures. The author assumed
that these skills were extensions of women's mothering role, making it
natural for women to produce poultry. He went on to describe successful
women poultry producers he knew. He cited a white widow near him
who kept 150 hens and sold eggs and broilers "as a sideline with her
household duties." Although the author did not seem to recognize it, this
widow was probably earning her entire cash income from her poultry
operation, thus confirming that lone women could survive and remain on
the land.[4]

Farm women had long earned money from the sale of their dairy
products, another activity that farm magazine editors saw as falling
within the farm wife's "natural" sphere. Advertising and articles touted
dairy production as an additional arena in which women could earn
some "extra" money. A 1929 *Farm Journal* ad showed a man handing a
cream check to a smiling, apron-clad white farm wife who was standing
next to a DeLaval cream separator. Similarly, in 1932 *Progressive Farmer*
editor Lois Dowdle profiled a Texas farm woman who earned $780 from
butter sales the previous year: "When the butter business was a casual
pin money affair, Mrs. Beavers tells how her husband laughed at her for
'fooling with it, taking the milk from the calves.' But it is a business
of family cooperation now, and everybody recognizes its importance."
Dowdle's comment reveals that even farm men tended to discount their
wives' earning power, at least until it proved to generate a significant

amount of cash. Mrs. Beavers' husband's comment that she was "taking milk from the calves" illuminates the tensions that women's market activities sometimes created within the farm family. Mr. Beavers produced calves for the market, and he needed milk to feed them. Mrs. Beavers' butter business created competition for scarce resources. In the Beavers household, this tension was resolved when Mrs. Beavers' business began to produce significant amounts of income, but in other households, farmers may have demanded that their wives stop their market activities.[5]

Advertisers in farm magazines encouraged farm women to experiment with other forms of market production. Appealing to farm women's desire to earn money with "work at home opportunities" and to their increased familiarity with technology, the Gearhart Company offered to pay *Farm Journal*'s female readers extra money to work in their "spare time at home." "In hundreds of American homes millions of hours are going to waste," the ad copy lamented. "These are golden hours which many women might well turn into money." The copy went on to promise that farm women could make hosiery at home with the Gearhart knitting mill and that the company would buy all "standard" hosiery they produced. Implicit in the ad copy was the message that labor that did not produce cash income was "wasted" time, a message that devalued much of farm women's productive and reproductive labor. The language masked the real intent of the ad, which was to sell Gearhart equipment. What the ad did not explain was that women would be required to invest in a Gearhart knitting machine before they could begin work. In a similar ad, the Steber Machine Company also offered wives knitting machines on which they could make socks at home. The ad directed women to send in an attached coupon with two cents for more details. Although it is not clear how many women in the upcountry engaged in this sort of long-distance contract textile work, the ads themselves promoted the idea that it was acceptable for women to make money at home.[6]

Although dozens of articles in farm magazines touted rural women's economic contributions, editors had to be convinced that farm women made significant contributions to farm incomes. In 1931 one ill-informed women's editor at *Progressive Farmer* discounted the idea that a farm woman might contribute large amounts to the family's income. She insisted instead that the farm woman's job, like that of her middle-class sisters, was spending, not earning. Her readers quickly disabused her of the notion that they were simply home purchasing agents. In the very next issue, the editor reported that she had received a flood of letters from women who were making significant contributions to farm families' incomes. Readers wrote in to say that they were earning money through the sale of dairy products, cooked products, handicrafts, cut flowers, fruit and vegetables, and poultry products. Although she was obviously surprised by the magnitude of farm women's earning power, the editor graciously admitted that she had misjudged farm women. The deluge of letters correcting the editor's false impression was ample testimony that, regardless of the limited role that some home economists saw farm women playing, the women saw themselves as partners in earning the family living. Women's vigorous response suggested that this role mattered to them sufficiently to protest publicly.[7]

Their beliefs that farm women's cash earnings were simply "pin money" may reflect the biases of farm magazine editors who sought to appeal to the most prosperous and commercially oriented farm families, families whose wives might have had the means to model themselves on the suburban housewife/consumer. These were, after all, the families who subscribed to farm magazines and who could afford to buy advertisers' products. Poor families could rarely afford the luxury of a subscription to a farm magazine. A 1935 study by the U.S. Department of Agriculture found that in Tennessee's rural Blount and Loudon counties there were only six to nine subscriptions to any type of magazine per one hundred residents. In the neighboring mountain county of Sevier, there were fewer than three subscriptions per one hundred residents. Yet the outcry sparked by the *Progressive Farmer* editor's comments indicate that even prosperous farm women, members of families with means enough to subscribe to farm magazines, envisioned themselves as farm producers.[8]

Low-Capital Routes to the Marketplace

As farm women's letters to *Progressive Farmer* suggest, the routes they most often used to enter the market were those that required little in the way of investment beyond the woman's own labor. Such routes allowed them to enter and leave the marketplace easily, based on their shifting needs for cash. Often the most effective of these low-capital routes were expansions of tasks already considered part of the farm woman's role. For example, rural women commonly earned money through poultry production. They usually raised chickens and eggs for family consumption and had long sold surplus production on the open market. Chickens and chicken feed were relatively inexpensive, and farm women could easily expand their production simply by raising a few more chicks. This made poultry production accessible to rural white women at all economic levels. During the 1920s and 1930s, many farm women, especially white women, expanded their poultry production to meet their families' needs for increased amounts of cash.

The amount farm women actually earned from poultry production has largely been obscured by the fact that women commonly bartered these items for things they needed from peddlers and storekeepers. Bartered eggs were usually not included in cash income figures even though they had purchased goods with cash values. East Tennessee storekeepers Mrs. Creed Proffitt and French Clark noted that eggs and butter had been just as acceptable as cash payments at their stores. Yet this earning power would have remained virtually invisible in farm records or other sources. Typical of women who engaged in these types of market exchanges was Jessie Felknor's mother, who kept 75–100 chickens throughout the 1920s, both selling and bartering the eggs. Felknor noted that her mother had not only traded eggs for household supplies, but she had also purchased Jessie's high school class ring with cash earned by selling hens.[9]

Like Felknor's mother, farm women commonly used this combination of bartering and selling poultry products for necessities and luxuries. Tennessee Valley Authority (TVA) records illustrate that many women earned a significant amount of cash over and above bartered products from the sale of poultry products. When the TVA began buying farms in the Tennessee River valley that were due to be flooded by TVA dams, they sent relocation workers out to do extensive interviews with the affected families. In order to determine the resources that a family would need to relocate, workers asked very specific questions about the families' cash incomes for the previous year. Although relocation workers' comments indicate that many families were frankly suspicious of the government workers and undoubtedly underestimated their incomes, reports on poultry production give us some sense of the amount of money farm women were earning from this activity. Oral histories from other areas of the upcountry paint a similar picture.

Wives of both sharecroppers and small farm owners sold their eggs and chickens, and for white women this was often quite lucrative. For example, Effie Shubert, the thirty-seven-year-old wife of a Loudon County, Tennessee, sharecropper, earned $150 from poultry sales in 1939. This was 19 percent of the family's cash income. The same year Martha Ray, the forty-two-year-old wife of a Roane County farm owner, reported that she had earned $55 from poultry sales. This was 12 percent of the family's $455 annual income. Gertrude Cyrus recalled that her mother sold fifteen to twenty dozen eggs every couple of weeks and supplied most of the groceries that the West Virginia family purchased. Her income enabled Gertrude's father to use the proceeds from the sale of his tobacco crop and his meager income as a deputy sheriff in Kanawha County to pay property taxes, buy farm equipment, and cover major family expenses. White women in female-headed households earned an even larger percentage of their income with poultry production. For example, Matty Leeper was a sixty-three-year-old widow who owned a farm in Loudon County, Tennessee. Her daughter and son-in-law assisted her with the farming and the support of three crippled grown sons. Leeper earned 42 percent of the family income from poultry production. For women whose families were toiling on marginal farms, poultry production often made the difference between paying property taxes or losing the farm; between keeping children in school or not; between calling a doctor in case of illness or not; indeed, between survival or starvation. For widowed farm women, poultry production was less physically demanding than many forms of farm work that allowed them to maximize the resource of inherited land.[10]

Struggling farm women, however, were not the only ones who sold poultry products. Even elite white farm women engaged in poultry production for the market, though their efforts proved to be less critical to the survival of their prosperous families. In Blount County Nellie Haddox and her grown daughters who lived at home earned $340 from poultry sales in 1939, a figure that amounted to only 3 percent of the family's $10,000 income from its commercial dairy operation. It is significant that Haddox and her daughters continued to engage in poultry production even though the family obviously did not need their earnings. The size and modernity of the Haddoxes' dairy farm indicated that Mr. Haddox reinvested much of his income in the farm, so the poultry income was probably money that the women themselves controlled and could spend as they wished.[11]

Although white farm women were able to earn significant amounts of cash from poultry production, the upcountry's elaborately articulated system of race relations kept most black women out of the marketplace. For example, Sudie Sherman was a Knox County, Tennessee, black woman who kept house for her sharecropper father-in-law after being abandoned by her husband. She earned $5 from poultry sales in 1939, only 3 percent of the family's cash income. In part, black women's lower profits from poultry production may have been due to their lack of capital to invest in proper feeds for maximum egg production and lack of access to the latest scientific production advice disseminated by farm magazine editors and by extension agents. Racial discrimination played a larger role, however. African American farm women recalled that white storekeepers and peddlers often refused to buy farm products from black women, both because of stereotypes about blacks' lack of cleanliness and because they were competing with white women. Southern whites did not want black women to gain a measure of financial independence that might make them resist providing domestic service in white households.[12]

Race also structured other opportunities for women to earn cash. Many white upcountry farm women expanded their market production throughout the 1920s and 1930s through other methods that required little capital investment, but black women found their access to these markets limited. For example, white women who had previously participated in the market in only a small way through the exchange of eggs and butter soon began to sell additional products for cash. Eva Finchum recalled that many women in her community picked and sold huckleberries found along roadsides and in woods in the area. Other women and children picked and sold blackberries and wild strawberries. Grace Sunbeam Ellis of Mingo County, West Virginia, remembered trading ginseng that she, her mother, and her siblings had gathered in nearby forests for fabric, overalls, and even candy at the crossroads store. In the 1920s many Landrum, South Carolina, farm women grew fresh grapes, which they packaged in small baskets and had their young children sell to railroad passengers when the train paused at Landrum station. A few women took advantage of nearby urban markets by growing and selling cut flowers. East Tennessean Elizabeth Jordan reported that she sold flowers from her two-acre garden from May to October. Some months she made as much as $150 selling flowers at a farmer's market in a nearby city two days a week. She also got orders to provide flowers for dinner parties, department stores, and hotel dining rooms in the city. Another white East Tennessee woman who sold flowers in the city reported earning about $200 a year in the early 1920s.[13]

The growth of the urban and rural nonfarm populations created new demand for farm produce, which spurred the development of new retail outlets. Roadside stands and local farmer's markets organized by white farm organizations and home demonstration clubs provided ready vehicles for distributing farm women's products. Farm magazines provided how-to articles for women's organizations that wanted to set up their own markets. *Farm Journal's* editors told women how to realize "Cold Cash From Canning" and urged them to try "Marketing Apples by the Jelly Route." An article in *Southern Agriculturist* in 1930 applauded several successful food markets established by Tennessee home demonstration clubs. In the 1920s, home extension agents encouraged women to become more active selling at regional farmers' markets and assisted farm women in establishing new cooperative markets. For example, a home demonstration club market in Spartanburg, South Carolina, provided dozens of local farm women with an outlet for their produce.[14]

But even in roadside markets, the racial structure of the economy in the upcountry South limited the options available to black women. Black vendors were not welcomed in the curbside markets run by white women's groups and farm organizations, thus limiting the markets available to them. African American women who lived on main roads sometimes tried to sell goods in their own roadside stands, but this practice provided a much smaller customer base than a busy downtown market. Some black women peddled to white and black neighbors on an ad hoc basis. But most black women found a limited market for substantial sales of garden produce regardless of the small investment such production would require. This practice worked to the advantage of white farm women. Not only did they have less competition in the marketplace,

FIG. 8. Sales of farm produce provided a substantial income for many farm women during the 1920s and 1930s. Women from rural areas around Knoxville, Tennessee, sold produce at the city's Market House. Here a farm woman sells vegetables and fresh flowers from the hood of her truck in 1928. (Photograph courtesy of McClung Historical Collection, Lawson-McGhee Library.)

but the limited options for black women to earn cash made them more amenable to working as domestics for the most prosperous rural white women.[15]

Dozens of white upcountry farm women took advantage of these new markets. For example, many women sold Appalachian crafts in the new venues. Lucy Quarrier of Kanawha County, West Virginia, learned weaving as a teenager working in a North Carolina girls' camp in the 1920s. She became an expert spinner and weaver and supported herself with the sales of her products. East Tennessean Mrs. Perry Keith sold surplus garden products in addition to eggs and butter. By the mid-1920s, she found the produce sales to be so profitable that she expanded her garden and began to can much of the produce for sale at the market. As

her daughters grew older, they began to help her, and she was able further to increase her production. In 1929 she took a booth "inside the
market house," that is, in the enclosed portion of the farmer's market
where booths were permanent and rental was more expensive. She told a
Progressive Farmer reporter that by 1932 she was clearing more than $300
per year, a very significant sum.[16]

Much to the approval of *Progressive Farmer's* editors, Keith explained
that she used most of her earnings for her children's education and for
home improvements. Like many farm women, Keith expressed discom-
fort at using her husband's meager farm earnings for home improvements. "If you help to make the money you feel comfortable using it for
home improvements and raising the standard of living," she told the
reporter. It was the freedom to spend money in her own way that provided Keith with the motivation to earn her own cash.

Most rural women's production for the market began with investments of very little capital, but middling or elite farm women were sometimes able to save surplus profits not needed to meet the family's needs.
They often reinvested some of their earnings to expand their operations,
indicating that they were ambitious and sought to earn more than "pin
money" through their efforts. For example, East Tennessean Ona Hale
used the proceeds from her turkey and chicken flocks to build a large
brooder house heated by kerosene. Not only did this undertaking indicate that she was willing to reinvest her profits to expand her operation,
but the size of the operation also demanded a huge amount of labor.[17]

Another of women's low-capital routes to the marketplace was keeping boarders. Farm magazine editors rarely acknowledged this common
practice, an omission that probably grew out of the editors' refusal to
recognize the mixed agricultural/industrial economies that created a
market for boardinghouses. Farm magazines and other representatives of
agricultural institutions, such as the USDA and the Farm Bureau, promoted commercial agriculture engaged in by businessmen-farmers. Part-
time farmers and a mixture of wage work and farming had no place in
their vision of agriculture's golden future; thus, these options for remaining on the land received no attention.

Nonetheless, for many farm women keeping boarders proved a lucrative source of income. Local miners, industrial workers, and construction hands from TVA projects created a demand for lodging space in rural

areas that outpaced employers' efforts to provide temporary housing, a demand that many farm women, mostly white women, eagerly filled. Like poultry and garden production, running a boardinghouse required little investment beyond a woman's own labor.

Yet even in this sphere, the racial organization of the upcountry economy shaped women's opportunities to be boardinghouse keepers. Most industrial and construction jobs in rural areas went to white men, not black men. In this way, whites were assured the best-paying off-farm jobs, while white landowners maintained a tractable source of cheap day labor among black men. Because most industrial workers were white, white women had far more opportunities to run boardinghouses than black women. For example, Pernie Branam's grandmother ran a boardinghouse for loggers near Jellico, Tennessee, in the 1920s and 1930s. West Virginian John T. Walton recalled a white widow who ran the boardinghouse for visiting mine officials in the Black Cat mining community. Maude Walker's father had contracts to do much of the rock and dirt hauling for several TVA projects, so in 1933, when her husband moved to Norris Dam to work for her father on that project, Walker moved with him and opened a boardinghouse for her father's other truck drivers. At the age of twenty-three, she kept nine or ten boarders in addition to caring for two small children. Because the men worked two shifts, she prepared two breakfasts and two suppers each day. Walker found that being a boardinghouse keeper was too big a job to furnish all the goods and services she needed herself. She bought most of her groceries because she did not have the time or the land to raise a large garden and keep livestock, and she hired a local woman to come in and do the laundry once a week. Walker saved a large portion of her earnings, which she and her husband later used to build a large two-story colonial house on the Blount County farm Walker's father had given them.[18]

Walker's experience points to another advantage of low-capital routes to the marketplace: not only was it easy to enter the marketplace, but it was also a rather simple matter to leave it when the need for cash earning disappeared. When the Norris project was finished and Walker and her family returned to Blount County, she simply closed down her boardinghouse, never entering the marketplace on any large scale again.

Not all boardinghouse keepers were young women trying to establish their families on sound financial footings. Carrie Smith, the wife of a wealthy Rhea County farm owner and miller, took an unusual approach to keeping boarders. Instead of keeping men in her home, she rented an adjacent house and kept fifteen boarders there. She and hired girls from the neighborhood raised poultry, milked cows, and worked a large garden to provide most of the food for these boarders, managing to clear $1,800 in 1939. This was 35 percent of the family's total cash income that year. For Smith, cash earning was not as essential as it was for women like Walker and Branam. Her husband's farming and business interests provided a very comfortable living for the family. This raises questions about why she would have engaged in the back-breaking labor involved in keeping a large boardinghouse. Although she left no testimony, Smith's husband told the TVA worker that his wife controlled her own income, making it likely that Smith preferred to earn a certain amount of cash that she could control.[19]

Although most of the women who kept boardinghouses in the region were white, black women occasionally kept boarders when single black men working in the area needed a place to stay. Because white women would never have kept black boarders, black women performed a vital service to their own communities as well as producing incomes for their own families by providing lodging for single black workers. For example, Evalena Rooker, the wife of a black Rhea County, Tennessee, sharecropper, told a TVA worker that she kept a boarder off and on through the late 1930s. However, she did not report her income from this endeavor. It is possible that she did not receive cash from this activity, but instead traded room and board for farm labor. There were few off-farm jobs available to black men in rural communities, so this seems likely.[20]

Just as the South's racial caste system created a need for housing for blacks who worked on TVA projects, it also created opportunities for some women in the coal fields. The segregated nature of coal town life limited housing options for both immigrant and black workers, who were refused housing in "white" sections of coal towns. This created opportunities for the wives of black and immigrant miners. Boomer, West Virginia, miner Dave Tamplin recalled that the recruiting of several hundred Italian workers created a housing crisis in the remote mining village. Most of the men arrived without families. "Maybe one out of every ten or fifteen would bring his wife," Tamplin explained. "[So she] would start a boardinghouse." He noted that the boarding men purchased their own food and paid her an agreed-upon fee each week to prepare it. Similarly Joseph Kovich's mother, a Croatian immigrant, ran boardinghouses for all the single immigrant men who worked at the Lorado Mine in Logan County where her husband was a night watchman. Her income enabled her to put several of her sixteen children through college. Black women also ran boardinghouses in coal towns.[21]

Another option for some women was manufacturing home work. The work-at-home schemes advertised in farm magazines were little different than the factory home work done by urban women. Some rural white women had access to this work because of the presence of industry within the region's rural hinterlands. For example, in the 1920s women in the Oak City community of Sevier County, Tennessee, made cane chair seats at home for the Oak City Mill, Chair, and Store Company. Most of these women were married with children. Again, the mixed economy provided opportunities for them to combine cash earning with their productive and reproductive work on the farm. The decline of the plant with the onset of the Depression had a significant impact on the cash income of these Sevier County families.[22]

Capital-Intensive Routes to the Marketplace

Not only were farm women selling poultry products and surplus garden vegetables and keeping boarders, but farm women all over the upcountry bartered their surplus milk, cream, and butter for household products as well as selling it for cash. In 1920 Miss Elizabeth Forney, a South Carolina Assistant Home Demonstration Agent, reported that one family "has been able to weather the boll weevil and present market conditions" through the wife's dairying. Nonetheless, dairying was a much more capital intensive operation than poultry production because it required the purchase of cows, an expensive investment. Wives of prosperous white farm owners were far more likely to have the capital for the large dairy herds (more than one or two cows) needed to produce substantial amounts of milk beyond the family's dietary needs than were poorer white or black women. West Virginian Ella Betler recalled that her mother, the wife of a prosperous landowning farmer and carpenter, pro-

duced substantial amounts of cheese for the market. She took the cheese
to the closest railroad depot, about five miles away, where it was shipped
to urban markets. Gene Randle, the daughter of a Loudon County, Tennessee, miller and farm owner, was reported to "show a rather unusual
interest in farm operations," apparently because she experimented with
the latest research findings in an effort to improve her dairy herd's production levels. She earned 17 percent of the family's income through the
sale of milk products. More prosperous tenant wives also produced substantial amounts of milk products. Tennessee tenant farm wife Virginia
Barger sold $150 worth of milk in 1939, 20 percent of family's income. In
1922 thirty-three Oconee County, South Carolina, women shipped butter
for sale at a market organized by state home demonstration agents in
Columbia. They averaged sales of $54 each.[23]

Dairy products, like poultry products, provided important income
for female-headed households. Bertha Badgett, a widowed white Blount
County farm owner, and her forty-one-year-old daughter Eula sold $50
worth of milk in 1939. This was 17 percent of their $295 income that year.
Similarly Ella Cooper, a black domestic servant living in the rural community of Louisville, Tennessee, reported that she earned $150 in 1939
from the sale of milk products. This was the same amount as she earned
from her work as a domestic, half her total income. Like the sale of
eggs and chickens, dairy production proved a lucrative activity for farm
women of both races, but particularly for white women. The activity also
allowed some widows to remain on the land and thus in their home
communities.[24]

The capital intensive nature of commercial dairy production, however, meant that women who had little up-front cash with which to buy a
herd could not benefit from the ready market for milk. For example, Sudie
Sherman, the black Knox County poultry producer discussed above,
earned no money from the sale of dairy products. The TVA worker's
report indicates that the family owned only one head of livestock, a cow,
making it likely that the family consumed all the milk it could produce.
Evalena Rooker, the wife of an African American sharecropper, also produced no milk for the market with her single cow. The same was true of
very poor white tenant farm women, like Elizabeth Rayburn. The sixty-
year-old wife of a two-thirds share tenant, Rayburn earned only $40 in

1939 from the sale of dairy products. This was only 9 percent of the family's total cash income that year, the rest of it coming from the sale of crops and from her husband's day labor.

Off-Farm Work

Farm women did not limit their cash-earning efforts to work that could be done in or near the home, however. Large numbers of upcountry farm women worked off the farm. White farm women's embrace of off-farm jobs in the face of opposition from the farm press, agricultural institutions, and, indeed, the general public, is indicative not only of families' dire need for cash incomes, but also of many women's ambitions to participate more fully in the family economy by earning a paycheck. Motivated by a desire to control a portion of the family's spending, to participate in the world beyond the farm, and often merely to survive, many rural upcountry women resorted to off-farm jobs in the years between 1920 and 1941.[25]

The racial structure of the upcountry economy also structured options for off-farm work available to white and black women. Textile mills, the most frequent employers of rural women, almost never employed black women. Cheap labor drew textile mills to nearly every small East Tennessee community located on the railroad line. By 1930 South Carolina had 239 textile mills employing 94,756 workers, mostly concentrated in the upstate counties of Anderson, Spartanburg, and Greenville. The opportunities were more limited for textile work in southwestern West Virginia, but a few mills existed, most notably the Kanawha Woolen Mills. There were also fruit and vegetable canneries in all three regions. Although many women worked reduced hours or suffered layoffs from these jobs at the height of the Depression, most returned to the factories as soon as they were able.

Mills generally employed young, white rural women. The female factory workers were most often single female heads of households or the wives of very poor farmers. Typical was forty-six-year-old Ora Russell, a widow, and her fifty-year-old sister Josie, who worked at the Charles Bacon Hosiery Company in Loudon County, Tennessee. Gladys Scott, the eighteen-year-old daughter of a disabled widow, supported her mother

FIG. 9. Although the wives and daughters of middling and elite landowners rarely chose industrial jobs, women in the poorest farm families often found factory jobs were the only way to supplement the farm's meager income. Sallie Collins, the daughter of an East Tennessee farmer, applies gold ink to fine book covers at Kingsport Press, a printer in northeastern Tennessee. (Lewis W. Hine photography, 1933. NWDNS-142-H-129. Courtesy of Still Picture Branch of National Archives at College Park.)

and two unemployed brothers with a job at the Loudon Hosiery Mill. In 1939 a TVA relocation worker reported that the wife of Gilbert Adcox, a desperately poor sharecropper who "lack[ed] ambition," had just gone to work for a local hosiery mill. Dolly Simmons worked in the Whitney Mills in Spartanburg, South Carolina. She and her brother supported their widowed mother and an orphaned nephew.[26]

Occasionally struggling rural women launched entrepreneurial ventures that were low-capital investments that involved working outside the home. Miss Jane Turner, a South Carolina spinster having trouble making ends meet after her parents died, became legendary in the rural

community of Landrum. Before World War I, she began buying vegetables, eggs, and butter from local farm wives and peddling them to the city
folks who summered in nearby Tryon, North Carolina, a mountain resort
town.[27]

Many poor rural women, both white and black, did traditional wom-
en's work as housekeepers and laundresses. For middling and elite white
women, the ability to hire domestic servants was symbolic of class privilege. Although census figures tell us only how many woman earned their
living through domestic service, not how many families hired domestics,
anecdotal evidence suggests that thousands of white farm women enjoyed domestic help at least occasionally. Middling white farm women
often hired African American women to come to the farm one day a week
to perform their most odious household tasks such as laundry. The southern system of job segregation reserved domestic and agricultural jobs for
black women, denying them higher paying work. This operated to the
advantage of white women, allowing all but the poorest to afford domestic help once in a while. For example, even after giving up her boardinghouse at Norris for a more cash-strapped existence on the farm, Maude
Walker was sometimes able to hire a black woman to assist with her
spring cleaning.[28]

Almost 40 percent of Tennessee's black women (compared to 12 percent of white women) were employed in 1920, and more than 50 percent of them were engaged in domestic service, mostly as cooks and
laundresses. In 1930 64.9 percent of Greenville County, South Carolina,
and 75 percent of Cabell County, West Virginia, black women were in domestic service. In 1939 Irene Russell, a forty-one-year-old African American from Tennessee, reported that she supported her disabled husband
and three teenage children by working as a housekeeper for Mrs. Leola
Cannon, a local white woman. Russell earned $3.50 per week. Her fifteen-
year-old daughter supplemented the family income with occasional
housework.[29]

Domestic service offered black women a complicated blend of privilege and exploitation. In 1939 Bessie Reed, an elderly upstate South Carolina woman, told a WPA interviewer about her years of domestic service
to white families. After her sharecropping father died, her mother sent
her out to work caring for white children. Bessie did this work for several
years before she married. She told the interviewer:

I had it easy kaise ev'y time the chilluns' 'et, I 'et too. De lady of the house gave me new clothes, when mine got frayed. . . . I never knowed nothin' 'bout no rugged times till I played a fool and took a black man to live wid. . . . Nursing I got sum'tin like a quarter or fifty cents now and den. I could save it up if I wanted to. De' entire worle knowed, except me, dat when you mar'res a black nigger all you gits fer' waitin' on him and workin' fer him, in his crop, is jes' mo' work.

Reed's account was probably colored by the fact that she was talking to a white interviewer and was very aware of the delicacies of race relations in the Jim Crow South, but her story was also shaped by the powerlessness and dependence she felt in her marriage. She implies that her husband controlled her labor and the proceeds from that labor ("workin' fer *him*, in *his* crop," author's emphasis). She found few rewards in married life, whereas she had enjoyed a better and more plentiful diet and a nicer wardrobe while working for white families.[30]

When Bessie returned to domestic service after thirty years of marriage, her husband resented her work. He saw her caring for a white woman's children and enjoying gifts of food and clothing from her employer that he could not provide. (Likely Bessie reminded him of this.) Resentful of her absence and believing that Bessie was putting on airs—that she "never did have no mind fer nothin' but settin' aroun' wid white folks"—he left her for another woman. A second marriage was happier, but Reed's new husband died. She continued to work for white families and took great pride in the fact that elite families hired her. "Ah sho' can beat 'em all a-cookin' and a-nursin' de way de white folks likes," she boasted. "White folks calls me a reg'lar nigger and 'dat make me feel ra'al proud of myself." Reed felt she gained more status from working for elite whites than from being a sharecropper's wife.

By the same token, she resented working for some whites whom she perceived as unworthy of her fine services. In the mid-1930s, unable to locate other work, she took a WPA job, but she soon quit. "The lady wanted me to nurse white folks up dar dat never had no quality," she explained. In this action, she emphasized her independence and her insistence on controlling the circumstances of her work life to the degree possible. She might be limited to serving white families, but she would choose the sort of families she served. Reed also took pride in the cleanliness of her home, again accepting white standards: "I lives clean like Ma did and I keeps my house jes' as clean as I does any white 'oman's." The interviewer remarked on the pure white sheets and embroidered bed-clothes in Reed's home. In Reed's life we see the curious blend of lim-its and status that the Southern racial caste system bestowed on black women.

White women who worked as domestics advertised their families' extreme poverty because there was no other reason white women would have stooped to perform domestic work. Most who did this were young and single. Two grown daughters of Oleta Reynolds, a poor white Ten-nessee woman, did domestic work in the community for $3 per week. Mary Jones, the thirty-nine-year-old white mother of several illegitimate children, worked as a laundress throughout the 1930s. The illegitimate daughter of a woman who struggled to make ends meet, South Carolina's Lucy Price cooked for summer folk in Hendersonville, North Carolina, before moving to Spartanburg to work as a boardinghouse cook. Wid-owed white farm women also did domestic work but generally only in the face of dire economic challenges. For example, Mabel Robinson, a twenty-nine-year-old white widow, reported to a TVA worker that she did housework for Mrs. Dode Smith for $2 a week from 1929 to 1933. Similarly, Elsie Crawford's mother became housekeeper and caretaker of an elderly lady in the neighborhood after the death of her coal-mining father left the family strapped for cash.[31]

While poor white farm women might take mill jobs and struggling women of both races might do domestic work, wives and daughters of middling or elite farmers were expected to engage in more genteel pur-suits. For these women, manual labor on the farm might sometimes be ac-ceptable, if not always pleasant. But factory work brought them into con-tact with men outside their families and with rougher sorts of people. This contact offended the sensibilities of many farm families who were devel-oping middle-class consciousness. It was far preferable for the wives of even struggling farmers to work at home, even if they had worked in factories before their marriage. For example, West Virginian Alice Hall worked in a tomato cannery for a year before her marriage. After that, however, she took jobs outside the home only when absolutely necessary, and when she did, she clerked in local general stores. She was emphatic that clerking was more appropriate work for a married woman.[32]

Instead of factory work, prosperous women had the option of investing in the capital-intensive, farm-based commercial ventures discussed
above. They also often had enough education to find more interesting, if
not more lucrative, alternatives. White farm women with more than an
elementary education used their need and desire for cash incomes to
move beyond farm production into other forms of work. Some parlayed
their creativity into cash income. For example, Marjorie Cole Smith was a
talented writer with a passion for sports. A letter to a newspaper editor
about a sporting event eventually led to a job as a weekly sports correspondent for four Tennessee papers. Similarly, Jessie Felknor, in spite of
her lack of college training, turned her love of music and her desire to
teach school into an almost full-time job as a music teacher. She taught
private students at a local school, a common practice throughout the rural
upcountry. These options required women to have considerably more
education than that of most upcountry farm women. Poor women would
not have education or opportunities for teaching music or working as
freelance journalists. These were ways that middling white women found
to work within a realm considered appropriate for their status.[33]

Daughters of more prosperous farmers were able to get enough education to qualify them for public school teaching. Although it paid about
the same as mill work, women with adequate education preferred teaching because it had a higher status in the community than factory work
and did not bring middle-class women into contact with rougher sorts of
men. Troy May Haddox, the daughter of a well-to-do Blount County,
Tennessee, dairy farmer, graduated from Maryville College and taught
school at Maryville Junior High. She still lived with her parents at the age
of forty-two. Her thirty-six-year-old sister Gladys, a graduate of the University of Tennessee, was a librarian at Everett High School. Like married
women who controlled their own earnings from farm production, many
young single teachers kept their salaries. The Haddox sisters' father told
the TVA relocation worker that the women did not contribute their salaries to the family fund, nor did they pay room and board. Instead they
were able to spend or save their salaries at their own discretion.[34]

During the Depression, female upcountry schoolteachers suffered
the same sex discrimination suffered by teachers all over the country. For
example, single female teachers were expected to work for smaller salaries than their male counterparts. Korola Lee became aware that she

suffered this brand of sex discrimination. "In 1933, I got $50 for teaching all seven grades in that old building," she recalled. "But I was [later] told that they offered it to [a male teacher] for $65, and he went down and seen it [the schoolhouse], and he went back and told 'em he wouldn't take it. I wish I had known it [at the time], that they offered it to him for $65 and gave it to me for $50. I might not have taken it if I had." Lee resented the discrimination, but she did not seem particularly surprised by it.[35]

Married upcountry teachers suffered a different types of discrimination. In 1939 a letter to the editor of *Farm Journal* from a farm wife decried local school board policies that, in order to free up a job for a man or a single woman, called for the firing of any female teacher if she married. Her ire indicates that such practices were awakening feminist sensibilities in some rural women:

Dear Editor:

Trying to legislate working wives out of paying jobs, a live issue nowadays, seems to me like playing with fire.

I'm not a wife with a salaried job, and never have been, but whenever a married woman can be told what she can do, or can't do, by law, not considering her wants, needs, qualifications, or such, because a single woman wants her job, we have come to a pretty pass.

To legislate against married women is class legislation and the beginning of the end of liberties. Soon any other liberty can be taken away.[36]

The author's position that married women had a right to work if they wanted to, regardless of economic necessity, was radical. This letter demonstrates that farm women were aware of the injustice of the discrimination they faced even though economic conditions and social pressures left them nearly powerless to address it.

In most upcountry counties during the Depression, there were regulations prohibiting the employment of married teachers. Mary Evelyn Lane lost her teaching job in Blount County, Tennessee, when she married in 1935 "because the men had to have the jobs." Lane did not think this practice was fair, and she noted that she and her husband could have used the additional income from her teaching. In fact, she returned to teaching as soon as regulations against hiring married women were abolished during World War II, and she continued teaching until her retirement.[37]

By the mid-1930s, New Deal programs offered occasional jobs to the upcountry's white farm women, but like the rest of the off-farm labor market, New Deal jobs were strictly segregated by race. White farm women received the highest paying jobs in projects that also offered them training in marketable skills. White East Tennessean Mabel Robinson was able to leave her domestic service job to become a school lunchroom cook on a WPA project in 1933. She retained this job for the full five-year limit of WPA employment. As was the case throughout the rural South, officials in New Deal agencies hired few black women, both because white women refused to work on an equal basis with black women on government work projects and because local whites feared that giving black women relatively well-paying relief work would lead to a shortage of cheap domestic and agricultural labor. The local elites who controlled Works Progress Administration (WPA) and National Youth Administration (NYA) boards restricted rural black women to the jobs traditionally reserved for black women, like Bessie Reed's nursing and domestic service WPA job. By restricting black women's opportunities, whites were able to maintain the racially structured labor pool, leaving poor black women available for domestic service and agricultural labor, a practice that benefited white landowners and their wives.[38]

"Lady Farmers"

As these examples indicate, employed women and farm women contributing to the family income with home production played key roles in the economic survival of farm families. Some women, however, farmed on their own without the help of a father, husband, or son. These women took full responsibility for all aspects of agricultural production, even tasks falling outside those considered part of the "natural" farm women's sphere. Even farm magazines recognized that these women existed. Occasional articles profiled "lady farmers." The *Farm Journal* ran stories with titles like "These Poultry Women Made Good" and "She Raises Karakul Sheep." Like the women in the 1930 *Southern Agriculturist* article entitled

"A Manless Dairy Prospers," the women farmers featured in the farm
press were always widowed or single women, never married women.
The editors apparently wanted to send a message that some women,
when forced to farm alone, could do so successfully, but they did not
want to encourage married women to tread into the male territory of
farm management.[39]

As was the case with poultry and dairy producers featured in farm
magazines, some upcountry widows did run their own farms. For example, Ella Craig, age fifty-six, managed to eke out a living on the sixteen
and a half acres she owned in Loudon County, Tennessee. She supported
her elderly mother and two teenage children on food from her garden
and livestock plus the $342 a year she earned from the sale of farm
products and from occasionally taking in laundry. Both children were in
high school, and Craig told the TVA worker that she had "no plans except
keeping . . . the children in school." The education of her children for a
better life was a powerful motivator for Craig. Similarly, seventy-year-old
white widow Elsie Badgett and her forty-one-year-old daughter subsisted on their farm products and the $295 a year they earned on their 104
acres. Minnie Bales, a fifty-five-year-old widow, did have the help of a
son-in-law and a hired laborer, but her statements to a TVA worker make
it clear that she made all decisions regarding the management of the
farm. Nor did having male help earn her more money than women who
worked without the help of men; she reported only $206 in farm income
for 1939, less than either Craig or Badgett. Likewise, single women often
farmed family land. Journalist Ben Robertson Jr. described his great Aunt
Narcissa, who farmed land inherited from her parents alone except for
the help of one hired man. Robertson noted that she despised domestic
work: "She cared nothing at all about the inside of a house." He said that
she refused to clean, cook, sew, or can, leaving these tasks to the last
living freedwoman left on her parents' place.[40]

It was not unheard of for the wives of prosperous businessmen to run
the family farm. For example, Ann Bell Cox Elmore, a fifty-three-year-old
Blount County, Tennessee, woman, told a TVA worker that she was the
"farm manager." In fact, the worker reported that "Mr. Elmore appears to
be less forceful while Mrs. Elmore assumes the position of leadership in
this family." F. A. Elmore ran the Dixie Maid creamery at Maryville, while
Mrs. Elmore managed a farm made up of land inherited from each of

their parents and from additional purchases. Mrs. Elmore ran a commercial dairy operation, presumably to supply her husband's creamery. In 1939 she reported that the farm earned $2,600, not including the creamery income. As the life of Ann Elmore demonstrates, some women did indeed define themselves as farmers rather than as farm wives.[41]

Yet these examples demonstrate that women who wanted to farm were only able to do so if they inherited land. Rarely did a woman earn enough to purchase her own land and begin a farming operation. Rather, women who inherited property, livestock, and equipment from husbands and parents were usually the only ones who were able to make such a choice. Widows frequently inherited land and ran farms until their children were grown, but Elmore was unusual. Daughters often inherited cash, while the land was passed on to sons. And even when daughters did inherit, they usually chose not to farm for a variety of reasons. For example, Naomi Banks Bridges' father purchased his sister's share of their parents' South Carolina farm in the 1930s. The sister was married to a farmer with significant landholdings in a distant county, and she did not want to pay taxes on land too far away for them to farm.[42]

Amounts and Uses of Farm Women's Incomes

There is no doubt that upcountry farm women made significant contributions to family incomes. Although records of their earnings are scarce, TVA files provide revealing glimpses of the size of farm women's incomes in East Tennessee. Of 111 randomly selected relocation records from TVA's Norris, Ft. Loudon, and Watts Bar dam projects, 45 white families reported income that can be verified as being earned by women. On these 45 farms, 27 women earned up to 25 percent of the family income, 10 earned from 26 to 50 percent, 5 earned 51 to 75 percent, and 3 earned 76 to 100 percent. There were not enough African American families in the sample to do an accurate comparison of their incomes. Female-headed white households earned considerably less than male-headed households. The 32 male-headed households earned an average of $1,385 each, while the 13 female-headed households earned an average of $625 each. This disparity in incomes is due less to a devaluation of the products that women produced than to the fact that, in a female-headed farm household, there was often only one adult engaged in market-oriented activities; while in male-headed households, at least two adults were producing for the market. Similarly, a 1933 study of South Carolina farm families found that farm woman earned an average of 25 percent of the family's income through various income-producing activities. Given that this survey included forty owner families and only six tenant families, this figure may have been high. As we have seen, women with access to more capital had the potential to earn larger incomes. Nonetheless, it is clear that many upcountry farm women at all economic levels were earning significant and irreplaceable portions of the family income.[43]

Women were not only providing a significant proportion of farm families' cash earnings, but they were also using these earnings to meet necessary expenses. Although farm magazine writers characterized farm women's income as "extra," women's cash earnings were definitely not "pin money." Only a few women reported using their earnings for home improvements. As the previous examples show, many women also exercised considerable control over those earnings, and they chose to use that money to benefit their families. They spent money on more basic needs: food that could not be grown at home, clothing, taxes, mortgage payments, and livestock. They also frequently invested their income in children's educations, demonstrating their commitment to a better future for the next generation. One Spartanburg, South Carolina, woman sold $1,000 worth of farm produce at the local home demonstration market in 1921, using the proceeds to keep her daughter in college.[44]

Women expressed great satisfaction with controlling their own money. Jefferson County, Tennessee, farm woman Della Sarten earned her own cash by selling butter and cream from her small herd of cows. She reported that she and her husband maintained separate checking accounts for all the years of their marriage. She paid the electric bill (after the arrival of electricity) and the grocery bill and bought the children's school clothing and books. Her husband kept his money for farm business and major family expenses. "I never did have to beg him for no money," she recalled. "I'm not a-bragging, but I never did have to. . . . I'd go to the store, and he never would grumble." The independence that Sarten felt at controlling her own income was a key motivator in her involvement in market-related activities.[45]

Some scholars maintain that farm women discounted their economic contributions as "helping"—as part of their household work and as secondary to their husband's incomes—perhaps in order to reflect idealized notions about gender roles within marriage. However, although some upcountry farm women did refer to their earnings as "helping," most saw their earnings as essential to the family's well-being. In recalling her Meigs County, Tennessee, grandmother's experiences during the 1920s and 1930s, Wilma Fisher noted, "Back then, the women sold their [eggs, butter, etc.] for survival. It was not looked upon as 'extra money.' It was regarded as very dear and used for important things. There was no such thing as 'extra money.' "[46]

Alta Scarbrough's family did not consider her income "extra money." As her grandson noted, it was her wage earning that enabled the family to survive as an economic unit: "We wound up there after my grandmother died in 1936, and Grandpa's family just went to pot then, you know. Scattered out." Without Alta as both an anchor and a provider, her husband was not up to the task of keeping the family together. Her youngest children were sent to live with her married children. The daughter and son-in-law who lived with her were left to make their way as best they could. The havoc wreaked on the Scarbrough family by the loss of Alta is ample testimony to the importance of her economic contributions.[47]

Four

Mixed Messages

Home Extension Work among

Upcountry Farm Women in the 1920s and 1930s

In 1925 Edna Howard, the Cabell County, West Virginia, home demonstration agent, reported on her efforts to run a women's camp for home demonstration club members in Cabell and Wayne counties. Much to her chagrin, although Wayne County women enthusiastically participated, not a single Cabell County woman attended. "This fact was a keen disappointment to me. It was a failure on my part not to have representatives from my county," she lamented. Howard noted that she had planned for this camp at the various women's club meetings and that she had made considerable effort to recruit participants. "My conclusion is that they were not sufficiently interested. The camp had been planned for them not with them," she summarized.[1]

Howard's experience and the rare record of her frustration speaks volumes about the interactions between home demonstration workers and the upcountry farm women they served. Home demonstration agents, most often young women who had some college training in home economics or education, saw themselves as social workers ministering to the needs of rural communities. They believed they were bringing a type of salvation to isolated farming folk (often the people they had grown up among) in the form of knowledge of "modern" housekeeping practices, instruction in subsistence and marketing strategies, and organization of community-based relief efforts. Agents also faced the demands of a USDA bureaucracy that aimed to separate farming from homemaking and to help prosperous white farm families adopt urban middle-class living standards.

Yet as Edna Howard discovered, farm women were not always receptive to agents' prescriptions for salvation. Farm women themselves had competing motivations for participating in extension work. Many desired to enter the mainstream of a mass culture and economy, to improve their own families' standards of living, and to engage in work that they themselves found meaningful and satisfying. They made intervention an interactive process, shaped as much by its subjects as by its leaders. Farm women's decisions about which projects they would participate in determined the shape of extension service programs as surely as did the dictates of extension agents and state officials. As Howard discovered, agents could not accomplish much without the cooperation of the women they served. In the end, the programs provided to upcountry farm women were products of a negotiated process.

In the interwar years, upcountry farm women experienced the direct intervention of the federal government in their daily lives as never before. New Deal agricultural and relief programs supplemented existing home extension education programs in attempting to reshape Southern agriculture and the farm home. Home demonstration work, the oldest of these government programs, was also the only intervention targeted directly at the farm wife. An exploration of home demonstration work reveals that agents' visions of appropriate behavior for women of a particular race and class shaped the type of programming they offered to upcountry farm women. In the upcountry South, agents sought to improve farm life for middling and elite whites by promoting the gendered division of labor and the consumption patterns advocated by the USDA and by helping farm women increase farm income and conserve family resources. Agents also sought to improve the living standards of African American farm families in more limited ways. This left poor white women in a problematic location: in spite of their desperate poverty and obvious need for this type of programming, as white women they were not considered appropriate targets for instruction in basic home sanitation and food preservation such as that directed at African American women. Yet they did not have the resources to adopt middle-class consumption and homemaking practices. A look at extension work in the upcountry lends insight into the dynamics of formulating coherent social service agendas, demonstrating that the messy realities of economic necessity, racial and gender politics, and individual preference often thwarted bureaucrats' neat plans to improve the "common people."

The Development of Home Extension Work

Throughout the interwar period, a number of factors shaped the extension service's vision of farm women's roles, which in turn helped to shape the design of home extension education. The first was the agency's roots in the Progressive movement, a movement that subscribed to the middle-class notion of separate spheres and of progress through the rationalization of daily life. Alarmed that the growing exodus of rural people to cities and industrial jobs might foreshadow a looming food shortage, urban overcrowding, and a breakdown in Jeffersonian agrarian values, progressive reformers believed that education in scientific farming methods might improve farm profits, which would in turn encourage farmers to remain on the land. Many reformers believed that farm women, fed up with the hard work and lack of modern conveniences associated with rural life, were leading the march to the cities. For this reason, reformers also sought to improve the lot of the farm wife. The Progressive Era's Country Life movement ultimately culminated in the passage in 1914 of the Smith-Lever Act, which sparked the development of an organized national program of extension education. The Smith-Lever Act funded not only agricultural education for farmers but also home extension education designed to make rural life happier and healthier for the entire farm family by teaching farm wives to improve the farm home. The gender division of farm labor promoted by extension workers inhered in the very legislation that established the program.

The bureaucracy established to implement this organized program of rural education also helped to shape its mission and goals. The Smith-Lever Act provided federal funds to match state and local dollars for the appointment of agricultural and home demonstration agents in rural counties. Local agents worked for a state agricultural extension office set up at the state land-grant college or university. The state extension office, in turn, reported to the U.S. Extension Service set up within the Department of Agriculture. Because federal funding was so critical to the extension work, the upcountry's state directors took special care to follow federal guidelines in developing county-level programming. The essential county funding depended on local politicians. At the local level, town-based businessmen and elite commercial farmers often dominated politics. These men shared the USDA's vision of women as farm homemakers and supported programs that reflected their own views of appropriate roles for women, powerfully influencing home extension programming. Theirs was a middle-class vision that did not address the needs of the poorest farm families.

The USDA's vision of the appropriate gender division of labor on family farms, with men engaged in commercial agriculture and women engaged in homemaking, shaped the agency's staffing policies and job descriptions. Although farm women often engaged in farm production activities, the gender division of labor among agents did not reflect this pattern. Agricultural agents were invariably men. They usually worked with male farmers on farming problems. Home extension agents were women who worked with farm women on home-related projects, such as clothing or food preservation. However, in counties where there was no home demonstration agent, male agricultural agents might work with women on poultry and dairy production projects; and in counties where there was no agricultural agent, a home demonstration agent took on this task.

Like the university-based specialists and the state administrators who guided home extension program development, home demonstration agents had usually studied home economics or education at the state's colleges and universities. Home economics, a new profession, based its claims to professional legitimacy on its role in teaching wives to be both homemakers and scientific housekeepers. While the term "homemaking" emphasized women's roles as creators of a refuge from a harsh public world, scientific housekeeping implied that housework was a skill requiring specialized knowledge and extensive training. Home economists taught women that scientific housekeeping was based on increased efficiency, and that efficiency could best be improved by using new household appliances and rationalizing the work process. This professional outlook meant that home demonstration agents were predisposed to teach white farm women that they should primarily be both consumers and emotional centers of the household rather than producers.

Gender hierarchies in extension work emanated from another source as well. Rural reformers struggled to gain professional recognition and legitimacy in a culture that saw rural life as backward and inferior to modern urban life. Their very contact with farm people was a sign of lower status. As a result, extension agents and other rural professionals sought to gain professional status by altering rural culture to fit urban standards. To accomplish this, agents focused on science and research as badges of academic legitimacy, preached the gospel of increased production to gain respect from commercial interests, and promoted a new farm gender hierarchy in order to increase their own status. Production issues were defined as largely the domain of male agents, while home and family issues became the province of females. In the process, agricultural institutions denigrated the importance of the "social issues" addressed by women agents in favor of "bigger" economic issues addressed by men.

While the outlook of home economists shaped home extension programs, race was a factor that further complicated the task of designing and delivering home extension education in the upcountry South, creating more tensions in extension service programming. Throughout the South, black farm families were served by African American agents who worked within the state extension service. In the upcountry, the black agent program received little or no funding from the counties because local governments failed to appropriate any funds for work among blacks. Nearly all of its funding came from the state-funded black land-grant institutions (Tennessee State University, West Virginia State University, and South Carolina State University), from the Rockefeller Foundation's General Education Board, and from the federal government. The lack of additional local funds meant that the salary and programming budget for African American agents was severely underfunded.

White Southerners did not see black women in the same roles as white women. Since whites considered African American women a source of cheap labor in white homes and on farms, they did want to encourage them to adopt the white model of the home-based farm housewife. This racial caste system made it difficult for white bureaucrats to envision black women in the same programs as white women. African

American women themselves preferred different programming than white women. Assumptions about the meanings of whiteness and blackness also shaped agents' interactions with women of both races. White agents focused much of their energy on helping white farm wives raise good rural citizens. In doing so, they believed they would help assure "the well-being of the race," in the words of one historian. At the same time, white administrators urged black agents to engage in "race improvement." By impressing upon black women appropriate values and behavior, agents could assist in managing local race relations.[2]

All these factors—the tension between the reality of farm life and the extension service's vision of the ideal farm wife, the institutionalized racism of the early twentieth-century South, and tensions within the home economics profession itself—combined to create a home extension service agenda rife with conflicting messages. In the upcountry South, then, home extension work in the interwar years was marked by tensions.

The Influence of Home Demonstration Work

Extension service programs never reached significant numbers of white farm women in the upcountry. Even at the height of club membership in 1929, less than 5 percent of all Tennessee farm women were enrolled in clubs. In South Carolina the peak year for membership was 1935, when 2.3 percent of all farm women belonged to home demonstration clubs. Fewer than 1 percent of West Virginia's farm women joined clubs throughout the 1920s and 1930s. For most farm women struggling to survive the economic crisis, home extension agents' agendas must have seemed far removed from the realities of their daily lives, a fact sometimes portrayed in popular culture. In her 1932 novel, *The Weather Tree*, Maristan Chapman wrote about life in a Tennessee mountain farming community. Chapman's characters were proud of their heritage of hard work and independence, and they were resistant to efforts by outsiders to make over their culture in the image of urban communities. They were also contemptuous of government officials who purported to help them improve their economic conditions. Mountain women were particularly skeptical of USDA officials who visited the community. Thelma, a young woman who had been keeping house for her brothers since her mother's death when Thelma was twelve, describes it this way to Barsha Lowe, the wisest and most respected farm wife in the community:

> "Thing that makes me just leaping mad is the folks they send spying to tell us what's amiss! There was a woman person come snooping around the store one day, claimed she'd been paid to come and count how much we ate. Who'd be paying to learn that? Claimed we'd ought to eat other than we do, but failed of saying where we'd get it."
>
> "Half of the folk government sends by to teach us farming is unknowen which side a cow is milked," Barsha said.[3]

Like the characters in Chapman's novel, many rural upcountry folk were suspicious of the abilities and motives of extension workers and other agents of the federal government. At times agents also severely miscalculated the type and method of programming needed by farm families. In 1935 the Cabell County, West Virginia, home demonstration agent discovered this. She noted that she had had little success with one new club because it "had several members who could not read and write and we made the mistake of starting out with a series of lessons that was far beyond their interests and abilities."[4]

Not only did many white women reject participation in extension work because of its lack of relevance in their daily lives, but many of those who did participate recalled doing so as a hobby and as a social outlet after their children were grown. For them, home demonstration work was a diversion, not a resource that aided them in surviving economic crisis. In 1935 the Cabell County, West Virginia, agent complained that one of her new home demonstration clubs suffered from this problem. She lamented, "We thought the women understood the work they were expected to do, but some of the leaders got the idea that the meetings were largely social." The women most likely to have time for such social activities were those at the top of the economic ladder. There is no demographic information on club members to indicate whether class was a factor in determining who participated. Anecdotal evidence from oral histories does suggest, however, that the wives of more prosperous farmers were more likely to be enrolled than the wives of poor farm owners or tenants.[5]

Although many white women viewed home demonstration clubs as purely social activities, others saw the extension service as only one of many strategies they used to cope with the economic crisis. Agents provided much-needed information on homemaking and subsistence production. Pearl Faulkner recalled that her mother joined the Brush Creek Farm Women's Club in Mercer County, West Virginia, in 1919. Raising a large family on an isolated mountain farm, she avidly read the pamphlets distributed by agents and tried to apply their advice in her home. "I don't believe it [home demonstration work] meant as much to me because I was able to get more information than she was," Faulkner recalled. "It was about the only information she had. . . . The lesson material in my mother's day was next to the Bible. She followed the Bible, and she followed the club lessons, all the instructions."[6]

Farm women's own testimony indicates that they joined for their own reasons and that they focused on their own projects. In 1935 West Virginia home demonstration agents were devoting 1,557 days to home furnishings and clothing projects and only 1,015 to food and nutrition projects. Yet one farm woman quoted in the state director's report said, "The most important [thing I learned] is my knowledge of food values and preparation. My little daughter was skinny and looked ill all the time. . . . I learned that foods contained different nutrients and that each of them has a special work to perform. . . . I set about correcting my child's diet and now she is the picture of health."[7] Like this West Virginia mother, many rural upcountry women picked and chose among the home demonstration programs that best fitted their needs and interests.

Home Extension Work: The Bureaucracy

The Agricultural Extension Service established by the Smith-Lever Act grew quickly. World War I created unprecedented demand for farm products and an all-time high in farm prices. During the war, the agency had successfully used education and propaganda to lead the effort to increase food production. Extension service funding had been increased to provide for additional personnel to meet the wartime emergency. Also as part of the food production effort, farm credit strictures were eased, enabling farmers to borrow large amounts of money to buy more land, livestock, and modern equipment. The advice supplied by agents helped increase farm yields just as high wartime prices helped farmers realize their most profitable years ever. Due partly to this wartime expansion and partly to the goodwill created by a booming agricultural economy, contemporary observers noted that the extension service had gained wider acceptance within farming communities during the war years.

The boom was over as quickly as it had begun. The end of the war proved disastrous for farmers as commodity prices plummeted. Farmers who had gone heavily into debt to modernize and expand found that they could not meet their financial obligations. The crisis in the farm economy had an impact, in turn, on extension work. State and local tax revenue collection declined due to the agricultural depression. As rural communities were squeezed by the fiscal crisis, local governments cut matching funds for extension agents' salaries in spite of the fact that farm families needed more help than ever in coping with the economic crisis. In Tennessee the numbers of agricultural and home demonstration agents working in the counties fell almost to prewar levels. In 1920 Tennessee had county agricultural agents in 45 of its 95 counties and home demonstration agents in 41 counties. By 1921 this number had fallen to 38 and 26 respectively, figures that would not significantly improve until the advent of New Deal funding supplements in the mid-1930s. Similar fluctuations in funding for agents' salaries occurred in South Carolina and West Virginia. Christine South noted a declining number of South Carolina home demonstration clubs in 1921 "due to some counties failing to appropriate funds." In those cases in which counties could not afford to fund both a county agent and a home demonstration agent, it was usually the home demonstration agent who was cut, because "women's work," defined as homemaking, was perceived as less critical to the local economy than "men's work," defined as production for the market. State extension service annual reports claimed that some county agents tried to work with farm women to make up for this loss, but specific examples are rare in the reports. Male agents occasionally reported helping women on such large-scale improvements as installing bathrooms and window screens and on dairying and poultry products. The reports make no mention of agricultural agents advising women on housekeeping issues, financial decision making, or home marketing initiatives.[8]

Home Extension Work Among African American Women

Home demonstration programs for the upcountry's black farm women were considerably different than programs for white women. Both the white bureaucracy and African American extension agents emphasized a different type of programming for African American women, but undoubtedly for different reasons. African American agents often found themselves torn between a commitment to Booker T. Washington's self-help philosophy and white benefactors' and administrators' pressures to teach black women minimal skills for self-sufficiency. While white agents could not envision black women in the role of consumer-homemaker, African American agents recognized that their constituents needed instruction on nutrition, health, and subsistence production far more than strategies for purchasing appliances or beautifying the living room. By electing to participate in some programs and avoid others, black farm women participated in shaping extension programs for themselves. Close analysis of the ways in which black home extension work differed from that of whites also illustrates how racial bias in the provision of government services limited the funding levels and the range of services received by African American farm families.[9]

In order to educate black farmers in better farming methods, officials at Tuskegee Institute in Alabama and Hampton Institute in Virginia had cooperated with the USDA to begin a "Negro Extension Program" several years before the 1914 Smith-Lever Act established a national system of extension education. In the upcountry regions, extension work for African Americans arrived later. It was 1916 before the Tennessee director of extension work felt the white program was sufficiently organized to turn his attention to Negro extension work. That year he appointed two African American women and three African American men as agents. By 1924 there were five black male agents and five black female agents, a number that was to remain fairly stable until 1936. Black agents made up about 10 percent of the state's extension agent staff, a number roughly equivalent to their 11 percent of the farm population. Yet this seeming equivalence is misleading. Unlike white agents, who had the luxury of devoting time and attention to the people of one county, Tennessee's African American agents had to serve several counties. The District IV black home agent served thirty East Tennessee counties. Because she lost much of the time that could have been devoted to working with farm women driving from county to county on rutted country roads, she only worked with African American women from ten to twelve counties in any given year.[10]

As in Tennessee, South Carolina's black extension program was not as well funded as white work. Negro work in South Carolina began during World War I, but it was discontinued in July 1919 when the federal emergency appropriation was withdrawn. The next year, the state extension service hired fourteen agents to work in fourteen counties during the summer months, not year-round as white agents worked. The following year, the appointment was increased to three and a half months. Occasionally local African American communities raised funds to hire agents for additional months. Similarly, in 1925 West Virginia was served by five black agents, about 10 percent of the state total of fifty-seven agents. Only two of these agents were women. By 1935, due to Depression-era cuts in state funding, there were only two black agents (one female) among the sixty-eight in West Virginia and only one woman.[11]

In general, reports in the three states indicated that African American farm families received extension agents cordially and welcomed the aid. Nonetheless, African Americans sometimes harbored suspicions regarding the intent of extension agents, particularly in the early years. In 1920 South Carolina home demonstration director Christine South noted that "the biggest obstacle to be overcome [in establishing the Negro work] was an occasional sign of the distrust among the colored people themselves. But this soon wore away." It was not only important for black women to accept home demonstration work, but it was also crucial that this work not threaten the dominance of the white community. Again and again state directors reported, as the South Carolina director did in 1920, that "the work was well received by white and colored."[12]

The white directors of the state home demonstration programs displayed considerable paternalism in their attitudes toward Negro extension work. Yet they also recognized the very real problems of poverty and poor living standards among rural upcountry blacks. In 1921 the South Carolina state director noted, "It has been our aim to strike at the fundamental problems in the life of our colored people, such as unsanitary home surroundings, poorly prepared food, and lack of a balanced ration." In her 1932 annual report, the Tennessee home agent for the eastern district noted that black home demonstration agent Sheilah Guess "feels very keenly that the health of the negro people must be guarded, so she emphasizes the growing of a year round garden, more poultry, and a cow for every home, homes kept in better repair, screened and made more sanitary and attractive." In West Virginia, African American agents arranged for immunization and health clinics in local communities, taught rural families how to raise diverse gardens and can their own food, and demonstrated techniques for improving home sanitation. For cash-strapped African American families, a garden was especially vital to providing the family with a balanced diet. In East Tennessee in 1926, 150 black women participated in the home garden project, growing a variety of vegetables. In South Carolina 1,482 black women participated in garden projects in 1922, producing over $20,000 of fruits and vegetables. Whites also participated in this program in large numbers, but blacks' participation in this program in larger numbers than in consumption programs indicates that they were again setting their own agenda for extension work.[13]

Black agents emphasized programs like home gardening and health, which improved the well-being of African American farm families, and food preparation and preservation programs, which improved family nutrition. Racial discrepancies in enrollment in this project also suggest that black women used the extension service help to meet their families' most basic needs. The discrepancy may also indicate that white women had more money with which to buy food. In 1925 African American women in Tennessee enrolled in the food preservation project preserved an average of 165 quarts of food each, while white women averaged only 48 quarts each. African American agents probably saw this project as more useful to clients, so they devoted more time to it.[14]

Although they focused the bulk of their efforts on projects related to farm families' health and diet, black agents did spend some time on consumption-oriented projects, such as home improvement, dispensing advice that was impractical for many black farm women to implement. How many African American women participated in home improvement programs remains unclear, although black agents did note that some black women made improvements to their homes. East Tennessee black agent Kate Gresham ran a Kitchen Improvement Program in 1925. The project emphasized the purchase of appliances and efficient kitchen design. Although eighty-seven African American women among her black home demonstration club members participated in the program in East Tennessee, the district agent's report does not specify the kitchen improvements they made as it does for white women. In fact, other statistics on participation suggest that African American women had few resources for the consumer items the extension service promoted. In 1928 black agents in Tennessee reported that among the 423 African American women enrolled in home improvement programs that year, only one woman reported installing a power washing machine, eleven installed kitchen sinks, one purchased a vacuum cleaner, twenty-four bought electric or gas irons, and eight purchased "iceless" refrigerators. These low numbers reflect not only the lack of resources to buy appliances, but also the fact that fewer African American farm homes had electricity.[15]

There is only one example in the annual reports of black home demonstration club members engaging in a major consumption-oriented home improvement project, and that example suggests that, when time and money permitted, African American women were eager to pursue the same projects as their white counterparts. Dozens of white home demonstration clubs decorated a "Better Homes Demonstration House," but there is only one example of a black club undertaking a demonstration home. In 1928 African American agent Kate Gresham led her Blount County, Tennessee, home demonstration club in turning the clubhouse loaned them by the Aluminum Company of America (ALCOA) into a demonstration house.[16]

It is significant that Gresham's club women were no longer rural residents. Most were rural natives of deep South states whose husbands had been recruited to fill the hottest, dirtiest jobs at the ALCOA's East Tennessee plant. In 1920 African American workers and their families made up almost half the population of the 3,200-resident company town, Alcoa, far outnumbering the population of the county's seventy-seven black-operated farms. These African American town dwellers enjoyed homes with running water, electricity, and indoor plumbing, a great improvement over the primitive conditions most had endured on farms. Although most of the black town women were not stay-at-home wives in the traditional white, middle-class sense, but rather were domestic workers for whites in Maryville, their jobs allowed them a modicum of free time to devote to such an involved project, something they would not have had if they had been working to eke out a living on a subsistence farm. They also used this opportunity to seek a level of respectability, as urban black women did through women's club activities. They were wage earners and full participants in the cash economy; unlike rural black women, they *had* money to spend. The existence of the black home demonstration house in Blount County suggests that, where funding and facilities were available, African American women may have been as interested in consumption-oriented programs as white women.[17]

Although most African American women did not make the home improvements emphasized by the extension service, it cannot be assumed that agents did not teach them other methods of home improvement that they did implement. The forms used to make agents' reports required them to quantify the number of women participating and the number making specific types of improvements, such as purchasing appliances and undertaking major remodeling projects. Significant home improvements that did not fall into these categories remained invisible. In a rare case, agent Kate Gresham's narrative report was excerpted in the 1926 Tennessee annual report. Her statement indicates that her own home improvement work stressed home sanitation. She emphasized the importance of installing window screens in homes, an improvement rarely mentioned by white agents, who usually worked with the most prosperous white families—families who already enjoyed window screens. As a result of her work that year, Gresham reported that fifty homes were equipped with wire screens and seventy-five homes with mosquito bar netting. Black agents used their limited resources to teach African American farm women to make relatively inexpensive home improvements that would significantly effect the health of the family rather than consumer improvements that remained out of reach.[18]

Home improvement programs were not the only extension programs for black women that emphasized consumption. The clothing project was also part of the black extension program. In Tennessee, Kate Gresham reported holding a clothing contest with twenty women in one African American women's club. Yet even in the clothing project, black women were less involved than white women. In 1925 the 1,037 African American women enrolled in the clothing project made 721 garments. In other words, only a little more than two-thirds of the black women made even one garment, a sharp contrast to the three garments per woman made by

white women participants. This disproportionate participation in the production of clothing points to the black women's more limited resources
for buying fabric and sewing machines as well as the greater amount of
time black women spent on farm work.[19]

With the onset of the Great Depression, African American agents
taught women enrolled in the clothing project new coping strategies. In
order to reduce the family's need for cash, black home demonstration
agents taught women how to remodel clothing and advised them to buy
mill ends from textile mills at 15 to 30 cents a pound. One African American woman reportedly made thirty garments for her family of five for
$1.05 by using "good serviceable" mill ends. This differed from the white
program, which taught women to turn men's suits into women's dresses,
possibly because white men were more likely than black men to have
extra old suits available for reworking.[20]

Black women's low level of participation in consumption-oriented
programs such as home improvement and clothing also indicates their
own efforts to select programs that filled their own needs and interests.
They participated in larger numbers in other programs that met their
more basic needs. In this manner, they helped to determine the types of
programming provided for them instead of simply accepting the agenda
set by the state extension service bureaucrats.

Not only did African American women engage in projects that improved family health, but they also participated in efforts to earn extra
cash. As with white women, home demonstration agents encouraged
black women to raise poultry for home consumption and for extra income. More than one thousand South Carolina black women participated
in the poultry project. Tennessee women of both races received funding
through a "return pullet" project that gave participants eggs or newly
hatched chicks to raise. The women kept the hens and sold a specified
number of pullets at a special sale in order to repay the sponsor. This program provided the capital women needed to get started raising poultry.
In 1925, 746 Tennessee black women statewide raised 16,184 birds. They
sold at least some of their hens, earning a profit of $2,673 or $3.50 each.
This contrasted sharply with white women's average earnings of $14.06
each. The lower profit levels do not necessarily mean that African American women were reaping lower benefits. It is likely that they were using a
higher proportion of their flocks to feed their families and were engaged

in bartering within the black community, an exchange that would have remained invisible to agents. It is also possible that black women deliberately underreported their incomes for fear they might be penalized by the white bureaucracy in the future for making too much money.[21]

With the stock market crash in November 1929, the bleak lives of southern African American farm families became desperate indeed. Plunging commodity prices further reduced the cash incomes of black farm families, while the general economic depression eliminated much of the off-farm wage work that blacks had long used to supplement meager farm earnings. Although African American home agents continued to engage in vital work, the number of African American women participating in extension programs declined sharply during the first years of the Depression, a pattern similar to that of white women. Although South Carolina and West Virginia did not keep consistent records of membership in black home demonstration clubs, in Tennessee membership plummeted from 859 in 1929 to 64 in 1932. The state report does not comment on the drop in participation by black women, but the fact that extension service staffing levels for black agents remained level suggests that the women themselves were too destitute to spare energy to participate in extension service programs. Many African American families were also being pushed off the land. Often they were forced to move frequently in search of steadily declining numbers of tenant farming slots, making it difficult for women to participate in home extension work. Enrollment climbed to 413 women in 1934, and additional funding and staffing from the 1936 Bankhead-Jones Act helped increase the numbers, but enrollment did not return to 1929 levels in the decade.[22]

With the onset of the Great Depression, black home agents apparently poured some of their efforts into helping farm families adjust production levels of various farm commodities to try to maximize their profits. There is no evidence that white home agents worked on these clearly agricultural issues at this point in the Depression, a fact that raises questions about why black home agents labored in this "male" domain. It is possible that many African American women were engaged in farm production work with their husbands, making it natural for female agents to work with them. More probably, the general understaffing of the black program led African American home agents to work on farm production problems. For most families, the need for cash income was an urgent

priority; thus, female agents serving counties not served by a black agricultural agents may have helped their constituents try to increase their
profits by assisting them with farm production issues. Whatever the reason, in 1931 Tennessee's black home agents across the state advised
twenty-eight farmers on how to adjust their production of wheat, corn,
potatoes, tobacco, truck crops, dairy cattle, hogs, and poultry, using the
Agricultural Extension Service's Economic Outlook, a prediction of commodity price levels for the coming year. In 1933 home agents assisted 124
black farmers in adjusting production.[23]

Although the Tennessee Extension Service Annual Reports repeatedly stated that "colored work was practically the same as white," there
was actually considerable variation in the type of work undertaken. As
we have seen, some of this variation was due to black agents' choice to
focus on the programs that would be most useful for farm families and to
African American women's choice to participate in programs that met
their most urgent needs. Other differences, however, were due to the lack
of funding provided for black programs and to racial biases that deemed
certain types of programs appropriate for only one race or the other.[24]

Among the programs virtually reserved for white women was the
farm marketing program. This program set up local markets at which
women sold their farm and home products. The university's home marketing specialist and local agents also assisted women in setting up their
own money-making enterprises, such as home-based tea rooms and bed-
and-breakfast operations. In a few cases, agents assisted women in setting up community businesses, such as cheese-processing plants and
crafts workshops. Except for the poultry project, there is little record of
involvement by African American women in farm marketing. This may
have been due to a lack of emphasis by black agents. Each of them served
hundreds of women in several counties, which would have left them
hard-pressed to find time to do more than assist farm families in meeting
immediate needs for food and clothing. Nonetheless, black women also
lacked resources to set up curb markets or to provide the small amounts
of capital they needed to begin producing enough for sale, help that the
extension service provided for white women. Another possible reason
that African American women did not participate in farm marketing
programs is that, in the upcountry, the small and dispersed black farm

population would have had a difficult time finding a sufficiently large market for their products among other poor black farmers.[25]

Racial biases were not only reflected in differences in programming and funding but also in the attention given to black extension work. Black work received less publicity from state extension service officials. Extension official Almon Sims devoted only two paragraphs in his 44-page 1939 history of Tennessee's extension work to the development of the Negro extension program. Similarly, each Tennessee annual report had approximately three hundred pages of narrative text, but black home extension work never merited more than four pages. In West Virginia the attention given to Negro work ranged from no space in 1921 to twelve pages of a 400-page annual report in 1925. South Carolina published a home demonstration work annual report separate from the one for agricultural work. Negro work generally received five to six pages of coverage in this 100-page report. Members of the state extension bureaucracy considered work with white families the central story, with token examples of African American work thrown in to prove that the work existed. Since the district agents who compiled these reports were being evaluated by white state extension service officials, who were in turn trying to obtain funding from a white legislature, they had plenty of incentive for emphasizing work with white women and for not turning African American farm families into economic rivals of whites.[26]

Racial bias among the extension workers was further evidenced in frequent overtones of racial condescension in these reports. In 1928 a Tennessee district home demonstration agent reported on the appointment of Sheilah Guess to replace Kate Gresham as the black home agent. In describing Guess's work, the district agent commented: "I was well pleased with the way she handled a group of twenty club girls [apparently young women] of different ages at Oakland, Knox county. She was able to keep every one busy all the time. . . . The girls seemed very much at ease yet very respectful toward her. I always find her calm and even tempered, well composed and always neatly dressed." The district agent's tone implies that she was pleasantly surprised to find such a competent African American agent. Similarly, in 1920 Christine South, director of South Carolina home extension work, reported: "We were fortunate in the colored women that we secured as agents. They were, without exception, sensibly practical women, all of them far above the average in education. Some of them were real leaders of their people." These comments were remarkable because state extension service employees did not comment on the professionalism of *individual* white agents.[27]

Other remarks by state extension service officials demonstrated this same racial condescension. In 1926 the Tennessee state extension service director noted that "most of the subject matter and project activity has to be simplified and modified to meet the needs of the negro county agent and home demonstration work." South Carolina's Christine South expressed surprise in 1922 that African American women embraced the learning opportunities provided by the extension service. She remarked, "It is a great pleasure to note the eagerness with which they receive new ideas."[28]

Even black agents were guilty of these types of remarks. In 1938 G. C. Wright, a black man who was the special agent for Tennessee Negro work (a new position funded with Bankhead-Jones dollars), remarked: "It was rather remarkable the interest shown in this campaign despite the fact that we have had Better Homes Campaigns for a number of years. Since the Negroes, as a race, are great imitators, the examples set by the whites serve to stimulate work among them."[29] The fact that Wright was reporting to a white superior probably influenced the condescending tenor of his remarks. Perhaps too, his statement reflects class tensions that were always present between better class and poor blacks. Nonetheless, the fact that his statement was excerpted by the white state home extension agent to appear in the annual report is indicative of the stereotypes and assumptions that underlay the white bureaucracy's attitude toward African American farm families and black home extension work.

Work among White Women: The 1920s

Programming for white farm women during this period falls into three distinct stages, though specific programming varied considerably from state to state. Although the extension service's vision of farm women's roles dictated the basic outline of programming, the shifts in programming thrusts grew out of the USDA's recognition of current farm economic conditions. From 1920 to 1929, agents emphasized the development of farm women's skills as consumers and as subsistence and market producers. From 1930 to 1935, the worst years of the Great Depression, agents tried to help rural constituents survive the Depression by adopting new production methods and coping skills as well as by organizing relief efforts in rural communities. Finally, from 1936 to 1940, agents' attention returned to consumption even as they maintained some emphasis on white women's production and coping skills.

The bleak agricultural economy of the 1920s provided home extension agents with an opportunity to help the poorest farm women improve their financial pictures. Even in the most prosperous rural counties, many farm families struggled with dire economic problems, and agents recognized the farm wife's productive work and her central place in the family economy by providing marketing projects. Yet agents and their bosses in state extension offices shared a vision of appropriate behavior for middle-class white farm wives—a vision modeled on the suburban homemaker. As a result, agents emphasized that the first goal of a good farm wife should be to improve the appearance and efficiency of the farm home and grounds.

Throughout the 1920s, home improvement projects were a major focus for home extension agents' energies. Home improvement programming reflected the extension service's belief that the farm wife should spend her time making a pleasant and attractive home for her family, leaving the productive, income-producing activities to her husband—a middle-class view. Agents stressed this program because of their belief (often accurate) that farm women were more unhappy with the substandard conditions of the farm home, conditions that compared unfavorably with middle-class homes, than farm men were with farm life. Because these programs were most appealing and accessible to farm women with the financial resources to make home improvements, agents spent most of their time with middling and elite farm women, leaving little time for those women needing assistance with more basic problems. But for the farm women involved, home improvement projects reaped tangible benefits.

Agents' belief that farm women envied the lifestyles of their middle-class sisters led them to advocate a model farm home that looked very much like the middle-class home. Agents promoted such improvements as paint and wallpaper, new curtains, and new appliances. Outside experts were brought in to help with the task of upgrading the farm house. In 1922 an East Tennessee district home demonstration agent reported, "Fortunately for Tennessee, Mrs. Wilmot, an interior decorator from New York, gave illustrated lectures to each of the four districts. . . . Many practical ideas were gained." The presence of a New York designer with her urban expertise lent prestige and credibility to the entire program. Women learned to improve floor coverings, rearrange furniture, and add wallpaper, pictures, and rugs to make the home more attractive.[30]

Agents' home improvement advice went beyond the interior aesthetics to focus on the efficiency of the homemaker's work space, another piece of the middle-class model. The kitchen, the very heart of efficient homemaking, was a central focus of improvement campaigns. In 1925, for example, the kitchen improvement contest was a major programming initiative. Home demonstration agents helped white women improve the arrangement, functionality, and appearance of their kitchens. Under the headline "What the Kitchen Campaign Meant to Me as a Club Member," a Sullivan County, Tennessee, farm wife reported on the benefits to many women of installing plumbing in the kitchen, building cabinets, improving ventilation, rearranging the work space for greater efficiency, and adding new paint, linoleum, and curtains. In 1921 South Carolina agents organized a Kitchen Improvement Contest, which offered a Hoosier kitchen cabinet as first prize and several small, labor-saving appliances as lesser prizes. As a result of the contest, they reported that 46 water systems and 132 sinks and drain boards had been installed, as well as 6 septic tanks and hundreds of improvements in flooring, lighting, ventilation, and arrangement of equipment. These figures suggest that most farm women could not afford the major expenses of the improvements most strongly advocated by agents but eagerly adopted suggestions they could afford.[31]

Farm wives found that more efficient kitchens lightened their work loads, a benefit that agents emphasized when promoting the kitchen improvement project. The regular extension service column in Blount County, Tennessee's *Maryville Times*, a weekly newspaper, described the local kitchen improvement campaign:

"BETTER KITCHENS" MAKE HOUSEWORK A PLEASURE
What could be more satisfying than to have a room you disliked changed into one in which you enjoy working. This [kitchen improve-

ment] "movement" recognizes that kitchens in countless homes are poorly planned as to lighting, placement of equipment, and decoration. Failure to appreciate the importance of these factors has placed a burden of extra work on many homeworkers.

This agent saw farm women being defined as workers, albeit as domestic workers. She went on to describe how home demonstration agents were planning more convenient and "cheerful" kitchens. All of these improvements were designed to make the farm homemaker happier and more efficient in her work space, implying that the reward would be less fatigue so that she could devote more time to her family.[32]

In spite of the emphasis on improved efficiency, agents seemed determined to separate the farmhouse from the barnyard. Agents' prescriptions for more efficient kitchens rarely included spaces for such farm production activities as separating cream or churning butter, activities that were often the responsibility of farm wives. Instead, they emphasized installing a sink on the back porch where the farmer could wash his work-soiled hands, and providing storage for work boots and coats smelling of the barnyard outside the kitchen, both attempts to remove evidence of farm production from the realm of the home. Again the agents' advice revealed that theirs was very much a "town home" vision. The white farm women themselves were more practical, however. Their descriptions of their own improvement projects often mentioned making space for processing separated milk and butter within the newly efficient farm kitchen.[33]

Home improvement did not stop with home interiors. Agents considered the appearance of the home grounds just as important. And as was the case with home interiors, the manicured and landscaped lawns of the suburban home were the model. Ironically, progressive reformers who urged city-dwellers to remove to suburbs had intended that suburbs would pastoralize the home—that is, create a bucolic existence removed from the squalor of city life, something resembling the mythic purity of the farm home. Of course, this ideology bore no relation to the reality of farm life.

Likewise, agents' efforts to make the farmhouse yard look like a suburban lawn also had no relation to the productive activity that was the very reason for the farm's existence. For white farm women, these well-groomed exteriors were symbolic of leisure time that could be spent on such genteel activities as gardening, long considered a pursuit of elite women. Only the wives and daughters of very prosperous farmers could afford to spend time in an activity that did not generate a cash income or food for the family table. Just as removing production from the farm home and re-creating it as a haven from a hectic world separated home life from farm life, so did elaborate home grounds separate the farm families' exterior surroundings from the business of the farm. Instead of kitchen gardens one step away from the back door and chickens scratching in the dooryard, agents promoted a more refined setting for the farmhouse—an elaborate, ornamental garden and a lush, green lawn—a formal entrance with the farm and barn invisible in the rear. To this end, agents taught farm women to plant shrubbery, flowers, and ornamental trees to beautify the area surrounding the farmhouse. At a Greene County, Tennessee, "Home Improvement Day," the director of the state extension service "told [farm women] of things to do in beautifying the home grounds" and showed farm women how to start cuttings for base plantings of shrubbery. Farm magazines ran reports on the successful efforts of home demonstration agents in leading white farm women to improve the home grounds. A 1929 *Progressive Farmer* story entitled "A Telling Campaign for Prettier Home Grounds" included photographs of lush gardens and well-landscaped farm homes that had been improved through the leadership of home demonstration agents. Photos of these homes and gardens offer little hint that the houses featured were located on farms. They could just as easily have been found in any suburban neighborhood. Yet, as with interior improvement projects, farm women were selective about where they spent their limited time and money. Significantly lower numbers of women enrolled in home grounds than in other projects. In Kanawha County, West Virginia, 200 women enrolled in canning and 300 in clothing in 1921, while only 125 signed up for house and lawn improvement. Very few adopted the more expensive practices enumerated in agents' reports. Two installed water systems, four repaired fences, and four seeded lawns, whereas over one hundred planted flowers and vines.[34]

By encouraging women to improve their homes inside and out, agents were in effect encouraging them to purchase more consumer products, another reflection of their use of the suburban model and of the consumerism of the 1920s. There was a measure of self-interest in agents' promotion of consumer purchases. Agents formed alliances with local businessmen, who not only provided much of the funding for special extension service projects but also formed the local political leadership that voted on county appropriations for home demonstration work. These alliances between agents and businessmen were apparent in various home improvement events assembled by home extension agents that subtly promoted the products of local businesses. In 1926 Greene County, Tennessee, agent Mabel Moore organized a "Home Improvement Day" especially for home demonstration club members from the county's farms and from the small town of Greenville. The event was cosponsored by Greenville's merchants. In the morning, specialists from the state extension service gave demonstrations on "Curtains and Draperies" and on "Making Lamp Shades." Following lunch, Miss Moore's report explained, farm women toured "the business places [which sold] utensils and furnishings which would lighten housework and make their homes attractive." Similarly, the *Maryville Times* described Blount County's Home Improvement Day, which included displays by local banks that assisted women in establishing savings and checking accounts, furniture and appliance displays by furniture stores, and housewares displays from dime stores. In all, twenty-seven merchants touted their wares and their services at the event, providing farm women with a source for all the products they could possibly need to improve their homes.[35]

In order to demonstrate the advantages of this improved farm home to as wide an audience as possible, several Tennessee home demonstration agents led their white members in developing a "Better Homes Demonstration House" similar to the one developed by Kate Gresham's black women already described. In the East Tennessee district alone, 2,650 people visited demonstration homes in 1928. Houses were usually loaned, and furnishings were loaned or donated by individuals and local businesses. Club members arranged the houses for "healthy, efficient, and comfortable farm life" complete with attractive furniture, indoor plumbing, electricity, appliances, and other amenities that most farm families could not afford. Furthermore, most of the demonstration houses were in the county seat rather than on farms. This meant that many of the farm women who were supposed to benefit from seeing the example of a model farm home were never able to get into town to see it. Instead, town women made up the bulk of the visitors. Once again, the model town home and the model farm home must have looked very much alike. The statements of women who participated in contests to recognize the "most improved" house or room also reflected farm women's acceptance of some elements of the middle-class model while retaining a sense of themselves as producers. The tensions between these two self-definitions were expressed by a Greene County, Tennessee, farm woman who described the Kitchen Improvement Contest this way: "What woman is there among us who does her own housework—and we are many—can go into a dingy, inconvenient, unattractive kitchen to do a half day's baking, or a whole day's canning, and keep a smile on her face and a song on her lips? . . . With our kitchens transformed into well-lighted convenient workshops, we enter on our work with renewed courage." Her emphasis on the psychological benefits of a beautified kitchen reflects the emotional language of middle-class homemaking advice—the construction of homemaking as a satisfying and important occupation. Yet this farm wife was not ready to discount her role as a farm producer. Calling a kitchen a workshop formed an explicit recognition of her role as producer, and her acknowledgment of the farm wife's need for "renewed courage" was an admission that farm life at that time required a tremendous amount of hard work and fortitude.[36]

In fact, many farm women used the proceeds of their farm-based work to make the improvements advocated by agents. In a typical alliance between farm magazines and the extension service, the Atlanta-based *Southern Ruralist* magazine cooperated with home demonstration agents throughout the South to sponsor a home improvement contest for Southern farm homes. Miss Mabel Worley of Hamilton County, Tennessee, one of 800 entrants from across the South, won the first prize of $500. The magazine featured photographs of Miss Worley's home before and after her extensive remodeling project. Worley sold flowers and butter, kept boarders, and did stenographic work to fund her improvements. She had invested considerable money and effort to transform her standard two-story farmhouse into a Colonial Revival dwelling reminiscent of plantation houses, complete with two-story white columns over the front porch and a balcony leading out from French doors on the second floor. Miss Worley had not only equipped her home with all the latest conveniences, but she also identified with a bygone South where white Southerners aspired to owning large plantation houses in which the domestic work would have been done by black slaves. In fact, owning such a fine home and commanding the aid of domestic servants was part of the very definition of the southern lady. One architectural historian has called the phenomenon of remodeling projects like Miss Worley's the "recreat[ion] in modern terms [of] the deferential social relations the antebellum plantation represented." In selecting Worley's home as the winner, the contest judges reinforced this model.[37]

By extension, Miss Worley's use of the model southern home for the southern lady indicated that she accepted the model that made the successful homemaker responsible for creating an emotionally satisfying home. She saw the nature of such a home as being visibly beautiful. She testified that "the winning of this prize is not only a great joy and satisfaction in receiving recognition of my struggles and hardships in making a 'real home,' but an inspiration to even greater effort to make it lovely—spiritually, mentally, and materially." For Worley a "real home" was a visually pleasing and materially substantial home. It contained all the latest conveniences. A "real home" belonged to white people. For African American women and white women who could not aspire to status as a white Southern lady, there would be no way to achieve a "real home." Here we see the emotional glorification of the home, interestingly enough from a single woman living in an inherited farm home.[38]

Home improvement projects were not the only consumption-oriented programs emphasized by home demonstration agents. They also put considerable effort into the clothing project, and farm women apparently found this project more accessible because it was more affordable. Home demonstration agents devoted much of their time to teaching the farm woman how to make herself more attractive for her husband and her neighbors. Home demonstration club sewing projects in the 1920s concentrated on helping farm women produce stylish and "appropriate" clothing for themselves. In 1926 "appropriate dress" received special emphasis in home demonstration programs. Women were taught that posture and line were more important to a stylish wardrobe than expensive fabric and fancy patterns. Perhaps this was an attempt to discourage women from adopting styles of dress—such as the styles adopted by working-class women—that were seen as gaudy. Agents had all club members make dresses from the same fabric and design to prove "that it is not the color or the fabric but the woman and the lines of her dress which gives her an air of distinction." Again, agents emphasized the middle-class standard of the stylish-yet-conservative matron. They ran fashion shows and dressmaking contests to encourage farm women to create more of their own garments, and women often adapted styles from fashion magazines or purchased patterns by mail from farm magazines in their efforts to outdo one another. They also showed women how to "remodel" old garments—that is, to spruce up a worn garment with new trim or to cut down a larger garment into a smaller one, for example by converting a man's wool coat into a woman's suit.[39]

The clothing project was one of the extension service's most popular programs in the 1920s. In 1925 the 3,192 Tennessee white women enrolled in the clothing project made 9,673 dresses and coats. This was a little more than three garments per woman. In 1921 South Carolina women remodeled 1,017 garments, while West Virginia women reported saving $635 by remodeling garments and making new ones. Perhaps the project's popularity was due to the fact that it was less expensive to make a few dresses than to install plumbing or redecorate a room. For women who controlled very little of the household's limited disposable income, this project would certainly have been more accessible. Since women were often unable to afford to improve their homes to the level of the suburban ideal, they may have found a stylish wardrobe one area in which they could compete with their sisters in town. The clothing project may also have appealed to farm women because, in a world where they made constant sacrifices for their families, they were eager to do something for themselves for a change.[40]

Home extension agents recognized that farm women often could not afford to engage in consumption, so they tried to help farm women find ways to earn additional money. Realizing that farm families needed additional income for necessities as well as for extras, they tried to address these needs through the home marketing project. Although this project explicitly recognized farm women's work as producers, many agents saw it as another means to the end of home improvement. In Tennessee, agents encouraged women to use their earnings to purchase laborsaving appliances and make other improvements rather than urging women to make a direct contribution to the family economy by spending earnings on necessities. In this way, agents promoted and yet trivialized farm women's work as producers while linking women's work with the purchase of consumer goods. But in West Virginia, always poorer, and South Carolina, where cotton farmers were being devastated by the boll weevil during the 1920s, agents touted farm marketing as a major means to assure family survival and raise the standard of living.[41]

Home demonstration agents' assistance in providing marketing opportunities had a significant impact on the white farm women who participated. One popular marketing effort was the establishment in a number of cities of curb markets, which sold garden produce, baked goods, plants, dairy products, and handicrafts. In Tennessee, individual white women reported annual curb market earnings ranging from an annual average of $254 to a high of $844 during the decade. Some agents started crafts workshops. Home demonstration women in Knox County, Tennessee, specialized in making hooked rugs, selling $2,500 worth of rugs between November 1927 and November 1928.[42]

Responding to the crisis precipitated by the boll weevil, South Carolina launched two important farm marketing efforts in the early 1920s. The first was a series of butter contests. Agents noted that much of the butter produced by farm women was "so poorly made as to be unsalable," so they gave demonstrations on butter production in eleven counties. Farm women learned the best temperatures for churning and ripening, proper sanitation, and even about feeds for cows that affected the quality of the butter. The demonstrations and the contests were open to home demonstration club members and nonmembers alike. These demonstrations were followed by contests offering prizes of cream separators, churns, and cash to producers of the best butter. The first year, 306 women participated, with increasing numbers thereafter. Farm women reported additional demand and higher prices for their improved butter.[43]

In 1921 the Home Demonstration Department of the South Carolina Extension Service expanded its efforts to help farm women market their goods by forming the South Carolina Home Producers Association. On behalf of this organization, agents negotiated contracts for the sale of particular farm products to retail outlets. Farm women signed contracts agreeing to produce specified amounts of these products according to a recipe provided by agents and to pack the products into standard containers for sale. Women sold butter, canned goods, soups, jellies, and relishes through this program. By 1922, 181 women throughout the state had participated, selling almost $14,000 worth of products.[44]

Home demonstration agents also encouraged farm women to raise and sell poultry for extra income, an activity that did not fit the suburban model. In South Carolina, clubs focused on culling inferior birds from the flock and educated women on building pure-bred stock. Agents organized community poultry associations to purchase birds in quantity. Tennessee home demonstration agents and extension service poultry specialists taught women about building proper poultry houses and using commercial feeds or mixing their own balanced rations at home. Women were encouraged to read poultry journals and to standardize breeds. Poultry associations and egg circles were formed for cooperative marketing efforts.[45]

Like the home marketing program, the extension service's food preparation and preservation programs were a more realistic recognition of farm women's central roles in the family economy than home improvement programs. These programs focused on teaching women to prepare nutritious and appealing meals and to can their garden produce for winter use. Before the introduction of self-sealing jars, many farm families had subsisted through the winter months on cornbread, dried beans and peas, pork, and root crops because they could not afford to buy green vegetables and fruits out of season. Canning programs provided a means to preserve the summer garden's bounty for a more diverse diet in the winter months. Agents taught thousands of women how to use the new self-sealing jars to preserve food for the winter months. In 1921 Tennessee home demonstration club members canned 112,413 quarts of fruits and vegetables. By 1925 this figure had risen to 184,062, and by 1928 to 691,149 quarts. In 1925 white women enrolled in canning projects canned an average of 48 quarts of food each. In South Carolina in 1922, 2,497 home demonstration club members reported canning over 600,000 quarts of fruits and vegetables, and in West Virginia over 300,000 quarts. These efforts significantly improved the nutrition and variety of the farm family's diet as well as saving them money.[46]

Not only did South Carolina agents help farm women to help themselves, but they encouraged them to help others. South Carolina's agents were by far the most activist agents in the upcountry. They not only engaged in limited outreach to poor rural women—even as early as the 1920s—but they led their home demonstration club members to conduct education and relief programs and lobbying campaigns. Several factors contributed to upstate South Carolina agents' activist bent. First, extension work in South Carolina was mature by the 1920s. South Carolina had been the home of the earliest home extension work in the nation, beginning with a girls' tomato canning club in Aiken County in 1904. By 1906 a state extension service was organized, supported jointly by the USDA, the Rockefeller Foundation's General Education Board, and Clemson College (now Clemson University). With its heavy dependence on cotton, South Carolina was also particularly hard hit by the arrival of the boll weevil. Agents could not have avoided the signs of rural poverty all around them. Finally, middling and elite white South Carolinians prided themselves on a long tradition of aid to their social inferiors.[47]

At the urging of home demonstration agents, South Carolina home demonstration club members engaged in a variety of activities designed to improve the quality of life for everyone in rural communities. They conducted milk campaigns, consisting of displays on the nutritional value of dairy products for store windows and speeches to schoolchildren on the importance of drinking milk. Agents organized baby nutrition clinics in rural communities in Spartanburg County. Public health nurses and pediatricians staffed these clinics, which screened babies for rickets and taught mothers about nutrition. Members in several upstate counties worked on beautifying school grounds and highways by planting flowers and ornamental shrubs. Clubs also conducted letter-writing campaigns to elected officials, lobbying them to take legislative action on behalf of compulsory school attendance laws, harsh punishments for violators of Prohibition laws, and funding for home and farm extension agents in every county. In 1929 home demonstration club members were successful in getting a bill passed to provide for the latter. Between 1926 and 1928 they also made a concerted effort to register farm women to vote.[48]

In the 1910s and 1920s, South Carolina also conducted home extension work among women in upstate mill villages. In 1912 Dr. D. B. Johnson, the president of Winthrop College, the home of South Carolina home extension work, secured an appropriation from the state general assembly to establish home extension work in mill villages. According to

Dr. Johnson, the object was "to arouse the residents of these communities to a keener interest in health, recreation, gardening, night schools for both sexes, and in home economics training." Mill owners provided salaries for local agents as well as a building that served as a clubhouse. Dr. Johnson told mill owners that this effort "would be a paying investment since such provisions would attract to their villages a more than ordinarily efficient class of mill operators." To state officials, this work seemed a logical extension of work with farm families. As South Carolina congressman A. F. Lever correctly observed, "Mill village people are just country people come to town." Like extension work among black women, state officials were probably motivated as much by a desire to establish some social controls and instill middle-class values in mill workers as by concern with their welfare. Mill workers had become a significant voting bloc—one that threatened elite control of state politics. Any activity that might promote ideas more hospitable to elite control was welcome.[49]

Mill village extension work paralleled much of that being done in rural South Carolina. Women were taught about growing gardens and canning in order to stretch mill wages and improve the family diet. Special classes were held for mothers to educate them about prenatal care, child nutrition, and health. Agents organized baby nutrition classes for mill families similar to those held in rural communities. Mill village agents gave limited attention to home improvement and clothing projects, but they did organize night schools in which mill workers could learn the "3 Rs" and participate in recreational programs.[50]

The Onset of the Great Depression: A Shifting Emphasis

As the extension service recognized the deepening of the farm depression brought on by the stock market crash of 1929 and the southern drought of 1930 and 1931, there was a shift in the emphasis of programs for farm women. Although the crisis had long been critical on upcountry farms, the USDA bureaucracy now perceived the economic situation as more serious. The annual reports soon began to reflect the depth of the crisis, and agents turned their attention to ways to assist farm families. "Live at home" became the motto of upcountry extension work, a slogan that referred to teaching farm families to produce as many of their needs as possible on the home farm and depend less on cash incomes.

This shift in extension service priorities was accompanied by a corresponding shift in the definition of the ideal farm wife. Now the farm woman was to devote most of her energy to helping the family survive the economic crisis by providing as many of the family's needs as possible with only minimal attention to the consumerist goals of the 1920s. In 1931 the Tennessee home demonstration director reported that the key emphases of home demonstration programs that year had been fourfold: the proper feeding of families; canning, with the surplus to be used for charity; the care of the farm flock; and the remodeling and renovation of clothes. All of these areas supported the "live at home" initiative.[51]

Agents used various strategies for reaching farm families to teach these skills. In Anderson County, Tennessee, the home demonstration agent organized canning clinics in three communities. She used a picture show as the attraction to draw crowds to meetings where, after the movie, she taught white families how to grow diversified gardens and can their produce. Although many people may have come to see the movie, the agent did not report a problem in getting families to stay for the canning and gardening demonstrations. In Kanawha County, West Virginia, agents organized a contest for gardens that provided "sufficient kinds and quantities of good quality [food] for use during all seasons of the year." They also arranged for tours of demonstration gardens cultivated by home demonstration club members who had used improved methods of cultivation and insect and disease control, and those who had introduced new vegetables. In Mercer County, West Virginia, seventy-five women grew at least two new kinds of vegetables in their gardens. West Virginia agents also gave educational demonstrations on various topics related to nutrition.[52]

In addition to teaching families how to stretch their food supplies, agents taught farm women how to conserve their clothing budgets. Agents believed, probably correctly, that it remained important to farm women to appear stylish in public, so they focused on helping women do more with less. White farm women, eager to maintain their images in the community in the face of economic strains, enrolled in the clothing project in large numbers. At the January 1933 home demonstration club meetings, agents all over East Tennessee taught women how to turn a man's gray suit into a "modern, one-piece dress with a six-gored skirt." In order to demonstrate to county officials the efficacy of spending for home extension work, Knox County women then wore their made-over dresses to the county court meeting where the appropriation for the home agent's salary was to be renewed. Agents also demonstrated attractive, easily-made clothing for children and devoted entire meetings to letting women cut out patterns from the agents' collection of master patterns so that they could save on the cost of purchased patterns. On another occasion, a USDA specialist spent two days giving demonstrations to East Tennessee club women on dying wool and cotton with homemade vegetable dyes made out of readily available items such as onion skins, broom sedge, sassafras, sumac heads, and goldenrod flowers. This helped with dying home woven fabrics and with handicraft work.[53]

Another project that was very popular with upcountry farm women during the Depression was the mattress-making project. This project provided a concrete way for women to improve the family's material conditions at a time when few had the money to buy manufactured mattresses. In 1933 the federal government began a program to distribute surplus cotton to farm families. Home demonstration agents taught farm women to make mattresses and quilts using the surplus cotton. Workers at WPA and NYA sewing rooms assembled mattress ticks that farm women then stuffed with surplus cotton. Many women who did not normally participate in home demonstration clubs became involved in this project. Articles in farm magazines encouraged widespread participation. Farm women responded eagerly to this program, replacing their straw ticks and feather beds with fresh clean cotton. A number of farm women reported their delight in making their first real cotton mattresses to replace straw and feather ticks. East Tennessean Ona Hale recalled that this was one of the most popular projects in her own home demonstration club. East Tennessean Agnes Greene recalled that her family had slept on straw ticks covered with feather beds before the extension service program made cotton mattresses available to them. "I thought, when we had a mattress, that we were on the up and up," she explained. The York County, South Carolina, home demonstration agent reported that the program was so popular with local whites that black farm women asked for their own mattress project.[54]

FIG. 10. The extension service organized mattress-making projects throughout the South during the late 1930s. Farm women used local cotton to stuff and tuft mattress ticks sewn by women and girls working for the WPA or the NYA. Here several African-American women complete a mattress at a South Carolina mattress center. (Ca. 1941. Photograph courtesy of Special Collections Unit, Strom Thurmond Institute, Clemson University.)

During the early years of the Depression, agents went beyond helping white farm families learn to "live at home." More than ever, agents recognized that farm families needed cash incomes with which to pay taxes and mortgages, purchase medical care, and buy the things that could not be produced on the farm. Farm women themselves were expanding their efforts to earn cash incomes. Agents responded by enlarging their own efforts to help women market home and farm products to generate extra income. Now agents talked about this income as essential to the family's survival rather than as the means to fund home improvements. In West Virginia, much of the programming at the 1930 state farm women's camp was devoted to teaching farm women how to market products of their home industries. Curb markets were expanded in the early 1930s to help increase farm incomes for home demonstration members. Women in McMinn County, Tennessee, opened a market for farm produce in the spring of 1932. That fall they moved to a heated location, where they sold hand-crafted gifts. Agents did not restrict their assistance with handicraft ventures to groups of women; they also aided individual women. With the help of her home demonstration agent in locating buyers, in 1934 one East Tennessee woman sold fifty-six dozen corn shuck dolls for $139.50.[55]

Agents' interest in promoting handicrafts among farm women was part of a revival of Southern Appalachian crafts that had appeared simultaneously in several locations around the Southern Highlands at the turn of the century. At Berea College in Kentucky and the Berry Schools in Georgia, officials seized on handicrafts as a way for students to earn their education. Crafts made by the students were marketed in cities around the region. This enterprise also caught on with adults. By the 1920s several handicraft schools across the South taught mountain women (and a few men) the crafts of their ancestors that had been forgotten with the advent of manufactured goods. Settlement schools, church-sponsored missions, and independent handicraft guilds marketed the crafts in the cities.[56]

The extension service was the first federal agency to get involved in the Appalachian handicraft movement. In 1937 Allen H. Eaton, a representative of New York's Russell Sage Foundation, which sponsored much development work in the Southern Highlands, wrote a history of the handicraft movement. Eaton reported that the extension service saw handicrafts as an important part of the agency's efforts to improve the opportunities of, and satisfactions with, rural life. Agents believed that handicrafts were ideal tasks to fill the time of farm families at slack agricultural seasons. Not only did agents teach women crafts and assist in their marketing, but they also promoted the standardization of the crafts. Eaton justified standardization as a necessity to meet the demands of the market. He explained, "Now in order to maintain the quality expected by outside purchasers and to guarantee the filling of orders, it has been necessary to subject the work to a degree of regulation by those sponsoring the revival." The process of standardization changed handicraft production from an art to a job for most southern craftswomen. A 1935 Labor Department study confirmed this, noting, "The workers in general are not expected to have creative ideas." Eaton admitted that some complained about their loss of creativity and autonomy, but he claimed that most simply welcomed the opportunity to earn additional income. The popularity of the extension service's handicraft programs suggests that Eaton was right: the need to earn an income overrode any concerns with artistic autonomy.[57]

More important than the loss of autonomy was the role of handicraft production in restricting women's cash-producing work to the home. Because agents believed that the farm women's place was in the farm home, they seized on handicrafts as an excellent way to help women earn money to supplement the farm income without entering the male realms of public work or farm production. Agents believed that handicrafts and other home-based production projects were important alternatives to off-farm jobs for desperate farm families, yet these handicrafts programs were limited to white women, again denying black women a valuable coping strategy.

Because they believed that farm women should remain on the farm and feared that they might flood cities with surplus laborers, agents expanded their efforts to assist women in marketing their crafts in 1934. That year the Tennessee Extension Service made various counties centers for the teaching and sales of traditional crafts. Hamilton and Knox counties became centers for hooked rug making, McMinn County for leather work, Hawkins County for hooked and braided rugs and corn shuck dolls, and Sevier and Sullivan counties for weaving.[58]

Agents helped women with other home-based moneymaking ventures as well. The Anderson County, Tennessee, home demonstration agent assisted one woman in opening a tea room in her home. She used her own homegrown food to cater parties for community people. In 1932 she served 116 parties (560 people) for a total income of $291.10. In 1933 she increased this income to $657. Similarly, the extension service's home management specialist assisted Mrs. H. B. Walker of Knox County in decorating the rustic tea room her husband built for her on their rural property. Mrs. Walker and her daughters cooked and served their farm products, doing $253 in business in 1932 and $211 in 1933. In West Virginia, agents encouraged rural women to establish tourist homes. As with the handicrafts marketing efforts, agents urged farm women to establish these home businesses so that they could confine their work to the home.[59]

Teaching farm women to maximize their food and clothing resources
and to produce cash incomes were not the only tasks that consumed the
time of home demonstration agents during the early years of the Depression. With the advent of New Deal programs in 1933, home demonstration agents became more active in assisting the federal bureaucracy. In
1934 Tennessee's male state extension service director reported: "The
women workers, also, greatly aided in bringing the public to a full appreciation of the value of AAA [Agricultural Adjustment Administration]
work." Women agents educated farm families about the functioning of
crop reduction programs, taking an especially active role in counties
where there was no male agricultural agent. In Claiborne County, agent
Lillie Oakley helped thirty farmers fill out the paperwork for receipt of
AAA payments for the wheat reduction campaign in 1933. West Virginia
agents assisted farm families with negotiating local and federal bureaucracies in seeking drought relief.[60]

Tennessee's home demonstration agents also assisted in the relocation of families displaced by the Tennessee Valley Authority's Norris
Dam project. Farm women eagerly seized on the opportunities created
by home demonstration workers to help integrate relocated families
into new communities even as they resisted the agency's more intrusive
forays into family life, such as efforts to examine the family's financial
records. Agents held meetings with relocated farm families to explain
TVA's relocation programs to assist with farm management, soil conservation, balanced livestock, cash crop production, and home management. They also contacted county agents in counties where families were
relocating to ask for assistance in getting the family settled in. Home
agents in the counties where families settled held meetings for relocated
women once a month to talk about home planning and farm records.
Although the agents themselves noted that farm women resisted their
efforts to systematize farm record keeping, attendance at the relocation meetings was good, suggesting that the meetings were important to
women facing the process of settling into a new community and that they
valued the education being offered.[61]

Besides helping farm families develop coping skills to survive the
economic downturn, home demonstration agents also engaged in various forms of relief work. They took applications for federal drought relief

loans from hard-hit farm families. They also advised local emergency relief administrators on work projects for women on relief rolls. Eight clerical jobs in county home demonstration offices were given to women on work relief. In 1934 the federal government provided funding for seasonal canning supervisors to teach larger numbers of women than agents could reach how to can. Agents trained the canning supervisors, marketed the program to farm women, and recommended women for appointment to the jobs. The state home demonstration director noted in 1931 that "the local community home demonstration clubs . . . have been the agencies through which home demonstration agents have been able to do the most effective relief work."[62]

In spite of the economic crisis and the press of administering New Deal programs, home improvement did not disappear from the agents' agenda, however. Agents' belief that the creation of an attractive and welcoming home was a central part of the farm wife's mission persisted, although the definitions of such a home were now considerably more modest. Given their continued participation, albeit in smaller numbers, farm women apparently valued efforts to create a more attractive home that may have provided some measure of psychological comfort in the face of great economic hardship. In 1932 a Tennessee home demonstration agent reported that home grounds remained the most popular program in terms of enrollment, with 1,831 East Tennessee women enrolled in the project. These numbers may be misleading, however. Women enrolled in projects by checking off the project on a form. Enrollment did not necessarily indicate that the women actively pursued projects to improve their home grounds. Many agents provided grounds beautification instruction along with vegetable gardening projects.[63]

The economic crisis permeated all the programming in the early years of the Depression. Even in home improvement, agents turned all their attention to improvements that required minimal cash outlays. The West Virginia state agent reported that the kitchen improvement contest remained one of the most popular, and that the living room improvement project focused on rearranging and refinishing furniture and "addition of more light through light finishes of walls and ceilings," a far cry from the expensive improvements emphasized in the 1920s. In 1932 the Tennessee home demonstration director noted that many women had learned to reseat old chairs with twine, cattails, and other materials readily available on even the poorest of farms. She remarked that "a few women are taking orders for this work and are adding something to their income."[64]

Agents also expanded efforts to organize relief and outreach to the poorest farm families, particularly in South Carolina, with its history of such work. In Spartanburg County, agents organized two health clinics for poor rural families; and in Anderson County, they held a clinic that gave typhoid and diphtheria inoculations. A group of officers from the South Carolina Council of Farm Women, the statewide organization of home demonstration clubs, met with federal officials in 1934, urging them to provide more WPA jobs for women. In Sullivan County, Tennessee, the General Federation of Women's Clubs of Bristol funded a canning kitchen run by the home demonstration agent. Two days a month, she supervised white farm women in the canning of surplus vegetables donated by farm families. That year 1,500 quarts were canned and given to the county's neediest rural families during the winter months. Cabell County, West Virginia, agents tried unsuccessfully to organize a relief credit association and to get the American Red Cross to assist destitute farm families.[65]

South Carolina home demonstration clubs continued other community service work, including beautification efforts along highways and at schools, churches, and parks. Club members wrote their state representatives, urging them to pass laws that would fight crime, reckless driving, "unwholesome motion pictures," and alcohol. They also lobbied the state to provide funding for rural libraries.[66]

One significant measure of the Great Depression's impact on Tennessee's farm women was the decline in the number of women participating in home demonstration club activities. At a time when the state's rural population actually increased by almost 10 percent, the number of women participating in home demonstration activities across the state fell dramatically. In 1929, 10,349 Tennessee white women belonged to organized home demonstration clubs. By 1932 this number had fallen to 5,177 women, and to 910 women in 1934. The District IV county agent observed the desperate straits of the area's farm families: "The diversified interests in East Tennessee have enabled the farmers to live, but they have had very little money to meet their obligations and buy necessities for the home and farm." He went on to note that many farmers who had previously worked part-time off the farm had lost their jobs. It was, he concluded, hard to keep the farm family's interest in regular demonstration work in the face of these keen obstacles to survival. There was also a decline in the number of counties served by home demonstration agents, a decline that would have had an impact on club enrollments. In 1931 five counties that had previously funded the salaries of home demonstration agents failed to make their annual appropriations. This meant that home demonstration work in those counties was discontinued.[67]

By contrast, South Carolina's and West Virginia's home demonstration club membership grew steadily until the late 1930s, largely due to these states' increased commitment to funding agents' salaries. South Carolina had 8,161 home demonstration club members in 1930. By 1935 this number had grown to 15,446. Similarly, West Virginia's 1925 membership of 3,900 women had swelled to 5,522 by 1935. Unlike Tennessee, which cut funding for home demonstration programs during the worst years of the Depression, these state legislatures seemed to understand the importance of maintaining and even increasing staffing levels in the face of the crisis.[68]

The Late 1930s: A More Balanced Approach

In 1935, as New Deal programs infused much-needed cash into rural upcountry communities, white agents perceived that the worst of the crisis had passed. Once again their definitions of the ideal farm woman shifted. Now the ideal white farm wife was both the center of the family economy and a consumer-homemaker. The live-at-home program remained a major emphasis of home demonstration agents. The South Carolina Council of Farm Women noted that over seven thousand home demonstration club members across the state raised year-round gardens in 1935, and many also had home orchards. The next year they reported that members had canned over eighty thousand quarts of fruits and vegetables. Agents maintained a particular emphasis on food preservation, recognizing that an adequate, nutritious food supply remained a key to a high quality of life for rural families. In 1936 the Knox County, Tennessee, home demonstration agent reported that "there seem to be too many families in the county buying a large part of their food, so the [food] project was adopted in the county as one of our major ones." She gave women suggestions on the types of food to produce on their farms, taught them to develop a canning budget (a plan for how much food they needed to preserve for the winter), and then taught them to can. She used educational circulars and radio talks on the topic to reinforce her message. Other agents reported similar efforts. A Tennessee district agent reported that in 1935 fifteen counties in East Tennessee had one-day canning demonstrations for women whose families received relief payments, with 624 attending. The canned food paid big dividends for farm families. The Jefferson County home agent reported that in 1936 323 of her home demonstration club members canned food with a value of $15,976. This represented a substantial savings in cash outlay for these farm families.[69]

Agents also continued to recognize white farm women's need to contribute cash to the family income. The West Virginia state home demonstration director noted in 1935 that "it has become necessary for women to help share the responsibilities of the family income, and, in many instances, they have had to bear the whole responsibility." The Tennessee home marketing specialist reported in 1935 that "since times have improved and people have more money to spend, it seemed the proper time to use every effort to place Tennessee home products before the public." Agents continued to work with women in running curb markets, special "one day" markets on important occasions, and other farm marketing efforts. In Clinton and Tazewell, Tennessee, small towns in Anderson and Campbell counties respectively, the home demonstration club curb markets served Civilian Conservation Corps camps. Tennessee club women also continued to sell traditional Appalachian crafts through the Southern Highlands Handicraft Guild and the Spinning Wheel organization, both located in Asheville, North Carolina; while West Virginia extension workers launched handicraft instruction for the first time.[70]

In spite of the continued emphasis on the farm woman's role in insuring family survival, the perception of an improving economy provided agents with incentive to renew attention to home improvement. But unlike the practical and inexpensive improvement projects of the early 1930s, agents now returned to the middle-class model home of the 1920s. Agents particularly emphasized a middle-class version of aesthetics, criticizing the cluttered and dark interiors of rural homes in favor of lighter, sparer rooms like those found in women's magazines that targeted the middle-class homemaker. Renewed attention was given to the addition of modern conveniences as well. In 1935 agents in five East Tennessee counties reported holding home improvement contests for best improvements to living rooms, kitchens, and bedrooms. Home agents visited the homes before improvements were made, urging women to get rid of extra furniture and to use light-colored walls and easy-to-clean floor coverings. In Cabell County, West Virginia, all but one meeting of the county Farm Women's Bureau (the organization of officers of local home demonstration clubs) in 1935 focused on home improvement.[71]

This return to the middle-class model was marked in 1936 by the resumption of the Better Homes Campaign. In Knox County, Tennessee, 200 women toured city and county homes where interior and exterior improvements had been made. Miss Ruby McKeel, the Anderson County home demonstration agent, reported that 1,041 of the county's women had participated in the Better Homes Campaign. (Not all these women were members of home demonstration clubs.) Among the improvements she noted were 740 improved yards, 215 freshly-painted houses, 135 new roofs, and 104 new homes. There were also 157 women who refinished furniture, 128 who made slipcovers, 115 who reseated chairs, 149 who installed kitchen water, and 40 who installed bathroom water. In South Carolina, improvements ranged from painting homes and planting lawns to installation of a handful of lily pools and rock gardens. As in earlier years, improvements ranged from relatively inexpensive to very expensive, based on families' means.[72]

Farm women eagerly installed modern conveniences when they were both available and affordable. The advent of the Tennessee Valley Authority made inexpensive electricity available in many rural areas, and Tennessee extension agents urged their subjects to capitalize on this. The Rural Electrification Act provided many farm families throughout the upcountry with access to reasonably priced electricity, while cash from New Deal programs and installment credit put appliances within the reach of many families for the first time. In contrast to the 1920s, when very few farm women purchased electrical appliances, significant numbers of women began to do so.

In Anderson County, Tennessee, one of the first counties to enjoy rural electrification, electrical cooking schools were held in five communities in 1936. That year, 325 Anderson County farm homes had installed electricity, and family members purchased 1,674 electrical appliances ranging from expensive stoves, refrigerators, and washing machines to less expensive irons and fans. In 1937 six Anderson County farm families worked with the extension service to become "Electro-Development Farm Demonstrators," a distinction requiring them to have both the farm and the home wired and electrically equipped. In 1939 East Tennessee District IV home demonstration agent Oma Worley reported that 1,163 homes in the region had installed electricity that year. In South Carolina, agents reported that 1,361 rural homes had installed electric lights, though only 48 had installed electric refrigerators. These numbers, however, represent fewer than 5 percent of the district's rural households. In West Virginia, agents made little mention of electricity until after 1940. Although access to electricity was steadily increasing, most farm families did not have electricity until the late 1930s or early 1940s.[73]

Home demonstration clubs continued their own efforts to provide education and relief to the poorest families in their own communities. West Virginia agents provided child-care training to club members and other rural women. West Virginia and South Carolina members organized traveling rural libraries. Clubs in both states also engaged in the beautification of rural school grounds. South Carolina clubs raised money for the rural poor. In Union County, South Carolina, club members raised $1,068 for poor relief in 1937, and Anderson County "support[ed] an orphan." Members in the upstate South Carolina district also raised funds for educational scholarships and loans for 4-H club girls. The Anderson County fund was helping five young women through college or commercial, beauty, or nursing schools in the 1930s; while Spartanburg County women helped nine young women.[74]

As we see from this analysis of home improvement work, home extension agents were torn between competing visions of the ideal farm wife: the farm homemaker and the farm producer. Agents recognized the necessity of women's contributions to the family income through production even as they encouraged white women to remove production from the household and as they rendered it invisible where it did exist. Agents were also unsure about the role black farm women should play. These mixed messages certainly made it harder for the extension service to achieve its goals of separating farm men's and women's spheres of work. Still, for many farm women, particularly white farm women, the mixed messages offered an opportunity to accept the educational benefits of extension work without fully internalizing its philosophies. Although the extension service's inability to articulate a program to serve the needs of poor farm women of both races shows how marginalized they were in U.S. agricultural policy, these women used extension work as one of many strategies to cope with the economic crisis.

In the final analysis, few upcountry farm women of either race were involved in home demonstration work. It would be a mistake, however, to assume that home extension work had no lasting impact on the shape of upcountry farm women's lives simply because of the low numbers of women it reached. Extension service policies assisted in the maintenance of a racially segregated rural society. The extension service's agenda of promoting a gendered division of farm labor and upgrading the farm home to suburban standards did prove popular with many prosperous farm wives who participated. These women were likely to be women who remained on the farm after the 1930s when their husbands made the transition to large-scale commercial agriculture. In the 1940s, 50s, and 60s, the lives of these commercial farm wives would resemble the home extension model; they were often more focused on homemaking and child rearing than on farm production. In this way, the extension service succeeded in shaping upcountry farm homes for generations to come through these women.

Five

Government Relocation and

Upcountry Women

People in the upcountry South experienced government intervention in many forms in the years between the two world wars. Not only did extension agents seek to assist farm women, but Agricultural Adjustment Administration programs provided cash payments to landowners for removing acreage from production, often forcing tenant farmers off the land. The Resettlement Administration attempted to place some of these landless farmers in subsistence homestead communities, while the Works Progress Administration and the Civilian Conservation Corps provided jobs for tens of thousands of rural folk and developed infrastructure in rural communities. But the most sweeping forms of intervention involved the relocation of rural families out of the path of federal construction projects.

This chapter examines relocation practices for two major federal projects: the Tennessee Valley Authority's 1930s dam construction program in East Tennessee and the U.S. Army's 1941 construction of the Camp Croft training facility in Spartanburg County, South Carolina. Like the Agricultural Extension Service, relocation projects left behind an ambiguous legacy for upcountry women. The economic transformation of the region provided both women and men with an improved standard of living and new earning opportunities. But at the same time, massive construction projects displaced thousands of families, some more than once, disrupting the community support networks that were so central to women's lives and to their power. The disruption of these support networks was much less traumatic for men, who were more easily able to enter impersonal new farm commodity markets than were women able to enter the informal networks of new communities. Particularly for families with few resources, this removal from mutual aid networks made it harder to remain on the land. Moreover, because maintenance of the family was a task seen as falling largely within women's sphere of responsibility, much of the work involved in relocating families fell upon the region's women.

The Tennessee Valley Authority— Regional Economic Development

On May 7, 1934, an enthusiastic *Knoxville News-Sentinel* reporter described the anticipated benefits of the Tennessee Valley Authority, gushing that Tennessee Valley housewives would soon have more time for their flower gardens because TVA electricity would "wash the dishes, heat the water, cook the meals, sweep the floors, and launder the clothes." The *News-Sentinel* reporter was not alone in his optimism. All over the valley, rural and town folk alike rejoiced at the promise of TVA. They envisioned a new era of economic development in the region. TVA electricity would lighten the housewife's load, improve the farmer's production levels, and draw new industry into the Tennessee Valley, creating jobs for thousands.[1]

TVA did transform the lives of East Tennesseans, particularly rural women. Within ten years of the agency's founding, most Tennessee Valley farm homes were equipped with electricity, which brought with it electric lights, household appliances, and the power to pump well water into the house. The TVA also improved the infrastructure of rural communities. In areas in which the agency constructed dams, it built better roads, making towns and trade more accessible and thus reducing the isolation of rural life. The massive dam building projects provided employment opportunities for the region's white men and for a few white women and black men, creating an alternative to life on marginal farms. Cheap electricity also drew some industry into the region, providing more employment opportunities for men and women. Moreover, TVA's vision of itself as a regional planning organization also led it to provide educational programs. Farmers participated in TVA's test demonstration programs, learning new and more profitable farming methods, while homemakers learned to use new electrical appliances at TVA-sponsored workshops. TVA's paramount educational effort, housed at its planned community at Norris, Tennessee, offered a unique program of adult education that functioned as job training for many of its participants. These new opportunities worked together to improve the region's standard of living dramatically in a relatively brief period. But the agency also relocated thousands of families from communities in which their ancestors had lived for generations.

These disruptions were not simply impersonal interventions meted out by an impartial government that treated all the affected parties equally. Like most New Deal programs, the TVA benefits were not evenly distributed. The agency maintained a policy of institutionalized segregation and discrimination against blacks that kept African Americans from deriving much direct benefit from it. TVA's programs, shaped by an agency policy of trying to remove marginal farmers from the land, were also structured in ways that favored prosperous, white land-owning families over poorer farm families of both races, and farm owners over tenants. Families who had some capital to invest were in a position to exercise considerable control over the shape of their lives after TVA. They could choose to stay on the land or move to towns and cities. Poor landowners and landless farm families often did not have this option. A shortage of land and a declining need for agricultural laborers drove these families into low-skilled industrial jobs. While factory work often improved their standard of living, the agency's policies forced many less prosperous farm families to give up a way of life that some would have preferred to keep. In either case, many women found these transitions particularly difficult. Town women and wives of commercial farmers found their old skills and contributions to the family economy devalued in the new order, while former tenant farming women were forced to make ends meet in alien industrial environments. TVA proved to be a mixed blessing for East Tennessee women.

To a region devastated by a long-term agricultural depression and drought, TVA provided real hope for a better life. Signed into law on May

18, 1933, the TVA Act marked the first time a government agency had been given the power to oversee the development of an entire region. President Roosevelt and other advocates conceived of the agency as a bold social experiment in the alleviation of poverty and regional under-development. Soon the agency drew up a comprehensive plan for the development of a system of dams along the Tennessee River and its tributaries. The dams were multipurpose: they were to provide navigability of the Tennessee River from its mouth at Paducah, Kentucky, all the way to Knoxville, Tennessee, by deepening the river channels; they were to eliminate spring flooding of river bottom farmland by controlling the flow of the rivers; and they were to produce inexpensive hydro-electric power that would in turn attract industry into a region ripe with cheap labor.[2]

In spite of opposition from private power producers, TVA's promise captured the imagination of the entire nation. The *New York Times*, in particular, offered enthusiastic coverage of the agency's progress. A 1936 Sunday magazine cover story entitled "A Dream Takes Form in TVA's Domain" described the transformation of the region in glowing terms, contrasting the grinding poverty of communities not yet touched by TVA with the "good land, well-cultivated . . . fields as rich and the common farmhouses as neat and comfortable as those of Iowa" in communities where dams had been built. The *Times* discounted the argument over public versus private ownership of utilities as far less important than this grand experiment in economic development. Reporters were particularly impressed with TVA's efforts to educate Tennessee Valley farmers in modern farming methods so that they could improve their own lives.[3]

In the early years, TVA's leaders believed that the regional transformation they were trying to effect would involve a balanced mix of agriculture and industry. Indeed, TVA director Arthur Morgan's modified Jeffersonian vision was a rural utopia in which prosperous commercial agriculture coexisted with small industrial facilities. Noting that there were more farmers in the Tennessee Valley than the region's farms could support, he believed that TVA's cheap power would encourage the development of more local industry, which would provide jobs for rural men without forcing them to move to cities. In this way, Morgan hoped to maintain the rural character of American life even as the region's farms were consolidated and agriculture was mechanized, leaving many farm

laborers unemployed. Although internal agency dissent, a limited budget, and circumscribed authority prevented the agency from acting to
implement much of this ambitious vision, it nonetheless shaped TVA's
policies for relocation of farm families.[4]

After years of economic depression, most Tennessee Valley residents
heralded the arrival of the agency as a long-awaited messiah to redeem
them from the evils of poverty. This was particularly true of the region's
farm wives, who rejoiced in the availability of electricity in their homes.
The first area to enjoy this new amenity was the five-county area affected
by the building of Norris Dam, where construction began in early 1934.
Compiling surveys of rural families taken by agency relocation workers
in 1934 before the arrival of TVA, historians Michael Muldowny and John
McDonald found that only thirty-one of the more than three thousand
families in the five-county area had electric lighting. Only twenty-two
families reported indoor toilets, a convenience closely linked to the presence of electricity because pumping water from farm wells into the house
required electricity. None of the families surveyed enjoyed central heat;
most used fireplaces and wood stoves. By the end of the decade, electricity was available to every family in the area, and more than three-
quarters of farm homes were so equipped.[5]

The testimony of farm women themselves speaks to the value they
placed on electric power and the credit they gave to TVA for the arrival of
electricity. When asked about obtaining electricity in the house, nearly
every Tennessee Valley woman interviewed declared that she got electricity when TVA arrived in the area. As East Tennessee homemaker
Tressa Waters put it, "When we got electricity, that was a big step. I guess I
got my stove right away. We were so proud of TVA." Although she remembers TVA as being the power distributor, Waters' electrical power
was probably installed by a local rural electrification cooperative. These
grass-roots organizations, made up of all rural electricity customers, received federal funding assistance in order to string electrical lines and
install service for customers, buying relatively inexpensive power from
TVA. Waters' conflation of TVA (the power producer) and the electric
cooperative (the power distributor) was indicative of her complete identi-
fication of TVA as the source of the Tennessee Valley's electricity. Moreover, her pride in the agency reveals the promise it held for many valley

families, who believed they were finally joining the national mainstream with the installation of electricity.[6]

TVA also improved the standard of living of the valley's farm women through their agricultural education programs. The agency's emphasis on grass-roots educational efforts provided new learning opportunities for thousands of Tennessee Valley residents, and this education often paid off in increased farm productivity and healthier, happier homes. Unfortunately for the valley's women, these programs, like those of the Agricultural Extension Service, promoted a model of commercial agriculture designed to remove women from farm production and poorer families from farming. For example, the agency developed an elaborate test demonstration farm program that provided selected Tennessee Valley farmers with fertilizer and cooperated with the extension service and the Soil Conservation Service to provide agricultural education. In return for these services, the farmers agreed to follow agency recommendations about production and to make their farms available to the extension service as a teaching site for other farmers. In this way, TVA was instrumental in shaping a new regional agriculture that focused on livestock raising and minimal cash cropping, a form of agriculture better suited to Tennessee's steep hillsides. In spite of the benefits some families derived from these new agricultural practices, TVA's policies helped remove women from farm production. In commercial livestock and crop production women were relegated to the world of the household. Moreover, because livestock farming required larger units of land than earlier patterns of mixed farming, these programs favored more wealthy landowners who had the capital to invest in additional pasture land and cattle.[7]

TVA's vision of the appropriate shape of modern agriculture influenced its distribution of these agricultural education programs. Indeed, as one historian has noted, TVA's early alliance with the Agricultural Extension Service and the Farm Bureau, an organization dominated by progressive commercial farmers, meant that the agency's agricultural policies were shaped by a vision of mechanized commercial farms. As a result, test demonstration work was rarely carried out among poor landowners, tenant farmers, or sharecroppers—the farmers who stood to benefit most from improved farming practices. Believing that it benefited the entire regional economy to move these inefficient poor farmers off the land and into industrial jobs in order to free up land and resources for those who remained in farming, TVA officials and their extension service colleagues instead sought out prosperous and better-educated farmers who were already well along in the transition to capitalist agriculture. As a result, poor farmers and their families benefited little from the agency's agricultural education programs.[8]

Moreover, in all its agricultural educational programs, TVA adopted a gendered model of education. Although its own relocation workers found hundreds of women managing their own farms throughout the Tennessee Valley, female-headed farms were rarely chosen for the test demonstration program. Farm women's statements indicated that they had an intimate knowledge of farming practice, yet they were not included in TVA's agricultural education programs. For many women, this was yet another way of pushing them out of farm production.[9]

TVA's educational programs for relocated families and other Tennessee Valley residents were also divided along gender lines. Given the structure of the programs, TVA officials seemed to assume that men would engage in earning a living, while women would keep house. For example, at the model community it built to house construction workers and other relocated families near Norris Dam, the agency built state-of-the-art schools that served the village's children during the day and its adults at night. The children enjoyed an ample library; vocational courses in agriculture, home economics, mechanical drawing, and shop; as well as college preparatory courses, all provided under the direction of a principal who had earned his doctorate at the University of Chicago. Here local students received a vastly superior education than the one previously provided by the cash-strapped local government. After school hours, job training classes in blueprint reading, mathematical analysis, carpentry estimating, arc welding, typing, shorthand, and bookkeeping were offered to the village's adult population. Residents of both sexes were free to enroll in all the classes, although men dominated classes that focused on mechanical skills, and women made up about half of the students in office skills classes. Officials with the Rockefeller Foundation's General Education Board (GEB) who visited Norris were impressed with the opportunities the agency was making available to the region's rural families. One GEB official noted, "In some of the shop courses there are people who are seeking recreational rather than job-training values. Thus in the furniture shop we saw several women, and a number of the men were engaged in making furniture for their homes." The GEB staffer shared TVA officials' gendered notions of appropriate job training for men and women. He assumed that women taking shop classes were only interested in making objects for their own homes, a worthy and appropriate goal for women, rather than in learning a job skill. TVA officials probably assumed the same thing, since they did not close these traditionally male courses to women at Norris.[10]

In spite of the positive benefits of rural electrification and education, the most important contribution TVA made to improving the lives of farm women was in the area of overall economic development. As historians have noted, TVA was a catalyst for much of the economic development that took place in the region over the next fifty years. Besides profiting from the long-term benefits of luring industry to the region, many women enjoyed short-term gain from the agency's building projects. For wives of farm owners and women who owned land themselves, the sale of a portion of their property that stood in the path of a dam-building project often provided cash used to improve the family's economic position or standard of living. For example, Peggy Delozier Jones recalled, "Oh yes, when TVA came, that's how we paid for this farm. They took our river bottoms." TVA paid a handsome price for the family's most fertile land that stood in the path of Watts Bar Lake, enabling the couple to pay off the mortgage on their land. The freedom from land debt helped the Jones family to complete a conversion to large-scale commercial farming that made them one of the most prominent farming families in Loudon County.[11]

White women benefited not only from the cash brought in from the sale of farmland to TVA but also from the new earning opportunities created by the transformation of the region. Many farm women in the region who had not formerly kept boarders opened boardinghouses for TVA dam project workers. For example, as previously mentioned, Maude Walker rented a large house in which she ran a boardinghouse for men working on the Norris Dam project, managing to save enough money to build her husband and children a house after the project was completed. Other women purchased or raised additional livestock in order to expand their butter and milk production to supply workers' dormitories at TVA construction sites. These women seized on temporary opportunities to earn cash, just as the region's women had done throughout the interwar years.[12]

Other white women found jobs with TVA. The agency required hundreds of clerical workers at dam sites across the state as well as at its Knoxville headquarters. Young farm girls from all over East Tennessee took business courses in high school and attended business colleges in order to qualify for these relatively high-paying jobs. The shortage of men caused by World War II opened up even more jobs to women. For example, Margaret Marsh, the daughter of a Blount County farm family, found a job in the blueprint department at TVA's Knoxville headquarters in 1944. After the war the agency fired most of the married women working in nonclerical jobs like Marsh's but kept the single women on. Marsh continued working at TVA until her retirement thirty-seven years later.[13]

Like white women, black women benefited from a generally rising regional standard of living after the arrival of TVA, though not nearly as much. One historian found that TVA did not adequately address the economic and social problems of the region's black residents but instead developed plans that would maintain the subordinate, segregated position of the race. TVA believed it had to get along with the local white governments and community organizations in order to succeed in its community planning efforts. In spite of giving lip service to providing equal opportunities and service to the Tennessee Valley's African American population, TVA caved in to local patterns of discrimination. Officially, the agency's policy was one of nondiscrimination based on a quota system designed to give black men the same percentage of TVA jobs as their presence in the local population. In practice, however, blacks were rarely hired for TVA projects, and when they were, they worked in unskilled, temporary reservoir clearance jobs. This meant that there were few work opportunities for rural black men looking for off-farm work in TVA project areas and that African American families did not enjoy the same improved economic opportunities as whites.[14]

The NAACP, sharply critical of TVA's policies regarding blacks, published two investigative reports in *The Crisis* on the agency's discrimination. Reporters John P. Davis and Charles H. Houston made three visits to the Norris Basin in 1934 and 1935 and reported that "the only function that the Negro has in the TVA, the only recognition which the TVA gives

him is as a labor commodity. And even this function is subject to certain exceptions." They complained that African Americans were confined to the lowest level jobs and that they were refused homes in the
nearby planned community of Norris, instead being forced to live in over-
crowded barracks and dormitories nearby. TVA claimed that this discrimination resulted from a shortage of black workers to fill skilled jobs and
from not having enough skilled black workers to make separate work
crews. Houston and Davis pointed out that there were plenty of skilled
black workers in southern cities and that "mixed crews work all over the
South without any clash, except where somebody wants to keep the Negroes out of jobs." TVA's policy of racial discrimination also extended to
its educational programs: black farmers were excluded from TVA's agricultural education programs and from the test demonstration program.[15]

Relocation Workers and Tennessee Valley Women

While women derived indirect and even direct benefits from the
enhanced economic opportunities TVA provided for them and for their
male relatives, the agency's building programs also had a devastating
effect on many of the region's rural women. Between its founding in 1933
and 1945, TVA built sixteen dams in East Tennessee. The agency would
complete seven more dams in the region by 1985. The lakes created by
these dams covered hundreds of thousands of acres and displaced thousands of families.[16]

For many Tennessee Valley women, the process of relocation first
brought them into direct contact with the massive fledgling federal
agency. TVA's Reservoir Family Removal Section was the division responsible for coordinating the relocation of affected families. The "Reservoir Family Removal Workers Manual" outlined the responsibilities of
removal workers. Their first task was to interview each family in order to
determine what relocation help was needed, making a thorough "case
study" of families who might need special readjustment help, most often
poor families or those with disabled members. After determining the
needs of the family, the worker was to refer the family to appropriate
federal, state, and local agencies. TVA offered little direct aid to relocated
families, preferring instead to put families in touch with local welfare

departments, the extension service, and other agencies that could assist them with specific needs. In addition, removal workers were instructed to work with appropriate agencies in an "attempt to prevent the lowering of the standard of living of population living adjacent to TVA property lines, wherever such population had been adversely affected by the programs of the Authority."

In practice, these instructions meant that relocation workers spent considerable time interviewing each family about their financial situation and their needs in a new home, advising them on salvaging building materials from their old property, and referring them to agencies that would help them locate new farms and homes. On rare occasions, relocation workers also helped wage earners find new jobs, registered children for schools in new neighborhoods, and established new relief and Old Age Assistance cases for families who qualified. For the poorest families, TVA sometimes provided trucking services to enable families to remove their belongings, and temporary shelter in TVA tents. Yet these services were rare. Fewer than one percent of the families relocated from the Norris Basin received these services, leaving some destitute families at a loss as to where to go or how to get there. In general, relocation workers were advised that TVA workers were not empowered to give direct benefits but rather "to interpret the needs of reservoir families to interested agencies, and likewise, to interpret outside agencies to the reservoir group." In sum, workers generally served as mediators between the agency and the affected communities.[17]

The relocation workers themselves played a powerful role in shaping TVA's relationship with residents. In the early years, TVA saw relocation as a logistical problem requiring relocation workers to be competent data gatherers. At the outset, most of the relocation workers were white East Tennessee natives, many of them among the few educated young people in the affected communities. On the earliest relocation projects, such as Norris Dam, TVA was as likely to hire female relocation workers as males. At this point, most of the workers had high school diplomas or a year or two of college, making them considerably more educated than most of their constituents, although still not professional bureaucrats in the eyes of TVA officials. Eventually, agency managers came to believe that the task of relocation was a highly technical one, requiring the skills to persuade, educate, and advocate. By the time of the Ft. Loudon and

Watts Bar Dams in the late 1930s, most relocation workers were men who held college degrees in sociology or agriculture, indicating that TVA was beginning to see relocation as the province of professional, and therefore mostly male, social scientists. Moreover, these workers were now primarily young men from outside the region, without the local person's understanding of, and sensitivities to, local culture and individual families' needs.[18]

Not only were some relocation workers insensitive to the local culture, but they often made assumptions about the gender division of labor on farms that were rooted in middle-class definitions of femininity, ignoring women's contributions to the farm operation. Relocation workers of both sexes presumed that men made all the farming decisions. They sought to obtain farm financial and demographic information from male household members but were willing to talk to women if men were unavailable. Yet male workers tended to discount women's roles in farm decision making. For example, if there was a male present on the farm, workers referred to all livestock, even livestock traditionally tended by women, as belonging to the man. A relocation worker visiting a farm belonging to Mrs. Matty Leeper of Loudon County recorded his own confusion about rural gender roles when he noted that "Mrs. Leeper is owner of the farm and seems to take a definite place in its management. However, Mr. Toole, the son-in-law, is probably the *real* manager of the farm" [author's emphasis]. Even when family testimony seemed to indicate that the woman was the primary farm manager, relocation workers were more comfortable with the assumption that an adult male was making the farm decisions, reflecting the agency's belief that men farmed, while women kept house. As a result, women's work remained invisible in decisions on relocation assistance.[19]

Displacing Families

The impact of the dislocations varied from project to project and from family to family. For example, TVA's first dam, Norris, also proved to be its largest in terms of the number of families displaced. In order to build Norris Dam, the agency purchased 153,000 acres and relocated over three thousand rural families in the Clinch and Powell River valleys of central

East Tennessee between 1933 and 1935. By contrast, only 249 families in Blount, Loudon, and Knox Counties were relocated for the Fort Loudon Dam project between 1939 and 1942. The size of the project, however, was not the only measure of its impact. The people removed from the Norris Basin were among the most isolated and economically disadvantaged in the entire state, which meant that these families had few of the financial or psychological resources needed for a successful relocation. By contrast, the people relocated for the Fort Loudon project were less isolated, living in close proximity to the major city of Knoxville. They were also able to benefit from the general improvements to the economy brought about by World War II, making relocation less traumatic than for many of the Norris folk.[20]

Economic class, race, family dynamics, and personal preference largely determined the impact of TVA's programs on East Tennessee's rural women and the degree of control these women were able to exert on the changes they faced. Wealthier families could choose among several more attractive options. Prosperous farm owners were in the best position to profit from TVA's purchase of their property because they could use the proceeds from the sale to buy good land in other locations. For example, Carrie Smith was the wife of a wealthy businessman and farm owner. The Smiths lived in a two-story frame Victorian house with gingerbread trim in the area of Rhea County affected by the Watts Bar Dam. Smith and her husband sold this property for $6,145, ample funds to allow them to buy another farm in the same community where they had spent a lifetime. For Smith, relocation was a matter of dealing with the disruption of moving and the details of rebuilding her house rather than of learning how to get along in a new community. Her old friends and relatives remained nearby, and they not only would have eased the psychic pain of the disruption but would also have provided physical help with the move.[21]

Sometimes these prosperous women chose to take a larger role in the farming operation as a result of changes in farming patterns wrought by relocation. Kate Simmons and her husband sold his family's Jefferson County home place to TVA in the late 1930s for the construction of Douglas Dam. TVA's removal of land from production had driven up land prices in Jefferson County, but prices remained low in unaffected East

Tennessee counties. With the proceeds of the sale, the Simmonses were able to buy a large, fertile farm farther south on the Tennessee River in Loudon County. Here they built a prosperous dairy operation that was far more profitable than the small general farm where they had eked out a living in Jefferson County. A young mother when she moved, Kate Simmons seemed to revel in the challenge of building a life in a new community, and she took an active role in the management of the dairy operation.[22]

While some women welcomed the opportunity to stay on the land and took an active part in farm management, others eagerly adopted the role of middle-class homemaker when their husbands took wage work in the cities. Tenant farm women seemed particularly happy to abandon the hard physical labor of farm life for the more genteel world of homemaking. For example, Willie Cottrell, the thirty-two-year-old wife of a farm laborer, told a TVA worker how happy they were with their new situation. As the worker noted, "Mr. Cottrell has secured a position with the Security Mills in Knoxville and has moved his family there. Mrs. Cottrell said they were well-satisfied with their change—living in Knoxville with its many advantages, being paid a higher salary, and in a growing business with opportunity for advancement." Indeed, TVA helped the Cottrell family in several ways. Not only did the agency provide relocation assistance for the couple, but it was the driving force behind the move to livestock production that was fueling the rapid growth of Mr. Cottrell's new employer, a livestock feed manufacturer.[23]

But for every woman who used the changes wrought by TVA to positive advantage in her life, many more had to make the best of a bad set of options. Relocation workers' assumptions about appropriate choices for families of a particular race or class led to flawed relocation decisions. The Removal Workers' Code of Ethics called for the worker to be respectful of, and patient with, clients. The worker was to observe the confidentiality of the families interviewed, to avoid making promises he or she did not have the authority to keep, to be punctual with appointments and thoughtful with advice, to find or render services to families whenever such services were available, and to treat all families the same, regardless of wealth or status. Although statements by relocation workers indicate that most workers believed they abided by this code of ethics, individual cases demonstrate that racial and class-based assumptions colored their dealings with families. Agents often assumed that black families were not being uprooted from settled communities and that poor farmers were eager to leave farming.[24]

For example, black farm owners had a smaller range of choices than white landowners. When TVA officials took over the small, fertile farm owned by Edna Spencer's great-grandparents in rural Anderson County, they offered the couple no choice in new homes. Instead of providing a fair cash settlement, as the agency had done for Carrie Smith and her husband, workers offered the black couple a poor clay farm that the agency owned elsewhere in East Tennessee in exchange for their productive farm. Spencer's great-grandparents apparently did not object to this arrangement, probably believing they had no choice. Although they tried for several years to scratch out a living on the marginal land, they ultimately gave up, selling their farm and joining family members in Worcester, Massachusetts. Although their fertile farmland might have formed the basis of their ability to fulfill the TVA vision of middle-class commercial farming, the agency's actions effectively pushed them off the land. The effect of TVA's population removal programs was to proletarianize many African American landowners, forcing them to move from rural middle-class property ownership to the status of unpropertied wage earners.[25]

African American landowners like the Spencers were also not candidates for referral to other agencies. TVA's workers failed to refer black families to other local, state, and federal offices that might have helped them locate new land or improve their farm's productivity. Indeed, TVA's policy of promoting mechanized commercial agriculture and discouraging the old mix of subsistence and general farming common to African American and poor white landowners meant that TVA workers did not see them as candidates for assistance from other agricultural agencies and did not refer them for relocation help. Again and again, workers commented that white landowners with financial resources were good candidates for help from other agencies, implying that other families were not good candidates. In detailing the case of one widowed Blount County farm owner, a worker noted, "Since the family has some resources, it will be an excellent family for the extension service to assist." Indeed, the extension service helped the woman locate several possible farms for purchase. This type of help would have been invaluable to poor farm owners or to prosperous tenants hoping to find affordable land in order to enter the ranks of farm owners, but agency policy instead gave preference to families who least needed additional assistance.[26]

The agency's actions also had a devastating impact on the region's poorest white farm families. TVA's rapid eviction policies often forced poor families with little capital to take whatever housing and jobs they could get, leaving the wives of tenants and sharecroppers almost entirely dependent on the largesse of landlords or the availability of jobs or other tenant farming situations. Sometimes families were able to move with large landowners to new locations nearby, so that the disruption was limited to that normally associated with moving a household. For example, May Babb, her sharecropper husband, her fifteen-year-old daughter, and her sixty-seven-year-old mother moved only one mile away to the new farm purchased by their landlord when Ft. Loudon Lake took their old farm. Although the disruption to their lives was relatively minimal, the TVA worker who declared, "There will be little if any change in the social and economic life of this family," did not recognize the potential impact of even a small move. The family was now one mile farther from the village of Concord and thus one mile farther from schools, churches, and stores. For a family who walked everywhere because they did not own an automobile, the extra mile made the move significant indeed.[27]

TVA's purchases soon led to a shortage of farmland and housing in rural East Tennessee, exacerbating the difficulties of poor families. Much of the best farmland was taken out of production. For example, in Blount County only 75 of 2,988 farms were affected by the building of the Ft. Loudon Reservoir, but 50 percent of the Class I farmland (land with no fertility or erosion problems) was taken out of production. This meant that farmers who were able to locate land were forced to choose among less fertile acres. Moreover, because the TVA projects were removing so much of the region's farmland from production, farm prices were rising at a rate faster than either off-farm wages, commodity prices, or the rates TVA was paying for land, making it difficult for families who wanted to remain on the land to find a place to go. This problem was most acute for tenant farm families being displaced by the mechanization of agriculture and the removal of marginal land from production, programs also encouraged by the Agricultural Adjustment Administration's acreage reduction programs. For these families, who had no capital to buy land of their own, the search for a new home and livelihood was often frustrating. Many tenant families were driven into towns and industrial jobs in spite of their preference for remaining on the land.[28]

Others were forced to take temporary situations, knowing they would face the wrenching process of moving to new communities more than once. For example, Lillie Stevenson, the thirty-one-year-old wife of a farm tenant, was forced to move from a farm near Kingston to another Roane County farm in mid-1940 because of TVA's Watts Bar project. Unfortunately, this situation proved to be only temporary. After they raised a crop on this land, the family was again forced to move, this time to a farm in Meigs County. The new landlord knew that TVA would soon be taking this farm as well, yet he hired the Stevensons in order to get his crops planted that year. Apparently the family knew that this situation would also be only a temporary solution, but they had found no other viable options. Nine months later, TVA took the Meigs County farm. The family located a new situation where John Stevenson was a day laborer on a dairy near the town of Sweetwater. After recording the saga of this family's three moves over three counties and three communities in less than eighteen months, the TVA worker stopped recording their movements. There is no record of the fate of the Stevensons or of Mrs. Stevenson's reaction to the multiple moves.[29]

The shortage of land was particularly devastating for landless farmers who found their work no longer in demand because farm owners were leaving active farming or were using the proceeds of sales to TVA to mechanize their farming operations. Relocation workers often recognized that the discriminatory racial caste system, combined with the shortage of land, created special hardships for black families. For example, a worker visiting Sudie Sherman and her family noted, "Being a Negro, it might be hard for this [family] to find a location as good as the one they have now." Ultimately the Shermans were able to move with their landlord to another farm he had purchased nearby. They benefited by staying in the community in which they had lived for the past twenty-eight years and by gaining a much better house than their previous home that had been "about to fall down," according to the relocation worker.[30]

The shortage of land and the dismantling of so much marginal housing also made available rental housing prohibitively expensive. The case of Addie Adcox dramatically demonstrates the desperation felt by many tenant farm women as they searched for new home. Adcox was the thirty-three-year-old wife of a white Loudon County sharecropper. The couple had four children ranging in age from two months to ten years. Addie Adcox provided most of the family's income through her job at the Loudon County Hosiery Mill. The mill did not provide housing, however, and while Mr. Adcox looked in vain for a new sharecropping situation or a rental house that the family could afford, their landlady was determined to sell her farm and rid herself of the family quickly. She began demolishing the Adcox's house while they still lived there. The TVA worker reported that "Mrs. Adcox seemed almost frantic over their inability to find another place." It is easy to imagine her panic as she watched her home coming down around her.[31]

Ultimately, the Adcoxes proved luckier than many tenant farm families affected by TVA. The sympathetic relocation worker suggested that the family apply for a subsistence homestead at Cumberland Homesteads in Cumberland County, Tennessee, and assisted them in completing the paperwork. This project, part of the Resettlement Administration's subsistence homestead project, aimed to provide the Tennessee Valley's poorest farmers with land for subsistence farming supplemented with part-time industrial employment opportunities for men. At Cumberland Homesteads, families were able to purchase farms of 35 to 50 acres with low-interest financing from the federal government. In addition, the Resettlement Administration set up small cooperatively run industries in which family members could earn cash. The aim of the community was to allow "farmers to gain from the soil an economic well-being and sense of security which are unknown along this rugged plateau today." Families like the Adcoxes had to apply for acceptance into the Cumberland Homesteads community, and Resettlement Administration workers selected them on the basis of their neediness, prior farming experience, likelihood of success, and "desire to become a homesteader." For the Adcox family, Cumberland Homesteads provided a chance at a new start. Moreover, for Mrs. Adcox, daily life would have been far more comfortable. The homes at Cumberland Homesteads were modern and were equipped with electricity and plumbing, vast improvements over the shack the family left behind in Loudon County.[32]

Nonetheless, for the Adcoxes participation in the project meant uprooting the family from the home community that had sustained the family over the years and moving to a new community nearly one hundred miles away. Most of the psychological burden for resettling the family and finding a niche in the new community fell to Addie Adcox. Rural communities were based on a complex web of relationships that provided exchanges of labor and goods as well as emotional support to the members of farm families. It was this mutual support network that enabled the old family farms to survive the ups and downs of the agricultural economy. By forcing families to move out of these communities and away from support networks, TVA disrupted families' traditional coping strategies. The impact of this process was particularly significant for rural women, who had played the central role in maintaining these networks.[33]

In contrast to the experience of the Adcox family, TVA offered few choices or referrals to other agencies for black sharecroppers. Evelina Rooker was a domestic servant, and her husband, Orville, a sharecropper in rural Meigs County. The family, which was being displaced by the Watts Bar project, worked 88 acres with their landlord's tools and lived in a white two-story frame house in good repair. Because they could find no other opportunity, they were forced to move to another farm owned by their landlord, knowing that they would have to move again when TVA took that land the next year. Their new house was smaller and in worse condition than the previous one. The family was able to locate another situation in Meigs County when TVA took the second farm, but TVA provided no support for the family in locating these new homes. Instead, they closed the case after the second relocation.[34]

TVA workers often blamed poor families for their inability to find permanent new situations. Naomi Reed, her sharecropper husband, and four children lived in rural Rhea County where the farm on which they worked was taken for Watts Bar Lake. Reed told the TVA worker that she was in poor health, but TVA offered no special assistance in finding the family a suitable new situation. First, the Reeds moved from one house to another on the same land. Later in the year, they moved to yet another house on the same landlord's property. Two months later, the TVA worker reported:

This family moved to Rockwood on November 26. Their new location is only temporary inasmuch as he [John Reed] was forced to move by the owner so that he could dispose of his buildings. All during this period this man has been very dilatory about making plans for permanent relocation, and he effected his removal without any very definite plans for his eventual readjustment and relocation. This case is being closed.

The TVA worker did not recognize the lack of financial or psychic resources this family had, instead blaming the situation on John Reed's lack of ambition. Part of the relocation workers' frustration may have been due to agency prohibitions on offering direct aid to affected families, but most of the exasperation stemmed from a class-based belief that poor families were to blame for their own poverty.[35]

Poor white and African American women also faced problems in navigating TVA bureaucracy because of discrimination against them and their own lack of education. Ella Cooper, a widowed black domestic servant in Blount County, owned a six-room weatherboard house, a barn, and a smokehouse on a half-acre of land. Here she kept a couple of cows and managed to earn half of her $300 annual income peddling milk and butter in the village. The worker reported that this "dear old colored woman" was most cooperative in her dealings with the agency, but that she ran into title problems with the sale of her land. The worker lamented:

It was a sad business trying to explain to this rather helpless creature why she was not being paid. The Land Acquisition Department had formerly promised her that Chancery Court would clear the whole problem and she would be paid immediately. This promise was made several weeks ago. Until today it had not been explained to her that a friendly condemnation suit was being brought in order to clear the title. The worker with great reluctance pointed out to her that it would probably be several months before she would receive payment on her small place. She was dumbfounded and in a hopeless dilemma as to what she could do about it.

It was indeed a dilemma for Mrs. Cooper, because TVA was unrelenting in its insistence that she must move in order not to delay the agency's construction schedule. Nonetheless, Cooper refused to move as the situation dragged on for three months. Finally, with TVA assurances that she would indeed be paid, she purchased a one-acre plot a mile further from the village and began the process of having her house moved. The worker noted that in the new location "she is hardly as well located as formerly, as she was a domestic servant with plenty of opportunities for work in the village of Louisville; however, she is not so far away that she cannot get all the work she is able to do. There will be no need of follow-up in this case." The worker made no notation as to whether Cooper ever received payment for her land. Nor did he comment on the impact of the move on her milk and butter trade. Once the relocation worker got Cooper off her land and out of the way of construction, his duty to her was finished.[36]

Other women with few resources and little education, particularly household heads, proved to be particularly victimized by the removal process and by impersonal government bureaucracies. Irene Watkins, a forty-one-year-old white domestic, supported a disabled husband, three daughters, and one son who lived at home. A second son resided in the state institution for the insane. In order to protect the interests of this institutionalized son, Mrs. Watkins had deeded her small house and lot in Loudon County to the son, believing that this would provide him with support after her death, while allowing her the use of the property during her lifetime. The arrival of TVA, however, exploded her careful planning. Loudon County insisted that the county government should receive the proceeds from the sale of the house and lot as compensation for the money it had given the state for Watkins' son's care. Although the TVA worker made some effort to take legal action to protect Mrs. Watkins, the law was fairly clear: any proceeds from the sale of property in the name of the institutionalized son would have to go to the county to pay for his care. Mrs. Watkins received no monies from TVA for the sale of her land. She moved her family to a rental house in the same community but farther away from town. The relocation worker closed the case with a notation that "an effort will be made to interest the State Welfare Department in her condition."[37]

Age as well as race and financial means shaped the relocation experience for women. Younger women might initially resist relocation, but they often grew to welcome the changes it brought to their lives. The experience of Ella Craig's family pointed to the crucial role of age in determining the ease of readjustment for women. For women trying to support a family, moving to town could make life easier. A TVA worker noted that Ella Craig "apparently, is well-satisfied with her new home although her mother was better satisfied out in the country." Craig was a fifty-six-year-old widow who owned and managed her 17-acre farm in Loudon County. She supported her teenage children and her eighty-one-year-old mother by raising tobacco and subsistence food crops and occasionally taking in laundry as well as by selling milk and eggs. With the proceeds from the sale of the farm, Craig purchased an eleven-room home in Lenoir City and moved the family to town, where she took in boarders. She was also able to get more steady work as a laundress and liked being closer to schools and stores. Craig's elderly mother lamented to the relocation worker that the conveniences of town and the access to steady work meant little; being wrenched from the way of life she had known for eighty years was overwhelmingly distressing.[38]

Relocation often upset careful arrangements that had enabled elderly widows a measure of independence. For example, seventy-five-year-old Mary Simpson had worked out an ideal situation that allowed her to live independently on her 150-acre farm. She rented her land to other farmers and shared her seventeen-room colonial house with a young couple who took care of her in exchange for housing. The arrival of TVA disrupted this arrangement. The TVA worker noted that Mrs. Simpson was in poor health and would be unable to live alone. He reported, "She states that she probably will not buy another home but will board with some of the children and use such funds as she needs to pay her way during the remaining days of her life." Later the worker reported that she had moved to the home of Charles Wasson a short distance away. Although the relationship between Simpson and Wasson is not clear, he was most likely a son-in-law. For Mary Simpson, the coming of TVA meant that she could no longer maintain her independent household. She became dependent on the good will of her family, a situation that left her with considerably less control over her circumstances than life in her own home.[39]

Indeed, for very old widows the adjustment was particularly difficult because they were often removed from regular contact with the friends and neighbors of a lifetime. This was especially true for women like Simpson who were struggling to maintain a farm alone. For these women, mutual aid networks, such as the arrangement she worked out with the young couple and the assistance she received from her neighbors, were essential to her ability to remain on the land. Moreover, in spite of the fact that women who were farm owners had more financial resources with which to shape the relocation experience, they also may have suffered more from being removed precisely because they were more rooted in local community life than women in more transient tenant families. These women paid a high emotional price when they were separated from the communities that had provided support in myriad ways. John Rice Irwin reported that his great grandparents had a successful readjustment from Norris to another 300-acre farm in a neighboring community. By contrast, his widowed aunt, who was forced to move to Sweetwater, nearly fifty miles away, did not fare so well. Irwin recalled:

> She had some children, but they were almost grown. I think they married and left, and I remember visiting her when I was a child, and she lived in this big rambling farmhouse by herself, with all the people she called strangers around her. And she was a very lonely lady, and I remember [she] was crying when I started to leave because all the good times and all the friends back in the valley were gone.

Irwin's recollection speaks poignantly of the importance of community in his aunt's life and the meaning of the loss of that community to her. In old age, some women found it impossible to construct social bonds in new communities, leaving them feeling isolated and alone.[40]

Similarly, TVA workers seemed oblivious to the impact relocation might have on black communities. In fact, as the case of the Goins family demonstrates, TVA workers often did not recognize the existence of a black community. Flora Goins and her husband, John, an employee of the Aluminum Company of America, lived with eleven children and grandchildren in Blount County. They owned a four-room house and a large lot in the village of Louisville. More prosperous than many black families because John Goins had been employed by ALCOA since 1928, they were characterized as a "high type Negro family" by the TVA worker. Apparently the worker judged their socioeconomic status by the fact that their house was clean and in good repair, that the family's men had steady jobs, and that the children attended school. According to the worker, Mr. and Mrs. Goins expressed considerable interest in moving to town where their children would have better educational opportunities. Ultimately they moved to Alcoa, the Aluminum Company's company town. The worker noted:

A very large percentage of the employees of the Aluminum Company are colored. Therefore it is fortunate that the Goins family can move into a section where they will be immediately adjusted. School facilities for the colored at Alcoa are superior to those in other localities. Much consideration has been given to housing and other comforts for employees of his race. Altogether this seems the very best move that could have been made.

Not only was the worker unconcerned with the way the loss of their land might affect the Goins' ability to supplement the men's wages with subsistence products, but he did not comment on the effects of giving up the independence of property ownership for the dependence of renting a company-owned house. The worker seemed unaware that the Goins family might have been tied into a closely-knit black community in Louisville (the presence of three black churches in the village indicates a large and active black community) and assumed that the family would experience instant adjustment simply by living near other black families.[41]

Indeed, the impact of relocation on black community life was barely recognized by many relocation workers. Again and again, workers commented that "this is a Negro family that takes no part in the affairs of the community." The assumption was that, because they were excluded from community leadership posts and from the white community, African Americans did not have a community of their own and did not suffer from community disruption when they were relocated. Workers used "community" to refer only to the white community and "affairs of the community" referred to participation in schools and other formal organizations closed to African Americans. (The fact that workers saw "community" as being defined by formal organizations also helps explain why they ignored the disruption to mutual aid networks created by relocation.) Yet relocation workers' own testimony pointed to the presence of vital African American communities in rural areas. A worker visiting Sudie Sherman, the black woman who kept house for her sharecropper father-in-law in Knox County, reported that "when the worker called, the room was filled with Negroes; and a corn husking party seemed to be in progress." In spite of his explicit testimony about the presence of a black community, the worker's other comments ignore its existence. This belief made TVA workers even less sympathetic to the impact of removing black families from their communities than they were for whites.[42]

Families' commitment to maintaining community ties can be seen in their resettlement patterns, particularly in the case of Norris Dam, the first TVA project. When Norris was built in the mid-1930s, there was not yet a shortage of land in counties unaffected by the dam building. Land in other East Tennessee counties remained plentiful and relatively cheap because of the agricultural depression. Yet the families affected by Norris were reluctant to leave their own neighborhoods. In the Norris Basin, a study of 2,587 removed families found that 62 percent remained in the five-county area of the Norris project. This indicates that families were simply refusing to leave their community ties behind. Only 176 of the families in this study left the state. East Tennesseans' fierce attachment to the local community appears in sharp relief to migration patterns elsewhere in the South. One historian estimates that 1.39 million people left the South in the 1930s. Yet Tennessee actually gained white and black residents during this period.[43]

This pattern may have maintained community ties, but it did little to help an already depressed economy. Like much of the South, the five-county region was already suffering from overpopulation, and farms were already too small to support the large concentration of people living on them. This resettlement pattern simply meant that the same number of families were crowded on less land. It was more than a decade before the economy of the five-county region developed sufficiently to support an industrial base that provided a significant number of off-farm jobs. Ultimately, efforts to maintain communities proved to be in vain for many families as economic pressures forced rural citizens of the five-county region off the land. Lack of money eventually won out over love of land. After World War II began, many families did finally leave the Norris Basin for better jobs in northern cities.[44]

Acceptance and Resistance

The reactions of families to the disruptions created by TVA were mixed. Some families sold quickly and gladly, while others sold grudgingly but without much resistance. A few families forced TVA to initiate condemnation proceedings in an attempt to get a better price for their land, while others sought ways to delay removal. Six of the nearly three thousand families at Norris had to be evicted forcibly when rising flood waters endangered their lives. A random look at the relocation records for the other dams reveals a similar pattern. Some families resisted openly, but more commonly, families found subtle ways to resist and delay removal. Perhaps because the ideology of southern womanhood dictated that men treat the wives of white landowners with respect in all situations, women often initiated this resistance, believing they would suffer fewer repercussions than their husbands. In this way, they sometimes succeeded in exercising more control over their removal than they might have had if they had been more compliant with TVA's demands. For example, Maggie Simpson rented a few acres from a farmer in the Watts Bar basin. She supported herself and a teenaged son with housework for the landlord and with subsistence gardening. The worker noted that "she had been to school but very little, [but] she seemed to be fairly capable and energetic." Indeed, she applied this energy to pressuring her landlord to build her a new house on some of his land that remained above the taking line (the elevation at which TVA condemned and purchased land). On the worker's second visit, he noted that "Mrs. Simpson, as yet has no plan. She seems utterly without concern, and repeatedly states she can manage all right." Mrs. Simpson resisted for several months, finding excuses not to move to another location and pressuring her landlord to rebuild her house above the water line. Eventually the landlord gave in, perhaps because he didn't want to lose his housekeeper. By dragging her feet and pretending to be oblivious to the situation facing her, Simpson succeeded in dictating the terms of her removal.[45]

Other women used similar passive tactics to resist TVA's often unreasonably short deadlines for vacating their property. Mrs. B. H. Armour, a sixty-one-year-old Roane County widow, lived with her grown son and daughter on the 34-acre farm she owned. TVA bought her farm on February 26, 1941, and planned to take possession on March 1. Upon appeal from Mrs. Armour, officials agreed to extend the deadline for vacating the property to April 1. Meanwhile, Mrs. Armour bought house lots in the village of Kingston, where she planned to build a house. On March 31 she told the worker that construction on her new house had been delayed and that she simply could not yet move. Moreover, she circumvented the relocation worker who was appointed to be her liaison with the agency, instead discussing her situation directly with the TVA foreman working on her land; and she obtained a verbal agreement from the foreman that only her outbuildings would have to be moved immediately. Reluctantly, the worker secured permission for Mrs. Armour to stay in the house until her new dwelling was completed. In early May, Mrs. Armour was stricken with an unidentified illness. It is not clear whether this illness was genuine, although her children told the TVA worker that she spent several days in the hospital. Certainly, the relocation worker may have shared general middle-class assumptions that women were more frail, making him more likely to believe this was not a ruse. Regardless of the authenticity of her illness, Mrs. Armour was successful in delaying her removal until her new house was completed on May 19, nearly three months after TVA's original deadline for vacating the property.[46]

Sometimes women's resistance took more direct form than feigning illness or playing dumb. Lou Emma Taylor's parents took legal action to try to force TVA to pay them fair market value for their farm in the Norris Basin. Taylor came to visit her parents one afternoon and found a TVA official badgering the elderly couple and offering them a very short time in which to vacate their home. Both of Taylor's parents were in tears, which infuriated their daughter. "That just flew all over me, that my old daddy and mother were being rooted out of where they had roots," she recalled. "And then somebody coming along there and treating them like they were simpletons that didn't know nothing and tearing [them] apart like that!" Taylor informed the TVA representative that her parents had engaged a lawyer to negotiate a fair price and ordered him to leave. "He didn't allow as how he would, and I said, 'There's a good shotgun setting inside that door there, and if you don't get off this hill, I'll use it on you.' . . . And boy, he got up an moved, and I said, 'Don't you come back up here anymore and disturb my daddy and mother! That's enough!' And he didn't come back." Although Taylor's parents ultimately came to an agreement with TVA and voluntarily left their farm, Taylor's vehement resistance and threats saved them from considerable harassment in the interim.[47]

Camp Croft—Meeting the Wartime Emergency

TVA was not the only federal agency to relocate rural upcountry people during this period, and other agencies were less inclined to worry about the needs of the relocated, especially relocated women. On November 8, 1940, readers of the afternoon *Spartanburg (S.C.) Herald* were greeted by a two-inch headline: "Army Camp for 16,500 Men to Be Located in Lower Part of County." The article described the massive construction project that was expected to occupy over 12,000 acres and employ hundreds of civilian construction and support workers. With an estimated cost of $5 to $7 million, the camp would pump millions into the strapped local economy. Chamber of Commerce leaders and city and county representatives had courted U.S. Army officials for months, lobbying to be selected for one of the installations the army was constructing to train the new recruits inducted under the Burke-Wadsworth Act of September 1940, the first peacetime draft in American history. Because of the looming wartime emergency, the army hoped to acquire land quickly and begin construction shortly after the first of the year. Local officials promised to assist the government by negotiating leases with landowners and providing some of the infrastructural improvements to support the military facility.[48]

More than local politicians' promises had helped secure the installation for Spartanburg county, however. The city boasted the infrastructural supports that a large training facility required. Long known as the railroad "hub city" of the Southeast, Spartanburg also had a municipal airport and regular bus service. A southern railroad line bordered the tract chosen for the military camp, and Duke Power's main electrical service line cut through the center of the site. In addition to fine infrastructure, Spartanburgers had some powerful friends in Washington. Democratic senator James F. Byrnes, a close friend of President Roosevelt and soon to become a Supreme Court justice and the head of the Office of War Mobilization, called the city home. So did Governor Olin D. Johnston, who would shortly succeed Byrnes in the Senate. Local leaders thus brought both an advantageous physical setting and the influence of political allies to their campaign for economic development via a government project.[49]

Local boosters were right about the need for a major economic development project in Spartanburg County, an area hit hard by the Depression. The county of 127,000 people stretched from the Blue Ridge foothills to piedmont in the state's northwest corner. Although it had been a railroad and textile manufacturing center since Reconstruction, 40 percent of the county's population still lived on farms, most of them less than 50 acres. In spite of the ravages of the boll weevil, Depression-era plunges in cotton prices, and some of the worst soil erosion in the nation, cotton remained the chief cash crop in the county. Sixty percent of the county's farmers were tenants, who were often hopelessly embroiled in the crop-lien system. Nor did the county's textile mills offer much of an escape from the dragging agricultural economy. The textile industry had been ravaged by the Depression, with thousands of workers unemployed and thousands more working reduced hours and wages, and was only just beginning to recover as thousands of dollars worth of federal war mobilization contracts began to come in in the late 1930s.[50]

County leaders had good reason to believe that a major military installation would boost the local economy. During World War I, the county's west side had been home to Camp Wadsworth, an army training camp. The project had poured millions into the local economy and improved the road system. Construction teams had built over a thousand buildings on the camp property during the summer of 1917. The road constructed to the camp had provided the basis for a new highway connecting Spartanburg to Greenville, thirty miles away. Local rents had soared as landlords took advantage of the influx of civilian workers and trailing wives. Downtown merchants reported that their soda fountains had overflowed and that they had actually had trouble keeping up with the demand for basic consumer goods. In spite of some minor friction between soldiers and local residents because of the strains the camp put on the local infrastructure and racial tensions sparked by local white fears of an infantry unit from Harlem, Camp Wadsworth had provided a brief but significant boost to the local economy.[51]

City fathers believed that a new federal installation would bring similar benefits. They were triumphant in November 1940 when they announced the successful completion of negotiations to bring the facility to Spartanburg County. Within days after the announcement of the project appeared in the local papers, a committee of county officials and Chamber of Commerce leaders began negotiating lease options on land in the camp district. Several of the largest landowners met one-on-one with local negotiating officials and were instructed to quickly submit proposals for the lease of their farms.[52]

Even as they negotiated for lease options, local officials conducted a massive propaganda campaign designed to generate support for the project. In the eyes of its boosters, Camp Croft was both an economic opportunity and a patriotic duty for Spartanburg County residents. Articles appearing in both local papers almost daily touted the number of construction jobs the project would create. The mayor broadcast a radio appeal over local station WORD, calling on citizens to cooperate in the national preparedness effort. The editor of the *Spartanburg Herald-Journal,* the Sunday paper, noted on November 17 that the negotiation of leases was the only thing holding up the beginning of construction and appealed for landowners to do their part in hastening the process so as to aid in war preparedness efforts and at the same time boost the local economy. On December 12, the editor of the morning paper, the *Spartanburg Journal and Carolina Spartan* (owned by the same company as the afternoon daily, the *Spartanburg Herald* and the Sunday *Herald-Journal*), admitted that such a massive project was bound to create problems and inconveniences. He called on citizens to do all they could to support the Camp Croft effort, including refraining from engaging in profiteering. "Spartanburg cannot afford to display a spirit of greed [and] avarice," he added. A photo in the December 11 *Journal and Carolina Spartan* showed a field full of cars and trucks used to ferry workers to the construction site. The caption read, "Ride or walk, but get to the camp." Sightseers jammed the roads around the project, leading state highway officials to close the road bordering the site.[53]

By early December, in the face of resistance from local farmers who expressed concerns that the army would ruin their leased land, the army decided to purchase the necessary acreage outright instead of signing long-term leases. But any hope of reducing resistance was soon dashed. Even though officials were able to secure title to some land and break ground on December 5, 1940, several landowners refused to sign agreements, insisting that they were not receiving fair compensation. Local newspapers avoided reporting on this resistance, referring only obliquely to the fact that it was taking officials longer than anticipated to secure title to all the land.[54]

Newspapers, local officials, and army brass alike seemed oblivious of the havoc that property removal was creating in the lives of folks who lived in the area. In fact, a *Journal and Carolina Spartan* reporter wrote on December 7 that "it is not known exactly how many persons now living on the site will have to move, but the number has been stated as comparatively small according to Chamber of Commerce officials." Likewise, army officials understated the project's impact until after completion of relocation, when one report to the army's constructing quartermaster noted that "the job was not accomplished without grief. Scores of farmers left homes that had belonged to their grandfathers, saw them razed or burned to the ground to make room for the new camp." At the same time, this officer reported that land was purchased from over sixty-three owners (an incorrect figure) but made no mention of the hundreds of tenant farm families living in the area. Another official report on the needs for defense-related housing in Spartanburg County stated that only 200 families had been relocated from the Camp Croft area. The number was probably closer to 500.[55]

For the families facing relocation, several factors made this relocation different than TVA's removal of Tennessee Valley families. For one thing, the sense of urgency created by the war in Europe meant that government's focus was on getting families out of the way in order to get a training camp up and running, not on serving the needs of relocated farmers. As the editorials indicated, the construction of Camp Croft was seen as a matter of patriotism by local and national officials alike, and by implication, resistant farmers were being unpatriotic. Another difference from the TVA removal was that the federal bureaucracy kept its distance from the local people, leaving it up to local real estate agents selected by the county to negotiate with landowners on the government's behalf. Unlike TVA's dam relocations, the Camp Croft relocation was significant because there were no relocation workers to assist families in locating new land, negotiating the labyrinth of government agencies, or making the transition to new homes.[56]

By January 1941 the War Department, in cooperation with a Spartanburg attorney, resorted to condemnation proceedings in order to seize im-

Fig. 11. Some of the poorer families relocated from the Camp Croft area were moved to small homes constructed nearby by the Farm Security Administration. Vienne White, her son William, and a farmhand eat lunch in their incomplete FSA house. (Jack Delano photography, LC-USF34, 43821. Library of Congress.)

mediate control of the property owned by resistant farmers. The agency announced that the farmer-property owners would be allowed to live in their homes "as long as their farm buildings do not stand in the way of construction. When it is found that it will be necessary to push the building program through any occupied area, notice for removal will be given the residents in sufficient time for them to locate elsewhere."[57]

This lip service to the needs of relocating families fell by the wayside, however, in the face of extreme pressures to get Camp Croft in operation. In March 1941, when a survey found that ninety-nine families were unable to locate new homes, the Farm Security Administration (FSA) built twenty prefabricated houses a few miles away from the Camp Croft site. The FSA built similar housing developments around new military installations throughout the South. These were not economic development projects designed to assist poor farmers but rather emergency military housing projects. Eight men could assemble these small houses in a day at a cost of less than $1,000. Most (but not all) of the people who moved into these houses were landless tenants with few options.

Still, FSA houses did little to alleviate a housing shortage exacerbated by the flood of construction workers into the county. By March 14, an army survey found over two hundred families still living in the 22,000-acre site (up from the originally projected 12,000 acres) acquired by the government. Frustrated army officials circulated the area on Good Friday, ordering families, tenants and landlords alike, to be out by the following Monday. "They came to the house on Good Friday. They said the area would be part of a firing range on Monday," recalled William White, son of one relocated landowning family. "We had to act quickly, moving all the [stored] corn and mules and our furniture. I will never forget passing the Methodist Church on Easter morning with all our possessions piled on Ed Hood's truck. As we drove by, all the women were out front in their Easter finery." White and his family temporarily moved into one of the FSA houses. The relocation must have been especially difficult for White's mother and father, knowing that they were leaving a community that provided important mutual aid networks, a community in which they had spent most of their lives, for the unknown of a new life.[58]

As with the TVA relocation, tenant farm families had a hard time finding new sharecropping situations. With 22,000 acres of the county's land off limits, there was a serious shortage of farmland, and the landless hunted in vain for new tenant and sharecropping positions. A serious shortage of rental housing exacerbated the situation. Even sharecroppers who could find jobs had difficulty finding houses suitable for their large families. Claude Lee recalled that he and ten brothers and sisters had assisted their parents in sharecropping 190 acres in the Camp Croft area. "When they told us, my dad went all over the place looking for someplace where we could stay," he explained. The older children found their own jobs and places to stay, breaking up the family unit. Claude Lee married and took a job at Beaumont Mills, a textile plant near Spartanburg.[59]

Lee's experience points to another significant difference from the experience of landless people relocated by the TVA: thanks to the prewar mobilization, tenants displaced by Camp Croft found increasing opportunities off the land. Local textile plants and other manufacturers were expanding their employment rolls to fill new military contracts, and men and women alike were able to find factory jobs that paid considerably better than sharecropping. Men also found constructions jobs on the Camp Croft project. Except for the poorly paying textile mill jobs, however, few rural women benefited from new jobs created by the construction of the camp. A few women were hired for civilian clerical jobs at the camp, and two Spartanburg women were hired to run the officer's club, but farm women rarely had the clerical skills or the connections to get the few jobs available with the army. Thus, while women's opportunities for work did expand somewhat in the 1940s, few of the displaced rural women were able to find the type of jobs that offered an opportunity for advancement.[60]

Job opportunities or no, Lee's family found the disruption of community disturbing. "People were real close back then," Claude Lee recalled. "We all helped our neighbors. Everybody helped bring in crops or any kind of work that had to be done." Still, he observed that the move from the farm was not as difficult for tenants as for landowners. "It didn't bother me that much. I was used to moving around every year or so," albeit in the same community.[61]

As Lee noted, the disruption of mutual aid networks was particularly distressing for landowning families, especially women who had depended on the networks for social contact and assistance in times of crisis. Mattie Lee Murph and her husband were living on his family's large peach farm when the Camp Croft removal notices went out. They hadn't been married long and were fixing up an old stone house on the Murph farm when they were told to move. Like the Lee and White families, they received notice on Good Friday. Her husband, the youngest in the family, was able to find a small farm to purchase, but he had to start completely from scratch because his brothers had taken the mules and tools from the family farm. In spite of these hardships, it was the loss of community that Mattie Murph remembered most vividly. She complained that the new neighbors were not too neighborly and that they didn't like to visit as the old neighbors had. This sense of distrust in the new community must have increased her sense of being plucked from her old world willy-nilly.[62]

Maude and M. B. Smith Jr. would have agreed with Lee's and Murph's assessments of the difficulty for landowners. Their sense of the loss of community was acute, but so was the financial loss. When asked who suffered most from the relocation, prosperous landowning families or poor folks, their son Sanford Smith said that both groups suffered equally if they had been living on the land or in the community for several generations. "It hurt them emotionally because of their attachment to the land," he noted. "Then people were attached to the land, to the 'place.' . . . Financially, of course, it was the big operators who never completely recouped their loss. Most of the poorer people went on to find good jobs in the opportunities created by the war."[63]

The Smiths were among the most prominent farm families to resist the forced sale of their land. Smith's grandfather had been the first in the family line to come to Spartanburg County. Some time in the late nineteenth century, he purchased several hundred acres of land southeast of the village of Spartanburg and began a general farm and sawmill. He also ran a store. Smith's father, M. B. Jr., went into dairying and expanded the operation. Four of his five brothers joined him in the dairy business in the 1920s. As M. B. Sr. moved into semi-retirement, M. B. Jr., the oldest son, became the tacit head of the operation that encompassed about 1,500 acres. They had a large pure Guernsey herd, known as Alameda Dairy, and were milking 150 cows in 1940. In addition, the Smith brothers had their own bottling operation, selling wholesale milk and delivering their "Baby Joy" brand milk to local schools.[64]

The family was given a month's notice, leaving Maude Smith nearly frantic about where they would move. Although the Smith family felt the price they were being offered was a fair estimate of the value of the land, they were angry that they were not being allowed anything for the loss of their business. The brothers had just installed a new water system, complete with a water tower and a pump as well as a new barn, and they wanted compensation for those items as well as for the damage done to their business by the disruption. The brothers searched the county for an intact plot of land large enough to house their large dairy and rebuild the creamery, but thanks to the Camp Croft project, the choices were slim. Demand drove up the price for the county's remaining farmland, and little of it was suited to the family's needs. Facing a looming deadline for vacating the land, the Smiths fought the matter in court, one of a handful of families to fight the acquisition through legal channels.[65]

As the matter dragged its way through the courts, the family tried to maintain some semblance of normal life, continuing their work routines.

FIG. 12. The extended family of M. B. Smith Sr. in front of the Smith farmhouse. Maude and M. B. Jr. are in the back row, second and third from left. M. B. Smith Sr. and his wife are the elderly couple seated in the center of the photo. The elder Mrs. Smith died before the Camp Croft relocation. (Smith family photo, ca. 1935. Courtesy Sanford N. Smith.)

But they also prepared for the inevitable. The brothers cut timber off their property and used their sawmill to saw it and stockpile it for use in barns on new land. Yet even in this effort, they were thwarted by Uncle Sam. An army official passing by noticed the lumber and stopped to tell them it was government property and that their cutting was illegal. The lumber would have to remain with the farm. The lumber was later used in the construction of buildings at Camp Croft, fortunately for the army, which was facing lumber shortages. The Smiths, however, were never compensated for the lumber or for the labor they expended in milling it.[66]

Sanford Smith remembered the day his father gave up the fight. One Sunday morning, as the family was drawing their baths to prepare for church, the water suddenly went off. Once again, the bulldozers that ran seven days a week on the nearby construction project had cut the water line. Although it was not the first time it had happened, Sanford Smith remembers it as the last straw for his father, M. B. Jr. "It was the only time I ever saw Daddy cry," he sighed. Shortly thereafter, the brothers sold their equipment and cattle. They informed their eight black and five white tenant families that they would have to move.

The forced move broke up the family operation because the acreage they were able to find was not enough to support four men and their families. Two brothers left the farm. Chauncey went to work for a rival bottling company, and Rupert joined brother Paul's Community Cash supermarket chain. M. B. Jr. and Newton found 100 acres a mile or so from their old land but outside the Camp Croft containment area and began a very small dairy operation. They had to build new facilities, including a milking parlor. They also rebuilt the herd with Holsteins and Jerseys, cows that produced less butterfat but more milk for the whole milk market. They sold this milk wholesale to another bottler because the price they received for their farm was not enough to cover the cost of building a new bottling plant. The family was also able to build three tenant houses on the new land so that three of thirteen tenant families had a place to go.

Sanford Smith recalled that the whole episode placed a huge burden on his mother. Whereas on the old place, M. B. Sr. and two of his daughters had lived in their own farmhouse, they now moved in with M. B. Jr., his wife, and three sons—eight people coexisting in a six-room house. Moreover, the house was not nearly as modern as the old farmhouse. It did not have running water or an indoor toilet. Although M. B. Jr. managed to install a pump system and pipe in water after a year or so, it took a couple more years before he was able to install a bathroom. Even then, the shortage of building materials due to the war emergency meant the family had to make do with a concrete bathtub, far inferior to the bathroom they had had in their old house.

Not only was the house far inferior to the family's old farmhouse, but Maude Smith had to readjust her work habits to accommodate two other women in the household. Moreover, one of her sisters-in-law was allergic to wheat flour, forcing the family to change its eating habits. She was able to eat muffins but not biscuits, a staple of the farm diet. Sanford Smith

recalled that he had watched his mother weep for months after the relocation and wondered why she was so sad. He now knows it was sad-
ness at the loss of the home she and her husband had built, frustration at
the hardships of the new life, and grief for the anger her husband felt; but
at the time young Sanford didn't understand. He noted, "It was a time
when children weren't told anything. We just kept quiet. It was really
hard on the adults, losing all you'd work[ed] for." The presence of so
many people in the household caused inevitable strains that were finally
relieved after a year and a half, when M. B. Smith Sr. was able to purchase
a 36-acre farm nearby, and he and his daughters moved into their own
farmhouse.[67]

The whole episode created tensions in the extended family as well,
some of them permanent rifts. Paul Smith, the only one of the Smith sons
not farming in the family operation, was a cofounder of the local Community Cash grocery chain and a prominent member of the Chamber of
Commerce. He had been instrumental in bringing the Camp Croft installation to Spartanburg county. M. B. Jr. accused his brother of "selling
his birthright" for his part in negotiating the deal.[68]

Sanford Smith believed the forced move from the Camp Croft area
did lasting damage to both his parents. He said it was something his
father never got over. The formerly close-knit community was dispersed
all over the county, disrupting old patterns of mutual aid and visiting. But
more than that was the disillusionment. Smith believed his father felt
betrayed by his government. He felt "like this was not how things ought
to be . . . like the system had not worked for him." In fact, his son believed
that the episode strained all of M. B. Jr.'s relationships, including his
marriage, as he became more withdrawn and, at times, bitter. He noted
that M. B. Jr.'s rift with his brother Paul never really healed, though it
became less important in later years. The brothers saw each other at
family reunions and were civil to one another, but they never visited in
each other's homes again.

As with the TVA relocation, some families did resist the move. Not
only did M. B. Smith Jr. refuse to move until his court challenge was
decided, but he looked the other way when his own sons interfered with
the army's construction project. His youngest son, Sanford, recalled that
the boys would wait until the surveyors left their land each day and then
remove the stakes. At the time (he was six), he thought the activity was a

game, but he later realized that his older brothers were harassing the officials forcing them off the family land.

Families who lived on the fringes of the camp were also able to resist moving. Bessie Millwood, in her thirties at the time of the removal, kept house for her tenant farmer father. They managed to stay in their home for thirteen months after receiving the eviction notice. Her father took advantage of confusion over jurisdiction among various government officials. She recalled, "One man [an army officer] was nice. He comes by and says to stay on. Then another one comes by and says to get out quick." The family stayed until Mr. Millwood could finish renovations on a small house he had purchased nearby. Millwood remembered those thirteen months as an "awful time." Although they were not forcibly removed from their home, the army conducted maneuvers around the house. She said the soldiers were "crawling through the yard, digging foxholes at the edge of the yard." She was relieved to finally leave the chaos behind.[69]

In the end, government-imposed relocation was a wrenching experience for upcountry families. TVA proved to be a mixed blessing for the rural women of the Tennessee Valley. The agency's positive effects—wide distribution of electrical power, improved educational opportunities, and a generally rising standard of living—certainly improved the lives of most of the valley's rural families. Yet there was a trade-off for these benefits, a trade-off that was particularly difficult for the valley's women. Wrenched from communities where they had spent their entire lives and forced to make new lives away from networks of kin and neighbors who had sustained them during earlier hard times, they had to develop new coping strategies to replace those traditional ones. Women were also removed from trading networks that had enabled them to earn and control considerable amounts of cash from sales of their butter and eggs. When women moved into established communities, they found it hard to break into the butter and egg trade already dominated by local women.

Class and race were the major factors shaping the experiences of Tennessee Valley women with TVA in this period. For wives of farm owners, substantial financial means eased the transition by offering the family considerable control and numerous options for relocation. Moreover, TVA and other government agencies offered these more prosperous families plenty of relocation assistance because they were more likely to adopt the mechanized commercial farming practices favored by the agencies. In other words, assistance to prosperous families translated to "success stories" that looked good in agency annual reports. Poorer women were not so fortunate. Wives of tenant farmers, widows, and black women found themselves at the mercy of an impersonal bureaucracy and cruel economic forces. Indeed, because landowners often used the cash from the sale of their land to mechanize, thus reducing their labor needs, many poor tenants were forced off the land. After several years of transition, these families often found easier and more prosperous lives in town, but still they were forced off the land rather than choosing to leave. Moreover, once in town, women found that the skills that were so vital to the survival of the farm family were not so central to family life in town. TVA's relocation efforts also reveal the ways in which the South's persistent and entrenched racial caste system undermined TVA's utopian vision of remaking the Tennessee Valley for the good of all of its people.

By contrast, in the Camp Croft area of upstate South Carolina, relocation was treated as a patriotic duty, and families who resisted were viewed as failing to do their bit for the war effort. Camp Croft provided a huge boost for the local economy, one that created thousands of jobs for rural and town folk alike. Nonetheless, many families lost prosperous farms and businesses in the process, and some never recovered financially or emotionally. The federal government provided little assistance to the relocated families. For many upcountry Southerners, the forced relocations of the interwar years cemented feelings of mistrust of federal intervention.

~~~ Six ~~~

Rural Women and Industrialization

In 1969 an official of the Aluminum Company of America's (ALCOA) Tennessee operations acknowledged that the arrival of the company in East Tennessee early in the century had been a difficult experience for the rural people of Blount County: "The early days provided a traumatic experience. . . . A basically farming community felt the impact of the importation of outsiders—Yankees, large numbers of Negroes and Mexicans, strain on the school systems, competition for workers and salaried personnel, changes in the transportation systems, and the over-all opening up of a relatively isolated part of the country."[1]

The arrival of a large industrial employer in rural Blount County changed the face of the entire community, launching the shift from a rural agrarian society to an urban industrial culture. In similar ways, coal mining transformed rural southwestern West Virginia. Few historians have looked closely at women's responses to the arrival of heavy industry such as aluminum manufacturing and coal mining. Unlike textile mills, which employed large numbers of women and children, heavy industry employed men almost exclusively, leaving rural women to make different types of adjustments than those made by women who entered the textile mills.

Aluminum Manufacturing in a Rural County

In many ways, ALCOA was a boon for the farming folk of Blount County, Tennessee. Marginal farmers scraping out a meager living on small holdings were now able to supplement farm incomes with wages from jobs at ALCOA or to leave the farm entirely for life in town. The company also added to the county's coffers with its property taxes, enabling the county court (as the county commission was then called) to improve schools and roads, and even to increase funding for local agricultural extension work. Yet, as the company official later acknowledged, these benefits were not without significant costs, particularly for the women of the county. Even as Blount County's farm women embraced material improvements brought about by industrialization, they resisted total dependence on the wage economy and the adoption of urban industrial values, clinging to aspects of their traditional culture.

In spite of the arrival of ALCOA, Blount County retained its rural character throughout the years before World War II. The county's agrarian lifestyle was reflected in its market habits, its politics, and its newspapers. As was the case with most trade centers for farming communities, Saturdays were market days when the streets of Maryville, the county seat, were filled with throngs of overall-clad farmers and their families, traveling by a variety of conveyances, including buggies, pickup trucks, and cars. They sold produce on the streets, haggled for provisions at the general stores on Broadway, and socialized in the town's public spaces, lending a distinctively rural atmosphere to the town on those days. Rural men also played a leading role in county politics. Many of the county's elected officials came from the ranks of elite farmers. Farm news figured prominently in the local newspapers. The semi-weekly *Maryville Times* included a farm column that highlighted local agricultural organizations and production records set by county farmers, a weekly rundown on local wholesale farm commodity prices, a regular extension service column, and reports on all 4-H Club and Farm Bureau events and local and regional fairs.[2]

Although nearly half of rural families had become dependent on wage labor for at least part of their income, most of the county's population still lived on the land. In 1930 students in the department of political and social science at Blount County's Maryville College conducted a detailed social survey of the county, finding that two-thirds of the county's population still lived on farms more than ten years after the arrival of ALCOA.[3]

Another sign of the county's rural character was its lack of an industrial infrastructure. Although it boasted four banks, ninety-eight miles of railroad, and a 90 percent literacy rate, all important components in the development of an industrial economy, other elements of its infrastructure were weak. Most of the county's roads were dirt, gravel, or macadam. Aside from the three paved state highways that connected the county to Knoxville, Loudon County, and the mountains, the county boasted only fifteen miles of asphalt roads in 1930, ten miles of that in the towns of Maryville and Alcoa. One rural woman recalled that the road that ran from Maryville to the prosperous Quaker village of Friendsville in the 1920s was maintained by local men who did annual road work in lieu of paying taxes: "There was always holes [in that road] that when you got in the car, you'd drag on 'em. The roads were very, very bad. . . . There were roads, but they weren't car roads." The weak infrastructure meant that industries moving into the county had to be prepared to build their own roads, power plants, and other facilities.[4]

The county retained its rural character in the early twentieth century, but its farms were becoming smaller and, as a result, less profitable. Although the number of farms in the county grew steadily between 1900 and 1920, the per farm acreage was falling. In 1900 there were 2,160 farms in Blount County, and the average farm size was 128.6 acres. By 1925 the number of farms had grown to 2,909, while the average acreage had fallen to 74.4. Although this fragmentation of farmland was the inevitable consequence of partible inheritance patterns, the reduction in the amount of cultivable land per farm forced more families to look off the farm for additional sources of income.[5]

The Arrival of ALCOA

In spite of the county's rural character, industry was not new to Blount County when ALCOA constructed its first plant in 1914. Local historians have noted that industry began as early as 1785 when the first white settlers established tub mills, a type of water-powered grist mill. Chartered by the General Assembly of the Territory South of the River Ohio in 1795, the county grew rapidly. Small industry developed alongside agriculture in this foothills county located between the Tennessee River and the Great Smoky Mountains south of Knoxville. By 1887 the county boasted woolen mills, saw mills, sash and blind factories, a machine shop, a cord and twine manufacturer, and harness makers. In fact, the county had 242 manufacturing wage earners by 1900. The early twentieth century brought new extractive industries, such as Little River Lumber Company in the mountains and marble quarries in the southern part of the county.[6]

Pittsburgh-based ALCOA chose Blount County because of its abundance of rushing mountain-fed streams and rivers, excellent locations for a network of hydroelectric dams that would provide cheap power. The county also offered an ample cheap labor force among its poor rural people. Officials believed, usually correctly, that these country folk would be grateful for the opportunity to man the gigantic aluminum smelting operation the company planned. In 1910 ALCOA began purchasing riparian rights on the Little Tennessee River, where it planned to construct a network of hydroelectric plants to power its factories. Although the first dam in the foothills thirty-five miles south of Maryville was not completed until 1930, the company went ahead with construction of an aluminum manufacturing facility. In 1913 the company selected a site north of Maryville, the county's largest town, as the site for its plant.[7]

At the time of ALCOA's arrival, the town of Maryville had a population of just over 2,500 people. This thriving trade center boasted seventy-five businesses, including four banks that served surrounding valley and upland communities. The presence of Maryville College, an institution founded by Presbyterian circuit rider Isaac Anderson in 1819, lent the town an air of sophistication. Enrolling about seven hundred students in the 1920s, the college provided educational opportunities to many Blount County natives, especially its men, producing numerous physicians, lawyers, ministers, and business leaders who settled in the town after graduation. These citizens valued education and established a good town school system, which boasted two public grammar schools and a high school for whites, as well as a private high school, known as Maryville Polytechnic School, where the sons and daughters of the town's elite and some of the county's wealthiest farmers were educated. Black children were educated at the Hale School, a public grammar school.[8]

ALCOA's plans to build a plant and a company town just beyond the town's borders alarmed Maryville's citizens, who feared an influx of new workers, many of whom were expected to be blacks, outsiders, and "riffraff." Nonetheless, the promise of additional jobs and tax dollars proved irresistible. In 1914 ALCOA purchased 700 acres in North Maryville and began construction of a smelting plant and 150 houses for workers. The factory commenced production in 1915. As plant operations expanded, the mill village that had been planned by ALCOA engineers grew too. The boom created by World War I soon sparked the company to add a rolling mill, a plant that rolled aluminum ingots into sheet metal. This new plant began operations in August 1920. By 1920 the city of Alcoa had 700 houses and 3,358 citizens: 1,708 whites, 1,482 blacks, and 130 Mexicans. ALCOA employed 3,672 men with a payroll of over $3 million. Residents of the company housing, most of them former farm families from Blount County and other rural areas throughout the South, enjoyed amenities not available on farms or in many parts of the town of Maryville—running water, indoor plumbing, and electricity. Hundreds of men commuted from farm homes to ALCOA jobs every day, tending the farm after work or leaving the operation to wives and children.[9]

The Company Town

From the beginning, ALCOA wanted to encourage a measure of self-government among its workers even as it retained some authority within the confines of the village. Not only did the company provide mortgages to all workers of either race who could afford to buy the company houses, but they also laid the groundwork for a municipal government. The company hired a city manager to serve as the chief operating officer of the mill village, but in order to allow for elected residents on a city commission, the company sought to create an independent city. Officials also sought political power at the state level. In 1918 Dr. J. Walter McMahon,

ALCOA's medical director, was elected to the Tennessee legislature. Seeking to consolidate the company town's autonomy from Maryville, McMahon introduced a bill in the Tennessee legislature the next year to incorporate the mill village into a separate town called Alcoa.* This action came as a shock to the citizens of Maryville, who had viewed the mill village with an eye toward future annexation. Dismayed at the loss of potential tax revenues, they protested. Nonetheless, the industrial lobby proved more powerful than local interests, and the bill passed the legislature. Alcoa was now a political entity as well as a company town.[10]

In the two decades between the incorporation of the company town and the outbreak of World War I, hundreds of farmers from Blount County and beyond took jobs at ALCOA and moved their families to the company town, leaving the farm behind forever. Historian Ronald Eller contended that the Appalachian farmer's dependence on the new industrial order was imposed upon him against his will by macroeconomic forces beyond his control, but Blount County residents' response to industry was more complicated. Rural citizens and some working-class town dwellers were eager to take advantage of new wage-earning opportunities. One farm woman recalled that many farm families couldn't wait to move to town: "Get us off [the farm] as fast as you can get us. Men and women both [felt that way]. Men liked to farm, but there just wasn't no money to be made on it. ALCOA has helped an awful lot of people that were at the very bottom of the bucket." For the poorest families, life in the mill village offered superior living conditions and access to commerce and entertainment only dreamed of from the front porches of isolated, ramshackle cabins beside dusty and rutted tracks. New jobs at "the plant," as it came to be known, offered employment opportunities that initially seemed more stable than a farm life that left families at the mercy of the elements. Lula Gatlin Ramsey's father moved his wife and five children to Alcoa from Walland, a community in the foothills of the Smokies, to take a job at ALCOA. With all those mouths to feed, Ramsey believed, "my dad was lucky to go to work for ALCOA."[11]

_____

*ALCOA, in all capital letters, is the acronym for the Aluminum Company of America, the corporation. Alcoa, in lower case letters, refers to the town incorporated from the mill village.

Transformations in Gender Roles

Yet all was not wine and roses in town. Farm families gave up considerable autonomy in exchange for nice houses and regular paychecks. This transition was difficult for farm men. Once used to controlling their own time and working at their own pace and direction, they had to become accustomed to the discipline within the factory walls where the days were structured by a time clock and a foreman. Men found that the unity between life and work was now disrupted. Yet the transition was often even more difficult for the farm women, who also found the rhythms of work and time profoundly affected by the move to town. For the rural farm wife, life had once revolved around the barnyard, the garden, and the kitchen. Now limited land for gardening and livestock production forced women to buy rather than produce most of their food and clothing, a task requiring a new and different set of skills than producing these items on farms.[12]

The move to town altered interactions between husbands and wives. On the farm, husband and wife had had frequent contact and often worked side by side during certain periods of the day. Women often considered themselves partners in the farm operation. In town, white men "worked" and white women "kept house," a profoundly different way of conceiving of the gender division of labor that tended to render women's work invisible. Because men's work earned a paycheck, it was defined as "work," whereas women's work was often referred to dismissively as "keeping house." For rural women, who had defined themselves by their work, this was a difficult transition.

For black families, the impact on gender relations was more subtle but no less transforming. Because black men's wages were so low, most wives of ALCOA's black employees had little choice but to work outside the home after they moved to the company town. This was not new for them. On the farm these women had often done day labor for local white farmers or occasional domestic work for white families in addition to working with their own families in the fields. Now, however, they were working as full-time domestics in the homes of plant supervisors or of Maryville's middle-class white families. Not only was their work separated from that of black men, but they worked under closer supervision from white employers.

Many women of both races resisted this devaluation of their work and the dependence on wages that resulted from increased consumption by maintaining rural coping strategies in town. Most of the former farm women who moved to Alcoa grew gardens and raised hogs and chickens in their small backyards. They also continued to sell and barter small amounts of farm produce for extra income. As on the farm, these efforts to earn cash were motivated as much by women's desire to control some cash and by their efforts to remain central to the family economy as by financial need. Women also wanted to avoid total dependence on the wage economy, fearing that paychecks might not always be regular.[13]

These fears were not unfounded. Blount County was very much a one-company region. Although there were numerous other small manufacturing concerns, there were no employers who could absorb the large numbers of displaced employees when ALCOA was forced to cut its work force. Corporate management was aware that this fact left their employees vulnerable to economic downturns in a way that they had not been on the farm. Managers further recognized that layoffs might induce rural families to return to the farm in order to survive the downturn, as Piedmont textile workers often did, and they feared that workers might not return to town when things improved. To avoid the loss of their labor force, ALCOA tried to recruit other types of industry to the county in order to diversify the opportunities. In fact, company officials recognized that farm women might lead this flight to the farms, so they sought to attract textile manufacturers that would, in the words of one company official, "employ the surplus female labor in order to better stabilize our own labor situation." Yet, largely because of a slump in the textile industry in the 1920s, the company's economic development efforts were not successful, which left the fortunes of the families in Alcoa tied to that of the company. For this reason, ALCOA officials made extraordinary efforts to assist workers in surviving slack periods. Although the plant closed entirely from August 1921 to February 1922, the company tried to keep as many men as possible employed. ALCOA put some men to work on construction projects in the company town. In order to keep the remaining families from returning to the countryside, company officials organized relief efforts and allowed families to stay in company-owned housing at reduced rents.[14]

In addition to making efforts to accommodate unemployed workers, in the early years the company encouraged women to maintain their rural subsistence patterns. ALCOA officials saw these as valuable efforts that would "tide families over" during slow business periods. But the use of women's unpaid labor also helped subsidize the company's wages. With the onset of the Depression, ALCOA not only tried to avoid layoffs by cutting workers' hours and stockpiling aluminum in anticipation of better days, but they also assisted families in maintaining or adopting rural subsistence survival strategies. In a pattern common to southern heavy industry during those years, the company provided a tractor, a plow, and a worker to plow residents' gardens. ALCOA also provided families with garden seed at cost. For Alcoa's women, the Great Depression years marked a temporary return to the days when their work was central to the family's survival.[15]

Shifting Definitions of Class Status

Town life not only changed the nature of women's work, but it also disrupted the old rural mutual aid networks, forcing women to build new types of networks in town. For women, the old networks were based on exchanges of labor and farm commodities and on assistance in times of crisis. In town, there was less need for this type of exchange because many goods and services were now purchased with cash, rendering the old exchange networks obsolete. Instead, town networks were based on church congregations, newly organized home demonstration clubs for town women, and other formal organizations. Women had to learn to negotiate this more formal world of organizations.

In striking contrast to the informal networks of rural communities, these formal town organizations were class-based. Many of the established town women's clubs did not admit wives of ALCOA workers in the early years because they saw them as being members of a lower class. Ironically, Maryville's affiliate of the General Federation of Women's Clubs, the Chilhowee Club, had funded rural schools and mountain settlement work since the turn of the century but did not want to include the wives of ALCOA's wage workers, many of whom were descended from these same rural families, in their own organization. Yet the Chilhowee

Club welcomed the wives of company managers and supervisors. Some of these women were also the wives of farmers who had advanced quickly in the company, but because they were married to salaried workers, they found ready acceptance where the wives of wage workers did not. Suddenly the class differences among rural women, which had been less overt and explicit in the countryside, came to the surface.[16]

In fact, the growing class differences seemed to be more pronounced among ALCOA's women than among men. One southern historian of the antebellum period has suggested that class differences may have been more acute among white women than men because "the ways in which men's lives were intertwined and thereby bound closer together seemed to serve poorly or not at all for women, and divisions that were present for all became more distinct in the eyes of women." In oral histories, Blount County's women focused more on class differences than did men, more often using such terms as "poor families" and "white trash" to delineate themselves from whites of lower standing, and terms like "big shots" and "company men" to refer to salaried ALCOA workers.[17]

Whatever the reasons for the development of women's organizations along class lines, most of the wives of both wage and salary workers in Alcoa relied on churches and social organizations as the center of their organizational lives. By the end of the 1920s, the Alcoa community news column in the *Maryville Times* was filled with reports of meetings of church women's circles, an Alcoa home demonstration club, and other women's organizations.[18]

Although these organizations provided women with a social outlet, they did not serve to bind the community together in the same way that the old mutual aid networks had done. In the countryside, the networks had cemented ties between neighbors and families, including both women *and* men. They gave women a vehicle through which they could wield some power in the community by using their relationships within the network. Men and women shared more power in the rural community. Town-based networks did not function in the same way. In the formal organizations, women built ties to other women, but these networks did not necessarily include their husbands. Now community decision making was in the hands of company officials or the city commission, leaving women with little opportunity to influence events or wield power.

Shifting Race Relations

Not only did farm women who moved to Alcoa have to negotiate
new relationships between whites of different classes, but they also confronted shifting racial relations. The debate over race relations in Blount
County had always been lively. Because geography dictated small subsistence farms rather than large plantations, the county never had a very
large population of slaves or freedmen. Like many upland counties, most
of Blount's citizens had been strongly pro-Union during the Civil War.
Because of the influence of Maryville's large Quaker population and
Maryville College, antebellum abolitionist debate in the town was intense. The college's northern founders made the institution a center for
abolitionism, and it was even reputed to be a stop on the Underground
Railroad. Legend has it that Quakers also ran Underground Railroad
stops in Maryville and in the south Blount County village of Friendsville.
As early as 1820, Maryville's New Providence Presbyterian Church had
raised the hackles of some white citizens by purchasing, freeing, educating, and ordaining two black men. Maryville College admitted free black
men even before the Civil War, and by the 1870s was "admitting both
sexes and both colors," in the words of a college historian. This action
created considerable conflict among students, faculty, and even towns-
people, culminating in 1901 with the passage of a bill drafted by a state
legislator and college alumnus that outlawed the education of blacks and
whites in the same classroom or building.[19]

In spite of all this debate about appropriate race relations, relations
between individual blacks and whites in the county remained peaceful. The county recorded no lynchings in the post–Civil War years, and
blacks worked as laborers, domestics, and craftsmen in the town of Maryville. Black men often worked side by side with whites on various construction projects and on farms, but they were not hired for industrial
jobs. The county's public institutions were segregated, as were residential
neighborhoods in town. In the country blacks and whites might live
interspersed in the same communities, but in town preference and discrimination worked together to keep blacks clustered in the area around
the Hale School, a few blocks from Broadway.[20]

The arrival of the aluminum company would change things.
ALCOA's stated policy was to adhere to local patterns of race relations in

developing company towns. Yet the hiring of blacks for factory work was a departure from local practice. Blacks had not been employed in the small local textile mills or other industries. The corporation also brought in black workers from outside the county, and in the 1910s it briefly experimented with a small number of Mexican workers to take on the dirtiest and most dangerous jobs. At Calderwood, its dam construction project north of Maryville, ALCOA also hired blacks and Cherokees to do the most dangerous tasks involved in dam building. At the plant these included positions in the hated hot and miserable "pot rooms," the rooms where the aluminum was smelted from bauxite ore. The company did, however, adhere to urban southern patterns of residential segregation. At Calderwood, the village to house dam construction workers south of town, and at the main mill village at Alcoa, the company segregated black and white workers' residences.[21]

The close proximity of black and white neighborhoods in Alcoa, especially among rural people not used to living very near other families, might have been expected to create racial tensions between Alcoa's blacks and whites. For the most part, however, this did not seem to occur, partly because the two races lived in communities that were almost entirely separate. The company provided a separate elementary and high school for black students as well as a separate commercial building to house black-run businesses. More important, however, was the lack of racial competition for jobs. Blacks did not protest their segregation into the dirty, dangerous "pot room" jobs or try to apply for the high-skilled, better-paying jobs whites held at the plant, perhaps because access to any type of industrial job was an improvement. These factors seemed to reduce tension between the races throughout the 1920s.

Instead, Alcoa's blacks experienced tensions in their relationships with other Blount County African Americans. When the ALCOA plant arrived in 1914, Maryville had a small but relatively prosperous population of 300 blacks. They saw the influx of black families as a threat to their monopoly on domestic work. Most of the wives of black men employed at ALCOA did take domestic jobs—both in Maryville and for supervisory white employees of the plant who lived in Alcoa. The antagonism, however, went beyond competition for jobs. The laborers, domestics, and businessmen among Maryville's blacks also generally saw themselves as, to borrow historian Janette Greenwood's term, "better class blacks," and thus a cut above the uneducated country bumpkins imported to fill the dirty jobs at the plant. There was hostility between blacks on both sides.[22]

Although the company proved to be satisfied with its use of black factory workers, its brief experiment with Mexican workers was short-lived. ALCOA officials felt compelled to place these workers in a separate community with its own facilities, a very expensive proposition for such a small group of employees. Apparently the Mexican workers were not well accepted by workers of the other two races either. In 1919 Alcoa's company-employed city manager wrote to his superior in Pittsburgh that "[the Mexicans] are not proving as desirable as the colored. . . . It is bad enough to have schools for two of the races without a third gumming up the situation." Most of the Mexicans left the company and the town during the 1920–22 recession. The company blamed their departure on conflict with blacks over jobs during the downturn, while local blacks maintain that the company fired the Mexicans and sent them packing. Whatever the case, the use of Mexicans proved an unsuccessful experiment.[23]

Varied Responses to Industrialization

For some women the racial and class tensions and other adjustments engendered by the move to town proved too hard to take. Many wives of ALCOA employees and other wage workers who had moved their families to town insisted on returning to the countryside after a few years. Maude Walker's father, an elite farmer in southern Blount County, built her a house in a newly developed section of Maryville when she married a road construction worker in 1929. But Walker hated living in town where she felt "crammed in next to everybody" and where she had to worry constantly about whether her young son was playing in the street. So her father gave her a small farm in her home community where she brought her two young children to live in the mid-1930s.[24]

For French Clark, returning to the countryside was the result of two concerns: the quality of life for her children, and the family's survival. Her husband was working at ALCOA when they married in 1924, and the Clarks set up housekeeping in Maryville. Concerned about the potential corrupting influences of town life, they moved back to the country at French's insistence after their second child was born in 1928. "I didn't want to raise [my children] up there," she explained. She also noted that there were more options for making a living in the country. Although her husband continued to commute to town and work at ALCOA, she recalled that "they was bad to get laid off up there, that's what made it so hard." So the couple bought a country grocery store, which they ran for eight or nine years. French tended store most of the time, except when her husband had been laid off and assisted her. The couple rented a home on a small farm where they grew a garden and had an orchard. Here, Ole Clark could also pick up farm work for $1 a day whenever he was out of work. (This compared to the $15 a week he earned at ALCOA during the depression years.)[25]

As the case of the Clarks shows, this brand of coping had its own special problems for rural women. Because husbands were no longer around during the day as they had been when they farmed, women's work patterns were changed almost as profoundly as when they had lived in town. There was no longer a man around during the day to help with heavy work or to look after the children for short periods while women visited other women. Women often took over field work for their husbands when men got jobs at ALCOA. For Hettie Lawson, this coping strategy was exhausting. The Lawson family lived with their four children on a small farm in Wear's Valley in the foothills of the Great Smokies. In the late 1930s, after years of trying to make a living by subsistence farming supplemented with wage work and WPA and CCC jobs, Oliver Lawson finally landed a job at ALCOA, more than thirty miles away. He took the "work bus," part of ALCOA's extensive network of buses to transport rural employees to the plant. This meant that Oliver was away from the farm for more than twelve hours a day. Hettie tried to maintain a large garden, care for livestock, and tend the tobacco patch with the help of her children. Years later, her daughter recalled Hettie's frustration with one particular cow who seemed bent on making her life hell: "Daddy bought this cow. And they had a bell around her neck so we could find her. She'd get somewhere and hide, and she'd stand so still that the bell wouldn't tinkle, and we couldn't find her. And mama would climb those hills [looking for the cow] till she was just give out [exhausted]." The work and the isolation took its toll. As soon as housing became available nearer to town after World War II, Hettie insisted that they move out of Wear's Valley to a village near Alcoa.[26]

Company town dwellers and the families of commuters were not the only ones in Blount County to face adjustments. The arrival of ALCOA also created changes in the lives of Blount County residents who never left the farm. One of the biggest changes was the development of a transportation infrastructure that reduced the isolation of rural life. For women who remained on the land, these improvements in transportation created closer ties to the wider world. Wives of middling farmers began to make infrequent treks into downtown Knoxville for shopping.

This transportation revolution created new economic opportunities for women and men alike. In 1923 the first paved road was built from Maryville in Blount County to Gatlinburg, a tourist village in Sevier County. This road drew visitors from Knoxville, who soon bought land along the Little River in Blount County's Townsend community and built summer cabins. The Great Smoky Mountains National Park, established in 1934, also drew thousands of tourists. These summer visitors brought money and city ideas to the county. Similarly, in the late 1920s a new Maryville to Knoxville highway was constructed, bringing easier access to the city, its entertainment, and its markets.[27]

Easier access to city markets created new economic opportunities for families who remained on the land. The growth of the town created a new demand for milk, a necessity formerly provided by the family cow on the home farm. Peggy Pollard's parents took advantage of this demand by starting a commercial dairy on the farm Mrs. Pollard had inherited from her parents. Preferring "outside work" to "inside work," Mrs. Pollard used the development of the commercial operation to extend the old gender division of labor that assigned the care of dairy cattle to women. She did much of the milking and barnyard work while Mr. Pollard raised feed crops, operated the bottling machine, and ran home delivery trucks into Maryville and Alcoa. For the Pollard family, the combination of capital in the form of inherited land, better roads that improved accessibility to town, and new opportunities to earn cash by serving growing town markets made it possible to remain on the farm.[28]

The presence of industry also made it possible for some middling families to remain on the land by taking advantage of the new mixed economy and adopting a new gender division of labor. One or two male family members might take off-farm jobs to provide the family with needed cash incomes, while other male or female family members remained on the land raising subsistence and cash crops. Elizabeth Goddard recalled that jobs at the Little River Lumber Company allowed many families in the Blount County village of Townsend to retain their farms: "The Lumber Company, of course, was the source of income for a lot of people at that time, plus their farming. . . . Some members of the family would maybe be at home farming and some at the Lumber Company." TVA workers found a similar pattern among Blount County families working at ALCOA. Wives often worked small farming operations with help on heavy jobs from husbands and sons. The mixed economy provided yet another strategy for remaining on the land and gave many women new and welcome autonomy.[29]

Rural-Urban Tensions

Reducing the isolation of farm life created positive effects such as economic opportunities, but improved access to town also had negative effects. Rural-urban tensions increased in the 1930s, both between farm and town people and between town people and the newcomers to Alcoa. People of rural origins became acutely aware of the poverty and cultural differences that set them apart from the middle classes in town. French Clark recalled an incident that took place when her husband worked at ALCOA. Her husband had only one denim work shirt, which she washed and ironed for him to wear to work each day. One day her young son attached an iron-on patch to the back of the denim work shirt, and French was unable to remove it. "I know Ole [O-lee] was embarrassed to death, he had to wear that shirt with that red fox on it every day to work. He did have a Sunday shirt, but he did not have more than one shirt to work in," she explained. In the country, appearances had mattered less; so long as clothing was clean, well-mended, and ironed, it was acceptable. Living within one's means was more admirable than fashion or appearance. This was not true in town. Although popular culture, visits to town markets, home extension agents, and other influences had long made rural folk aware of a new standard of living, a standard based not on what you could afford but on appearing to have the same resources as one's peers, regular contact with town folk made it seem imperative to achieve that new standard.[30]

Town people also saw themselves as different, and quite probably superior, to country folk, even their own relatives at times. One resident of Alcoa stated emphatically, "I never considered myself 'rural'; I lived in a city. I knew I was different than country people." Increasing rural-urban tensions began to be reflected in high school athletic rivalries and to a lesser extent in county politics. Although elite rural families retained a foothold among the county's elected officials until the 1970s, middle-class professionals from Maryville were beginning to dominate the local political scene.[31]

Increased contact with the world beyond Blount County made even townsfolk sensitive about their image as country cousins, and the portrayal of women was a particularly sensitive issue. In 1927 a *Maryville Times* editorial indignantly responded to a *Knoxville Journal* reporter's description of rural women he saw in a Blount County courtroom. The city correspondent had noted only that the courtroom was filled with "old ladies . . . wearing old fashioned shawls with the years of toiling their hands and taking care of their menfolks, plainly showing on their features. They are a hardy and hard-working group of people." This passage raised the ire of the *Times* reporter, who was furious that his town might be painted as the sort of place where women were forced to do physical labor. The rural values of hard and honest work by adults of either sex, once so highly lauded by Blount County people, were now a source of embarrassment, a mark of the local people's difference from the "real city folk" in Knoxville and beyond. Contact with the world beyond the county's borders had forever changed the way Blount County residents saw their rural heritage.[32]

The 1937 Strike and the Crystallization of Social Tensions

A violent strike at the ALCOA plants in 1937 provides a lens with which to examine the crystallization of many of the tensions created by the transition to industrial life in town. The uncertainty of life in Alcoa during the depression years exacerbated worker dissatisfactions with factory life and work. Despite the fact that employees were not entirely satisfied with the company's efforts to address their problems during the hard times, they were hardly united in their ideas about how to achieve more benefits.

Unlike labor actions elsewhere in the 1930s, which tended to divide workers along lines between skilled and unskilled workers or race, the earliest strikes at ALCOA initially divided workers and their families along lines between commuting employees and those who lived in the company town. Despite these initial divisions, the company's violent response to the strikes eventually united workers, leading to the development of a very strong union in the 1940s. Workers who continued to live on the land and were not completely dependent on ALCOA's wages for a living were also less likely to want to risk their jobs by striking. They actually used their cash income from ALCOA to preserve their traditional way of life on the land. Losing their jobs at ALCOA would have upset this delicate balance and endangered their position on the land. By contrast, workers living in the company towns, who were most dependent on the good will of the company, were also paradoxically more supportive of the union. These lines were often more clearly seen in interviews with wives than with male workers themselves. The wives of commuting workers were silent on the issues of the union and the strike until specifically asked about them, and then they often had little memory of that time or dismissed the union as something they knew little about. They spoke of the 1937 strike as "a shame" and "a great tragedy." By contrast, wives of town dwellers were more likely to see the 1937 strike as having been successful in the long term in spite of its short-term failure because it laid the groundwork for later successes and unity.[33]

Scholars are just beginning to grapple with the meaning of silence in women's constructions of the past. Literary scholar Carolyn Heilbrun has suggested that silence and nostalgia are both "mask[s] for unrecognized anger."[34] Certainly Alcoa's women may have been angry on some level at their exclusion from union organizing in the years after the 1937 strike. Silence among the wives of commuting workers may mask marital conflict over the entire issue of union membership and striking. Because they did not live in the company town, they did not enjoy the camaraderie of the other workers' wives, nor were they subject to pressure from organizers. Unlike organizing efforts in major cities where workers' wives were part of the same community, wives of commuting workers were not connected to the union and their neighbors in the same ways as women of the company town. They may very well have seen the strike as a greater threat to their own delicately balanced way of life than did their husbands, and these fears may have contributed to their persistent silence about the union.

In the 1930s, the new interest in organizing among ALCOA's workers came on the heels of the passage of the National Industrial Recovery Act in June 1933, guaranteeing labor's right to organize and bargain collectively through representatives of its own choosing. Following 10 percent wage reductions in 1931 and 1932, ALCOA's Tennessee workers were dissatisfied with abortive attempts to negotiate with management. They welcomed an American Federation of Labor organizer with enthusiasm in late 1933, forming Aluminum Workers Local 19104, an organization nominally backed by the AFL but not part of any national craft union organization because it included hourly workers from all job categories, even unskilled jobs. Determined to make a strong show of worker solidarity and to fend off company attempts to use black workers as strike breakers, local organizers decided to enroll blacks as well as whites. In 1934 Local 19104 staged a 26-day strike that gained them nominal recognition from the company. Negotiations in the following two years also produced small gains in recognition and pay.[35]

In spite of these gains, the union was unable to break down the regional wage differential. At issue was the fact that workers at ALCOA's New Kensington, Pennsylvania, plant were being paid eighteen cents more per hour than those in Tennessee. The union called for equal wages for all ALCOA workers unless the company could prove that the Tennessee workers enjoyed a lower cost of living; the company insisted on its right to pay the going wage rate in a given geographic area, regardless of the cost of living. By the spring of 1937, when negotiations over the regional wage issue broke down, over half of ALCOA's workers had joined the union. In May Local 19104 voted 2,156 to 238 in favor of a strike. The local union president called for a walkout in the fabricating unit on May 18. Although he did not state his reasons for striking at only one plant, the plant where he himself worked, the president may have been trying to put pressure on the company without taking the drastic and expensive (to the company) step of shutting down the smelting operation, which would take several days to restart. All the workers at the fabricating plant heeded the strike call and walked out. In return, they received modest strike pay from the union, partly drawn from local dues and supplemented by the AFL. At the behest of the union, workers at the nearby smelting operation continued to work. In response to the strike, the company brought in 138 private security officers to guard plant gates from angry pickets.[36]

Among ALCOA's black workers, the 1937 strike seemed to hold out the promise of greater equality in the workplace and in the company town. Rhetoric about union solidarity and efforts to keep black workers solidly behind the union gave African Americans hope for larger changes. In later evaluating the impact of unionization on southern race relations, Mary Laurance Elkuss, a labor organizer sent to Alcoa from the Highlander Folk School, a grass-roots organizing and educational center then located in Monteagle, Tennessee, maintained that the unionization movement of the 1930s contributed to the reduction of racial tensions in the South:

> I felt very early . . . that the unions were playing a tremendous role in developing better race relations just from a standpoint that they were getting blacks and whites together in the same union hall, and, as far as I knew at the time, this was the only place where the little people [working class people] were getting together. . . . Within the union itself, when blacks and whites came to the meeting, they would often segregate themselves, but at least they were starting to talk to one another.[37]

Blacks and whites did have increased contact on a more equal footing as a result of union organization, and this may have played a long-term role in improving race relations in the South. In Alcoa, however, this contact only served to raise and then dash the hopes of black workers. Although they did not enjoy equal opportunities within the union, nor were they guaranteed equal rights in union contracts, they did benefit from the establishment of minimum job qualifications and wage scales for each job that prevented the company from making individual decisions about pay rates. Yet this very benefit made blacks less desirable to management. After the union contracts of the 1930s established set wages for each job classification, blacks could no longer be depended on to do only the dirty work in the plant or to work for less than whites, so ALCOA's management lost its enthusiasm for hiring large numbers of black employees. Blacks were frustrated by continuing racist behavior from union leaders who refused to make integration of company facilities a strike issue. After the 1937 strike, the union hall was integrated, but restrooms, water fountains, and cafeterias at the plant remained segregated. By 1940 many black workers began leaving ALCOA for better-paying, less segregated defense jobs in the North and the West.[38]

Not only was the 1937 strike marked by continuing racial discrimination, but it brought into sharp focus the class tensions that had first appeared among women's organizations in the little town. The outcome of the dispute stimulated the development of a working-class consciousness among women and men of both races. In East Tennessee's rural communities prior to World War I, class differences had existed, but class conflict remained minimal. Rather, tolerance and periodic cooperation marked relations between farm families of different socioeconomic classes. In the country, lines between landowner and tenant were blurred because tenants sometimes worked for landowning relatives and because landowners often supplemented their landholdings by renting from other landowners. In rural communities, respect from one's peers was earned through hard work and adherence to community moral standards more than through wealth or ascribed status. This was not the case in the company town, where lines between supervisors and workers were reinforced and made visible with differentiated housing and employee benefits. With the outbreak of labor actions, tensions between hourly and salaried workers escalated, creating class-based bonds among workers who were vividly aware that salaried workers not only enforced inequitable company rules and kept the plants going during prolonged strikes, but also benefited from the inequalities. One Alcoa resident recalled the tensions: "My father still owned and operated the Springbrook Grocery in Alcoa. We tried to remain neutral in the strike controversy, having friends and customers among [both] the hourly and salary workers. Much bad feeling developed between factions."[39]

This class awareness created new bonds among the wives and daughters of hourly workers, who drew on traditional coping mechanisms to provide for their families and help make the strike a success. For the wives of Alcoa's workers, the strike briefly revitalized their mutual aid networks, allowing them to reassert their centrality in the community and in the family economy for a time. For ALCOA's women, the strike brought new uncertainties and challenges—the loss of income, the fear of being evicted from their homes, the necessity of supporting their husbands' efforts to organize, and the struggle to keep the family fed in the interim. Labor organizer Mary Laurance Elkuss recalled that the town's women supported the strike through their subsistence activities and their behind-the-scenes organizing but made only rare appearances on the picket lines. Unlike textile mill strikes, where women were also workers and claimed a rightful place in the picket lines, Alcoa's women did not feel they belonged in the forefront of public protest, a pattern similar to strikes in other male-dominated industries in the South in the 1930s. Lula Gatlin Ramsey recalled that, while her husband spent many days and nights on the picket line, she did not. Rather, she focused on the family's day-to-day needs: "It took a lot of good management [by the women] to make ends meet. We helped each other."[40]

The women of Alcoa saw their worst fears realized in July 1937, when the strike turned violent. Negotiations had dragged on with little progress since May until July 6 when, determined to break the strike, local ALCOA officials announced that the fabricating plant would resume operations the next day with or without striking workers. The company made this move when Fred Wetmore, president of the local, was in Pittsburgh negotiating with company officials. Desperate after nearly six weeks of living on the minimal strike pay, and fearful of losing their jobs, a significant number of men decided to return to work. ALCOA's hired guards succeeded in opening up the picket line as the returning strikers and some strikebreakers arrived for work. Accounts of the violence are conflicting, but apparently a scuffle broke out between the security force and union pickets, followed by the retort of gunfire.[41]

A young storekeeper was minding the store when he heard shots fired. "The strikers and the company guards had started a war," he recalled. He soon learned that one striker and one of the security officers hired especially to "keep the peace" during the strike were killed that day. At least twenty others were shot. To quell the violence, the governor

mobilized the National Guard and placed the company town under martial law. Meanwhile, local president Wetmore rushed back from Pittsburgh to resume negotiations, but the strike was essentially broken.
"Some people were getting pretty hungry by this time, having run up big
grocery bills at my father's store," noted the storekeeper. The shooting
finally broke the will of the striking workers. Operations at the fabricating plant resumed, with the company claiming that 2,000 employees had
returned to work before the union officially settled the strike. The union
insisted that only 550 had returned and that the rest were scabs hired by
the company. Given that the newspapers did not report significant numbers of strikebreakers being laid off when workers returned to their jobs,
the company's number may have been more accurate. Since striking employees had returned to work peacefully, the National Guard went home
after less than a week on patrol.[42]

While the men were returning to work, Wetmore and the AFL's representative were clashing in the negotiating room. Wetmore wanted to
hold out for concessions; the AFL negotiator insisted that the strike was
broken and that there was little alternative but to settle and continue
organizing and negotiating. In order to avert a divisive union vote, Wetmore resigned. The AFL negotiator struck a deal with ALCOA officials
without the approval of the local leadership or the rank and file, agreeing
to settle the strike with only minor concessions from the company, including maintenance of the jobs of striking workers.[43]

In spite of this setback, the violence of the company's response to the
strike had the effect of galvanizing the support of workers and their wives
for unionization and collective bargaining. Commuting workers over-
came much of their resistance to union membership. Furious that the
company granted the wife of the slain security officer a pension, while the
wife of the striking worker got nothing, Alcoa's women organized fundraising efforts to raise some money for the worker's widow. She became
symbolic of women's dependence on their men and thus their relationship to the company. In this way, wives of workers were justified in
making claims on the company. Their support for unionization grew.
They urged their husbands to join the unions and later formed a union
auxiliary that would provide crucial material support in future strikes.
Looking back, many of them realized that the 1937 strike had laid the
groundwork for all of these gains. Lula Gatlin Ramsey noted that the 1937

strike and subsequent labor actions "took a lot of patience and long hours, but it was worth it for all the benefits gained and still being used."[44]

Meanwhile, feeling betrayed by the AFL, the workers turned to the rival Congress of Industrial Organizations (CIO) for future organizing leadership. By the late 1930s, the CIO increasingly based union organization in the workplace instead of the community. This policy, combined with the Alcoa women's willingness to accept a less visible role in organizing, worked together to marginalize women's place in organizing when the strike was over. In the end, the development of a strong workplace-centered union rendered women's essential support of organizing invisible and marginalized their place in the family economy. In later strikes the union became more firmly centered in the workplace, with women's activities confined to an organized union auxiliary.

The outbreak of World War II sparked a boom at ALCOA's local plants and allowed workers to negotiate from a position of strength. The aluminum ingots manufactured and stockpiled to keep workers employed during the depression years were soon devoured to feed the nation's insatiable war machine. Production at the company's Tennessee operations increased 600 percent during the war, and the plants were expanding, swelling the work force to 12,000. For the first time, the company recruited local single women of both races for plant jobs. Women handed out tools in the machine shops, learned to grind machine parts, drove forklifts, and took on countless other light industrial jobs. Yet these new opportunities for women within the plant were short-lived. As was the case in most industries, women were pushed out of these jobs when veterans returned from the war.[45]

By this time, the face of Blount County had changed forever. A new pattern was firmly entrenched: hundreds of landowners farmed part-time and worked full-time at ALCOA, enabling them to stay on the land in spite of economic downturns. For other families, in a pattern shaped by the county's one-industry character, "the plant" became a genuine family affair, dominating their economic lives. Lula Gatlin Ramsey's father, husband, two brothers, a sister, three brothers-in-law, and a son worked for ALCOA, most of them retiring from the corporation. Similarly, Frances Dunn's husband, five brothers, a son, a daughter, and a son-in-law worked for ALCOA. In this way, ALCOA ruled the lives and the economic fortunes of much of the county until the 1980s.[46]

Mining Communities in Southwestern West Virginia:
Different Industry, Similar Patterns

The wives of southwestern West Virginia coal miners shared strikingly similar experiences with the wives of Alcoa's aluminum workers.
Well into the twentieth century, farm families found themselves moving
to mining towns in search of economic opportunity and better lives. Once
there, they survived by maintaining rural subsistence patterns and mutual aid networks, by maximizing women's and men's earning potential,
and by moving back and forth between the mine and the farm according
to an individual family's preferences and needs. Yet they found that
mining life transformed their culture forever, creating in them a new class
consciousness that was at odds with the more fluid class boundaries of
the countryside. And like the folks of Alcoa, mountain families struggled
to preserve their traditional way of life by accommodating themselves to
change.

Mingo County was typical of southwestern West Virginia counties
transformed by mining. Once almost entirely agricultural, by 1940 there
were only 2,040 farmers (only two of them black) among the county's
40,802 people. Over 67 percent of them reported working off the farm at
least some during the year, for an average of 169 days each. Landowners
reported working off the farm more days than tenants, suggesting that
off-farm work was allowing landowners to hang on to their acreage. The
average farm size in Mingo County had steadily declined from 125.6
acres in 1920 to 37.9 acres by 1940. According to the 1940 Census of
Agriculture, 1,961 Mingo County farm households reported home use of
farm products, but only one household reported that poultry products
were a major source of income. Three farmers reported that dairy products were a major source of income, and only one farmer named the sale
of field crops as a major source of their income. These figures suggest that
farm families were producing a subsistence on the land, supplemented
by cash earned in mining and other off-farm jobs.[47]

Coal mining in southwestern West Virginia was much older than
ALCOA's Tennessee operations. Although geologists, explorers, and settlers knew about unusually rich coal deposits in the mountains of southwestern West Virginia as early as colonial times, there were only 185
mines employing less than 1,600 workers in the entire state by the time of

Civil War. The difficulty of transporting coal out of the rugged mountain terrain retarded the growth of mining until the 1880s when large-scale railroad construction opened up the mountains to the outside world. During those years, outside capitalists began to buy mineral rights on many of the small farms tucked into the mountains. In fact, coal mining and railroads developed hand in hand. Often the syndicates of business-men who owned mining rights built railroads in order to haul their coal. Conversely, railroad owners often opened mines to provide business for their railroads. The Chesapeake and Ohio Railroad, completed in 1873, connected the old Virginia Central Railroad to steamboat shipping on the Ohio River. The Norfolk and Western Railroad connected the Chesapeake Bay with the Ohio River. All these provided new avenues for hauling coal to urban markets.[48]

The 1880s were boom years in the West Virginia mining industry, largely because of the growing demand for coal in the burgeoning indus-trial cities of the East and Midwest. Dozens of mines opened in the south-western mountains, and their construction sparked a shift in the state's population from the northern part of the state to its central and southern counties, as struggling subsistence farmers left the land seeking new opportunities in the mines. In fact, the mines themselves helped push farmers off the land. Many had supplemented their subsistence with hunting, but railroads drove the game further into the mountains, reduc-ing the stock of game. The acquisition of land by coal companies led to a decline in farming.

As in Blount County, Tennessee, the development of mining brought a flood of newcomers to southwestern West Virginia. Thanks to a short-age of native-born white laborers, mine owners looked further and fur-ther afield for miners. They recruited new immigrants from the mining regions of central and southern Europe as well as southern blacks seeking to leave behind the poverty and oppression of the deep South. In 1880, there had been no black miners in West Virginia, and only 924 of the miners had been born in Europe. By 1920, there were 12,000 black miners and 28,000 Europeans. By 1910, only 83 percent of the state's population was made up of native-born whites.[49]

The importation of immigrant and black miners complicated racial and ethnic relations in mining communities. Certainly black and im-migrant miners experienced considerable discrimination and prejudice

from native-born whites. Both groups lived in segregated sections of
company towns and in the least desirable housing. Virginia Giacomo
noted that Italian immigrants at Boomer lived in a section of town known
as "Little Italy." "When we were growing up, we weren't allowed to mix
with them," she recalled. "But later we mixed and went to school together and they was treated better." She claimed that only one member of
her family, a brother, expressed any objections when she later married an
Italian miner. Dave Tamplin grew up in Boomer about the same time as
Virginia Giacomo. He claimed that the Italians "mixed fine." Joe Kovich
recalled that immigrants in Logan County tended to cluster by national-
ity, but he did not attribute this practice to discrimination. Rather they felt
more comfortable in ethnic enclaves because "their English speaking
wasn't too good" and "due to their customs and their language and so
forth." Apparently native-born West Virginians were ambivalent about
the white immigrants but ultimately tolerant.[50]

Similar ambivalence greeted African American miners who came to
West Virginia. One southwest West Virginia native noted that mine re-
cruiters had made "many rosy promises" to attract black miners. Black
miners found economic opportunity in the state. Although they were
rarely advanced to supervisory positions in the mines, they found better
wages and more independence than they had had as sharecroppers, and
they experienced less political and social discrimination. West Virginia
did segregate its schools and social welfare institutions but not its common carriers. Neither did the state disfranchise African Americans. Although racism existed in West Virginia, it was less overt and stigmatizing
than in many areas of the deep South. And in segregated coal town
communities, blacks were gathered in significant enough numbers to
develop religious and fraternal organizations and businesses. A black
middle class, which helped black miners gain additional services and
rights from mine operators and some level of recognition from the United
Mine Workers of America, emerged in coal towns by the 1910s.[51]

The growth of coal mines stimulated the building of company-
owned towns to house miners. Because of the difficulty in traveling long
distances on the rocky roads and rough trails of the southwestern mountains, mine owners felt compelled to provide miners with housing close
to the mines in order to assure themselves of a large and reliable work
force. A 1925 study by the U.S. Coal Commission found that 80 percent

of the state's miners lived in coal towns. Mine owners quickly discovered that these company towns gave them tremendous power over their miners. Not only did the company own most of the housing in the mining town, but they also owned the retail stores, barbershops, and school and church buildings. The companies often organized baseball teams for miners and ran saloons, pool halls, and theaters. Miners were paid in coal scrip, metal and paper vouchers that could only be redeemed at stores owned by the company that printed it. Numerous studies found that prices were higher in the company stores than elsewhere. The company even employed doctors, nurses, and dentists to serve its mining families, charging miners for this medical care through weekly payroll deductions. Every aspect of the organization of mining towns was calculated to provide mine owners with maximum control over their workers and to enable them to retain a large percentage of their payroll in the form of payments for goods and services to company-owned businesses.[52]

Not only did the mine owners exert extraordinary power over the social and economic lives of miners, but in sharp contrast to Alcoa, they also controlled politics in the unincorporated coal towns. Because the towns were owned and controlled by mine owners, there were no local political officials who might cater to the interests of miners. Even in state elections, miners had trouble getting information about candidates. Newspapers hostile to mine owners and their hand-chosen candidates were banned from the company towns. Company mine guards served as pollsters and inspected the ballot of each voting miner. By controlling the votes of their workers and by handing out federal patronage appointments to influential citizens around the state, mine owners managed to establish powerful political machines that served their own business interests. Logan County native Roscoe Spence noted that "political machines drowned out the efforts of those who would clean up the elections and give the people of the area an even break. Judges were elected and controlled by the coal companies; sheriffs protected their property and enforced their policies . . . to such an extent that the people were helpless to fight back, and when they did, [they] faced financial ruin." Another West Virginian recalled that "each company had a man that was a police on their property, and he was appointed by the sheriff. He didn't get any salary from the county, but he got a salary from the coal company." These tactics would leave organized labor with little political

power as the United Mine Workers of America (UMWA) began to organize in the state.[53]

Women in Mining Towns

Women found life in mining towns hard, but perhaps no more physically arduous than life on the farm. Life in primitive company towns had
some of the same drawbacks as farm life, such as the lack of plumbing
and electricity. As on the farm, the dearth of labor-saving devices made
housework exhausting. Giacomo recalled her house in the mining town
of Boomer, a house not much different from most West Virginia farmhouses of the day: "They were old wooden houses. . . . We had wooden
floors, uncovered. We scrubbed on our knees. We carried water and split
kindling. We had open grate fires and washed on a wash board and living
conditions was hard back in them times." Living conditions may have
been similar to farm life, but gender differences became more sharply
drawn in coal towns just as they had in Alcoa. Women had worked beside
their husbands on the farms, something they did not do in the mines.[54]

One historian has called mining families "existence oriented"—that
is, they worked to exist from day to day. Black and white families living in
mining camps coped with an uncertain economy by combining industrial
work with rural coping strategies. They often pooled multiple incomes,
with several males in a single household working in the mines. Women
also worked at home to produce incomes. Some took in laundry, some
sold produce, and some sold milk to the families of mine officials. But
the most common strategy among women was to keep boarders. Mary
Davis operated a boardinghouse for black miners to support her family of
sixteen children after her husband was disabled in a mining accident.
John T. Walton recalled a white woman who ran a boardinghouse for
mine officials. Another miner recalled that Italian miners occasionally
immigrated with their wives and that those women often ran boardinghouses for other Italian miners. Black women were usually able to find
domestic jobs in the homes of white mine managers. Margaret Moorman
recalled the experience of her mother in the 1920s: "No matter how poor
white people are, they can always find a little change to hire a black

woman in their home, and [my mother]. . . would work occasionally for some of the bosses."[55]

Rural subsistence strategies were transported to mining towns. A 1924 study by the West Virginia Coal Association estimated that 50 percent of the state's mining families planted gardens and kept livestock to supplement the family's diet. In some counties the percentage was higher. In 1923 the Children's Bureau of the U.S. Department of Labor found that 70 percent of mining families in Raleigh County raised crops and livestock. One West Virginia miner noted that his wife and daughter "worked harder in the fields than any man ever did and that's why we grew more stuff in the [company] towns than the farmers on their farms." Not only did women supplement the family's subsistence with their agricultural produce and canned goods, but they also gathered environmental resources, including berries for the family diet, and wood and coal for fuel.

When women's subsistence efforts were not enough to meet the family's needs, women in mining camps turned to another strategy of rural life: mutual aid networks. They swapped products with other women, worked together on cooperative efforts like quilting and canning, and helped each other out in times of illness. One McDowell County miner recalled that "if anybody got sick the whole community knowed it and they helped him out." Whole families pitched in on some projects like hog killings, bean stringings, and corn shuckings. As on the farm, these activities also served as social activities. When misfortune befell one family, the community's women often collected money and household goods for them.[56]

Women in mining towns coped with stresses unknown on the farm, stresses that increased the hardships of their lives. They lived with the constant fear that a mining accident would rob them of loved ones and of economic support. Giacomo recalled one cave-in that killed 123 men and trapped her father in the mines for four or five days. The stress and boredom of life in coal towns may also have increased alcoholism and its accompanying family problems. One historian has noted that the consumption of alcohol provided miners with a coping mechanism for dealing with the dangers of the mines and the uncertainty and boredom of mining town life. Many miners made moonshine whiskey for their own consumption and to supplement their incomes. Virginia Giacomo recalled that most of the miners she knew drank and "half of them made the old moonshine whiskey they drank." She went on to recount her father's abuse of alcohol and its effect on the family: "He loaded ten and twelve cars of coal a day. And on the weekends he drank and he would come in and break up all the dishes in the house. Then he would go right back out on Monday morning and work the whole week. He would tell my mother to go buy and replace what he had destroyed. . . . He just drank a lot on the weekends. He was a mean man when he drank."[57]

Not only did many mining families use rural coping strategies in the mining towns, but many miners of both races continued to live on farms and commute to work or moved back and forth between their own farms and the mining camps. Burl Collins walked six miles each way from his farm to his mining job. Southwestern West Virginia was a region of small farms. Joe Kovich recalled that many farmers would work in the Logan and Mingo County mines "during the week and then on weekends go to their homes on farms." Although the region received ample rainfall, the difficult terrain meant that the land was suited to livestock farming, a pursuit more easily combined with off-farm work than large-scale crop farming. Most farmers in the area also grew gardens for their own consumption and feed crops of corn and hay. Farms were small. In 1920 the average farm in the nine southwestern counties was 85 acres, significantly smaller than the state average of 109 acres. Because of the terrain, large portions of the farms in the southwestern counties were not arable. One West Virginia farmer/miner's son recalled that only 20 acres of their 100-acre farm was cleared for pasture and cropland. Mining wages allowed many families to preserve their rural way of life by providing the income needed to subsidize the farm.[58]

In fact, many of the native-born whites were so intent on returning to a family farm or on saving money to purchase their own farm that they saw mining as a temporary expedient—a means to an end. Bertha Holton's husband mined for a few years in Lincoln County. Although Bertha maintained that he made "good money," he disliked mining life so much that, after accumulating some savings, he became a sharecropper. The couple raised tobacco and truck crops, peddling the latter to Charleston retail establishments. By the early 1930s, they had saved enough money to buy their own farm. Many other miners held on to their farms and returned to them during slack periods in the mines or strikes. Matt Hanna's farmer father worked in the mines during the winter, and the family accompanied him and lived in mining camps during those months. Like subsistence strategies practiced within the company towns, holding onto one's own farm was a way to decrease dependency on the company. Similarly, mining allowed many farmers to remain on landholdings too small to support a family. William Payne recalled that his father's job in the mines supplemented the subsistence his mother raised on their 5 acres.[59]

Miners' Wives and the West Virginia Mine Wars

Although mining was well established in West Virginia before the twentieth century, World War I set in motion a series of events that would profoundly reshape life for miners and their families. As had been the case in Tennessee, labor conflicts threw class and racial tensions in mining towns into sharp relief and drew miners' wives into the fray. Early attempts at unionization in the coal fields had enjoyed limited success. Mine owners used the police forces and local governments they controlled as well as the economic power they wielded over miners to thwart efforts to organize strong unions.

The United Mine Workers of America, an AFL-affiliated industrial union, was organized in West Virginia in 1890. That union led a violent and unsuccessful nationwide coal strike in 1894. Another strike in 1897 ended with the first of a series of anti-labor injunctions issued by West Virginia judges. Periodically thereafter, the UMWA led organizing drives in the coal fields of the southwestern portion of the state, including the Paint Creek/Cabin Creek strike in the Kanawha coal field in 1912–13, one of the most violent events in American labor history. This action, known throughout the state as the earliest of the West Virginia "mine wars," was marked by the imposition of martial law in the area and the governor's negotiation of a strike settlement that conceded little to the union. Though miners achieved little in these early labor actions, they began to learn the value of collective action and to develop a working-class consciousness. Unfortunately for the miners, the Paint Creek/ Cabin Creek strike also united the state's coal operators, who began to see the union as a destructive force that was out to destroy the southwest West Virginia coal industry. These developments would prove crucial in later labor actions.

The coming of World War I temporarily changed labor's fortunes in West Virginia. During World War I, the tremendous demand for coal exempted miners from the draft. Federal officials called for miners and owners to work together to support the war effort and backed off to some extent on their hostile approach to the labor movement. Thanks to the unprecedented profits of the war years, mine owners were willing to make some concessions to unions for the sake of keeping the mines running. Most of the state's mines were unionized during these years, and UMWA membership in the state increased from 7,000 in 1913 to 50,000 by the end of the war. By 1920 about 90 percent of the miners in the southwestern coal fields had achieved the eight-hour day. That year the Supreme Court dealt a serious blow to the labor movement in the Hitchman case, which ruled that a company could operate its mines on any terms it saw fit without union interference or even allowing union organizing. But mine owners did not immediately exploit this decision to ward off unionizing.[60]

These gains were not to last, however. Predictably, demand for coal fell off precipitously with the signing of the Armistice, and huge stockpiles held by major coal-consuming industries further reduced the market. Prices plunged. Mine operators struggled to stay afloat in an atmosphere of fierce competition. Now mine owners turned to the Supreme Court decision in the Hitchman case to combat the unions.[61]

World War I had also altered the character of the mine work force. Many immigrants left the mines during the war for better and safer jobs in manufacturing. Those who remained had always been active in the union movement, and now they supported it more strongly than ever. Mine owners also used wartime profits to mechanize, firing many black workers who had once done the unskilled tasks now completed by machines. The black miners who were left found increasing racial stratification in coal towns. During the war years, many black miners developed a working-class consciousness that politicized them and drove them to join unions. Interracial and interethnic solidarity would be a major feature of post–World War I labor actions in the southwestern coal fields.[62]

Meanwhile, the UMWA was seeking to organize the remaining

37,000 of the state's 91,000 miners who did not belong to a union. They decided to focus their efforts on Logan and Mingo Counties in southwestern West Virginia, coal fields that accounted for about one-third of the nonunionized work force. Mine operators in these counties fought back, seeking injunctions against the unions. They also resorted to yellow-dog contracts, which required men to agree not to join a union in order to retain their jobs. Owners hired mine guards to try to keep union organizers out of the coal fields and paid county sheriffs to employ anti-union deputies. Don Chafin, the sheriff of Logan County, was the most infamous of these sheriffs and one of the most hated men in southwest West Virginia. Chafin employed forty-six active-duty deputies whose salaries were paid by the county and by the coal companies. He also deputized as many as five hundred men who were not on active duty but were vested with full legal authority to make arrests.

In the fall of 1919, as the UMWA prepared for a strike, operators in Logan and Mingo Counties tried to prevent union organizers from coming into those counties. Rumors, mostly unfounded, circulated that mine guards were beating and killing miners and their families. On September 4, about four thousand miners from the Kanawha coal fields gathered to march on Logan County. Their goals included the hanging of Sheriff Chafin, the abolition of the mine guard system, and the unionization of all of the southwestern coal fields. Only a call for federal intervention by the governor convinced the miners to disperse. Meanwhile, waves of strikes swept the coal fields.

As had been the case in Alcoa, mining had changed the socioeconomic structure of the southwestern counties. In mining towns, most farming folk became wage-earning proletariat, some of them landed and some of them landless, but all dependent on mine wages. A few farming folk, those who landed jobs as mine officials and supervisors, became a self-conscious middle class. These newly middle-class families often felt caught in the middle during labor conflicts. John T. Walton's parents ran a store for a mining company. He recalled that they often felt torn during labor confrontations when former neighbors and friends were on the opposite side. "The fact [was] that. . . the store man was in between the company and the men all the time," he explained. "[Y]ou had to please the company and you had to please the people." He noted that "having been poor all of our lives, our sympathy was definitely fifty-fifty with the people. We realized their problems, mother and dad were very very good to them, they. . . shared their milk and the butter and eggs. . . . [W]henever sickness hit the camp, why mom was up there to help somebody." Walton's parents coped with their ambivalence about their own upward mobility by sharing personal resources with miners' families, but their own dependence on the company determined where their loyalties lay during the strike. For their part, miners and their wives resented fellow farm families who moved into the middle class, scorning them as "company men." Strikes brought these class tensions out into the open.[63]

Miners' wives played an important role in these strikes. A *Century* reporter noted that "if miners are slaves of coal, the women are the slaves of slaves." As with the United Steelworkers in Alcoa, the UMWA did not recognize the women as workers, but they did harness women's actions in support of the strike. And much of the burden for surviving strikes fell on the women of the coal camps. As one of them told the *Century* reporter, "It's us has to put the children off till next day without food. It's us has to hold rags together to cover our bodies and our men's and babies'. It's us has to cook meals with nothing fit to cook, an' make bread with water an' salt an' moldy flour. The men set an' jaw while we work our arms loose: that's what a strike means." Women increased their subsistence and mutual aid activities during the labor action. They also often suffered the violence and indignities of coal operators' actions against striking miners. They were often evicted from company-owned housing. The *Century* reporter interviewed one woman who, with her eleven children, was living with three other families in a village of tents near a creek. She was surrounded by her household goods, many of which had to be left in the rain.[64]

Mining town women's persistent support of unions in the face of evictions, near-starvation, and violence is strong evidence of their belief that unionization was a key to improving their lives. As one woman told a reporter,

> If we don't live real good or eat real good, we know what we're doin' it for, an' we'll stick as long as we got to. . . . I'd rather see this baby die as see the union die. If we lose this strike, he might as well be dead. They ain't going to be no security for him, nor for any of us, if they kill our union like they're setting out to do. . . . My babies may be hungry now

while the trouble is on . . . , but if we don't fight now, they'll be hungry all their lives.

The wife of a black miner echoed her sentiments: "Might as well go hungry fer to strike as go hungry fer to be out of work." For women in mining towns, unionization offered the possibility of a more secure future; doing nothing meant the perpetuation of the status quo.[65]

Not only did mine women support the strike with their subsistence efforts and their moral support, but they sometimes put their bodies on the line, taking an active role in organizing and fighting. A San Francisco reporter noted that "women fought side by side with men" in the coal fields. At the Paint Creek strike in 1912, when mine guards had outfitted a train with machine guns and used it to fire into tent cities of evicted families camped along the tracks, women prevented the guards from making a return run by tearing up the railroad tracks. Mobs of women often attacked strikebreakers with broomsticks and other household implements. Dave Tamplin remembered that women and children sometimes joined marchers on the picket lines. In a World War II era strike, miners were prevented from picketing by court order, so their wives walked the picket line while the men cared for the children and "kept house." West Virginia miners' wives were more willing to join the fray than the Alcoa women for at least two reasons: they had been targets of violence themselves, making them feel the need to defend themselves and their families; and many had also been evicted from their homes, again a direct attack on the family.[66]

Perhaps miners' wives and daughters were inspired by the presence of UMWA organizer Mother Jones during so many of their strikes. Mary Harris "Mother" Jones, an Irish immigrant who taught school for most of her young adulthood, learned about trade unionism from her husband, a Memphis iron molder. In 1867 a yellow fever epidemic killed her husband and all four of her children. Grief-stricken, Jones moved to Chicago, where she worked as a dressmaker until the Chicago Fire of 1871 left her homeless and unemployed. In the fire's aftermath, she stumbled into a Knights of Labor meeting and found her new career as a union organizer. In the 1890s Jones shifted her efforts to the UMWA, first coming to West Virginia in 1897. Jones expressed shock at the wretched conditions she found in the coal fields of the state she called "medieval West Virginia."[67]

Jones proved to be very effective at convincing West Virginia miners to join the union, partly because of her practical appeals to miners' wives. One biographer noted that Jones "spoke earnestly and colorfully and in terms and anecdotes which they [mining folk] understood." Ollie Jane Mullins recalled that Mother Jones tried to feed striking miners' families. Mullins' husband, Eli, a retired miner, recounted an incident when Jones helped harvest a mine family's garden even as company mine guards rained bullets around her ankles to try to scare her away. "She went, fit [fought], and organized," Mullins noted with admiration.[68]

Jones participated in five major strikes in West Virginia. Mine operators were so convinced at her effectiveness that they hired spies to follow her around, waiting for her to say something inflammatory. She was arrested for conspiracy to commit murder during the Paint Creek strike in 1913, but the charges were eventually dropped. A West Virginia prosecutor once called her "the most dangerous woman in America. She comes into a State where peace and prosperity reign. She crooks her finger—20,000 contented men lay down their tools and walk out." Eventually mine owners recognized that their opposition to Jones was only intensifying miners' resistance. As the son of one miner put it, "The company folks didn't like [her presence] very much but they didn't try to do too much about it either. They'd write bad things about her in the paper, but . . . sometimes she said 'um and sometimes she hadn't."[69]

In 1920, the spring after the first march on Logan, the union organizers' attention turned to neighboring Mingo County, where miners had just been dealt a wage cut. A few small mine owners signed contracts with unions, but the large operators continued to resist and hired private mine guards to fend off organizers and to evict union miners from company housing. This action led to a series of bloody confrontations, a new round of mine wars. In Matewan, an independent incorporated town in Mingo County, Chief of Police Albert Sidney "Sid" Hatfield promised to protect miners who joined the union. On May 19, 1920, thirteen guards from the Baldwin-Felts security company got off the train in Matewan and began evicting union families from houses owned by the Stone Mountain Coal Company just outside town. When the guards returned to the station that afternoon, they were met by Sheriff Hatfield and a band of armed miners. Each group tried to arrest the other, and shots rang out.

Seven Baldwin-Felts men and two miners were killed, as was the mayor of Matewan, a bystander not involved in the confrontation.[70]

Hatfield and fifteen others were charged with murder, but they were acquitted by a local jury, who claimed there was not enough evidence to convict them. However, on August 1, 1921, seven men hired by the Baldwin-Felts agency killed Hatfield and a friend on the steps of the Mingo County courthouse. These murders sparked fresh violence and wildcat strikes throughout the coal fields. Governor Ephraim Morgan declared martial law, ordered the arrest of union organizers, and dispatched all one hundred of the state police to Mingo County. The insurrection then took on a life of its own.

In late August, five thousand miners, many of them veterans of the Paint Creek strike, massed near the northern border of Logan County, planning to march to Mingo County to free miners who had been jailed for union activity and to lift martial law in Mingo. Mother Jones urged miners to use caution on the march. Sheriff Don Chafin declared that the miners would not march across his county. Coal operators gave him funds for a private army to "protect" business and to stop the march. Chafin recruited three thousand volunteers, including doctors, lawyers, and businessmen from West Virginia's cities and towns—an indication of the class conflict inherent in the labor confrontation. Chafin positioned this "army" in trenches on Blair Mountain, along the route to Mingo County. Meanwhile the miners commandeered cars and trains at gunpoint, raided farms for food, and proceeded across Logan County. Many farm women voluntarily gave the marchers food. Miners' ranks swelled to over fifteen thousand in a line twenty miles long. A reporter for *The Nation* noted that the miners' contingent included one carload of women in nurses' uniforms, each wearing a cap emblazoned with the UMW logo, the wives of miners with some nursing experience.

The armed confrontation began on Blair Mountain on August 31. Fighting spread along a ten-mile line and lasted for three days. Governor Morgan appealed to President Harding for help, and two thousand federal troops and a squadron of bombers were sent. The president also sent UMWA organizers a telegram in which he promised to get rid of the mine guards if the miners would disperse. Mother Jones presented this telegram to miners and appealed for their retreat. Chafin's army disbanded, and the miners laid down their arms, not willing to shoot at soldiers of the United States Army. In all the fighting, only twelve miners and four of Chafin's men had been killed.

In the end, the Battle of Blair Mountain was a defeat for the miners. Hundreds of miners and union officials were arrested, and fifty-four were charged with treason. Several were convicted of murder and served prison time. In October of 1922, making little progress, the UMWA called off the strike in the southwestern coal fields. Mines began hiring large numbers of nonunion miners, and union membership dropped from 50,000 to 600 by the end of the decade. With the continuing downturn in coal markets, miners struggled to find jobs.[71]

At the same time, the federal government stepped in to prevent further outbreaks of violence. On June 21, 1921, the U.S. Senate had ordered an investigation of labor conditions in the mines of West Virginia. The study found that coal operators dominated local governments and that their practice of paying deputy sheriffs was "un-American." Investigators recommended that that practice and the use of mine guards should cease, even as they condemned the unlawful violence of the miners. In the end, little was done, and the issue of the miners' right to belong to a union was not settled until the passage of the Wagner Act during the New Deal.

The onset of the Great Depression in 1929 exacerbated miners' problems and further undermined union strength. Unemployed miners crowded soup lines in southwestern West Virginia and swelled the relief rolls and WPA projects. Virginia Giacomo recalled that her husband worked on WPA projects during periodic layoffs from the mines. Eli Mullins recalled that only the subsistence he and his wife raised on the farm allowed them to survive the infrequent day labor he found in the mines. Miners' wives who had supported the strikes once again found themselves struggling and disappointed.[72]

The lives of ordinary upcountry women changed dramatically with the arrival of the Aluminum Company of America in Tennessee and the coal mines of southwestern West Virginia. Industry sparked economic development and enabled formerly marginal farm families to move into the cash economy. But life as a wage worker's or a supervisor's wife differed from the independent life of a farmer's wife. Some women resisted the transition to urban industrial values by insisting on remaining on the land or returning to the land, while others attempted to maintain rural subsistence patterns in town.

Life in town transformed rural definitions of class, and thus relationships among upcountry folk. The exigencies of town life, the Great Depression, and subsequent labor actions sparked the development of a working-class consciousness among the wives of wage earners. Former neighbors and friends, who had worked side by side in rural mutual aid networks, found themselves divided by these class factors. This new consciousness led to successful union organizing even as it ultimately undermined women's traditional coping strategies and marginalized women's place in the family economy. Although the arrival of heavy industry provided material improvements for most of the women affected, they paid for these improvements at the cost of their traditional position in the family.

Seven

Farm Wives and Commercial Farming

Between 1920 and 1950, southern agriculture underwent a massive transformation. In the early years of the twentieth century, most upcountry farmers were general farmers; that is, they grew a wide variety of crops and raised livestock, some for home consumption and some for sale in the market to generate cash. During the years between the world wars, many of these farmers began to make the transition to the specialized, profit-oriented commercial agriculture promoted by the U.S. Department of Agriculture (USDA), the Tennessee Valley Authority (TVA), and other governmental agencies. Using modern equipment and agricultural techniques to maximize production, commercial farmers began to specialize in one or two agricultural products produced largely for sale in the market. For most East Tennesseans, this process of commercialization was gradual. At first, farmers shifted their general farming efforts to produce larger amounts for the market, even as they continued to produce some products for home consumption. Slowly but surely, they began to devote most of their efforts to one or two crops and to production for the market.

Although they also produced some subsistence products, the farmers of upstate South Carolina were already producing primarily for the market. Yet here too, dramatic changes would occur between 1920 and 1950. In the cotton belt, including the counties of upstate South Carolina, farming methods had changed little since the days of slavery. The labor-intensive nature of cotton cultivation, the lack of mechanized tools to ease the process, and the availability of plenty of cheap labor—black and white—combined to discourage cotton planters from adopting many modernizations in cotton farming or diversifying their crops. All that would change between the wars when soil depletion, the flight of agricultural workers to the cities in search of better jobs, the devastation wrought by the boll weevil, and the agricultural depression made mechanization and diversification a matter of survival for the upstate's commercial farmers. Already dedicated to producing for the market, many cotton belt landowners began to supplement and then replace their corn and cotton with truck crops, orchards, and livestock. They also mechanized operations and applied the latest research findings in order to maximize productivity.

Agricultural change was a protracted process. Commercialization was a capital- and land-intensive shift that transformed rural communities from networks of farm families sharing resources to a complex of "independent small businesses" run by the most prosperous white families. The process of change also gradually displaced poor black and white landowners and farm laborers, who began an equally protracted transition into the wage economy or to wage work combined with part-time farming. Moreover, the shift to commercial farming profoundly changed the lives of upcountry farm women. Wives of commercial farmers found their roles in farm production and in the community's mutual aid networks transformed, while women who were displaced faced the same difficult choices and adjustments seen among the women displaced by the TVA and Camp Croft. This chapter compares the impact of the rise of commercial dairy farming on the lives of white rural women in Loudon County, Tennessee, with white landowning women's responses to the shift to peach farming in upstate South Carolina.

Upcountry farm women were not passive victims of the commercialization of agriculture. Although the nature of farm women's work changed, the wives of commercial farmers did not automatically adopt the role of farm homemaker promoted by the USDA. Rather, they made a variety of choices about their roles on the new commercial farms, choices that were influenced as much by their personal preferences, family dynamics, and economic needs as by the advice given by the USDA. Many women saw themselves as farm managers and as full partners in the farm decision-making process. Others used the need for an influx of cash to support the commercial farming operation as an excuse to take off-farm jobs. In any case, the transformation of the lives of wives of commercial farmers was a highly complex and negotiated process.

Women's work was not the only thing that changed with the shift to commercial farming; mutual aid networks were also transformed. In contrast to the Midwest and the mid-Atlantic states, informal mutual aid networks persisted in the rural South, albeit in a transmuted form, well into the 1950s. This persistence was largely due to chronic economic problems that left even the most prosperous commercial farmers struggling to purchase enough land and equipment to operate without occasional community aid. During and after the transition to commercial farming, women remained the glue that bound together the system of mutual aid networks in the rural community, subsidizing capitalist agriculture with their unpaid organizational efforts. Nonetheless, the commercialization of agriculture transformed these networks, entwining them with formal farm organizations such as the Farm Bureau. The gendered organization of the Farm Bureau and other groups reinforced a set of class and gender hierarchies very different from those embedded in earlier informal networks.

Commercial agriculture demanded labor and capital; it attracted those with the means to compete in the market. Therefore, it was difficult for poor white landowners and tenants to make the transition to commercial farming, and it was virtually impossible for black farm families. A few black farmers did become commercial peach growers, but no woman interviewed—white or black—recalled a black family among the ranks of those who made the transition to commercial dairy farming in Loudon County, Tennessee; and indeed, there are no black dairy farmers in the county today. Some blacks managed to maintain jobs as tenants or farm laborers or to continue subsistence farming. Nonetheless, the lure of better jobs in cities, especially Northern cities, proved far more attractive than life on the margins of an increasingly middle-class, white farming community. The *Census of Agriculture* found that the number of black farmers in Loudon County declined from 74 in 1925 to 31 in 1945. (In the same period the number of white farmers actually increased from 1,278 to 1,445.) Perhaps more significant is the fact that only 6 of these 31 farmers (fewer than 20 percent) were tenants, predictably indicating that black landowners were able to remain on the land longer than their landless counterparts. The manual labor required in peach farming provided jobs for black agricultural workers in Spartanburg County long after they lost their place in Loudon County, but even here the number of black farmers declined from 5,220 in 1920 to 2,687 in 1950. (More than 78 percent of the remaining black farmers were tenants.) Because black farm women were rarely found among commercial farming families, they are not examined here.[1]

Loudon County, Tennessee—An Emerging Dairy Farming Center

Like many counties in the upcountry South where cotton farming had not exhausted the land, Loudon County was an ideal location for the development of successful commercial farms. First settled in the seventeenth century by Englishmen who established a fort on the Tennessee River, Loudon County had the highest percentage of tillable land of any county in East Tennessee. The Tennessee and Little Tennessee Rivers cut a swath through the 219-square-mile county, creating miles of fertile river bottom farmland. Although small family farms dominated the county throughout the nineteenth century, the river provided seasonal transportation to markets in Chattanooga and Knoxville, facilitating the development of a handful of large grain and livestock plantations in the antebellum years. In 1799, for example, James and Jane Carmichael Blair obtained 560 acres along the Tennessee River at present-day Loudon. They established "Blair's Ferry," a well-known river landmark, and practiced general agriculture, a practice that continued among later generations of the family until the twentieth century. Most of the county's small twentieth-century black population were descended from slaves who worked large operations like the Blairs'. In fact, as was the case in other areas of the South, some of the freedmen continued to work on their home plantations as sharecroppers and wage workers after emancipation.[2]

By the early part of the twentieth century, Loudon County was a thriving combination of general farms and small industry. Twenty-eight miles of railroad owned by the Louisville and Nashville Railroad and by Southern Railway criss-crossed the county, providing transport routes for the small industry located in the little town of Lenoir City. This company town was founded to house the employees of the Lenoir Car Works, manufacturers of railroad and street cars. The railroad and the company town proved to be magnets for other manufacturers, including a candy maker, two chair factories, Calloway Lumber Manufacturing Company, Old Hickory Brick Company, three hosiery mills, several machine shops, and other small industries. Wage work provided an alternative for a few of the farm families who were unable or unwilling to convert to commercial agriculture, allowing them to hang on to the family land. Many part-time farmers were among the 3,321 wage earners in the county, and industrial wages of $2.1 million in 1930 pumped much-needed cash into the local economy. The hosiery mills often provided work for the daughters and wives of poorer farmers, while farm men sought periodic employment in the car works and the lumber mills. Although these industries helped rural folk remain on the land by allowing them to supplement farm incomes with wage work, the jobs in Loudon County were not as highly skilled or well-paying as the jobs at ALCOA in neighboring Blount County. As a result, commercial farming appeared much more attractive than factory jobs to Loudon County farmers with the capital to make it work.[3]

Because of the importance of commercial farming, Loudon County retained its rural character even as its industrial base grew. By 1930 the county had grown to 17,128 white residents and 677 African Americans, with more than half of the residents living in the countryside. Feed stores and farm equipment dealerships shared Main Street storefronts with clothing and general stores. As in most upcountry counties, the local newspaper reflected the rural interests of citizens. Regular coverage of outstanding local crop and livestock production, producers' group meetings, and a column written by the county agent shared the front page with national and world news, local Republican Party announcements, and the "Tennessee Weekly Industrial Report."[4]

Thanks to the rich river bottoms and gently rolling hills, Loudon County's farms had always been more prosperous than most in the state and in East Tennessee. In 1920 the average farm in the county was valued at $5,010, as compared to a state average of $4,054 (see Table 7.1) The onset of the Depression caused farm values to plunge, with the average value of a Loudon County farm falling to $2,610 by 1935, a decline of almost 50 percent but still well above the state average of $2,029 that year. These rural residents enjoyed relatively comfortable lives. Government officials found living conditions in the county's farm homes were gen-

TABLE 7.1 Average Farm Values:
Tennessee, Loudon County, and Nearby East Tennessee Counties

Average value*	1920	1925	1930	1935	1940	1945
Tennessee	$4,054	$3,005	$3,025	$2,029	$2,863	$3,715
Blount County	$5,339	$3,504	$4,339	$2,724	$3,392	$3,715
Loudon County	$5,010	$4,318	$4,011	$2,610	$3,824	$5,215
Sevier County	$3,266	$2,993	$3,225	$1,768	$2,288	$3,692

Sources: Fifteenth Census of the United States: Agriculture, 1930, 894–902, 870–76; Census of Agriculture, 1935, 593–94, 598, 600; Census of Agriculture, 1945, 18–19, 29, 34.
*Total—land, livestock, and equipment.

erally better than those in most East Tennessee counties. In 1930 government workers surveyed 109 of the county's farm homes, finding that the vast majority were "modern" or "in good condition." Only 22 percent were "in need of repairs" or "in bad condition." Over half of all farms fronted on improved roads, that is, regularly maintained gravel or paved roads.[5]

The county's low tenancy rates and relatively high tenant farm values were also indicative of its farm prosperity. Only 36 percent of Loudon County's farmers were tenants in 1925 as compared to 41 percent statewide. These tenant farmers were often more prosperous than farm owners, suggesting that heavy indebtedness for land prevented some of the county's farm owners from accumulating valuable cattle and equipment. In 1925 the average white tenant farmer in the county worked a farm whose land, livestock, and equipment were valued at $4,684; while farms owned by white operators averaged a value of only $3,829. A similar pattern characterized the county's 74 black farmers. Black tenants worked farms valued at $2,099, while black owners worked farms valued at $783. Paradoxically, this tenant prosperity did not translate into a fighting chance for tenant farmers who wanted to establish commercial operations. Land remained the most valuable asset necessary for the transition to capitalist agriculture, and the decline of commodity prices and opportunities for off-farm work during the depression years, followed by the sharp increase in land prices in the late 1930s after TVA displaced many families, meant that tenants were unable to afford this land.[6]

The development of Loudon County as a commercial dairy farming center proceeded slowly in the 1920s and 1930s. Those who chose to specialize faced several obstacles. Modern dairy farming not only required large amounts of pastureland for herds, but also a significant infusion of cash to invest in milking equipment that enabled the efficient milking of sizable herds and the storage of milk according to increasingly strict health department regulations. Still, in spite of the enormous amount of capital required, Loudon County was an opportune place to establish a dairy farm because its land was well suited to livestock farming, it had excellent access to railroads, and farm owners had some unusual opportunities to accumulate cash for capital investment. Not only did some local farm families use industrial jobs to supplement farm incomes with wage labor, but the arrival of TVA in the late 1930s led to the federal purchase of portions of river bottom farms within the flood plains of Fort Loudon and Watts Bar Lakes. These purchases provided the cash many families needed to expand their land holdings and to purchase cattle and equipment. TVA's own farm demonstration program further encouraged commercial agricultural practices. For instance, Joseph Alexander's farm north of Lenoir City was a TVA Test Demonstration Farm from 1938 to 1948. Moreover, New Deal agricultural price supports raised milk prices, increasing the potential for profitable dairying. Finally, TVA power and New Deal rural electrification initiatives brought affordable electricity to farms, a necessity for the proper refrigeration of milk and dairy products.[7]

Cash was not the only requirement for the development of commercial dairy farming. Successful dairying demanded readily accessible markets. Full-time wage workers in Lenoir City provided one market. Several farmers started their commercial operations with local milk delivery routes that served town customers. The county's rail connections also provided easy access to population centers in Knoxville and Chattanooga. Improving federal highways like U.S. 11 (the Lee Highway) generated more truck traffic. But the arrival of Scott's Cheese Factory in nearby Sweetwater in 1927 provided most Loudon County farmers with the needed incentive to expand their dairy production. Started by an expert Wisconsin cheese maker, who moved South to take advantage of expanding southern markets, the plant was the largest buyer of Loudon County's raw milk until it closed in the late 1940s.[8]

In response to incrementally expanding markets and the slow pro-

TABLE 7.2 Loudon County Dairying

Value*	1920	1930	1935	1940	1945
All dairy products	$140,486	$136,320	n/a	$144,830	$288,200
Whole milk	n/a	$93,446	n/a	$177,491	n/a

Sources: *Fifteenth Census of the United States: Agriculture, 1930,* 953; *Sixteenth Census of the United States: Agriculture, 1940,* 467; *Census of Agriculture, 1945,* 115.
*In dollars.

cess of accumulating capital, the growth of the dairy industry in the county was gradual at first. Between 1929 and 1949, the number of cows milked on Loudon County farms increased from 2,920 to 5,928. Perhaps a more telling statistic is the rapid increase in the sales of whole milk and a corresponding decline in the sales of butter (see Table 7.2) In the same period, the number of farms selling butter, a commodity usually produced in small amounts by farm women, actually decreased from 422 to 180; while annual sales of whole milk increased from 373,782 gallons to 1,226,853 gallons. This shift indicated that the sales of large quantities of whole milk, the backbone of commercial dairy farming, were becoming more important. The number of farms reporting dairying as their major source of income more than doubled, from 45 in 1939 to 94 in 1949. World War II particularly spurred production, with high wartime prices and heavy demand from cities outside East Tennessee. Oral histories with dairy farm families reveal that the 1920s, 1930s, and 1940s were a period when families consolidated landholdings and built herds while gradually reducing production of other cash crops and livestock as the first stage in their shift to commercial dairy farming. Farm women were central to this process of transition.[9]

Commercial Farm Wives

The USDA—largely through the Tennessee Agricultural Extension Service located at the nearby University of Tennessee—promoted the transition to commercial agriculture. Moreover, federal and state agricultural officials had a distinct view of the role women should play on commercial farms: the ideal farm wife would devote her time to creating a domestic haven for her hard-working farmer husband. Wives of general farmers were involved in multiple productive activities, including vegetable and livestock production for home use and for sale on the market, assisting with field work, and even sharing in farm decision making. Although Tennessee's extension agents and other agricultural officials did recognize women's critical role in small-scale farm production, they did not see women playing a significant part in farm decision making or in the "real" work of commercial production. Agents continued to see women as producers, but they saw their efforts as focused on the home rather than on the farm operation. It is difficult to determine how much exposure Loudon County farm families had to this USDA prescription. To be sure, the county agent's weekly newspaper columns consistently referred to the farmer as "he" and did not address the role of the farm wife in production issues except for occasional advice to farm women on poultry husbandry. In the wake of post–World War I federal budget cuts, Loudon County lost its home extension agent, so that for a time, Loudon County's farm wives were not regularly exposed to this USDA ideology via home demonstration clubs. Nonetheless, male agents continued to meet with, and provide assistance to, farmers, spending most of their time helping the county's largest producers. Once a home extension agent was again assigned to the county in the late 1930s, home demonstration work focused on home improvement, housekeeping, and child rearing. Such programs served to reinforce the idea that the farm wife's domain was the farm home, not the barnyard or the field. A similar message came from the professional experts with TVA's farm demonstration programs.[10]

Loudon County's commercial farm wives did not necessarily recognize this split in roles, however. Not only did they continue to play their traditional roles of producing the family's food and clothing and supplementing the family income with the sale of farm produce, but they also actively participated in commercial production and farm decision making, resisting efforts to marginalize their role as farming partners.

Mabel Love was one such farm wife. Her experience illustrates the multifaceted roles of the women on Loudon County's commercial dairy farms. The daughter of a middling tenant farmer, Love married the son of a middling Loudon County farm owner. After her in-laws died, Love's husband and brother-in-law ran the family farm as a general farming operation for about fifteen years. Then Love and her husband borrowed the money to buy out his siblings' share and began a dairy operation. Love described the process of accumulating the farmland needed to run a large dairy:

> [First] we bought out the rest of his brothers. Then we got this place here. Then we just kept on buying a little bit more land. [laughter] The first one I guess that we bought [after the home place] was that area right up where you go around the curve up there. . . . And we bought that and paid on it a while and then decided to try to buy some more. Then we bought where the grandson lives. . . . Then after we got that paid for, which was quite a job to get that done, then we bought where that field is right over there on top of the hill.

This slow process of amassing acreage was typical of families expanding their commercial farms. Land, however, was not the only commodity the Loves needed to establish their commercial operation. They also needed to build a dairy herd and to buy equipment. At first they milked their herd of fifteen cows by hand. They also saved money and managed their profits carefully, repeatedly reinvesting in new livestock and equipment. As electricity became available in the early 1940s, the Loves increased the size of their herd and added equipment.[11]

As Mabel Love's use of the pronoun *we* to refer to land purchases indicates, she never saw herself as simply a housewife. Rather, she considered herself a full partner in the farm operation. "I always had a big garden, but I did help on the farm," she recalled. "I would drive the tractors, and I milked." In addition to this farm work, she raised most of the family's food supply in her large garden and earned cash to buy groceries from the sale of chickens and eggs, thus stretching the family's resources so that more farm profits were available for reinvestment.

Love also shared in farm decision making. Historian Nancy Gray Osterud has argued that the way farm women present events when recounting their lives reveals much about their sense of agency. Women who feel little control over events recalled that things "happened" to them, while women who had a sense of agency referred to events as things they chose. This observation provides a revealing look at Mabel Love's sense of herself as a farm partner. She spoke of decisions to buy cattle and equipment as decisions "we" made and of farming accomplishments as "ours." Moreover, neighbors credited Mabel with being the savvy money manager who made it possible for the family to accumulate one of the largest farms in the county.[12]

Profits alone did not motivate Mabel and her husband. As had been the case when she grew up in a tenant farm family, Mabel Love saw farming as a family affair. She also envisioned the accumulation of land as a source of financial security and as the means with which to build a legacy for her three sons. Today, Love proudly notes that her grandson is the third generation of the Love family to farm the land she and her late husband so painstakingly accumulated. Mabel Love measured her family's success not only in terms of profits and their ability to make a comfortable living farming, but also in their ability to pass the farm on to their children.[13]

Like Mabel Love, Ethel Davis and her husband built a commercial dairy operation from their handful of milk cows. The Davises married in the 1920s and struggled for several years to turn the land he inherited from his parents into a viable commercial dairy. Davis's husband often drove a milk truck to supplement the farm income. While he was away from the farm on his milk route, Ethel and a brother-in-law shared the farm work. She recalled, "I once had fourteen [cows] that I milked . . . by hand." Once the couple was able to install electricity and obtain milking machines, Davis was happy to give up the burden of milking. Instead, she focused on her garden, the sale of her surplus produce and eggs, and assisting with field work. The Davis's dairy is still in operation under the management of the couple's only son.[14]

Harriet Delozier also took an active role in the productive work of her family's dairy farm, but she focused her efforts on the processing and marketing of milk rather than on milking and field work. Delozier's in-laws had lost the farm to foreclosure in 1931, so Harriet and her husband Arthur obtained a mortgage to repurchase the family land. Here they turned the corn and wheat operation into a commercial dairy farm. Their proximity to Lenoir City created a large market for home delivery, and they sold most of their milk this way in the 1930s. "We peddled buttermilk and eggs and everything just to try to make a living," Arthur Delozier recalled. "My wife, she'd take an old T-model and go all over the county and town delivering buttermilk and eggs."[15]

Milk delivery was the last step in Harriet Delozier's participation in the family dairy. Her work began with the bottling of the milk in her farmhouse kitchen. Here she and her mother-in-law also churned the butter and washed the eggs they sold. The family gradually built a prosperous operation. In 1947, when the Tennessee Health Department established more stringent standards for milk production, the Delozier family was able to build a Grade A dairy barn and expand their production. At this point, Harriet Delozier withdrew from the farm operation, leaving most of the work to her husband and her sons, who were now grown. Her withdrawal suggests that, like Mabel Love and Ethel Davis, Harriet Delozier was determined to create a stable dairy operation to pass down to her sons. But unlike Love and Davis, who also enjoyed farm work, Delozier was content to leave that work to the family men once they were old enough to meet its labor demands. The family operated the dairy until 1986.[16]

The productive work of women like Love, Davis, and Delozier played a key role in the development of commercial dairy farms that were a legacy for their children. For many, it was the influx of cash from an outside source that made this legacy possible. Peggy Delozier Jones and her family used cash received from the sale of some river bottom land to TVA to help build their commercial farming operation. In their case, the proceeds from land sold for Watts Bar Lake in the late 1930s paid off the mortgage on their farm land, freeing up more cash with which to invest in equipment and cattle.[17]

Peggy Jones never expected to be a farm wife. As with Mabel Love, her language in describing her life is very revealing: "My husband wasn't a farmer when I promised to marry him [in 1922]," she recalled. "I always said I wouldn't marry a farmer; it was too hard. But his father bought a farm, and put Jim on it farming. He [her husband] hadn't had too much experience; he'd helped on his grandfather's farm some. So when the Depression hit, we had a right hard time." In some ways, her experience illustrates the lack of control she felt over decision making that profoundly changed her life. Her father-in-law decided to buy his son a farm, which sealed her fate. Moreover, her husband had few farming skills and found it hard to survive the hardships of the Depression. Life was difficult in the early years of her marriage, and Jones's major commitment was to the well-being of her two young sons. To that end, she settled into the traditional mold of farmer's wife. During those years, Peggy assisted with the family's support by providing food from her garden, canning produce for the winter, and selling eggs and turkeys.

Once her sons were older, Jones found off-farm opportunities that better fit her education and inclinations. The daughter of a Loudon County landowner who had prized education for his children, Jones had earned a degree in home economics from Mary Washington College in Virginia and taught high school for a while before her marriage in 1922. In 1941, when both of her sons were in high school, a family friend active in local politics offered her a job supervising the WPA school lunch programs in Loudon, Roane, and Monroe counties. When Congress did not renew the WPA program a couple of years later, the Loudon County Welfare Department hired Jones. She justified her work outside the home as a means to provide for her family's material well-being and to aid in capitalizing the farm operation. This income proved valuable in providing the family with cash to expand the dairy operation and sustain itself as well as to send their sons to college. Jones was not motivated entirely by the good of the farm, however. She enjoyed her work immensely, particularly because it got her out into the community every day and away from the almost exclusively male world of the farm. She reveled in interacting with women in her work, and in fact worked for almost thirty years.

Although Jones's husband was never very interested in dairy farming, preferring to raise cash crops, her sons found livestock farming appealing. In the 1940s, with the sharp rise in milk prices due to World War II, her sons started a small dairy, which eventually grew into one of the county's largest operations. Jones provided much of the productive farm work for this operation in her later life. She recalled, "I didn't do too much out in the field [until] after I retired." At that point, she often assisted her sons by driving tractors for planting and harvest. "I'd work from daylight to dark with [my son]. I liked to drive a tractor, and I'd help him," she explained. "[My daughter-in-law] was cooking, and I'd work with the boys. . . . I'd rather work outside." This shift from mere tolerance of the farm early in her life to active and eager involvement after her retirement may say something about the dynamics of Jones's relationship with her husband. Although she never criticized him in her interview and maintained that he did not object to her farm work, she was considerably more active in productive farm work once it was under the management of her younger son.

The Transformation of Mutual Aid Networks

The wives of commercial farmers were not only central to the process of building profitable dairy operations, but they also remained central to the process of building mutual support networks. Yet these networks were changing as class lines became more rigid. In the early part of the century, class lines certainly existed in rural Loudon County, with clear distinctions between elite, middling, and poor farming families. Nonetheless these lines were fluid, and there was considerable interaction among members of all groups. For example, Mabel Love, a tenant farmer's daughter, was able to marry the son of a farm owner. This fluidity had extended to mutual support networks, which often found elite, middling, and tenant families working side by side to help each other at harvest or times of personal crisis.

All this changed as class lines became hardened with the development of commercial farming. While some poor landowning families found it possible to remain on the land, farming in limited ways, few were able to buy the land, cattle, or equipment they needed to start a commercial dairy. It also became difficult for most tenant farm families to find good farm-based employment, although a few found opportunities on the new commercial dairy farms. As farmers mechanized, they had less and less need for traditional farm laborers who worked next to them in the fields. Yet dairying had its own peculiar labor demands. Dairy farming is unique among most types of commercial farming because it requires a disciplined routine much like industrial work. Cows have to be milked twice daily every day, confining farm families to the drudgery of milking seven days a week, three hundred sixty-five days a year. While there are slower times in the winter when feed crops do not have to be tended, dairy farming is less seasonal than most types of farming. Many dairy farmers, particularly those with no children or children too young to assist with farm chores, find this grind too difficult to bear alone, so they hire "milkers." The milker's responsibility is to feed and milk the cows, a highly skilled but poorly paying job. In the middle years of the twentieth century, farmers usually offered a salary and a house to the milker and his family.[18]

Yet the very restructuring of farm labor precipitated by the rise of commercial dairying reinforced new class hierarchies in the rural community by further separating farm management from farm labor. On Loudon County's old general farms, farmers and their hired hands had a much more personal relationship. Day laborers were often single sons of other local farm owners seeking to earn some extra cash on a seasonal basis. Other hired hands worked on a more permanent basis but still had a similar informal relationship with the farmer, often living with the farm family or at least on the farm. Farmers' relationships with share tenants were also vastly different. Most of the time, share tenants worked their own plots with little day-to-day supervision from the farmer. The shift to the use of hired milkers transformed the farmer-laborer relationship into something that more closely resembled the industrial employer-employee model. Low pay and loss of autonomy made the job of milker much less desirable than many factory jobs, leading many men to take their families to the cities where industrial jobs with comparable supervisory practices offered better pay.[19]

Although this transition to an employer-employee relationship lightened the workload of some wives of commercial farmers who no longer had to feed and house hired hands, it had profound consequences for the wives and daughters of these employee farm laborers. The widening social separation between commercial farmers and their laborers meant that daughters of laborers would have few opportunities to move up the class ladder by marrying a farm owner as Mabel Love had done. Moreover, the wives of these laborers now found themselves excluded from mutual aid networks that had provided vital support for them. Mabel Love described the large work parties that took place during threshing and "siloing" (the cutting of corn silage as cattle feed) during the 1920s and 1930s. Rural people moved from one farm to another helping each other complete the harvest. The neighborhood men gathered to share in the field work, while the neighborhood women shared the cooking. Women's work was visible and necessary at these work parties. "We just had such a good time being together that it didn't seem like work," Love noted. "Everybody helped everybody else. It was real good." But "everybody" no longer included all the members of the farming community.

The development of commercial farming meant that these occasions, which had once included most of the families in the neighborhood, were becoming class-based. The families that Love recalled participating in her own threshing parties were other prosperous commercial farmers from the neighborhood. Male farm laborers and tenants might work for wages at their employers' threshing parties and eat lunch with the other workers, but their wives and children were not included in the communal cooking and feasting as were the wives and children of landowning commercial farmers.[20]

Moreover, as wage earners, these new agricultural workers did not participate in an exchange of labor for labor, but rather exchanged their labor for cash. Because agricultural laborers who owned farmland were usually too poor to hire farm laborers for their own harvests, they were forced to make do with family labor in cases where they once would have turned to the mutual aid network. Not only did this leave many of them unable to expand their production in order to develop a commercial operation, but it also left their wives with fewer strategies to cope with economic hardships because they could not ask more prosperous farm wives for help.

The development of commercial farming also saw the undermining of informal mutual support networks, even for commercial farmers, as farm families placed mutual aid functions in the hands of formal farm organizations like the Farm Bureau. A national organization, the Farm Bureau began in 1911 as a committee on agriculture within the Broome County, New York, Chamber of Commerce. Although organized for the sole purpose of hiring a county agricultural extension agent, the organization developed quickly among commercial farmers across the nation. Due to its roots in extension work, it had close ties to the USDA from the beginning, adopting the USDA's gendered view of farm family life. The organization also developed close ties with agribusiness. From the beginning, the Farm Bureau was made up mostly of middling to elite farmers who were not looking for radical social change but rather for a vehicle for political and economic power.[21]

To tie the scattered Farm Bureau chapters together, organization leaders formed the American Farm Bureau Federation in 1919, establishing, in the process, a bureaucracy capable of taking on a number of mutual aid functions for its members. Farmers often had trouble obtaining

fire, life, and crop insurance from insurers reluctant to take on the unpredictable risks of rural life. The Farm Bureau offered its members affordable group insurance policies. The organization also grew into a powerful
congressional lobby, playing a significant role in shaping U.S. agricultural
policy that benefited commercial farmers to the detriment of subsistence
and tenant farmers during the 1920s and 1930s.

In Loudon County, Peggy Delozier Jones's older brother, George Delozier, and several other local landowners founded the Farm Bureau in
the late 1930s in order to provide for "the support and encouragement
of agriculture." One of their key motivations was to take advantage of
group insurance benefits offered to members by the state Farm Bureau
Federation. Two women were among the seven founders of the local
organization. They were wives or widows of prosperous landowning
farmers. Their presence was in keeping with the fact that many women
saw themselves as partners in the farm.[22]

Yet their central role in the policy-making side of the local organization would not last. If farmers were businessmen, then organizational
ideology saw farmers' wives as supportive helpmates, not as partners in
the organization. This ideology was reflected in the national organization's gender-segregated structure. Gradually full voting Farm Bureau
membership became restricted to men, by custom if not by rule. Women
joined Farm Bureau Women, an organization designed to function as an
auxiliary to the real work of the male group. In 1936 the Associated
Women of the American Farm Bureau Federation noted that the "purpose of this association is to assist in an active, organized way in carrying
forward such phases of the American Farm Bureau Federation programs
as inevitably enlist the creative interest of women." These activities included promoting educational, social, and spiritual opportunities for
rural people, and support for home demonstration work.[23]

In Loudon County, although the local Farm Bureau Women's organization was not formalized until 1949, farm women quickly found their
work restricted to the "women's sphere." As they had done with community harvest rituals, Farm Bureau officers called on their wives to organize events and to provide the food and fellowship that proved so attractive in organizing. Peggy Delozier Jones recalled that she organized the
meals for Farm Bureau events for years. As had been the case with mutual aid networks, the organizing that women did was crucial to the

success of the Farm Bureau. Yet men did not see this work as central to the organization's work. Female neighbors remembered Peggy Jones as a Farm Bureau leader, while male neighbors remembered only her husband's and brothers' leadership. When prompted, men conceded that Jones had organized their meals, but they saw this work as only peripheral to the real work of setting local Farm Bureau policy, something that was done by men.[24]

Rigidly prescribed gender roles were not the only negative aspect of the development of the Farm Bureau. As was becoming the case with informal networks in neighborhoods, the new Farm Bureau was very much a class-based organization. The American Farm Bureau Federation saw farming as a business and farmers as businessmen, a middle-class vision that was a departure from the old hands-on approach to farming that was traditional in East Tennessee. Apparently the leaders of the Loudon County Farm Bureau felt the same way. The organization's rolls were filled with the names of the county's most prosperous landholding families, who clearly saw farming as a business, not with the names of its tenant farmers. Marginal landowners might belong to the organization, but they were not among its leaders or even its active participants. Many of them belonged only for the privilege of buying cheap insurance.

Social Life and Consumption

The increasing class consciousness among commercial farming families seen in the organization of mutual aid networks and farm organizations was also reflected in the organization of social life. The names of commercial farm families began to appear with greater frequency in the social columns of the local newspaper that reported on social activities in many communities. Throughout the 1930s, the wives of Loudon County's rising dairy farmers began to appear with greater frequency in these pages—visiting other neighbors, hosting church circle and women's group meetings in their homes, and even traveling to the distant cities of Maryville or Knoxville for "shopping." Moreover, the details of these social events began to resemble urban society pages. Farm wife Mrs. Ora Mae Russell hosted the Missionary Society of the Methodist Episcopal Church at her farm home on an April evening in 1938. The reporter to the *Loudon County Herald* noted that "during the social hour an ice course was served. A handkerchief shower was presented Miss Mary Sue White who will soon leave for Starrett College in Nashville." An "ice course," a very elegant dessert, was not inexpensive in the days before electricity was common on farms. For rural families, ice was a precious commodity used to chill milk and butter until they could be taken to market. The rural household's use of ice to eat was therefore an act of conspicuous consumption designed to display the Russell family's growing affluence. The fact that a young woman from a rural church was going off to college was also a sign of rising expectations and class-based aspirations for children. In fact, a disproportionate number of the wives of commercial farmers were college-educated, a sign of their birth families' aspirations for them as well their husbands' visions of appropriate qualifications for farm wives.[25]

Newspaper coverage of farm wives' social activities also points to another way in which the wives of commercial farmers were beginning to imitate their middle-class sisters in town. For businessmen, the ability to support wives who could engage in conspicuous consumption and leisure activities was symbolic of wealth and affluence. This was also the case for Loudon County farm families. Although persistent economic problems meant that it would be years, if ever, before farm owners could spend all their time managing the farm and supervising laborers to do the so-called dirty work, commercialization and mechanization made it easier for farm wives to find a few hours a week to engage in social activities. In the late 1940s, Peggy Jones and seven high school classmates formed a bridge club which met regularly.[26]

Social activities were not the only activities unrelated to farm production to claim the attention of the wives of commercial farmers, which suggests that, even as they held on to their role in farm decision making, they were selectively adapting characteristics of the USDA's ideal farm wife. For them, consumption was the tangible proof of their success, evidence that their farms were generating profits large enough to spare some money to improve the farm home. Many of them adopted consumption patterns advocated by home extension agents they met through involvement in home demonstration work. The home demonstration club provided not only an opportunity to mingle with farm wives of a similar standing, but also the chance to learn new homemaking skills. With the reinstatement of home extension programs in Loudon County in 1939, commercial farm wives eagerly learned new techniques for making fashionable clothing and for adapting extension agents' decorating advice to the farm home as well. As time went on, commercial farm women became more involved in consumption-oriented projects such as home improvement. An active member of Farm Bureau Women and the local home demonstration club, Kate Simmons eagerly engaged in home improvements, seeking to make her home more attractive and to lighten her own work load. She recalled that after the family obtained electricity, "the first thing I bought was a stove, which I loved. I was ready to give up on that [messy] wood stove." She also began collecting Victorian antiques and expanding a doll collection begun by a family friend in her childhood. In September 1954, her farm home was featured in a *Progressive Farmer* article as an example of innovation, good taste, and practicality in decorating the farm home.[27]

Of course, relatively few of Loudon County's rural landowners were able to adopt these trappings of middle-class life. Fewer than 10 percent of Loudon County's farm families established commercial dairy operations or large commercial farms of any type. Families who decided to become commercial farmers generally came from the middling or elite classes of rural citizens. Many, such as the Delozier family, had long held positions of influence in the county. Others, such as the Loves, were ambitious hardworking folk lucky enough to start with a modicum of capital in the form of rich farmland. For families unable or unwilling to become commercial farmers, the changes were less positive. The mechanization that was inherent in commercialization gradually made the labor of tenant families unnecessary. At the same time, the need for large plots of land and TVA's removal of thousands of acres of farmland from production created a market for small farms that bordered larger operations and caused land prices to skyrocket. Many small landowners found it increasingly difficult to earn a living on general farms. Most eventually gave in to the temptation of high land prices and sold their holdings to commercial farmers, perhaps retaining a house and lot, or moving to towns in search of better lives and more work opportunities. This disruption could be devastating for farm women who were not prepared for the very different demands of town life.

Others chose to remain on the land without trying to make a living as commercial farmers. In these families, men often took off-farm jobs in Lenoir City or in neighboring Blount County, depending on wives and children to keep a small farming operation going. Everett Hobbs tried full-time farming for a few years during the 1930s. He kept a small dairy herd, selling milk to Scott's Cheese Factory in Sweetwater, and raised small grains and tobacco. Nonetheless, when he had the opportunity to take a job at the Aluminum Company of America (ALCOA) in Blount County, he jumped at the chance. His wife, Irma, maintained the farm during his absence. For many years, she and their daughters raised beef cattle and the tobacco crop with help from Everett at night and on weekends. Although this arrangement created a heavy work load for Irma, it also left her free to spend her days at home with her daughters. She preferred ordering her own work without interference from Everett and probably enjoyed the feeling that she was contributing to the family's income. As a result of their combined efforts, the Hobbs family enjoyed considerably more prosperity than they would have experienced from farming alone. They were able to send all three daughters to college or secretarial school and to retire to the farm.[28]

Peach Farming in Upstate South Carolina

For upstate South Carolina farmers, the interwar years brought a different set of transitions than those experienced by Loudon County's rural folk. Kline Cash recalled that his grandfather had been the first landowner in the community of Cowpens, South Carolina, in northeast Spartanburg County, to devote a few acres to peach farming. John Cash planted his first orchard in 1925. "I really don't know why he decided to plant peach trees," speculated his grandson. "Probably because somebody [in the region] had done it, and it looked like it was a good thing to do. That's usually what farmers do. They see somebody else making money on something and say, 'Well, I can do that.'" John Cash did see other people making money on peaches. The first railroad carload of peaches was shipped from the county in 1924, inspiring a number of farmers to convert some of their depleted cotton and cornfields into orchards. As in Loudon County, this conversion was a shift to a new type of farming that would slowly but steadily transform the lives of the county's women. Yet several things made the shift to peach farming very different from Loudon County's adoption of dairy farming.[29]

Perhaps the greatest difference was that Spartanburg County farmers already focused most of their energies on producing for the market, albeit through labor intensive, unmechanized cotton and corn farming. In the years after the Civil War, the white yeomanry in the upstate, attracted by the high price of cotton, had abandoned self-sufficient subsistence farming and committed most of their resources to raising cotton for the market. Spartanburg farmers quintupled their cotton production between 1860 and 1880. In 1850 Spartanburg County farmers had produced 3 pounds of cotton for every bushel of corn they grew; by 1900 they were producing 24.47 pounds of cotton for every bushel of corn, a figure that bespeaks an enormous shift in resources. Cotton fever was an unfortunate affliction for upstate farmers. The soil in the upstate was the poorest soil in the state, primarily a thick red clay that was low in nutrients and prone to erosion. Cotton is one of the worst crops to grow in marginal soil because it quickly depletes nutrients. Continual cotton production combined with poor farming practices to nearly destroy the county's agricultural land. By 1933 a Southern Regional Commission study found that six of the seven upstate counties (all but York County) had some of the worst erosion in the nation. Based on these findings, the Soil Erosion Service of the U.S. Department of the Interior chose Spartanburg County for the nation's pilot erosion prevention project.[30]

Poor soil and an unpredictable market were a devastating combination for the upstate's yeomen farmers. Abandoning self-sufficient practices that had allowed them to feed their families and hold onto their land throughout the antebellum period, they had turned to cotton farming hoping to get rich. They had converted garden space and livestock pastures into cotton fields, often buying much of their food in stores. Of course, purchasing the farm family's food increased their need for cash. By the 1890s, overproduction led to a decline in cotton prices, a problem that would recur periodically in coming decades. In addition, rapid declines in soil fertility caused a marked decrease in per-acre yields. Lacking the cash to purchase chemical fertilizers that would combat diminishing yields or to buy additional acreage, some farmers borrowed money to operate and to meet expenses during poor years. Soon they lost their mortgaged land. The cycle of overproduction, declining cotton prices, and continual indebtedness sucked many white upstate farmers into the crop lien system. When they lost their own land to foreclosure, they turned to sharecropping as a means of survival. Thus, they joined hundreds of black farmers who had never been able to buy land because of poverty and discrimination, and black landowners who had lost their land to the same cycle of indebtedness. By 1920 nearly 68 percent of the county's 8,260 farmers were tenants, a figure even higher than the appalling state average of 63 percent. Most white farmers (landowners and tenants) operated farms that averaged about 49 acres (black farmers averaged 38 acres), hardly enough to raise a cotton crop profitable enough to support a farm family.[31]

The crop lien system was an insidious trap. Farmers indebted to their landlords were forbidden by law from leaving that farm until they paid their debts. Many farm families did manage to climb out of debt and leave their farms to take jobs in local textile mills, and some chose to stay in the mill towns. But the ties to the land were strong for many others. Landowning families often worked in textile mills for a few years in order to pay off mortgages and then returned to farms. Sharecroppers used mill jobs to save enough money to buy mules or tools before returning to the land. Historian Allen Tullos interviewed a family in neighboring Greenville County who worked in the Poe Textile Mill for a few years. After paying off the mortgage, the parents returned to the farm for the rest of their lives, but several of the grown children preferred to stay on in the mill.[32]

Even when they remained on, or returned to, the land, upstate farmers remained tied to cotton. Landlords, who furnished seed and tools as well as acreage, usually insisted that sharecroppers produce cotton, and landowners stubbornly persisted in growing the same crop. The reasons were complicated. Some of it was the hope for profit. In a good year, cotton was enormously profitable. But cotton was also part of the upstate way of life. World War II journalist Ben Robertson, who grew up on an upstate cotton farm, put it this way, "Cotton is a state of mind with us, a philosophy, and we continue to plant it in spite of the fact that we have not made money on cotton more than once in about every ten years.[33]

During the first third of the twentieth century, events were conspiring to convince upstate farmers to abandon cotton, though most still

TABLE 7.3 Average Farm Values: Spartanburg County
and Surrounding Counties

Average Farm Values*	1920	1930
South Carolina	$4,222	$2,401
Greenville	$6,041	$3,285
Spartanburg	$5,951	$3,141
Cherokee	$4,912	$2,453

Source: Fifteenth Census of the United States: Agriculture, 1930,
470–75.
*Total—land, livestock, and equipment.

resisted change. In 1917 the boll weevil arrived in South Carolina, deci-
mating cotton yields. Some years the insect destroyed as much as 50
percent of the cotton crop. Nonetheless, cotton prices remained high due
to the disruptions and demands of World War I, so most Spartanburg
County farmers persisted with their cotton crops. Then in 1920, with the
postwar decline in demand from European and domestic markets, cotton
prices plunged from 40 cents per pound in the spring to 13.5 cents by
December. Prices recovered to 28 cents by 1923 but plunged again to less
than 10 cents in 1930 with the onset of the Great Depression. These problems were exacerbated by several dry growing seasons in the mid-1920s.
The value of crop production in the state of South Carolina fell from $446
million in 1918 to $63 million in 1932, with cotton leading the losses. Farm
values also fell; in Spartanburg County, the average value of land, livestock, and equipment per farm plunged from $5,951 in 1920 to $3,141 in
1930 (see Table 7.3). Declining cotton prices combined with a reduced
demand for textiles to bring on a depression in upstate South Carolina
years earlier than the rest of the nation felt it.[34]

In anticipation of the boll weevil, agricultural extension agents based
at Clemson University had begun to preach crop diversification as early
as 1912. They found a few converts among the upstate's more progressive
farmers. Ben Robertson's grandfather, a respected leader in the Pendle-
ton community, urged his fellow farmers to diversify. Worried about the
boll weevil and about creeping industrialization, he exhorted that diversified farming was "our only hope of fighting off the machine civilization,

our one chance of resisting the complicated insecurity of an industrial world." After the boll weevil arrived, Robertson's family, in the face of community ridicule, planted orchards and began to rotate a boll weevil-resistant strain of cotton with corn and winter wheat. Their efforts proved successful, and eventually neighboring farmers like John Cash followed their lead.[35]

Other progressive upstate landowners were listening to the men at Clemson as well. One of them was Ben M. Gramling Sr. Gramling's grandfather had founded the north Spartanburg County community that bore his name in the 1850s, and Ben and his family were among the most influential members of that community. The Gramling family were jacks of all trades, working as wheelwrights, selling timber from their own property, and engaging in diversified farming. When Southern Railway built a main line through the area in the 1880s, family members convinced railroad officials to construct a spur connecting Gramling family land to the main line so that they could move their substantial cotton and timber crops to market. By 1920 the Gramlings owned several hundred acres in the vicinity and employed dozens of sharecroppers who raised corn and cotton. They also ran a general store business, selling everything from clothing to caskets. Local folks noted that the Gramlings seemed to have a knack for making new ventures work.[36]

Ben Gramling Sr. had inherited the family's willingness to take risks. He was concerned about the effects of the boll weevil and declining cotton prices on his own and his neighbors' fortunes. On January 11, 1921, he gathered a group of neighboring landowners together to meet with a Clemson extension agent who tried to convince them that the climate and soils of the upstate were well suited for peach farming, a profitable crop for which there was a growing demand. Peach farming seemed a gamble to these men. Although peaches were grown commercially in neighboring Georgia, large-scale production of peaches was new to the upstate. A Greer farmer, J. Verne Smith, had planted a successful commercial orchard in 1898, but the men in the Gramling community feared this was an isolated success. Peach trees would not begin producing until their fourth year. The producers feared that they might take cropland out of production for four years in order to grow a commodity that might never prove profitable. Nonetheless, the boll weevil and falling cotton prices had taken their toll, so these farmers agreed to a cooperative arrangement in which they could share the labor and some of the risk.[37]

The cooperative agreement adopted by the Gramling men was similar to thousands of grower's associations formed by Southern truck farmers between 1880 and 1930. These arrangements not only allowed them to share labor and growing expertise, but also to cooperatively market their products and to regulate their production levels through mutual agreement. Most cooperatives were short-lived, but the efforts helped farmers overcome many of the obstacles to beginning successful truck farming. The Gramling farmers set aside varying amounts of acreage for their orchards—from 5 to 30 acres each. They worked together to plant their trees and all planted the Elberta variety. Each morning the men met at some central location, probably the Gramling Brothers' General Store, and shared their work plans for the day. They often assisted each other with pruning, spraying for pests, and picking. At harvest time, the peaches were picked and brought to the Gramling depot where they were placed on a boxcar and shipped to Spartanburg. Most were then shipped to wholesale produce markets in neighboring states. Extension service officials assisted the farmers with brokering the peaches—that is, finding buyers.[38]

The Gramling farmers' experiment was a success. They shipped their first four carloads of peaches in July 1924. Other farmers, such as Kline Cash's grandfather, took note of their success and began to plant orchards as well. Soon small farmers all over the upstate were planting peaches. The county's production of peaches for the market swelled from 133,758 bushels in 1929 to 963,967 bushels in 1939. Soon wholesale distributors were demanding fruit that was sorted in order to assure uniformity, so several growers built packing houses where they sorted their own fruit and that of neighboring growers. The Gramlings were probably the first to build a packing house. The family also branched out into other areas of the peach business, distributing and installing packing house equipment for other growers. Other local businesses emerged to make peach baskets and crates. By 1939 the county boasted 233 packing sheds of varying sizes clustered in the northern end of the county. They packed peaches from 872,000 bearing trees in 2,000 orchards, also clustered in northern communities. Success bred independence. By the end of the 1930s, the peach pioneers' cooperative efforts were tapering off as these farmers built their own packing houses and began to function as individual businessmen, hiring wage laborers for their peach harvest. In 1938 the peach industry employed 7,000 part-time workers in Spartanburg County.[39]

Peach Farm Wives

As the shift to dairy farming had done in Loudon County, the shift to commercial peach farming would bring gradual but significant changes in the roles of landowning farm wives. On the old cotton farms, the division of labor had resembled that found on East Tennessee's general farms. The wives of the most prosperous landowners assisted in decision making and engaged in small-scale production for the household and market. The wives of poor landowners and tenants combined these activities with frequent field work. Tenants considered it a badge of honor if their wives and daughters did not have to plow (the heaviest field work), but hoeing and picking cotton were tasks that exempted no tenant farming women, white or black, because of the huge investment of labor the cotton and corn crops required.[40]

Some wives were an integral part of the decision to gamble on peach farming. John Culbertson and his wife planted their first orchard in 1922 at the urging of the Spartanburg County extension agent and Ben Gramling. The boll weevil had taken most of their cotton crop in 1920 and 1921, and only the bank's agreement to let them pay the interest while delaying the principal on their mortgage had enabled them to hold onto his land. Culbertson explained to a WPA interviewer in 1939 that his wife had been a partner in the agonizing decision to plant 10 of his 30 acres in peaches: "At home I talked the situation over with Mary. It seems funny now, but it was a serious problem then. It meant giving up acres of land that I had been using for cotton, my money crop, for five or six years, with no return from the land and a lot of expenses in taking care of the trees. We discussed it for days."[41]

Not only did Mary Culbertson share in the decision to shift some of the family's cropland to peaches, but she subsidized the effort with her own production. She produced much of the family's food supply on the farm, shouldering responsibility for the family's garden and for milk and poultry products. She also sold surplus milk, butter, eggs, chickens, and garden produce on Saturdays in nearby Landrum or just across the border in Tryon, North Carolina. "That extra money helped out lots," John Culbertson reported. Presumably Mary also helped with picking and packing peaches.

The Culbertsons shipped their first peach crop in 1929 and found peaches profitable over the years. They purchased additional land and expanded their orchards. Thanks to their joint efforts, they were able to build a new farmhouse "with all the modern conveniences" in 1935, in spite of the Great Depression. They put two of their four children through college and one through law school. Of his wife's contribution, John Culbertson concluded, "Whatever I may be today, I owe any success that I have had to Mary."[42]

In addition to subsidizing the family with home and market production and assisting in decision making, landowners' wives often contributed to growing orchard operations by keeping the books or running other family enterprises. Kline Cash noted that his grandmother had run the small general store that his family owned in the Chesnee community, while his mother later kept the farm books for many years. Landowners' wives often picked peaches and supervised packing houses at harvest time.[43]

As in Loudon County, the ways that landowners' wives helped with the commercial peach operation were often determined by economic necessity and by personal preference. Vada Cash Sellers and her husband raised peaches for a few years in the 1930s. She recalled, "I remember one Fourth of July when we had our peach field . . . and I got on my long-sleeved shirt and went out and picked peaches all day. . . . I remember being so glad when we finished. I've never picked peaches again." Although she pitched in and helped with the crop when her labor was needed, she did not like the work. A few years later, possibly at Vada Sellars' urging, she and her husband gave up their orchards and built a mattress manufacturing plant. By contrast, Ruth Hatchette McBrayer loved the peach business. Before her marriage she had worked as a schoolteacher, but she took over the family orchard and packing house after her husband's early death. "This orchard became my life," she said. "I just absolutely lived it. . . . I worked all the time. I helped to prune in the wintertime. I worked with the men. Driving tractors if they were shorthanded." She noted that she had to learn the business, educating herself by reading and attending extension service lectures. She bought land and gradually expanded her operation which she ran until the late 1980s.[44]

Unlike in Loudon County, peach farming did not transform the mutual aid networks of Spartanburg County's farmers. Due to the high rate of tenancy in the area and the extreme poverty of tenants, mutual aid networks were already largely class-based. Landowners helped each other, as the names they list among their networks attest. A landowner helped his own tenants, but only rarely did he assist the tenant of another landowner. When tenants assisted a landowner, they did so in exchange for wages. It was not a system of mutual obligation.[45]

Peach farming accelerated the process of turning tenants and sharecroppers into wage laborers, as it had among dairying families in East Tennessee. In the 1930s, 40s, and 50s, as landowners expanded their orchards, they reduced their cotton acreage. Often they allowed tenants to remain in existing housing on the farm, paying them a weekly wage to assist with peach farming. Nonetheless, seasonal lulls in peach farming and the low pay made city jobs much more attractive. Many left the land, especially after World War II created better opportunities elsewhere. Some poorer rural women found seasonal work in picking and in packing houses, but like their men, they found more appealing work off the farm. By the 1960s, local peach growers began to experience shortages of local labor and turned to migrant work forces to harvest the peach crop.[46]

In the final analysis, most of the families who made the transition to modern commercial farming in the upcountry South were those who started out with material advantages: land and access to capital for investment in equipment and additional land. The development of commercial agriculture rigidified class lines and ultimately pushed most blacks out of the agricultural economy. The wives of commercial farmers embraced the material improvements wrought by the shift to dairy farming. They saw themselves as key players in the transition. For most families, turning to commercial farming was a means of gaining middle-class status, and they achieved this status through a variety of decisions about the allocation of family labor and cash resources. Farm women committed themselves to commercial farming as a means of enhancing life for their children and gaining status for themselves.

Yet the fruits of the transition were more ambiguous than they seemed at the time. Although the wives of part-time farmers sometimes continued to have a central place in farm production, wives of commercial farmers ultimately found that the recognition of their central role on the family farm was diminished. Most maintained some influence over decision making within the farm household even as that influence was discounted and rendered invisible in the larger farming community. The positing of mutual aid networks within the formal boundaries of middle-class farm organizations reduced women's roles in community decision making and also men's recognition of their roles. Formal organizations separated male and female work as well as separating the physical labor of farming from mental labor of farm management. The metamorphosis of mutual aid networks also served to hasten the exclusion of poor land-owners and tenant farmers from commercial farming. For many rural upcountry women, the coming of progress proved a bittersweet victory.

Eight

"The Land of Do Without"

The Changing Face of

Sevier County, Tennessee, 1908–1940

Sevier County, Tennessee, provides a lens through which to view the multiple causes of early twentieth-century change in one rural county and the residents' profound ambivalence about this change. Before the arrival of the lumber industry in the first two decades of the century, most of the citizens of mountainous Sevier County had lived largely independent and self-sufficient lives in isolated enclaves. The timber cutters brought the first round of change from the outside world. In their brief stay in the mountains, lumber companies changed the face of the mountains and encouraged many of the mountain people to become dependent on wage labor. By the late 1920s and early 1930s, the mountains were logged out, and the Depression was taking its toll on the timber industry. In those years the federal government brought a new wave of change with the creation of the Great Smoky Mountains National Park, a development that brought a new outside influence—tourists.

Like their neighbors in the lowland counties, upland Sevier County folks had mixed feelings about all these changes. While they welcomed many improvements that brought more comfortable lives, they mourned the passing of old values and old ways of living. Historians examining the lives of Southern Appalachian citizens during the early part of the century have focused on the region's economic history without examining the gender implications of these economic changes. Yet the transformations wrought by the arrival of the outside world had different effects on women than on men and provoked different responses from them. The work of men and women changed profoundly, and women found their old work marginalized as wage labor came to be defined as the "real work." Moreover, men and women embraced different types of changes. Although women welcomed the arrival of electricity, modern roads, and education for their children, they resisted total dependence on wage labor by maintaining many of their traditional subsistence activities whenever possible. By contrast, men seemed to welcome the transition to a cash economy even as they resisted moving out of old mountain cabins and watching their children choose other ways of living.

If Sevier County people's responses to change were molded by gender differences, they were also shaped by class factors. The creation of the National Park forced many mountain people off land owned by their families for generations. The most prosperous relocated families were often able to buy property in the county's new tourist centers and start thriving businesses, while poorer families were unable to afford land and were forced to take wage-earning jobs inside and outside Sevier County. Some chose to leave the mountains for economic opportunity in industrializing lowland counties or even outside the region. For the families who remained, class differences would become more pronounced, and the gap between the haves and the have nots would widen perceptibly. This growing economic gap left women at the bottom of the economic ladder with fewer options for coping and improving their lives than those at the top had.

A Mountain Society

Geography dictated that change would come later to Sevier County and other mountain areas than to the lowland communities. Situated high in the Great Smoky Mountains on the Tennessee–North Carolina border, Sevier County's first settlements sprang up in the 1780s in the fertile river bottoms and rolling hills of the northern third of the county. By the beginning of the nineteenth century, additional settlements appeared in the steeper and less fertile land drained by the French Broad and Little Pigeon Rivers and their tributaries. Settlers came last to the steep mountains in the southeastern portion of the county. One local observer called the river gorges settled by the earliest white pioneers "valley[s] of luxury and poverty"—luxurious in their natural beauty and peaceful solitude, poor in their difficult and isolated way of life.[1]

The mountain terrain created a difficult existence for most of its settlers. Those who obtained land in the northern part of the county built large farms that became balanced commercial and subsistence enterprises. Most people, however, lived on more marginal land, eking out a subsistence living with farming, hunting, and trapping. Yet even the mountaineers were not entirely independent of the market. Rising property taxes, mortgages, and other obligations required cash. Sevier County's farmers had long produced a few goods for the market, mostly by selling some livestock and farm products in Sevierville and Knoxville. In 1920, of the 3,450 farm operators in Sevier County, 71 percent were tenants farming an average of 80 acres each (see Table 8.1). Given that much of this land was not arable, most tenants were poor and were largely dependent on the goodwill of landowners. Nonetheless, the children of mountaineers did not remember life in Sevier County as being poverty-stricken. "We always had plenty to eat," one woman recalled. "Even during the depression years of the early 1930s, we fared just the same as before."[2]

Mountaineers accepted the only way of life they had ever known—a life rich in natural beauty if not in material things. In spite of the stereotype of the mean mountain cabin with its dirt yard, most photos show the porches of these cabins covered with flowering plants. Missionary John C. Campbell described them this way: "The yard is bare of grass, swept smooth and pretty like the palm of your hand, but there is bloom for the summer through—a snow-ball and a rosy bush, flowering quince and coral-berry." Mountain women devoted much time to their flowers, and family members were often photographed next to prized flowering bushes, belying the image of a bleak mountain existence.[3]

Perhaps mountaineers prized beautiful surroundings because they rarely left them. Scattered villages sprang up among clusters of farms along the Little Pigeon River, but town life was extremely limited. By 1920 Sevierville, the county seat, had fewer than one thousand inhabitants.

TABLE 8.1 Sevier County Agricultural Statistics

	1920	1930	1935	1940	1945
Number of Farms					
Total	3,450	2,931	3,079	3,422	3,148
White operators	3,410	3,916	3,058	3,387	3,064
Black operators	40	15	21	35	14
Number of owners	2,483	1,800	1,964	n/a	2,354
Tenancy rate	71%	61%	63%	n/a	75%
Average Farm Size (in acres)					
All farms	80	76.7	68.7	65	68.4
White operators	80	76.9	68.8	n/a	n/a
Black operators	44.1	46.8	43.4	n/a	n/a

Sources: Census of Agriculture, 1930, vol. 3, pt. 2, pp. 618–19, 870, 902; *Census of Agriculture, 1935,* vol. 1, pt. 2, p. 604; *Census of Agriculture, 1940,* vol. 2, pt. 2, p. 480; *Census of Agriculture, 1945,* vol. 1, pt. 20, pp. 34, 51, 132.
Where n/a is given, figures are not available in easily comparable form to other years.

Residents of the more isolated mountain enclaves visited the county seat only a few times a year. Moreover, poor roads and rough terrain made visits to urban centers like Knoxville very rare. Men usually made one or two trips to Knoxville each year to sell produce, but grown women rarely ventured beyond the mountains. In mountain ideology, women belonged at home caring for the family. In 1935 a mountain woman told a *National Geographic* writer that she was twenty-eight years old before she ever visited Knoxville and that it took her over a week to make the round trip. Given the isolation of mountain life, much of daily survival depended on good relationships with one's family and neighbors. Neighborliness was valued above all else. As in other rural communities, elaborate informal mutual aid networks organized by local women provided support for families in times of crisis as well as social opportunities during good times. In this closed world, outsiders were often perceived as a potential threat to be evaluated carefully before they were trusted.[4]

Paradoxically, in spite of mountain folks' mistrust of outsiders, they were a generous people. Horace Kephart, a librarian who went to live in the Great Smokies in the early part of this century, wrote *Our Southern*

Highlanders (1913), arguably the most famous account of mountain life. Kephart called the mountains "the land of do without" and marveled that these poor people readily shared their limited resources with anyone who seemed to need them. He found that he was always greeted politely and given food and shelter wherever he went. Mountain etiquette demanded that no traveler be denied hospitality even if he was greeted with suspicion and caution.[5]

The mountaineers' deep distrust of outsiders was due not only to their isolation but also to their confrontations with federal revenue officers. Often mountaineers found it more profitable to turn their corn crops into moonshine whisky, a product easier to transport than grain and much in demand even before the days of Prohibition. As one mountaineer explained to Kephart, "Corn juice is about all we can tote around over the country and get cash money for. Why, man, that's the only way some folks has o' payin' their taxes." This fact gave rise to a thriving trade in illegal alcohol, which the locals called "blockading" (as in blockade-running), and led to many conflicts with federal revenue agents who came to collect the excise tax on whisky. Shook's Gap, a mountain pass through which the road to Knoxville passed, became notorious for gun battles between revenue officers who had blocked the roads and mountaineers transporting moonshine to city customers. As one contemporary journalist noted, the mountaineer came to view "the Government representative, no matter to what branch he belongs, [as] merely a 'feller that'll git ye inter trouble.'"[6]

Isolation and opposition to moonshining were the primary reasons Sevier County people distrusted outsiders, but they were not the only reasons. The extreme homogeneity of the county's citizens left them with little prolonged exposure to people who were different. Most Sevier County folks were direct descendants of the original white Scots-Irish settlers. In fact, the 1930 census recorded only five foreign-born people among county residents. Moreover, the county's population was more than 98 percent white. Most of the original Cherokee residents had been forced out of the mountains by President Andrew Jackson's troops in the mid-nineteenth century Indian removal known as the "Trail of Tears." Many of the Native Americans who had remained moved to North Carolina in the late nineteenth century when the government established a reservation there. By 1910 only forty-five Cherokees were left in Sevier County.[7]

Like the Native American population, blacks made up a minuscule proportion of Sevier County's citizens. Only 318 blacks lived in Sevier County in 1920, a number that declined steadily through the 1950s, while the white population remained stable. Of the 77 blacks who lived on farms in 1930, 60 percent eked out a subsistence living on the small parcels of land they owned. Most of the county's blacks worked in domestic jobs and day labor in Sevierville. A few even worked side by side with whites doing the lowest level jobs on lumber crews. Yet their small numbers left them isolated in the tight-knit world that was Sevier County.[8]

The departure of most Native Americans and blacks and the lack of in-migration created the ethnic homogeneity of the county. For Sevier County people, to be a mountaineer *was* to be white. Nonmountaineers, including nonwhites who resided locally, were sometimes regarded with mistrust or at the least with ambivalence. Historian John C. Inscoe has noted that much of the famed Appalachian antislavery sentiment was actually class hostility toward slaveholders. Many mountaineers avoided contact with blacks whenever possible, identifying African Americans with slavery, a submission to authority that no mountaineer could fathom. Kephart described it this way: "[The mountaineer's] dislike of negroes is simply an instinctive racial antipathy plus a contempt for anyone who submits to servile conditions. A neighbor in the Smokies said to me: 'I b'lieve in treatin' niggers squar'. The Bible says they're human—leastways some says it does—an' so there'd orter be a place for them. But it's someplace else—not around me!'"[9]

For the most part, however, this antipathy manifested itself in segregated schools and communities rather than in violence. The minuscule black population, itself created by out-migration due to the lack of opportunities for blacks, meant that blacks and whites were rarely confrontational. One study found no racial violence reported in the county during the first thirty years of the twentieth century. It is not clear whether any unreported violence took place, but it seems doubtful. At best, whites tolerated the blacks in their midst; at worst they discriminated against them and otherwise ignored them.[10]

Just as Sevier County residents were ethnically homogeneous, class differences were also less pronounced before the arrival of wage labor. This is not to say that there was no local elite, however. There was a resident ruling class of large landowners and lawyers from Sevierville that dominated local politics and the economy. There were also differences in the material wealth of citizens, of course. Large landholders fared better than small landowners or the landless. A few Sevier County residents, such as Gladys Russell's father, were skilled craftsmen, and they also earned a little more than their neighbors. Yet there was less sense of opposing class interests than there would be after outside capitalists arrived. Even families with money could not live materially much better than their neighbors, because the isolation of the county made it difficult to import consumer goods or to travel out of the mountains. As one woman recalled, "You know, we all grew up together like that. One person didn't have more than the other. You didn't feel better than somebody else. And, in fact, everybody was in the same boat." This perception of relative class equality led to tightly knit mutual support networks that included most white citizens regardless of means. Elites may have been motivated to help their poorer neighbors by paternalism, but there was little hostility between the classes.[11]

Partisan politics also did not divide Sevier County folks very much. Although elections might be hotly contested, they were contested within the Republican Party, not between parties, and after balloting was complete, voters usually rallied behind the elected Republican until the next election. Sevier County was even more solidly Republican than most of East Tennessee; there were only three registered Democrats in the entire county in the early 1930s. Legend has it that as a motivational tool one lumber boss promised, "You boys work hard all week, and we'll go to Sevierville Saturday and see a Democrat."[12]

Before the arrival of lumber companies in the late nineteenth century, Sevier County residents had maintained a largely barter economy based in mutual aid networks. They raised most of their own food and traded labor and supplies with neighbors. On the mountain slopes, farmers commonly ranged hogs and cattle that were driven overland to Knoxville for sale. Livestock and livestock products formed the largest sources of the county's agricultural income because poor roads and the lack of railroads limited the transport of cash crops. Usually farmers also took apples from the home orchard and a few other products to Sevierville or Knoxville once a year (see Table 8.2). Even after the arrival of the lumber companies, many families maintained subsistence farms and earned cash from a combination of sources. Gladys Trentham Russell's family made a

TABLE 8.2 Sources of Income: Sevier County Farms

	1920	1930	1940	1945
Crops	n/a	$419,686	$438,519	$1,100,000
Livestock and livestock products	n/a	$888,544	$624,444	$1,200,000
Forest products	n/a	$78,893	$25,187	$26,883

Sources: Census of Agriculture, 1930, vol. 3, pt. 2, pp. 618–19, 870, 902; Census of Agriculture, 1935, vol. 1, pt. 2, p. 604; Census of Agriculture, 1940, vol. 2, pt. 2, p. 480; Census of Agriculture, 1945, vol. 1, pt. 20, pp. 34, 51, 132.
Where n/a is given, figures are not available in easily comparable form to other years.

living in a variety of ways in the 1920s. Her father sold corn, timber, and tanning bark; shod mules and horses; did surveying; repaired wagon and buggy wheels; and operated a gristmill; while her mother raised a garden, sold chickens and eggs, and practiced midwifery.[13]

As the lives of the Trentham family suggest, the gender division of labor on mountain farms was similar to that on other rural upcountry small holdings. Men did the heavy fieldwork as well as the hunting and trapping; while women cared for the garden and house, preserved the family food supply, and made the family wardrobe. Horace Kephart described the mountain family as "patriarchal," noting that "about family matters, [the mountain man] consults with his wife, but in the end, his word is law." Gender relations in the mountains were more overtly patriarchal than in many of the upcountry's counties. At mealtimes, women in some families stood at the table and served the men, eating only after the men were finished, a concrete symbol of women's subservient status. Yet Kephart's reading of gender relations was influenced in part by social practice, which dictated that mountain men interact with strangers while women hovered in the background. In reality, women did exercise considerable influence over family decision making behind the scenes. Children of mountaineers often recalled that their mothers "made" their fathers choose a particular course of action, indicating more shared power than Kephart's observations suggested.[14]

Not only were family power relations dynamic, but the gender division of labor also seemed to be flexible in some families. Women sometimes took on men's work. Since providing for the family's subsistence was a major component of mountain women's work role, women's moves into traditionally male spheres of activity could be justified on these grounds. Mary Brackin Whaley, born in 1889, recalled that she liked to farm and hunt alongside her husband. "I put as much meat on the table as he did," she boasted. "I'd go up one hollow with a rifle and he'd go up another, and I'd come back with as many squirrels as he would." Through farming and hunting, Whaley contributed to the family's subsistence, making her participation in traditionally masculine activities tolerable, if peculiar, in the eyes of her community.[15]

Flexible gender roles or no, life for mountain women was filled with hard work. Contemporary visitors noted that the women were often very pretty in their youth; but they aged quickly due to hard work, early marriage, frequent childbearing, and poor diet and hygiene—an observation borne out by photographs. Kephart noted that mountain women were often stoop-shouldered by the age of thirty-five due to the hours spent bent over a fireplace to cook. (Mountain families rarely had cookstoves because of the difficulty of transporting them from town.) Women frequently married at fourteen or fifteen, and they commonly had between seven and ten children. John C. Campbell observed that marriage provided the only viable means of support for most mountain women. Few had enough education to be school teachers, and in any event, teaching did not pay enough. Women couldn't earn a living bartering garden and livestock products unless they had access to land, something they gained only if they were widowed or, more rarely, they inherited property. Most of the county's farmers were tenants, and landowners would not choose childless women as tenants. Furthermore, Sevier County boasted little wage work, and few of those jobs would have been open to women. Thus marriage seemed a far brighter option than the marginal dependency of being single. As Campbell put it, "There is little comfort for the spinster relegated to the hard tasks of life yet dependent for support upon her male and her married women kindred, all of whom are agreed in thinking her a failure." To an even greater extent than in lowland counties, marriage was a given for mountain women.[16]

When the lumber companies arrived in Sevier County in the early twentieth century, the mountain woman was living a life very much like that of her grandmother. Her days were dominated by hard work, and she spent almost all her time with family and neighbors. Exposure to new people and new ideas was rare indeed. But all that was about to change.

The Lumber Companies

By 1920 when the agricultural depression commenced, Sevier County had a population of 22,384. The Census Bureau classified the entire population as rural and found that more than 75 percent of citizens lived on farms. The rural character of the county was apparent in the local papers, where farm news and advertisements for agricultural products dominated the pages. Sevierville, the only incorporated town at that time, served as the trading center for the whole county. Although farming and small-scale logging dominated the economy, the county also boasted some lumber-related industries, such as sawmills, a planing mill, and furniture factories, as well as a seasonally operated vegetable canning plant and a hosiery mill. Sevier County was connected to Knoxville by the Tennessee and North Carolina Railway (formerly the Knoxville, Sevierville and Eastern), which carried passengers and freight into town once a day.[17]

The logging industry brought the first round of sweeping change into this rural setting. Although private companies and local landholders had done small-scale logging in the late nineteenth and early twentieth centuries, the first major logging operation was established in 1908 by Little River Lumber Company, which grew out of Knoxville lawyer and businessman John English's 1890s timber acquisitions in the mountains of Blount and Sevier counties. English's loggers cut virgin timber along the mountain rivers and floated batches of logs downstream twenty miles to his Rockford sawmill in a process known as a "river drive." An 1899 flood destroyed much of the infrastructure of English's operation, prompting him to sell his mountain landholdings to a Pennsylvania-born businessman, W. B. Townsend, in 1901. Townsend called his company Little River Lumber Company, and he quickly turned it into a very profitable business. Rather than depend on the unpredictable river to transport his logs, Townsend constructed railroads to haul the lumber out of the mountains. After first logging on the Blount County side of the mountains, Little River Lumber Company built a railroad from Sevierville up the Middle Prong of the Little Pigeon River to Elkmont in Sevier County in 1908. Here in this mountain valley, the company constructed a logging settlement that included a commissary, a boarding house known as the "Hotel Elkmont," machine shops, and small houses for supervisors and skilled workers. Shortly thereafter, Little River Lumber Company would be joined by Champion Paper Company, which acquired land in Sevier County's Greenbrier Cove. Lumbering had arrived in earnest.[18]

Logging quickly took its toll on the beauty of the mountains. Not only were thousands of acres of primeval forest denuded by clear-cutting, but the rivers were damaged by the floating of logs to railroad points. Logs were also moved to the railroad tracks with skidders, large machines that "skidded" the logs down the mountains. This process created erosion, which in turn caused further damage to streams and rivers. Trains and other equipment sometimes started devastating fires. A 1917 fire at the Higdon Creek area of Sevier County temporarily put hundreds of loggers out of work and destroyed hundreds of acres of timber.[19]

In spite of the environmental damage caused by logging, Sevier County residents welcomed the timber industry. For white (and a few black) mountain folk, logging provided their first opportunity to enjoy the benefits of wage labor. Loggers earned 65 to 90 cents per day plus lodging and meals in a crude bunkhouse or, in more established camps, family housing. This was more money than many had earned in a month, much less a day, and the paychecks proved seductive. For the first time, families had access to consumer goods, carried by log trains to the company store, as well as money with which to buy them. Many mountain men eagerly sought logging jobs. Throughout the 1920s, between 20 and 30 percent of Sevier County's men were employed in logging at least part of the year.[20]

In addition to enjoying a better standard of living due to men's logging jobs, many women found ways to make money from the new industry, usually by taking advantage of seasonal earning opportunities that required little capital and could be combined with child care and housekeeping duties. The most common strategy adopted by mountain women was running boardinghouses. Logging settlements were often several miles over narrow mountain tracks from the nearest villages, necessitating that workers live on site. Laverne Massey recalled that in 1921, Little River Lumber Company paid her $100 a week to feed eighteen workers who lived in company-owned barracks at the Hood Siding Lumber Camp. Although she had to buy her supplies and pay her kitchen help out of this, she managed to clear $50 most weeks. Together with her husband's salary as a log train engineer, the Masseys netted $75 to $100 a week, a huge amount of money for rural Sevier County residents. Although most other women who kept boarders did so on a much smaller scale and earned less than Massey, for a time the arrival of the lumber company made it possible for them to earn more money than they had dreamed was possible.[21]

In spite of the economic opportunities, life in the lumber camps brought adjustments, particularly for women. A look at the experiences of one family is instructive in understanding the new hardships and complexities that lumbering brought to women's lives, particularly the wide generational gap in women's experiences. Delilah Woodruff and her daughter, Dorie Cope, had vastly different experiences. For Woodruff and her husband, logging provided a means for securing their future. They used his earnings from lumbering and hers from boarding lumber camp workers to pay off the mortgage on their Sevier County farm in the 1920s. Although Woodruff and her children often joined him in the lumber camps, the farm provided the family with a place to go during periodic layoffs. Moreover, owning a farm provided a means of avoiding complete dependence on wage labor for a living. Woodruff and her family were able to raise most of their own food as well as earn some cash through commercial farming efforts during the lean periods in the lumber industry.[22]

Things were more complicated for Dorie Cope and her younger peers. Like many young mountain men of his generation, Cope's husband entered logging instead of attempting to establish his own farm. When he married, he brought Dorie to live with him in a company house at the lumber camp. Here the couple started a family. They spent much of their time living at temporary logging camps deep in the mountains. In many of these camps, houses were no more than boxes set off flatcars by the side of the railroad tracks, facilitating easy moving of the camp when the area was logged out.

For Cope and other young women, the task of feeding a family became more difficult in the remote camps. There was little space for gardens on the steep mountain slopes and only infrequent passenger service into the larger lumber camps for grocery shopping. They could not range livestock in the path of loggers, and men working in the logging operation had little time to augment the family diet with hunting. Unlike her parents, Dorie Cope and her husband did not have a farm of their own with which to supplement their lumber camp earnings. Gradually young mountain families like the Copes produced less of their own food, making them more dependent on logging wages. In this sense, the very structure that was creating earning opportunities for some women was also making families dependent on these opportunities.[23]

Young couples like the Copes soon learned that lumbering was a fickle way to make a living. In spite of the fantastic earnings reported by Laverne Massey and her husband, most workers did not fare so well. Lumbering was a seasonal industry that provided six months of employment at best. A USDA study found that in 1934 timber workers' average annual income was only $240. The seasonal nature of logging and the uncertain wages made life particularly difficult for women trying to maintain some semblance of family stability in the face of these changes. Like many women without their own farms, Dorie Cope moved her family back and forth between the lumber camp and her parents' farm numerous times during the 1920s and 1930s because various logging operations shut down, leaving her husband temporarily unemployed.[24]

This process of moving back in with the older generation put stresses on both families and the land. Young families often crowded back onto farms owned by parents who sometimes were still raising younger children. When the Copes moved back to live with the Woodruffs, Delilah Woodruff still had elementary-school-age children at home. This overcrowding was bound to create tensions, especially between adult women struggling to realign their own familial roles. Much of the burden for getting the family through the transition fell on Dorie Cope and her mother. Both women were faced with burden of integrating two households in one small house and adjusting personal work routines to incorporate all the additional family members. Many tiny small holdings were hard-pressed to support so many people, forcing some young families to leave the mountains temporarily or permanently in search of work. In 1921, after being unemployed by the Higdon Creek fire and finding it too hard to eke out a living on her parents' farm, Dorie Cope's husband moved the family to Gastonia, North Carolina, where he found work as a supervisor in the Cramerton Textile Mills.

Outside the mountains, the Copes briefly tasted prosperity. Here Cope earned $8.50 per day, a small fortune even compared to his excellent wages as a logging supervisor. In spite of the disruption of moving and the pain of being far from her natal family, Dorie Cope delighted in her mill town house, which came complete with electricity and running water, unheard of luxuries in the mountains. Yet this too proved to be an unstable opportunity. In 1922 the mill closed in the wake of the postwar downturn in the textile industry, sending the Copes back over the mountains to her parents' farm in Sevier County until a lumbering job was available again.

Life in Sevier County had changed irreversibly with the arrival of the lumber companies. Not only did young rural families become dependent on wage labor, leaving them vulnerable to fluctuations in the economy, but life in the lumber camps also awakened them to the larger world, changing their expectations and altering their hopes and dreams. As Dorie Cope put it, after Little River Lumber Company closed, "The isolation of the farm bothered me. There were days when we didn't see anybody but the mailman. . . . The lumber companies had opened the door to the outside world. We became aware of 'things'—things that money could buy, things that made life easier (or harder), things to see, things to do. Our isolation had ended." More than any other force, the timber industry had exposed Sevier County folks to the wider world. Now nothing would be the same.[25]

The National Park and the Development of Tourism

The 1930s brought a new series of changes to Sevier County. The Depression hit the lumber industry hard, making the timber companies receptive to the federal government's efforts to buy their mountain holdings for a national park. The sale of land and the establishment of the park brought a new wave of government intervention to mountaineers who already distrusted the government. It also brought a new industry—tourism—which wrought drastic changes in Sevier County. Tourism, with its low-wage and low-skill jobs, particularly for women, proved to be almost as exploitive as the lumber companies.

Tourism preceded the arrival of the Great Smoky Mountains National Park by decades. Several springs and spas, popular for health reasons, operated in Sevier County between 1870 and 1935. Hunting aficionados had also long known the beauty of the Great Smokies. In the early years of the century, avid hunters began weekend expeditions to the mountains, and a handful of lodging facilities sprang up to serve them.[26]

Sevier County's fledgling tourist industry received a shot in the arm with the construction of a few auto roads and railroads in the first decade of the twentieth century. The Little River Lumber Company operated a scenic excursion train to Elkmont on summer Sundays. Trains were filled to capacity with Knoxville's middle-class families, who traveled to the mountains to enjoy the scenery. Their destination was usually lunch at the Wonderland Hotel, a tourist attraction near the Elkmont lumber camp noted for its delicious country-style meals. The Wonderland Hotel with its fifty rooms and the adjacent Appalachian Club also catered to Knoxville people looking for longer stays. Tourists relaxed on the porch of the big frame hotel, reading or chatting with other guests, or hiked scenic trails and swam in icy mountain streams. Visitors frequently approached landowners around Elkmont about the possibility of buying small plots of land in order to build "cabins" for vacation use. As a result, a summer mini-resort grew up around Elkmont in the 1910s and 1920s, seasonally reducing the isolation of some mountain communities.[27]

Mountain scenery was not the only attraction that drew tourists. The *WPA Guide to Tennessee*, written by Federal Writers' Project workers in the late 1930s, noted that "[m]any of the early visitors came to find the products of the handicraft revival." Settlement workers and missionaries had initiated Sevier County's handicraft revival beginning in the 1910s. As the media and local color writers brought mountain folk into popular culture in the late nineteenth and early twentieth centuries, missionaries and settlement workers became aware of the tremendous levels of poverty in the Southern Appalachians and turned their attention to solving these problems. One of the first settlement houses in Sevier County was sponsored by Pi Beta Phi, a service organization for college women and alumnae. In 1912 a small group of Pi Beta Phi members, mostly northern middle-class college graduates, arrived in the tiny village of Gatlinburg to open a school and settlement house. At the time, Gatlinburg consisted of six houses, three general stores, a blacksmith shop, a Baptist church, and the abandoned building that became the first schoolhouse. About two hundred families who lived in the surrounding mountain coves formed the community the settlement workers hoped to reach.[28]

The settlement workers at Pi Beta Phi tried to meet some of families' material needs as a way of gaining acceptance. Discerning that a steady income was the greatest need of most families, the settlement workers sought ways to help mountain folk earn money. In addition, workers hoped to revive old handicraft traditions being lost with the arrival of mass-produced goods. Although they planned to offer some handicraft instruction to mountain men, the settlement workers believed that men would spend most of their time in farming and possibly logging, while women would have more free time to engage in craft work. In 1916 Pi Beta Phi established a handicraft workshop at the school where school-girls and interested mountain women were taught to weave cloth and make baskets. In the words of Allen Eaton, a northerner sent by the philanthropic Russell Sage Foundation to look over the operation, the women of Pi Beta Phi "strove to develop initiative and independence among the mountain people and to foster home industries which might become a means of livelihood."[29]

Always distrustful of outsiders, mountain women were at first reluc-tant to participate in handicraft programs, so Pi Beta Phi workers visited with community people and gradually convinced some of them to par-ticipate in the workshops. They also persuaded older mountain women to teach both Pi Beta Phi crafts teachers and local female students the old handicrafts. Spinning had not been done in the area for nearly thirty-five years when the settlement workers decided to have local people spin their own yarn for use in weaving. One of the women they enlisted in the project became legendary, both for her for her weaving, spinning, and teaching at Pi Beta Phi and for her extraordinary personal saga. Aunt "Liddy" (Lydia) Whaley had raised her children on a rough mountain farm alone after the death of her husband in the Civil War. Aunt Liddy cultivated her crops, sewed coats by hand in order to earn cash to pay her land taxes, and became well known for her beautiful hand-woven cloth. She raised and sheared the sheep; washed, carded, and spun the wool; and wove the cloth. She also made beautiful baskets. In her old age, the settlement house teachers convinced Aunt Liddy to share her skills with her neighbors. She taught spinning and weaving to dozens of women and girls before her death in 1926 at the age of 86.[30]

Settlement workers did not stop at teaching mountain people to make crafts. They also found buyers. Crafts were marketed in cities by local Pi Beta Phi chapters and later through the cooperative efforts of the

FIG. 13. Many Sevier County, Tennessee, farm women supplemented their incomes by making handicrafts that were marketed by the Pi Beta Phi Settlement School in Gatlinburg. Aunt Lizzie Reagan, a 75-year-old widow who lived near the school, taught weaving there in 1933. (Lewis W. Hine Photograph, NWDNS-142-H-145. Courtesy of Still Picture Branch, National Archives at College Park.)

Southern Highland Handicraft Guild. The Pi Beta Phi workers also designated one building in their growing complex as a gift shop called the Arrowmont Gallery. This small gallery served Gatlinburg's embryonic tourist trade. As Appalachian handicrafts found an audience among collectors all over the country, the demand for products grew, helped along by such nationwide publicity as an exhibition of Appalachian crafts at the Corcoran Gallery of Art in New York City in 1933.[31]

Over the years the potential for income drew more and more women to the handicraft program, particularly as the agricultural depression of the 1920s worsened. Many women saw the handicrafts as an appealing alternative to the hard physical labor of farming. One local historian recounts the story of a mountain woman who appeared with her daughter at the Arrowmont shop on a cold winter morning, having walked five miles from their home. She told the workers:

> I've worked hard all my life. I started to hoe corn and 'taters when I was a little 'un and I been hoein' ever since. I've had nine chillun, seven are livin' and two air dead. I've lived in the same holler twenty year— sometimes I think I'd like a sight to change. When I heerd of this weavin' I thought I'd quit workin' in the field and let the young 'uns do hit. I'm forty-four year old and I'm tired, so I aim to work inside now.

The account does not tell us whether this woman had a husband to share the burden of making a living farming, but her comments suggest that she did not. Whatever the case, her motivation is clear: she is simply tired of the exhausting physical labor involved in farming, of the hours of backbreaking work and the exposure to the elements. For her, weaving was an opportunity to make a living in an easier way.[32]

In spite of the hopes of settlement workers and mountaineers, the return from crafts work proved disappointing. The writers of the *WPA Guide to Tennessee* noted that a government survey found the results of the crafts movement disappointing for several reasons. First, because mountain crafts workers worked for middlemen who supplied raw materials and marketed their products, they were not allowed much artistic freedom to experiment with new designs. Second, said the investigators, "The market for primitive handicrafts is limited; the average customer cannot, or will not, pay much more for goods produced by long hours of handwork than he pays for a machine-made imitation. The average income of the Appalachian handicraft producers is $52 a year."[33]

Although there is no doubt that handicraft work never provided mountain women with the earning potential of other types of jobs, the women themselves were never so critical of the handicrafts movement. Unlike the Pi Beta Phi workers, they did not see handicrafts as a key to cultural revival; rather, they saw it as another means to financial survival. They did take pride in the aesthetic side of their work, enjoying making "pretty things," but their primary concern was with the income they derived from handicrafts. Again and again they recounted how they and their relatives had supplemented the family income in important ways through work for the Arrowmont Gallery or by working on their own.

For the mountain women, handicrafts provided a way to earn an income without leaving Sevier County and work that was flexible enough to accommodate housekeeping, gardening, and child care. Dorie Cope's sister hooked rugs for one tourist shop, while a cousin wove placemats for the Arrowmont Gallery for over fifty years. Cora Owenby Morton began weaving for Pi Beta Phi in 1926 at the age of twenty-three. She wove towels, placemats, and coverlets for them for forty-seven years in between the demands of raising seven children. Other women made and sold their handicrafts independently of the Pi Beta Phi Settlement and a Methodist settlement house in the nearby village of Pittman Center. Gladys Russell's grandmother twined cornshucks into seats for the ladderback chairs produced at O. J. Mattil's Woodcarving Shop.[34]

In the 1920s tourists began to discover the beauty of the Appalachian crafts being produced at Pi Beta Phi's workshop and by other regional craftspeople, sparking the development of tourist amenities in Gatlinburg. Several new hotels and crafts shops joined Pi Beta Phi's Arrowmont Gallery in serving the tourist trade in and around the village in the 1920s and 1930s. The names of the owners of these shops and lodgings read like a who's who of Gatlinburg's largest landowners: Ogle's Broom Shop, where Hattie Ogle sold brooms her husband made; Josie Maples's and Allie Ownby's gift shops; and Reagan's Woodworking. The largest hotel, Mountain View Lodge, was run by Andy Huff, a wealthy lumber company owner. These shops sold crafts produced by the shop owners as well as the products of neighbors made on consignment.[35]

The early tourist trade brought the beautiful Smokies to the attention of Tennesseans and others who feared that logging was going to destroy the beauty of the area. As far back as the 1880s, naturalists had been promoting plans for a national preserve of some type in the mountains on the Tennessee–North Carolina border. In 1900 interested citizens formed the Appalachian National Park Association, which immediately began to lobby the U.S. Congress for the purchase of a park in the area. Tennessee and North Carolina senators and representatives were avid spokesmen for the project, but general congressional support built slowly. Meanwhile, books by regionalists, such as Horace Kephart's *Our Southern Highlanders* and Margaret Morley's *The Carolina Mountains*, both appearing in 1913, kindled interest in a national park among people well beyond the Appalachians. Following another twelve years of persistent lobbying, in 1925 Congress authorized the Department of the Interior to determine the boundaries of a national park in the Smokies. The legislation did not, however, provide funds for purchase.[36]

Unlike the national parks in the American West, which were mostly carved out of existing government landholdings, virtually all of the land in the Smokies was in the hands of private owners. This fact made establishing the park an expensive proposition, particularly since 85 percent of the 6,600 acres designated for the park was in the hands of lumber and pulpwood companies, which were reluctant to lose their lucrative landholdings. Yet supporters were not discouraged by the daunting task of raising funds to acquire parklands. After the congressional authorization, grass-roots support for the park movement swelled into a fundraising effort. Knoxville school children collected $1,391.72 in pennies, nickels, and dimes. The States of Tennessee and North Carolina issued bonds to fund a total of $4 million in land purchases, and conservation groups subscribed close to $1 million more. By 1927 more than $5 million had been raised for the purchase of parklands, but supporters still only had half of the money needed to establish a park.

At this point, John D. Rockefeller Jr. came to the rescue. Conservationists approached the wealthy oil heir and philanthropist about the project, bringing him to visit the Smokies. Impressed by the beauty of the area and the commitment of Tennessee and North Carolina conservationists, Rockefeller followed the precedent he had set in Maine with Acadia National Park and pledged an additional $5 million for land purchases. The money was to come from the Laura Spelman Rockefeller Memorial Fund, which honored his late mother. With all the money pledged, the Department of the Interior set about surveying boundaries and buying up property.

In contrast to North Carolina, where most of the vast tracts owned by corporations were located, land in Tennessee was in the hands of 6,200 separate property owners. This land included over one thousand small farms and five thousand summer homes and lots. One thousand tiny parcels, clustered around Sevier County's Elkmont, totaled only 52 acres. The state of Tennessee's appropriation bill for land purchases included a provision for the creation of a seven-member property acquisition commission for the Tennessee side of the park. The Tennessee Great Smoky Mountains Park Commission, made up primarily of conservation-minded businessmen from Knoxville and Nashville, had power to take land by condemnation. In other words, when landowners resisted sale of their lands or balked at accepting the commission's price, the commission could initiate condemnation proceedings. The court would then set a price that was almost always lower than the landowner believed was fair. With the help of mountain guides and temporary surveyors, the commission completed the massive purchasing project in the late 1920s and early 1930s.[37]

Reaction to the establishment of the national park was mixed in Sevier County. One-third of the county's land was within the park boundaries. In spite of their general mistrust of federal intervention, the Great Depression and the closing of the lumber camps made many citizens welcome the economic opportunities the park would bring as well as the cash from the sale of their farms. A few county leaders complained that they would rather have better roads to North Carolina than a national park. The governor responded by pledging state funds for the construction of a road from Gatlinburg to the North Carolina border at Newfound Gap, a highway completed in 1929. Still, some were angered and resisted selling through court action. Only those with means and connections were able to resist with any effectiveness. The landowners at Elkmont, most of whom were middle-class Knoxville residents, succeeded in getting Elkmont excluded from the area in which the Great Smoky Mountain Park Commission had the right to take land by condemnation. This enabled the owners of summer homes to hold out for higher prices than most farmer-landowners. Similarly, W. O. Whittle, the owner of the 660-acre Cherokee Orchard tract near Gatlinburg (a profitable apple orchard) used his statewide political connections and a savvy public relations initiative to avoid selling until 1938. In neighboring Blount County, wealthy landowner John W. Oliver challenged the U.S. Park Service in court and ultimately lost. The Champion Fibre Company's challenge to the condemnation of its land made the front page of the *Sevier County Republican and Record*. Champion indicated that it was happy to sell the tract provided the price gave it the fair value of the uncut timber on the property. A jury awarded the company $2.35 million, a figure within a few thousand dollars of its asking price.[38]

Although those with means resisted through legal channels and many mountaineers drove hard bargains for their land, violent resistance was apparently rare to nonexistent. In the end, the sense that they had no choice and the appeal of cash from the sales ultimately won out over many mountaineers' strong attachments to their home places. Gladys Trentham Russell recalled, "Most folks were happy with the prospects of selling their rocky fields and hillsides for more money than they estimated it to be worth, but some felt they didn't want to be driven from their old homeplaces at any price." Many of these holdouts were appeased in 1932 when Congress granted them the right to sell at a reduced price and retain lifetime leases to their mountain farms. Some mountaineers were crafty bargainers. One land buyer was told by an elderly landowner's adult sons that their parents might not survive the shock of leaving the family home place. The land buyer relented, giving them a fair sale price *and* a lifetime lease for the parents. A few weeks later, the land buyer passed by and was shocked to see the young sons and their wives and children moving. He confronted the young men, who admitted they had used the elderly status of the parents as a bargaining chip to gain the lease for their parents and money for themselves to buy better land outside the park. Many landowners commented that a lack of resistance brought them a more favorable deal for the sale of their land. By 1934 all the land that had been purchased was turned over to the Department of the Interior to manage.[39]

Like the lumber companies, the national park brought new economic opportunities to the people of Sevier County. Not only did the publicity about the new park immediately increase tourist traffic, but mountain men also found jobs working for both the state and the U.S. Park Service. They guided surveyors and occasionally worked as surveyors themselves. They worked on roadbuilding projects and constructed hiking trails, campgrounds, and picnic grounds. Mountain women supplemented their incomes by boarding construction and surveying teams. The county's remaining farmers also found expanded markets for their products among tourists eager to buy farm-fresh produce and mountain honey, temporarily creating a revival of interest in farming among those families who remained on the land and altering the character of the county's agricultural base by shifting their emphasis from corn to livestock and truck crops.[40]

At the height of the Depression, the federal government combined the development needs of the Great Smoky Mountains National Park with the economic needs of the people, establishing several public works programs in the park. Unfortunately, as was the case with New Deal programs elsewhere, most of these programs gave jobs to men on the assumption that men had families to support, whereas women were being supported. For jobless local men, the Works Progress Administration (WPA) provided jobs building roads throughout the national park. Young men stationed at Civilian Conservation Corps (CCC) camps throughout the park built bridges, fire watch towers, and hiking trails; reforested logged-out areas; and constructed additional picnic areas. One of the most enduring contributions of the CCC was the construction of 113 kilometers of the Appalachian Trail in the Smokies. These camps provided jobs for local boys as well as for young men from all over East Tennessee. Many of the young outsiders working at the CCC camps met and married local girls and took them to live outside the mountains, providing them with opportunities for a very different life than they might have had before the Depression.[41]

The only Sevier County New Deal program that employed significant numbers of women was a National Youth Administration program that hired young mountain women to do clerical work at park headquarters. For the women who participated, this experience provided clerical training that was later marketable locally in the tourist industry and outside the mountains in dozens of types of businesses.[42]

The national park brought more than economic opportunity to the people of Sevier County. As had been the case with lumber bosses and settlement workers, contact with increasing numbers of tourists brought news of the world beyond the mountains, news that caused many young people to aspire to a different kind of life than their parents had lived. Gladys Trentham Russell, a young woman inspired by the settlement workers to obtain a college education, vividly recalled a wooden trinket box given to her grandmother by a Knoxville woman who visited the Elkmont area year after year. The lady brought the box from Jerusalem, and young Gladys remembered that the object fired her own imagination about faraway places that she longed to see someday. These contacts were important in changing the expectations of mountain youth, especially mountain girls, who often met outside women who had seen and done things once unimaginable.[43]

Although it was not dedicated until 1940, the Great Smoky Mountains National Park got national attention almost immediately, and this attention drew tourists to see the strange mountain people. In 1935 a *National Geographic* reporter characterized the formation of the Great Smoky Mountains National Park as the "development of a national playground." Predictably, most of his attention was on the scenic natural beauty of the park, and the accompanying photos showed spectacular mountain peaks and scenic vistas. Nonetheless, he also gave some attention to the rustic charm of the ignorant and isolated mountaineers. The reporter's tone and style, the photos he used, and the stories he chose to tell emphasized the "otherness," the foreignness of the mountaineer to the average *National Geographic* reader. He described cabins where every item was handmade and the self-sufficient life of the mountain farm family, a lifestyle already vanishing as he wrote. Photographs of mountain men engaged in sorghum grinding and hauling logs appeared alongside shots of rustic cabins. The grizzled farmers in their old-fashioned clothing indeed looked like people from another country. The reporter also described the hard physical work done by the mountain women, work unfathomable to most of *National Geographic*'s middle-class readers.[44]

Journalists' inviting tales about the quaint mountain village of Gatlinburg and the charming highlanders drew tourists to the region. The *National Geographic* writer waxed eloquent about his experience of watching the village in the morning:

> The village was just awakening. A few hikers and horseback riders emerged from the hotels and roadside cabins for a day's outing on the trails. Men born and reared in the hills, drawn to the village by visitors' dollars, hurried to their filling stations to catch the early morning trade.
> Proprietors swung open the doors of their curio and craft shops, displaying stacks of linen, rugs, tapestries [probably weavings], furniture . . . all made by native craftsmen.

Soon the publicity and the increased traffic swelled the little village and shattered the quiet of this idyllic scene. Gatlinburg's population swelled from 75 people in 1930 to 1,300 by 1940. This population jump was largely a redistribution of the county's population. Many of the families displaced by the national park settled in Gatlinburg in order to remain close to their extended families and friends as well as to take advantage of the economic opportunities ensuing from the growing tourist trade.[45]

Famed journalist Ernie Pyle was among the million annual visitors drawn to the Smokies in the 1930s by publicity about the park's beauty. He noted that the tourist trade benefited the local economy. After several vacations in the area, in 1940 he described the economic development of Gatlinburg: "Today Gatlinburg, thanks to tourists, has a population of 1,300 and is rolling in wealth. And what is unique about it—and delightful too—is that the money is going into the pockets of the old original families here, who for so long had almost nothing." Pyle was correct in saying that mountain families were benefiting from the tourist trade, although few were getting rich.[46]

The mountaineers devised many ways to profit from the tourist trade. For a people who distrusted strangers, Sevier County people soon learned to exploit every opportunity to make money. Savvy mountaineers were quick to recognize the appeal of that "otherness" promoted by the *National Geographic* reporter. To urban dwellers, a visit to the park and contact with the mountain people was one way to return to rural roots. Rather than trying to become more like their urban visitors, mountaineers became great actors, exaggerating their eccentricities in order to encourage tourists to spend their city dollars. Sevier County's men ran "shootings"—events at which they invited tourists (for a fee, of course) to come test their marksmanship against the mountaineers. "Shootings" climaxed with rollicking picnics for the whole family, complete with mountain music and games. Each June, Gatlinburg celebrated "Old Timer's Day," another event at which tourists were invited to practice various mountain traditions. The most popular were "old-fashioned" hog, wife, husband, cow, and dog calling contests designed to demonstrate the most effective vocal techniques for summoning these various mammals. There were also ballad, hymn, and "old harp" (shaped note) singings. Young and old alike enjoyed storytelling, fiddling, horseshoes, and, of course, mountain food. Even the retail shops began to exploit the "myth of the mountaineer." The Mountaineer Museum charged admission to view its collection of household and agriculture tools, furniture, guns, and even bear traps. The Barnes Cherokee Indian Museum (which was run by whites) charged admission to see "authentic" Cherokee artifacts.[47]

As they had with the revival of Appalachian crafts, mountain people sought to exploit the romantic appeal of stereotypes about the mountaineer by staging these "hillbilly" events. Many of the tourist attractions were designed to allow male visitors to keep in touch with traditional masculine outdoor activities that they were distanced from in urban life. "Shootings" allowed them to prove prowess at a masculine skill. For a brief time, mingling with the "hillbilly" provided middle-class male visitors a chance to do the unacceptable. Several scholars have suggested that people of mountain background often deliberately paired positive stereotypes about the competent and masculine mountain man with negative ones about the uncouth hillbilly in order to simultaneously profit from and rebel against the standards of urbanized middle America. The process of romanticizing "traditional" mountain culture for a tourist audience also appealed to urban audiences longing for a "simpler" past.

Tourism provided opportunities for people who wanted to remain in the mountains. Although most Sevier County residents did benefit economically from the tourist industry, some benefited more than others. In spite of the romantic picture he painted, journalist Pyle himself noted that five families dominated the burgeoning tourist trade in Gatlinburg. Four of these families—the Ogles, the Whaleys, the Maples, and the Reagans—were among the county's earliest settlers and had long been its largest landholders and wealthiest citizens; while the fifth, the Huffs, were descended from a small-time lumber baron who had arrived in the mountains in the first decade of the century. Pyle commented that "[f]our of these five families [all but the Reagans] control Gatlinburg. They reap most of the profit, and they likewise take the responsibility and do the good deeds." The major means of control for these families was their refusal to sell land to outsiders or even to local people. They used their own landholdings to gain control of most of the profits from the tourist industry. These families owned hotels, general stores, tourist courts, filling stations, gift shops, saddle horse concessions, and restaurants.[48]

As a result of this increasing concentration of wealth, poorer Sevier County residents, particularly those forced off their land when the park was established, were often left with few options. Like the poorest families displaced by the TVA, they suffered the most. The minimal relocation assistance offered by the U.S. Park Service, combined with rising land prices and a growing need for cash, made it very difficult for them to recreate their old lifestyles in new mountain locations. They often crowded onto even smaller farms and tried to eke out a living on marginal farms. Others chose to work for the tourist entrepreneurs at low-paying, low-skilled jobs or sought work outside the mountains.

Tourism provided many new opportunities to the mountain women, who often found they enjoyed contact with people as much as the wages they earned. Gender relations among mountain families had dictated that men and sometimes children might travel to Sevierville and occasionally to Knoxville for trading trips. Mountain women, however, had rarely had contact with people beyond the few dozen families in their home communities. Now, however, cooking and cleaning in hotels brought them into contact with a diverse group of people and with new ideas. Perhaps more important than the contact with the wider world was the sense of satisfaction many women found in earning money through labor that had some value to outsiders. This was one reason so many stayed in the hotel business their whole lives. Occasionally women started tourist endeavors, such as the women shop owners in Gatlinburg mentioned above and Mrs. Belle Caton, the founder and proprietress of the Line Springs Hotel.[49]

Women also occasionally found a career ladder in the tourist industry. For Pauline Parton, a kitchen helper's job was the touchstone to a lifelong career managing and owning hotels. In 1929, at the age of twelve, Parton began cleaning rooms at the Wonderland Hotel, then considered the Smokies' poshest attraction. The next summer she was promoted to "making salad, cutting pie, and slicing bread" at the Wonderland. Parton spent the rest of her life in the hotel business, gradually accumulating enough savings to buy a Gatlinburg hotel.[50]

Women like Pauline Parton who went on to manage and own hotels and restaurants were the exception rather than the rule, however. Much of the tourism labor force was made up of women who worked as cooks, motel maids, and waitresses. Long hours, low pay, and hard physical labor characterized their jobs. The gender split in tourist jobs not only followed the traditional division of labor on local farms, but it also reflected women's lack of capital to invest in their own enterprises. Sociologists studying the rise of tourism in developing nations have concluded that the industry depends on exploitation of women in low-skilled, low-wage service jobs. This pattern was certainly true in the developing Sevier County of the 1930s. Women did the cooking and the cleaning for tourists, while men worked on the higher paying construction jobs.

Although men and women entered the tourist industry in similar numbers, men were concentrated in better paying jobs. They owned retail shops, service stations, and hotels. By contrast, mountain women and girls, many of them in the paid labor force for the first time, were concentrated in low-level service jobs. According to the Bureau of the Census, between 1930 and 1940, the number of white Sevier County women engaged in tourist-related occupations swelled from zero to 91. By 1950 this number had grown to 457. Similarly, in 1930 no men reported working in tourist-related occupations; in 1940, 117 men were in these jobs; and by 1950, 758 men made their living in the tourist industry. More than two-thirds of the men were proprietors of retail shops and other tourist businesses; while two-thirds of all women were working as hotel maids, cooks, and waitresses. There were few jobs for working-class men in tourism beyond a few positions for young men as handymen and gas station attendants; most men owned businesses, worked in construction, or held better jobs outside the mountains. In other words, Sevier County's men participated in the tourist economy as middle-class owners or skilled craftsmen, while most women participated as low-paid wage laborers.[51]

The demand for land for development gradually drove up local housing prices, increasing the cost of living and reducing the chance that families could hold on to enough land to farm. Many families gradually sold off their acreage for tourist enterprises, so that they depended even more on the off-farm wages earned by women and men. The tourist jobs that initially seemed to offer an additional option for women gradually became their only option if they remained in the mountains.

Still, as was the case with the handicraft movement, Sevier County's women embraced tourism jobs, partly because they allowed them to make a living without leaving Sevier County. As Wilma Williamson recalled, "Most women thought it [the development of tourism] was the best thing to happen to Sevier County." And tourism did bring material improvements, including better housing and more consumer goods, while reducing the isolation of mountain life. Middling women whose husbands thrived in the new economy benefited, but single women who stayed in Sevier County resigned themselves to a future bereft of material opportunities.

The trade-off for material improvements was that something was lost from mountain life. The spirit of community that grew out of mutual aid networks was diminished. Declining emphasis on subsistence activities also left people less able to survive economic downturns. Growing class distinctions also brought a nostalgia for the days when, in Wilma Williamson's words, "we were all in the same boat." The gaps between rich and poor families were more pronounced, and the poorest citizens became more aware of their poverty.[52]

Leaving the Mountains

In order to cope with the changing economy, many families developed a new gender division of labor. Because mountain culture dictated that women stay close to home and family, most women who worked outside the home joined the tourist industry, while men preferred to find better paying jobs outside the mountains. The construction of good roads enabled many mountain men to seek work in Knoxville or in nearby Blount County, where industrial jobs were available. Many Sevier County men spent long hours commuting to jobs in these places in order to remain in their beloved mountains.

This new pattern took its toll on family life. Many families eventually gave up the grueling pattern of the husband commuting long distances while the wife worked in the mountains and moved to valley towns where the men worked. For a number of years Wilma Williamson's husband commuted to a job at ALCOA, but eventually the grind became too much. After World War II the family moved to Blount County. The same economic changes that left Williamson and her husband dependent on a wage economy made it more attractive for them to leave the mountains. Similarly, Betty Hayes and her husband left the mountains for a job at ALCOA after logging ended at Elkmont in 1938. Yet the Hayes family clung to the old ways, purchasing land in the Ellejoy community of Blount County, an area nestled in the foothills of the Smokies well outside the bounds of the park.[53]

While women seemed to welcome the opportunity to move to cities and towns where there were more contact with people, better housing, and good schools for their children, men often bitterly resisted leaving the land they loved. After Gladys Trentham Russell's father sold his land to the U. S. Park Service, her mother, Mary Jane Trentham, insisted that the family move to town so that her youngest children would get a better education. Her husband, however, delayed the move. Russell recalled that "it took Ma a few years to persuade Pa to arrange for the move. On the day we moved, Pa had business in Knoxville. He hired my cousin, Arthur Oakley, and his truck from Gatlinburg, to do the hauling. Then Pa insisted that he didn't move, we did." Like many mountain men, Russell's father welcomed the money brought by the new order but resisted severing his ties to land that had been in his family for generations.[54]

The experiences of the Trenthams was common. Many mountain families were not able to stay in the mountains or even in East Tennessee. One researcher found that between 1940 and 1950 the Appalachian counties of East Tennessee had a net out-migration of 62,162 people. Another study, this one done by the federal government, found that between 1935 and 1940, eight of every one hundred citizens in the mountain counties of East Tennessee migrated out of the area. More than one-third of those migrating had previously been employed in agriculture. These mountain folk tended to migrate to metropolitan areas where relatives and old neighbors were already living. Many East Tennesseans went to midwestern industrial cities or to Atlanta. Large numbers also went to the coal mines of Virginia and West Virginia and to factories in Tennessee's cities.[55]

Whether they moved to Tennessee's cities or to northern states, mountaineers faced culture shock as they tried to adjust to urban life. Florence Cope Bush expressed this shock humorously in an essay about her own family's transition to life in Knoxville. After her father's job with the Little River Lumber Company ended in 1938, he joined the Knoxville Utilities Board (KUB) as an electrical lineman. At first he installed electrical lines in distant counties, so the family remained on his in-laws' Sevier County farm and later in the village of Pigeon Forge. But in 1943 the family made the big move to Knoxville, where Mr. Cope was working on KUB's local crew. For the Copes, the move to Knoxville brought an opportunity to own property, something they had never been able to do when moving from lumber camp to lumber camp. Here the family bought its first house in a neighborhood that was less than thrilled to see mountain people moving in next door. Although the neighbors eventually accepted the Cope family, largely as a result of relationships between their children, other adjustments were harder. Family members

clung to many of their old ways, setting themselves apart from Knoxville people. The Cope boys disdained the "fancy pants" worn by neighbors and by their city cousins, preferring their own overalls instead. In
fact, Bush noted that the family "didn't associate much" with their city
cousins "because we still had too many rough edges to smooth down
before we could be seen with proper folk." This type of separation from
family was difficult for people who had valued family connections above
all else.[56]

In the city, Dorie Cope too faced the challenges of adapting to a new
culture. Her unfamiliarity with urban social patterns made the transition uncomfortable. Her daughter recalled that "the natural shyness
of the mountain woman was the most difficult problem she had to face.
Her quiet reserve was sometimes misunderstood in a neighborhood full
of coffee-klatching women." The behavior appropriate for a mountain
woman proved unnerving to her new city friends, who were used to
much chatter and gossip, and her reserve was sometimes mistaken for
snobbery or disapproval.[57]

More threatening than the gossip of new neighbors were the challenges to her parental authority. The traditional mountain values that
Dorie Cope was determined to instill in her children were called into
question by the urban materialistic culture of Knoxville, where social
success was often based on economic factors. In the words of her daughter, "[She] felt it had been easier to raise a family in the mountains than in
the Knoxville suburbs. Peer pressure and the need to conform were problems faced by the younger children every day. In the logging camps,
everyone was equal to everyone else. Poverty for one meant poverty for
all; prosperity for one meant prosperity for all. . . [In the city, t]heir role as
parents was challenged in new ways."[58]

Dorie Cope's determination to hold onto her old values even as she
welcomed the economic opportunities of the city was embodied in an
incident regarding the family cow. Dorie had refused to move unless the
cow came along, so Mr. Cope had made arrangements to stable the animal near their new house. But on moving day the stall was not yet ready,
leaving the family to grapple with the problem of what to do with the
cow. They tied her up to the back fence, where the poor animal was
frightened by passing trains on a nearby railroad track causing her to

bawl and "fertilize" the future lawn all day. This caused great consterna-
tion among the neighbors, some of whom complained loudly.

The cow was Dorie Cope's bridge between the old life and the new.
Her insistence on bringing the cow to the city illustrates both the ambivalence many woman felt about coming to the city and their determination
to maintain some control over the family's subsistence. Although they
were anxious to give their children city advantages, they also feared
the corrupting influence of urban life. As her daughter remembered it,
"Momma simply couldn't picture herself in a hat like [her city cousin]
wore, and her children were not going to become pawns of city society to
be molded and changed into stiff-necked wimps. By insisting that the
cow come, Momma thought she had won this one." The cow was indicative of Mrs. Cope's reluctance to give up the self-sufficiency of the farm
and her central place in the family economy. Her ability to produce the
family's food had often made the difference between starvation and survival. Her work had been essential to the family's well-being. For Mrs.
Cope, the cow was a tie to the old way of life and old values, a way to
teach her children the discipline of hard work and of raising one's own
food.[59]

For Dorie Cope and other Sevier County women—indeed for all rural
upcountry women—adapting to the changes of the early twentieth century was a negotiated process. The most prosperous women still had the
greatest range of choices. Yet, as in the other counties, individual preference and family dynamics also shaped women's responses to outside
forces. Believing that any economic opportunity was an improvement
over the poverty of earlier times, mountain women expanded their role
of providing for the family to include all sorts of cash-earning activities.
They also embraced changes that reduced the bleak isolation of mountain
living or gave their children opportunities for a better life. Although they
sometimes lamented the loss of family and neighborhood ties or the
development of more rigid class boundaries, they rarely longed for a
return to the old life.

The Persistence of Rural Values

Change was perhaps the only constant in the lives of rural women in the twentieth century. By 1941 multiple agents of change increased the pace of the transformation from a rural agrarian to an urban industrial culture in the upcountry South. In the World War II and Cold War years, shifts in government policy, mechanization, and structural changes in the agricultural economy encouraged the development of specialized commercial farms at the expense of small general farms. A few families successfully adopted commercial farming practices, but thousands of rural folk left the land for jobs in the region's small towns, while thousands more managed to stay on the land only by taking off-farm jobs. The development of manufacturing and the transformation of rural upcountry locations into tourist destinations offered new opportunities for those pushed out of farming by economic changes and federal agricultural policy.

All this change transformed gender relations. Some women who remained on farms carved out new niches in the family economy by becoming partners in farm management or by taking off-farm jobs. Others chose to model themselves after middle-class homemakers. Wives of the region's new wage earners tried to maintain their centrality to the family economy even as they found their productive work marginalized in a world that increasingly defined "work" as wage work. Although the transformation was never complete, the seeds of change sown in the period between 1919 and 1941 continued to bear fruit in the lives of the region's women throughout the remainder of the century.

World War II hastened the pace of change in the upcountry. A boom in farm prices created prosperity for the region's commercial farmers, encouraging expansion and further modernization. Defense industries in the region flourished, creating more off-farm jobs to lure rural citizens, particularly women, away from farming. Thousands more upcountry southerners left the area for well-paid defense jobs in the Midwest, and many of them stayed, at least until retirement returned them to the South. For women, the move to northern cities brought a new round of adjustments—to urban life and to the unfamiliar culture of the North. Many of these transplanted rural women entered the paid labor force for the first time. Others continued to practice their own coping strategies—taking in boarders, keeping gardens on narrow urban lots, and "making do."[1]

For those who remained in the region, the war brought new challenges and new hardships. Rural folk found that the cash generated by higher farm prices and high-paying off-farm jobs did little good because of wartime shortages and rationing. One woman recalled that, during the war years, "money wasn't so scarce, but there was nothing to buy." Families were forced to walk to church and to work because of gas and tire shortages. Modernization of homes, delayed because of lack of money, was further postponed because of lack of materials. Many families could not install running water until the end of the war made plumbing fixtures available. In some areas the installation of electrical lines had to wait because the war effort placed heavy demands on supplies of copper and other metals. In the 1940s, farm women were often frustrated because the return of prosperity did not greatly change the material conditions of their lives.[2]

Not only did industry expand and agriculture decline throughout the region during the war, but the federal government became a strong presence in daily life in the upcountry. The Oak Ridge facility in Anderson County, Tennessee, built components of the first nuclear bomb. After the war, this installation, as Oak Ridge National Laboratory (ORNL), provided highly skilled and high-paying jobs for local citizens, many of whom got college educations on the GI Bill. ORNL employed thousands of skilled workers—male and female—from all over the region during the

Cold War. Military bases and other federal facilities dotted the landscape, employing thousands of upcountry workers. The descendants of those once displaced by the Tennessee Valley Authority worked at its headquarters in Knoxville and at TVA power plants scattered throughout the region. Upcountry folk remained distrustful of big government and resistant to higher taxes into the 1980s, consistently voting for conservative Republicans, but they nonetheless embraced the jobs federal spending brought with it.[3]

While most upcountry southerners, especially African Americans, left the land in the decades after World War II, white women who remained on the land tell us much about the extent of the transformations in the agricultural economy and in gender roles in the last half of the twentieth century. East Tennessean Eva Finchum told an interviewer that in the early years of the twentieth century, "there was nothing but . . . farming, that's all there was." Eva, however, lived to see many alternatives to farming. When the United States entered World War II, Finchum's husband joined the armed forces, and Eva and her three children moved in with her parents. "Me and Dad farmed just like we was big farmers," she recalled. After the war, Finchum's husband, A. D., worked at a factory in Morristown while Eva "farmed right on" on land the couple bought in Sevierville. She milked twenty-two cows and raised tobacco. "Two or three years in a row, I made more off them cows than he made at the plant," she explained. Her income made it possible for the family to remain on the land and to achieve something approaching a middle-class standard of living. Like many upcountry people, the Finchums shifted gender roles and combined a small commercial farm with factory work in order to hang on to their rural lifestyle. Producing farm income enabled Eva to maintain her central place in the family economy.[4]

Like Eva Finchum, Ruth Hatchette McBrayer farmed in the postwar years, but she did so for different reasons. A South Carolina school teacher who gave up her job upon her marriage in 1933, McBrayer found herself widowed and childless fourteen years later. The peach farming operation started by Gene Hatchette's late father "was just dumped on me. . . . I didn't know what to do really, but fortunately I learned." McBrayer discovered that her inheritance was encumbered by substantial debt, which she worked to pay off. After the debts were gone, McBrayer said, "If I can make that much money, I'll make some for myself." She explained that she soon became deeply interested in the work of peach farming.[5]

Hatchette's male farmer neighbors doubted that she could make a go of farming on her own and hoped to buy her land cheaply. She recalled that this made her even more determined to succeed. In order to learn the peach farming business, she attended Agricultural Extension Service workshops and even hosted them at her own farm, inviting her skeptical neighbors. Eventually, neighbors accepted her as a fellow farmer. "After the men in the community saw that I had the determination and the courage and the ability, instead of conniving against me, they began to try to help me," she reported. As an active member of the local and state Peach Growers Association, Hatchette learned of new techniques and technology that she applied to her own operation. She purchased an air cooler for her packing shed and installed the first irrigation system in the county. A profitable grower, Hatchette farmed until 1985.

Not all women who remained on the land after World War II chose to be active in the farm operation. Mary Evelyn Lane, born in 1912 in Blount County, Tennessee, saw her father lose his dairy farm during the Depression. Although he later resumed crop farming on a small scale, he never achieved the same level of prosperity again. Her husband struggled to make a go of farming on his father's land, trying various commercial farming ventures, such as growing seed corn for a national agribusiness firm. Mary Evelyn's home production grew less critical to the family's well-being as cash income gained importance to the Lanes. A teacher before her marriage, she returned to the classroom as soon as the wartime labor shortage again opened jobs for married teachers. When asked how rural Blount County residents felt about farm life after surviving the depression years, she exclaimed, "'Get us off the farm as fast as you can get us.' Men and women both [felt that way]. Men liked to farm, but there was just no money to be made on it."[6]

Like many farm women in the postwar years, Lane continued to subsidize the farm operation with her off-farm work. She taught school for twenty-nine years and then, upon retirement, campaigned for a seat on the county school board. She served eight years in that capacity, helping to oversee the construction of new schools for the county's growing population. Yet she believed that her work remained marginalized because she was female, even in the 1970s and 1980s. Colleagues on the school board often ignored her suggestions and concerns because "I was a woman, and I didn't have any sense." Lane also witnessed the enormous growth of industry that offered materially better opportunities to Blount County's rural people and thus helped hasten the decline of farming. After her husband's death, she sold the family farm for a county industrial park and moved to a condominium in town. Although she still reads *Progressive Farmer* regularly, she doubts that farm life is a viable option for most people born without what one historian has called an "equity head start." As Lane put it, "You've got to have capital or you can't do anything on a farm. . . . When you look around, there aren't a whole lot of people on the farm today unless their parents began it, and they got their foot in the door."[7]

Lane's statement points to perhaps the most significant change in the lives of rural upcountry people: the shift to a cash-based society. Commercial farming and life in an increasingly consumption-oriented society both demanded large amounts of cash. This new world, where disposable income increasingly determined social status, pushed the old community-based mutual aid networks to the margins of social relationships. Prosperous farm families now purchased the goods and services once provided by mutual aid networks. Unable to afford to replace the products of mutual aid networks, poorer families also interacted less frequently with the most financially successful farm families in the community—families who might have provided resources that would make the difference between staying on the land or leaving the farm. As class boundaries became more rigid, former rural dwellers developed a more overt class consciousness, making it difficult for women to improve their economic positions by marrying up the class ladder. Firmer class lines actually diminished the options of the poorest white and black upcountry women.

The shift to a cash-based economy also diminished women's pivotal role in organizing and maintaining mutual aid networks and thus reduced their control over, and visibility in, community life. Wives of commercial farmers and rural nonfarm wage earners took charge of most family spending and thus had increased control over the allocation of family resources. At the same time, many felt more dependent on their husbands. In the past, farm women engaged in petty market production such as the sale of eggs and butter not only controlled the disposal of that small income but also felt they were making contributions to the family's well-being. After World War II, as increasing numbers of rural women entered the middle class, wives of wage earners and commercial farmers felt increasingly dependent on those husbands. To avoid this dependence, many women stubbornly refused to give up their own income-producing activities. Laura Tate recalled that her grandmother continued to sell her eggs in the 1940s, long after her husband's success as a commercial farmer and road-building contractor rendered this income superfluous. "A woman should always have her own money," she advised. By contrast, women who no longer had an independent source of income sometimes felt they "had to ask" their husbands for money, an uncomfortable trade-off for material prosperity.[8]

Federal farm policy, industrialization, tourism, and the growth of the service sector all interacted to shape a rural economy based on commercial agriculture and to reshape gender relations among the area's rural people. Materially, the lives of rural upcountry women improved dramatically in the mid- and late-twentieth century, and women who remained on the land believed they had a wider range of options than their grandmothers faced. Still, their contributions to the farm grew less critical than before, their work more marginalized. Even as they had more opportunities to hold official positions, their role in community life was less visible and less central. Becoming middle class broadened—and circumscribed—their lives.

Abbreviations

BTC   Broadcast Television Collection, Archives of Appalachia, Library, East Tennessee State University, Johnson City, Tennessee

BMC   Burton Manning Collection, Archives of Appalachia, Library, East Tennessee State University, Johnson City, Tennessee

CA   U.S. Bureau of the Census, *Census of Agriculture* [year]

CGC   Charles Gunther Collection, Archives of Appalachia, Library, East Tennessee State University, Johnson City, Tennessee

DL   Dacus Library, Winthrop University, Rock Hill, South Carolina

EHOHP   Extension Homemakers Oral History Project, Dacus Library, Winthrop University, Rock Hill, South Carolina

ESAR   U.S. Department of Agriculture Extension Service Annual Reports [state, year]

FERA   Federal Emergency Relief Agency

GEB   General Education Board Records, Record Group 1, Rockefeller Foundation Archives, Rockefeller Archives Center, Tarrytown, New York

KC   Kennedy Local History Collection, Spartanburg County Public Library, Spartanburg, South Carolina

MHC   McClung Historical Collection, Lawson-McGhee Public Library, Knoxville, Tennessee

NA   National Archives and Records Administration, College Park, Maryland

OHA   Oral Histories of Appalachia, Library, Marshall University, Huntington, West Virginia

OHSA   Oral History of Southern Agriculture, National Museum of American History, Smithsonian Institution, Washington, D.C.

SASC   Charles S. Johnson et al., comps., *Statistical Atlas of Southern Counties: Listing and Analysis of Socio-Economic Indices of 1,104 Southern Counties* (Chapel Hill: University of North Carolina Press, 1941)

TVA   Record Group 142, TVA Reservoir Property Management Division Population Removal Records, National Archives-Southeast Region, Atlanta, Georgia

USDA   U.S. Department of Agriculture

WPALHC Works Progress Administration Life Histories Collection, Library of Congress, Washington, D.C.

YA   U.S. Department of Agriculture, *Yearbook of Agriculture* [year]

Notes

Introduction: "All We Knew Was to Farm"

1. Maristan Chapman (pseud. of Mary and John Stanton Higham), *Homeplace* (New York: Viking Press, 1929).

2. Ibid., 73.

3. Ibid., 5.

4. Howard W. Odum, *Southern Regions of the United States* (Chapel Hill: University of North Carolina Press, 1936). See also Robert Tracy McKenzie, *One South or Many? Plantation Belt and Upcountry in Civil War–Era Tennessee* (New York: Cambridge University Press, 1994).

5. The first scholar to examine the power of "Appalachia" as an ideal was Henry D. Shapiro in *Appalachia on Our Mind: The Southern Mountains and Mountaineers in the American Consciousness, 1870–1920* (Chapel Hill: University of North Carolina Press, 1978). David E. Whisnant adds texture to this study in *All That Is Native and Fine: The Politics of Culture in An American Region* (Chapel Hill: University of North Carolina Press, 1983). Mary Beth Pudup, Dwight B. Billings, and Altina L. Waller, in *Appalachia in the Making: The Mountain South in the Nineteenth Century* (Chapel Hill: University of North Carolina Press, 1995), have illuminated the diversity of the Appalachian mountain region.

6. Della Sarten, interview by LuAnn Jones, May 1, 1987, OHSA.

Chapter 1. Rural Life in the Upcountry South

1. William Bruce Wheeler and Michael J. McDonald, "The Communities of East Tennessee, 1850–1940: An Interpretive Overview," *East Tennessee Historical Society Publications* 58–59 (1986–87): 3–38; Wilma Dykeman, *Tennessee: A Bicentennial History* (New York: W. W. Norton, 1975), 3.

2. Wheeler and McDonald, "Communities of East Tennessee," 3–38.

3. WPA Writers' Program, *West Virginia: A Guide to the Mountain State* (New York: Oxford, 1941), 8–11; John C. Campbell, *The Southern Highlander and His Homeland* (New York: Russell Sage Foundation, 1921), 347–48.

4. Campbell, *Southern Highlander,* 343–44.

5. Ibid., 57–58; WPA, *West Virginia,* 40–46.

6. "Class, Section, and Culture in Nineteenth Century West Virginia Politics," in *Appalachia in the Making: The Mountain South in the Nineteenth Century,* ed. Mary Beth Pudup, Dwight B. Billings, and Altina L. Waller (Chapel Hill: University of North Carolina Press, 1975), 210–32.

7. Otis K. Rice, *West Virginia: A History* (Lexington: University Press of Kentucky, 1985), 188–98.

8. Ibid., 198.

9. Wheeler and McDonald, "Communities of East Tennessee," 7–8; Robert E. Corlew, *Tennessee: A Short History,* 2nd ed. (Knoxville: University of Tennessee Press, 1990), 284–301; Lester C. Lamon, *Blacks in Tennessee, 1791–1970* (Knoxville: University of Tennessee Press, 1981), 3–25.

10. V. O. Key quoted in David D. Lee, "Rural Democrats, Eastern Republicans, and Trade-Offs in Tennessee," *ETHS Publications* 48 (1976): 108.

11. Wheeler and McDonald, "Communities of East Tennessee," 7–8.

12. Samuel D. Mobley, interview by W. W. Dixon, undated, WPALHC.

13. Don H. Doyle, *New Men, New Cities, New South: Atlanta, Nashville, Charleston, Mobile, 1860–1910* (Chapel Hill: University of North Carolina Press, 1990), 8; David L. Carlton, *Mill and Town in South Carolina, 1880–1920* (Baton Rouge: Louisiana State University Press, 1982), 18–25.

14. Wheeler and McDonald, "Communities of East Tennessee," 58–59.

15. U.S. Bureau of the Census, *Census of Agriculture,* 1930 (hereafter, *CA*), vol. 2, pt. 2, figures compiled from pp. 870–84, 894–902.

16. Jessie Felknor, interview by LuAnn Jones, May 2, 1987, OHSA; *CA,* 1930, vol. 2, pt. 2, compiled from pp. 870–84, 894–902; USDA, "Economic and Social Problems and Conditions of the Southern Appalachians," 1935, 46, 73–76.

17. *CA,* 1930, vol. 2, pt. 2, compiled from pp. 470–75. Similar patterns were found in all the other upstate counties. For example, in Spartanburg County, the average farm size was 49.4 acres with a 67.7 percent tenancy rate. Owners farmed 66 acres compared to tenants' 42.2 acres, and blacks farmed 38.4 acres compared to whites' 54.7 acres.

18. *CA,* 1930, vol. 2, pt. 2, figures compiled from pp. 470–75; Archie Vernon Huff Jr., *Greenville: The History of the City and the County in the South Carolina Piedmont* (Columbia: University of South Carolina Press, 1995), 292. Even in Greenville County, where blacks made up only 28 percent of farmers, they farmed an average of 15 fewer acres than whites.

19. *CA,* 1930, vol. 2, pt. 2, figures compiled from pp. 296–99.

20. Ibid.

21. Ronald L. Lewis, "Railroads, Deforestation, and the Transformation of

Agriculture in the West Virginia Back Counties, 1880–1920," in *Appalachia in the Making*, ed. Pudup, Billings, and Waller, 297–320.

22. Mary Lou Brown Barton, to author, March 15, 1995; Lisa E. Brown Widener, to author, March 24, 1995.

23. Ryan Alexander Page, *Our Way of Life: The Odyssey of a Farm Family* (Fairfax: Wallace and Sons Printing, 1982), 17.

24. Lessie Shiveley, interview by Gary A. Jarrett, undated ca. 1972–74, OHA.

25. "Arthur Delozier," interview by author, July 21, 1994; Bill Lewellyn, interview by author, August 10, 1993, MHC; Della Sarton, interviews by LuAnn Jones, May 2 and May 7, 1987, OHSA; "Peggy Delozier Jones," interview by author, July 21, 1994.

26. *Census of Population*, 1930, vol. 3, pt. 2, pp. 915, 918. In Sevier County, Tennessee, in 1930, roughly 7 percent of white women and 11 percent of black women had off-farm jobs as compared to Blount County, Tennessee, where 34 percent of black women and only 18 percent of white women were employed.

27. *Spartanburg Journal and Carolina Spartan*, October 22, 1940; lynching figures are compiled from *SASC*, 197–204.

28. *SASC*, 207–22; Michael J. McDonald and William Bruce Wheeler, *Knoxville, Tennessee: Continuity and Change in an Appalachian City* (Knoxville: University of Tennessee Press, 1983), 56–58.

29. Joe William Trotter Jr., *Coal, Class, and Color: Blacks in Southern West Virginia, 1915–1932* (Urbana: University of Illinois Press, 1990), 68–85, 102–11.

30. Lucille Thornburgh, interview by June Rostan, April 30, 1978, *Twentieth Century Trade Union Women: Vehicle for Social Change*, Oral History Project, Institute of Labor and Industrial Relations, Michigan State University and Wayne State University; Edna P. Spencer, "What Color is The Wind?" (master's thesis, Clark University, 1985); Edna P. Spencer, interview by author, January 26, 1995.

31. Mary Beth Pudup, "The Boundaries of Class in Pre-Industrial Appalachia," *Journal of Historical Geography* 15 (1989): 139–62. See bibliographical essay for an extensive list of sources on rural class structures.

32. Joel Williamson, *A Rage for Order: Black/White Relations in the American South Since Emancipation* (New York: Oxford University Press, 1986), 239.

33. Compiled from *Abstract of the Fourteenth Census of the United States*, 1920, 815; and *CA*, 1925, pt. 2, pp. 736–45; *CA*, 1930, 870–82; U.S. Department of Agriculture, *Yearbook of Agriculture (YA)*, 1931, 19.

34. *YA*, 1922, 1002.

35. Ibid., 6.

36. *YA*, 1923, 539; C. E. Lively and Conrad Taeuber, *Rural Migration in the United States* (Washington, D.C.: Works Progress Administration, 1939), 22; Wheeler and McDonald, "Communities of East Tennessee," 27.

37. Jack Temple Kirby, *Rural Worlds Lost: The American South, 1920–1981* (Baton Rouge: Louisiana State University Press, 1981).

Chapter 2. Making Do and Doing Without

1. Hildegarde Kneeland and Hazel K. Stiebeling, "Readjustments in Family Living Are as Drastic as Those Effected in Farming," in *YA*, 1933, 389.

2. Tennessee figures compiled from *CA*, 1925, 736–45; *CA*, 1930, 870–82; *CA*, 1940, pt. 2, 472–82; *YA*, 1931, 19. The same sources reveal that in the relatively prosperous valley county of Loudon, the total value of crops sold or traded in 1924 was $913,891. By 1929 this figure had fallen to $333,649, and by 1939 to $286,993. Nonetheless, as in Sevier County, the number of farmers selling crops had increased 6 percent. Thus the average value of crops sold or traded per Loudon County farmer dropped from $353 in 1929 to $287 in 1939.

3. P. G. Beck and M. C. Forster, *Six Rural Problem Areas, Relief, Resources, and Rehabilitation: An Analysis of the Human and Material Resources of Six Problem Areas With High Relief Rates* (Washington, D.C.: WPA, 1935), 1, 5.

4. FERA, "Rural Problem Areas Survey Report No. 32, Bledsoe County, Tennessee," November 1934; and "Rural Problem Areas Survey Report No. 3, Grainger County, Tennessee," October 1934, Tennessee State Library and Archives, Nashville, Tennessee; Beck and Forster, *Six Rural Problem Areas*, 1, 5.

5. Carrie Jerome Anderson, interview by Mary Long, June 9, 1977, EHOHP.

6. Wilma Williamson, interview by author, July 18, 1994, MHC.

7. Ibid.; Florence Cope Bush, *Dorie: Woman of the Mountains* (Knoxville: University of Tennessee Press, 1992).

8. Edna P. Spencer, "What Color is the Wind?" (master's thesis, Clark University, 1985); Edna Spencer, interview by author, January 26, 1995.

9. One local historian recounted that in the last half of the nineteenth century, there were thirteen potteries in the northwest corner of Spartanburg County, which were kept busy turning out white clay jugs for whiskey produced by local moonshiners (James Walton Lawrence Sr., *Shadows of Hogback* [Landrum, S.C.: *News Leader*, 1979]).

10. Bill Lewellyn, interview by author, August 10, 1993, MHC.

11. "The Relation Between the Ability to Pay and the Standard of Living Among Farmers," USDA Bulletin No. 1832, January 1926, 8–9. A 1939 study of farm family diets reached similar conclusions. See Hazel K. Stiebeling and Callie Mae Coons, "Present Day Diets in the United States," *YA*, 1939, 296–303.

12. Gilbert W. Beebe, *Contraception and Fertility in the Southern Appalachians* (Baltimore: Williams and Wilkins, 1942).

13. A. D. and Eva Finchum, interview by LuAnn Jones, April 30, 1987, OHSA; Maude Walker, interview by author, August 17, 1993; Maude Chadwick, interview by Marianne Brewick, October 10, 1973, OHA. Wilma Williamson interview.

14. Korola Lee, interview by author, August 10, 1994, MHC.

15. Watts Bar project, Box 126, TVA; LaVerne Farmer, interview by author,

August 9, 1993, MHC; Robert R. Madden, *Walker Sisters Home: Historic Structures Report* (Great Smoky Mountains National Park, Department of the Interior, 1969), photocopy located in MHC; Jessie Felknor, interview by LuAnn Jones, May 2, 1987, OHSA.

16. America Jarrell, interview by Gary Miller, ca. 1975, OHA; Hettie Lawson, interview by author, August 16, 1993, MHC; Gladys Trentham Russell, *Call Me Hillbilly: A Personal Account of Growing Up in the Smokies Near Gatlinburg* (Alcoa, Tenn.: Russell Publishing Co., 1974), 9–10; Wanda Brummitt, to author, March 1994.

17. Della Sarten, interview by LuAnn Jones, May 1, 1987, OHSA; A. D. and Eva Finchum interview.

18. Alice Hardin, quoted in Allen Tullos, *Habits of Industry: White Culture and the Transformation of the Carolina Piedmont* (Chapel Hill: University of North Carolina Press, 1989), 256–63; J. W. Joseph et al., "Agrarian Life, Romantic Death: Archeological and Historical Testing and Data Recovery for the I-85 Northern Alternative, Spartanburg County, South Carolina," South Carolina Department of Transportation, April 1, 1991, 109–113; John C. Campbell, *The Southern Highlander and His Homeland* (New York: Russell Sage Foundation, 1921), 128.

19. J. C. Kessell, interview by Jeanann Leone, ca. 1973, OHA; Florence Cope Bush, "The Boy Who Liked To Quilt," *If Life Gives You Scraps, Make a Quilt* (Concord, Tenn.: Misty Cove Publications, 1992) 55–57, 71.

20. Evelyn Lewellyn, interview by author, August 10, 1993, MHC; Lizzie Broyles, interview by Lon Broyles, November 16, 1975, CGC.

21. Effie Temple, interview by LuAnn Jones, May 8, 1987, OHSA; "Arthur Tipton," interview by author, July 19, 1994; Jessie Felknor interview; Margaret Marsh, interview by author, July 18, 1994; "Mabel Love," interview by author, July 19, 1994, MHC; Edwin Jones Best Sr., *A Place Called Greenback: An East Tennessee Town at the Turn of the Century, 1870–1917* (Maryville, Tenn.: Blount County Genealogical and Historical Society, 1994).

22. "Everett Hobbs," interview by author, July 19, 1994, MHC; Fay Ball, interview by Karen Handley, July 6, 1974, OHA.

23. Mrs. Bonnie Faulkner, to Eleanor Roosevelt, Record Group 69, WPA Central Files, States, Tennessee, 661.1 to 663, Box 2594, National Archives, College Park, Maryland; Wilma Fisher, to author, March 22, 1994.

24. "Arthur Delozier," interview by author, July 21, 1994, MHC.

25. Georgia Thomas, to author, March 1994.

26. Evelyn Lewellyn interview.

27. Drawn from the following oral histories: "Ethel Davis," interview by author, July 19, 1994, MHC; "Mabel Love," interview by author, July 19, 1994, MHC; Laverne Farmer interview; Mary Evelyn Lane, interview by author, August 8, 1994, MHC.

28. Fay Ball interview; Ruby Booth, interview by Marianne Brewick, October 23, 1973, OHA; Sylvia Sowards, interview by Karen Handley, August 8, 1974, OHA.

29. Naomi Banks Bridges, interview by her daughter, December 6, 1980, EHOHP; Laverne Farmer interview; French Clark, interview by author, July 22, 1994, MHC; Korola Lee interview.

30. Laverne Farmer interview.

31. *Maryville Times*, December 22 and 29, 1924; "Ethel Davis" interview; Wilma Williamson interview.

32. French Clark interview; Lucy B. White, interview by David White, undated, ca. 1973, OHA.

33. Laverne Farmer interview; Everett Hobbs interview; Hettie Lawson interview; McDonald and Muldowny, *TVA and the Dispossessed*, 29–50; Mary Evelyn Lane interview; A. D. and Eva Finchum interview.

34. Russell, *Just Call Me Hillbilly*, 21.

35. John West, interview by author, August 12, 1993, MHC.

36. Carrie Jerome Anderson interview.

37. French Clark interview; A. D. and Eva Finchum interview.

38. Bertha Mae Asbury, interview by Barbara Redman, March 5, 1973, OHA; Etta Grigsby Nichols to unknown interviewer, June 28, 1970, BMC; Lizzie Broyles interview.

39. Edna P. Spencer, "What Color Is the Wind?"

40. Etta Grigsby Nichols, interview by unknown interviewer, June 28, 1970, BMC; Lizzie Broyles interview, CGC; Minnie Conley to unknown interviewer, ca. 1975, BTC.

41. Mrs. Arthur Smith to unknown interviewer, June 27, 1970, BMC; Etta Grigsby Nichols interview. One study found that in 1920 the upland county of Sevier had between five and ten doctors to serve its 20,480 people, while more developed Blount County had between ten and fifteen doctors to serve a population about the same size (USDA, "Economic and Social Problems of the Southern Appalachians," 157–161, 166).

42. Mrs. Arthur Smith interview; "Granny Woman," unidentified midwife to unidentified interviewer, BTC; Etta Grigsby Nichols interview.

43. Richard E. Herrmann, "Tennessee Churches During the 1930s," *Tennessee Historical Quarterly* 44 (1985): 59–71; "Records of New Hope Methodist Church, Philadelphia, Tennessee," undated typescript in the author's possession; French Clark interview; Russell, *Just Call Me Hillbilly*, 31.

44. Alice Hall, interview by Karen Hall, July 7, 1974, OHA.

45. Bill Lewellyn interview.

46. Alice Hall interview; Bill Lewellyn interview; Mickey Crews, *The Church of God: A Social History* (Knoxville: University of Tennessee Press, 1990), 1–18, 92–93; North Callahan, *Smoky Mountain Country* (Boston: Little, Brown, 1952), 92–94.

47. Bill Lewellyn interview.

48. Herbert Douglas to Irene Lamb, in "Claiming Our Economic History, Jellico, Tennessee," Oral histories collected by the Rural Community Exchange Cooperative, Jellico, Tennessee, Spring 1987, in Special Collections, University of Tennessee, Knoxville.

49. Madden, *Walker Sisters Home;* Alice Hall interview.

50. *Maryville Times,* January 15 and 19, 1931; March 5 and 9, 1931; *Spartanburg Journal and Carolina Spartan,* October 2, 3, and 13, 1931.

51. *Farm Journal,* December 1931, 15; Kneeland and Stiebeling, "Readjustments in Family Living," 389.

52. *Maryville Times,* January 17, 1929, 1; Mary Evelyn Lane interview; Paul Reagan, to author, March 17, 1994; "Minutes of the 16th Annual Convention of the South Carolina Council of Farm Women," Winthrop College, June 11 and 12, 1936, p. 26, Mrs. W. E. Cochran Papers, box 1, folder 5, DL.

53. Mary S. Fitzgerald, "A Rural Woman's Contribution to Her Community," *Progressive Farmer,* February 1933, 16–18; Charlotte M. Temple, "Rural Club Women Lead," *Farm Journal,* April 1934, 11, 25.

54. Bill Lewellyn interview; FERA, "Rural Problem Areas Survey Report 32."

55. William R. Payne, interview by Ella Gibson, November 3, 1973, OHA; Hettie Lawson interview; Bessie Reed, interview by Caldwell Sims, January 9, 1939, LC; Lessie Shiveley interview.

56. ESAR, Cabell County, West Virginia, 1930.

57. Minnie Adcock, to Franklin Roosevelt, December 2, 1938, and H. G. Reynolds to Minnie Adcock, December 13, 1938, RG 96, Records of the Farmers Home Administration, correspondence relating to complaints, 1935–42 (PI 118, Entry 6, Box 3). For similar letters see Record Group 69, WPA Central Files, States, Tennessee, 661.1 to 663, Box 2594, National Archives, Washington, D.C.

58. Mary Evelyn Lane interview; Margaret Marsh, letter to author, August 1994 and interview.

Chapter 3. "Grandma Would Find Some Way to Make Some Money"

1. Bill Lewellyn, interview by author, August 10, 1993, MHC.

2. Jessie Felknor, interview by LuAnn Jones, May 2, 1987, OHSA.

3. Florence E. Ward and Katherine Glover, "The Farm Woman Goes Into Business and Successfully Reconciles a Home and a Career," *Woman's Home Companion* 53 (October 1926): 4, 89.

4. *Farm Journal,* February 1923, 47, and December 1923, 87; Michael K. Byer, "The Woman in Poultry Culture," *Farm Journal,* January 1926, 55.

5. *Farm Journal,* June 1929, 37; Lois P. Dowdle, "The Home," *Progressive Farmer,* January 1–14, 1932, 8.

6. *Farm Journal,* January 1923, 63, and February 1924.

7. Lois P. Dowdle, "Can the Farm Home Earn $500? At Least It Can Spend That Amount for Improvements," *Progressive Farmer,* October 15–31, 1931, 20; "Ten Dozen Money Making Ideas: How Farm Women Can Help Add That $500 More," *Progressive Farmer,* November 1–14, 1931, 3.

8. USDA, "Economic and Social Problems of the Southern Appalachians," 1935, 167.

9. "Mabel Love," interview by author, July 19, 1994, MHC; Mrs. Creed Proffitt, interview by Connie May Valentine, October 12, 1974, CGC; French Clark, interview by author, July 22, 1994, MHC; Jessie Felknor interview.

10. Ft. Loudon project, boxes 133–135, Watts Bar project, boxes 75–80, and Norris project, boxes 11–25, TVA; Gertrude E. Cyrus, interview by Greg Cyrus, August 5, 1974, OHA.

11. Ft. Loudon project, box 133, TVA.

12. Dorie Sanders, conversation with author, December 3, 1994.

13. A. D. and Eva Finchum, interview by LuAnn Jones, April 30, 1987, OHSA; Grace Sunbeam Ellis, interview by Linda May, June 28, 1974, OHA; James Walton Lawrence Sr., *Shadows of Hogback* (Landrum, S.C.: *News Leader,* 1979), 65; Elizabeth H. Jordan, "Dollars Grown in Her Garden," *Farm Journal,* August 1932, 7, 18; "Some Ways for Farm Women to Make Money," *Southern Agriculturist,* June 1, 1921, 7.

14. Mary R. Reynolds, "Marketing Apples by the Jelly Route," *Farm Journal,* September 1930, 20; Sarah Umoselle, "Cold Cash From Canning," *Farm Journal,* August 1934, 5; Maude Guthrie, "Food Markets for Tennessee Club Women," *Southern Agriculturalist,* June 1, 1930, 12; ESAR, Tennessee, 1933, 223; ESAR, South Carolina, 1922, 19, School of Home Economics Papers, box 1, folder 8, DL.

15. Edna Spencer, interview by author, January 26, 1995.

16. Lois Dowdle, "The Home," *Progressive Farmer,* October 15–31, 1931, 20; Michael Frome, *Strangers in High Places: The Story of the Great Smoky Mountains* (Knoxville: University of Tennessee Press, 1966), 231–40; Lucy Quarrier, interview by Barbara Woerner, April 20, 1971, OHA; Inez Lovelace, "She Adds $300 to Family Income," *Progressive Farmer,* June 1–14, 1932, 16.

17. Ona Hale, to author, March 24, 1994.

18. Pernie Branam, "Claiming Our Economic History, Jellico, Tennessee," oral histories collected by the Rural Community Education Cooperative, Spring 1987, Hodgson Library, University of Tennessee, Knoxville; John T. Walton, interview by Michael Galgano, undated, ca. 1974, OHA; Maude Walker, interview and letter to author, March 1994.

19. Watts Bar project, boxes 75–80, TVA.

20. Ibid.

21. Dave Tamplin, interview by Stephen W. Brown, April 2, 1973, OHA; Joseph Kovich, interview by Anna Laura Kovich, undated ca. 1974, OHA.

22. Effie Temple, interview by LuAnn Jones, May 8, 1987, OHSA.

23. Ella Betler to unidentified interviewer, April 30, 1976, OHA; Ft. Loudon

project, boxes 133–135, and Watts Bar project, boxes 75–80, TVA; ESAR, South Carolina, 1920 and 1922, Christine South Gee Papers, box 1, folder 2, DL.

24. Ft. Loudon project, boxes 133–135, and Watts Bar project, boxes 75–80, TVA.

25. Opposition to the employment of married women during the Great Depression was rooted in the ideology of separate spheres and, more importantly, in the belief that married women were taking jobs from men who needed to support their families.

26. Watts Bar project, boxes 75–80, and Ft. Loudon project, boxes 133–135, TVA; Susie Simmons, interview by Elmer Turnage, January 6, 1938, WPALHC; Mary Beth Pudup, "Women's Work in the West Virginia Economy," *West Virginia History* 49 (1990): 7–20.

27. Lawrence, *Shadows of Hogback*, 52.

28. "Ethel Davis," to author, September 1994; Mary Evelyn Lane interview; Maude Walker interview.

29. Watts Bar project, boxes 75–80, and Ft. Loudon project, boxes 133–135, TVA; *Census of Population, 1920,* vol. 4, pp. 126, 362; *Fifteenth Census of Population, 1930,* vol. 2, pt. 2, pp. 802, 1287.

30. Bessie Reed, interview by Caldwell Sims, January 9, 1939, WPALHC.

31. Watts Bar project, boxes 75–80, and Ft. Loudon project, boxes 133–135, TVA; Elsie Crawford, "Claiming Our Economic History," Jellico, Tennessee. Oral History Collection, Spring 1987. Special Collections, Hodges Library, University of Tennessee, Knoxville; Lucy Price, interview by David A. Mathews, December 14, 1938, WPALHC.

32. Alice Hall interview; *Farm Journal,* April 1939, 48.

33. Jessie Felknor interview.

34. Ft. Loudon projects, boxes 133–135, TVA. The *Maryville Times,* January 7, 1920, contained advertisements for girls to be knitters at Ideal Hosiery Mills in Blount County for a salary of $10–$15 per week. In the same issue, county school superintendent Gordon Miser reported that the average teacher's salary was $51.60 per month.

35. Korola Lee, interview by author, August 10, 1994, MHC.

36. *Farm Journal,* November 1939, 60.

37. Mary Evelyn Lane, interview by author, August 8, 1994, MHC.

38. Watts Bar project, boxes 75–80, TVA.

39. Bertha Snow Adams, "These Poultry Women Made Good," *Farm Journal,* March 1924; Edwin Larson, "She Raises Karakul Sheep," *Farm Journal,* 1921, 57–63; *Farm Journal,* March 1930, 24; "A Manless Dairy Prospers," *Southern Agriculturist,* June 1, 1930, 9, 15.

40. Ben Robertson Jr., *Red Hills and Cotton: An Upcountry Memory* (New York: Alfred A. Knopf, 1942), 177–88; Watts Bar project, boxes 75–80, and Ft. Loudon project, boxes 133–135, TVA.

41. Ft. Loudon project, boxes 133–135, TVA.

42. Naomi Banks Bridges, interview by her daughter, December 6, 1980, EHOHP.

43. Compiled from Norris project files, Watts Bar project files, and Ft. Loudon project files, TVA; Mary E. Frayser, "Cost of Living of Farm Family Found Very Low," undated clipping from unnamed newspaper, Mary E. Frayser Papers, Box 19, Folder 165, DL.

44. Agnes B. Green, to author, March 25, 1994; Lois P. Dowdle, "The Home," *Progressive Farmer*, June 1–14, 1932, 16, and "Educate Your Boys and Girls," October 1–14, 1931, 12; ESAR, South Carolina, 1921, 43–47, Gee Papers, box 1, folder, DL.

45. Della Sarten, interview by LuAnn Jones, May 1, 1987, OHSA.

46. Wilma Fisher, to author, March 22, 1994.

47. Bill Lewellyn interview.

Chapter 4. Mixed Messages

1. ESAR, Cabell County, West Virginia, 1925.

2. O. B. Martin, "A Decade of Negro Extension Work, 1914–1924," USDA Miscellaneous Circular 72 (Washington, D.C.: Government Printing Office, 1926); Earl W. Crosby, "The Struggle for Existence: The Institutionalization of the Black County Agent System," *Agricultural History* 60 (Spring 1986): 123–36; Karen J. Ferguson, "Caught in 'No Man's Land': The Negro Cooperative Extension Service and the Ideology of Booker T. Washington, 1900–1918," *Agricultural History* 72 (Winter 1998): 33–54.

3. ESAR, Tennessee, 1929, 4; *CA, 1930*, vol. 2, p. 878; ESAR, South Carolina, 1935; ESAR, West Virginia, 1920–1940, Johnson, *SASC*, 197; Maristan Chapman, *The Weather Tree* (New York: Viking, 1932), 64.

4. ESAR, Cabell County, West Virginia, 1935.

5. Ona Hale, to author, April 4, 1994; Wilma Fisher, to author, March 30, 1994; Korola Lee, interview with author, August 10, 1994, MHC; Mary Evelyn Lane, interview with author, August 8, 1994, MHC; ESAR, Cabell County, West Virginia, 1935; "Kate Simmons," interview with author, August 5, 1994, MHC.

6. Pearl Faulkner, interview by Margaret McKenzie, March 11, 1982, EHOHP.

7. ESAR, West Virginia, 1935.

8. ESAR, Tennessee, 1921, 28–29, and ESAR, Tennessee, 1925, 33–88; *YA, 1925*, 1400–1; ESAR, Tennessee, 1926, 95, 100, 103, 111; ESAR, South Carolina, 1921, 33.

9. Ferguson, "Caught in 'No Man's Land,'" 35.

10. O. B. Martin, "A Decade of Negro Extension Work, 1914–1924"; Earl W. Crosby, "The Struggle for Existence"; General Education Board Records, Record Group 1.1., Tennessee Series, Rockefeller Archive Center, North Tarrytown,

New York; ESAR, Tennessee, 1921, 28–29; compiled from ESAR, Tennessee, 1921–39; *Sixteenth Census of the United States: 1940*, 162–63.

11. ESAR, South Carolina, 1919 and 1920; and ESAR, West Virginia, 1925 and 1935.

12. ESAR, South Carolina, 1920, 45–46.

13. ESAR, Tennessee, 1932, 122; ESAR, South Carolina, 1921, 57; ESAR, West Virginia, 1925 and 1940; ESAR, Tennessee, 1927, 159; ESAR, Tennessee, 1926, 172; ESAR, South Carolina, 1922, 86.

14. ESAR, Tennessee, 1925.

15. ESAR, Tennessee, 1925, 241; ESAR, Tennessee, 1928, 389, 398. These numbers do not include the thousands of farm households whose members did not participate in extension service programs.

16. ESAR, Tennessee, 1928, 161, 164.

17. *CA*, 1930, compiled from pp. 870–84, 894–902.

18. ESAR, Tennessee, 1926, 135.

19. ESAR, Tennessee, 1926, 123–24; ESAR, Tennessee, 1925, 22, 128.

20. ESAR, Tennessee, 1933, 283; ESAR, Tennessee, 1934, 144; ESAR, Tennessee, 1937, 199, 201.

21. ESAR, Tennessee, 1925, 28; ESAR, South Carolina, 1922, 89.

22. ESAR, Tennessee, 1929, 369; ESAR, Tennessee, 1931, 121, 238–70; ESAR, Tennessee, 1932, 385, 187, 391; ESAR, Tennessee, 1934, 344; ESAR, Tennessee, 1936, 13, 225.

23. ESAR, Tennessee, 1931, 121; ESAR, Tennessee, 1933, 283.

24. ESAR, Tennessee, 1925, 31.

25. ESAR, Tennessee, 1932, 287; ESAR, Tennessee, 1933 and 1934.

26. ESAR, South Carolina, 1922; ESAR, West Virginia, various years; Almon J. Sims, *A History of Extension Work in Tennessee, Twenty-Five Years of Service to Rural Life, 1914–1939* (Washington, D.C.: USDA, May 1939), 31–31, in the Virginia Moore Papers, Special Collections, Hoskins Library, University of Tennessee, box 1, folder 1. Though many white agents were mentioned by name and featured in photographs in the publications, not a single black agent was named or pictured.

27. ESAR, Tennessee, 1928, 164; ESAR, South Carolina, 1920, 45.

28. ESAR, South Carolina, 1922, 87.

29. ESAR, Tennessee, 1936, 13; ESAR, Tennessee, 1938, 137.

30. ESAR, Tennessee, 1922, 186; ESAR, Tennessee, 1926, 307; ESAR, Tennessee, 1928, 156; ESAR, South Carolina, 1921, 43–44; ESAR, South Carolina, 1920, 43; ESAR, West Virginia, 1921.

31. ESAR, Tennessee, 1925, 97, 128, 241–44; ESAR, South Carolina, 1921.

32. *Maryville Times*, January 28, 1929.

33. ESAR, Tennessee, 1928, 156; ESAR, Tennessee, 1925, 97, 128, 241–44; *Maryville Times*, January 28, 1929.

34. ESAR, Tennessee, 1926, 126; *Progressive Farmer,* July 27, 1929, 7; ESAR, Kanawha County, West Virginia, 1921, 11.

35. ESAR, Tennessee, 1926, 126; *Maryville Times,* March 21, 1921. In Blount County, the county court (equivalent to a modern county commission) that voted on funding for home extension work was made up of prominent farmers, educators, and local merchants. Local histories and newspaper accounts speak of local merchants funding home demonstration work contest prizes and projects (*Maryville Times,* March 22, 1923; Blount County Extension Homemakers Council, "A History of Blount County Home Demonstration Work," undated typescript, copy in author's collection).

36. ESAR, Tennessee, 1928, 161, 164.

37. ESAR, Tennessee, 1929, 308, 928–29; *Sevier County Republican,* March 10, 1930, 1; Catherine Bishir, "Landmarks of Power," *Southern Cultures* 1 (1993): 5–45.

38. ESAR, Tennessee, 1929, 308.

39. ESAR, Tennessee, 1926, 123–24; ESAR, Tennessee, 1925, 22; ESAR, Tennessee, 1928, 388, 397; ESAR, South Carolina, 1922, 14–16.

40. ESAR, Tennessee, 1926, 123–24; ESAR, Tennessee, 1925, 22; ESAR, Tennessee, 1928, 388, 397; ESAR, South Carolina, 1921, 33; ESAR, West Virginia, 1921.

41. ESAR, South Carolina, 1921, 43–47, and 1920, 22; ESAR, West Virginia, 1925.

42. ESAR, Tennessee, 1926, 117–18; 1925, 22; 1928, 118; and 1929, 110; ESAR, South Carolina, 1921, 59–64.

43. ESAR, South Carolina, 1920, 18–23; 1921, 27–30; and 1922, 20–23.

44. ESAR, South Carolina, 1921, 43–47; and 1922, 33–39.

45. ESAR, South Carolina, 1921, 56–59; ESAR, Tennessee, 1921, 289, 267–269, 282; ESAR, Tennessee, 1926, 112–13; ESAR, Tennessee, 1922, 262; ESAR, Tennessee, 1925, 27–28; ESAR, Tennessee, 1929, 352, 380. In 1925 2,469 white women in Tennessee raised 98,828 birds for a profit of $34,714 from the sales of eggs and chickens; this was an average of $14.06 per woman. By 1929 there was a decline in commercial poultry raising by home demonstration women. The individual profits of the women who continued to participate increased, however. That year 2,054 white women raised 58,499 birds for a profit of $14,507, or an average of $28.48 per woman. These earnings were probably not evenly distributed, however, as the size of the poultry operation would have varied according to individual woman's time, resources, and inclinations. At a time when over half of all farmers earned less than $800 per year (USDA considered $1,200 the minimum subsistence level), the sums earned by some farm women on these projects were a significant contribution to the family income. (Figures for 1929 from *CA, 1940,* vol. 2, pt. 2, p. 482; *YA, 1928,* 280–82; *CA, 1920,* 439.)

46. ESAR, Tennessee, 1921 and 1928; ESAR, South Carolina, 1922, 25; ESAR, West Virginia, 1921, 41–2.

47. "History of South Carolina Extension Homemakers Programs," un-

dated typescript, South Carolina Extension Homemakers Council Papers, box 1, folder 1, DL.

48. ESAR, South Carolina, 1921, 39–41; 1922, 19; 1926, 8–9; and 1920, 33–36; Jane Ketchen, "South Carolina Home Demonstration Council," typescript, June 1959, South Carolina Extension Homemakers Council Papers, box 1, folder 1, DL.

49. "Typescript biography of Mary Frayser," (n.a., n.d.), Mary Frayser Papers, box 2, folder 9, DL; "The Origin and Development of Home Economic Extension Work by Winthrop College," undated typescript, Mary Frayser Papers, box 2, folder 10, DL.

50. "Origin and Development," Frayser Papers, box 2, folder 10, DL.

51. ESAR, Tennessee, 1931; ESAR, West Virginia, 1930; ESAR, Cabell County, West Virginia, 1930; "Minutes of the Thirteenth Annual Convention of the South Carolina Council of Farm Women," June 26–27, 1933; "Minutes of the Tenth Annual Convention of the South Carolina Council of Farm Women," June 7–8, 1930, both in South Carolina Extension Homemakers Council Papers, box 2, folder 10, DL.

52. ESAR, Tennessee, 1931, 86–87; ESAR, West Virginia, 1930; ESAR, Kanawha County, West Virginia, 1930.

53. ESAR, Tennessee, 1933, 283; and 1935, 327

54. ESAR, Tennessee, 1933 and 1934, 325, 141; "Making a Cotton Mattress," *Progressive Farmer,* November 19, 1932; Ona Hale letter; Agnes Greene, to author, April 6, 1994; Mary Evelyn Lane interview; "Reports of Home Agents on the Mattress Project, South Carolina," August 9, 1940, Papers of the School of Home Economics, box 1, folder 8, DL.

55. ESAR, Tennessee, 1931, 95; and 1934, 144; ESAR, West Virginia, 1930.

56. Allen H. Eaton, *Handicrafts of the Southern Highlands* (New York: Russell Sage Foundation, 1937).

57. Eaton, *Handicrafts of the Southern Highlands,* 292–94, 264; "Earnings of Handicraft Workers in Southern Mountain Regions," *Monthly Labor Review* 41 (July 1935): 146–49.

58. ESAR, Tennessee, 1934, 142; and 1936, 425; Eaton, *Handicrafts of the Southern Highlands,* 223.

59. ESAR, Tennessee, 1932, 256–61, 335, 120; and 1933, 224; ESAR, West Virginia, 1930.

60. ESAR, Tennessee, 1934, 2; and 1933, 121, 75; ESAR, West Virginia, 1930; ESAR, Cabell County, West Virginia, 1930.

61. ESAR, Tennessee, 1934, 98–99; and 1935, 351, 191, 404–05.

62. ESAR, Tennessee, 1934, 2, 144.

63. ESAR, Tennessee, 1932, 117.

64. ESAR, Tennessee, 1932, 85; and 1934, 325; ESAR, West Virginia, 1930.

65. "Minutes of the Tenth Annual Convention of the South Carolina Council of Farm Women," June 7–8, 1930, and "Minutes of the Fourteenth Annual Convention of the South Carolina Council of Farm Women," July 9, 1934, both in

South Carolina Extension Homemakers Papers, box 2, folder 10, DL; ESAR, Tennessee, 1931, 86–87; ESAR, Cabell County, West Virginia, 1930.

66. "Minutes of the Tenth Annual Convention of the South Carolina Council of Farm Women," June 7–8, 1930, "Minutes of the Thirteenth Annual Convention of the South Carolina Council of Farm Women," June 26–27, 1933, and "Minutes of the Fourteenth Annual Convention of the South Carolina Council of Farm Women," July 9, 1934, all in South Carolina Extension Homemakers Papers, box 2, folder 10, DL.

67. *Sixteenth Census of the United States: 1940,* Agriculture, 3:37; ESAR, Tennessee, 1929, 4; 1932, 374; 1933, 67; 1931, 8; and 1934, 333. The Tennessee farm population increased from 1,215,452 in 1930 to 1,308,420 in 1935.

68. "History of South Carolina Council of Farm Women," undated typescript, South Carolina Extension Homemakers Council Papers, box 1, folder 1, DL; ESAR, West Virginia, 1925 and 1935.

69. ESAR, Tennessee, 1936, 237, 239; 1937, 135; and 1935, 427; ESAR, West Virginia, 1935; "Minutes of the Sixteenth Annual Convention of the South Carolina Council of Farm Women," June 11–12, 1936, 28, and "Minutes of the Seventeenth Annual Convention of the South Carolina Council of Farm Women," June 7–8, 1937, 33, both in Mrs. W. E. Cochran Papers, box 1, folder 5, DL.

70. ESAR, Tennessee, 1935, 324, 326, 332; ESAR, West Virginia, 1935.

71. ESAR, Tennessee, 1935, 432–33; ESAR, Cabell County, West Virginia, 1935; ESAR, West Virginia, 1935.

72. ESAR, Tennessee, 1936, 235–36; "Minutes of the Eighteenth Annual Convention of South Carolina Council of Farm Women," June 6–7, 1938, South Carolina Extension Homemakers Papers, box 2, folder 10, DL.

73. ESAR, Tennessee, 1936, 181; 1937, 136; and 1939, 271; Korola Lee interview; Oliver and Hettie Lawson, interview with author, August 16, 1993, MHC; Mary Evelyn Lane interview; "Minutes of the Seventeenth Annual Convention of South Carolina Council of Farm Women," 33, South Carolina Extension Homemakers Papers, box 2, folder 10, DL; West Virginia ESAR, 1935 and 1940.

74. Jane Ketchen, "History of South Carolina 4-H Scholarship Loan Funds," 1937, typescript, South Carolina Extension Homemakers Council Papers, box 1, folder 1, DL; "Minutes of the Seventeenth Annual Convention of South Carolina Council of Farm Women," 30–31, and "Minutes of the Sixteenth Annual Convention of South Carolina Council of Farm Women," 27, both in South Carolina Extension Homemakers Papers, box 2, folder 10, DL; ESAR, Cabell County, West Virginia, 1935; AES, ESAR, West Virginia, 1935.

Chapter 5. Government Relocation and Upcountry Women

1. "More Time for Flowers," *Knoxville News–Sentinel,* May 7, 1934.

2. Marguerite Owen, *The Tennessee Valley Authority* (New York: Praeger Publishers, 1973), 14–17.

3. R. L. Duffus, "A Dream Takes Form in TVA's Domain," *New York Times Magazine,* April 19, 1936.

4. *New York Times,* April 19, 1936; Michael J. McDonald and John Muldowny, *TVA and the Dispossessed: The Resettlement of Population in the Norris Dam Area* (Knoxville: University of Tennessee Press, 1982), 268–70; *New York Times,* May 11, 1934. The other two TVA directors, however, had somewhat different views of regional planning. Arthur Morgan's vision dominated agency policy in the first five years of its existence; nonetheless, internal wrangling contributed to the agency's limited effectiveness. Unfortunately, TVA's limited budget and power also made it difficult for the agency to achieve these ambitious objectives. Moreover, the massive changes that would have been needed to bring this degree of change to the poverty-stricken Tennessee Valley may have been more intrusive than the Congress or the people of the region would have accepted.

5. *Maryville Times,* August 14, 1939, 1; McDonald and Muldowny, *TVA and the Dispossessed,* 109–10, 114.

6. Korola Lee, interview by author, August 10, 1994, MHC; Tressa Waters quoted in Eleanor Arnold, ed., *Voices of American Homemakers* (Bloomington: Indiana University Press, 1985), 177.

7. "Ethel Davis," interview by author, July 19, 1994; *YA, 1938,* 284–85.

8. Edwin C. Hargrove and Paul K. Conkin, eds., *TVA: Fifty Years of Grass-Roots Bureaucracy* (Urbana: University of Illinois Press, 1983).

9. For example, Loudon County farm woman "Ethel Davis" gave a detailed description of the soil conservation practices her family adopted at the urging of TVA and Soil Conservation Service officials. "Ethel Davis" interview.

10. "Report on the Norris Community," 1935, and Walter B. Hill, "Norris Follow-Up Report," 1936, typescript, both in folder 1486, box 159, Tennessee series 137, GEB.

11. "Peggy Delozier Jones," interview by author, July 21, 1994, MHC.

12. Maude Walker, interview by author, August 17, 1993.

13. Margaret Marsh, interview by author, July 18, 1994.

14. Nancy L. Grant, *TVA and Black Americans: Planning for the Status Quo* (Philadelphia: Temple University Press, 1990), 19–20, 45–69.

15. Charles H. Houston and John P. Davis, "TVA: Lily White Reconstruction," *The Crisis* 41 (October 1934), 290–91, 311; John P. Davis, "The Plight of the Negro in the Tennessee Valley," *The Crisis* 42 (October 1935), 294–95, 314–15.

16. McDonald and Muldowny, *TVA and the Dispossessed,* 125.

17. Ibid., 176; Tennessee Valley Authority, "Family Removal Workers Manual," undated typescript, TVA, box 1.

18. "Reservoir Family Removal Worker's Manual," TVA; Norris Project, boxes 25–35, Ft. Loudon Project, boxes 133–140, and Watts Bar Project, boxes 79–80, TVA.

19. Ft. Loudon Project, box 133, TVA.

20. McDonald and Muldowny, *TVA and the Dispossessed,* 4–7; TVA, "Popula-

tion Readjustment, Ft. Loudon Area, Final Report," February 1, 1943, typescript, 3–4, TVA Technical Library, Knoxville, Tennessee.

21. Watts Bar Project, box 80, TVA.

22. "Kate Simmons," interview by author, August 5, 1994.

23. Ft. Loudon Project, box 135, and Watts Bar Project, box 76, TVA.

24. "Reservoir Family Removal Workers Manual," TVA.

25. Edna Spencer, interview by author, January 26, 1995.

26. Ft. Loudon Project, box 134, TVA.

27. Ft. Loudon Project, box 133, TVA.

28. *Maryville Times,* March 18, 1940, 1; Frederick E. Ketchen, "TVA Reservoir Property Management Department Community Readjustment Studies of Blount County, Ft. Loudon Area," June 4, 1941, typescript, TVA Technical Library, Knoxville, Tennessee.

29. Watts Bar Project, boxes 79 and 80, TVA.

30. Ft. Loudon Project, box 133, TVA.

31. Watts Bar Project, box 75, TVA.

32. Ibid.

33. Ibid.; *Knoxville News Sentinel,* February 4, 1934; Patricia Barclay Kirkeminde, *Cumberland Homesteads as Viewed by the Newspapers* (Crossville, Tenn.: Brookhart Press, 1977); D. F. Folger, "The History and Aims of Cumberland Homesteads," *Mountain Life and Work* 11 (July 1935): 5–7.

34. Watts Bar Project, box 79, TVA.

35. Watts Bar Project, boxes 79 and 80, TVA.

36. Ft. Loudon Project, box 135, TVA.

37. Ft. Loudon Project, box 134, TVA.

38. Ft. Loudon Project, box 133, TVA.

39. Watts Bar Project, box 80, TVA.

40. John Rice Irwin quoted in McDonald and Muldowny, *TVA and the Dispossessed,* 62.

41. Ft. Loudon Project, box 135, TVA.

42. Ft. Loudon Project, box 133, TVA.

43. McDonald and Muldowny, *TVA and the Dispossessed,* 236–62; Jack Temple Kirby, "The Southern Exodus, 1910–1960: A Primer for Historians," *Journal of Southern History* 49 (November 1983): 585–600.

44. McDonald and Muldowny, *TVA and the Dispossessed,* 236–62.

45. Ibid., 62; Watts Bar Project, box 80, TVA.

46. Watts Bar Project, box 80, TVA.

47. Lou Emma Taylor quoted in McDonald and Muldowny, *TVA and the Dispossessed,* 62–63.

48. *Spartanburg Herald,* November 8, 1940; *Spartanburg Journal and Carolina Spartan,* November 9, 1940.

49. "Special Souvenir Edition of the Fiftieth Anniversary Celebration of Camp Croft, South Carolina: From Wartime Heritage to Peaceful Community,

1941–1991," 1991, Camp Croft files, KC; U.S. Army Corps of Engineers, "Ordnance and Explosive Waste Archives Search Report for Former Camp Croft Army Training Facility," 1994, pt. 2, Appendix L–3, KC.

50. Archie Vernon Huff Jr., *Greenville: The History of the City and the County in the South Carolina Piedmont* (Columbia: University of South Carolina Press, 1995), 292–94; Howard W. Odum, *Southern Regions of the United States* (Chapel Hill: University of North Carolina Press, 1936), 38, 56; *SASC*, 204; *Spartanburg City Directory*, 1942, 18, KC; figures compiled from *CA*, vol. 1, pt. 3, pp. 422, 438–44, and *Census of Population*, vol. 2, pt. 6, p. 394.

51. Camp Croft Press Section, "Camp Croft's First Year," undated typescript in Camp Croft Records, KC; Dwain Pruitt, *Things Hidden: An Introduction to the History of Blacks in Spartanburg* (Spartanburg: City of Spartanburg Human Relations Office, 1995), chap. 7; and Kristen L. Bruch, "'Riot' in Spartanburg?" (student paper, Converse College, May 1998).

52. *Spartanburg Journal and Carolina Spartan*, November 12, 19, 20, 21, and 23, and December 2, 1940.

53. *Spartanburg Journal and Carolina Spartan*, November 12, 19, 21, 23, and December 2, 11, and 12, 1940; *Spartanburg Herald–Journal*, November 17, 1940; Camp Croft Press Section, "Camp Croft's First Year," KC.

54. *Spartanburg Journal and Carolina Spartan*, November 20 and 21, December 2, 7, and 10 1940.

55. *Journal and Carolina Spartan*, December 7, 1940; Thomas A. Boynton memo to Major Neal R. McKay, Constructing Quartermaster, undated typescript ca. 1941, Camp Croft Records, KC; George L. Walling to J. W. Cramer, Memorandum, "Advisory Committee to the Council of National Defense," February 21, 1941, Record Group 207, Records of the Housing and Home Finance Agency, Division of Defense Housing Coordination, Geographical Dockets, 1941–42, box 10, PI–164, NA.

56. *Journal and Carolina Spartan*, January 31, 1941, February 6, 1941; *Spartanburg City Directory*, 1940, "Camp Croft," typescript, Army Corps of Engineers Archives Search Report, pt. 1, Appendix D–3; George L. Walling memo to J. W. Cramer, February 24, 1941, RG 207, Records of the Housing and Home Finance Agency, NA.

57. *Spartanburg Herald–Journal*, January 12, 1941.

58. "Camp Croft," undated typescript, U.S. Army Corps of Engineers, Archives Search Report, pt. 1, appendix D–3, KC; Mattie Lee Murph, telephone interview by author, September 24, 1997; William White quoted in Gary Henderson, "Images of Home," *Spartanburg Herald–Journal*, September 27, 1997, B–1.

59. Claude Lee quoted in Henderson, "Images of Home."

60. Camp Croft Press Section, "Camp Croft's First Year," KC.

61. Claude Lee quoted in Henderson, "Images of Home."

62. Mattie Lee Murph telephone interview.

63. Sanford N. Smith, interview by author, September 17, 1997.

64. Sanford N. Smith interview; *Spartanburg Journal and Carolina Spartan,* November 23, 1940.

65. Sanford N. Smith interview; *Spartanburg Journal and Carolina Spartan,* November 21 and 23, 1940.

66. Sanford N. Smith interview.

67. Sanford N. Smith interview; Suellen E. Dean, "Camp Croft," *Spartanburg Herald–Journal,* September 12, 1991.

68. Sanford N. Smith interview.

69. Bessie Millwood quoted in Nancy Atkins, "Camp Croft Remains Vivid Experience for Area Woman," *Spartanburg Herald–Journal,* September 13, 1977.

Chapter 6. Rural Women and Industrialization

1. Roy Fisher, Tennessee Operations Manager, Speech to Maryville Kiwanis Club, August 12, 1969, as quoted in Russell D. Parker, "Alcoa, Tennessee: The Early Years, 1919–1939," *East Tennessee Historical Society Publications* 48 (1976): 84–103.

2. *Maryville Times,* February 22, 1925, 1; May 18, 1925, 1; July 2, 1925, 4; October 3, 1927, 1; August 14, 1933, 1; and September 12, 1934, 1; Durwood Dunn, *Cades Cove: The Life and Death of a Southern Appalachian Community* (Knoxville: University of Tennessee Press, 1988), 85–88, 125, 143, 224–25; Inez E. Burns, *History of Blount County, Tennessee* (Nashville: Tennessee Historical Commission, 1957, rev. 1988), 330–32.

3. Maryville College Departments of Political and Social Science, "Social Survey of Blount County, 1930," 10, 13, Special Collections, Hoskins Library, University of Tennessee, Knoxville.

4. Maryville College, "Social Survey of Blount County," 17, 24; Mary Evelyn Lane, interview by author, August 8, 1994.

5. Maryville College, "Social Survey of Blount County," 15, 17.

6. *Goodspeed's History of Tennessee* (Nashville, Tennessee: Charles and Randy Elder Booksellers, 1887, repr. 1972), 828; Burns, *History of Blount County,* 31, 217–50; Adele McKenzie, "From Agriculture to Industry," *Bicentennial Years in Blount County, 1776–1976* (Maryville: Maryville–Alcoa *Daily Times,* 1976), in Special Collections, Hoskins Library, University of Tennessee, Knoxville, Tennessee; Maryville College, "Social Survey of Blount County, 1930," 11–17.

7. Parker, "The Early Years," 85.

8. Maryville College, "Social Survey of Blount County," 5; Parker, "The Early Years," 86; Carolyn L. Blair and Arda S. Walker, *By Faith Endowed: The Story of Maryville College, 1819–1994* (Maryville, Tenn.: Maryville College Press, 1994), chap. 7; Tindall, *Blount County: Communities We Live In* (Maryville, Tenn.: Brazos Press, 1976), 13–21.

9. Parker, "Alcoa: The Early Years," 85–91.

10. Ibid., 87, 91. Tennessee's counties have a dual property tax system. All landholders in the county pay county taxes. In addition, landholders within the limits of an incorporated town or city pay additional city property taxes. Maryville had hoped to annex the county territory, which included the company town, in order to add to its own tax base.

11. Lula Gatlin Ramsey, to author, June 28, 1995; Mary Evelyn Lane interview; Ronald C. Eller, *Miners, Millhands, and Mountaineers: Industrialization of the Appalachian South, 1880–1930* (Knoxville: University of Tennessee Press, 1982).

12. Harriet Arnow's classic novel, *The Dollmaker,* recounts the experiences of one family who moved from the Appalachians mountains to work in a midwestern factory during World War II. Although the transition was neither as abrupt nor as complete for Blount County natives, there were similarities.

13. Bill Lewellyn, interview by author, August 10, 1993; Lula Gatlin Ramsey letter.

14. Parker, "Alcoa: The Early Years," 94–98; Bill Lewellyn interview.

15. Parker, "Alcoa: The Early Years," 94–98.

16. Tennessee Federation of Women's Clubs, *Woman's Work in Tennessee* (Nashville: Tennessee Federation of Women's Clubs, 1916), 95.

17. Jennifer K. Boone, "'Mingling Freely': Tennessee Society on the Eve of the Civil War," *Tennessee Historical Quarterly* 51 (Fall 1992): 144–45.

18. *Maryville Times,* May 12, 1920, 1, and February 12, 1934, 1; Parker, "Alcoa: The Early Years," 86.

19. Dunn, *Cades Cove,* 124–25; Blair and Walker, *By Faith Endowed,* 100–12.

20. *SASC,* 207; John McKenzie, to author, August 12, 1993; Bill Lewellyn interview.

21. John McKenzie letter; Parker, "Alcoa: The Early Years," 88.

22. Parker, "Alcoa: The Early Years," 89; Janette Thomas Greenwood, *Bittersweet Legacy: The Black and White "Better Classes" in Charlotte, 1840–1910* (Chapel Hill: University of North Carolina Press, 1994).

23. Parker, "Alcoa: The Early Years," 96.

24. Maude Walker, interview by author, August 17, 1993.

25. French Clark, interview by author, July 22, 1994.

26. Oliver and Hettie Lawson, interview by author, August 16, 1993; Wilma Williamson, interview by author, July 18, 1994.

27. Betsey Beeler Creekmore, *Arrows to Atoms: The Story of East Tennessee* (Knoxville: University of Tennessee Press, 1959), 105–6; Burns, *History of Blount County,* 52; Korola Lee, interview by author, August 10, 1994; *Maryville Times,* March 2, 1936, 1.

28. Peggy Pollard, interview with author, July 16, 1994. Similar accounts were given by other Blount County people. See Laverne Farmer, interview by author, August 9, 1993; Korola Lee interview; John MacKenzie letter.

29. Laverne Farmer, interview by author, August 9, 1993.

30. French Clark interview.

31. William K. Webb, letter to author, June 3, 1995; Burns, *Blount County, Tennessee,* Appendix, list of officeholders.

32. *Maryville Times,* February 10, 1927, 1.

33. Parker, "The Early Years," 98–100. French Clark interview; Mary Evelyn Lane interview; Bill Lewellyn interview; Lula Gatlin Ramsey, letter to author, June 28, 1995.

34. Carolyn G. Heilbrun, *Writing a Woman's Life* (New York: Ballantine Books, 1988), 14–15.

35. U.S. Statutes at Large, XLVII (Washington, D.C.: Government Printing Office, 1934), 198; Craig Billingsley, *A History of Local 309, United Steelworkers of America, AFL-CIO-CLC, Alcoa, Tennessee, 1933–1977* (Alcoa, Tenn.: Local 309, 1976), 11–15.

36. Parker, "The Early Years," 98–100; Billingsley, *A History of Local 309,* 15–27.

37. Mary Laurance Elkuss, interview by Gloria Gordon, October 21, 1976, The Twentieth Century Trade Union Woman: Vehicle for Social Change Oral History Project, Institute of Labor and Industrial Relations, University of Michigan and Wayne State University. The AFL held that all workers were eligible to belong to the union but did not interfere if its locals excluded blacks.

38. Parker, "Black Community," 203, 218; Parker, "The Early Years," 101;

39. William K. Webb letter; Parker, "The Early Years," 98–100.

40. Mary Laurance Elkuss interview; Lula Gatlin Ramsey letter; Mary Evelyn Lane, to author, July 2, 1995.

41. Parker, "The Early Years," 99–101; Parker, "Alcoa: Years of Change," 101; Sammy E. Pinkston, "History of Local 309: United Steelworkers of America, Alcoa, Tennessee" (master's thesis, University of Tennessee, Knoxville, 1970), 14–19; Billingsley, *A History of Local 309,* 22–27; *Knoxville News–Sentinel,* July 7, 1937, and July 8, 1937; *Knoxville Journal,* July 8, 1937.

42. Pinkston, "History of Local 309," 30–40; *Maryville Times,* July 8, 1937.

43. William Webb letter; *Maryville Times,* August 13, 16, 20, 23, and 27, and September 6, 1934; *Knoxville News Sentinel,* July 7 and 8, 1937; Parker, "Alcoa: The Early Years," 98–101.

44. Pinkston, "History of Local 309," 30–40; Parker, "Years of Change," 102; Lula Gatlin Ramsey letter.

45. Evelyn Lewellyn interview.

46. Lula Gatlin Ramsey letter; French Clark interview; Parker, "Alcoa, Tennessee: The Years of Change, 1940–1960," *East Tennessee Historical Society Publications* 49 (1977): 99–115.

47. Figures compiled from *Sixteenth Census of Population, 1940,* vol. 2, pt. 7, p. 473; *CA,* vol. 2, pt. 2, p. 123, and vol. 1, pt. 3, pp. 220–24, 265; *CA, 1930,* vol. 2, pt. 2, pp. 296–99.

48. WPA, *West Virginia: A Guide to the Mountain State* (New York: Oxford University Press, 1941), 70–75.

49. David A. Corbin, *Life, Work, and Rebellion in the Coal Fields: The Southern West Virginia Mines, 1880–1922* (Urbana: University of Illinois Press, 1981), 8.

50. Virginia Giacomo, interview by William Giacomo, April 16, 1973, OHA; Dave Tamplin, interview by Stephen W. Brown, April 2, 1973, OHA; Joseph A. Kovich, interview by Anna Laura Kovich, undated ca. 1974, OHA.

51. Roscoe Spence, interview by Ann M. Berry, December 3, 1973, OHA.

52. Ibid.

53. Ibid.; Dave Tamplin interview.

54. Virginia Giacomo interview.

55. John T. Walton, interview by Dr. Michael Galgano, undated, ca. 1974, OHA; Dave Tamplin interview; Joseph Kovich interview.

56. Burl Collings, interview by Claire Cipolaro, August 3, 1974, OHA.

57. Virginia Giacomo interview.

58. WPA, *West Virginia,* 70–75; Burl Collins interview; Joseph A. Kovich interview; figures compiled from *CA, 1930,* vol. 2, pt. 2, pp. 296–99; Matt L. Hanna, interview by J. Kraft, August 6, 1973, OHA.

59. Bertha Holton, interview by Ellen Stephens, August 4, 1974, OHA; William R. Payne, interview by Ella Gibson, November 3, 1973, OHA; Matt L. Hanna interview.

60. Otis K. Rice, *West Virginia: A History* (Lexington: University Press of Kentucky, 1985), 227–28.

61. Ibid., 228.

62. WPA, *West Virginia,* 63–64.

63. John T. Walton interview.

64. Freda Kirchway, "Miners' Wives in the Coal Strike," *Century* 66 (November 1919): 83–90.

65. Kirchway, "Miners' Wives," 89.

66. Dave Tamplin interview.

67. Mary Harris Jones, *Autobiography of Mother Jones,* ed. Mary Field Parton (Chicago: Charles H. Kerr and Co., 1925), 235.

68. John T. Walton interview; Eli and Ollie Jane Mullins, interview by unnamed interviewer, ca. 1974, OHA.

69. Dave Tamplin interview.

70. Rice, *West Virginia: A History,* 229.

71. Ibid., 229–33.

72. Virginia Giacomo interview; William R. Payne interview; Eli and Ollie Jane Mullins interview.

Chapter 7. Farm Wives and Commercial Farming

1. *CA, 1925,* 712; *CA, 1945,* 29, 140; *CA, 1930,* 461; *CA, 1950,* 419. For example, South Carolina author Dori Sanders' father developed a 250-acre peach

orchard on his farm in York County. See Jim Auchmutey, "Tasting the South: Peaches and Prose," *Atlanta Journal–Constitution,* July 6, 1997, sec. M, p. 1.

2. *Goodspeed's History of Tennessee* (Nashville: Charles and Randy Elder Booksellers, 1887, repr. 1972), 825–26; Carson and Alberta Brewer, *Valley So Wild: A Folk History* (Knoxville, Tenn.: East Tennessee Historical Society, 1975), 273–78; "James Blair Farm, Loudon County, Tennessee," Tennessee Century Farms Collection, Center for Historic Preservation, Middle Tennessee State University; "Kate Simmons," interview by author, August 5, 1994; "Arthur Delozier," interview by author, July 21, 1994.

3. W. R. Woolrich, *Agricultural-Industrial Survey of Loudon County, Tennessee* (Washington, D.C.: Civil Works Administration, 1935), 1–4, 10–11, 53.

4. Woolrich, *Agricultural-Industrial Survey,* 8, 109–17. For a glimpse of the character of the local newspaper, see for example, *Loudon County Herald,* September 27, 1928; May 21, 1931; November 22, 1934; June 18, 1936; April 7, 1938; October 10, 1938.

5. Figures compiled from *CA, 1925,* 11, 14, 699, 710–12, 718; *CA, 1935,* 593, 594, 598, 600, 602, 604, 608.

6. USDA, "Economic and Social Problems of the Southern Appalachians," 1935, 79, 98. Figures compiled from *CA, 1925,* 11, 14, 699, 710–12, 718; *CA, 1935,* 593, 594, 598, 600, 602, 604, 608.

7. Woolrich, *Agricultural-Industrial Survey,* 3–4; "Arthur Delozier" interview; "Peggy Delozier Jones," interview by author, July 21, 1994; "Alexander Farm, Loudon County," Tennessee Century Farms Collection, Center for Historic Preservation, Middle Tennessee State University.

8. Mary A. Powell, untitled history of Scott's Cheese Factory, June 23, 1994, photocopy in author's possession; "Arthur Delozier" interview; "Mabel Love," interview by author, July 19, 1994; "Ethel Davis," interview by author, July 19, 1994.

9. Figures compiled from *CA, 1930,* 953; *CA, 1940,* vol. 1, pt. 20, pp. 459, 467, 477, 495; *CA, 1945,* vol. 1, pt. 20, p. 115; *CA, 1950,* vol. 1, pt. 20, pp. 86, 161. "Arthur Delozier" interview; "Peggy Delozier Jones" interview; "Kate Simmons" interview; "Ethel Davis" interview.

10. See ESAR, Tennessee, 1920–1940, especially 1936, 230–31, and 1939, 416, 419; *Loudon County Herald,* assorted issues, 1920–1950, e.g., September 27, 1928, p. 1, November 22, 1934, p. 1, and June 18, 1936, p. 1.

11. "Mabel Love" interview.

12. "Mabel Love" interview; "Ethel Davis" interview; Nancy Gray Osterud, "Land Identity, and Agency in the Oral Autobiographies of Farm Women," in *Women and Farming: Changing Roles, Changing Structures,* Wava G. Haney and Jane B. Knowles, eds. (Boulder, Colo.: Westview Press, 1988), 73–87.

13. "Mabel Love" interview.

14. "Ethel Davis" interview.

15. "Arthur Delozier" interview.

16. "Arthur Delozier" interview; John Rousseau Browder, to author, June 4, 1995.

17. "Peggy Delozier Jones" interview.

18. "Mabel Love" interview; "Kate Simmons' interview.

19. "Arthur Tipton," interview by author, July 19, 1994; Ft. Loudon and Watts Bar Project, both in Box 121, TVA.

20. "Mabel Love" interview.

21. Samuel R. Berger, *Dollar Harvest: The Story of the Farm Bureau* (Lexington, Mass.: D. C. Heath, 1971); Mary E. Neth, *Preserving the Family Farm: Women, Community, and the Foundations of Agribusiness in the Midwest, 1900–1940* (Baltimore: Johns Hopkins University Press, 1995), 133.

22. John Browder letter; "Charter and By-Laws of the Loudon County Farm Bureau," Loudon, Tennessee, photocopy in author's possession, 1.

23. "By-Laws and Charter," 1; "Report of the Associated Women of the American Farm Bureau Federation at the Third Triennial Conference of the Associated Country Women of the World," Washington, D.C., June 1–6, 1936, in the Papers of Laura Lane, box 2, folder 16, Schlesinger Library, Radcliffe College, Harvard University, Cambridge, Massachusetts. The structure of today's American Farm Bureau Federation is more egalitarian.

24. "Peggy Delozier Jones" interview; "Arthur Delozier" interview; "Everett and Irma Hobbs," interview with author, July 19, 1994; "Ethel Davis" interview; "Charter and By-Laws." The Loudon County Farm Bureau By-Laws defined "voting farmer members" as those deriving 50 percent or more of their income from farming or devoting 50 percent or more of their time to the production of farm products. Since women's productive work was often discounted as "helping out," they could easily be relegated to the category of "associate members."

25. *Loudon County Herald,* April 7, 1938.

26. "Peggy Delozier Jones" interview.

27. ESAR, Tennessee, 1939, 416–19; "Kate Simmons" interview; "Peggy Delozier Jones" interview; "The Ideal Farm Home," *Progressive Farmer,* September 1954.

28. "Everett and Irma Hobbs" interview.

29. Kline Cash, interview by author, October 4, 1997.

30. Kline Cash interview; Howard W. Odum, *Southern Regions of the United States* (Chapel Hill: University of North Carolina Press, 1936), 38; Soil Conservation Service, *South Carolina Soil and Water Conservation Needs Inventory, 1970,* pamphlet in Spartanburg County Public Library, Spartanburg, South Carolina.

31. Figures compiled from *CA, 1930,* vol. 2, pt. 2, pp. 458–62.

32. Allen Tullos, *Habits of Industry: White Culture and the Transformation of the Carolina Piedmont* (Chapel Hill: University of North Carolina Press, 1989), 175–77.

33. Ben Robertson, *Red Hills and Cotton: An Upcountry Memoir* (New York: Alfred A. Knopf, 1942), 157.

34. *CA, 1930*, 470–75.

35. Robertson, *Red Hills and Cotton,* 162, 270.

36. James Walton Lawrence Sr., *Shadows of Hogback* (Landrum, S.C.: *News Leader,* 1979), 69; Mike Corbin, "A Year in the Life of an Upstate Peach Farm," Exhibit, Spartanburg County Museum of Art, September-October 1997; WPA, *A History of Spartanburg County,* (Spartanburg: Bond and White, 1940), 277–78; Henry E. Gramling II, interview by author, October 10, 1997.

37. WPA, *A History of Spartanburg County,* 277–78; Emory V. Jones, "The Agricultural Life of Greenville County, 1850–1950," *Papers and Proceedings of the Greenville County Historical Society, 1991–1994* 10 (1994): 74; Henry E. Gramling II interview; John Culbertson, interview by R. V. Williams, January 27, 1939, WPALHC.

38. Henry E. Gramling II interview.

39. Henry E. Gramling II interview; Kline Cash interview; *CA, 1930,* vol. 2, pt. 2, p. 495; *CA, 1940,* vol. 1, pt. 3, p. 487.

40. Ryan Alender Page, *Our Way of Life: The Odyssey of a Farm Family* (Fairfax: Wallace and Sons Printing, 1982), 5–30; John Culbertson interview.

41. John Culbertson interview.

42. Ibid.

43. Vada Cash Sellars, interview by Mike Corbin, September 4, 1996; Kline Cash interview; Henry Gramling II interview; Ruth Hatchette McBrayer, interview by Mike Corbin, July 7, 1997.

44. Vada Cash Sellars interview; Ruth Hatchette McBrayer interview.

45. Ruth Hatchette McBrayer interview; Henry Gramling II interview.

46. Henry Gramling II interview.

Chapter 8. "The Land of Do Without"

1. Carson and Alberta Brewer, *Valley So Wild: A Folk History* (Knoxville: East Tennessee Historical Society Publications, 1975), xx; "Sevier County Saga," 1976, pamphlet in the History Collection, Sevier County Library, Sevierville, Tennessee.

2. "Sevier County Saga"; Gladys Trentham Russell, *Call Me Hillbilly* (Alcoa, Tenn.: Russell Publishing Co., 1974), 20, 58; Wilma Williamson, interview by author, July 18, 1994; Florence Cope Bush, *If Life Gives You Scraps, Make a Quilt* (Concord, Tenn.: Misty Cove Publications, 1992), 143; Horace Kephart, *Our Southern Highlanders: A Narrative of Adventure in the Southern Appalachians and a Study of Life Among the Mountaineers* (1913, reprint Knoxville: University of Tennessee Press, 1976), 265–69, 308.

3. John C. Campbell, *The Southern Highlander and His Homeland* (New York: Russell Sage Foundation, 1921), 123; Bush, *If Life Gives You Scraps,* 143; Robert R. Madden, "Walker Sisters Home: Historic Structures Report, Part II and Furnishing Study," Office of Architecture and Historic Preservation, Department of Interior, 1969, copy in MHC.

4. Leonard C. Roy, "Rambling Around the Roof of Eastern America," *National Geographic* 70 (August 1936): 249.

5. Kephart, *Our Southern Highlanders*, ix–xi, 16–17; Roy, "Rambling Around the Roof of Eastern America," 243.

6. Kephart, *Our Southern Highlanders*, 126, 199–220; WPA, *WPA Guide To Tennessee* (Knoxville: University of Tennessee Press, 1939, repr. 1986), 337; Louise Rand Bascom, "Uncle Sam in the Appalachians," *Outlook* 111 (October 27, 1915): 483–89, quote on 484.

7. *Census of Population*, 1930, vol. 3, pt. 2, pp. 895, 901; 1940, vol. 2, pt. 6, pp. 594, 672; and 1950, vol. 2, pt. 42, pp. 19, 33, 96, 138; Russell Thornton, *The Cherokees: A Population History* (Lincoln: University of Nebraska Press, 1990), 123–33.

8. Gladys Trentham Russell, *It Happened in the Smokies* (Alcoa: Russell Publishing Co., 1988), 60; figures compiled from *Census of Population*, 1930, vol. 3, pt. 2, pp. 895, 901; 1940, vol. 2, pt. 6, pp. 594, 672; and 1950, vol. 2, pt. 42; pp. 19, 33, 96, 138.

9. Kephart, *Our Southern Highlanders*, 454; John C. Inscoe, "Race and Racism in the Nineteenth Century Southern Appalachians: Myths, Realities, and Ambiguities," in *Appalachia in the Making: The Mountain South in the Nineteenth Century*, ed. Mary Beth Pudup, Dwight B. Billings, and Altina L. Waller (Chapel Hill: University of North Carolina Press, 1995), 103–31.

10. *SASC*, 220.

11. Wilma Williamson interview.

12. Vic Weals, *Last Train To Elkmont: A Look Back at Life on the Little River in the Great Smoky Mountains* (Knoxville: Olden Press, 1993), 63.

13. Kephart, *Our Southern Highlanders*, 330–33; *CA, 1930*, vol. 3, pt. 2, pp. 618–19; *CA, 1940*, vol. 2, pt. 2, p. 480; *CA, 1945*, vol. 1, pt. 20, p. 132; *CA, 1950*, vol. 1, pt. 20, p. 163; W. R. Woolrich and John L. Neely Jr., "Agricultural Industrial Survey of Sevier County, Tennessee, 1934," Tennessee State Library and Archives, Nashville, Tennessee, 3–6; Russell, *Call Me Hillbilly*, 61–62.

14. Kephart, *Our Southern Highlanders*, 289, 330–33.

15. Weals, *Last Train to Elkmont*, 55–57.

16. Kephart, *Our Southern Highlanders*, 289, 333; Campbell, *The Southern Highlander*, 127–29, quote on 127.

17. *WPA Guide*, 338–39; *Census of Population*, 1930, vol. 3., pt. 2, pp. 895, 901; *Sevier County Republican and Record* and *Montgomery's Vindicator*, scattered issues, 1920s.

18. Weals, *Last Train to Elkmont*, 1–7, 21.

19. Florence Cope Bush, *Dorie: Woman of the Mountains* (Knoxville: University of Tennessee Press, 1992), 132–36.

20. Michael Frome, *Strangers in High Places: The Story of the Great Smoky Mountains* (Knoxville: University of Tennessee Press, 1966), 161–69.

21. Weals, *Last Train to Elkmont*, 103–5.

22. Bush, *Dorie*, 132–55; Wilma Williamson interview.

23. Bush, *Dorie,* 132–55; Wilma Williamson interview; Laverne Farmer interview by author, August 9, 1993.

24. Woolrich and Neely, "Agricultural and Industrial Survey of Sevier County," 8; Bush, *Dorie.*

25. Bush, *Dorie,* 213, 220–21.

26. "Sevier County Saga"; *WPA Guide,* 339.

27. Weals, *Last Train to Elkmont,* iv–v, 27, 46; Russell, *It Happened in the Smokies,* 59–60; "Sevier County Saga."

28. Frome, *Strangers in High Places,* 231–37.

29. Allen H. Eaton, *Handicrafts of the Southern Highlands* (New York: Russell Sage Foundation, 1937), 72.

30. Eaton, *Handicrafts of the Southern Highlands,* 73; Frome, *Strangers in High Places,* 241–42; Russell, *It Happened in the Smokies,* 60–61; "Sevier County Saga."

31. Eaton, *Handicrafts of the Southern Highlands,* 72; "Sevier County Saga"; Frederic Allen Whiting, untitled editorial, *The American Magazine of Art* 26 (October 1933): 441–42.

32. Frome, *Strangers in High Places,* 242.

33. *WPA Guide,* 339–40.

34. Wilma Williamson interview; Russell, *Call Me Hillbilly,* 8–10, and *It Happened in the Smokies,* 18; *Gentle Winds of Change,* 100–101.

35. *WPA Guide,* 339; Russell, *It Happened in the Smokies,* 18; "Sevier County Saga."

36. Frome, *Strangers in High Places,* 174–79.

37. Carlos C. Campbell, *Birth of a National Park in the Great Smoky Mountains* (Knoxville: University of Tennessee Press, 1960; rev. 1978), 53–54.

38. *Sevier County Republican and Record,* November 14, 1928; July 31, 1929; November 19, 1930; December 5, 1930; and November 4, 1931; Dan Pierce, "The Barbarism of the Huns: Family and Community Removal in the Establishment of the Great Smoky Mountains National Park," *Tennessee Historical Quarterly* 57 (Spring/Summer, 1998): 62–79.

39. Russell, *Call Me Hillbilly,* 63; *Gentle Winds of Change,* 239; Campbell, *Birth of a National Park,* 70.

40. Roy, "Rambling Around the Roof of Eastern America," 249–50; *Sevier County Republican and Record,* July 16, 1930.

41. Wilma Dykeman and Jim Stokley, *Highland Homeland: The People of the Great Smokies,* undated booklet by the National Park Service, ca. 1970, 119–65; "Civilian Conservation Corps Recollected," *Knoxville News Sentinel,* June 18, 1995, E10; Wilma Williamson interview.

42. Wilma Williamson interview; Russell, *It Happened in the Smokies,* 129; Bush, *If Life Gives You Scraps,* 71.

43. Russell, *Call Me Hillbilly,* 11.

44. Roy, "Rambling Around the Roof of Eastern America," 242–66.

45. Ibid., 244.

46. Ernie Pyle, "Gatlinburg and the Great Smokies" (Gatlinburg: G. C. Callaway, 1951, reprint of 1940 Pyle newspaper columns), 15, Special Collections, Hodges Library, University of Tennessee, Knoxville.

47. Roy, 250–51; *WPA Guide to Tennessee,* 341.

48. Pyle, "Gatlinburg and the Great Smokies," 15–18; Russell, *It Happened in the Smokies,* 128–29.

49. "Sevier County Saga"; Wilma Williamson interview.

50. Weals, *Last Train to Elkmont,* iv; "Sevier County Saga."

51. *Census of Population,* 1930, vol. 3, pt. 2, p. 918; 1940, vol. 2, pt. 6, p. 624; and 1950, vol. 2, pt. 42, p. 107.

52. Wilma Williamson, to author, undated, mid-July 1995.

53. Weals, *Last Train to Elkmont,* 74–78.

54. Russell, *Call Me Hillbilly,* 63–64.

55. Donald J. Bogue, Henry S. Shyrock Jr., and Siegfried A. Hoermann, *Subregional Migration in the U.S., 1935–1940,* Vol. 1 (Oxford, Ohio: Miami University and Scripps Foundation, 1957), 95, 98–103.

56. Bush, *If Life Gives You Scraps,* 155–62.

57. Bush, *Dorie,* 224.

58. Ibid., 225.

59. Bush, *If Life Gives You Scraps,* 156.

Epilogue: The Persistence of Rural Values

1. Bill Lewellyn, interview by author, August 10, 1993, MHC.

2. French Clark, interview by author, July 22, 1994, MHC; Maude Walker, interview by author, August 17, 1993, and letter to author, March 1994.

3. For an account of the development of Oak Ridge, see Charles W. Johnson and Charles O. Jackson, *City Behind a Fence: Oak Ridge, Tennessee, 1942–1946* (Knoxville: University of Tennessee Press, 1981).

4. Eva Finchum, interview by Lu Ann Jones, April 30, 1987, OHA.

5. Ruth Hatchette McBrayer, interview by author, August 20, 1998.

6. Mary Evelyn Lane, interview by author, August 8, 1994, MHC.

7. In *American Farmers: The New Minority* (Bloomington: Indiana University Press, 1981), historian Gilbert C. Fite coined the phrase "equity head start" to refer to those twentieth-century farmers who enjoyed an advantage over others by inheriting significant land, cattle, and equipment, thus reducing their need to go into debt as they launched commercial farming operations. The lack of debt allowed them to survive bad weather, economic downturns, and farm credit crunches when many of their peers could not.

8. Laura Tate, interview by author, December 26, 1998; Della Sarten, interview by LuAnn Jones, May 1, 1987, OHSA.

Bibliographical Essay

Wherever possible, I have allowed farm women to speak for themselves and have drawn my interpretations from their own words. To this end, I conducted oral history interviews with upcountry women (and men, in some cases). I have deposited transcripts of the following interviews in the McClung Historical Collection of the Lawson-McGhee Public Library in Knoxville, Tennessee (names in quotation marks are pseudonyms as requested by the interview subject): French Clark, "Ethel Davis," "Arthur Delozier," Laverne Farmer, "Everett and Irma Hobbs," "Peggy Jones Delozier," Mary Evelyn Lane, Oliver and Hettie Lawson, Korola Lee, Bill and Evelyn Lewellyn, "Mabel Love," "Kate Simmons," John and Margaret Alice West, and Wilma Williamson. The following interviews were not archived because of technical difficulties or at the request of the interviewee: Kline Cash, Henry Gramling II, Margaret Marsh, Ruth Hatchette McBrayer, Mattie Lee Murph, Peggy Pollard, Sanford N. Smith, Edna Spencer, "Arthur Tipton," and Maude Walker.

I also drew on interviews placed in archives by other scholars. The Oral History of Southern Agriculture collection at the National Museum of American History is a rich source of information on early twentieth-century southern farm life and agricultural transformation. The Archives of Appalachia at East Tennessee State University (ETSU) in Johnson City, Tennessee, holds three collections that are useful to researchers on Appalachian life in the twentieth century. The Broadside Television collection contains videotapes from television interviews done with elderly mountain folk in the late 1970s. The Burton-Manning and Charles Gunter collections include oral histories gathered by ETSU professors and their students in the late 1970s and early 1980s. The Oral History of Appalachia collection at Marshall University in Huntington, West Virginia, contains hundreds of interviews done by Marshall students and professors in the mid-1970s, mostly in Kentucky, Virginia, and West Virginia.

I also used letters and published and unpublished memoirs of the region's women. The growth of the tourist industry in the mountains of East Tennessee has sparked a cottage industry in self-published memoirs of "hillbilly" life in the "old days" before the development of the Great Smoky Mountains National Park. These books, cited in chapter notes, provided a wealth of information on life in rural East Tennessee during the period I studied.

Unfortunately, these sources do not tell the whole story. Silences are often as significant as words, and people's stories about the past are shaped and colored by many factors, including their present lives. I often had to look beyond women's own words to decipher the meanings of their reticence. Contemporary newspaper and magazine accounts and government documents filled some of these gaps, providing information on those who left no records and offering the perspectives of government workers, missionaries, journalists, and other outsiders as well. The population removal records of the Tennessee Valley Authority were particularly useful in this regard. Moreover, popular culture, especially articles and advertising in farm magazines, shed considerable light on the messages that farm women were receiving from agricultural institutions, particularly the federal agencies.

In writing this book, I have benefited from a recent explosion of publications in the field of rural history, especially the history of rural women. I have drawn on much of this work to place my own study in context, but I have also used the work of scholars in many other fields, including urban social history, labor history, and rural sociology.

The best overview of American agricultural history is David B. Danbom's *Born in the Country: A History of Rural America* (Baltimore: Johns Hopkins University Press, 1995). Some of the most important work in agricultural history in the past ten years has refocused our thinking on the transition to capitalism by demonstrating that the transition was a protracted and complicated one. Along the way, rural people combined subsistence and commercial agriculture in order to meet their own goals of independence and family persistence on the land. Several historians have pointed out that this transition to rural capitalism brought about a crucial shift in the gender division of labor. See Allan Kulikoff, "The Transition to Capitalism in Rural America," *The William and Mary Quarterly* 46 (January 1989): 120–44, and "Households and Markets: Toward a New Synthesis of American Agrarian History," *The William and Mary Quarterly* 50 (April 1993): 342–55; and Nancy Grey Osterud, "Gender and the Transition to Capitalism in Rural America," *Agricultural History* 67 (Spring 1993): 14–29.

Historians of southern agriculture note that southern farmers, unlike their midwestern counterparts, were not able to successfully turn to capitalist agriculture until the 1930s, 40s, and 50s when New Deal price support programs, expanding regional markets, the development of adequate transportation systems to tie them to national markets, the availability of farm credit, and new agricultural science and technology combined to support their efforts. See Gilbert C. Fite, *Cotton Fields No More: Southern Agriculture, 1865–1980* (Lexington, Ky.: University Press of Kentucky, 1984); Pete C. Daniel, *Breaking the Land: The Transformation of Cotton, Tobacco, and Rice Cultures Since 1880* (Urbana: University of Illinois Press, 1980); and Jack Temple Kirby, *Rural Worlds Lost: The American South, 1920–1960* (Baton Rouge: Louisiana State University Press, 1987). Daniel and Kirby portray the lives of the South's farm women before the transformation but do not examine the changes in farm women's roles wrought by the shift to commercial agriculture. For a comprehensive look at twentieth-century southern economic transformations, particularly in agriculture, see Pete Daniel, *Standing at the Crossroads: Southern Life Since 1900* (New York: Hill and Wang, 1986).

Recent works have demonstrated the variety of agriculture in the both the antebellum and postbellum South. See Jeanette Keith, *Country People in the New South: Tennessee's Upper Cumberland* (Chapel Hill: University of North Carolina Press, 1995); and Robert T. McKenzie, *One South or Many? Plantation Belt and Upcountry in Civil-War Era Tennessee* (New York: Cambridge University Press, 1994).

Articles in James C. Cobb and Michael Namorato, eds., *The New Deal and the South* (Jackson: University of Mississippi Press, 1984) provide an overview of New Deal programs and their implementation in the South. Robin D. G. Kelley's *Hammer and Hoe: Alabama Communists During the Great Depression* (Chapel Hill: University of North Carolina Press, 1995) lends insight into the effect of New Deal programs on both black and white tenant farmers and on the possibilities and limitations for interracial grass-roots organizing and resistance. Harvard Sitkoff's *A New Deal for Blacks: The Emergence of Civil Rights as a National Issue* (New York: Oxford University Press, 1978) is highly critical of the New Deal's failure to address the problems of blacks nationwide.

The strength of the works of Daniel, Fite, and Kirby is their attention to the impact of the transformation on poor blacks and whites at the bottom of the economic ladder. Other works that look at these powerless people are Steven Hahn, *The Roots of Southern Populism: Yeoman Farmers and the Transformation of the Georgia Upcountry, 1850–1890* (New York: Oxford University Press, 1983), and J. Wayne Flynt, *Dixie's Forgotten People: The South's Poor Whites* (Bloomington: Indiana University Press, 1979) and *Poor But Proud: Alabama's Poor Whites* (Tuscaloosa: University of Alabama Press, 1989).

Historians, rural sociologists, and other scholars have long tried to understand southern rural class relations. Much of the work on antebellum class relations is useful for understanding rural class status after the Civil War as well. Frank Owsley's landmark early work *Plain Folk of the Old South* (1949, reprint Baton Rouge: Louisiana State University Press, 1982) presented a world of white interclass harmony because of his reliance on the testimony of elite whites. In recent years, historians have taken a more nuanced approach. Stephanie McCurry's study of relationships between yeomen and elite households in antebellum South Carolina looks at sources of interclass tensions and the forces that ultimately bound the two groups together during the Civil War (*Masters of Small Worlds: Yeomen Households, Gender Relations, and the Political Culture of the Antebellum South Carolina Low Country* [New York: Oxford University Press, 1995]). Stephen V. Ash, "Poor Whites in the Occupied South, 1861–1865," *Journal of Southern History* 57 (February 1991), also looks at class in this period. Fred Arthur Bailey provides another corrective to Owsley's idealistic picture in his article "Tennessee's Antebellum Common Folk," in *Tennessee History: The Land, The People, and the Culture,* ed., Carroll Van West (Knoxville: University of Tennessee Press, 1998): 80–100.

Other studies that carried the examination of rural class structure beyond the Civil War include Flynt's work; I. A. Newby's *Plain Folk in the New South: Social Change and Cultural Persistence, 1880–1915* (Baton Rouge: Louisiana State University Press, 1989); and Steven Hahn's *The Roots of Southern Populism: Yeomen Farmers and the Transformation of the Georgia Upcountry, 1850–1890* (New York: Oxford University Press, 1983). Janette Thomas Greenwood's study of post-Reconstruction Charlotte also provides an insightful look at the development of black and white class definitions (*Bittersweet Legacy: The Black and White "Better Classes" in Charlotte, 1850–1910* [Chapel Hill: University of North Carolina Press, 1994]).

Sociologists Jess Gilbert and Carolyn Howe, in "Beyond 'State vs. Society': Theories of the State and New Deal Agricultural Policies," *American Sociological Review* 56 (April 1991): 204–20, note that there are distinctly different rural class systems in various regions of the country. However, they assume that all southerners fit into a class hierarchy based on sharecropping. This two-tier system does not fit the complexities of the upcountry's class structure, nor does it explain how class status was determined there. An analysis that more closely resembles the rural class structure in the upcountry is Mary Beth Pudup's study of middle class formation in Appalachian counties of Kentucky. She found that class status was based on family lineages, residence in county seat towns, land ownership, and occupational groups ("The Boundaries of Class in Pre-Industrial Appalachia," *Journal of Historical Geography* 15 [1989]: 139–62). A recent work by Marilyn Irvin Holt, *Linoleum, Better Babies and the Modern Farm Woman* (Albuquerque: University of New Mexico Press, 1995), also maintains that rural class structure was based on a series of cultural factors such as "cooperation with neighbors, church attendance, or interest in education" (p. 7). Holt does not, however, examine class differences in great depth, focusing instead on the rural "middle class," which she defines as farm families who aspired to participate in the "general culture" that, by her description, closely resembled middle-class urban culture. Elizabeth Anne Payne explores the complexities of rural class relations, where distinctions between prosperous and poor were a matter of degree and status was conferred as much by personal characteristics as by land-owning status ("The Lady Was a Sharecropper: Myrtle Lawrence and the Southern Tenant Farmers Union," *Southern Cultures* 4 (Summer 1998): 5–27, esp. 17–18).

The work of labor and social historians examining urban and suburban women has also been useful for conceptualizing transformations in class consciousness. See Mary P. Ryan, *Cradle of the Middle Class: The Family in Oneida County, New York, 1790–1865* (Cambridge, UK: Cambridge University Press, 1981); Jeanne Boydston, *Home and Work: Housework, Wages, and the Ideology of Labor in the Early Republic* (New York: Oxford University Press, 1990); and Stuart M. Blumin, *The Emergence of the Middle Class: Social Experience in the American City, 1760–1900* (Cambridge, UK: Cambridge University Press, 1989).

The development of scholarship in women's history has led to a wealth of research on rural women, most of it focused on regions other than the South. These works have often focused on the way the transition to commercial agriculture or industrialization have transformed rural women's lives. For more on women and the transition to commercial agriculture outside the South, see Mary Neth, *Preserving the Family Farm: Women, Community, and the Foundations of Agribusiness in the Midwest, 1900–1940* (Baltimore: Johns Hopkins University Press, 1995); Jane Adams, *The Transformation of Rural Life: Southern Illinois, 1890–1990* (Chapel Hill: University of North Carolina Press, 1994); Katherine Jellison, *Entitled to Power: Farm Women and Technology, 1913–1939* (Chapel Hill: University of North Carolina Press, 1993); Adams, *The Transformation of Rural Life*; Deborah Fink, *Open Country, Iowa: Rural Women, Tradition and Change* (New York, 1986); Joan Jensen, *Loosening the Bonds: Mid-Atlantic Farm Women, 1750–1835* (New Haven: Yale University Press, 1986), and *Promise to the Land: Essays on Rural Women* (Albuquerque: University of New Mexico Press, 1991); Sally McMurry, *Transforming Rural Life: Dairying Families and Agricultural Change, 1820–1885* (Baltimore: Johns Hopkins University Press, 1995); and Nancy Grey Osterud, *Bonds of Community: The Lives of Farm Women in Nineteenth Century New York* (Ithaca: Cornell University Press, 1991), "The Valuation of Women's Work: Gender and the Market in a Dairy Farming Community During the Late Nineteenth Century," *Frontiers* 10 (1988): 18–24, and "Land, Identity and Agency in the Oral Autobiographies of Farm Women," in *Women and Farming: Changing Roles, Changing Structures*, ed. Wava G. Haney and Jane B. Knowles (Boulder: Westview Press, 1988), 73–87. Osterud's work is particularly important in illuminating the blending of public and private spheres in rural life.

Women's history scholars have often maintained that the transition to a cash-based economy resulted in the devaluation of women's traditional work. See, for example, Jeanne Boydston, *Home and Work*. This urban model does not fit an agrarian world, however. Rural people did not understand women's work or the gender division of labor in this way. Wages did not determine the value of a farm family member's work; thus, men's work was not necessarily more highly valued than women's. Rather, farm folk recognized men's and women's work as qualitatively different. For more on the ways men and women understood the shift in the gender division of rural labor, see Osterud, *Bonds of Community*, 202–27; Jane M. Pederson, *Between Memory and Reality: Family and Community in Rural Wisconsin, 1870–1970* (Madison: University of Wisconsin Press, 1992), chap. 7; Mary Neth, *Preserving the Family Farm*, 24–27, and "Gender and the Family Labor System: Defining Work in the Rural Midwest," *Journal of Social History* 27 (March 1994): 563–77.

Agricultural extension work has inspired a wealth of research, partly because of historians' fascination with the gap between the activist ideal and the bureaucratic reality in extension work, and partly because the records are so readily available. The earliest work is a good place to start. See Gladys L. Baker, *The County Agent* (Chicago: University of Chicago Press, 1939); Wayne D. Rasmussen, *Taking the University to the People: Seventy-Five Years of Cooperative Extension* (Ames: Iowa State University Press, 1989); and Wayne D. Rasmussen and Gladys L. Baker, *The Department of Agriculture* (New York: Praeger, 1972). For a cogent synthesis of the development of all agricultural institutions, including land-grant colleges, the extension service, and other USDA agencies, see Mary Neth, *Preserving the Family Farm*, chap. 4. For more on home extension work among women in other regions during this period, see Dorothy Schwieder, "Education and Change in the Lives of Iowa Farm Women, 1900–1940," *Agricultural History* 60 (Spring 1986): 200–15; Cynthia Sturgis, "'How're You Gonna Keep 'Em Down on the Farm?': Rural Women and the Urban Model in Utah," *Agricultural History* 60 (Spring 1986): 182–99; and LuAnn Jones, "Re-visioning the Countryside: Southern Women, Rural Reform, and the Farm Economy in the Twentieth Century" (Ph.D. dissertation, University of North Carolina at Chapel Hill, 1996). A recent account that explores home extension work as part of Progressive-era domestic reform in the South, noting connections between the broader rural improvement movement and home extension work, is Mary S. Hoffschwelle, *Rebuilding Rural Communities: Reformers, Schools, and Homes in Tennessee, 1914–1929* (Knoxville: University of Tennessee Press, 1998).

In the South, segregation complicated delivery of extension service programs. For accounts of the segregated extension program in the South, see Earl W. Crosby, "The Roots of Black Agricultural Extension Work," *Historian* 39 (February 1977): 228–47, "Limited Success Against Long Odds: The Black County Agent," *Agricultural History* 57 (July 1983): 277–88, and "The Struggle for Existence: The Institutionalization of the Black County Agent System," *Agricultural History* 60 (Spring 1986): 123–36; Gladys L. Baker, *The County Agent*; Gary Zellar, "H. C. Ray and Racial Politics in the African-American Extension Service Program in Arkansas, 1915–1929," *Agricultural History* 72 (Spring 1998): 429–45; and Allen W. Jones, "The South's First Black Farm Agents," *Agricultural History* 50 (October 1976): 636–44. LuAnn Jones has shown how the work of a black female AAA agent served to bolster African American extension work in the Southeast ("In Search of Jennie Booth Moton, Field Agent, AAA," *Agricultural History* 72 [Spring 1998]: 446–58). Jeannie M. Whayne extends the study of black extension work into the post–World War II years in "Black Farmers and the Cooperative Extensions Service: The Alabama Experience, 1945–1965," *Agricultural History* 72 (Summer 1998): 523–51.

Three recent studies examine the ways in which agents' conceptions of appropriate race and gender roles shaped extension service programming. Kathleen C. Hilton found that USDA officials assumed that white "men and women filled separate, unequal roles within the rural household." Because USDA officials' conceptions of gender roles were more flexible for rural blacks, African American agents had more freedom to develop programs that met their constituents' needs. Nonetheless, black agents were hindered by funding constraints and by the extension service's general indifference to the home demonstration program for black women. Similarly, in a study of home demonstration work in Alabama, Lynne A. Rieff found that the extension service's efforts at rural reform fell short of their goals precisely because of the assumptions that USDA officials and agents made about gender and racial hierarchies. See Hilton, "'Both in the Field, Each With a Plow': Race and Gender in USDA Policy, 1907–1929," and Rieff, "'Go Ahead and Do All You Can': Southern Progressives and Alabama Home Demonstration Clubs, 1914–1940," both in Virginia Bernard et al., eds., *Hidden Histories of Women in the New South* (Columbia: University of Missouri Press, 1994), 114–33 and 134–49, respectively; Lynne A. Rieff, "'Rousing the People of the Land': Home Demonstration Work in the Deep South, 1914–1950" (Ph.D. dissertation, Auburn University, 1995).

Historians have tended to focus on the institutional or political history of the TVA, but only a few studies have examined the agency's impact on rural people, generally concluding that the agency was the catalyst for the Tennessee Valley's modernization, but that it nonetheless failed in its broad-based planning responsibilities. Richard Lowitt maintains that the agency led the way in transforming valley agriculture from a self-defeating cycle of crop production to livestock production better suited to East Tennessee's hilly landscape. He calls the agency a "catalyst for modernization," but recognizes the TVA's failure as a master planning agency. Rather, he says the TVA took practical actions that were quite successful in improving specific areas of life in the region ("The TVA, 1933–45," in Edwin C. Hargrove and Paul K. Conkin, eds., *TVA: Fifty Years of Grass-Roots Bureaucracy* (Urbana: University of Illinois Press, 1983): 35–65. Michael McDonald and John Muldowny, *TVA and the Dispossessed: The Resettlement of Population in the Norris Dam Area* (Knoxville: University of Tennessee Press, 1982), are generally less positive, noting that the agency was successful as the "Valley's educator" and in its efforts at water management and recreational planning, but that it dismally failed in its efforts at regional development planning, resulting in the uprooting of thousands of rural people without providing them with real improved options. Wayne Clark Moore argues that the agency's policies were predicated on the belief that too many people lived on farms and needed to leave the land. He blames TVA for the decline of many farm communities that were already weakened by structural decline and "the modernization of the farm economy" ("Farm Communities and Economic Growth in the Lower Tennessee Valley: Humphreys County, Tennessee," Ph.D. dissertation, University of Rochester, 1990). Michael Rogers gives a more positive evaluation of the agency in his study of attitudes toward removal, finding that responses to removal varied according to the age and educational levels of those effected ("TVA Population Removal: Attitudes and Expectations of the Dispossessed at the Norris and Cherokee Dam Sites," *Journal of East Tennessee History* 67 [1995]: 89–105).

Southern historians have analyzed the effects of industrialization on rural people. Jacqueline Dowd Hall and Allen Tullos provide in-depth analyses of the impact of textile mills on the South. See Hall, et al., *Like a Family,* and Allen Tullos, *Habits of Industry: White Culture and the Transformation of the Carolina Piedmont* (Chapel Hill: University of North Carolina Press, 1989). David L. Carlton's *Mill and Town in South Carolina, 1880–1920* (Baton Rouge: Louisiana State University Press, 1982) provides a revealing look at relationships between textile barons and traditional rural and town elites, and between textile workers and other locals. Nancy MacLean illuminates southern whites' reluctance to have white women work under the supervision of unrelated men ("The Leo Frank Case Reconsidered: Gender and Sexual Politics in the Making of Reactionary Populism," *Journal of American History* 78 [December 1991]: 917–39). Ronald Eller, J. Wayne Flynt, and Jacqueline Jones examine the South's poor whites and poor blacks and the opportunities and problems that industrialization created for these groups. See Eller, *Miners, Millhands, and Mountaineers: Industrialization of the Appalachian South, 1880–1930* (Knoxville: University of Tennessee Press, 1982); Flynt, *Dixie's Forgotten People;* and Jones, *The Dispossessed: America's Underclass From the Civil War to the Present* (New York: Basic Books, 1992). Don H. Doyle's *New Men, New Cities, New South: Atlanta, Nashville, Charleston, Mobile, 1860–1910* (Chapel Hill: University of North Carolina Press, 1990) explores the dynamics of New South industrial development. John C. Hennen, *The Americanization of West Virginia: Creating a Modern Industrial State, 1916–1925* (Lexington: University Press of Kentucky, 1996), provides a similar view of development in West Virginia.

For background on labor organizing in the upcountry South, see Robert H. Zieger, ed., *Organized Labor in the Twentieth Century South* (Knoxville: University of Tennessee Press, 1991). In her article in that collection, "Heroines and Girl Strikers: Gender Issues and Organized Labor in the Twentieth Century South" (84–96), historian Mary Frederickson says that in southern textile and steel mill towns, the reality of most women's involvement in union organizing was day-to-day maintenance of members and contributions as auxiliary union members. Although many female textile workers did play roles in organizing and picketing, they were more active behind the scenes in the same ways that they worked on steel mill strikes where they were not workers. Jacqueline Dowd Hall, however, found that where women were workers, they took a very active part in picketing and organizing in the textile industry. See Jacqueline Dowd Hall et al., *Like a Family*, and Jacqueline Dowd Hall, "Disorderly Women: Gender and Labor Militancy in the Appalachian South," in Vicki L. Ruiz and Ellen Carol DuBois, eds., *Unequal Sisters: A Multicultural Reader in U.S. Women's History*, 2nd ed. (New York: Routledge, 1994), 348–71. W. Calvin Dickinson and Patrick D. Reagan assess the reasons for the failure of women's early efforts to organize in the Harriman, Tennessee, hosiery mill strike in "Business, Labor, and the Blue Eagle: The Harriman Hosiery Mills Strike, 1933–1934," in Carroll Van West, ed., *Tennessee History*, 391–412.

Russell D. Parker, in "Alcoa, Tennessee: The Early Years"; "Alcoa, Tennessee: The Years of Change, 1940–1960," *East Tennessee Historical Society Publications* 49 (1977): 99–115; and "The Black Community in a Company Town: Alcoa, Tennessee, 1919–1939," *Tennessee Historical Quarterly* 37 (1978): 203–21, focuses on the institutional history of the town of Alcoa rather than on the citizens' responses to industrialization. Richard M. Buckner provides a similar study of another ALCOA company town in Blount County in "A History of Calderwood, Tennessee" (master's thesis, University of Tennessee, Knoxville, March 1982). On the development of coal mining towns and the culture of mining camps, see Crandall A. Shifflett, *Coal Towns: Life, Work, and Culture in Company Towns of Southern Appalachia* (Knoxville: University of Tennessee Press, 1991); David A. Corbin, *Life, Work, and Rebellion in the Coal Fields: The Southern West Virginia Mines, 1880–1922* (Urbana: University of Illinois Press, 1981); Joe William Trotter, *Coal, Class, and Color: Blacks in Southwest West Virginia, 1915–1932* (Urbana: University of Illinois Press, 1990); and Janet W. Greene, "Strategies for Survival: Women's Work in the Southern West Virginia Coal Camps," *West Virginia History* 49 (1990): 37–54.

Recently scholars have acknowledged that whiteness, like blackness, is a socially constructed category that carries particular social meanings. Whiteness also bestows particular privileges on those designated as white. Shelley Fisher Fishkin provides a survey of the literature on whiteness in her article, "Interrogating 'Whiteness,' Complicating 'Blackness': Remapping American Culture," *American Quarterly* 47 (September 1995): 428–65. Other scholars examining this issue include David R. Roediger, *The Wages of Whiteness: Race and the Making of the American Working Class* (New York: Verso, 1991), and *Towards the Abolition of Whiteness* (New York: Verso, 1994); George Lipsitz, "The Possessive Investment in Whiteness: Racialized Social Democracy and the 'White' Problem in American Studies," *American Quarterly* 47 (September 1995): 369–87; Marilyn Frye, "On Being White: Thinking Toward a Feminist Understanding of Race and Race Supremacy," in Frye, *The Politics of Reality: Essays in Feminist Theory* (Freedom, Calif.: Crossing Press, 1983), 110–27; Ruth Frankenberg, *White Women, Race Matters: The Social Construction of Whiteness* (Minneapolis: University of Minnesota Press, 1993); and Patrick Huber, "A Short History of 'Redneck': The

Fashioning of a Southern White Masculine Identity," *Southern Cultures* 1 (Winter 1995): 144–66.

The wealth of research on African American history, especially in the South, has added immeasurably to this study. Jacqueline Jones's *Labor of Love, Labor of Sorrow: Black Women, Work and the Family from Slavery to the Present* (New York: Vintage Books, 1985) describes black women's labor history. Robin D. G. Kelley's work has been very helpful in understanding rural black resistance. See *Hammer and Hoe* (1995) and *Race Rebels* (New York: Free Press, 1994). On African American migration, see Earl Lewis, *In Their Own Interests: Race, Class and Power in Twentieth Century Norfolk, Virginia* (Berkeley: University of California Press, 1991), and Louis M. Kyriakoudes, "Southern Black Rural-Urban Migration in the Era of the Great Migration: Nashville and Middle Tennessee, 1890–1930," in Van West, ed., *Tennessee History*.

The best overviews of West Virginia history are John Alexander Williams, *West Virginia: A History* (New York: W. W. Norton, 1984, 1976) and Otis K. Rice, *West Virginia: A History* (Lexington: University Press of Kentucky, 1985). The Works Progress Administration's history of the state provides a brief historical account and a snapshot of the state at the end of the Great Depression (*West Virginia: A Guide to the Mountain State* [New York: Oxford University Press, 1941]). Other important sources on West Virginia history include Mary Beth Pudup, "Women's Work in the West Virginia Economy," and Shirley C. Eagan, "Women's Work, Never Done: West Virginia Farm Women, 1802–1920s," both in *West Virginia History* 49 (1990): 7–20 and 21–35, respectively.

On South Carolina history, see Walter Edgar, *South Carolina: A History* (Columbia: University of South Carolina Press, 1998). Local South Carolina histories that were helpful included Works Progress Administration, *A History of Spartanburg County* (Spartanburg: Bond and White, 1940); Archie Vernon Huff Jr., *Greenville: The History of the City and County in the South Carolina Piedmont* (Columbia: University of South Carolina Press, 1995); and Dwain Pruitt, *Things Hidden: An Introduction to the History of Blacks in Spartanburg* (Spartanburg: City of Spartanburg Community Relations Office, 1995). A recent master's thesis by Marianne Elizabeth Julienne lends insight on rural upstate South Carolina women ("A Woman's World: A Female Household in Spartanburg, South Carolina, 1880–1900," University of South Carolina, 1997).

The standard work on Tennessee history is Robert E. Corlew, *Tennessee: A Short History*, 2nd ed. (Knoxville: University of Tennessee Press, 1990). The *WPA Guide to Tennessee* (1940, reprint Knoxville: University of Tennessee Press, 1986) provides a contemporary snapshot of the state. Lester C. Lamon gives an overview of African American history in the state (*Blacks in Tennessee: 1791–1970* [Knoxville: University of Tennessee Press, 1981]). Michael Frome furnishes an account of the changes taking places in the Great Smoky Mountains, making creative use of oral histories, in *Strangers in High Places: The Story of the Great Smoky Mountains* (Knoxville: University of Tennessee Press, 1966). Durwood

Dunn's study of a Blount County mountain community lends insight into the process of property removal for the national park (*Cades Cove: The Life and Death of a Southern Appalachian Community, 1818–1937* [Knoxville: University of Tennessee Press, 1988]).

Much work on the history of Appalachia has attempted to explore how distinctive this region is and how much its identity has been socially constructed by outsiders. See, for example, Henry D. Shapiro, *Appalachia on Our Minds: The Southern Mountains and Mountaineers in the American Consciousness, 1870–1920* (Chapel Hill: University of North Carolina Press, 1978). A recent collection of articles on the region illuminates the diversity of the region known as Appalachia and explores patterns that are not necessarily unique to Appalachia or general to the entire region. See Mary Beth Pudup, Dwight B. Billings, and Altina L. Waller, eds., *Appalachia in the Making: The Mountain South in the Nineteenth Century* (Chapel Hill: University of North Carolina Press, 1995). Jane Becker traces the cultural politics of the development of the Southern Appalachian handicraft revival and the construction of categories of "folk" and "tradition" (*Selling Tradition: Appalachia and the Construction of an American Folk, 1930–1940* [Chapel Hill: University of North Carolina Press, 1998]). David E. Whisnant's fine study of settlement workers in Appalachia was useful in understanding the role of culture workers in rural areas (*All That Is Native and Fine: The Politics of Culture in an American Region* [Chapel Hill: University of North Carolina Press, 1983]).

Other work explores the economy of the Appalachian region. Historian Paul Salstrom, *Appalachia's Path to Dependency: Rethinking a Region's Economic History, 1730–1940* (Lexington: University Press of Kentucky, 1994), maintains that first extractive industries, then the federal government, created a culture of dependency among the citizens of the Southern Appalachians by making them dependent on cash. Other scholars have called Appalachia a colonial economy. Explorations of this theme and of economic development in general include Helen M. Lewis, Linda Johnson, and Donald Askins, eds., *Colonialism in Modern America: The Appalachian Case* (Boone, N.C.: Appalachian Consortium Press, 1978), and Mary Beth Pudup, "The Limits of Subsistence: Agriculture and Industry in Central Appalachia," *Agricultural History* 64 (1990): 61–89. In a provocative recent work, Wilma Dunaway argues that Appalachia has always been dominated by absentee capitalists (*The First American Frontier: Transition to Capitalism in Southern Appalachia, 1700–1860* [Chapel Hill: University of North Carolina Press, 1996]). Ronald L. Lewis, *Transforming the Appalachian Countryside: Railroads, Deforestation, and Social Change in West Virginia, 1880–1920* (Chapel Hill: University of North Carolina Press, 1998), describes the transformation of Appalachia from a rural agricultural society to a twentieth-century society embedded in capitalism and world markets, all a result of the arrival of the timber industry in the late nineteenth century.

Index

Library of Congress Cataloging-in-Publication Data
Walker, Melissa.
   All we knew was to farm : rural women in the upcountry South, 1919–1941
/ Melissa Walker.
   p. cm. — (Revisiting rural America)
   Includes bibliographical references and index.
   ISBN 0-8018-6318-X (alk. paper)
   1. Women farmers—Appalachian Region.   I. Title.   II. Series.
HD6073.F32U69   2000
331.4'83'0974—dc21   99-38678
                                                              CIP

CINDERELLA'S HOUSEWORK:

FAMILIES IN CRISIS, HOUSEHOLDS AT THE EDGE OF CHAOS!
Paul Meinhardt

Turn the Page
PUBLISHING

Published by Turn the Page Publishing LLC
P. O. Box 3179
Upper Montclair, NJ 07043
www.turnthepagepublishing.com

Distributed by
First Edition Design Publishing
www.firsteditiondesignpublishing.com
May 2012

LIBRARY OF CONGRESS CATALOGING IN PUBLICATION DATA
Meinhardt, Paul
Cinderella's Housework:
Families in Crisis, Households at the Edge of Chaos

ISBN: 978-1-62287-002-8 (PRINT)
ISBN: 978-1-62287-003-5 (EBOOK)

Library of Congress Control Number 2012935880

Set in Times New Roman
Cover Design by Mark Delbridge, Delbridge Design LLC

ACKNOWLEDGMENTS

Joan Alevras Meinhardt, my wife and muse ... and a tough one at that.

Michael Minton and Jean Libman Bloch, authors of *What Is a Wife Worth? The Leading Expert Places a High Dollar Value on Homemaking,* whose work was a major inspiration for *Cinderella's Housework.*

Those who provided guidance:
Roseann, Kirk, Eloise, Tony, Ken, Denise and Jim.

Family survivors permitting interviews and conversations about their families: Cindy, Mary Ann, Kim, Amanda, Aja, Donna, Heather, Eloise, Kelly, Anita, Christine and my family.

Most of all, a mountain of gratitude to my publisher and friend, Roseann S. Lentin.

INTRODUCTION
In the Beginning, Mother and Child!

Cinderella's Housework offers family-centered solutions to the 21ˢᵗ Century Economic Crisis. Families are shaped to fit the mold of the global economy. Shrinking family income is the problem, the reason **families exist in crisis mode ... at the edge of chaos.**

Families are the engines driving the global economy. Family-households are the core of endless human and environmental change. This book suggests a family-based analysis and solution for the global economic crisis.

The household is Mother Nature's "factory," producing humanity. This is the reality hiding in plain sight. The 21ˢᵗ Century political-economy needs to consider the human family in terms of **income-consumption**, as well as environmental change. Just as income and consumption are two sides of the same coin, human and environmental costs must be considered as part of any enterprise budget.

I suggest that Crisis Economics and shrinking family income are the result of shortsighted leadership, both in government and in corporations. Some suggest that economic crises result from surging testosterone. While hormonal imbalance may be part of the problem, I suspect the problem is far more complex than our body chemistry. The 21ˢᵗ Century question is: **Can humanity survive economic globalization, as well as cycles of environmental and economic crisis?**

My wife asked, "Paul, what is this book about? Look at the goulash you are writing ... you put everything in your book but the kitchen sink. You have stories about moonshine ... commentaries about *Cinderella* and children stories. Along with serious economic analysis, you've shoved in speculative physics and philosophy. You weave in genetics, computer networking, DNA, food, auto and drug industries, health, global terrorism, cosmic energy, political economy, marriage and divorce, jobs and income. Did I miss anything? A better question is, did you miss anything? So with all the stuff you've crammed into the book, how do you connect the dots? **You give the impression that everything is about family**."

I chuckled, "Yes, I know. That's the point ... the connecting thread. **Family *is* about everything and everything is ultimately about family ... because it's about people ... and family is where it all begins.**"

TABLE of CONTENTS

Essay 1

HOUSEWORK HELL

The poor child was given all the rough housework.
(*Cinderella*, Charles Perrault, 1697)

Cinderella was written to entertain and educate. Stories such as *Cinderella*, *Puss in Boots*, *Tales of Mother Goose*, *Beauty and the Beast*, and *Red Riding Hood* were more than bedtime stories. They were written to instruct children in the virtues of the society they were born into, namely the new market society.

Cinderella, in particular, is a parable of early market society. It is also an example of how market society transforms the extended cooperative family into a competitive corporate family. The death of Cinderella's mother and the remarriage of her father, create the conditions for household struggle. The merchant father, away on business much of the time, leaves control of the household to the stepmother.

1) ***Isolated Household***: Cinderella is the household drudge. Prior to the step-family, Cinderella was the focus of her father's attention. In the step-family, Cinderella is degraded from the family "trophy" to a servant in the household. She is a prisoner of housework inside her own home, while the step-family enjoys "stepping out in society."

Cinderella bridges the isolated household and social life outside. The reality of the story is that Cinderella "produces" the household, while the step family "consumes" it. The story is as much a prophecy as a fairy tale.

If the *Cinderella* story seems oddly familiar, it's because it brings to mind the 21st Century household. In fact, the nuclear family of parents and children, continue to reflect establishment priorities. Families increasingly become single parent households. The carefully watched servant of yesterday is transformed into the 21st Century homemaker, either male or female.

Deeply rooted conflicts are revealed in the "Cinderella" story. Cinderella represents family cohesiveness, while the step family represents household deconstruction. Cinderella is physically and personally beautiful. She represents the cooperative tribal family. The tribal family is the totality of all social and economic activity.

The stepsisters are ugly, despite their lavish clothes. Cinderella is beautiful, even in her rags and grime. The suggestion is that the new middle class family, in spite of its material trappings, needs a rebirth to the beauty of an extended, cooperative family, with family members and with community.

As we move through the essays, I will use the story of my family, a line of cattle breeders, to highlight the message of this text: how family members banding together for the good of all breeds success. The following is a short excerpt from *Breeders, My Family Story:*

In ancient Sumer lived a tribe of cattle breeders. Their skill at breeding livestock was widely known. Invited by neighboring tribes, the breeders traveled widely in the Middle East. In those times, wealth was reckoned in tribal increase of people and livestock, as well as trade goods. By those standards the breeders were a tribe of great wealth and importance.

The birth of children was of primary importance, and so women, mothers, wives and daughters were the decision-makers and planners. In my ancestry, women controlled the means of production by controlling the birth of children. Therefore, women were the true leaders, even as men held titles of chiefs and kings. Today women are still in household control.

2) ***She Who Must Be Obeyed:*** Like prisoners of war, it is our duty to escape our income prison, if we can't correct it. Many of us become impoverished as the economy disintegrates. We feel hopeless to change it. As with Cinderella, people begin to realize that a system of greed and mendacity is a dead end.

The death of Cinderella's mother and remarriage of her father, create conditions of household struggle. The merchant father, away on business much of the time, leaves control of the household to the stepmother.

Cinderella's fairy godmother is the household goddess. She is the spirit of household fertility. In extended families, the senior mother plays this part, often a grandmother. "She who must be obeyed" is the great African witch … the Good Woman, Woman of Wisdom, Healing Woman and Good Wife. She is the woman of power and wisdom in H. Rider Haggard's novel *She*.

"She" is the: "woman of the house," tribal matriarch … Great Goddess, Mother Nature, Gray Goddess of prehistoric Greece, Hestia of the hearth, household Goddess in ancient Crete, Healing Woman, Conjure Woman, Cosmic Mother, Hecate, Mary the Sea Mother, Goddess of All Waters, Matron Chief in tribal societies, and countless others.

Sea Mother transforms fetal sea water into infant blood, the miraculous water of life. In this regard, all mothers are Sea Mothers … literally and figuratively. Fetal water is similar to sea water. It contains the same proportions of ionized salts such as sodium chloride, sodium bicarbonate (baking soda), calcium, potassium, magnesium, manganese, iodine and most of the other trace metals found in sea water … primarily iron. Human blood is similar.

In ancient times, the household goddess was often the Water Spirit, widely known as the Virgin of the sea, later called Mary. 'Mare' is Latin for sea. "She" is the Virgin Spring, providing the water of life, breaking the water of birth. "She" creates life.

"She" washes away our sins, and drowns our sorrows in tears of grief and joy. In the household, "She" purifies everything and everyone. "She" transforms ordinary household chores into sacred hearth rituals.

"She" is midwife, household priestess, and purifier. She holds the power to create and transform life. She is the Water of Life, transforming, creating, growing, purifying, cleansing, and washing away the tears of loss.

"She" who purifies the household earns new respect, appreciation and awe. The "cleaning woman" not only washes away our sins and tears, but does the laundry, the dishes, and windows. "She" is the household bread-winner. "She" is house-worker and wage-worker. "She" is the household deity.

Housework is an "action-prayer" performed by the family deity … who daily purifies and sanctifies the household. The family deity and muse-mother must receive offerings of attention and respect for the continual sacrifices they make.

Cinderella summons Hestia of the Hearth, her fairy godmother. The godmother instructs her to fetch the largest pumpkin from the garden, and the mice from the trap. Cinderella knows what must be done. With help from her godmother, Cinderella takes control of the household. She reasserts her power over life and society, with the aid of household magic.

It is as if Cinderella is transformed into the Goddess of Life. The pumpkin and mice suggest Cinderella's power over family and nature. The home-maker is a fountain of creation and destruction. Like the deity, Shiva, household power is both creative and destructive ... male and female ... testosterone and estrogen ... two sides of the same coin.

She holds the power to turn pumpkin into food or garbage. She can turn a household into heaven or hell ... often both. She can create a household of angels or devils. There is a bit of Cinderella in all of us. People have the power to create a passive household of compromise and acceptance or an active household of renewal and liberation.

What is greater than the power to create a child? Every child is a new birth of freedom and hope. Young or old, male or female, the struggle for personal freedom begins in the family-household.

3) ***Cinderella's Message***: Cinderella's message is that the old tribal household is a better deal; but she is stuck with the market system, as we all are. She can't change the system, but in a fairy tale all things are possible. With a little help from her godmother, Cinderella fights back.

Today, people see themselves ripped from jobs, careers, family, retirement, and society. We lose income. We lose homes. Families disintegrate. People and households are ground down. People cry out in pain. Government tries to control the beast, but it is too little, too late.

Victims fight back with empty pockets. We no longer have the income for shopping trips to the mall. Restaurants and entertainment are cut out of shrinking budgets. Vacations and holiday escapes become distant memories. Gasoline and heating oil costs eat up more of our shrinking income.

Most families cannot afford new cars, appliances, and big-ticket purchases. Banks hoard their money. Personal credit and business loans are difficult to obtain. The social-economic system implodes, collapsing in on itself.

Economic crises affect families in many ways. Not only does reduced income stress families economically, but psychologically as well. In crisis economies, anxiety and depression become unwelcome members of the family. **Rather than resist the injustice, drugs are pushed to help us "adjust."**

Cinderella represents the family confrontation between housework and wage-work. The present economic crisis is causing a not so "cold-war" between family need and establishment greed. Increasingly, wage-workers and house-workers are the same people. In crisis economies, family income implodes, not with a bang but with a whimper.

In summary, Cinderella's message is:

1. Irresponsible banking holds families, nations, and the Earth hostage to greed and deception.
2. More low-pay wage-work usually means less time for housework, further diminishing families.
3. Crisis economies result from irresponsible investors gambling public funds and family income.
4. Corporations 'socialize' wage-workers; while households 'isolate' unpaid housework spouses.
5. Family anxiety and impoverishment are the result of shrinking family income.

Essay 2

FAMILY SHOPPING

*Along with children, shopping is the most humanizing part
of housework. Shopping provides for human needs,
as well as social, trade, and corporate contact.*

At first, I could find no mention of shopping in the *Cinderella* story. Then I thought about the final part of the story. Cinderella and her godmother planned her appearance at the prince's ball. It's obvious. I realized at last that Cinderella and her godmother were shopping for a prince.

Cinderella and the prince were both seeking a happy and prosperous life. Many of the guests at the princely ball were the families and daughters of successful entrepreneurs. We might say that all at the ball were shopping for reproductive success.

At the ball, the jealous sisters were shopping for clever dressmakers, in the hope that a gown like Cinderella's would help them catch a prince. One lesson of the Cinderella story is that **to escape housework isolation, we must get out into the social whirl of enterprise and trade.** Shopping gets us into that world.

Shopping is the modern equivalent of *hunting and gathering,* minus the drudgery and brutality. The goal of shopping is to provide the needs and desires of life. Most people consider shopping a pleasant experience. The opportunity for socializing is far greater when shopping than being at home.

1) ***Bringing It All Together:*** Shopping enables family survival, providing both *re-creation* and *recreation*, as well as facilitating social relations, enterprise, and trade. **Gesamtkunstwerk** is the German word for "unifying all aspects of culture." That's what shopping does for the family. It brings it all together. Shopping extends the family domain outside and beyond

the household confines. In effect, **shopping may reduce social barriers and is the most vital part of housework.** Shopping is a socially unifying experience. It is Gesamtkunstwerk.

As a behind the counter deli worker, I see many opportunities for Gesamtkunstwerk—talking to customers, teaching children the metrics of what a half pound costs if a pound is $3.99, and chatting with co-workers. When I was a teen, Dad had a market at the edge of our cattle ranch in south Florida. Later, we opened a toy store next to the market. I was active in both businesses. While at university, Dad needed me in his moonshine network. These venues provided years of experience interacting with customers, suppliers, and the broad range of the shopping experience.

2) ***Shopping For a Life:*** Life is a shopping trip. That's the way I see it. In this life, we are always searching, pursuing, and shopping for stuff. We shop for adventure, knowledge, wisdom, love, friendship ... and some sort of epiphany. The **lure of hidden knowledge** is my shopping pursuit.

Process, change and transformation are what life, the family, household, Cosmos and shopping are all about. I suggest that seeking what is missing from our lives is of more value than reaching the goal. Every time I studied for another degree, the process of working my way toward the degree was more enjoyable than actually getting the degree.

Fortunately, we never find everything we shop for. I say 'fortunately' because life would lose its zest if we were too easily satisfied ... if all our needs, hungers, desires and fantasies were realized with little or no effort. **Experience tells us that the process of shopping is more important than the objective. I suspect that life is more about "process" than reaching an imagined goal.** I spent many pleasant years working toward various degrees. Adding one degree to my resume only prompted a new quest for yet another. The pursuit of academic stature was becoming a fixation.

It was the **lure of hidden knowledge,** and discovering my spouse and kids along the way, that brought me to the realization that it was my family, my **reproductive success** that satisfied me, not another piece of vellum. **The ultimate shopping trip is seeking a mate and reproductive success.**

What happens to us when life's shopping trip is too successful? Millionaires and billionaires can provide some answers to this question. Many of the rich live a non-stop super-saturated shopping trip. Some of the super-rich are less concerned with "run-of-the-mall" shopping and more concerned with shopping for investments and power.

When the super-rich shop for power, they sometimes shop for lobbyists and legislation, which, at times, when used for the good of the few, curtails the rights of the majority.

The effectiveness of the "**Billionaires' Pledge**," to donate at least half their wealth to charity, is a case in point. "A total of 69 of America's richest families have so far joined the pledge, meaning that 17% of the 403 U.S. billionaires have joined the effort.[1]

If we view the "billionaires' pledge" philosophically, we may suppose that 69 billionaire families arrived at an epiphany. It's understandable that people can reach a point in the process of shopping for wealth and power when they pause to reflect on their direction, and may arrive at a point of discovery. At that point the **angel of our better nature** (as Lincoln suggested) takes charge to direct our lives onto the path of human kindness. These blessed 69 now travel a path that may lead us all to more humane pursuits.

Who shops for power? Egotistical entrepreneurs shop for power. These include banking moguls, financial traders, and speculators. They shop for the laws they want. All it takes is the right price. That's why the old cliché so aptly applies, "We have the best Congress money can buy."

When the super-rich go shopping, they buy legislation, governments, and the birthright of 99.9% of families.

Few of us will ever enter the power brokers' shopping mall. The dues for that exclusive club are beyond our reach. Whenever a new attack on family income is launched, we need only follow the "money trail," to learn the "who" and "why" behind the attack.

The super-rich have a hunger that only power can satisfy, but never for long. The cost-cutting dollars extracted from family income feeds the power-hungry beast. But for some, there is never enough money or power to satisfy that addiction.

While most of us shop for life, the super-rich shop for power over our lives. The many wars and "police actions" that the majority fought and died for did not provide the hoped-for freedom and equality. Rather the war machine enriches the super-rich to the point where they are "out of control."

A contingent of the super-rich have become **loose cannons**, careening around the globe, wreaking havoc on people and the Earth at every turn. The results of the super-rich wrecking ball are the revolutions in Iran, Iraq, Egypt, Libya, Tunisia, Syria, Yemen, Bahrain, and the others like Greece, Spain, Portugal, Ireland and Italy … waiting in the wings.

The terrorism unleashed and financed by the oil-barons, has already begun to fester and metastasize in Iran, Iraq, Afghanistan and Pakistan. Money is at the root of most terrorist acts, and vast sums of wealth are amassed by the world-wide security-military establishment. The military industrial complex uses various security agencies, such as the CIA, to shop for global opportunities.

Is there a connection between terrorism and the wealth created by terrorism? In the computer industry, it is well known that the first creators of anti-virus software were the authors of the first network virus. Now, millions of information workers must shop for virus protection.

The super-rich fear for their wealth and power. They use **their** multimedia to spread **their** fear and create a multi-billion dollar security industry. Employment for millions of police, military and other security workers necessitates laws to break, and people to break them. The result is millions of prisoners and thousands of prisons throughout the world. **Fear-mongering fosters fearful shopping.**

Fear is a timeless motivation for shopping. Fear of hunger and death started us hunting, gathering and shopping for food and protection. Our unpredictable environment makes Mother Nature the prime mover for all shoppers. We shop for food, love, protection and power. **What Mother Nature gives with one hand, the super-rich take away with the other.**

3) ***Shopping Is My Life, My Family Story:*** My earliest shopping memory is of Grandma taking me to the corner grocery. I noticed the big red and white tomato soup sign in the window. I was four years old and recognized

the large gilt letters. Grandma asked, "Now Pauli, what do those golden letters spell?" I recall sounding out T-O-M-A-T-O-S-O-U-P and with the aid of the red and white soup can, joyously shouting, "TOMATO SOUP." Grandma exultantly crooned, "Such a clever lad you are."

From that time on shopping was always a happy learning experience. I loved the trolley rides with the wind on my face. I would pull out loose straws in the seats, until Ma told me to stop. On the corner of St. John's and Ralph Avenues we transferred trolleys. There was a bar on that corner and I loved the smell of beer. Poking my head in the open door, I would and wave to the men. Ma pulled me away.

In my grammar school years, I loved shopping for soda, bubble gum, jelly beans and especially comic books. I'd write on my calendar when the next issue of Buck Rogers would arrive on the news stand. I would pay my ten cents and read every word, including the ads. The "Charles Atlas" ads were burned into my mind. I believe comics were my key motivation for learning to read.

Comic books were shopping catalogues for kids. The ads were hypnotic for me. "Boys, grow mushrooms in your basement … ." We didn't have basements in south Florida. "Kids, sell flower and vegetable seeds to your neighbors … win BB guns and bikes."

I drove Ma nuts with these requests. It got to the point where I had to hide my comic books. When Ma found my comics, she shredded them, adding the shreds to the cattle feed. Finally, Dad got her to stop by saying the comic book ink was bad for the cattle.

At the reservation school, teachers would trash any comic book they saw. But when we moved to Miami Beach teachers would take our comics and return them at the end of the day. Dad was Glades County sheriff then. He was also an "enterprise chief." An enterprise chief manages tribal businesses.

We lived at the edge of the reservation, on the shore of the Lake. We fished almost every night for perch and catfish. Okeechobee is the perch capitol of Florida, America, the world … I forget which. In any case we hunted fish, snakes and frog legs as much as we shopped … loved frog legs and fish pan-fried in olive oil, lemon and garlic.

Sometimes dad would skin and cut-up snakes to pan fry in chicken fat. Snake meat tasted like meaty chicken necks...at least to me. The tribe raised gators for the leather. The matrons cured and made alligator belts, hand-bags, wallets and custom-fit shoes.

The only part of the gator that was eaten was the fatty tail. Along with other meats and cold cuts, dad sold fresh and pickled fish, frog legs, barbeque snake meat and smoked gator tail in his market.

Dad would say, "You love fish and fish love you ... it's great that we don't have to do much food shopping." I still love fish, but don't eat frog legs anymore. Fish is my main protein source. I eat no other meats and my meat shopping is exclusively, canned salmon, sardines, tuna, anchovies and pickled herring.

The ranch was transformed into 20,000 cinder-block veteran homes. The Federal Housing Authority bartered with the tribe. The FHA got the ranch land, and in exchange the tribe received ten acres at each of twelve on-off ramps of the new federal highway that cut through the reservation. This was a great trade, as the FHA was shopping for suitable land near the new highways, close to the fresh water of Lake Okeechobee and near the urban center of Palm Beach.

With Sheriff Joe's help, the tribe sold ten-year leases to shopping center builders at each of the twelve on-off ramps. In addition to supermarkets, the shopping center leases provided 20,000 square feet of store space for the tribe at each pair of on-off ramps, five miles apart.

They put in medical-dental store-front clinics at each of the shopping centers. Most of the square footage became tribal trading centers for liquor, gasoline, car repairs, tribal crafts, sundries, toys, newspapers, magazines and tourist stuff.

Much of the cash flow came from shoppers eager for home-brew moonshine. "Sunshine Juice" was twice as good and half the cost of the best commercial liquor. Since it was produced and sold on tribal land, it was 100% legal. Distributing moonshine throughout the South helped me get through college.

These days, as a deli clerk, I can happily serve shoppers and socialize with them. In fact, shoppers and supermarket shopping provide an excellent laboratory for the study of family shopping practices. I can honestly say, "Some of my best friends are shoppers." In fact, everyone is a shopper for one thing or another.

We arrive full circle, back to the point where hunters and gatherers are now shoppers. Just as with our first mothers, those who provide successful reproduction, and do the family shopping, hold the power. As it was in the beginning, is now, and ever will be...those who reproduce and provide the provisions remain in control. As I observe shoppers and their shopping methods, they impress me increasingly with their skill and intelligence. Here are some key observations:

Savvy shoppers...
1. **Plan** ahead in considerable detail;
2. Take an **inventory** of household supplies and **schedule** shopping according to need;
3. Tend to buy mostly what is on **sale**, according to store ads;
4. **Buy limited amounts** of fresh or unpackaged foods on sale, such as bananas;
5. Shop as if it is an income preserving game … to **spend the least and get the most**;
6. Keep **coupons** to buy, trade or donate to **charities** for tax deductions;
7. **Shop in groups**, car pool and take turns minding shoppers' kids;
8. **Teach kids** shopping skills;
9. Give shopping lists to **working spouses**, to pick up after work;
10. **Smile** at store clerks to energize both clerks and shoppers.

4) ***Born To Shop, Family Story:*** Until the last few years, I did not think of shopping as the primary housework activity. This family story presents remarkable shopping activities as defining moments in the lives of remarkable people:

When his dad opened the Trading Post, Doc had just turned fifteen. This was about a month before the adjacent on-off ramps opened. Next to the Trading Post was the huge new supermarket. It opened a few weeks before the Trading Post, and was doing "sell-out" business. The medical-dental clinic did not open until a month after the "grand-opening" celebration of the federal highway ramps.

The first part of the Trading Post to open for business was the liquor store, where the featured brand was "Mik-Sem Liquid Sun-Shine." It was the first legal moonshine sold in Florida. It was smoother, purer and more potent than any other liquor, and at half the price.

The tribal "shine" was fermented from citrus pulp and sugar cane molasses. Triple refluxing produced triple distilled high quality liquor. It was, by far, the finest shine anyone had tried. Actually, it was more like fine brandy, than moonshine.

There was a large Marine base west of the highway with 10,000 families and 20,000 new veteran's homes behind the strip-mall east of the highway. These new residents, west of North Miami, doubled the population of the town. In the early 1950's it was a veteran's world, with plenty to spend, and even more to buy.

The day the liquor store opened, the fruit juice bar and cafe also opened in the Trading Post. A well-known Cajun band was hired to play country music from noon until closing that night. Teaspoon size samples of "Liquid Sun-Shine" were provided all day, along with fruit juice chasers.

By three in the afternoon, the throngs filled every parking space on the five-acre parking lot. The supermarket provided 10¢ hotdogs and burgers. The Trading Post and Supermarket teamed up to provide two-dozen portable toilets, one dozen huge open tents with picnic tables, and the Cajun band. Thirty moon-lighting state troopers and twenty Marine MPs were hired for crowd control security.

Doc and twenty other tribal folks served customers. Quarts were $2 and gallon jugs were $5. A huge 18-wheeler, jammed with cases of "Liquid Sun-Shine," was backed-up flush with the back door. Gallon jugs of orange juice were provided by the Trading Post Cafe for 10¢. Huge signs were posted:

It is against the law to open liquor bottles anywhere on these 5-acre premises. Law enforcement is here for your safety and protection. You are strongly advised to keep all liquor bottles sealed until you are home.

By eight that evening the "Liquid Sun-Shine" was completely sold out, and by nine the parking lot was almost empty. That Saturday was a grand success. There were thousands of happy shoppers.

With the thousands of people from the surrounding area on both sides of I-95, there was no trouble, in spite of the supermarket selling cold beer and the Trading Post providing "Liquid Sun-Shine" samples.

5) ***Shopping For the Next Wave:*** Michio Kaku, *Physics of the Future, How Science Will Shape Human Destiny and Our Daily Lives by the year 2100*, provides a technology shopping list for the rest of this century.

He suggests that waves of innovative technology stimulated human progress since we first learned to control fire. In the last 200 years, we have played technology leapfrog, with shorter periods of time between each new technology wave.

Technological innovation is moving rapidly. The problem is that the next wave is being "high-jacked" by a huge imbalance of global wealth. For the next wave of innovation to move the wheels of human progress, income producing jobs must grow along with a new wave of technology. Economic and job planning must accompany technology planning; **"As crisis bites, the rising wealth gap becomes key."**[2]

In the U.S. a mountain of wealth controlled by 8% of families, deprives the 92% of lower income families with the income needed to shop, buy and support the next technology wave. If there are now 117 million U.S. households, each new hi-tech product is purchased by only a few million well-to-do "innovator-shoppers."

Given the current pace of wealth accumulation, by 2100 less than 1% of Americans will control more than 99% of all wealth. But of course the great cosmic lesson is that energy is perpetually in a state of flux. Everything, all conditions, economies, and technologies are constantly changing, not because we want things to change, but because Mother Nature rules.

It's unlikely that the imbalance of wealth will be tolerated much longer. The point of "wealth critical mass" is already playing itself out in revolutions throughout the world.

* * *

Here's my theory of how energy perpetually "shops" for the next change: At the end of space-time, **black holes** gobble up weakened energy, and each other, until only a single explosively unstable **singularity** remains. The **singularity** expands into the next **big bang** cosmic cycle. Each cosmic cycle is likely to be different from the one that came before or will come after.

Cosmic dynamics suggest that immense concentrations of energy and wealth, sooner than later, reach a point of terminal instability. Highly concentrated "crystallized" energy, such as wealth and nuclear stockpiles, make for a frightful future.

Along with the immensity of scientific and technological change, the antiquated social-political-economic environment must soon de-construct. Likely, a new unpredictable configuration will change the entire scenario. An orderly de-construction is my hope; better to have the change come with a whimper than a bang.

Imagine some form of global commonwealth, even if it is just wishful thinking. Certainly the falling dominoes of revolutions in Africa and the Middle East, together with the bailouts of Greece, Ireland, Portugal and soon Italy and Spain, suggest that whatever change is in the works is starting now. In the U.S. these changes are voiced by the **Occupy Wall Street** movement.

To date, the revolutions and radical leadership changes that are in the works include: Iraq, Afghanistan, Pakistan, Tunisia, Egypt, Libya, Bahrain, Yemen, Syria, Jordan and a new unification agreement between the two major Palestinian factions.

Neighboring nations such as: India, Morocco, Algeria, Iran and Israel are likely to experience major changes. The Cosmos, Earth and humanity is in flux. We either go with the flow or get crushed by it. Like the 1960's Bob Dylan song said, the times are a 'changing!

What all this means is that people are constantly shopping for a life.

6) ***Shopping for a Global Commonwealth:*** There may be one last devastating global depression, triggered perhaps by a disaster of global proportions, or a series of exploding economic bubbles. If a "terminal"

crisis were to trigger a wave of global misery, it will likely be followed by a global uprising that clears away the old global economy. What will replace it depends on our imagination.

The series of revolutions in North Africa and the Middle East, the Occupy Wall Street movement, along with the world-wide debt crisis, may be the prelude to a global economic disaster or miracle. Rebuilding will necessitate a more equitable distribution of global wealth.

Imagine a **global commonwealth,** federation, cooperative or union of nations, picking up the pieces after the global economy collapses. Someday soon, it will be necessary to empower a global economic-environmental salvage agency, with the clout to over-ride local politics and salvage what is beneficial from the old order and deconstruct what is harmful. In broad strokes, a **global commonwealth** might provide:

1. A **Base economy agency** established for the global environment and the basic needs of all people. The primary objective of a **Base economy** is to optimize the human condition and the global environment. **Base economy** provides health care, education and the necessities of life for all people.

2. A **Global commonwealth** is the global umbrella that provides freedoms, family rights and human rights, along with education sufficient to provide a high level of professional-technical education, personal entitlements, public participation and civic responsibility.

3. An **Enterprise economy** fosters enterprise, art, science, research, industry and the necessary commerce to support society. Family-household shopping and consumption, while regulated, can access a substantial level of goods, services and comforts. **Enterprise economy** contributes to the **global commonwealth** 80% of its surplus value; that is, net surplus after net cost.

4. **Global commonwealth** insures the wellbeing of the global environment and people. This is the primary responsibility of the **Global Commonwealth**. Vital sectors of the economy, such

as investment, finance, insurance, housing, transportation, basic commodities, education, public safety and security are regulated much as they are now, but with built-in "over-sight" at all levels.

5. **People work as they are able, and receive support as needed**. All have global commonwealth accounts credited for birth, education, preventative healthcare and basic family support and debited for consumption above and beyond the **base economy** amenities.

6. The **supply-demand** side of basic necessities are closely regulated by an adjustment agency. All forms of gambling affecting the overall economy must be treated as felonies. All public abuses resulting from addictive behavior may be subject to "Addictive Behavior Treatment Clinics." Damage adjudication may involve work indenture to injured parties.

7. **Conspicuous consumption,** injurious practices such as financial speculation are strongly discouraged, but still permitted, as are gaming casinos, within the confines of strictly controlled "reserves."

8. Violations of the public good and welfare, resulting in public harm or damage, may be judged and sentenced by **Commonwealth Defense Committees, CDC**. The CDC consists of volunteers representing the local neighborhoods, or zip code areas.

Victimless activities, such as sex, drugs and extreme recreations are no longer considered crimes and are not regulated, unless valid complaints of abuse, harm or damage are submitted to the CDC. The death sentence, torture, imprisonment, as well as other cruel and unusual punishment is abolished.

CDC's may pass sentence in the form of public-private fines, indenture, public service, compulsory wage-work and/or mental health treatment. Prisons are abolished. Civil and public suits for damages are referred to CDCs. Only certified public adjudicators may represent the interests of defendants and plaintiffs. All other professionals or representatives have no legal standing before the CDCs. However, those without legal CDC standing may be summoned as witnesses by public adjudicators.

9. All **elections are compulsory**; permitting one vote per household by home computer.
10. **Media** are free of censorship, but are libel for broadcasting false or harmful information.

8) ***Shopping For Energy:*** As in the beginning, is now, and is likely to continue, all critters need energy. We are always shopping for energy. It may be our ancestors hunting red meat to replenish lost blood-iron during menses and child bearing, or gathering wild food. We now hunt for sales, bargains, specials, coupons and only buy when "it's on sale."

Household-family formation began as trading food for mating privileges. We continue to shop for sex and reproductive success.

We always shop for energy. When we buy stuff at the market, we are sustaining the energy of our family or household. A household may consist of one person. In any case, all shopping, families, households and economies are based on energy exchange. **The value of housework is to transfer and recycle human energy.**

As we enter the 21st Century, the **most important pursuit is the quest for energy**. Our use of carbon-based energy provides more problems than solutions. Before the end of this century, non-destructive renewable energy is likely to replace current sources.

Most research is dedicated to energy technology. The search for ways to save the environment and replace destructive energy sources amounts to a rapid hunt for environmentally efficient energy. We are on a global shopping trip. **Shopping for energy promises to be endless. Energy is at the root of reproductive success and securing our environment.**

9) ***Shopping for A Woman's Smile:*** One form of energy that I have invested in since my earliest years is a **woman's smile**. Early on it was kin-folk mostly. Now in my prime, any woman's smile sends a rush of energy

surging through my body. If you want to get technical about it, we can attribute it to adrenalin, testosterone, growth hormone, dopamine, oxytocin and pheromones stimulating certain neural pathways.

We can talk about a wireless optical network that is established when we look into each other's eyes, as we both smile. But I believe a tangible contact occurs that is far more than the sum of its electromagnetic and hormonal parts. It feels like an exchange of energy.

Most of my deli customers are women. When I'm able to give them what they want, my reward is a sumptuous smile and eye contact that energizes my mind and gladdens my heart. All my life I shop for a woman's smile. As lame as this sounds, it works for me.

Of course, there's genetic code behind these pleasantries. Somewhere back in time the genetic code for reproductive success evolved to include **trading food and protection for sex**.

We spend our lives "shopping" for energy in one form or another. But we only know energy from a personal and narrow view point. The essence of "energy," like "reality," is as remote from our understanding, as a galaxy at the other side of the Cosmos. As we speed the pace of human comprehension, genetic change speeds up, much as cosmic expansion accelerates.

In *Physics of the Impossible*, Michio Kaku relates the *Star Trek* episode in which a capsule is found with a frozen human body. After thawing and healing, the man is revived. He discovers that he is 400 years older, and immediately tells Captain Kirk, that his **investments** must be worth a great deal of **money** by now.

Kirk asks, what are **investments** and **money**? The man responds by asking, how people get what they want? Kirk replies, "We just ask for what we want and we get it." Kirk is referring to **replicators** that can reproduce all human wants.

Of course Mother Nature, that is to say the Cosmos, is the ultimate replicator. She provides all our needs and requires only what we are able to give. And what can we give? We can give our seed and eggs for reproductive success.

We can shop for immortality as we recycle our energy and genes in our children. We can shop for opportunities to be stewards of the Earth. We can shop for opportunities that beneficially recycle Earth's energy resources.

10) ***Shopping for Real Solutions:*** As mentioned, the ultimate shopping trip for me is the **"lure of hidden knowledge."** Hidden knowledge, like family, includes all possibilities. Most everyone wants to know something … about their origin, about their reality. Where are they going and why are they here? How do we make the best of the human condition and a fickle environment?

No matter what anyone says or how convincing the proposal, we all choose what is worth believing and pursuing. Primarily, **we are on a life-long shopping trip to reproduce** as a way of preserving our lives.

It amounts to shopping for some small measure of immortality. The creative urge and inspiration of writers, artists, inventors and those "driven" to preserve ideas is part of this life-long shopping trip.

Being aware that all energy is part of cosmic energy recycling just doesn't "cut-it" for most of us. Physicists repeat the mantra, "Energy is neither created nor destroyed, but is endlessly transformed." As intelligent people, we may agree with this "law" of thermodynamics; but I for one cannot take it to heart.

Playing with the grandkids provides me with a greater sense of immortality than the certainty of energy recycling. Knowing that genetic code "programs" all life (including our own) and that geometric energy code is the foundation of the Cosmos still has me seeking, shopping for the switches and buttons to press for more answers. But there will always be more questions than answers … of that I'm sure. My kids and grandkids are answers enough, for now.

11) ***Summary of Why We Shop:*** The objective of housework is **successful reproduction,** and that's what we all shop for. We may be financial gurus or sanitation engineers, but whatever we do in life, it is ultimately for family, kids, kin or merely a household of one. Maintaining and caring for one-self is part of the successful reproduction process.

Family-households **produce people.** The more people families produce the better the chance for family continuance. We shop for knowledge of how we can perpetuate ourselves. And family kinship groups comprise a tried and true method of forwarding reproductive success.

Essay 3

LIFES, Low Income Family Economic Support

A deprived family is neither free nor productive.

In a collapsing economy, the most desirable action is to reverse the collapse and restore a positive economic pattern as rapidly as possible. Employment statistics don't distinguish between full-time, part-time, temporary, reduced hours and no longer seeking a job. If any wage is reported, the worker is considered employed.

The basic problem is the accumulation of wealth at the expense of family income. Those who accumulate wealth do so by exporting American jobs and an assortment of so-called "cost-cutting" measures that reduce employment, income and purchasing power.

As of December, 2011, A FRESH account emerged ... about the magnitude of financial aid that the Federal Reserve bestowed on big banks during the 2008-09 credit crises. The report came from Bloomberg News, which had to mount a lengthy legal fight to wrest documents from the Feds that detailed its rescue efforts ...

Billions are secretly showered on troubled financial institutions to stave off disaster. Individuals get little or no help. Here are some of the new figures ... . Among all the rescue programs set up by the Fed, **$7.77 trillion** in commitments were outstanding as of March 2009 ... ."[3]

If we needed fresh evidence of banks controlling government, here it is: Dictatorship by the banks. Why didn't the government demand bank-stock ownership worth $7.77 Trillion? That would have given our government effective ownership control of American banking. A similar bailout-stock trade worked with General Motors ... why not with banks?

As the corporate economy improves, family income continues to decline. Families with unemployed and under-employed workers include:

1. Workers no-longer seeking employment;
2. Temporary workers;
3. Part-time workers;
4. Workers forced to accept reduced work hours;
5. Workers forced to accept income rollbacks;
6. Workers in the underground economy.

While government, Security Exchange Commission, SEC, provides $7.77 Trillion, interest-free, to the banks, the American middle class pays for it. Now it may be seen how falling income destroys the American family. If someone took your money without permission, you would call that theft. What is it called when the SEC takes our money without permission?

* * *

It's likely that half of all families, in all income groups, have some economic stake in the underground "off-the-books" economy. Americans are resourceful. If jobs are not available Americans will find alternative income, and of course greed knows no limits regardless of income.

1) ***Neglect of Family Income, LIFES***: The 21st Century economic crisis is the result of neglecting family income. The result is that consumers can no longer afford to buy the way they did during the last 60 years. Real wages for real work slowly erodes to the point where low paid retail service work replaces high paid industrial work.

Abusive government, banking, housing, insurance, and stock market practices have further victimized the most vulnerable families. How much longer can the financial vultures be allowed to pick over the bones of our economy?

If low-income families received bail-outs, support, depreciation allowances and subsidies, as do American banks, the economic crisis might be reversed. Imagine low-income-families receiving monthly checks for $1,600 for the poorest, and less for the groups with more income.

The one-year cost of such a program would be $750 Billion. This is far less than the bank bailout money paid by the same low-income tax-paying families, via the SEC. A long-term Low-Income-Family-Economic Subsidy, LIFES, is unlikely to happen under government egis. **Low-income-families do not have lobbyists with deep pockets. Why not a LIFES lobby?**

By 2012 it is likely that fewer than 10% of U.S. families will control over 90% of U.S. wealth. That's where the money may be found. U.S. income in 2012 is likely to exceed $50 trillion. The cost of a "Family Income Support Program" is about 1.5% of the annual net worth of wealthy Americans. A long-term family bailout is less than 10% of the bank bailout.

A family support program might be in the form of a private commercial bond sales program, modeled after the successful World War II, 1940's, Victory Bond sales. All bond sales would be pooled into a Family Support Program, based on income tax returns.

There is a precedent for such surcharges in time of war, and this is war. It's time that those who have profited from this economic crisis start paying a share of the costs. The rationale for a family repayment program has as much to do with sustaining the overall U.S. economy and enterprise well-being, as supporting low-income families. In effect, it introduces into the enterprise economy a new game plan. This game plan provides something for everyone.

The corporate economy and wealthy families would gain the added security and support of moderately higher and sustainable consumption by all families. All families would have access to interest bearing investment bonds. Low-income families gain a sense of security and support resulting in a rise in consumer confidence and sustainable consumer spending.

Some of the benefits of support for low-income families:

1. Enable major consumer **spending**, on big-ticket items such as **autos**, **homes** and **health care**.
2. Smooth-out business **sales-cycles** and, smooth-out drastic swings in the economy.
3. Permit better **planning** for employment, distribution, and manufacturer purchases.
4. Economic **cycle consistency** provides for smaller and more manageable financial swings.
5. Increased consumer spending increases **job creation**.

Family deprivation plagues low income families. People that are deprived of life's amenities are not as productive as they could be. Deprived people are not free people. Not only do they hinder production and consumption, but also threaten the established order of society.

The revolutions throughout the world are by deprived people. The Occupy Wall Street movement is by mostly well educated people deprived of jobs. **It is the accumulation and poor distribution of wealth that is the real global problem.**

2) ***LIFES, Real Solutions to crisis economics***: A basic solution to low income families is a **Low Income Family Economic Support** program **(LIFES)**. **LIFES lottery-bonds** could be sold by private-commercial agencies. All **LIFES** proceeds may be designated for low income family support. A LIFES program can improve wealth distribution and increase family consumption, as well as jobs. Cycles of crisis economics may be reduced with a **LIFES lottery-bond** program.

A commercial approach involves a voluntary "Victory Bond" program like the successful 1940's World War II program. **Ten-year Bonds might pay 2.5%** annual interest. Lottery-bonds could be attractive investments, as well as a way to benefit the economy and low-income families.

1. **Victory Lottery Bonds** could be sold as lottery tickets are sold in the same retail outlets. A single denomination of $25 on maturity, would sell for $18.75, in unlimited multiples. **Victory Lottery Bonds** might be test-marketed first in counties or zip codes with the lowest family income and expanded based on the test-market results.

2. Such a program may **solve the problem of bouncing from one economic crisis to another**. A privately operated lottery bond program could eventually supplement or replace government tax or "surcharge" programs.

3. Funding might be via executive order, placing a **Surcharge on all financial trading**, derivatives, mortgages and insurance transactions. The "Commander-in-Chief" might declare an "Economic Crisis Emergency."

4. As with U.S. government majority ownership of General Motors, the model of a **Commonwealth economy** may have already begun. Holding majority ownership of principal industrial and financial companies, in escrow by the government, may be an option similar to stocks, but the taxpayers have to own an interest in the bailouts.

5. Perhaps a **fully private-commercial lottery-bond program** is the best approach. As government is now controlled by billionaires and millionaires, the more philanthropic of these might be persuaded to initiate a **LIFES** lottery-bond agency, for the benefit of low-income families and the economy as a whole.

3) ***What Happened To Family Income?*** According to the U.S. Census Bureau, "Median Household Income Dropped 3.6% in 2008" and as much as 5% in 2009. Now, toward the end of 2011, economic prospects continue to be dismal, suggesting further declines in household income.[4]

Median U.S. household income fell to $50,303 in 2008, the most drastic drop on record. This compares to the median family income of $50,046 in 1999. It's as if we lost ten years of income growth. U.S. Census projected median family income of $64,400 for 2010, but at the rate household income is dropping we are not likely to even see 1999 income levels.

While family income is falling, the poverty rate is rising, to 13.2% in 2008, up from 12.5% in the previous year. Nearly 40 million Americans were living in poverty in 2009. If current trends continue, over 20% of the U.S. population will be impoverished by 2012.

"Official" unemployment exceeds 9%. "Unofficial" unemployment is closer to 25%, when part-time and disillusioned workers are included. Comparisons to the 1930s Great Depression are therefore in order.

Falling consumer demand is the result of falling family income. Families can't afford big-ticket purchases and certainly can't afford credit for such purchases, assuming they could get the credit. Establishment economists entertain the fantasy that families are saving and paying off debt, as if that reduces the money available for necessities.

The biggest expenditures are housing, healthcare and transportation. Families have cut back on these "big three" purchases because job, wage, credit and income roll-backs are poisoning the economy. Narrow-minded investors are destroying the middle-class goose that lays the golden egg.

Ask, "Who is responsible for reducing family income and destroying the middle-class?" The answer is the narrow-minded of global finance and banking. Their criminal neglect lies in not recognizing the **"family-house-hold" as the root of all profit**.

If families cannot afford big-ticket purchases, it may be a mercy that access to credit is severely cut back for the average American. Banks are deservedly "taking the heat" for destroying the home mortgage, auto and healthcare industries. The crushing debt of these necessities remains high, while family income continues to fall.

One solution is to provide sustained and adequate national support for low-income families. Time and again, we've seen low-income families spend whatever money they get on consumer goods and services. This triggers a **"multiplier"** whereby upwards of $10 may be generated in the economy for every $1 spent.[5]

It's likely that a LIFES, "Low Income Family Economic Support," program providing $750 billion a year, could generate $7.5 trillion spent on necessities, such as long delayed healthcare, housing and transportation. Local elected "adjusters" could decide eligibility, based on ability to work.

4) ***What Is A Low-Income Family?*** A 2010 family income report projects the highest median income of $71,744 for a New Jersey family of two earners, and the lowest of $42,606 for Mississippi. As events now unfold in 2011, it looks like 80% of households will have income under $71,744 and 20% above.[6]

The 20/80 split in 2010 seems to be widening. This means that 15.6 million families have annual income of $71,744 or more, and 62.4 million have income of under $71,744. Government economists consider a family "wealthy" if their annual income is $250,000 and over. States such as Oregon add a tax surcharge on income of $250,000 and over.

In terms of economic support, low-income families provide the work, and buy the stuff that keeps America prosperous. The only solution to this economic crisis is a more equitable distribution of wealth. The inertia of wealth resists any interruption of class comfort. As low- income families strive to improve their income, they make the wealthy increasingly anxious.

The number of "taxed family households" is projected to increase to 78 million in 2010, while the total number of U.S. families is expected to reach 115 million. I suggest that the number of families will reach 120 million by 2012. This estimate is based on data provided in the 2007 U.S. Census Table 674, the most recent data available. I've added my own estimates for 2008 through 2012, in the following table:[7]

Annual Family Income As a Percent of 78 Million Families		
Year	High-income is$71,744 and Over	Low-Income is Under $71,744
2007	42%	58%
2008	35%	65%
2009	25%	75%
2010	20%	80%
2011	15% projection	85% projection
2012	10% projection	90% projection

It's the objective of careless cost-cutting corporations to extract resources by ripping apart nature and family. Economic "lose-cannons" continue the rampage through the mortgage industry. Destruction of families continues as home mortgages are divided into prime, sub-prime, toxic assets, and further divided into "derivatives."[8]

The point is that by dividing property and assets into more diverse and complex financial instruments, understanding is lost in a maze of obscurity. The reality of wealth loses its objectivity and becomes abstract, insubstantial, regressive and destructive. Accounts of financial transactions are dispersed and obscured. This is criminal fraudulent behavior.

Income inequality is the basis for the global economic crisis of the 21st Century. Families are woven into the fabric of inequality. The cost of this crisis will be extracted, as always, from families that can be taxed. The lesson for our children is that narrow-minded entrepreneurs shirk social responsibility by tax avoidance, and middle and low-income families are stuck with the tax burden.

Essay 4

FAMILY SURVIVAL

Housework is the vital link between all social and economic activities. The Cinderella story dramatizes this connection. Examining the development of this process, we may see it as a vast mix of conflict between work inside and outside the home.

Both wage-work and housework contribute to the family. But conflict grows from the confrontation between irresponsible enterprise and household production. It is war on the home front. Housework produces people in the family. Irresponsible enterprises and myopic corporations employ wage-work to produce commodities, things. Wage-work sometimes separates us from our humanity while housework literally produces our humanity.

Irresponsible corporations victimize wage-workers and, in effect, house-workers. In an effort to increase profits and cut costs, corporations may produce work that is dreary, repetitious and dehumanizing. Social and environmental costs are seldom on the balance sheet. Such conditions reduce all workers to a new type of serfdom. Workers in the 21st Century have daily freedom, but in the long run we are all servants of the global marketplace. Mother Nature fashioned us to be stewards of the Earth and not destroyers. The cosmic family creates households and people for this purpose. **Human households produce people, the most important of all products.**

1) ***Families Speak, How It Feels***: As the global economic crisis deepens, it affects low income wage workers most severely. Millions of people have little choice but to accept part-time low-wage jobs. While the food industry is not the bottom of the labor market, it consists of millions of low-wage jobs and hard-working wage-workers. This I know from first-hand experience.

I'm one of the low-income wage-workers lucky enough to find a job. Working with other food workers over the last few years provides an insight and appreciation for the work we do. We talk every day about work and family issues. Repeatedly, we talk about our families and the difficult time we have supporting them.

A constant theme is money, hourly pay, cutting work hours, how many hours on this week's schedule and what about next week. Most of us part-time workers belong to a minimally supportive union. Between holidays we are lucky to get 20-25 hours of work each week. To keep costs down most companies seldom hire full-time workers. Many of us are forced to seek out second and third part-time jobs. Still it is difficult to make ends meet.

The companies I work for are among the best and still they try all sorts of gimmicks to extract more work in fewer hours, resulting in lower income. But this is the accepted practice for all companies. **There are thinkers and accountants, and the accountants rule.**

2) ***Tools of the Trade:*** The nature of housework and wage-work involve special tools. Housework tools such as cooking-stove, fridge, vacuum cleaner, dishwasher, clothes washer-dryer, automate and isolate solo houseworkers. In deli work, the same housework tools render the housework experience a more satisfying prospect.

What makes family housework chores so different from housework chores on the job?

1. On the job, workers are **paid a wage**, however low.
2. Wage workers are paid by the hour and receive **paid breaks**.
3. Hourly work has a **start and end time**, even with the indignities of a time-clock.
4. Enforced work **safety rules** reduce danger to wage workers.
5. Criticism and reprimands are usually limited to more **civil periodic reviews**.
6. Wage work crews provide gentle instruction, support and a **friendly work place** environment.

Certainly, such wage-work experience is far from universal, or ideal. When the housework experience is compared to similar wage-work, the results are distinctly different. In many respects, housework and wage-work antagonistically confront each other.

Housework tends to expand to fill the available time. This is the "make-work" effect. Since housework is usually unpaid solo work, it tends to be poorly defined, unplanned, excessively or minimally done. Criticism of housework is typically misdirected, diffuse, unkind, and ill advised. The only part of housework that is often planned is the shopping list.

Most important, housework can be isolating and unsatisfying. The tools of housework in the household and in the workplace are far less significant than the organization of the actual work. For many customers, especially the elderly, the highpoint of the day could be talking with a deli counter person, customers, or service people.

3) ***Cult of Isolation:*** The public world of wage-work tends to oppose the private world of housework. As Cinderella realized, the more deeply involved she was in housework, the more difficult were the prospects for a satisfying life outside the home.

The teamwork of corporate production is made public by the commodities displayed in stores, outlets and malls. Except for the children we show-off, housework is usually hidden. From this point of view corporate work is public and housework is private.

What is satisfying about housework? Most parents are pleased with their children and the affection received from their spouse. In most surveys of house workers, children are considered the only satisfying part of family housework.

In the privacy of the home, the house-worker spouse may prod, and "dramatize" seemingly trivial household concerns. In contrast, corporate rules of workplace privacy, dignity, safety and productivity encourage diplomatic correction of errors by the experienced work crew.

There persists a sense of individualism in both housework and wage-work. Before work in the household and the workplace was separated, farming and tribal society performed cooperative and communal work.

While tribes maintained separate "societies" for men, women, veterans, and healers, these were all supporting the welfare of the tribe.

Why are household and workplace separate? Charles Nordhoff, in his 1875 classic *Communistic Societies of the United States*, described the communal societies that built the common wealth ideals of America over the last three centuries. A more complete survey of American economic societies was compiled by William A. Hinds in his 1902 survey of *American Communities.*[9] This work is of special interest as it documents the "co-partnership" agreements arranged by "certain gentlemen of London" for the 1607 Jamestown, Virginia Charter and the 1620 Pilgrim colony of Plymouth, Massachusetts.

The Jamestown Charter authorized colony members to "trade together in a common stock" for five years, but the colonists abandoned this agreement before the five years expired. The Pilgrim Colony entered into a "co-partnership" where "all profits and benefits that were gotten by trade, trucking, working or any other means, of any other persons, were to remain in the common stock" for seven years.

All colonists' material needs were supplied out of these common stocks. At the end of the seven years each colonist was paid ten pounds sterling, while the Charter investors in London received 100 pounds sterling. This is perhaps the earliest documentation of a worker-enterprise agreement in North America. One 1600's pound would be worth about $1,000 today.

What about the first Jamestown colonists? Archaeological evidence suggests that they walked out on their five-year agreement with the "Gentlemen of London." It is likely that they enmeshed themselves in the surrounding tribal societies of that time. Recent genetic evidence suggests this.

What of the Plymouth Colony? After seven years they went "walk-about" to create their own independent societies in Massachusetts, Connecticut, Rhode Island and the rest of New England. From these early records, it might be said that the American dream is built on the prospect of escape, "walk-about."

Like the first immigrants from Siberia, perhaps 30,000 years ago, early colonists walked away from undesirable situations, such as rapid climate change, toward more promising prospects. (Climatic fluctuations usually produced key changes in human evolution.)

In the 21st Century there's no place left to escape. We must take back our human heritage from those who would own us. **The reality of wealth held in common is the exception, while closed-minded cost-cutting is the global rule.**

How does corporate control by the few, of the many, occur? It is well documented that corporate-dominated nations first send diplomatic missions and missionaries to convert the natives living on land coveted by enterprises. Next come trade agreements that favor the native people. Just as gamblers allow a new player to win, at first, native people get hooked into "trade."

Enterprise representatives, advisers, tax collectors and trade councils soon follow. The next step in tribal destruction is to charge fees and taxes for transporting trade goods, protection, advisers, and finally a governing bureaucracy.

At first, the tribe and especially the tribal leaders benefit from the new trade. Later, the "costs" of trade are increasingly put on the backs of the tribal people. Tribal leaders that continue to benefit will support enterprise impositions. These questionable tribal leaders compromise tribal welfare for personal gain.

Corporate aggression is repeated by the oil, diamond and gold enterprises in Africa. The slave trade, as well as telephone, railroad and fruit enterprises in America are well documented. They followed the examples of the Dutch East Indies Company, East India Company and the Hudson Bay Company, of the 1600's ... engulf and devour.

People diminished by unequal exchange often resist. The corporations will then "hire" the able-bodied to work in mines, plantations and factories.

The World Revolution, I suggest, began in America in 1776, in France in 1789, continued in Germany in 1848, in the U.S. War Between the States in 1861, the Paris Commune of 1871, in the Russian Revolution of 1917, the Chinese Maoist Revolution of 1949, the Cuban Revolution of 1959, and continues globally now in the 21st Century, as Crisis Economics. **At the heart of all conflict is the human will to survive by preserving the family in a free and equal environment.**

4) ***Heart of Darkness:*** **Family is the nursery of humanity.** As the household creates people, it also creates the conflict between house-workers and wage-workers. Most global problems are rooted in the arrogance of the super-rich attempting to buy unlimited power.

Getting into enterprise metaphysics is a waste of time and energy. The environmental and human destruction continues, and deepens, after more than 500 years of progressive market enterprise.

The super-rich are in the saddle, riding the human family into the dust. Wealth is hoarded, rather than distributed, as in a commonwealth of human families. A commonwealth of all production and profit would go a long way toward minimizing war, impoverishment, gluttonous wealth and pestilence.

I suggest that the family is a true commonwealth, to the extent that family members give what they can, and receive what they must.

Essay 5

LABOR PAINS

*And while her step-sisters were surrounded with every comfort
and luxury and lived a life of ease, the younger girl swept and dusted
their rooms, washed the dishes, scrubbed the floor and steps
and worked from morning till night.*
(*Cinderella*, by Charles Perrault, 1697)

At the level of survival, people need food, clothing, shelter, entertainment, sanitation, social contact, love and sexual satisfaction. The expenditure of energy needed to meet these needs can be summed up as housework.

Every type of work involving the care of people is the domain of housework. Every task, from birth to death, to the extent that work is done to care for people, is part of the housework process. If we care for ourselves, then we are doing housework.

**HOUSEWORK IS REAL WORK. IT IS THE MOST VITAL
WORK OF ALL, SINCE BY DOING HOUSEWORK
WE PRODUCE OUR CHILDREN AND OURSELVES.**

Housework is vital because it produces our own lives. Housework is productive because it produces people. Producing people is the most important work of all. All other work, such as wage-work, merely supports the family indirectly.

Housework is an evolutionary advance, genetically determined, to the extent that people consciously work to care for kin, as well as themselves. All living things perform these same essential functions instinctively, genetically.

1) ***Worst of Housework:*** Ann Oakley, in her book, *The Sociology of Housework*, explores the dehumanizing character of housework in a series

of interviews with Englishwomen.[10] While the study was not representative of a large population, the results mirrored interviews carried out in Western countries.

Monotony, repetition and boredom were the worst of housework, while raising children was the best. Most house-workers, parents and family, consider children a reward, a blessing, a joy.

It's suggested that households are centers of scarcity. Time is scarce. Too few people to do too much work create a scarcity of energy. Most important is the scarcity of rewards. Rewards, like corporate profits, are plentiful. It's the unequal distribution of these that is the problem.

Contrasting household "scarcity" is the embarrassment of riches flowing into corporations. The only part of corporate wealth that house-workers see is the overflowing shelves of commodities, services, and stuff in the malls.

The reality is that wage-work creates all the stuff on those overflowing retail shelves. The irony is that housework and wage-work create all the wealth; yet most of us who create the wealth suffer from scarcity.

The conflict between household and corporation can be reduced to a war between crushing scarcity and obscene wealth. Household scarcity is made intolerable by millions of lost jobs, lost income, and a criminal mortgage conspiracy.

2) ***Cinderella's Household:*** The connection and the split between housework and wage-work begin with small industry manufacture in 1600's market society. Cinderella is a symbol of this split and connection. While her father was a merchant outside the home, and Cinderella worked in the home, they shared important functions. Both took responsibility for maintaining the family.

There is a remarkable similarity between the *Cinderella* and *Beauty and the Beast* stories. Both stories suggest alliances between merchant fathers and local princes. Both Cinderella and Beauty are coerced into housework by sisters who are social upstarts. Since both women end up marrying princes, the impetus to form families is as important a message as the merchant-prince alliance.

Both Cinderella and Beauty cared for people. They maintained the family by caring for household needs. To the extent they attended to household needs, they maintained and "produced" the family members. Their work was as specialized as their merchant fathers.

I suggest the objective of these stories of the time was to foster popular support for the rapid growth of the mercantile economy, at the expense of family self-sacrifice, and its eventual reward.

Housework depends on the organizing and planning skills needed to perform an unbroken chain of routine and disconnected tasks. Most important, Cinderella and Beauty had the love and wisdom to motivate their struggle to preserve deteriorating families. And that is the true magic of those stories.

Both housework and wage-work start and end in the household. The wage-worker and boss typically start the day at home, nurturing and nurtured by housework. Household nurturing may begin with sex, toiletry, feeding, childcare, clothing, sanitation and transportation.

The wage-worker and boss then spend the better part of the day working to support the family-household. The end of the day is framed the way it began, with the addition of rest and recreation.

3) ***Social Aspect of Housework:*** Because wage-work produces commodities under factory conditions, different work standards are involved compared to housework. Gathering workers together, to labor cooperatively in the same workplace, results in a strong social environment.

Equally important is the need to socialize. Economic household support is as important as keeping up social contacts. The social isolation of housework may be as dehumanizing as the social cohesion of the work place is humanizing. Our goal should be to humanize both housework and wage-work.

The word "re-creation" has a special significance. Within the framework of household and family, re-creation is the figurative and literal "re-creation" of the family. Recreational sex, play, affection, attention, and love between family members bind them together reproducing and recreating household ties.

There are important exceptions to household isolation. There may be socializing with neighbors such as the "coffee klatch." Shopping trips with neighbors and kids provide powerful socializing. Chats with store clerks may be the social high points of the day, especially for the elderly.

4) ***Subversion of Housework:*** The stature of housework is changing. Housework is gaining respect as the economic crisis worsens. Spouses who lose jobs or have their work hours cut discover that substantial savings are realized when they do their own housework.

Often a well-paid spouse loses a job, while the spouse doing housework must work at a low-paying job. When the wage-worker becomes the house-worker, the value of housework becomes obvious. With our income reduced, I'm content to clean our 1,700 square-foot condo, knowing that $80-$100 is saved by not hiring outside cleaners.

Some have said that the war against the family is a war against women. But men are women's children. All the men I know have mothers. It's more a matter of short-sighted greed than actual hostility to women and families. Greed hurts women, mothers, children, elderly and the infirm … greed harms everyone.

* * *

It's no accident that "Hestia of the Hearth" is the first Goddess in Greek and Roman traditions. Hestia, goddess of hearth and household, did not fool around. She did not traipse between heaven and earth to cause all sorts of mischief, as did other deities.

Any household kitchen or fireplace is Hestia's shrine. She has no temples or sacred places, as do other deities. Hestia stays put in the household. She is recognized as the last of the old Greek (Pelasgian) deities, and the first of the classical Greek (Hellenic) Olympians.

Like Hestia of the hearth, family caregivers are not covered in glory, but they have a permanent, secure place in the household. Cinderella is an updated incarnation of the Hearth Goddess. Cinderella, like Hestia, does not rebel, but does the housework and bides her time.

Being born into a family is far from a one-time act of birth. Rather, people born of women are reborn daily. People recreate themselves every day and every year of their lives. The process of creation and re-creation begins in a person's family and household of birth.

People later find mates, and continue the process of re-creation in new families of their own creation. As kids are born, educated, work and grow, the household creation process endures, because mothers endure.

5) *21st Century Crisis:* The purpose of the nuclear family, I suggest, was primarily to create a sustainable surge of consumption and production. For over 60 years that surge succeeded in creating a prosperous middle class that continued to expand its ranks to include 85% of American families, at least until 2008.

In the 21st Century, the family household continues its "devolution," triggered by inhumane activities, such as home mortgage speculation, derivative trading fraud, global terrorism and global economic crisis. The victims of corporate inhumanity are families, households, nations, all people, as well as the global environment. We are told there are corporations too big to fail. Are there frauds too big to correct?

In 2011 a surge in single mother-child and single spouse families are the fastest growing family formation. The surge in condo building in the last twenty years reflects the increase in smaller families. The remnants of the 21st Century family are further crushed, minced, diced and mined to extract additional profits, by means of narrow-sighted "cost-cutting."

In spite of the degradation, the family continues to create people and re-create households. The amazing resiliency of family households continues to provide enough energy to re-create society. With all the transformations, and re-creations, the family household survives.

Family households survive monotony, fragmentation, boredom, loneliness, isolation, underdevelopment and devaluation. Household caregivers are lovers, teachers, mothers, fathers, social workers, scientists, psychologists, pharmacists, technicians, doctors, nurses, sanitation workers, cooks, gardeners, purchasing agents, accountants, bookkeepers, judges, jury, clergy, chauffeurs, coaches, stewards, domestic workers and public servants.

Family tasks are re-created outside the family, as a multitude of trades and professions. **Every activity outside the family begins in the family. Global corporations depend on family skill and energy.** Predatory corporations continue to parasitize families. If corporations had to create all family tasks, let alone pay for the labor, the corporate system would be far different from what it is now.

Liberating the global family depends on curbing the disastrous activities of antisocial enterprise. Specifically, we need to correct the genocidal damage to the family and the Earth caused by: Global wars, police actions and terrorism, as well as threats to family and individual security. The damage to the global environment must be reversed. Most important, we must end the cycles of "Crisis Economics," that is the main cause of human misery.

Narrow-minded enterprise wages war against all families. Hopefully, we can stop the war, heal the family and heal the Earth?

FAMILY RE-CREATION

Cinderella's rest and re-creation was sitting in the chimney corner after her workday. It's important to understand the value of "re-creation" as a means of renewing household energy, re-creating the family, and re-creating ourselves. Re-creation means to create again. We continually re-create ourselves, and as natural beings we recreate nature, at least our small part of nature.

As we re-create ourselves at home, the home is vulnerable to attack. The family household is always challenged. Now the threat is from fraudulent bank mortgages. It was noted on National Public Radio, July 15, 2010 in their "401K State of the Economy Report" that the mortgage derivatives market totaled 16 trillion dollars and that one million mortgage foreclosures were expected in 2010.

The speculators destroy, while families create. By threatening our homes, the financial perpetrators threaten the household, family and the production of people. Here's a modest proposal to offset this threat:

Initiate an "Economic Crisis Surcharge" of 5% on mortgage derivative market sales for a national "Family Income Support Program." That amounts to $800 billion. In fact, the entire financial and investment industry might be included in this program.

1) ***Social Production:*** This Family Story illustrates aspects of re-creation and social production:

The women in his life say Doc is a party animal. The intent is partly a complement and partly a critique. Doc was usually anxious and introverted, but at parties he achieved a temporary release from anxiety. He often said it was women's smiles that energized and inspired him.

At parties Doc was happy, smiling, talkative and even charming. For the most part he was this way with women. Doc and his wife Kel both loved parties, and even more they loved to flirt. And flirting occasionally led to brief love affairs for both of them.

They played the "1970's Game ... share your love." It was their favorite sport and was a constant source of amusement for them. Included was a sometimes gentle and sometimes sarcastic repartee with each other. Often the comments started fits of laughter and ended in passionate love-making. Until her cancer death after 41 years of marriage, they remained lovingly loyal to each other.

* * *

After the death of his first wife, Doc and his new wife sold the old ranch and bought a new condo. Doc's anxiety and self-isolation worsened, but the condo people became friends.

They too were party animals. They often talked about their prime years in the 1970's. After all, it was the 70's they said. The 70's attitude is "anything goes ... and usually does."

There were many parties and Doc enjoyed them all. He sometimes got involved in party planning. The party people agreed that they were growing into a large extended family. The condo folks were over 50 with kids gone and time on their hands.

Partying was not just recreation, but was the re-creation of a new condo extended family. Some parties were in the condo clubhouse and some were in the separate condo buildings. Doc and the party crew moved chairs, tables and furniture, decorated and cleaned.

He spoke with the party crew as they made measurements for the next party. Doc explained his theory. "As we party we create a new condo family." It's as if the clubhouse becomes the tribal center for each of the five "clan" buildings. In some ways, it's similar to the Iroquois long house. The party crew thought that was an interesting insight ... about how the condo is evolving.

A few years later, due to budget cutbacks, Doc lost his well-paid teaching job. There were only low paid part-time jobs to fall back on. Doc and his wife had five part-time jobs between them. Unable to pay the condo fees, they were no longer welcome at the clubhouse.

Recreation is re-creating people. Most people think of recreation as TV, movies, cable, games, eating out, dancing, sports, socializing and other forms of entertainment. Recreation is of course all of these. In addition, recreation contributes to the process of physically, mentally and socially re-creating people and family households.

2) ***Recreation and Re-creation:*** Re-creation is a physical process. All activity, change and transformation are part of the re-creation process. Maintaining the household, raising children, housework, wage-work, genetics, socializing and environmental change ... all are part of the re-creation process. Housework energy is also a matter of curved motion, recharging our energy to get work done.

Energy recycling re-creates the cosmos. Earth spins on a constantly changing magnetic axis. Planets rotate around suns. Solar systems rotate around galaxies. Galaxies rotate around the Cosmos. Spinning, orbiting, rotation, cycling and recycling are all curved motion, transforming and re-creating all energy ... in our cells, in us and in our families. Some consider curvature a fifth dimension, along with length, width, height and time.

Re-creation is: Fun and games, as well as re-creating ourselves, family and household; household support, maintenance and renewal of household energy; nutrition, exercise, health and socializing; recreational sex, having children and domestic care-giving. Re-creation is socializing in the workplace, in the household and in the world. Re-creation is all activities that contribute to the family good and welfare.

The ancient Vedas of India say that the **Cosmos is the Deity**. The latest cosmic explorations suggest that the **Cosmos is energy** and is constantly recycling, self-recreating ... with no foreseeable beginning or end. The **human family is part of the cosmic family.**

It is self-evident that housework is productive, at least to mothers and parents. If you grew-up in a household, then you are the product of house-work, as most all of us are. **Hiding in plain sight is the undeniable fact that families and housework produce people.**

This might be called an "existential truth," referring to the fact that we exist as individuals, but we also exist in family households, and importantly, we exist as "products" of housework. The reality of survival is that conscious awareness predisposes people to consider their individual existence as primary. That conscious awareness makes us survivors.

* * *

The 21st Century economic crisis forces more people to share the burden of wage-work and housework. **To the extent that we feed, clothe, house and clean, we produce the family**. The family is often one person living alone. (Toward the other extreme, family can consist of 100's or 1000's of members, as in tribal, Hutterite, Mennonite, Amish and Mormon societies.)

In spite of her condition, or because of it, Cinderella was socially pro-ductive. She maintained her step-family by feeding, cleaning and a mul-titude of household activities. Cinderella dressed their hair, made their clothes and cared for the family by supporting the complex social life they demanded. **Beneath the charming children's story of Cinderella is a depth of housework**.

The care and nurturing in a family is far more complex than any type of wage-work. If wage-work is considered productive then housework is super-productive. The reality is that wage-work cannot exist without housework. Wage-work is only possible when housework precedes it. **Wage-work cannot be productive unless housework is sufficiently productive to first produce the wage-worker.**

4) *Family-Corporate Production:* Why is housework super-produc-tion? The household is the flesh-and-blood factory producing flesh-and-blood people. **People are the products of the household "factory."** At

times the corporation functions as an economic slaughterhouse, stripping people of family, energy, labor, productive effort and human dignity.

More often the corporation provides a socializing function that benefits both wage-workers and families. As previously stated, **corporations and most enterprises provide a vital social framework that benefits most people.** Corporate managers often refer to co-workers as a "family." However, as with most family groups, there are excesses that need correction.

Certainly corporations can automate production, and to a large extent they do. Robotic workers replace millions of working people. **Auto corporations are brilliant robotic factories, but they have yet to program robots to buy autos. Families buy cars, not robots.**

The secret of corporation vulnerability is that social production never gets out the warehouse door. Family production is purely social, woven into the energy fabric of Earth, stars and Cosmos.

On the other hand, corporate production is driven by the urge to profit by selling goods and services to families. Through mechanization and increased production, corporations create their own vulnerability by cutting wages and employment. The result is reduced family income and reduced purchases of corporation products and services.

Cinderella is the poster child of household drudgery, but she is productive on many levels:

1. Producing a **merchant** by caring for her father's household needs;
2. Producing a **house-worker** by caring for herself; and
3. She produces a **social class** by caring for her stepmother and step-sisters. Cinderella functions as a **parent** caring for her father, herself and stepfamily.

Most enterprises sidestep the issue of including family housework in the national economy by classifying housework as a biological process, rather than an economic process. We know that **families produce the people who produce the corporations**.

Perhaps corporations are actually biological processes, rather than economic entities? It makes more sense to include all forms of production, all forms of work, housework and wage-work, as part of the economy.

5) ***Commonwealth Society:*** If child-bearing housework is a biological process, excluded from the economy, how should we classify the biological production of grain, vegetables, fruit and livestock? Why not subtract National Environmental Costs from the Gross Domestic Product? Accounting for all environmental costs and subtracting total costs from Gross Domestic Product would provide a Net National Product.

What are the costs of Crisis Economics? They are corporate fraud, oil spills, and hurricane losses due to cost-cutting engineering, financial-bank mortgage fraud, derivative industry fraud, the cost of the unemployed millions, and insurance health-care fraud.

Detailing Gross Domestic Costs is a book in itself. While environment, health, education, transportation and social costs reduce gross product, the industries created to ameliorate these costs add to the Gross Domestic Product. Human survival necessitates the treatment of these environment-energy issues as part of a Global Energy Budget, rather than a list of corporate damage.

The 21st Century economic crisis knows no borders. From a corporate viewpoint, people living and reproducing in a subsistence environment, gleaning enough from their surroundings for survival is not economically productive because subsistence living does not contribute to the global economy.

When corporations cut down rainforests to produce cattle for burgers, then the socially unproductive subsistence farmers are transformed into wage-workers for the corporations and are counted as socially productive. The narrowness of such corporate thinking does not take into account the social and environmental costs.

There is still another meaning to "socially productive." Social production produces solutions and not problems. Ant colonies are both socially and biologically productive in the global environment. Unlike some corporations, ants can learn, plan and intelligently function for the good and welfare of the ant colony as a whole.

The fundamental failure of the corporate system is that it simultaneously produces "development" for a few and "underdevelopment" for many. Cinderella worked to produce development for her social climbing family and underdevelopment for herself. Maybe ants have the answer. Why can't corporations be more like ants? Is it possible that ants are more intelligent than people? Ants certainly seem more intelligent than many corporate leaders.

Much of the effort to "teach kids" involves making certain that children accept the rules of society. Cinderella must have been socialized in this way or she could not have accepted her degraded position in the family. Imagine the years of "teaching" at the hands of stepmother and stepsisters needed to produce Cinderella's life of self-degradation and servitude.

Social, economic and political events often enter into family planning. Over the last few decades families decided to have fewer children and marriages, at least in the "developed" nations. At the same time, divorce rates continue to rise. We Cinderellas have no prince waiting to rescue us. We can only rescue ourselves.

In the 21st Century global economic crisis, families respond with fewer marriages and births, and as a result, fewer purchases. Human reproduction is directly linked to commodity production, which is based on the availability of house-workers and wage-workers. In terms of the social environment, the viewpoint of many corporations tends to be self-serving and near-sighted. With some notable exceptions, many corporations are not known for their sense of social or environmental responsibility.

When the frenzy of greed ends in disaster, enterprises beg for bailouts. As with GM majority ownership by the U.S. government, the model of a "Commonwealth economy" may already have begun. Holding majority ownership of principal industrial and financial enterprises in escrow by the government, as commonwealth for the people, may be the only viable solution to crises economics.

6) ***Shopping as Recreation:*** "When the going gets tough, the tough go shopping." This cliché is often used to trivialize shopping, and make a joke out of it. But shopping is no joke. I suspect shopping is the modern equivalent of "hunting" for food and resources.

Energy renewal and transfer is what the hunter and shopper have in common. As the most vital part of house-work, shopping is much more than a hunt for family sustenance. Shopping is probably the most important activity contributing to family recreation and re-creation.

The shopper is shopping to resupply family needs. In the shopping process, shoppers are also socializing with people, exercising as they walk and talk, even if it's talking on a cell phone. A walk through the mall, window shopping, is a common type of recreation. And now it appears that shopping may improve our health and longevity.

Frequent shopping among the elderly may not always be about buying things, but about seeking companionship or taking exercise, which is easier than more formal exercise. The conventional view of health promotion focuses on physical activity, but engaging in social and economic activities in later life may also contribute to better health.[11]

FAMILY BILL OF RIGHTS

The prince was constantly at her side, paying her compliments
and speaking tender words to her. But it was twelve o'clock!
Cinderella jumped up and ran, swiftly as a deer.
(*Cinderella*, by Charles Perrault, 1697)

**On January 11, 1944 U.S. President Franklin Delano Roosevelt,
FDR, proposed a "Second Bill of Rights." In his State of the Union
address, FDR announced a social-economic plan as an addition
to the United States Constitution and the Bill of Rights.**

The plan would be implemented politically rather than judicially. FDR
suggested that previous guarantees "proved inadequate to assure U.S.
equality in the pursuit of happiness." The plan provides an "economic bill
of rights" to guarantee what might be considered family rights. These would
guarantee:

1. A living wage job
2. Freedom from unfair monopoly competition
3. Home
4. Medical care
5. Education
6. Recreation

This economic bill of rights is effectively a "Family Bill of Rights." It's
designed to back up political freedom with vital family economic security.
FDR contended that the freedom, peace and security of America and the
world depended on these guarantees.

In that message to Congress, FDR argued:

> It is our duty now to begin to lay the plans and determine the strategy for the winning of a lasting peace and the establishment of an American standard of living higher than ever before known. We cannot be content, no matter how high that general standard of living may be, if some fraction of our people—whether it is one-third or one-fifth or one-tenth—is ill-fed, ill-clothed, ill-housed, and insecure.

FDR contended that **personal freedom cannot exist without the guarantees of economic security. Needy people are not free people**. People that are hungry and lack family income look for any help they can get, be it Hitler, Stalin or some other tyrant. Most of Europe adopted a "family bill of rights" over the last 60 years, while America is locked into an economic limbo.

1) ***Family Rations:*** Family rationing refers to the fact that income, consumption, healthcare and education are all rationed, based on cost. With high unemployment and dwindling family income, resources such as housing, healthcare, jobs and transportation are effectively rationed. The following Family Story dramatizes the nature of family rationing:

> Doc turned 75 in June. In this year of worsening economic conditions the state had cut back all advanced computer courses in the public school system to save funds. Doc had taught advanced computer networking for 12 years.
> Although his instructor job was part-time, it paid enough to support a condo lifestyle. Fortunately the year before, after much cajoling from his wife, Doc got a part-time job in the appetizer department of a major supermarket. Doc was now the "Deli-Doc" and enjoyed the work even though it paid a fraction of what teaching did.
> After a year of deli work Doc, doing family economics research, noticed changes in the way his customers purchased deli products. Even though suppliers had constant "rolling sales," customers ordered ¾, ½,

¼ pound and even separate slices. In better times they would buy much more. "Rolling sales" are reduced prices on different deli items each week. Cold-cuts, especially sliced turkey and cheese, became a high-point in the food rationing process.

Now serving number 45 ... Hi! What can I get you ... Lebanon baloney? Fine, how much would you like ... half-pound? Yes ma'am, it's on sale this week for $3.99 ... and if there's any remaining, it will still be on sale Saturday.

Doc always showed the customer the first slice and sometimes samples to taste, especially if the thickness of the slice did not suit them. Joking with them, saying that his goal in life is to feed the hungry, was sure to bring a smile to the most hardened face.

How's that slice? You want it thinner ma'am? No problem ... the slice you want is what I'll give you. How's this next slice? Thinner still? Sure-enough ... do you want the meat shredded ... just before shredding? That I can do! Thin enough to read the newspaper through? Give her what she wants. It took me fifty years of marriage and two wives to teach me that.

Family housework and corporate excess are at opposite ends of a "value spectrum." At one end is the corporation, socializing people and their tools by bringing them all together, concentrating them in one workplace. At the other end of the "value spectrum" is housework, producing and caring for people.

Family housework maintains and nurtures our needs, creating-maintaining humanity. The objective of housework is people. Global corporations, companies, investors, speculators, financiers and bankers are all the products of families-households. The antisocial among them act as if they are "self-made." But we can safely assume that all corporate leaders had mothers.

One hundred years ago most people lived on family farms, consuming most of what they grew or created. A portion of the produce would be brought to market. For the most part, family farm production, and market proceeds, benefited the farm family.

This form of "natural production" is production for the family, clan or tribe. The more successful family farms grow into factory farms. Corporations bring together a pre-existing mass of hands, resources and tools. By centralizing workers and all resources, corporations "socialize" the workplace.

In this process people become wage-workers, and labor is extracted from workers in exchange for wages. The value of the "extracted" labor and production must exceed the wage paid or there can be no **surplus value**, and therefore no profit.

People who work for wages are provided with income reflecting only a small portion of their labor. In reality, the paid wages are rations for the wage-worker family. What becomes of the 95% of labor that's not paid as wage-worker income? This excess labor, or **surplus value**, is transformed into value that is now completely outside and separated from the wage-worker family.

This Family Story provides a perspective of the moonshine industry after WWII:

When the war ended the lucrative military contracts for food-stuffs also ended. For most growers and ranchers the end of the war meant that rationing was over. The dam of consumer demand burst. People saved a great deal of money from high-paying jobs during the war years.

From 1942 to 1945, nearly everything was rationed, so there was little to buy. Fresh fish was not rationed, but all canned fish was rationed. The "black market" supplied rationed items at exorbitant prices. The Office of Price Administration, OPA, functioned as the rationing police, fining and jailing violators. But that did not stop the demand for goods or the supply.

In a way, the black market was an escape valve for pent up demand and amassed savings. This was particularly true with liquor. Smuggling from Cuba and clandestine liquor brewing of: Shine, Moonshine, White Mule, White Dog, Juice and White Lightning were significant sources of income for the Mik-Sem tribe.

Dad and his partners referred to these activities as "importing cattle feed." Dad handled sales and distribution. Tommy headed up the tribal council and managed the actual Moonshine production.

Soon after the War, Sheriff Whalen died in a moonshine still explosion. This was a common occurrence, especially when the copper coils are clogged with mash and insects. Dad took over Whalen's job as Sheriff. Now Sheriff Joe, my dad, directed security, sales and transport.

The first thing dad insisted on was still safety and sanitation. Cooper coils were scoured clean with wire brushes before and after each batch. Steel 42-gallon molasses drums with removable copper inserts replaced the old copper stills. After each batch, the spent mash was sold as cattle feed and the thin copper inserts were melted down and poured into molds for new inserts.

Old barns, smoke houses, tobacco drying sheds and warehouses soon housed all the moonshine stills. The stills were nestled below ground level, but among the livestock, curing meat and curing tobacco leaf. Old gasoline pumps functioned at ground level to fill and empty the stills. As methane gas from livestock manure was fed from above ground level to fire the stills, minimal hands-on was needed with the stills.

Above the stills, lofts were built to support large amounts of hay. In this way odors from the stills were neutralized and absorbed. Substantial monthly payments to the local owners provided much of the on-site maintenance and security, so that the local moonshiners were able to make fast pickups and deliveries on set routes. They called it the "milk run."

At first, stills were run on charcoal instead of open fire. Soon after, the stills were fueled with methane gas piped directly from livestock manure fermenters near the stills. Automatic thermostats registered still heat and regulated the flow of methane. The raw liquor, collected by the moonshiners, was now triple distilled and finally filtered through charcoal. Spent charcoal was compressed and recycled as bar-B-Q bricks, for sale at dad's market.

Since water supply was a major issue, mineral-free water was trucked in from natural fresh-water springs on Mik-Sem tribal lands. The springs were linked to a huge underground aquifer that included Silver Springs and Crystal Springs. Tanker trucks served double-duty by collecting and delivering the finished Moonshine. Smaller dairy pump trucks delivered mash slurry for fermenting, cooking, and raw shine collection.

These changes vastly improved the quality, economics, safety and sanitation of moonshine production. The huge increase in production necessitated hundreds of workers instead of the dozens previously employed. This further improved tribal employment, farm economics and overall county income.

The quality of the moonshine was far better than commercial liquor and could easily sell for half the price. Bootleggers were selling it with the label, "Liquid Sun Shine." Moonshine enterprises were so successful in boosting the local economy that dad was elected for two terms as sheriff.

Dad's political power did not depend on moonshine. He was a tribal patriarch, tracing his origins back to the original family in Europe. In a time of virulent racial segregation, dad as a tribal chief stressed that Mik-Sem tribal success was based on "hybrid vigor."

My school teacher said that dad feeds the whole county. As a result, dad's tribal market had the lion's share of county business. Dad said, "The whole county is family and we take care of family, no matter what."

Drinking water supply is a perpetual problem in South Florida. While the soil contains few nutrients for agriculture, ground water is either heavily laced with sulfur and iron, resembling orange soda, or else the water was crystal clear with no mineral content, as in Silver Springs.

In the 1920's dad established contacts in Cuba to supply rum, molasses, sugarcane waste (bagasse), fermentation by-products and other nutrients to feed South Florida cattle. Waste from the canneries and breweries in South Florida were also used as livestock feed.

But there was never enough supplemental feed to significantly improve the quality of meat and milk. Local people and livestock lived on short rations.

When the war ended in 1945 people wanted fresh, high quality meat. They did not want the low quality canned meat that was produced in South Florida. After the war, people demanded "choice" and "prime" cuts. With the end of rationing, the market for "canner-packer" and "good" grade meat was finished.

The result was that most livestock producers switched to growing sugarcane or other crops. Those in the moonshine business kept a low profile by attempting to preserve a semblance of their livestock business.

2) ***Family Transition:*** Family and household structure constantly change. Up and down the evolutionary ladder, offspring are born in a vast variety of species and habitats. Family transition keeps pace with the evolution of life.

It makes sense that families change as offspring change. As humanity evolves over millions of years, so have human offspring and the human household. Even in the 21st Century the family has changed since the time of Cinderella's family.

The Cinderella story marks the change from the extended farm, clan and tribal family to the smaller family of merchant society. It's the story of nuclear family formation. The nuclear family refers to the basic mother, father and child/ren pattern.

With crisis economics, the family is further changing to little more than a mother and child ... the new nativity, created by crisis economics. While the extended family had some control of its own work, the nuclear family has little. **The smaller the family, the less internal control it possesses. As families transition, shrinking in size, smaller families become weaker families.**

As family size is reduced, the fragmented family loses people and independence. Family values are replaced by market values. Global corporations absorb family resources, while family deprivation results in family rationing. **Family control is now largely replaced by corporate control.** Corporate control consists of:

1. **Organizing** and socializing household labor for the benefit of the corporation;
2. **Management** of household production;
3. **Control** of household labor via wage-work;
4. **Authority** over household consumption by means of limiting wages.

As people were forced off farms and into factories, as crafts were extracted from the family into factories, as people are now more heavily taxed, disintegration of family and household are inevitable. The single-person family is now a pitiful fragment of the once extended family.

In fact, the family loses power and control as it loses people. More people in a family result in more skills to draw upon, greater security, and more sources of income.

Cinderella is a classic example of the decline and fall of the family. The artificial character of the nuclear family is that it is little more than an economic fabrication. As a matter of economic survival, Cinderella's father spliced a step-family onto the remnant of his own family. This created a monstrous parody of family transition, but also created an ageless story.

Every aspect of the Cinderella story seems to stress the conflicts, misery and ugliness resulting from the creation of the step-family, which is of course a gross exaggeration for purposes of the story. Cinderella, however, provides many insights into family formation, especially the formation of nuclear families.

3) *__Family Disintegration:__* Even in cities, large families have more power, especially where there is a strong sense of kinship. This Family Story dramatizes the point:

Throughout his life Doc had vivid memories of Grandma Burke, his ma's mother. There were eight grown children and their mates living together in three adjacent houses of three floors each. The family myth involved the death of Grandpa Patrick. He was a leather craftsman who made custom shoes. Everyone was told that he fell down a flight of stairs one night and cracked his head open on a cast iron stove.

Aunt Francis, the oldest sibling, lived to 102, but before she died she told Doc's father that Grandpa Patrick was an Irish revolutionary, called back to Ireland by his old brigade. Grandpa Patrick died in a British prison. The Brits returned the ashes and 36 pair of shoes Grandpa made for the family while a prisoner of war.

As a small child Doc remembered that the five aunts and three uncles had jobs that contributed to the extended family income. After Grandma Burke died, the married aunts and uncles set up separate households, but remained close and mutually supportive.

The onset of World War II, and the prosperity it brought, split the family into smaller households. The faster economic pace and plentiful jobs encouraged the formation of nuclear families consisting of parents and children.

Doc remembers the warm, almost suffocating sense of security, with the bustle of loving relatives constantly about. Any time someone talked about Grandpa Patrick, Grandma would hush them up saying, "Leave the "Trouble" in Ireland, we're all Americans now." Doc heard this often as a small child, and would shout it when he heard an argument. The aunts and uncles were amused by this childish admonition, but the argument did stop. For a moment they looked sad, and his ma shed some tears, but soon the cheerful banter would resume. His dad would whisper in Doc's ear, "Good boy."

* * *

Living in a society on short rations encourages social and economic competition. Families often fight in any way they can to generate income. Often, families are forced into the underground economy, as the only way to survive.

SHRINKING FAMILIES

The human family has evolved for eons, first as mother and child, then primal hordes, bands, clans, tribes, extended families, nuclear families and often back again to a single mother and child. If a father is present, it is usually for brief periods between escapes. But it must also be said that mothers often use their children as an escape.

The economic crisis of the 21st Century fosters the greatest unemployment since the great depression of the 1930's. Massive job loss reduces family income and forces household workers into minimum wage-work. With under-employment and unemployment at record levels, people are forced to move back with family.

I suggest that family destruction results in crisis economics; and crisis economics destroy families. The destructive cycle begins with rapacious power brokers.

The trend toward single parent households tends to create impoverished households. Single person households include single parent, usually a mother and child, separated couples, elderly and young people. Single person households are often low-income households. Do corporations benefit from fragmented households? With lower income, reduced buying depresses the entire economy.

* * *

Cinderella is a victim of 'loving' extortion. Her father, stepmother and stepsisters trained Cinderella for a servile life of housework drudgery. In a real sense, all members of the Cinderella family are separated, estranged from household labor, Cinderella most of all. The more families are split, the more family members suffer.

Changing economic conditions, especially in market society, catalyze internal family splits and suffering long before the family physically fragments. Market societies, by reducing and rationing income, create smaller families.

In the Cinderella story, the nuclear family is seen as an archetype for the new merchant family. The merchant-father is the family 'owner.' Stepmother and stepsisters are 'foremen' and Cinderella is the 'domestic worker.'

For the next few hundred years, the family 'foreman' is the wife-mother-housekeeper, managing children and servants for the husband-father-owner, who is usually 'away,' like an absentee landlord. The husband-father is only a peripheral part of the Cinderella story. In fact, the husband-father from antiquity to the present seems to remain at the periphery of the mother-child family.

Cinderella is the main player performing her role against a backdrop of merchant society. The dramatic plot plays out with Cinderella and family demonstrating how the nuclear family malfunctions more than it functions.

There is something in nature and in our genetic system prodding humanity to go "walk-about;" to see what's over the next hill. For mothers, children are the natural focus of attention, resulting in a deficit of attention for wage-worker fathers, who may then seek attention elsewhere.

Extended tribal family members control what they produce even though productivity does not measure up to corporate standards. Enterprise views the productivity of extended family, tribe, guild, union, cooperative and commune as less productive than corporate wage-work.

There is no question that corporate wage-work is more productive than other production systems. There is no doubt about the profits that corporations produce. **Economic crises are not the result of profits, but of the unequal distribution of profit.**

The antisocial corporation hoards profit. The essence of economic crises is the unequal distribution of profit. Workers and families produce the most, but get the least. Corporation owners produce the least and hoard the most.

Hoarding, greed and a socially destructive view of the world, I suggest, characterizes the antisocial entrepreneur.

The idea of 'profit' had little meaning in the old extended family. Concepts of 'gain' were a natural part of family and household relations. There is a significant difference between 'gain' and 'profit.' A raise in wages 'gains' more goods and services for the family. 'Gain' can strengthen families and households.

Tribal people exchange gifts to strengthen social ties. Gift exchange assures strong social bonds and satisfies material needs. 'Gain' was part of the tribal household to the extent that it contributed to social exchange and allowed tribal people a 'gain' in status and prestige. On the other hand profit is what remains after all value is extracted from wage work and the costs are subtracted.

"Surplus labor" and "surplus value" result after the costs of wage-work are subtracted. A family might 'gain' from housework labor, but families do not 'profit' since housework does not produce "surplus labor." Family housework only 'gains' when the necessary amount of housework is performed and no more. In tribal society, producing and constantly cultivating social bonds is the primary value.

1) ***Cinderella's Society:*** To see Cinderella as just a household drudge is a small part of the picture. The total Cinderella perspective depends on understanding the forces outside the household, namely the market economy in relation to the household.

Cinderella's servile role results from outside social forces that affect her step-family. The step-family aspires to social position in merchant society. That reality shapes Cinderella's role in the household.

In the merchant society of the 1600's, Cinderella and step-family realize that their security and social ties depend on making the 'right connections.' The prince's ball provides an important social opportunity. The prince's ball is a key-stone in the edifice of the alliance between the emerging merchant class and the local prince. Such alliances throughout Europe helped end feudalism.

* * *

Recall that the Spanish Armada, and the expanding global power of Spain, suffered a permanent setback in 1588. As a result, English aspirations were able to expand economically throughout the world as Spanish power declined, especially in North Europe and North America.

The Mayflower landing in 1620 initiated English economic expansion in North America. With the decline of Spain, the English alliance with Dutch and other North European trade powers permitted explorations and acquisitions in rapid succession.

The explorations of Walter Raleigh and Henry Hudson initiated enterprises such as the Hudson Bay Company and East India Company, forerunners of global enterprise. The English-Elizabeth alliance with Russian-Ivan opened the White Sea trade routes into Russia, at the expense of the Hanseatic League and the feudal Boyars.

Social ties can be stepping-stones to wealth. Success for the Cinderella sisters depended on marrying into wealthy families. The prince's invitation may signal the new alliance between merchants and royals. The old static society of feudal landed lords and church posed a serious threat to the new dynamic merchant class, as well as to the power of princes.

Nicolò Machiavelli's master work, The Prince, published early in the 1500's, provides a comprehensive survival manual for royals. Most local princes (royals) were threatened from all sides by other royals, feudal lords, church and the growing wealth of merchant traders.[13]

The quest for power in the 1500-1600's was at its core a struggle between moribund feudal estates and successful, more enlightened merchant princes. The success of Portuguese Prince Henry the Navigator (1394-1460) is a prime example. Henry remained rich and powerful his entire life, suggesting that Henry may have inspired Machiavelli's *The Prince*.

Feudal lords attempted to keep a stranglehold on landed wealth and serf labor. Merchants viewed the landed gentry as an impediment to their progress and prosperity. Vulnerable royals attached themselves to the rapidly rising merchant class, permitting the survival of royalty in much of North Europe.

The human quest for reproductive success is seldom a matter of the 'best' choice, but of the 'better' choice ... the more progressive option. In the 1600's, the merchants were more progressive than the feudal landlords.

Queen Elizabeth I, daughter of Henry VIII, and a chip off the old block, sprinted ahead of the pack. She seems more aggressive than her dad. Certainly she was the tiger of global exploration, trade, and power. Elizabeth I was arguably the inspiration and force initiating the expansion of English global trading enterprise for the next 400 years.

'Gain' is far more than the acquisition of wealth. More important are the social ties that develop within and between families and governing royals. Cinderella's princely conquest is a metaphor for the rising class of merchant entrepreneurs and their alliance with royals. Similarly, Elizabeth provided royal charters to promising merchant allies.

2) ***Complex Transformations:*** Families, like societies, governments, and economies, change through a series of complex transformations. The story of Cinderella may be viewed as a significant signpost along the path of family transformation. I suggest that families, environments, power structures and economies form a mutually interactive pattern of complex transformation.

The first 500 years of the 'modern' era saw the dissolution of Roman dominance of Europe, Middle East, Asia Minor and North Africa. The Roman Empire withered away first at the frontiers. Pensioned Legionnaires and wealthy Romans acquired small kingdoms throughout Europe. The residue of Roman power was transformed into the feudal estates of Europe.

The Roman Legion border guards established families and local tribal loyalties. After stabilizing their border kingdoms, they did an about face, backtracking toward Rome to grab what was left of Roman power. Like Rome, they had a global perspective and worked closely with local Celts, Germans, and other power groups, to engulf and devour the remains of Roman Empire.

* * *

World Wars I and II were true global trade wars, ending in 1945 with shared global control by both Soviet and American spheres of influence. Trade war continued in the form of a 'Cold War' between the Soviet alliance and the American alliance. And the winner appears to be ... Communist China, the new global economic power broker.

The United States is now the clear victor in the war for corporate "freedom." In the 21ˢᵗ Century, global corporations are in financial debt to Communist China. Relatively cheap labor and manufacture continue to attract global corporations to the Peoples Republic of China.

As the principal global debt holder, China is now pivotal in the world economy. But no nation is immune from global crisis. China is now experiencing the "fall-out" from global reduction in family income and shrinking consumption-demand. Trade wars continue, fought with stealth, terrorism and electronic network attacks. **This is less a history lesson, and more an account of family transformation through trade.**

3) ***How Do Families Benefit?*** In the tribal family, a household or tribe realized gain by gift exchange. **The purpose of gift exchange is to build social ties.** This is the case throughout the centuries. With a gift of breeding livestock, one tribe might gain permanent access to a salt deposit belonging to a neighbor tribe.

To acknowledge new social ties, the salt tribe would 'gift' the livestock tribe with half of the offspring. This gift arrangement provided a permanent social link between the two tribes. Inter-tribe marriages provided similar ties. The point is that while both tribes benefit there is no gain in the sense of trophy, wealth or profit. There is no "my-gain-is-your-loss," as is typical in corporate economies.

What is established with gifts and barter, that equally benefit giver and receiver, is a "just exchange." Tribal society based on "**just exchange,**" benefits all persons. A generalized statement of "just exchange" might be: **From each according to ability; to each according to need.**

Ideally, tribes and families hold all wealth in common. From the concept of "**just exchange**" arises the idea of "**commonwealth.**" This means that people do what they can, and share what's available. From the viewpoint of nations, "just exchange" has a 21st Century equivalent in the idea of a "commonwealth."

The "commonwealth" ideal is an extension of tribal and family values. In a traditional family, members contribute as they are able. Family members are cared for, depending on their needs and the availability of resources. **In a "commonwealth" all wealth is held in common, willingly contributed and justly distributed. The ideal family is a commonwealth.**

Aristotle described the Greek "Oikonomia" of 2,500 years ago. Our current word 'economy' is derived from that ancient word. In those times, the tribal-family-household was the entire economy. All societal functions were performed in the "Oikonomia." It included tribe, family, household, large numbers of kin, retainers, servants and slaves.

The "Oikonomia" extracted a livelihood on large tracts of land, inherited from tribal-family ties, and functioned as self-sufficient households, and as small trading city-states. "Oikonomia" were early commonwealth formations.[14]

4) ***Origins of Corporate Society:*** Thousands of years ago the idea of 'gain' split into two forms. The older practice of 'just exchange' as a social and tribal sacrament, changed into a second form of 'gain.' In the second form of gain, gifts were reckoned as tribute, trophy, booty and slaves from conquered people. In this version of gain, wealth was an "I win, you lose" game.

Today, a residue of tribal gift exchange survives in the form of: The United Nations, European Common Market, Foreign Aid, the Berlin Airlift, Most Favored Nations Trade Agreements, NATO, and various other security-aid pacts between nations.

The global enterprise may, from time to time, collapse under the weight of its own greed and mendacity. Global corporations now control governments, family income, and that's the problem. Corporations pressure governments to further bleed family income to save the economy from its own failure. This is the current 'complex transformation' in the 21st Century economic crisis.

5) _Down-sizing the Family:_   When corporations need workers, the family household is the first and last stop in the search. During World War II (1941-1945) women homemakers were recruited and trained by military industries. The War created opportunities that would not occur without it. While full employment was achieved, the family fragmented.

With over 16 million Americans in military service, war production was in desperate need of workers, any workers. The War served to get America out of the Great Depression of the 1930's. Before the War $20 a week was a living wage. During the War, unionized war industry workers earned $50-100, and more a week.

Wars helped to liberate women, people of color, and hundreds of millions from the worst abuses of totalitarianism. But in the process, the global family was the victim of genocide. There were over 100-million combatants and more than 70-million war-related deaths between 1939 and 1945.

Since the 1940's, global corporations created a permanent war economy. Corporations can only survive by expanding their power and profits through global trade. Global wars are the only tried-and-true way to break-out of economic crises. Now Iran looms large as a dangerous solution to the global economic crisis.

Sucking income out of families characterizes short-sighted entrepreneurs. The family creates workers and soldiers for the global corporations. Pathological corporations function like parasites. Successful parasites live off the energy of their hosts. The host grows weaker, but a **successful parasite must keep the host alive or die along with its host. Similarly, many financial interests live off middle income families.**

In this regard, Cinderella represents the stress and fragmentation of the family. When stepmother and stepsisters needed many services "to go out in society" they did not look outside the family for these services. They did not need to look far to find help. There was Cinderella, the most vulnerable member of the family, with little real choice in the matter.

The 21st Century family has little choice. Families need income. In the new world economy of corporate instigated rationing, income like healthcare are rationed. **Pricing of food, clothing and housing are the primary method of rationing in the corporate world.**

6) *__Families and Super-Profits__:* To illustrate the role of family housework, in creating corporate super-profits, a real example is examined:

A chemical company sales rep has annual sales averaging $1,000,000. The full cost of maintaining the sales rep is $50,000 per year including sales expenses, salary, benefits and   overhead. Total "cost of sales," as a percent of gross profit is $50,000/$1,000,000 or 5%. In terms of hours worked, the sales rep is paid for one hour out of every 20 worked. The sales rep is paid 5% of her sales.

The chemical company would break even if the sales rep works only two hours a week instead of 40. In reality, the sales rep works two hours for her, and 38 hours for the company. The two hours amount to cost of maintenance, and the 38 hours are "surplus labor."

The sales rep worked at least ten hours daily, Monday through Thursday, including travel between sales calls … reserving Friday to set-up sales calls for the following week and paper work.

The point is to show how surplus labor from wage-work relates to the extraction of corporate profit from housework. The amount of work expended to support, maintain and re-create the sales rep is housework.

Over the last century, research shows that housework time ranges from 40 hours a week for single person households to over 84 hours for large households. Housework hours include all the hours needed for support, maintenance and recreation.

For a single person household, the time devoted to housework includes recreation, travel, socializing, dating, shopping, grooming, eating, and cleaning … probably in that order. Sales rep work-days average out to 8 hours of wage-work, 8 hours of housework and 8 hours of sleep.

Some economists say sleep time is a necessary part of wage-worker maintenance, and should be included in the housework total. Certainly, sleep provides necessary revitalization, and that's part of housework.

Included in housework is the need to maintain a "class acceptable" life style. The way we groom, dress, shop, as well as the car, and the people we associate with, form of recreation and type of restaurants … all serve to maintain our social status, or "class acceptable" life style.

Such a life style is a necessary part of being considered a "team player" in the corporate world. Cinderella's housework provides the labor necessary to maintain the step-family in a "class acceptable" life style for climbing the social status ladder.

If the sales rep costs the company $50,000 on sales of $1,000,000, then the cost of sales is 5%. Two hours per week of sales work covers the cost of sales (2/40=5%). The peculiar demands of corporate society create the extra housework needed for family survival:

Two hours of **paid** wage-work are needed to maintain the sales rep, plus 38 hours of **unpaid surplus** wage-work contribute to company gross profit. Add to these 40 hours of **unpaid socially necessary housework,** for a total of 80 hours of housework/wage-work each week.

In this regard, corporate profit depends on unpaid housework and unpaid wage-work. Two hours of paid necessary work support 78 hours of unpaid work. In the case of the chemical sales rep, two hours of paid work supports 78 hours of unpaid work. So 2.5% (2/80) is paid work and 97.5% is unpaid work.

Corporations cannot survive without workers and workers cannot survive without housework. More profitable drug companies need more housework than say, low profit garment producers. A well cared-for wage-worker, on the job and in the home, is a more productive worker. The sales rep is highly productive because she receives a relatively high wage.

Corporations constantly reduce the cost of production by automating manufacture and reducing wage-work. Early in the 20th Century a union contract was negotiated between Henry Ford and Walter Reuther, President of the United Auto Workers, UAW. Ford asked Reuther what his union would do when all the workers are replaced with robots. Reuther replied by asking Ford how he planned to get his robots to buy cars.

In their frenzy to reduce costs, corporations neglect the consumption side of the equation. Now in the 21st Century, the global enterprise is on a suicidal path. By down-sizing, out-sourcing, furloughing, and part-timing wage-workers, antisocial corporations have not only cut-back millions of workers, but also cut-back millions of worker purchases. This is especially true in the auto industry. The immediate result of cutting-wages is to reduce income and family purchases … especially of new cars.

Economically blind corporations cry out for workers' tax dollars to bail them out. Government is forced to use tax money to prevent mega-corporation bankruptcy, and mega-unemployment. We are told by corporation sob-sisters, "To save the economy, tax payers must save the corporation."

While family income and consumption shrink, imprudent corporations beg for more handouts, while cutting more jobs. In effect, short-sighted corporations hold the American tax-payer hostage. Lobbying legislators for laws that further victimize families and governments, amounts to extortion.

Profit is not the problem.
It is the uneven distribution of profit that is at fault.

Essay 9

What's a Spouse Worth?

The facts of life are hidden in plain sight.
Family-households are flesh and blood factories.
House-work produces the most import product of all, PEOPLE.

There are six significant issues developed in this and later chapters:

1. Housework performed to "produce" the family earns an **inadequate income**;
2. **Unpaid housework jobs** are at times the same jobs that earn wages outside the household;
3. To survive, many low-income families are coerced into the **underground illicit economy**;
4. Globally, "low-family-income" leads to social, **political and economic instability**;
5. **Crisis economics** is both the cause and effect of "low-family-income;" and
6. **Global wealth concentration** ignites economic crises and "low-family-income."

In spite of the platitudes about housework and family values, those doing house-work are the most under-valued and under-paid people in society. If this situation is to change, and I think it must, any significant change will be the result of the pioneering efforts of family law professionals, such as Michael H. Minton and Jean Libman Bloch, leading the way in the struggle for equitable family support.

The basic problem is providing adequate income support for family care-givers. Toward this end, people facilitating family mediation and divorce have established the legal basis for recognizing **marriage as an**

"economic partnership." Most states and many nations now follow some form of "uniform marriage and divorce act" guidelines to support home-makers.

Mothers are the chief engineers of reproductive success. If housework is the production of humanity, then the foundation of humanity is motherhood. Mothers are the great cosmic energy transformers.

In the process of "birthing" humanity, mothers use their genetic code to create more of us. That's what housework is all about … producing people. But you knew that!

It is by our own hands and minds that amorphous energy crystallizes into housework, wage-work, resources, products and services ... all produced by, and consumed as human energy. Housework is people producing people, insuring the continuance of humanity.

Cinderella's Housework treats the "energy exchange" of housework and wage-work as part of a network of global housekeeping. When "energy" is considered, it's in terms of the "work" people do.

Rather than being a national or global issue, I suggest that "housework" is an issue of cosmic importance. In our approach to family housework, I try to integrate both human and physical aspects of the energy needed to be human. I further suggest that **energy used in family housework is the human side of cosmic housework.**

The core household is the mother and child. Mother and child are the true nativity of human creation. Successful reproduction and rearing offspring *is* "productive work" that the human race depends on. **That is where housework and family efforts are directed ... to the care and nurturing of family members. In short, housework creates and nurtures humanity.**

Hours of work and wages are part of the energy-budget that provides family income. Most people doing family housework do not keep track of the hours they put in. And few keep track of the energy spent doing house-work. **To the extent that energy expenditure supports our lives, it is housework.**

1) ***Pricing Housework:***   In 1983 Michael Minton and Jean Libman Bloch, published *What Is a Wife Worth? The Leading Expert Places a High Dollar Value on Homemaking.* The book analyzes the value of a spouse in terms of the housework performed and the replacement cost of such housework.

The key premise is, "a replacement cost is incurred if someone outside the family is hired to perform the services of a housekeeping spouse." Wages paid to replacement workers would equal the value of a spouse's housework. In wealthy households, the "help" are paid to do housework.

In the Minton-Bloch book, 24 household jobs are listed. The jobs range from food buyer, nurse, waitress, bookkeeper, dietitian and child psychologist. The prevailing hourly wages are used to calculate the value of each job. The total is over $40,000 per year for the housework performed by a spouse in the early 1980's.

In April, 2012, a survey of 8,000 moms indicated that a stay-at-home mom handles almost 95 hours per week of work, worth almost $113,000 per year [$22.87 per hour]. A working mom should add approximately 58 hours of work at home, about $67,000, to her current salary (*"What's a Mom Worth?"* (Market Watch.com).

While compensation and support of all people is of vital concern, the emphasis in *Cinderella's Housework* is on the need for a "Low Income Family Economic Support" LIFES program, rather than compensating an individual spouse. The original *Cinderella* story of 1697 describes the social-economic-political family.

Cinderella's story-book ordeal inspires a comprehensive approach to family well-being. Not that homemaker support is less important, rather family income support offers a firmer prospect for long-term economic support. Support of the homemaker is vital. Equitable compensation for work performed is the foundation of a truly just society.

Minton and Bloch establish a realistic economic foundation, not only for the support of a housekeeper-spouse, but also to establish a legal basis for family support. The rationale provided by a multitude of divorce settlements, points sharply to the overwhelming injustice suffered by most divorce families ... particularly low-income families.

Deprivation in low-income families is both the cause and effect of economic crises. Since low-income families can only exist if there are high-income families, the vast income inequality that results, stands like an economic beast on a feeding frenzy ... consuming low-income families in its path.

A July 28, 2010 *New York Times* article, *"An Unexpected Drop in U.S. Durable Goods*," is the result of a "... sputtering economy [dragging] down demand." The point is that low-income families are not able or willing to buy, thus dragging down demand. In this way, crises economics cause low-income families, and low-family-income causes economic crises.

Low-income means low demand for goods and services.
Falling income means falling consumption and falling economy.

The day after Thanksgiving, "Black Friday" 2011, there was an unexpected surge in retail sales. Retailers offered huge price reductions. Millions of savvy shoppers lined-up hours before retailers opened for business. The media hailed this as a dramatic economic "recovery." As a retailer, I suggest the Black Friday so-called "recovery" is little more than shoppers buying when there are savings to be had, and retailers reporting high sales to drive sales and not mentioning the returns.

The deprivation of low-family-income can be considered economic terrorism. While falling consumer demand is serious enough in wealthy societies, in the most deprived societies, low-family-income supports social-political unrest, revolution, and perhaps even terrorism.

In the *New York Times*, July 30, 2010 article, by Alissa J. Rubin, *"Taliban Exploit Openings in Neglected Province,"* she notes that "Deprived of jobs and government services, people in Baghlan Province [Afghanistan] are turning to the Taliban for speedy **justice** and **work**.

Each new economic crisis is poised like a beast devouring whole families and nations. The unavoidable conclusion is that income inequality is the cause of economic crises, and economic crises cause further income inequality.

The U.S. Government lists 168 coded jobs that are performed both inside and outside the home. This is hardly surprising considering that most occupations begin as home-based crafts.

Looking at market development since the time of the *Cinderella* story, it may be seen how all tasks, jobs and endeavors originate in the family. The leaders of the corporate world all began as "mother's children." The products and services of world commerce are rooted in the household and nurtured by family imagination. Below is a list of 24 jobs that are basic parts of both family housework and the overall economy.

Jobs That Are a Basic Part of Housework

Shopper-Buyer	Family Advisor	Interior Designer
Nurse-Health Worker	Maintenance-Repairs	Caterer
Tutor-Educator	Child Care Worker	Child Psychologist
Food Handler-Waiter	Cleaner-Janitor-Hygienist	Dishwasher
Tailor-Seamstress	Cook-Chef	Dietitian-Nutritionist
Laundress-Clothier	Errand Messenger	Secretary-Social Planner
Chauffeur-Deliverer	Bookkeeper-Budgeter	Public Relations Host
Gardener-Florist	Technician-Engineer	Computer-Networking

"Computer-Networking" was added to my updated list of housework tasks because electronic networking and cell phones provide access to a vast range of household services, especially shopping, e-mail/communication, school websites/blackboards, books, libraries, films, medical references, food/health information, and many additional "on-line" services.

Central to housework is "communication." If you look at the above 24-item chart, you will notice that all of the items involve motion-movement, work-energy and some type of communication networking. **These days, housework includes Microsoft Windows as well as window cleaning!**

2) ***Economic Partnership ... Valuing Housework Jobs:*** data indicate a 70 hour work week for housework. That figure will vary, depending on the size of the household, number of people in a household and other factors. In one instance, the weekly value totaled $774.77, with a yearly value of $40,288.04. (*What is a Wife Worth?*)

In 2007, the following job categories and related wages were compiled:

Selected U.S. Occupations and Wage Rates in 2007, Adjusted 2009

Occupation	Number Employed	Average Hourly Rate	Annual Income
All Occupation	135,185,230	$20.32	$ 42,270.00
Managers	1,697,690	$51.91	$107,973.00
Public Relations Managers	51,730	$48.66	$101,220.00
Personal Home Care Aids	614,190	$9.47	$ 19,690.00
Recreation Workers	282,680	$11.81	$ 24,570.00
Models	1,660	$14.50	$ 30,160.00
Office/Administration Support	23,231,750	$15.49	$ 32,220.00
Information Record Clerks	215,780	$16.78	$ 34,910.00
Computer Operators	107,450	$17.82	$ 37,070.00

The recognition of marriage as an "economic partnership" passed into federal law statues as the "Uniform Marriage and Divorce Act." While providing legal guidelines for mediation and divorce, it paves the way for placing a monetary value on all housekeeping tasks and jobs.[15]

3) ***What Is Your Mom Worth?*** The family-household is the fundamental means of human change and survival. Since there were human households it has been our heritage to exist within the "turmoil of endless transformation." On a human level, Crisis Economics is the way we experience most change.

Certainly we experience enough turmoil in our lives, and much of it is due to our constantly changing social and natural environment. Many of the changes we experience are a response of our genetic code to changes in our environment. This is adaptation.

To fully understand the "family," we need some knowledge of energy-housework interactions. The housework we do is intelligently coded to such an extent that we need not take much time to think about each housework chore. While housework is planned, it's also semi-automatic.

* * *

Think of how you and your spouse, or maybe just you, juggle all the household tasks each day. It's all housework … coded intelligence … from the time you awake, wash, run a comb across your head, dress, get breakfast, brown-bag lunch, race to work … it all depends on genetic code. That code is in the lists we make, in our genes and in the little gray cells between our ears.

How can we put a price on the love and affection between mother and child? In the early 1800's plantation owners in the American South insisted on a similar relation between master and slave. Yet, accounting records of that time show that a strong slave could be purchased for $1,000, produce more than $10,000 per year in goods and services, while the costs of maintaining a slave could be as little as $20 per year. Yet, only 8% of Southerners owned slaves.

And now we still wax rhapsodic about family, and especially mom. Less well known are the government and corporation actuarial accounts of worker value, the cost of children, the costs of health care, and the cost-benefit analysis of a person's life.

Somewhere in the accounting ledgers are the cost-benefits of wages paid and family income, according to each family member. Mothers, children and fathers are valued beyond price, but it is still possible to calculate their value in the corporate marketplace.

* * *

A financial services group studied the variety of household jobs mothers perform. Keeping in mind that there are no typical mothers, just as there are no typical families or households, the assumption can be made that a number of well-documented jobs are common to most families, at least those with children.

The U.S. Bureau of Labor Statistics suggested seventeen primary jobs with their wage values. From this, the financial services group estimated a mother's monthly value at $42,400, or $508,700 yearly. The jobs and annual values were:

1. Animal Caretaker, $17,500;
2. Executive Chef, $40,000;
3. Computer Systems Analyst, $44,000;
4. Financial Manager, $39,000;
5. Food and Beverage Service Worker, $20,000;
6. General Office Clerk, $19,000;
7. Registered Nurse, $35,000;
8. Management Analyst, $41,000;
9. Child Care Worker, $13,000;
10. Housekeeper, $9,000;
11. Psychologist, $29,000;
12. Bus Driver, $32,400;
13. Elementary School Principal, $58,600;
14. Dietitian/Nutritionist, $41,600;
15. Property Manager, $22,600;
16. Social Worker, $30,000;
17. Recreation Worker, $15,500.

While the financial group correctly considered motherhood a full-time 24/7 job, all seventeen jobs are not performed 24/7. In a similar vein, we are paid for the actual work we "clock-in." Unless you are a corporate officer, you are not likely to be paid for a 24/7 job.

Those whose pay scale is up in the clouds somewhere, I suspect, dictate their own pay. Nevertheless, the financial study is correct in these points:

First, housework performed by a mother or spouse is more valuable than any wage job.

Second, no attempt has been made to pay wages reflecting the importance of producing people.

Third, motherhood-housework is praised as long as it has no effect on actual family income.

Fourth, that is why most of us live in low income families.

4) ***Underground Economy Families:*** Low family income is a national and global threat. Inadequate family income threatens the prospects of rich and poor in all societies. In an attempt to survive, low income families create and maintain a global underground economy.

It's estimated that the underground economy may comprise half of Gross Domestic Product in all nations. Much of the underground economy is not included in government accounting.[16]

While the global economic crisis threatens families, it significantly impacts our security. The more immediate threat is from increasing numbers of low income families throughout the world. Families enmeshed in the political-economy of highly stressed societies have little choice. Families living in vulnerable regions are coerced into supporting those in power, be they terrorists, war-lords, local despots or landlords.

The message is clear. When we estimate the dollar value of housework, we often find that the value of housework exceeds family wage income. In 2010, the economic crisis forced a modification. The new dividing point between low and high income families is $72,500, with 80% of families below and 20% above.

It is the 27% of families with annual income under $35,000 that are "most at risk" of being drawn into the underground economy. As for the 17% of families with annual incomes under $25,000, I reckon they are already part of the underground economy, as a matter of survival. These figures are based on families that file income tax returns, are counted in the census and leave a paper trail.

What about "off-the-books" income? The millions of Swiss and "off-shore" hidden bank accounts ... the millions of safety deposit box hoarders

... the Madoffs and other thefts of millions, billions and trillions can only hint at the size of the "off-the-books" underground economy.

Tax evasion and avoidance is perhaps the leading method of depriving all families of a fair share of the wealth we all produce. A *New York Times* article about tax evasion and avoidance reveals the tip of the underground economy: "Billionaire Brothers Long Suspected of Tax Evasion," July 30, 2010, by Edward Wyatt.[17]

If most families produce more "house work value" than the actual income needed to support the family, how do families make up the income short-fall? If families cannot make ends meet with "legitimate" wage income, then families will find other means of support that do not appear on the official Labor Department list of jobs.

The "underground economy" is avoided in most economic discussions. Illegal occupations are often the last resort in the struggle for survival. Most illegal income sources are declared illegal because corporations and governments attempt to stifle competition. In times of economic crisis underground income sources are life preservers for low-income families.

The first economic crisis was initiated by the new U.S. Federal Government in the late 1700's. The first president of the U.S. initiated the "legitimate" liquor industry in the new United States. "Home" liquor production became the first family survival system in America. Converting grain to liquor was often the only way of transporting crops for markets.

This writer's family was active in the moonshine industry for over 100 years until the 1950's. I worked my way through university in the moonshine industry. Among the rural people of the South, moonshine was, and still is, a semi-respectable livelihood. The moonshine industry is alive and well throughout America. Crisis economics has made moonshine a growing underground industry in most urban areas.[18]

Since no data on the size of the underground brewing industry are available, I suggest a figure of $350 billion annually, which is about equal to the size of the "legitimate" liquor industry. My estimate is based on the fact that both the underground and "legitimate" liquor industries grew up together over the last two centuries and established themselves in parallel markets.

The other "higher profile" underground markets are: **Marijuana** $142 billion; **Prostitution** $108 billion; **Counterfeit technology** $100 billion; Counterfeit **pharmaceutical drugs** $75 billion; **Prescription** drugs $73 billion; **Cocaine** $70 billion; Opium and **heroin** $65 billion; Web **Video piracy** $60 billion; **Software piracy** $53 billion; and **Cigarette smuggling** $50 billion.[19]

Who are the real mega-thieves? Those listed above are "small-time" compared to the financial-banking "industry." The real "champs" of crisis economics are the financial bankers and brokers who created the **$370 Trillion Derivative Market**. The rest of us are the "chumps."

And the point of all this is? To show you how valuable your spouse is. Don't blame yourself or your spouse for the condition of your family income. No matter how much housework you do or how many low-wage jobs you juggle, remember there's a 370 trillion dollar beast out-there with its grubby paws on the scale of income justice.

5) *Moonshine:* Millions of deprived families cannot wait for government reforms. Many families hard pressed for income discover their latent enterprising spirit. They find ways to meet their family needs. The underground economy provides many opportunities for the economically challenged.

My family's moonshine industry is the same enterprise that captivated the father of our country, George Washington, the "Moonshine Patriot." The story of moonshine in America "… is the first instance of the have's manipulating the laws of this country to benefit themselves and to put the have-nots in a position of not being able to compete."[20]

Once again it may be said, "There's nothing new under the sun." The descendants of the Norman Conquest built an empire, "On which the sun never set." They are the parents of the American "Tidewater Aristocrats," who wrested part of the British Empire from their parents. The grand old tradition of our founding mothers and fathers continues in the form of global corporate society.

6) *Do Your Own Family Work Chart*
Here's a Blank Chart to Copy and Apply to Your Family
Check the latest government data at
http://www.bls.gov/oes/2008/may/oes_nat.htm#b00-0000

U.S. Labor Dept. Job # and Defined Job		Spouse(s) Hours/Week	Spouse $ Value of Housework/Week	Spouse $ Value Total/Week

Value per Week of Spouse 1, $_____ + Spouse 2, $_____ = _____

(Value per Week x 52) = Year Value = Spouse 1, $_____ + Spouse 2, $_____

Essay 10

FOLLOW THE MONEY

"Go into the garden and fetch me a pumpkin. Her godmother
scooped out the inside, leaving nothing but the rind and then
touched it with her wand. "I'll go and look in the rat trap,"
said Cinderella, "if there is a rat in it, we'll make a coachman
of him." "You are right," said her godmother, "go and see."
(*Cinderella*, Charles Perrault, 1697)

Prior to the market economy, property in the current sense did not exist.
The economic power of markets and property first became viable in Europe
2,500 years ago. Trade in flint and obsidian tools date back over 100,000
years. Trade at territorial borders is as old as humanity.

Five thousand years ago Egyptians were shipping honey-cured ducks
in wax-sealed clay jars throughout the Mediterranean. Greek, Persian and
Trojan tribal city-states were fighting over trade routes 3,000 years ago.
International market trade is as old as tribal border trading.

The Trojan War survivors influenced the Latin tribes of Italy, especially
the Etruscans. By the time Julius Caesar was assassinated in 44 BC, the
decline of tribal society in Italy was well along. I wonder what history
would write if the Etruscans succeeded in dominating, rather than Rome.

Seven kings maintained Etruscan tribal market dominance until a sex
scandal, the rape of the Sabine women, involving the last king, Tarquin,
ended Etruscan tribal power. Tribal raiding for mates was not unusual.
Early household formation was far from being kind and gentle. **Failed
reproductive success has ended many dynastic families.**

The first Roman Republic was born out of Etruscan tribal tyranny 2,500
years ago. Before the abstract idea of "property" took hold, it was necessary
to reduce the power of tribal market control. The Roman Empire expanded
under the first emperor, Caesar Augustus, and especially his wife, Empress
Livia, matron-chief of the Julian tribe of Julius Caesar.

The age of Augustus, 2,000 years ago, was an age of rapidly expanding international markets and trade. Tribal commercial interests and land holdings were the domains of the Roman Senate. More than subjugate Europe, Caesar's Gallic Wars opened a vast network of market trade by coercing commercial alliances with hundreds of local tribes.

The first century "Pax Romana" achieved perhaps the first truly global market economy, with its mercantile center of one million people in Rome. The Roman market economy extended land and sea Silk Routes to Africa, China and India. Even the Basque cod fisheries of the North Atlantic Grand Banks were integrated into the Roman market economy.

Barter continued to be a major part of international trade. In fact, the balance and imbalance of world trade still functions as a barter system. Western nations provide "AID" in the form of foodstuffs, weapons and "pay-offs," in exchange for goods, services and "alliances" from recipient nations.

1) ***The Billionaire Pledge?*** The wealthiest families are at risk today and they know it. We now arrive at a point when the concept of "wealth" is seriously threatened. Unthinking investors have put the wealthiest families in danger from global terrorists, extortionists and especially the millions of deprived low-income families.

As of December, 2011, we are in the fourth month of the Occupy Wall Street protest. The protest has spread to cities across America. An international outcry of anger against the inequality of wealth is spreading and deepening. While the majority of Americans experience the economic fall-out of shady financiers, the super-rich remain untouched ... for now.

What helped to expand the protest were the police abuses with pepper spray and the arrests of protesters. In the New York Times article, one of the people interviewed stated, "I'm not sure how our democracy is going to work if our votes are drowned out by money." A second said, "In my opinion, corporate overreach is the source of our problems." Another "... suggested that protesters might one day unite with the Democratic Party. Others said Occupy Wall Street might spawn a left-leaning equivalent of the Tea Party."[21]

Similar protests are spreading in Europe. Greece is in bankruptcy. Greek family structure is disintegrating as a result of high unemployment among well-educated people less than 35 years of age. Many are immigrating to nations in need of their skills. Australia is holding job fairs in Greece for engineers, doctors, dentists and health care workers. The events in Greece, Europe, Middle East and America are sending world financial markets into a tail-spin.

The wealthy have not felt themselves so threatened since the Great Depression of the 1930's. With these events in mind, a number of U.S. billionaires have pledged to donate at least half their income to charity.

* * *

In a recent news release, "Dissing Bill Gates: Who's Missing from His Billionaire 'Giving Pledge' Club" by Michael Corkery, 40 Billionaires list their names in pledging half their fortunes to charity. As of May 11, 2011 the number of pledgers reached 69;[22] "The list includes billionaires who have pledged more than half of their fortunes to charities. Started by Bill and Melinda Gates and Warren Buffett, the "Giving Pledge" could prove to be the next ultra-status symbol for the super-rich."[23]

It may be the "next ultra-status symbol," but behind the hoopla there is real and deep-seated fear. Since the 1930's Presidents Franklin D. Roosevelt, John F. Kennedy, Bill Clinton and, recently, Barak Obama provided temporary "fixes" for economic crises. These "fixes" provided something of a release valve for the massive anger directed toward corporations and the wealthy.

Now, in the first years of the 21st Century Economic Crisis, billionaires seem to be taking some preventative measures. It is likely that the "Billionaire Pledge" will spread to millionaires. If this were to happen, it could alleviate some of the antagonism between low-income and high-income families.

By shifting perhaps $500 to $1,000 billion to low-income families, consumer spending and consumption could raise the entire economy out of crisis mode. If there is one thing that establishment economists agree on, it is that falling consumer demand and reduced spending are the most dangerous parts of this economic crisis. As employment and income continue to drop, consumers can only respond by curbing consumption.

The problem with the "Billionaire Pledge" is that it is another charitable gesture. It serves only to preserve the antiquated ritual of hoarding wealth. It is more appropriate in a Cinderella fairy tale than in the 21st Century global economy. This gesture of the wealthy says much about enterprise mentality that sees itself as some sort of bogus royalty, rather than responsible leaders in a democracy.

Throwing some cash to charities, assuming that there will be some indirect aid to low income families, is an extension of the old "trickle-down" theory. That is, by passing generous billions through notoriously tight-fisted red-tape charities, some of the wealth will actually help low-income families.

Most charities are more concerned with *public relations* than *relations with the public*. Only direct, long-term aid to low-income families can make a difference. By the time "charitable institutions" subtract their "overhead" costs from the donated billions, and find "qualified" low-income families, the "trickle-down" has become an angry "drop-in-the-bucket."

True leaders offer substantive programs, not fairy-tale gestures. Solutions to global economic crises need to be addressed within the framework of the global political-economy. The "Billionaire Pledge" is a nervous, guilty admission of failure in leadership.

Unconscionable leaders rigged the political-economy by hoarding wealth. The result is that "low-family-income" becomes an economic Frankenstein about to destroy the enterprise system that created it. The "Billionaire Pledge" not-withstanding, it will take more than a few panic gestures to correct the cycle of crisis economics. The "Billionaire Pledge" might be a step in the right direction if we were still living in feudal Europe. Instead of donating to charity, billionaires would be better advised to establish a Low Income Family Economic Supplement private agency or something like it.

2) ***Wealth and Family-income:*** Family-household-income is of primary importance as families provide all workers and consumption. It's family

work that maintains the corporate global economy. The energy of our work produces the goods and services needed at all levels of society.

Albert Einstein divided "energy" into two parts: Energy moving at **light speed**, such as sunlight, X-rays, Cosmic rays and Gamma rays. These he called **Fast Energy**. Energy at **less than light speed** Einstein called **Crystallized Energy**. People, earth, air, water and all material stuff is **Crystallized Energy** since it moves slower than the speed of light. Crystallized Energy might better be referred to as **Slow Energy** as compared to **Fast Energy**.

People working for wages are paid money that becomes part of family income. Money is effectively Crystallized Energy. It is income paid in exchange for our hours of work. Money is also the Crystallized Energy that corporations receive when the goods and services we produce are purchased by family members.

If you think about it, we burn our body energy in the hours that we work. We are compensated for our expenditure of work-energy with wages. Crystallized Energy provides family-income so we can work some more, and buy some more. The point is that the Crystallized Energy we get back as wages and income is only a small part of all the energy we put into wage work.

You've thought of money in many ways, but I'll bet you never considered money as Crystallized Energy. In this regard, economic exchange involves the constant transfer of Crystallized Energy in the form of money. As with all energy in the Cosmos, Crystallized Energy needs to be in constant circulation for the maximum benefit to all people, households and families. **Imbalances of human wealth are imbalances of human energy**.

A cosmic rule about energy is that "energy tends to spread itself out more or less evenly, regardless of the energy form." As we are all parcels of cosmic energy, using Crystallized Energy in our daily lives, it stands to reason that concentrations of Crystallized Energy, as with all energy, must be dynamically distributed to maintain a human balance, as well as a balance of nature.

If crystallized energy, the money in our economy, does not circulate at a certain rate of transfer, economic crises occur. Jobs and wages are declining, as is family income. The effect is to reduce family purchases of goods and services. I suggest that **money is a form of human energy**. Therefore, the distribution of money, as with all energy, needs to adhere to the laws of nature.

The drop in family consumption is a direct effect of the drop in family income. Economic energy transfer is now dangerously reduced, resulting in the 21st Century Economic Crisis. The gross imbalance of wealth is the main cause of economic crisis and household chaos. Looking at the current economic crisis in terms of energy transfer, it may be seen that these dismal times are the result of Crystallized Energy (money) transferring at a glacial pace. **In prosperous times, the flow of money and energy is rapid.**

The reasoning is that more and better jobs can generate higher family income. Increasing low-family-income will increase spending on consumer goods and achieve an overall speedup in the flow of money. Increasing the speed and equalizing money distribution increases the speed and distribution of human energy.

3) ***Low-Middle-Upper Income Families:*** Low-income families now account for 46% of U.S. families; 40% are middle income, and 14% are upper income. Since the onset of the economic crisis in 2008, significantly more families have fallen into lower income groups. Income imbalance grows ominously.

In the 2010 Income Table, below, the group with income under $21,855 increased to 20%. Prior to 2008 that figure was under 15%. The U. S. Government now defines "Low-income" as 150% of the poverty level. So "Low-income" is now officially defined as $21,855 or less.

More than 17.5% were unemployed or underemployed in October 2009. The previous recorded high was 17.1% in December 1982. This includes the officially unemployed, who have looked for work in the last four weeks. Included are discouraged workers, looking in the past year, as well as millions of part-time workers seeking full time work.[24]

Income Tax Filing for Two Income U.S. Families, Estimated for 2010[25]

Income in 2010	78 Million Families	100% of Families
Less than $21,855	15.6	20.0%
$21,855 to $47,499	20.7	26.6%
$47,500 to $71,743	18.9	24.2%
$71,744 to $99,999	11.4	14.6%
$100,000 to $999,999	6.0	7.7%
$1,000,000 and over	5.4	6.9%

A more realistic "Low-income" is based on state median income. In February 2010 median income was reported as $71,744 for a two-earner family in New Jersey. The data affirm that actual income is rapidly declining. The two earner $71,744 income is included since New Jersey shows the highest income of any state.[26]

If this inequality of family income were viewed as a pyramid of wealth, the middle and low-income base would change from 74% to 85% (2007 to 2010) of all families supporting the 26% to 15% (2007 to 2010) of all families at the peak. **Low-income Families Support a Pyramid of Wealth in America.**

In 2011, low to middle-income for 85% of all families is likely to support the 15% of high-income families. By 2012 income inequality is likely to be 90% versus 10%. Is anyone surprised by this contrast? What is not surprising is that the low income 85% pays the bulk of welfare for the rich and poor. Welfare for the rich is in the form of "depletion allowances" and industry tax subsidies. Subsidizing the record profits of global oil corporations is paid out of our taxes.

In 2007 there were 3 million U.S. millionaires with a net worth averaging $4.3 million. That amounts to a total net worth of $12.9 trillion and constitutes 30% of global net worth. This was a 9.4% increase over 2006.[27]

The number of U.S. millionaires rose to 7.8 million in 2009, 16% increase over the 6.7 million in 2008. Affluent households, with net assets of $500,000 or more, increased 12% to 12.7 million. In the same period there were 980,000 households with over $5 million in net worth, a 17% increase over 2008.[28]

This year the World's Billionaires have an average net worth of $3.5 billion, up $500 million in 12 months. The world has 1,011 10-figure titans, up from 793 a year ago but still shy of the record 1,125 in 2008. Of those billionaires on last year's list, only 12% saw their fortunes decline … Americans account for 40% of the world's billionaires, down from 45% a year ago. The U.S. commands 38% of the collective $3.6 trillion net worth of the world's richest, down from 44% a year ago.[29]

That's a one-year increase of 19% in the number of billionaires and an increase of 35% in their net worth during a time of increasing poverty. Severe poverty is at its highest point in three decades. The point of these dry statistics is to demonstrate the immense burden shouldered by the average American family. We will see why these millions, billions and trillions add up to a monstrous abuse of democracy and power.[30]

4) *Family Wealth Table:* The income data in the previous Table were averaged in each category. "Less than $22,500" is now an average of $11,250; "$22,500 to $47,499" averages $35,000 and so on, for each income group:

U.S. ANNUAL INCOME of 78 MILLION FAMILIES in 2010
(Estimates are based on U.S. Census, New York Times, Bloomberg News Service and Forbes)

Income Class	Average Income	Million Families	Income $ trillions	% of U.S. Wealth
1) Poor	$ 11,250	12.0	$ 0.14	0.34%
2) Low-Middle	$ 35,000	20.0	$ 0.70	1.72 %
3) Middle	$ 60,000	18.0	$ 1.08	2.66 %
4) Upper-Middle	$ 86,250	15.3	$ 1.32	3.25 %
5) Rich	$ 500,000	4.9	$ 2.45	6.03 %
6) Millionaires	$ 4,300,000	7.8	$ 33.54	82.53 %
7) Billionaires	$ 3.5 billion	404 individuals	$ 1.41	3.47 %
	Totals	**78**	**$40.64**	**100.00%**

Consider that 65 million families, 84% of tax paying families, work and support the other 16%, with average incomes of $500,000. The injustice of this arrangement is that families, comprising 84% of America, must live on less than 8% of the wealth we create. The rich control 92% of wealth. In 2010 American families created over $40 trillion in wealth for the rich, millionaires and billionaires, who controlled 92% of that total. What's wrong with this picture?

Wealth sits precipitously like a huge sand castle. The slightest instability or scrutiny hastens the fall of the fragile corporate edifice. We see this process unfold in the daily gyrations of the stock market, and we live through the destruction caused by periodic economic crises. Global corporations have become crisis corporations. This is what Occupy Wall Street is all about.

5) ***Family Values:*** Here are some family values, and the ways in which families support the economy and corporations. **When we produce our families, we produce the economy**:

1. Family-households are the factories that **produce people**.
2. Family-households produce **house-workers**, and they produce all working people.
3. Family-households produce **wage-workers**, and they produce the economy.
4. Families **purchase and consume** the goods and services produced by corporations.
5. Family members are **volunteers** for the good and welfare of society.
6. Families sacrifice sons and daughters to **secure & protect** their nation.
7. Families produce **scientists**, **technicians**, **teachers**, and all skills, even corporate managers.

I experience the effects of income reduction almost daily, in my work as a deli clerk. A woman came to my counter for half a pound of our $3.99 per pound ham. When I handed her the package of ham, she points to the $12.99 per pound prosciutto ham and tells me, "That's what I really want, but it costs more than my jewelry."

6) ***Family Equilibrium Experiment:*** A group of Princeton mathematicians were in the habit of bar-hopping on weekends. The objective was to score with the most attractive gals. By the time they realized that the most attractive gals were taken, the other less attractive gals were also unavailable. No matter how many bars they frequented the same thing happened.

As they were mathematicians, they reduced the dilemma to mathematical terms and discussed it exhaustively. One of them, John Forbes Nash, proposed a solution. Nash suggested a real life experiment. "Let's agree that next weekend, when we go seeking gals, we all ignore the most enticing gals and make a play for the less attractive gals. We'll see how we score with the second rank gals."

A real life math experiment is irresistible to mathematicians. They all agreed it was a great idea. After a few weekends into the experiment, they discussed their results. Of ten participants, nine scored by the third bar, on the first night. Ninety-percent success with gals by the third bar impressed the mathematicians.

This compared to a 10% success rate with the most attractive gals. **The experiment suggests that cooperation between competitors could result in moderate gains for most, with no big winners or losers. In this game plan, all are winners as it eliminates the extremes of 'I win, you lose.'**

An arrangement of this type is referred to as a **Nash Equilibrium**. Likely, it was the strategy used by our ancestors who migrated out of Africa eons ago. The success of a cooperative strategy, in view of environmental challenges, was genetically embedded in the offspring of survivors.

Cooperative agreements in tribal and market societies became more the rule than the exception. The first human hordes, bands, clans, tribes, households and families prove the long-term effectiveness of the **Nash Equilibrium.**

The most famous of these equilibrium agreements went into effect between the Eastern and Western bloc countries in the 1960's. The first East-West nuclear non-aggression agreement was the result of the Cuban

Missile Crisis of October 1962. Leaders on both sides agreed to put "Red Phones" in place, permitting instant direct contact in the event of a crisis.

The result of this equilibrium is that while there is no winner or loser, we are alive to tell the tale. In that respect we are all winners. It may be said that the Nash Equilibrium prevented a nuclear holocaust. Cooperation, in and between the earliest human families is a survival strategy that works. That we survived thousands of years of conflicts suggests a powerful genetic factor favoring cooperation and social equilibrium.[31]

The equilibrium of the 21st Century, such as it is, makes itself evident in the multitude of nations, states, provinces, governments, corporations, societies and the civil communication within and between each. The objective of all organizations is the security, good and welfare of people, or at least it should be.

A world out of balance is in a cycle of constant environmental stress. Planetary orbits affect the magnetic polarity of planets. Magnetic forces unleashed by slight orbital disturbances affect the Sun and our Earth. The polar angle of the Earth has changed frequently in the billions of years of existence. Shifts in the magnetic pole have resulted in frequent changes in Earth's climate.

These points suggest that neither physical nor social equilibrium is constant. Likely, there is dialectic between extremes, as there is between positive and negative magnetic opposites, providing constant transformation. Transformations may result in temporary equilibrium, or synthesis, until new stresses upset the equilibrium. This is the cosmic reality impacting our Earth and human families.

In 21st Century America, the economic equilibrium is out of balance. An untenable imbalance has developed between the massive amount of wealth controlled by a few and the deprivation experienced by the many. The U.S. was not formed as a 'winner-take-all' nation. Rather, this nation is the result of a revolution to liberate us from the 'winner-take-all' abuses of Britain.

The current crisis results from a 'winner-take-all' economy imposed by the rule of wealth. In this state of affairs the plutocracy has the wealth to buy legislators, lobbyists, and the media. This land of equal opportunity has degenerated into rule by the super-rich.

The cooperative equilibrium is broken. Conflicts between rich and poor dominate the global landscape. Global revolutions are the responses of people saying NO to crisis economics.

WHAT IS TO BE DONE?

"So he made Cinderella sit down and hold out her foot,
and the little slipper went on easily and fitted as perfectly
as if it had been molded to her foot in wax."
(*Cinderella*, Charles Perrault, 1697)

In Lewis Carroll's *Through the Looking-Glass*, the Red Queen could represent many women. She said, "It takes all the running you can do, to keep in the same place." Certainly mothers of small children feel that way. The Red Queen might just as well be referring to life in the 21st Century Economic Crisis.

The previous essays examine the problems of housework, household and family from various perspectives, posing more questions than answers. Major emphasis is placed on social, environmental and economic roots, from antiquity to the 21st Century.

From the beginning of humanity, the changing environment has shaped the changing human household and the people produced in the household. And now the reverse is occurring. That is, the human family seems to be accelerating environmental change. The feedback effect is firmly in place.

The human family and the global environment are locked in a cosmic tango. Every step one partner takes is answered by the other.

If it is true that humanity is switching on and off parts of the environment, then it is also true that the environment is doing the same to the human family.

Family households are the living "factories" that produce people. That is the reality hidden in plain sight. Not thinking about it or trivializing it does not make it less true. It is the imaginative and energy coding power of the household that creates people, and by means of our offspring we imagine and recreate the Cosmos and ourselves.

1) ***Family and Class:*** In contemporary American society, the family household is a unique creation of global enterprise. Consider the global reach of international enterprises.

One level of the power hierarchy are the so-called cultural institutions (communication media), linking the image and voice of authority with the eyes and ears of the family. Government authority exercises power through taxation, police and media propaganda (lobbying, public relations, "news," TV programming and advertising).

All these are "guided" by a small group, controlling global corporations and most of U.S. wealth. Too many trillions are in too few hands. And the power of those trillions continues to resist a fair distribution among the millions of families who helped create all the wealth.

These are just a few of the methods the super-rich use to oppress families. It is the hierarchy of wealth that transforms the family household into a factory that processes and produces people. Global corporations care about wage-work and consumption, not the families of people who do the work and consuming.

The fundamental premise in corporate society is that human labor can be bought and sold just like any other commodity. Global corporations provide access to anything that can be bought and sold: corn, computers, entertainment, homes, mortgages, bogus derivatives, politicians, legislators, governments and wage-workers.

Corporations don't pay for housework, environmental damage, pollution, unemployed, underemployed and certainly don't pay for the diminished lives of people in families. Corporate victimizers don't pay their fair share in the short run, so in the long run we all must keep paying.

The long run results in periodic economic crisis. Here again shady corporations can pay-off officials and slither away with little or no damage. And the rest of us, the 92% of American families that the U.S. Census does not list as statistically wealthy, we pay for corporate bailouts, subsidies and tax breaks, using our hard earned tax dollars to pay for corporate welfare.

The market system is designed to create both abundance and scarcity. The scarcity of commodities raises prices until consumption falls resulting in lower prices to encourage more consumption. This is how families become victims of market scarcity. The fluctuation of gasoline prices at the pump is one form of scarcity and price manipulation we all experience.

Unemployed wage-workers can't afford to buy as much as when they were employed. This results in large inventories of unsold commodities, such as autos. Government pumps our tax dollars into car price reduction to increase sales ... when the subsidy ends, so do auto sales.

WNYC, National Public Radio, October 2, 2009, aired the extent of unemployment, which statistics in 2011 have shown little change. Surveys of families resulted in 57% reporting a relation that was unemployed in the last year.

Now, in 2012, official unemployment is below 9%. Key economic indicators such as housing and new car sales are improving. American auto corporations are reporting impressive profits. The American economy shows some signs of recovery. However, the underlying conditions causing economic crises remain unchanged.

Of 78 million U.S. tax-filing families, over 45 million (57%) are impacted directly by job loss. In my own family, four relations lost their jobs in the last year. But lobbyists, establishment economists, and the financial community push for more aid to corporations, not families. Why is corporate welfare acceptable when aid to families is not?

Congressional "talking-heads" vote billions in bailouts for corporate casualties. In an under-handed way it makes sense, since banking-corporate contributions pay for congressional elections. This is why we have the best congress money can buy.

Corporate manipulators hold the power. They shed crocodile tears for the millions of workers they will fire ... unless they get the bailouts. Some moguls brag publicly about the joy or firing workers. Taxpayers get the pain of paying billions in extortion to the corporations that deny people an adequate income.

The bottom-line is that enterprise narcissists fire millions of workers anyway. They say, "Pay-up or we'll shoot the dog." We paid and they still shot the dog. This form of extortion amounts to economic terrorism. How should we respond to terrorism of any kind?

Let's not forget the pitiful aid to families that do not earn six-figure incomes … a few hundred dollars in a one-time "family aid" payment and a pathetic subsidy for trade-ins on new car purchases.

Those earning less than $100,000 annually are the "cash cows" that normally consume the stuff that corporations produce. Global corporations "downsize" American workers, while "up-sizing" foreign workers.

Who are the real American traitors and why don't Americans consume their way out of this crisis? Is this a great mystery? My nine-year-old granddaughter has the answer, she tells me,

"We can't buy all the stuff we want because daddy lost his job."

"Yes, they stopped feeding the "cash cow," and there will be no ice-cream for a while."

"But why did they do that, she was a hard working cow?"

"They said because it's cheaper to feed the bull on the other side of the world."

"Everyone knows that you can't milk bulls."

"Well, they didn't know that … they never did understand cash cows."

"How does this story end?"

"You decide … should we nurse the cow back to health, or keep feeding the same old bull?"

"I think she was a good old cow, everyone loved her milk, and I want ice-cream again. I want the cow back. It cost too much to keep feeding that old bull, so let's stop it. Can we take the feed from the bull and give it back to the cash-cow again?"

2) ***Economy On The Edge Of Chaos***: A society in crisis must restore itself. A society that reports 57% of families with relations that lost jobs is a society in crisis. The problem is that 90% of U.S. families experience falling income. These are "low-income-families." Unemployed and under-employed are the victims of :

1. **Obsolete skills** and lack of realistic retraining;
2. **Exporting jobs** to low wage nations;
3. Competitive pressure to **reduce wages**;
4. **Falling consumption** due to reduced income;
5. Cutbacks, rollbacks, furloughs, benefit cuts and **reduced work hours**.

Families with reduced income do not suffer in silence. When no other income is available people migrate into the underground economy. The underground economy has been embedded in the pores of society since the first apple was forbidden, and the first people began migrating.

**Humanity is a family of immigrants and refugees,
with one objective: reproductive success.**

When family needs are not met by the "lawful" economy, the underground economy provides income for those in need. What is "lawful" is defined by those in power, be they the liquor industry, drug corporations or the legislators supported by them. Newly arrived immigrants often depend on the underground economy for their survival. Like it or not, both underground and corporate economies exist to meet human needs.

The corporate system keeps changing the rules … to suit its need and greed. In corporate America, if you are wealthy enough you can violate the rules and prosper. If you are not wealthy, you can follow the rules and suffer the consequences, or seek income in the underground economy. This is symptomatic of an economy on the edge of chaos.

The 21st Century economic collapse is the result of shrinking family income. It's about millions of families that follow the rules, pay their taxes, and suffer the consequences. When family income shrinks, so do family purchases. The downward spiral of shrinking income shrinks consumption. It's a symptom of an economy on the edge of chaos.

Some years ago, I had a summer job compiling an Internet database for a news magazine. Most of us were local teachers and students when the work began. A few weeks into the job, workers from India replaced some of us. In another few weeks, Chinese replaced the Indians. By the end of the summer, we were all replaced with Vietnamese. The rules changed weekly. The only option was to work or leave. This is symptomatic of an economy on the edge of chaos.

The only major construction project in our region since 2005 is an investor's bank. This is a symptom of a crisis economy.

3) ***Wealth Inequality Fallout:*** How has the growing inequality of wealth affected the American family? The most dismal change over the last 50 years is the declining quality of food available to families. The decline in food quality keeps pace with a decline in health over the same period.

A recent example of food quality decline I experienced involved a deli customer and friend. I had just cut him a half pound of high quality ham. My friend, laughing as he took the package says, "Hey, Pauli, did you hose the ham I bought last week? It was dripping wet when I got it home. What gives?"

I replied, "You know they pump water into the cheaper sale hams. That's why we can sell it so cheap. What you saw was "water-fallout." The low quality processed ham often "perspires" excess water when cold ham is warmed. What I gave you now is naturally smoked ham … from smoke houses … no water is pumped in."

Since 1960 there's been an increase in heart disease, stroke, cancer, diabetes and especially obesity. Paradoxically, longevity has improved since 1960. We may be living longer but enjoying it less. Morbidity increases while mortality declines.

As food quality declines, families typically spend half-as-much of their income on food in 2010, compared to the amount of family income spent on food in 1960. During this time, the cost of health care has doubled. This is symptomatic of an economy on the edge of chaos.

Over the last 50 years I've worked in the food and chemical industries. In that role, I must admit to being a willing part of the problem by my contribution to agribusiness. Most of my involvement was with the nutrition of people and food animals. This amounted to an attempt to replace the natural nutrients in animal and human diets with commercial substitutes.

For both livestock and people, the appearance and taste of foods are equally important. Lest we think cattle are less discerning than people in their taste preferences, a major problem in cattle feeding has been the ability of cattle to blow bitter-tasting riboflavin out of the feed trough. Part of my research required formulating special feed-flavor disguises for unpalatable nutrients such as riboflavin.

With people, the appearance and flavor of food is as important as the price families are willing to pay. The quality of food depends on substantial changes in food chemistry over the decades, and not always for the better.

The poultry industry used small amounts of arsenic in the form of arsenilic acid as an additive to broiler-fryer chicken feed. This helped improve "feed efficiency," increasing chicken weight gain on reduced amounts of feed. The arsenic also added to the "golden" skin color of chickens, suggesting to the consumer a healthy bird. I believe this feeding practice has ceased.

A significant example of food chemistry impacting the quality of food and the health of families is the increase in salt, fat, sweeteners (corn syrup), texturizing agents (starch and gelatin), nutrients, coloring agents, preservatives and a vast array of other chemicals. All of these describe processed foods; but even "fresh" foods present problems.

The health of families and the quality of food is greatly diminished by the mix of salt, sugar and fat added to processed food and family diet. As do many families, we check the percent of sodium, fat and sugar in the processed foods we buy. We try to avoid products with labels listing more than 10% of these.

If you pay attention to the ingredient labels on processed food, especially delicatessen items, it is quite easy to find products where water, fat, salt, sugar, starch and gelatin total over 50%. The actual "food" in processed food is often far less than 50%. In many processed foods, such as processed ham, we are paying for water adulteration. One popular brand of salami totals 86% fat, salt and cholesterol. In such products there's not much room for meat.

In my family, ranching-farming practice attempted to conserve the energy of feedstuffs. This amounts to reducing the costs of production. As in most businesses, cost-cutting is easier to control than sales.

Periodically, cattle, hogs, poultry, horses and mules were moved to new grazing fields. Once that field was "grazed-out," livestock were moved to a fresh field. Livestock "droppings" were not wasted. Typically, hogs were herded into the field to feed on the large animal waste after the large animals were moved to a fresh field. The energy in these food wastes was recycled.

When the hogs were finished feeding, they were herded out and only hog waste remained. Geese and ducks were then admitted to the hog-waste littered field, to be followed in turn by broiler, roaster, stewing and frying chickens. Whatever "fertilizer" value remained produced new grazing for the next large animal rotation. Feeding costs were reduced by a succession of livestock grazing.

By the time the grazing cycle ended, new grazing was ready for large livestock again. This form of energy recycling is now referred to as "natural-organic-free-ranging" meat production. This recycling practice is thousands of years old and has been in effect since grazing animals were domesticated.

At the age of twelve, it was my job to "rotate the stock" following dad's rotation plan. Cattle and dairy farming in South Florida had reached a dead-end by 1950. The sandy soil lacked enough nutrients for grazing and that's why animal waste recycling was a necessity. The cost of importing high quality animal feeds from Georgia and other states was not economically viable.

About that time I began to lose my taste for meat and milk. In fact, my stomach would not easily tolerate meat and milk. I could never figure out if it was psychological or genetic intolerance. In any case, fish has become my main source of protein. I eat no other animal protein and my overall health has improved over the decades.

The point of all this is to provide specific details showing how cost-cutting and wealth imbalance has impacted the health and wellbeing of families. Just as we are all part of the problem, we can all become part of the solution.

Up until the 1960's a major food additive was monosodium glutamate, MSG. While glutamates occur naturally in foods such as soy and meats, a major source of MSG naturally occurs in wild truffles. In fact, what makes truffles so valuable a culinary addition is that it is perhaps the most powerful of all flavor enhancers. Small amounts of MSG can make almost anything taste better.

MSG is Generally Recognized as Safe (GRAS), by the Food and Drug Administration (FDA). There are plenty of objective pro-health reasons for adding more MSG and far less salt.[32]

If you are seniors, you will recall how great food used to taste when "eating out," especially Chinese food. Why has MSG been removed from most processed foods? One reason is that salt is cheaper than MSG and cost-cutting "rules" in virtually all enterprises. Not that I'm selling MSG … it's just one example of how cost cutting is affecting the chemistry of food and health.

Glutamate is safer than salt. It's an amino acid building block in proteins. Glutamic acid is an important nervous system neurotransmitter. "In neuroscience, glutamate is an important neurotransmitter that plays a key role in long-term potentiation and is important for learning and memory."[33]

4) ***An End to Economic Brinksmanship:*** A workable solution exists, but it is not likely to be popular with the wealthy. U.S. 2010 data indicate 80% of tax-paying U.S. families, with an annual income under $72,500, were classified as "low-income-families." By 2012, 90% of American families are likely to fall into the "low-income" family category.

Imagine low-income-families getting monthly support checks of $1,600, $1,200, $800, $400 or $200, depending on income. That amounts to $10 an hour for 40 hours of housework each week, or $20,800 annually for the lowest-income (poverty) households:

2010 Average Annual Income With and Without a Family Supplement

A=Class	B=Average Income	C=Annual Support	D=B+C Income Support	E=78 Million Families	F=C*E Cost in $ Billions
Poor	$ 11,250	$ 20,800	$ 32,050	12.0	249.6
Low-middle	$ 35,000	$ 10,400	$ 45,400	20.0	208.0
Middle	$ 60,000	$ 5,200	$ 65,200	18.0	93.6
Upper-middle	$ 86,250	$ 2,600	$ 88,850	15.3	39.8
Rich	$ 500,000	None	Not applicable	4.9	0.0
Millionaires	$ 4,300,000	None	Not applicable	7.8	0.0
Billionaires	$ 3,500,000,000	None	Not applicable	404 individuals	**Total $ 591.0**

In the proposed plan, only the first four groups receive a downward graduated family supplement. The cost of this program would be $591 billion annually. Now, 84% of U.S. Families, the first four groups, live on 8% of U.S. annual income.

Rising unemployment, abusive mortgages and falling income result in reduced purchases. Falling consumer demand worsens the economic crisis.

It seems obvious that employment can only improve if consumption increases. The reverse is also apparent; that is, employment and family income must increase before consumption will increase. It's hard to imagine consumer spending increasing if family income continues to decline.

Spending will not increase until family income increases. This is why some type of family income support program is needed. It is the only sure way to jump start massive family consumption. A family support program costs far less than the corporate bailout money paid by the same tax-paying families benefiting from this family support program.

The above Table shows that 12.7 million families are likely to have incomes averaging $500,000 or more in 2010. Those 12.7 million families account for $40 trillion in 2010. That's where the money may be found. The cost of a "Family Support Program" is less than 2% of total wealthy family income, even assuming the rich lost one-third of their income in 2008-2010.

The "Commander-in-Chief" may have no choice but to declare a "National Economic Emergency," and levee a 1-10% graduated "surcharge" on the monthly income of all families with an annual income of $250,000 and over. There is a precedent for such surcharges in time of war, and this is war. It's time that those who profit from this economy start paying a fair share of the costs.

5) ***Family Equilibrium:*** The Family Support Program is an economic application of Nash Equilibrium. In the 1960's it prevented a nuclear holocaust. The Nash Equilibrium could prevent a global economic meltdown. A "Final Solution" to the threat of global instability might be in the form of a United Nations Global Family Support Outreach.

The rationale for a family support program has as much to do with sustaining the overall U.S. economy, as supporting low-income families. In effect, it introduces into the corporate economy a new game plan. This is a "win-win" game plan providing something for everyone, according to the guidelines of the Nash Equilibrium.

The corporate economy and wealthy families gain the added security and support of a moderately higher and sustainable level of consumption by all families. Low-income families gain a sense of security and support resulting in a rise in consumer confidence and sustainable consumer spending.

Those who buy into a "Victory Bond" program invest in the nation, the national economy and their own security, as well as a relatively high yield financial investment. Specific benefits expected from a family support program include:

1. Rapid increase in consumer goods **spending**, especially on items such as **health care**;
2. Business **sales-cycles** "smooth-out," with a reduction in drastic swings in the economy;

3. Permitting better **planning-savings** for employment, distribution and manufacturing;
4. Allowing banking/finance/investing a **moderate but sustainable profit**;
5. As **financial stability** grows, credit, loans and mortgages become more available;
6. Sustainable **employment** is encouraged with steady increases in consumer spending;
7. **Energy and environment** technology support increases with an improving economy;
8. The "**Market Multiplier***" can multiply the effect of family consumption ten-fold;
9. Investing $591 billion in a family support program could return **$5.91 trillion**;
10. As a "**Surcharge**" and/or a "**Victory Bond**" initiative, less than 2% of wealthy family income can support a national family subsidy;
11. The lure of speculative bubbles and **economic brinksmanship** can be moderated.

The proposed family support program applies the **Nash Equilibrium** as an economic security game plan. While there are not likely to be big winners or losers, all families will enjoy moderate gains. The major benefit is in family, national and global security.

Americans will feel safer and more comfortable with themselves and others. As national security improves, the status of American leadership in the world will recover its reputation as a force for peace, freedom and progress.[34]

6) *__Subsidized Wage-workers:__* Environmental change works its way over millions, thousands and hundreds of years. It is likely that genetic adaptation and human learning is a slow process. Yet, from the perspective of geological-environmental change, human progress is quite rapid. In fact, the rate of change seems to speed up in terms of genetic change, and human technology.

I was talking to a librarian about a family subsidy plan to provide up to $400 per week for the lowest income group filing income tax returns. She was upset about government in general and was especially concerned that subsidized wage-workers would have new disincentives for wage-work.

This is an issue I had not considered. Talking to supermarket co-workers, I decided to test this issue. I was especially interested in talking to workers who are mothers. I asked, "How much extra each week would you need to quit your job … $100, $200, $300, $400 a week, or more?"

The answers surprised me. No one was prepared to leave their job for a few hundred dollars a week extra. Everyone I work with complains about their job. They complain that as part-time workers they don't get enough hours. Fewer hours means less pay. They need their jobs for union medical-dental benefits.

They would miss socializing with fellow workers, customers, neighbors, relatives and friends. After all, most people we know make frequent trips to the market. They like to have a few hours away from the kids. They like getting out of the house and they like getting away from the household chaos … and into a more disciplined supermarket chaos. Most had someone to care for the kids while they worked.

I asked what amount of money they would need to quit work. The response was that there was so much they wanted to buy that it would take thousands, like winning the lottery, before they would even consider quitting.

One mother said, "If I had the money, I'd take a long leave of absence and take the kids on a round-the-world cruise, but not my husband. He needs to stay home and take care of the house and his relatives. But I think after a few weeks I'd get tired of loafing, and I'd miss everyone, so we'd hop on a plane with loads of presents for everyone … fly home first-class, and take a limo home … that would be enough for me."

It seems that people need more income rather than less work. Socializing on the job, and brief vacations from family are also important. In subsequent talks, I asked if they knew of any people who would not work if they got a subsidy. By the way, these were not formal surveys; rather these were simply casual conversations during breaks, before and after work.

The people who would not work at legally acceptable jobs comprise a rather short list:

1. People who don't file tax returns or are working in the **underground economy**; When I was in college, working my way through via the family moonshine business, and earning $500 a month, I still liked working Saturdays selling shoes in down-town Atlanta. If I made $10 on a Saturday that was a lot, but I did it for the socializing.
2. People with **disabilities** that already get worker-compensation, public support, disability, social security and pensions are not likely to work.
3. **Retired** Senior citizens, getting a **pension** or are **disabled,** seldom are inclined to work. To conclude, "low-family-income" workers prefer to keep working, regardless of outside support.

Essay 12

A Way Out of Crisis Economics?

Cinderella, who was watching and who knew her own slipper
said lightly, "Let me see if it will fit."
(Cinderella, by Charles Perrault, 1697)

Income inequality is suggested as the root of economic crises. Both the wealthy 10% and the low-income 90% of American families present a constant threat to national economic security. Actually, it's more like 1% and 99%, as our president suggests. The problem is that families are not fairly compensated for their housework and wage-work.

1) ***War on the Home-front:*** We are in an economic war. Global corporations are at war with each other, as well as with families of house-workers and wage-workers. Instead of innovative competition, corporations fight a war of attrition by cost-cutting. Families are forced into the front lines of economic combat, competing for income and trying to survive economic crises.

Far removed from the economic onslaught of family survival are the corporate generals, launching their economic weapons of family destruction. Corporate weapons are job cuts, out-sourcing to the lowest wage nations, wage cuts, cutting work hours, job furloughs, temp and part-time jobs.

Reduction of job benefits reduces overhead costs, as well as responsibility to workers. Loyalty to America is replaced by loyalty to the global corporation. Victimizing corporations out-source American know-how, jobs and innovation. Corrupt corporations betray the nation and the family. It's a "cold-war" that's becoming a "hot-war" of global revolution.

Where is corporate loyalty and responsibility now that America needs it? The work and consumption of all 120 million American families are needed to create 404 billionaire families and 7.8-million millionaire families.

**It's the collective productivity and buying power
of all families that create all wealth.
It takes the global village to raise the global family.
It takes the global family to create global wealth.**

Undeniably, the wealthiest families make immense contributions to charities. It is well publicized that some families have set up foundations and trusts consisting of billions of dollars to serve the good and welfare of families. I for one will not minimize the enormous sense of responsibility demonstrated by dozens of America's wealthiest families.

Some pioneering, cutting-edge technologies have demonstrated great social and economic responsibility. In fact, most American families have repeatedly shown an unfailing willingness to risk their lives and wealth in the face of national crises.

We are now in the midst of a global economic war. In the 21st Century, the USA is the battlefield. Thousands of Americans are at war suffering and dying in Middle East battlefields. In any case, welcome to World War III. Like all wars, WWIII is the product of monstrous greed, extravagant bribery and a global fabric of lies.

It only takes a hand-full of irresponsible leaders to create a global crisis. But it takes all global families to avoid and prevent global crises. Perhaps that's what the "Arab Spring" and "Occupy Wall Street" are all about.

American families, once again, practice those ancient savage rites of child sacrifice. This time the "dark deities" demand human sacrifice for wars of greed and tax tribute from all low-income families. The "dark deities" are financial gnomes, acting through bought and rigged elections, providing the best government money can buy.

The ancient Romans, victors in the Punic wars against Carthage, 2,300 years ago, wrote that Carthage practiced child sacrifice to their god, Mammon. We too sacrifice our children in wars to make the world safe for global corporations. Whatever the rationale may be, we need only "follow the money" to find the real cause of any war. When we "round up the usual suspects" they are always hiding at the end of a money trail.

2) *__Aide To Low-income Families:__*   I suggest providing aide to the families in need, from the families buying lottery-bonds. A private agency **"Low-Income Family Economic Support, LIFES,"** is suggested that "sells" interest-bearing lottery-bonds. Elected local "monitors" can determine families who qualify for aid.

Lottery-bonds may be sold like lottery tickets, providing local zip-code or county based funds for distribution to local qualified families and lottery winners. It is suggested that all LIFES aid be localized and generated by the sale of lottery-bonds.

LIFES may be a private, non-profit or for-profit agency chartered to sell long-term interest-bearing bonds. LIFES would distribute all net income to low-income families on a monthly, long-term basis. This is not another governmental agency. It is not a banking, financial or insurance group, though LIFES could perform similar activities.

The objective of LIFES is to redistribute income in order to build a more innovative, secure, stable and just economy. I do not propose replacing any public or private enterprise, or employment. LIFES lottery-bonds would provide monthly lottery-bond winners to keep up public relations.

All lottery-bond purchasers, winners or not, would have a bond that they pay \$18.75 for and returns 2.5% a year for ten years. At maturity, the bond may be cashed for \$25. Effectively, everyone wins: lottery winners; lottery-bond buyers; families in need; local business sales increase because people are buying more; with increasing sales, more jobs are created. And local politicians can take the credit for creating a modest local economic and social improvement.

I propose building an entirely new localized agency that provides investment opportunities, hires employees, is publicly regulated and functions in the local and national interest. LIFES might function like zip-code based post offices, serving local needs by selling LIFES lottery-bonds locally ... to serve needy local families.

The specific purpose of LIFES is to provide continuing supplemental income to low-income families reporting annual taxable income of less than the 2010 median income of \$71,744 (for a two-earner family in New Jersey). For most other states the median income is lower.

3) ***Low-Income Family Economic Support, LIFES:*** Expanding on this proposal, **LIFES** depends on an enterprise, initiative, rather than government. To qualify for income support, families would need to apply to local LIFES "monitors" with notarized copies of tax filings or some other form of income verification. **It is reasonable to assume that millions of families with high or "underground" income will not apply to LIFES.**

The purpose of an agency for **Low-Income Family Economic Support, LIFES,** is to provide supplemental family income assistance to low-income families, so that a family filing tax returns and reporting annual taxable income of:

Under $24,500 would qualify for a monthly LIFES check of $1,200 ($14,400 annually);

$24,500 to $34,499 would qualify for a monthly LIFES check of $1,000 ($12,000 annually);

$34,500 to $44,499 would qualify for a monthly LIFES check of $800 ($9,600 annually);

$44,500 to $54,499 would qualify for a monthly LIFES check of $600 ($7,200 annually);

$54,500 to $64,499 would qualify for a monthly LIFES check of $400 ($4,000 annually);

$64,500 to $71,743 would qualify for a monthly LIFES check of $200 ($2,400 annually).

4 - ***Cost and Funding:*** The cost of a LIFES program is projected at under $600 billion annually. LIFES is proposed as a private agency-company, chartered and insured by the same regulatory agencies that regulate banks and other private financial enterprises.

LIFES might sell bonds, fund shares, and other financial products. The bonds may be due in ten years. Using 1940's World War II U.S. Victory Bonds as a starting point, and as a promotional model, LIFES Bonds might be created along the same lines.

Consider that the U.S. is embroiled in a global economic war. The global economic crisis is undermining the security of the U.S. It could be considered our patriotic duty to support LIFES Bonds. By providing economic support for U.S. low-income families, we are securing our nation and reducing the terrorist threat. LIFES could be a model for securing nations throughout the world.

Following the model of 1940's Victory Bonds, the basic denomination is suggested at $25. LIFES Bonds might be sold as lottery tickets, with unique serial numbers and in multiples. Ten-year LIFES Bonds might sell for $18.75, paying 2.5% annually to a maturity value of $25. Monthly lotteries for bond holders, by county or zip code, could build long-term popularity.

To promote bond sales, local zip-code based monthly lotteries for those purchasing lottery-bonds could provide small monthly wager-investments for people who wish to aid the local economy.

Merchant sponsorship of LIFES bonds would provide patriotic support and enterprise advertising. As with the old Works Progress Administration (WPA), LIFES Bonds might provide a national rallying point for a "grand patriotic effort."

5) ***$600 Billion Family Subsidy:*** Just as there are depreciation allowances for corporations, we might consider a family subsidy as a "Family Depreciation Allowance." Families depreciate as do all production facilities.

What can be expected from a LIFES family subsidy program?

1. The family subsidy is likely to be **spent on consumer goods** and postponed health care.
2. Rapid spending of LIFES subsidy may produce up to ten times the subsidy, or **$6 Trillion**.
3. $6 Trillion in consumer spending would **lift the economy** out of crisis mode.
4. The subsidy can create an **"Economic Gyroscope"** to stabilize swings in the economy.

5. Trillions in consumer spending can speed **major job creation**.
6. Improved family security, morale, health and education can provide **increased productivity**.
7. The cost and quality of **health care** is likely to improve.
8. Upgraded **educational and technological** skills can improve U.S. world standing.
9. A technological speed-up in **energy innovation** is likely to benefit all families and nations.

6) *__Family Bill of Rights__:* In his **FAMILY BILL OF RIGHTS,** Franklin Delano Roosevelt's 1944 proposal for a "Second Bill of Rights" was introduced. FDR's plan provides an "Economic Bill of Rights" to guarantee what might be considered family rights. FDR's proposal is the inspiration for the **LIFES** plan.[35]

FDR said that **needy people are not free people**. People that are hungry and lack family income look for any help they can get. In 1944 FDR was referring to the attraction of Soviet Communism, which indeed became a magnet for the starving nations of Europe, though it could not be sustained. Today we can truthfully say that lack of family income forces needy people into the "underground" economy, and more ominously into the arms of global revolution, social unrest, and terrorism.

FDR's economic bill of rights is effectively a "**Family Bill of Rights.**" It is designed to back up political freedom with vital family economic security. FDR contended that the freedom, peace and security of America, and the world, depended on these guarantees.

Personal freedom could not exist without the guarantees of economic security. A lasting peace, FDR argued, required the establishment of an American standard of living, freedom and accomplishment that serves as a beacon to the world.

In the 21st Century we reach the point where these economic truths are accepted as self-evident. I suggest that the American people are ready to empower a Second Bill of Rights, providing for a significant, all-encompassing security and prosperity for all—regardless of our differences.

FDR further elaborated the Second Bill of Rights:

1. Right to a useful-remunerative **job** in the nation's industries, shops, farms, or mines;
2. The right to earn enough to provide adequate **food**, clothing and recreation;
3. The right of every farmer to raise and sell products at a return which will provide the farm family a decent living (**freedom from commodity price speculation**);
4. The right of every business person, large and small, to trade in an atmosphere of **freedom from unfair competition** and domination by monopolies at home or abroad;
5. The right of every family to a decent **home**;
6. Right to adequate medical care and the opportunity to achieve and enjoy **good health**;
7. Right to protection from economic fears of old age-sickness, accident, **unemployment**;
8. The right to a good **education.**

Footage of Roosevelt's Second Bill of Rights was believed lost until it was uncovered in 2008, in its entirety, in South Carolina by Michael Moore while researching for the film *"Capitalism: A Love Story."*

The dire need for a Family Bill of Rights is compounded by the current economic crisis:

1. **Reduced family income** due to cutting work hours, lack of jobs, layoffs and outsourcing;
2. **Fall in consumer buying**, reflecting falling family income;
3. Lack of income and reduction in sales **reduces the public tax base** for public services;
4. Oregon voted to keep the tax increase **surcharge** on family income of $250,000 or more.
5. **Home sales** are at the lowest level in 15 years;
6. Home **mortgage** rates dropped to 4.0%, lowest in 50 years;

7. Banks refuse most business and **home mortgage loans**;
8. **Birth rate** and population growth are falling in the United States.

These events point to "Low Family Income" as both cause and effect of economic crises. The global economy is teetering at the edge of chaos.

We need to emphasize FDR's key point, and that is " … a clear realization of the fact that true individual freedom cannot exist without economic security and independence. Needy men are not free men. People who are hungry and out of a job are the stuff of which dictatorships are made."

7) Share Our Wealth, Huey Long Speaks: Some believe the foundation for a Family Bill of Rights was provided by Huey Long in the 1920s. Note the similarity of FDR's "Second Bill of Rights" to Huey Long's "Share Our Wealth" proposal.

Huey Long received national attention as governor of Louisiana in 1928 and U.S. Senator in 1930. In a time of weak economies, weak national prospects and weak politicians, Huey Long stood as a tower of strength. In short, he was loved by the poor and hated by the rich. The corporations that Huey Long regulated called him corrupt and the poor people he helped called him their savior.[36]

Some considered him a virtual dictator, but he also initiated massive public works programs, improved public education and public health, and initiated substantial restrictions on corporate power in the state. Most important, Huey Long rapidly and decisively raised living standards in Louisiana, and promised to do the same for the rest of the nation.

Huey Long: Now in the third year of his [FDR's] administration, we find more of our people unemployed than at any other time. We find our houses empty and our people hungry, many of them half-clothed and many of them not clothed at all [Resembles 2011].

[There were] … twenty-two millions on the dole [U.S. population was less than 100 million], a new high-water mark in that particular sum, a few weeks ago. We find not only the people going further into debt, but that the United States is going further into debt. The states are going further into debt, and the cities and towns are even going into bankruptcy. The condition has become deplorable … .

And with it all, there stalks a slimy specter of want, hunger, destitution, and pestilence, all because of the fact that in the land of too much … our president has failed in his promise to have these necessities of life distributed into the hands of the people who have need of them.

Now, my friends, you have heard me read how a great New York newspaper, after investigations, declared that all I have said about the **bad distribution of this nation's wealth** is true. But we have been about our work to correct this situation. That is why the Share Our Wealth societies are forming in every nook and corner of America. They're meeting tonight. Soon there will be Share Our Wealth societies for everyone to meet. They have a great work to perform.

8) ***Huey Long's Family Entitlements:*** When we focus in on Huey Long's program, there are a number of points that cannot be ignored. FDR could not ignore the family entitlements and neither can we.

1. He proposed a **redistribution of wealth** via sharply graduated income and inheritance taxes.
2. Distribute the **necessities of life** into the hands of the people who have need of them.
3. Every family in America should **own a home** equal in value to at least one-third the average.
4. No family shall own more than three hundred times the **average family wealth**.

A private agency selling **LIFES** "Victory" lottery-bonds, to provide a family subsidy to low-income families, is a good start. Since **LIFES** is suggested as a private endeavor, it would not be subjected to emasculation by a dysfunctional congress.

9) ***Fed Has a Spare Trillion:*** The comment below was posted to the on-line August 27, 2010 *New York Times*, in response to a front-page article, "Bernanke Signals Fed Is Ready to Prop up Economy:[37]

> Excess reserves ... $1 trillion that banks have been keeping at the Fed. How about that? With that spare Trillion lying around why not distribute that money to tax-payers with income tax returns of under $71,744? That Trillion is probably tax-payer money originally.
>
> Giving it to low-income families as a "Low-Income-Family-Supplement" would certainly see consumer spending rise like a 4th of July rocket. And think of the "multiplier effect."
>
> Every $1 spent could generate up to $10 more for the economy. If the problem is consumer spending … give consumers something to spend instead of constantly reducing consumer income.

Speaking of financial initiatives, as this is written, the G-20 "wrote-off" half of the Greek debt to relieve the Greek financial burden. The **Group of Twenty Finance Ministers and Central Bank Governors** is a group of finance ministers and central bank governors from 20 major economies: 19 countries plus the European Union.

This was done to influence the Papandreou vote of confidence, which he won on November 5, 2011. The G-20 nations represent 85% of global wealth, and they strive to keep a lid on the global crisis, about to boil-over.[38] The G-20 managed to keep the lid on Greece, for the time being. Where the global crisis will erupt next is anyone's guess.

10) ***Predatory Mortgages:*** It's important to examine the human phenomena of land ownership, landlords, and especially the more recent aberrations of mortgages. Some of the reasons for a close analysis are:

> *First*, I have a personal interest in this subject since I am on intimate terms with the overwhelming burden of a mortgage. As my family migrates **from comfortable "middle class" to anxious "low-income"** status, my concern with mortgages becomes a matter of survival.

Second, the 21st Century Economic Crisis, I suggest, is rooted in the **vast inequality of wealth** that is largely fed by an antiquated system of Landlord Feudalism. This feudal relationship has not changed significantly in 2,000 years.

Third, from the perspective of "family," a **home mortgage effectively mortgages the family**. While family members support and work for each other, ultimately the family is beholden to a landlord. As family income falls, families tend to disintegrate and become impoverished or seek refuge in the underground economy.

Fourth, looking at the national and global results of mortgage wealth, the **vast imbalance in wealth is ultimately destructive to people, families, nations and the Earth**. The rich are motivated to **maximize** rather than **optimize** their wealth. The few who **optimize** wealth benefit the Earth and serve humanity. The real "bottom line" for benefactors and destroyers is the current condition of the global environment.

11) ***Mortgage Leveraging:*** We need to concern ourselves with global property ownership and mortgage control. If you imagine that global corporations instigate global land grabs, you are probably correct. North America, with 5% of world population, controls 33% of world wealth. Census data suggest only 2% of Americans had incomes exceeding $250,000 in 2010.

To "follow the money," we'll examine derivatives, the organs separated from the bodies of mortgages, debts, notes and interest bearing assets. By June 2008, the Bank for International Settlements, BIS, stated the total amount of global outstanding debts and notes was **$684 trillion; 67% of the total world debt was mortgage debt** and interest notes.

World debt has increased substantially since 2008. BIS is an intergovernmental organization of central banks fostering international monetary and financial cooperation and serving as a bank for central banks, **not accountable to any national government, but only to bank owners.**[39]

To profit from owning property, a price must be set and rent or interest charged. For this purpose, the interest rate derivatives market provides a marketplace for most global corporations. "The [BIS] estimates that the [amount of outstanding debts] in June 2009 was US $437 trillion for OTC (Over The Counter) interest rate contracts, and US $342 trillion for OTC interest rate swaps.[40]

As ridiculous as these puffed-up figures sound, **the OTC market size poses a threat by its mere existence**. OTC markets are an economic hall-of-mirrors.

In a world of rational economics, OTC markets would cease to exist. Governments of the world fear to tread on these economic monstrosities. Derivatives are economic nuclear warheads, as the 2008 melt-down has shown. **Like radiation, derivatives poison all people in contact.**

These $437-684 trillion are not real wealth. Global wealth was estimated at $118 trillion in 2010, with the U.S. share $40 trillion. The hugely inflated speculative OTC bubbles and leverage of real wealth triggered the 21st Century Economic Crisis and the current world financial meltdown.

How does global banking create $437-684 trillion? Traditionally, banks kept reserves of $1 for every $10 loaned. Since the 1990's, and "relaxed" bank regulations, reserves have shrunk. The crash of 2008 is characterized by leveraging up to $50 in mortgage loans for every $1 dollar in reserve. The **leveraging "scam" stole money from millions of mortgaged families.**

It's of value to see how global wealth is classified according to asset management. The following table provides an insight into global wealth management. Global asset managed wealth was estimated at $118.5 trillion in early 2008.

The Economic Crisis significantly reduced global wealth late in 2008, and by late 2009 the total declined to $111.5 trillion. These totals are as close to assessing real wealth as we are likely to get.[41]

In the following table, notice that almost 28% of global wealth is in **private** control. Various **funds** control over 36%. **Insurance** companies control nearly 16%. That accounts for 80% of global wealth, or at least "declared" wealth. We have good reason to ask, how much wealth is hidden and undeclared?

Global Asset Management[42]

Rank	Type of Fund		$Trillion	Dates
1	Private wealth	27.7%	$ 32.800	2008
2	Pension funds	20.3%	$ 24.000	2008
3	Mutual funds	16.0%	$ 18.900	2008
4	Insurance companies	15.7%	$ 18.700	2008
5	Real-estate	8.4%	$ 10.000	2006
6	Foreign exchange reserves	6.2%	$ 7.341	2008
7	Sovereign wealth funds	2.8%	$ 3.300	2007
8	Hedge funds	1.3%	$ 1.500	2008
9	Private equity funds	1.0%	$ 1.160	2007
10	Real Estate Investment Trusts	0.6%	$ 0.764	2007
	Total		**$118.465**	

Notice in the above chart that private wealth is the leading asset. This suggests that most of the other assets are controlled by Private wealth. If you are wondering how the global imbalance of wealth stacks up, this is one starting point. Imagine a Global Social Assessment of 10% per year on this total, distributed according to global social need.

12) ***Mortgage Default:*** The ongoing U.S. mortgage foreclosure epidemic, starting late in 2006, initiated a domino effect throughout Western Europe, mostly in Ireland and England. Property ownership is a key factor in the global economic crisis, primarily because it drains income from family ability to purchase goods and services, draining the overall economy.[43]

At the start of 2008, 5.6% of all mortgages in the United States were "delinquent." By the 2nd quarter that rate jumped to 8.9%, including residential properties and home "foreclosure." Most of the damage was caused by sub-prime adjustable rate mortgages and mortgage loan leveraging.[44]

For the first time since 2006, the number of loans in the process of foreclosure fell in the second quarter of 2010. The problem is no longer high-interest sub-prime loans. The critical area now is prime loans, where delinquencies and defaults are driven by stubbornly high unemployment. Since it takes a paycheck to support a family and make mortgage payments, falling employment and reduced wages now severely affect the middle class homeowner.

Mortgages that are in serious default, which means at least 90 days past due, fell to 9.11% of all loans from 9.54% in the first quarter of 2010. The peak was 9.67% in the fourth quarter of 2009. The percentage of loans moving from default to full-fledged foreclosure also dropped in the second quarter.

This rare good news coincides with a time when forecasts for housing are bleak. Sales of <u>existing homes</u> in July 2010 fell by 26% from the same month the prior year. Sales of <u>newly built homes</u> dropped during the month by 32% from 2009. It was the slowest July for new homes in records stretching back to 1963.[45]

The point is that the middle class, the foundation of the U.S. Economy, is crippled. In 2010-2011, 85% of Americans became low-income families. Most were part of a robust middle class. Poor employment prospects, severely reduced income, together with the destruction of home equity, have sent consumer demand and spending on a downward spiral.

13) ***Fraudulent Mortgages:*** Over the last few weeks of October 2010, the media was sniffing the trail of mortgage fraud. The gist is that in a rush to sell millions of mortgages, mostly Adjustable Rate Mortgages (ARMs), over 70% of mortgages written in the last decade are so full of errors as to create a mass of fraudulent mortgages.

Most of the mortgage fraud victims are low-income families. Availability of federal mortgage **guarantees for banks** (rather than for home owners), together with "easy terms" attracted millions of first-time home buyers, and an assortment of predatory speculators. All such **federal laws and guarantees are the result of intense financial industry lobbying,** paid for by financial industry customers.

This fed the housing bubble to the bursting point. Fannie-Mae and Freddie-Mac do not sell mortgages, but purchase mortgages from banks and sell them to investors in the form of mortgage-backed securities.

Fannie and Freddie provide (sell) guarantees to cover losses in the event of default. It must be emphasized that the **"guarantees to cover losses" are only for the banks and lenders, not for the home owners.**

It's up to the bank-financial firms to service and manage guaranteed mortgages, providing approved vendor lists to handle all aspects of mortgages, from selling homes to filing foreclosures. **Banks get guarantees and bailouts, while homeowners take the fall.**

ARMs were easily available, with enticingly low "bait-and-raise" interest rates, low or no down payment, and often little or no verification of buyer or seller documents. The explosion in unemployment and falling income broke millions of families.

What had previously been millions of middle-class families supporting the American economy, in just two years, became low-income families without enough income to "buy" the economy out of the doldrums.

Low-income families are now the collapsing pillars of an economy built on a fraudulent mortgage industry. The scope of this economic debacle is evident in the foreclosure turmoil that is rapidly enveloping the entire economy.

By 2012, the U.S. judicial system determined that 85% of all mortgages are fraudulent. As of March 2012, a $25 billion settlement is in the works. This is not yet a certainty.

Still to be determined is how this money will be distributed to defrauded home owners and if individual defrauded home owners can sue banks issuing fraudulent morgages.

For all these reasons, LIFES, Low-Income Family Economic Security program is suggested as a solution that can restore the U.S. Economy. Some form of non-governmental initiative is needed as soon as possible. Hopefully, LIFES can lift the U.S. economy.

THE OTHER FAMILY VALUES

The only family constant is perpetual change, adaptation and transformation. Since the great transformation, from primate to hominid, the human family continues to live in "code red" crisis mode. People in the 21st Century witness extremes in science, technology, culture and economic wealth.

The vast army of low-income families grows. The ranks of high-income families shrink, and most of the middle class now comprise the bulk of low-income families. Both low-income families and global corporations are central to the current economic crisis.

Families and corporations direct the transformation of humanity. This is the economic reality. Families produce people. That is an obvious, if ignored truth; but it bears repeating since it is too easily taken for granted. **Families are "factories" producing all of us; families produce everything people create and accomplish.**

The all-encompassing importance of "family" must be boldly stressed. This is necessary as economic victimizers are at work destroying the family. At the same time, the wealthy shed crocodile tears for the "mom-and-pop-apple-pie-family" that they destroy. For this reason we need to clearly and precisely understand the importance of "family" in the continuing transformation of humanity.

Families consist of households and the housework performed in households. Families: produce, maintain, re-create, nurture, support, feed, clothe, shelter, educate, and secure family members.

Corporations depend on families for wage-work, housework and consumption of corporation-produced consumables. **Families produce corporations and the people that run them**. Families depend on corporations for income to buy what they need. Corporations grow out of the ever-widening trade of family-based cottage crafts and manufactures.

As the *Cinderella* story dramatizes, family needs are always determined by the current state of the environment and society. Human needs are not absolute. The point is that families and corporations are mutually dependent. Any economic system will always depend on the family.

"**Corporation**" is used in the sense that global corporations are currently the dominant global social, political and economic power. For better or worse, we need to accept this reality.

Antisocial industries, such as banking, liquor and tobacco, function in a socially harmful way, producing fraudulent mortgages, toxic assets and deadly products that destroy families and economies.

"**Family**" is a reflection of current society, and includes all people who support and are supported by each other. Families both determine, and are determined by, the dominant social system. While the family-household is communal and cooperative, it is forced to comply with current social-political-economic norms.

The only constant in these definitions is that the forces of transformation, change and adaptation are perpetually at work. Reality and Mother Nature never rest. The Cosmos is in a state of constant flux, transformation, and so are we. **Cosmic transformation IS cosmic housework.**

Corporations are engines of enterprise, built on a base of family-household stability, technology, science and social cohesion. The great contribution of corporations is to mobilize, centralize, train, and socialize family members to become productive workers and consumers.

Most human skills are learned at our mother's knee, in family-households. These include corporate skills. Family households are often trivialized and swept under the economic carpet, but certain existential truths cannot be denied:

1. **Families** produce all **people**, wage-workers and house-workers, as well as non-workers.
2. **Families** are the source of all human **ideas and creativity.**
3. **Corporations** grow out of families and families grow as parts of corporate society.
4. **Corporations and political leaders** are mothers' children; they are all members of families.

1) ***Three Faces of Reality:*** Byron Katie's *Loving What Is* discusses a view of reality that comes in three flavors: **my reality**, **your reality**, and the **reality outside** of us. I certainly have 'my' own reality and it is as real for me as 'your' reality is for you. My reality is how I see and know the world.

It's unlikely that my reality is identical with the reality "outside." At best, our personal view of reality is only a partial reflection or shadow as Plato suggested, of the reality outside us. We are 'forms' of the 'essence,' like shadows on a cave wall.[46]

What is outside us is only outside our understanding. Certainly, we are part of the reality outside and it is part of us. People have named the great outside reality: Mother Nature, Cosmic Mother, God, Allah, Great Mother, Great Spirit, Creator or Cosmos.

The outside reality, the Cosmos, consists of all energy, every possible universe, and all dimensions, including you and me.

By the way, the next time you find yourself "going round in circles" or "spinning you wheels" consider that circles and circular motion may constitute a fifth dimension, along with length, width, height and time. Think about that the next time you do housework. Isn't that a comfort?

As part of the outside and inside reality we are **"Da-Sein,"** or **"beings-there-in-the-world,"** as Martin Heidegger suggested. We must learn to accept our existence for what it is and no more. **"Ich bin mit meinem Da-Sein züfrieden,"** meaning, "I'm pleased with my existence." Like it or not, we are in the Cosmos, and the Cosmos is in us, so make the best of it. It's the only game in town.[47]

We are constantly learning more about the Cosmos, the reality outside and our genetic reality inside. In the process, we learn more about ourselves. Science reports new discoveries daily. Radio telescopes receive radio frequency spectra images of galaxies, magnetic stars, black holes, frozen water, and carbon spectra from the beginning of time.

The Genome Project continues to study the reality of our genetic code. DNA genetic code determines the reality of animals and plants. Geometric code is the plan of the entire Cosmos, all stuff, even us. We learn that inner and outer reality is energy, and energy is part of family code.

Inner and outer reality consists of all energy and all code, known and unknown. We are real. We exist because we are aware of, imagine or dream our reality. In this regard, **reality is the Cosmos. Reality is a totality of all awareness, imaginings, dreams, energy and code.**

Regardless of the amount of code, all stuff, including us, share the same cosmic reality. Cosmic reality is a unity, in which there's room for all of us. There is a **cosmic equality** in that all stuff is energy, code, living and intelligent, in various forms, degrees and amounts.

Reality accepts us without condition, judgment or limits, simply because we exist. Regardless of whether or not we realize it, or even care ... there's room for all of us.

Our existence is enough to qualify all people as global citizens.

2) ***Repairing Reality:*** Byron Katie suggests, " ... love and accept the world for what it is, without conditions." Recognize cosmic reality, the world, families, and corporations without judgment. **We can accept and still change what does not work.** Just as early humans moved out of the East African heat, so too families and corporations in disrepair can be repaired and made whole.

If corporations fail, examine the reality of the failure, do what is needed to fix them. If families lack the income to meet their needs, examine the reality of falling family income, and repair it. Repair abusive mortgages. Repair family health care. We have no choice. We must have faith in our ability to repair what is in disrepair.

If families lack needed income, both the quantity and quality of family production will fall. Families may produce more people, but without adequate income family needs are not met and the quality of life declines. Lacking adequate care and love, children become unhealthy, ill-educated, and unprepared for wage-work, housework or life.

**It's our duty to save low-income families that are failing.
Failed families become burdens rather than assets. But you knew that.**

The social costs of poor health, poor education, unemployment, prisons and social instability, as well as family and corporate welfare, exceed the cost of providing adequate family income. The cost of imprisoning one person exceeds most family income. Both families and corporations pay. Both families and corporations need repair.

What is the point of saying Social Security and Medicare are too costly? The people who point their finger fail to recognize our tax billions paid for corporate bail-outs, or was it corporate welfare? Why single out family welfare and ignore welfare to oil and factory farm corporations?

What is corporate welfare? It's the billions credited to corporate taxes for various depletion allowances, depreciation, tax breaks, cavalier accounting, "benign neglect" and lack of adequate regulation.

And yes, a corporate bail-out is tax-payer money paid to corporations to recover from the damage caused by a failure in corporate leadership. Corporate welfare is the fine print on bank credit card statements, insurance policies, health insurance mendacity and the thousands of hidden corporate lobby-influenced legislation. Corporate welfare is a government run by corporate lobbyists and power brokers.

3) ***Reality of Surplus Value, Family Story:*** Corporations produce consumables to meet family needs. Corporations sell their stuff to generate profits, wages and family income. Surplus value results when corporations can sell goods and services at a price that exceeds all costs.

A measure of corporate success is transforming surplus value into shareholder dividends. Corporate **Surplus Value** is:

1. Paying higher **dividends** to shareholders;
2. Keeping **prices** and sales above costs;
3. Providing **wage income** commensurate with worker productivity and family needs;
4. Paying the **social-environmental costs** that are part of corporate productivity.

Families and corporations each have their story their reality:

Corporate story: "When workers are better educated, motivated, more productive, and buy more of our stuff, we will pay higher wages. Our competitors reduce their costs by using lower-cost foreign workers and production. To compete we must do the same."

Family story: "When corporations act responsibly to workers, families, environment, and society, higher family income will generate greater purchasing power and productivity, benefiting both families and corporations."

Both families and corporations say the others "out there" cause the problem. As long as families and corporations insist that forces outside themselves are responsible for all problems, there is little chance of a solution.

Families point to advertising media. Not that these stories are untrue, rather the reality of unfair foreign competition and media propaganda advertising are only part of the reality. How can we take responsibility for failures we all share? Families and corporations are dependent on each other. It's not "us or them." All must "own" the success and failure.

Perhaps it's time to think about a completely different approach:

Truthful Reconciliation ... Responsible Redistribution ...
an American Commonwealth;   Share the Wealth We All Produce
and Earn; America, right or wrong ... but if it's wrong make it right.

The blame-game does not work. Problems must be identified and resolved. If the biggest corporation in a vital industry is going bankrupt, then it's in the national interest to provide the billions needed and in exchange take a controlling share of the company for the taxpayer. Since it is our tax dollars that provide the bailout, "we the people" should own the controlling shares.

Those with a controlling share of corporations make the rules, hire and fire corporate management. As with any owned shares, shareholders may sell or purchase shares as they see fit. Government taxpayer-shareholders can vote to end obscene bonuses-salaries and other management excesses.

If this works for the auto giants like GM, it may be extended to other vital parts of the national economy, such as home mortgages, health care, insurance, finance, and banking, especially if they seek public funds.

In today's economic crisis, falling family income threatens survival of families and nations. How that contradiction will be resolved, we can only speculate. But families survive; in one form or another, we are always here.

4) ***Benefits of Corporations:*** Corporation and enterprise capitalism bring vital benefits to the human family:

1. **Corporations Liberated** serfs, peons and slaves: In his book *Civil War in the United States*, Karl Marx suggested that the liberating value of corporate capitalism is to free slaves for wage-work and to buy the products produced in factories.[48]
2. **Corporations** increase **Social wealth** by providing relatively higher income, quality of life and wage-worker consumption, as compared to earlier social formations.
3. **Corporations** improve the **Health and education** of society. Corporations need public health and education to create and maintain productive house-workers and wage-workers.
4. **Corporations** provide the **Family support** needed to produce, maintain, and re-create wage-workers. Corporate workers receive wages to support families and consumption. The growth of the American middle class between 1945 and 2005 is the result of enterprise and small business expansion of employment opportunities.

During the 1945-2005 period, the **middle class expanded to include 85% of all U.S. families**. The unique level of U.S. prosperity and world hegemony rests on the foundation of middle class family income. These gains are disappearing, as a result of fraud and corporate-banking expansion.

5. Launching the **Multiplier** involves wages paid and consumables purchased with wages. At the level of basic wages and consumption, **each dollar spent for goods and services may generate up to ten dollars in social wealth.** Therefore, LIFES subsidies to low-income families may generate a ten-fold multiple of new purchases.[49]

6. **Liberation of Resources** is achieved by mobilizing, ordering and centralizing masses of workers, tools and resources. This was especially important in liberating serfs from feudal estates, and slaves from the American South. Far more than industrialization is involved here. Industrialization depends not only on resources, but even more important, **industry requires the vitality of a large number of consumer-families.**

In the War Between the States (Civil War), 1861-1865, Lee mounted an invasion of the North at Gettysburg, Pennsylvania. One reason for targeting Gettysburg was the concentration of factories near the Mason-Dixon Line. Lee's troops lacked the essentials of war, especially boots, and Gettysburg held a number of boot and ordnance factories.

Southern States lacked industrialization simply because a consumer society that buys the stuff industries produce was missing. Planters and slaves are poor consumers. At the same time, the Northern States were building a vibrant enterprise and consumer economy.

7. **Surplus value** (surplus remaining after all costs are paid) provides government funding, family income, investor profit and fuels the global corporate economy. **Without a large middle class receiving a living-wage, falling family income results in falling consumer purchasing.**

A large number of middle class families with adequate family income purchased large amounts of goods and services, generating a large consumer economy. This was the American experience between 1945 and 2005. By 2005 over 85% of the 78 million American families were middle-class, middle income families. By 2010 this same 85% became low-income families living below government defined median income levels. Of course, median income is now declining.

8. **Corporations** create a fertile environment for advances in **science, technology** and the **arts** by lobbying the government and contributing to these endeavors. **The benefits of global corporations are real and progressive**. The corporate political economy provides a great leap forward for humanity.

Preserving what works and changing what does not, has always been the key to human transformation and survival. In this regard, it is necessary to preserve the benefits of global corporations, just as we do with genetic traits, and breed-out the faults.

5) ***Migrating Families:*** Nicholas Wade's *Before the Dawn* integrates recent genetic DNA data and clues unearthed in archeological digs to describe human transformation from primate bands to "modern" families. The human family is rooted in the hunting-gathering primate band of five million years ago. In many ways it appears that global corporations are a continuation of the hunting-gathering tradition.[50]

These migrations of "modern" humans probably occurred in the last 100,000 years. A dry hot environment likely forced the migration of small groups of 150 or so, over thousands of years. Homo erectus, Homo habilis, Neanderthal and earlier humans migrated into Europe and Asia perhaps one million years ago. Likely they followed hunted herds as climate changed.

Up until the last 10,000 years, much of earth's water was frozen in glaciers throughout the Northern Hemisphere. At the peak of glaciation, oceans were 200 feet lower than they are now. Land bridges connected continents. Early migrations probably followed waterways and herds searching for food and water.

Fishing along rivers and coasts developed early on, reducing dependency on migrating herds. As ruminant herds tend to follow grazing and waterways, raft and boat building may have eased the migratory burden.

The first "successful" modern people were probably nomadic herders, and the more settled were fishing people. In the 21ˢᵗ Century, Samies still lead and follow reindeer herds across the Arctic latitudes of Scandinavia, Finland and Russia (Laplander is considered a derogatory name for Sami).

Sometime in the last 100,000 years, herders noticed that ruminants favored grazing certain grasses, plants and fallen fruit. Eventually, our ancestors noticed that grass seeds sprouted when wet, as did fallen fruit. These observations may have provided a first step toward crop cultivation. Eicorn, emmer, barley, rice, millet and rye grew wild. These grasses were early cultivated grains.

Herders, growers and fishing folk set up trading posts as the early vestiges of civilization appeared. Jericho (Arïhā) in Jordan, and Çatalhöyük on the Anatolian Plain in Central Turkey were likely the first substantial settlements. As world climate warms the glaciers retreat. The global warming process continues 10,000 years later. As the earth warmed, glaciers released increasing amounts of water, favoring crop cultivation and irrigation.

Nomadic herders traded cattle for grain, and later traded breeding cattle for the use of cropland. These were tribal, rather than individual trades. The trade negotiations often continued for generations, as tribes intermarried and settled neighboring land. The use of breeding cattle might continue as long as cropland remained productive. This was tribal trading of useful resources, often cemented by marriage. Tribal trade was based on mating and social ties, not property.

Tribal trade might continue for generations, as long as both tribes remained satisfied with the value of trade, or as long as marriages remained productive. Changes in trade agreements were usually negotiated successfully, but if not then a complete break might evolve into warring camps.

6) _**Market Economy Invades Europe:**_ Vacuums, especially political vacuums, tend to fill rapidly. There are always advanced "trade missions" preparing the way for migrating people, enterprises and armies. Population depletion due to plagues in Europe attracted skilled craft people and enterprising traders to centers of opportunity.

European seaports were emptied of half their people by various plagues. The replacement people were a polyglot of traders, crafters and entrepreneurs traveling with Celts, Mongols, Saracens, Huns, Magyars, Danes, Vikings, Normans, Angles, Saxons, Ostrogoths, Visigoths, Canaanites (into Greece) and other migrating-trading-marauding people.

The roots of the market economy were established in Europe one thousand years ago. Traders traveled as households, tribes and clans. The few that traveled without family usually established households in new trading areas. Mercantile families consisting of established traders and manufacturers began their rise to political power in the last 500 years.

For thousands of years there were enterprising artisans, traders, fabricators and merchants. These enterprising people were a small minority, and were careful not to antagonize those in power. Up until the 1600's they had a limited role in a largely self-sufficient agrarian society.

Linkage is the key. Enterprise and trade organized the world through exploration in the Americas, Africa, Middle and Far East. Organized religion sent out missionaries. Governments sent trade missions, provided royal licenses and households supplied skilled people.

Once enterprising merchants gained power, by allying with local princes, they gradually curtailed the power of the feudal landlords. Merchant companies and trading enterprises soon organized with royal licenses and charters. The *Cinderella* story dramatizes these transformations (merchant's daughter marries prince).

Early factories and enterprises provided a substantial benefit by freeing large numbers of people from feudal serfdom. For the most part, merchant society was far more liberating than the landlords and created opportunities for individuals, markets, family farms and crafts.

Most important were the elaborate networks of canals connecting major waterways. Canal networks were constructed since the time of ancient Sumer and Babylon, 5,000 years ago. A frenzy of canal building in Europe over the last 500 years created an entire industry.

The canal industry in Europe and the Americas amounted to a major "jobs program," employing thousands of workers, up until the 1800's.

Additional armies of workers gained "spending power" with the world-wide construction of telegraph and railroads.

These 19th Century communications industries followed canal "right-of-ways," until a worldwide network of trade expanded in the wake of the market economy. In the 20th Century networks of telephones, postal delivery, auto roadways, air lanes, gas-oil pipelines, electric power lines and computer networks, supplemented and gradually replaced the old canal system.

In the 21st Century fiber-optic and wireless communication networks provide a global web of trade that vastly expands and speeds the world economy. Soon we will see networks of wireless electrical power grids eventually replace electrical wire lines.

For over a decade, I taught my introductory computer networking classes about communication networks. I began by detailing the global network of rivers, seas and oceans that continue to provide the most economical shipping system. Wild cattle such as deer pounded out the first overland roadways. The first hunters followed the wild herds across these trails.

Hunters, traders and human migrations followed the water ways with canals, telegraph and railroads followed the canals. All other communication networks followed these "right-of-ways." By the end of the 20th Century, fiber-optic lines were strung into existing gas pipelines. Fiber-optic lines were mounted on under-sea phone cables, linking all the continents.

The center of Atlanta, my home town, is called "Five-Points." It's where deer trails intersected Northwest Georgia for eons. This is where cattle were driven to and from markets and farms in the early days of Atlanta.

The whole point is to demonstrate how, over millions of years, Mother Nature set the pattern for networks of trade, commerce and human communication. People have taken-over this job only in the last few thousand years. In the last few centuries of network building, families and the people produced by families were in great demand to build the global economic infrastructure.

Thousands of Irish were contracted for the canals in the United States. The first federal construction project in the U.S. was the canal system along the Delaware River, beginning in 1790 and continuing over fifty years, followed by the Eire canal in Pennsylvania, Morris canal in New Jersey and many others.

Families of immigrant workers built the telegraphs, railroads, electrical lines, gas transmission pipe-lines, motor vehicle roads, and recently fiber-optic and microwave (cell phone) wireless networks. Consider the evolution of communication networks: first, follow grazing herds, then water ways, canals, telegraph, railroads, highways, fuel lines, air-sea lanes, computer networks, wireless-optical networks, and now space lanes to the stars.

From a nation over-populated and impoverished, Ireland supplied the world with skilled-intelligent workers. In the U.S., canal laborers were in such demand that in the early 1800's it was reported, falsely, that they were paid "a dollar and a dime a day," which at the time would have been a fantastic wage.

8) *__Nuclear-Middle-Low-Income Families:__* While trading families are as old as humanity, the middle-class family of the 21st Century is the result of transformations over the last 700 years. The 14th Century immigrant-invaders of Europe were probably the more intelligent, enterprising and dynamic people from Asia, Africa and the Middle East.

Newcomers filled the vacuum created by plagues that wiped out half of the European population. Disposal of the dead became a major industry for the European survivors. Survival of body disposal workers is attributed to the "Good Women" supplying burial crews with wine containing crushed garlic cloves.

Water supply, sewage and waste disposal also became major industries. When the first statistical studies of profession longevity, in the 1840's, were carried out, it surprised everyone that sewage and waste disposal workers outlived all other skilled workers.

We now know that inhaling small amounts of hydrogen sulfide, the odor of rotten eggs, contributed to the life-span of sewage workers. Humans still have genes inherited from the earliest hydrogen sulfide breathing organisms that lived billions of years before the arrival of oxygen breathers.

New arrivals provided a much needed addition of "hybrid vigor." The newcomers and the European survivors formed families creating the genetic capacity to survive and prosper in a severely depopulated Europe.

My wife is of Finnish background on her father's side. Some of the elder Finns harbor a dislike for Hungarians. None of the younger Finnish descendants understood this dislike. They know that the Finnish language is unique and unrelated to European languages, except there are some similarities to Hungarian; yet they were convinced that Finns and Hungarians had no connection.

After some research, I found that the invading Huns, founders of Hungary, included a group of Central Asian tribes known as the Turanian family. The Turanian Huns continued on from Hungary and later settled Estonia, Finland and Lapland about 1,000 years ago.

I searched and found that " … there is a Turanian family of languages … beginning with the Samoyed and Tungus of Siberia, taking up the Mongol and Manshu, passing across into Europe with the Turkish, following on the Hungarian, and ending with the Estonian, Lapp and Finn." [51]

This elaboration is provided to illuminate part of the complex series of migrations into Europe. The process that forwards the conversion of self-sufficient tribal-farming communities to nuclear, middle-class and low-income families works on the following pattern:

1. For skilled labor to "produce" in centralized factories, **people must "need" to work for wages**. This "need" must be based on a series of strong carrot and stick incentives.

2. To establish this need, the **self-sufficiency of the family must be deconstructed**. Usually the first step was the destruction of the value or market for household produce. A well-documented example is the destruction of cottage weaving by 19th Century textile factories throughout Europe.

3. A further step for establishing family "need" was to **tax the family home, lands, people, cattle**, and looms. Since the 1960's, in New Jersey, fruit trees and farmland were heavily taxed to drive farmers off their land. New Jersey had the highest per acre farmland tax of any state.

4. The **real estate-landlord lobby** is notorious for the demise of farming in New Jersey and the entire USA. The building boom that ended in the housing bust of 2008-2012, destroyed the retirement and life savings of millions of middle-class Americans.

5. Public land or commons were rendered inaccessible or too costly by means of enclosures, access fees, beach fees, parking fees, tolls, taxes, license fees, insurance and liens. Taxing farmland out of existence has gone so far as to force legislation to preserve farmland and "nature reserves." In reality these "preservation" measures function primarily to protect wealthy landlords, who can afford to lobby such legislation into existence, and only on a secondary basis is any significant land preservation enacted.

6. The cost to families for supporting abusive mortgages and government "services," force formerly self-sufficient families to earn outside "underground" income. Half of all American families are seriously affected by unemployment and reduced income. Many of these "low-income" families are forced into the "underground" economy.

7. To survive, the family farm must adapt to market demands, get farm loans and transform into factory farms. The alternative is to sell the farm and opt for other income sources. Farmland tax abatement in New Jersey requires 5 to 10 acres or more of contiguous farmland. Each year the amount of land qualifying as "farmland" increases. These legislative "adjustments" are lobbied by and for the real-estate industry.

8. Over the last 100 years, the rural population of the U.S. vacated most farms for urban wage work. This resulted in depopulating 90% of rural America and overpopulating the 10% of urban areas. In 1900 the reverse was the case.

9. Exporting high paid jobs to impoverished foreign workers further destroys the income and family of both American and foreign workers. Global corporations become antisocial when they cease to take responsibility for the environmental-social-economic consequences of their actions, as is the case in the current global crisis.

10. The extended family splits into nuclear families as grown children marry and set up separate households. Smaller families often fragment into a parent and child household. Young or old single person households are becoming a large portion of all families. Now with vast unemployment, large numbers of young and old workers are forced to move back with whatever family is available. This further shrinks consumption by reducing the number of households needing new furnishings.

As a producing-consuming unit, the nuclear family seems to be the most efficient form of family for the current global market. From the viewpoint of the current market economy, family fragmentation, as well as an increasing number of families and households may be desirable.

This is not to imply that market society invented the small nuclear family, of parents and child/ren, but global entrepreneurs found it beneficial to harness and promote the type of family mythologized in the *Cinderella* story.

MOTHER'S WORK

Until you've gotten down on all fours to scrub toilets, or unrolled tangled threads from a vacuum cleaner roller-brush, you can't possibly appreciate what is involved in housework.

Watching young kids and cleaning up after them, entertaining, educating, feeding and even providing affection is easily a full-time job.

1) Mothers Know: Most housework is still done by mothers and women; but increasingly males are learning first-hand the "joys" of housework. This is the trend in the midst of the 21st Century Economic Crisis. One spouse may hold a low-paying job when the other loses a high-paying job.

As the burden of housework and wage-work strikes a double blow, all that remains is imagining and fantasizing. I imagine automatic, programmable house-cleaners. As I toil over toilets and bust the dust, I dream of gadgets and technology that will provide an electromagnetic solution to my drudgery.

While the rich can afford housekeepers, the rest of us must make do as best we can. I've reduced the cleaning of our 1,700 square-foot home to about three hours every few weeks. I still imagine a technological rescue in the next commercial. That is my true faith, that commerce and Cosmos will save the day.

Decades of commercial propaganda have conditioned us to expect the next scientific miracle, as if it is our birthright. More than an expectation, "faith" in a rescue by science and technology has become the most popular American religion. I suppose this is what comes of believing in "human progress." If there is only one lesson we learn from our earliest schooling, it is that we are part of the great, never-ending drama of "human progress."

At the very least, we house-working spouses believe that human progress will appear like a star in the East, in the form of the next household miracle. I want to believe that the next generation of house cleaners will include programmable sonic-vibrating cleaners so we won't have to "make-love" to the toilets, or scrub bath and shower stalls. After all, it wasn't that long ago that indoor plumbing and electric lights became household miracles.

The point is that unless you are highly imaginative, or a little crazy, housework tends to trap and ossify the house-worker. A multitude of small stop-and-start tasks consume the time available for housework, fracturing mental focus. That may be part of the "training" needed to create a family muse.

House-workers are forced to run on an increasingly more complex treadmill of fragmented and unnerving household tasks. The daily grind further grinds-down parents, especially mothers.

Certainly love and pride of children provide an overpowering sense of satisfaction. Undoubtedly it is that love and pride that renews the energy needed to continue the daily household struggle.

2) *__All work is real__.* To be human is to consciously feel ourselves. At times, and for many people, work of any kind may seem unrewarding, uncreative and uninspiring. With the proper attitude, work can be liberating. People with long-term family or personal concerns may find physical and mental work pleasantly distracting … or not.

3) *__Mothers' Work on the Prairie__*: Back in the 1960's, Betty Friedan wrote that she could never find anyone to fit the advertising image of the "happy housewife." Rather she found certain peculiarities about the time housework takes.

Work that took six hours could be polished-off in one hour as soon as some other outside interest developed, such as a job or school. The more a spouse is deprived of meaningful functions in society, the more housework seems to expand to fill the empty hours. Time required for housework expands as the challenge of other work and activities declines.[52]

Assuming that the point of all labor is to create and preserve people, the natural objective of housework emerges as the labor expended toward this objective. These values have not changed in millions of years, whether consciously aware of self-preservation drives, or not.

From the primate band, to the human band, to the kinship clan, to tribe and corporate families, the objective of human labor is the same ... create and preserve people ... reproductive success. **Reproductive success becomes increasingly a challenge. But the rapidly evolving human brain becomes increasingly adept at coping with challenges.**

In many farming families, the division between housework and wage-work blurs. The description of a Kansas prairie subsistence family of the late 19th Century provides a vivid picture of household patterns ... before the separation of wage-work and housework:

> In the early years, when her home was a dugout with roof and front wall of ... sod, she worked ... with her husband, planting, harvesting, building, fighting grasshoppers [locust] and prairie fires ... other farm tasks remained in her hands. These included the entire care of the kitchen garden and much of the work of caring for cattle, pigs, hens and calves, milking and churning and doctoring.
>
> Most of what she needed for housekeeping she had to provide herself. She made brooms, mattresses, and floor mats from straw and corn husks; soap from lye and tallow; lye from ashes ... she made almost all the clothing for the family which eventually included eleven children.... The butter she churned and the eggs she gathered.... Vegetable, fruit, berries and melons she grew or gathered.
>
> On a typical Kansas farm ... the work of women provided almost all that was necessary for keeping house, feeding, clothing and otherwise sustaining the family.[53]

A picture emerges of prairie life as an **exhausting array of small and large tasks requiring extra labor because the house worker must continually switch tasks.** The constant transition from rest to motion must be compensated for by a prolonged workday.

Shaped by the market economy, most families experience a prolonged workday. The above quote reveals how housework is connected to what is today wage-work. Early homesteading may be seen as an intimate economic and survival partnership between parents, children and family. With all the necessary work, many children were a real asset. This is the case on most farms.

The point is that work at home and work outside the home are two sides of the same coin. Housework and wage-work are so interdependent that it's a deception to credit wage-work as part of the Gross Domestic Product and not housework. To judge one type of work as "economically real" and the other as merely a "biological" process amounts to political propaganda and establishment "suck-up."

Prolonging the workday matters little to corporate management. The reason is that corporations think of profit as a direct result of wage-work, and only indirectly dependent on housework. Corporations may even be willing to reduce the workday of the wage-worker, but this can only occur because the **labor of the wage-worker rests firmly on the back of the house-worker**.

The house-worker's day is limited only by the number of hours in a day. In other words, prolonging the day for housework continues because the cost of maintaining a house-worker is far less than that of the wage-worker.

4) **_Mothers' Work and the GDP_**: A person doing housework for wages is officially part of the labor force and the Gross Domestic Product (GDP). According to the May 2009 U.S. Department of Labor occupation statistics, over 130 million workers were employed in 800 occupations.

The various workers employed in housework "Management Occupations" codes include many more occupations than listed below:[54]

11-9031 Preschool and Child Care, $23.16 mean hourly wage, 51,140 workers;

11-3042 Training and Development Managers, $45.37 mean hourly wage, 29,320 workers;

11-3061 Purchasing Managers (shoppers) $46.59 mean hourly wage, 65,080 workers;

11-9051 Food Service Managers (meal prep) $24.71 mean hourly wage, 190,250 workers;

11-9111 Medical/Health Services (Dr. Mom) $43.74 mean hourly wage, 271,710 workers.

Only "Management Occupations" are listed above, but I'm sure you get the idea. Moms are certainly household managers.

If family income reflected the value of the actual work done in a home, you can well imagine the impact on the overall economy. Family purchases would vastly increase, especially in healthcare, housing and childcare. Overall consumption of goods and services would raise the sinking economy, as well as raise the sinking ship-of-state.

If a wage-earning housekeeper marries the boss, wages may cease or if wages are still paid the wages will no longer be acknowledged by the Internal Revenue Service (IRS) and will no longer be included in the GDP. Once the housekeeper marries, the housework becomes "private" and is no longer a part of the GDP economy. Yet, housework performed for wages is considered part of the Gross Domestic Product. Who made these rules and why? You can probably guess.

What's wrong with this picture? **What's needed is a strong "Family Income Lobby."**

Such determinations make no sense, unless we realize that these rules are the result of corporation lobbying. Corporations avoid the costs of housework. **In the final reckoning house-work is performed to provide wage-workers for corporations.** Thieving farmers used to say, "Why buy a cow when you can get milk through the fence." Corporations say, "Why pay for housework when we can change the laws to get it free."

[By the magic of the marriage contract a woman is]...excluded for life from independence and activity recognized as socially useful. Her skills as cook, nursemaid, decorator, manager, marketer, teacher, tailor (her total housekeeping talents and skills) earned her wages prior to marriage. She agrees (and her husband agrees also) [that her professional housekeeping skills] cease to have social value under the marriage contract (Beatrice Fernyhough, *On Confinement of Women to Housework as an Exclusion from Social Production*).

One might ask, "If housework, like marriage, is such a private matter, why is there so much governmental concern with the formalities of marriage: licenses, birth registration, compulsory education, divorce and other legalities?"

The legalities point to the "socially" productive nature of housework. More importantly, the legalities suggest that marriage may be a government-corporate way of coercing housework without paying wages. **Since most U.S. state law considers marriage an "Economic Partnership," perhaps families should have the same economic and tax privileges as corporations.**

By now it is abundantly clear that the super-rich buy elections. They buy legislators; they buy lobbyists, as well as laws and regulations. In effect, the super-rich buy governments. Don't blame the government for our problems. Government is merely the creature of the super-rich.

Early in the 1900's, many anarchists kept marriages and births secret from government. To avoid governmental control, marriages and births were not registered. This provided a degree of freedom from military conscription and taxation. Anarchists maintained a separate economy and social life.

The 2010 U.S. Census has income data on 78 million families. Unofficial estimates put the actual number of families at 120 million. Where and who are these uncounted 42 million families?

Household workers are actively seeking new status and income by organizing. Here is one example:

Executive Order 09-15 set into motion an effort that would allow home healthcare workers who care for their own family members to collectively bargain and select with which union they would prefer affiliating–either the Service Employees International Union or the American Federation of State, County and Municipal Employees.

Both union options were rejected. Here's **why 66% voted for NO UNION Representation:**

Because they need help during private activities of daily living, a majority of individuals hire family members as personal support workers. A trusted and familiar person in this role promotes safety and comfort. Families do not want a third party interfering in their relationships in the privacy of their homes. Both the Federal Social Security Act and Illinois statute cap HBSSP funds [are included in current support]. Unionizing personal support workers will reduce critical supports because $60-$75 for union dues or fair share will be deducted out of the capped total monthly stipends.

The psychological impact that any threat or actual reduction of assistance has on individuals in the HBSSP and their families is serious. Money earned by families via this program is often used to further support the individual. A loss of funds could force institutionalization;

Organized labor recruits in-home caregivers...3,000 who receive Illinois stipends are targeted....Union advocates have promised families that they will find a way to increase monthly stipends from the state, which change annually because they are based on federal Supplemental Security Income [SSI] payments.[55]

Services and materials produced in the home are largely "use" values contributing to the reproduction and maintenance of people. Producing people includes both the maintenance and procreation of family. Raising children, who later become wage workers, includes "exchange" value since housework produces wage-workers.

While trained in the halls of academia, I am not now, nor have I ever been an "establishment" economist. As such, I am not subject to the rules of "peer-review," nor academic rectitude. Not subject to those rules, I am free to research and write on any subject that I consider of merit in regard to the economy of family households.

Economics of family, household and housework is definitely not a serious part of establishment economics. That is what makes this *Cinderella's Housework* book important. This book is the result of exploring the dark and dusty out-of-way corners of our American economy that the establishment would prefer to ignore.

The only reason that housework is not included in the Gross Domestic Product, I suspect, is due to establishment economists "cooking-the-books" when it comes to placing a value on housework. And if you follow the money, it is a short trail leading to corporate-financial-banking support and control of government and academia.

Instead of evaluating each type of work comprising housework, as some divorce lawyers and judges so aptly do, establishment economists live in a state of denial. That is, they deny that housework has any calculable economic value. Concerning the value of housework, consider this:

> The ability to labor resides only in a human being whose life is consumed in the process of producing. First, it must be nine months in the womb, must be fed, clothed and trained; then when it works, its bed must be made, its floors swept, its lunch box prepared, its sexuality not gratified but quieted, its dinner ready when it gets home.
>
> This is how labor power is produced and reproduced when it is daily consumed in the factory or the office. To describe its basic production and reproduction is to describe women's work [housework].[56]

5) *__Contrary Goals:__* To say that families and corporations have contrary goals is a vast understatement. Families, well mothers anyway, want the best for their families. Mothers, and most parents, want all family members to be happy and successful. That is what "reproductive success" amounts to. **Assuming that everyone wants the best for "their" family, does that justify ignoring all other families? The answer to that question divides the humane from the inhumane.**

A civilized person contributes to family well-being to the extent possible; the savage grabs as much as possible today, with no thought for tomorrow. It also means that each person in the family receives what they need to be happy and successful. It may be said that the family objective is, from each according to ability, and to each according to need.

Family is the communal core of society. Family cohesion is based on mutual love and caring … one hopes. I suggest that mothers are the social glue that holds families and all society together. Further, I suggest that the ultimate human incentive is love of family.

When we examine all our actions, we will discover that everything we do is ultimately for those we love and care for, our family.

While the goal of the family household is reproductive success, the corporate objective is to maximize profit. We could say that **profit is the measure of corporate reproductive success**. Similarly, it might be said that **reproductive success profits the family**.

Viewing the family and corporation relationship in terms of economics, both require a production and consumption cycle. Families must consume goods and services to successfully produce family members. Corporations must consume goods and services to produce profits.

The primary resource that corporations consume is the labor of wage-workers, produced by family housework. Similarly, families consume resources supplied by corporations. This is shopping. Shopping is a hunt for supplies needed to sustain the household. Our ancestors hunted and gathered food. Now we hunt down the latest bargain and gather money-saving coupons.

6) ***Consumption-Production Cycle***: The rapid concentration of wealth brings the global economic crisis to a head. Cosmic energy, like money, tends to clump-up, but to make proper use of energy and money, we need to unclump them. An economic "black hole" is needed to create new beginnings from the energy of old wealth.

Every production cycle must have a consumption cycle. It may be the family consuming food energy to produce children, or corporations consuming workers' energy to produce autos. It may even be the Cosmos consuming-recycling weakened energy at the "event horizon" of "black holes," to produce renewed energy in the form of new stars.

Consumption is part of the production cycle, and production is part of the consumption cycle. Energy consumption and production, at all levels, form a perpetual cosmic energy recycling system. In this regard, families and corporations are part of the greater cosmic family.

Just as home-building consumes wood, steel, brick, mortar and human labor, parents consume household resources to produce children and themselves. In this way **consumption is indispensable for producing families, workers and corporations.**

When corporations pay workers as little as possible, workers must consume as little as possible. In this way corporations minimize family income. At the same time, managers expect workers in other venues to consume as much as possible. This corporate "near-sightedness" effectively denies the reality of a sustaining production-consumption cycle.

Early in the 20th Century, the first large-scale auto company decided to pay thousands of workers $5 a day. It guaranteed that auto workers could afford to buy the cars they manufactured. This became the corporate model for most of the 20th Century. The result was a prosperous middle-class, comprising over 80% of American families.

By the end of the 20th Century, corporate treasurers replaced corporate thinkers. As the treasurers focused on cost reduction, they lost sight of corporate and overall economic objectives. Corporate treasurers are now cashing in their chips, instead of exercising corporate imagination. Corporate leaders have retreated into a 19th Century Dickens-like mind-set.

CONTRARY GOALS OF HOUSEWORK AND WAGE-WORK

Housework Produces:	Wage-work Produces:
1-People	1-Goods, services and corporations
2-Social and public values	2-Private profit
3-Social networks of use value	3-Exchange value
4-The family household	4-Low-income families
5-Houseworkers	5-Commodity speculation
6-Wage-workers	6-The global economic crisis

The 21st Century Economic Crisis pits the contrary goals of housework against wage-work. Corporations view wages and family income as a bottomless money source, treating workers and families like cows to be milked. The amount and quality of milk a cow produces depends on the quantity and quality of care and feeding. If corporations treated cows like they treat families, there would be no milk.

Lobbying buys legislation and tax "reform" to increase corporate profits, while reducing family income. Attempts at progressive taxation, to provide a greater share of wealth for the public good, are usually defeated, delayed, or shelved … to corporate advantage.

7) ***Undoing Mothers Work***: In the tribal society household, there is far less division of labor than in corporation society. Typical of these extremes in social organization is the way in which labor is performed.

Families and tribes tend to operate communally. In contrast, the nuclear family (parents and child/ren), is in the process of further fragmentation and isolation. This is largely due to corporation cost-cutting, resulting in reduced family income.

Family households, built by mothers, are being dismantled and destroyed by corporate shortsightedness. With the growing pattern of single parent households, and reduced household income, parents and children are forced to combine households with other kin. This trend further reduces housing demand and consumption.

As corporate society unravels, mother-based kinship groups replace the dismantled remnants of nuclear families. This process is economically driven by the global reduction in family income. In the U.S. this results in the destruction of the middle class. Typical of this process is the break-up of the middle-class family caused by wage-cuts, job loss and falling income.

Results of De-constructing the Family-household:

1. **Families and people are isolated** from the community and each other.
2. **Social-economic barriers** are built between housework and wage-work.
3. Households break-up due to income and spousal conflict.
4. **High-low-income social isolation** between families and classes intensifies.

5. Deserting rural areas and crowding into cities destroys both family and environment.
6. **Enterprise-financial-banking wealth** lobbying controls government at all levels.
7. Seeds of "Class Warfare" are sown as extremes in wealth deconstruct the family.

Over the last 1,000 years, trade, commerce and enterprise continue to be the most progressive and civilizing human force. During this period human mortality and morbidity gradually declined. Life expectancy has doubled in the last century.

Quality of life advances via increasing family income, public health, education, science and technology. Human benefits grow at a quickening pace. I suggest that it is the global impetus of trade, commerce and corporations that weave the fabric of progress ... and then there's the down-side.

The table below compares the differences between pre-corporate rural households and nuclear family urban households:

Comparing Pre-corporate Rural and Nuclear Urban Households[*57]

Point of Comparison	Rural Households	Urban Households
Social Economic Structure	Communal Sharing	Isolated Hoarding
Home and Work Divisions	Little Separation	Large Separation
Division of Labor by Sex	Usually Equal	Large Separation
Ownership of Tools	Usually Equal by Sex	Women/Men Own House/Wage Tools
Dominant Work Form	Equal for Family	Wage-work Dominate
Ownership	Communal/Shared	Individual and Private
Mating and Marriage	Extended Clan-Family	Pair-bonding
Value System	Social Kinship	Individualistic-Materialistic
Cultural Development	Simple-Land-Based	Complex-Urban-Enterprise

*Based on *The Origin of the Family, Private Property, and the State: in the light of the researches of Lewis H. Morgan,* comparing rural and enterprise household labor factors.

Keeping pace with human progress is the increase in fear, deception and greed. These dehumanizing attributes seem to be part of the human condition. Ultimately, these negatives are survival tools necessary in stressful environments. Often, the charismatic power of leaders masks their fear and greed. **Most *features* provided by Mother Nature are accompanied by *faults*.**

It was once said that "power comes out of the barrel of a gun." It may now be said that "power emanates from electronic wealth." There is a wild beast scratching at your door ... it is wealth- out-of-balance. The beast threatens all families, all households and all people. This beast is now a global threat.

**Wealth-out-of-balance must be tamed
or the human family will be devoured.**

FAMILY ENDINGS

A disturbing trend in the last century is the shrinking household. The euphemism for shrinking families is the "nuclear" family, consisting of parents and offspring. If not created by the global marketplace, nuclear families are dependent on it.

Families are embedded in the global market economy, and the global market economy is rooted in families. The code of corporation cost-cutting treats the family as a cash-cow to be milked. When the family loses its breadwinner and can no longer supply suitable wageworkers or consumers, the family is dismembered like the cow that's no longer worth milking.

1 - *__Family Breakdown__*: The code of the global market economy is to impose cost-cutting on low-income family wage-workers. The result is to reduce families into smaller household units. The final result is a return to the mother-child household … the single parent household.

Single parent households are the end result of family destruction. This is but one way that the periodic cycles of economic crises impact families. Family-households are the bottom rung on the economic ladder; yet all our pursuits are for the sake of loved ones, our families. From the perspective of corporate accounting, families are merely units of labor and consumption.

Living in a crisis economy means that we experience radical changes in the global and local economy, and most importantly in our families. Crisis economics affects most families. While the structure of the family continues to break-down and fragment, so too does the conscious awareness of family members change radically.

Living with the constant threat of physical and economic terrorism, many families try to break out of the prison of fear. In the mid-1970's many

American families were vocally, publicly, "in-your-face" opposed to the Vietnam War. Millions of people were radicalized by the Vietnam War.

Thousands of families and religious groups provided draft counseling, draft resistance and sanctuary for the victims of the military-corporate complex. As the military was desperate for recruits, draft counselors persuaded drug addicts to volunteer for service in Vietnam. This provided a drug paradise for the addicts, filled the recruitment ranks, and helped end the war.

While Vietnam was a dramatic military defeat for the U.S. market economy, it was at the same time a victory for human awareness. Families began to question government leadership. Serious opposition took root. Opposition grew … resisting the destruction of families and the loss of offspring. I smile when I see the "Made in Vietnam" label in some of my clothes.

"Occupy Wall Street" (OWS) is the 21st Century protest, venting the anger of millions of families. The core of this anger is the obscene global concentration of wealth in a few families, taken from the vast majority of families deprived of income. This explains the spread of similar protests throughout America and the world.

In 1962, the Cuban Missile Crisis threatened a nuclear holocaust. Americans woke up in the morning thankful that they could experience a morning to wake up in. Fear grows from war to war and from crisis to crisis. Depressions, recessions and economic crises, punctuated by wars and threats of annihilation, create deep, pervasive fear and anxiety.

The crisis economy is a growing irritant made endurable only by escapism. Global corporations continue to expand vast economic interests throughout the world. As individual and family awareness changes, so does the corporate outlook.

Global corporations now realize that military expansion is far more costly than economic expansion. That's why American's will not be told the real costs of the Iraq and Afghan wars. If the true costs of these 21st Century wars were made known, it would likely set off "**Occupy Wall Street**" protests like Fourth of July rockets.

If you are looking for the trillions in the national debt, I found one trillion for you. Those "tax and spend" corporations have the dis-honor of creating much of our debt. "According to the Center for Defense Information, the estimated cost of the wars in Iraq and Afghanistan will reach $1.29 trillion by the end of fiscal year 2011."[58]

One consequence of corporate economic expansion is the realization that power depends more on economic than military control. The most significant result is the People's Republic of China (PRC) debt holdings. The PRC supplies global corporations with cheap labor and consumer goods. In return China accepts as payment trillions in bonds from global corporations and their client governments.

The reduction in military actions is one fortunate result of enterprise cost-cutting. Corporations are slow learners. It took corporations decades to realize that bribes and consulting fees greased the wheels of economic expansion far more efficiently than wars.

This awareness resulted in the Common Market, European Economic Community, World Bank, International Monetary Fund (IMF), G-20 and a multitude of related global agencies.

Nations that attempt to share the wealth with all families are labeled by the G-20 as "living beyond their means." Egalitarian nations are driven to the point of national bankruptcy. The nations of south Europe are "rescued" with billion dollar bribes to their so-called leaders. In the process, families are sacrificed to the insatiable greed of the super-rich and the investment bankers that represent them.

The infamous "National Debt," at least a good part of it, can be credited to corporate inspired wars in Iraq and Afghanistan, $1.29 trillion, U.S. corporate debt to China $2.2 trillion and the hidden $7.7 trillion the Securities and Exchange Commission so generously and secretly provided to the financial-banking community.

There you have it, $11.19 trillion in tax-payer dollars, taken out of our pockets. Now did that hurt? You bet it did! As our global "pocket-pickers" gleefully say, "A trillion here and a trillion there, and pretty soon you're talking about real money." Once again, the joke's on us ... the 99%. And the merry pranksters having their bit of fun are the other 1%. The "debtor" nations are coerced, with economic threats, back into the crippling arms of global bankers. The cost of these extortions is ultimately paid by families.

Global corporations must expand or wither away. The cost of expansion can only come from family households and wage workers.

The huge income inequality in 2010-2011 results in a virtual economic war against 85% of U.S. families (ranked as low-income). There are regions of the U.S. where income inequality varies widely. Viewing 2010 state income, New Jersey shows the highest median income, $59,812; while Mississippi is the lowest, $31,954. Even greater extremes are expected in 2012.[59]

Of the 117.5 million U.S. households in 2009, the 20% of lowest income households had an average income of $14,860 while the highest 20% averaged $142,577. Such extremes in family income, ten-fold between highest and lowest quintiles, indicate gross inequality. The difference between average income of 80% of U.S. families with the highest average income of $76,500 and the upper 20% is detailed below:[60]

Households	Average Income	Multiples of $76,500
6 million Rich	$ 500,000	6.5 times
5.4 million Millionaires	$ 4,300,000	56.2 times
About 385 Billionaires	$ 3,500,000,000	45,752 times

In the above table, 6 million "Rich" households with income between $100,000 and $999,999 had an average income of $500,000. If the highest average income of the fourth quintile (60-80%), $76,500 is divided into $500,000 the "Rich" had 6.5 times more income than the highest average middle-income group with $76,500.

Similarly, 5.4 million "Millionaires" averaged 56 times more income than the highest "Middle" income group with $76,500. And the 385 "Billionaires" averaged nearly 46,000 times more income. Forbes lists 385 billionaires in 2011.[61]

If we take the above table and calculate the wealth of each group as a percent of total households, some interesting extremes are revealed.

117.54 Million 2009 Households	% of All Households	Average Income	Total Income $31 Trillion	Income % of Total
106 million under $100K	90.3%	$ 34,104	3.62	12%
6 million Rich	5.1%	$ 500,000	3.00	10%
5.4 million millionaires	4.6%	$ 4,300,000	23.22	74%
385 Billionaires	< 0.001%	$3,500,000,000	1.35	4%

The only part of income that is equal is that ALL income groups are not reporting large portions of their income. Unreported income is probably equal to the average income of each group. These inequalities are becoming more extreme as the 21st Century Economic Crisis continues.

The big problem, as the falling dominoes of revolution indicate, is lack of jobs, huge unemployment and underemployment. And still, even people with jobs experience continued income reduction, mostly by cutting work hours, unpaid "days-off," Personal Holidays and worker furloughs. The word "furlough" further suggests that we are in the midst of an economic war.

The point is that as family income inequality becomes more extreme, the pressure of family deprivation throws the spotlight on hidden income, revolution and terrorism throughout the world.

It is understandable that the CIA maintains a "World Fact Book" of national income inequality. High income inequality may indicate regions ripe for revolution.

3) ***Capital and Low-Income Families***: When "capital" is discussed, it is as a catch-all for the power of wealth in a global political-economic environment. "Capital" is the central power supply distributing wealth. The source of "capital" wealth is primarily our labor, the work we do.

In the 21st Century, global corporations command the material resources and energy of the Earth. Global corporations replace feudal lords. The nations of the Earth are now the new semi-dependent vassal states, subject to the irresponsible influence of corporate wealth.

At the level of townships and villages, each with its "feudal" mayoral fiefdoms, economic orders filter down from global corporations, to national governments, to provinces and states, to counties and parishes, to cities, towns and villages and finally to families.

The economic orders are in the form of budgets, bond issues, taxes, state and federal laws ... all determined by the influence of wealth. Throughout the world, global corporations buy elections, buy legislation and buy the enforcement apparatus. In this way, a few corporate owners have reduced planet Earth to a global plutocracy.

The decades-long reduction in family income results in economic crisis. Corporate cost-cutting reduces family income and buying power. This is what happens when accountants replace thinkers. The conflict between corporations and working people crystallizes into severely reduced family income. The results are boom and bust economic cycles.

Conflicted households may shift housework roles. Breadwinners become housekeepers and housekeepers become breadwinners. This is one way increased corporate cost-cutting leads to fragmented families.

Corporations unify resources and labor. Each corporation strives to unify and coordinate all its resources. In terms of the overall economy, corporations compete, but at the global-level corporate "associations" and cartels set prices, cut costs and cut worker income. This amounts to a global corporate conspiracy against families.

Corporation cartels are dictatorships by the largest corporations. Smaller companies are coerced to "fall-in-line" or be acquired by larger companies. Global corporate cartels are industry monopolies that dominate raw materials, labor, technology, markets and political power.

Corporate cartels permit the mass marketing of household equipment designed to expand and automate housework, while creating fragmented, repetitive household tasks. Global corporations continue to expand and unify their activities. The fall-out from corporate collaboration is to fragment households and families, by means of reduced income.

Corporate "freedom" means that corporations are free to expand and to realize obscene profits, while wages and family income are constantly reduced.

"Freedom" for women, children and men declines as family income shrinks. Yet, corporations and profit are impossible without families, natural resources, and global social-political-economic control.

Like it or not, we all have invested our lives in the corporate system. Just as stockholders are paid dividends, families are the true corporate underwriters and have earned, but not received, a fair share of corporate profits.

While it may take a village to raise a child, it takes a nation of families to create and maintain the corporate system. There's nothing wrong with profit. It is the inappropriate distribution of profit that is at the root of every economic crisis.

Just as the mother feeds the child, the child must eventually feed the mother. It's time for the corporate system to start feeding the millions of families that created and nurtured the corporations.

4) ***First and Last Family Value***: In the midst of the global Economic Crisis, I begin to wonder … if the "best and the brightest" led us into this global debacle, and we did nothing about it, then perhaps we are a hopelessly stupid species.

Faith in our leaders and experts has paved the way for an endless chain of economic crises. Add to this the threat of nuclear holocaust, as well as global warming, and it becomes increasingly evident that some major changes are in order.

If your family is threatened, you would do everything in your power to protect your loved ones. Now we are at the brink of global disaster. Low-income families throughout the world are falling through the "safety net." Millions of Middle East and North African families are doing something about the global crisis.

Occupy Wall Street has a message for us all:
Stop-Look-Listen-Think-Organize-Act!

Keep in mind that the **first and last family value is reproductive success**. This means we protect our families from inhumane leaders. We may need to "take-to-the-streets" and have our own "Arab Spring" if major changes are not forth-coming.

The survival of the American family demands that we do the impossible ... Share Our Wealth, Our common-wealth, before it's too late! To do the impossible, we must believe in the possible.

Remember what *Alice in Wonderland* advised, to stretch the mind
**"Try to believe something impossible every day,
preferably before breakfast."**

**And as a final message, remember:
ALL CHANGE IS HOUSEWORK!**

END PAPER 1

Household Economy

Household economy is the organization of people living in clans, tribes, nations, families and households. **Households** are daily living arrangements, preceding families by millions of years. A mother and child comprise the basic household.

The way our environment is formed, ranging from abundance to scarcity, determines the social and economic aspects of our lives. Whether abundance-scarcity is natural, fabricated or both, it is difficult to find a society not shaped by environmental conditions.

Mother Nature is the final arbiter in all matters, from the genetic environment **inside** to the cosmic environment **outside**. We are all part of the society we live in and it is extremely difficult to separate our family from the surrounding society.

The *Cinderella* household dramatizes this idea of social "embedding." The step-family embodies the environmental pressures on Cinderella, effectively making her a servant in her own household. The resulting class structure of mistress and servant characterizes the middle-class nuclear family in much the same way as in the Cinderella household.

In contrast, the extended family tends to equalize people and work. Urban market society began to affect self-sufficient farming-craft society in the 1600's. If, after her mother died, Cinderella could have relied on her father her interests might have been protected, resulting in a less interesting story.

A key aspect of Cinderella's problem is the isolation and loneliness so typical of small households. Cinderella, the household drudge, does the housework to support the family position in society. In a way, Cinderella is a hostage of her social climbing step-sisters. The step-sisters, in turn, are victims of a market society that demands the trappings of social class.

1) ***Household Scarcity and Plenty:*** People, who live by gathering, without hunting, herding or farming, experience an entirely different life-style from hunters, herders and farmers. A key factor is the abundance or scarcity of food. With natural abundance people gather daily only what they need that day.

Many tribal people living in equatorial regions enjoy just such "easy living." Lush forests can supply daily needs with a few hours of gathering. Before and after the American Revolution, North America, east of the Mississippi, was just such a lush and plentiful land. That may explain why the Iroquois moved east from their original home in the Dakotas, hundreds of years before the colonies were established.

In 1700's to early 1900's North America, landlords and factory owners had great difficulty recruiting tenants and workers. The physical basis for American freedom allowed people to migrate to the West for free homestead land and to escape eastern domination.

* * *

Benjamin Franklin's later years were spent in Paris representing the fledgling American Revolution. Reports of North American abundance preceded Franklin by at least 100 years. Franklin's job was to sell the American Revolution as an investment opportunity.

As the ambassador of the American Revolution, Franklin's primary job was to obtain aid for the revolution, recognition for the new republic, and independence from the English trade monopoly. Toward this end Franklin needed to "sell" the idea that great fortunes could be made in North America. As it turned out, this was not a hard sell.

The major impediment to world trade with North America was England's monopoly and exclusive commerce control of North America. Force of arms gave England control of the lush and abundant North American lands.

A decade prior to the American Revolution, England forced France out of Quebec in the "French and Indian War." The peace treaty between France and England denied direct French commerce in North America.

England became the sole trade broker for North America. This was a painful economic pill to swallow for Europe and especially France.

Fur and cod fish were plentiful in North America and enjoyed a lucrative market in Europe. American maize, potato, sweet potato, tobacco, sugar, ground nuts (peanuts) indigo and cotton helped to revolutionize European industry and nutrition. The novelty of pemmican (smoked-dried berry-cured wild meat) provided a long-lasting portable source of protein for Europeans.[62]

France craved revenge for the loss of Quebec. What France and the rest of Europe craved most was unimpeded access to the wealth of North America. For this reason alone France provided virtually unlimited support for the birth of a free and independent trading republic in North America.

Since the 1600's the merchant class in Europe became the power behind the royal heads of state. European merchants provided the "royals" with addictively-lucrative investments. Royal heads and merchants would fall together if trade expansion were stifled. In fact, the royal head of France did fall, largely due to Louie's profligate support of the American Revolution.

For these reasons, Franklin was greeted as the darling of Paris and all Europe. His scientific discoveries about electricity made Franklin the "discoverer of electricity." In addition to his scientific genius and widely acknowledged charm, the investors of France and Europe endlessly pursued Franklin. Franklin's key diplomatic weapon was his "knowing silence."

The arms industry of France together with hundreds of financiers and merchants had their representatives crowd Franklin's offices in Paris for years. So much "private" aid was shipped to American ports that even with the English embargo and shipping loses, the new republic was deluged with materials. Yet, little of the aid reached Washington's troops in a timely way.

Battalions of veteran officers and soldiers from the French and Indian War volunteered at their own expense to aid the revolution. Some like Lafayette, Kosciusko and von Steuben paved the way to American victory. Many more arrived in the colonies to cause chaos and contention for the leaders of the revolution. Most visiting officers spent months maneuvering for commissions, status, rank and recognition.

Louis the Sixteenth was perhaps the most ardent of all the supporters of the American Revolution, providing many millions of his "personal fortune" as loans, "to be repaid as convenient." The bitter truth was that Louis' "personal fortune" was bled from the French people.

A decade after American independence, Louis and many of the royals lost their heads, literally and figuratively. One might imagine the American Revolution giving birth to the French Revolution and French royalty unintentionally conceiving both revolutions.

The head count continues. Merchants of death and greed are counted. Their names and crimes are knit into the fabric of society. Every age has a Madame Defarge and her thousands of sisters, daughters, granddaughters and great granddaughters. They continue to count the heads of the billionaires and millionaires. **Today the Internet counts heads.**[63]

2) *Çatalhöyük, Fertility Economy:* Mother Nature speaks to us across the ages. She speaks of what was, what is, and what will be. She tells us that we have some freedom and flexibility in daily actions, but in the long run, environment, acting through the household and family, is the final arbiter.

No discussion of households is complete without considering the earliest known "city." Digs since the 1950's indicate that a substantial "city" existed at the site of Çatalhöyük, on the central Anatolian Plain in Turkey.[64]

The area of excavation reveals structures joined together, somewhat like Pueblo cliff dwellings. Some of the Pueblo site artifacts were carbon dated as 30,000 years old. The Clovis people of that period were forced, by hot dry conditions, to abandon their Southwestern American site.

It is thought that Çatalhöyük was abandoned for similar reasons. There appeared to be no hostile invasion or catastrophe. Active volcanic mountains eight miles north, site of the much-prized obsidian, left no evidence of destruction.

The outside mud-brick stucco walls were high and thick, approachable only by ladders. Since all structures join with common access to all areas within the buildings, a cooperative communal life-style is suggested. Streets and public areas appear limited to roof-tops. As all openings are in the roof, the hundreds of adjacent rooms provide ample wall space for decorations.

There are no windows or doors in evidence. All internal walls are white-plastered and rooms are free of debris. Sewage, ashes and other waste are found in large outside mounds. Location on a fertile flood plain may explain the unusual architecture of Çatal Höyük.

From the internal wall decorations and artifacts it's evident that thriving hand-crafts, household life, and social-religious activities were all closely integrated. The first textiles were found at this site. Perhaps the single most important trade item was obsidian, a black volcanic glass, harder and sharper than steel, obtained from volcanic mountains a short distance to the north. Obsidian blades are still used in surgery.

Wall decorations and sculptures depict mostly women and horns of bulls. Other décor included bee hives, red and black net designs, leopards, vultures, boar's lower jaws, cruciform flowers resembling butterflies or labrys, the double ax composed of back to back, ⸙· half-moons.

These fertility symbols suggest a fertility-based society, with a belief in reincarnation. Numerous wall reliefs and votives showing mostly pregnant women, but also joined female-male artifacts suggest, if not a matriarchal fertility-based society, then at least a gender equal society.[65]

3) **_Iroquois Household:_** In Iroquois society the power of women was largely based on an environment that favored relatively easy food gathering. Such conditions favored the status of women, as the people who gathered most of the food. It is estimated that as much as two-thirds of calorie intake was supplied by women and children gathering food.

Judith Brown (*Toward an Anthropology of Women*) noted that it is not only the woman's contribution to productive labor, but their "**control over the distribution**" of what is produced that forms the basis for female domestic and political power. **Distribution** is the key.

Social status is often determined by the extent of control over food production and distribution. In most societies the breadwinner holds the most status and power. Most remarkable is how, on the basis of their household power, Iroquois women were able to hold religious, political, economic and social power.[66]

The Iroquois were by no means a minor tribal group. They were one of the most powerful people in North America. Originally they migrated east from the Dakotas, conquering and absorbing lesser tribes along the way. At its peak, their influence ranged from the Hudson Bay to the Gulf of Mexico and from the Mississippi to the Atlantic.

The most important feature of the Iroquois Federation was the economic power of women, based on an environment providing ample food for gathering and trapping. The social effect was that Iroquois women had total control of food. It was woman's power over fertility as well as food that gave them key social positions.

It was the decision of the matron-chiefs almost entirely that permitted raids and war parties. They did this by controlling food distribution. Providing the necessary food and supplies when favoring a war and refusing the staples when opposed. Aside from provisioning, it was customary for warriors to consult the matrons concerning the auspices of raiding and war parties.

Based on an abundant gathering environment and the "power-to-the-bread-winner" it is not difficult to understand how woman's power could be institutionalized as fertility religion. Fertility, religion and culture, expressed as totems, taboos, breast and genital fetishes, are natural outgrowths of the need to identify **life spirit** in a practical way.

Fertility religion in tribal society is an extension of the environment and is daily maintained by the household economy. Imagine the strength of such communal-fertility tribes. Everyone: men, women and children, build their status on the basis of relatively equal contributions. **It was household equality built on a plentiful environment, where both bread-winners and meat-winners contribute appropriately.**

The stability of people depends on the level of confidence in their society. For the Iroquois, faith in their society was based on the smooth functioning of a plentiful environment and a tribal economy.

Animal totems and taboos were Iroquois cultural-religious expressions of dependence on natural fertility. The political economy of households and nations depend on the availability of environmental resources. To a large extent, Mother Nature is in charge of fertility.

4) ***Political Economy In Market Society:*** The household function of producing, maintaining and creating people includes: communicating **social values** between people; providing anchors of **social stability**, such as household and income; managing environment, **income** and social stress. Households may also **teach** confidence, security and equality.

In market society, time not spent working is referred to as leisure or re-creation. Actually, leisure is the time needed to recuperate from work. Leisure time is restful re-creation time. It allows people to re-create themselves, their households and families.

In pre-market societies, prior to corporations, people did not differentiate between the time spent working and the time given to social pursuits. The Iroquois made no distinction between work and leisure. **Re-creation may be work and work may be re-creation**.

Anyone who frequents social gatherings attended by "status-challenged" social climbers will understand why "socializing" can be hard work. Similarly, Native American ritual dances such, as the Green Corn Dance or Veterans Dance can be harder work than harvesting crops.

Shopping may be both re-creation and housework. For full-time or part-time housekeepers, the isolation of housework can be broken by the social interactions of shopping. As with the work in tribal society, there may be no differentiation between housework and re-creation for many people when they go shopping. **Recreation is the process of re-creating people.**

Market economy classifies society into wage-work and activities that are not done for wages. The social effect of this arbitrary definition is to toss aside and degrade housework as "not real work," since no wage is paid. **Physical science defines work as any activity that requires "energy in motion," and both wage-work and housework require motion energy, and plenty of it;**[67]

If and when people live in a society based on "common sense," the new leaders will re-define the nature of "work." When the "wise women" gather to set new standards, family-household economy will of course come first.

They will ask, one hopes, **"How is everything produced?" The answer must be, "People produce everything." And the wisest of the wise will ask, "Ah, yes, but who produces the producers?" The answer is that people, families and households produce all people.**

So the wise folks in our fabled "common sense" society will agree that all people should be valued and compensated by their contribution to society as a whole. Since they will agree that it is in their self-interest to value people most highly, those who produce and nurture people must be valued and compensated. **Naturally, most of these "valued" people will be mothers, as well as those devoting themselves to the work of nurturing people.**

As all families, households and house-workers produce all people and all of society, so all families will receive a realistic income. At least in this fable, common sense reigns supreme.

Just as we value the producers of factory tools, we must value mothers as the producers of the people who produce the factory tools. Mothers, therefore, are the ultimate producers and should be valued as such.

Returning to our ill-defined world, we need to look at the process that separates people from their work. In the world that most of us wake up in each morning, few of us feel the effects of nirvana-like self-integration, at least not until we have our first "cup-of."

Establishment economists insist that the housework I do is not really work and I should not be paid a wage for my housework. Political economists say that my housework produces the people who produce everything. We earn our wages fair and square, as do all wage-workers. So what is the value of housework? The answer is **people, the most valuable of all products.**

We live by the social values of the society we are part of. That is the social effect, and that is the concern of political economists. Whether we are born in, or immigrate to the USA, we swim comfortably in the social waters of America, or not. Most people learn to live comfortably in the society in which they find themselves. Both above-ground and underground societies provide opportunities for generating household income and a sense of comfort.

After all, income is income, and when household needs must be met, we "catch-as-catch-can." **The hunt for income is an extension of ancient hunting and gathering skills.** Eat first and the human spirit will take care of itself. You must feed the body first before you can feed the soul.

In most American households, the people who do the housework take it for granted that they receive no formal wage, because that is the current social value. Most people who do the housework also manage the family income. **Families may agonize about low-income, but few consider their housework worthy of a wage, except when they pay others to do the housework.**

End Paper 2

Stages of the Family

Family households reflect the social environment they find themselves in. While the household corresponds to the smallest unit of people living together for purposes of reproduction, support and security, the family also exists as a result of kinship relations.

During the earliest period of human antiquity, the household and family were identical. In Engels' *"Origin of the Family,"* various stages of human progression are suggested. While this arrangement is questioned among establishment academics, it provides a theoretical model to build on for economists outside the establishment.

Engels considered the **Consanguine Family** as the **first stage** of humanity. This may have been the Neanderthal household arrangement perhaps 700,000 years ago. In this earliest stage, **mating groups were separated solely by age**. Except for mothers with children, all other mating combinations were permissible within the same age group.

Grandparents in one marriage group, parents in a second, children in a third, and grandchildren in a fourth. This form of mating no longer exists, but remnants are found in the Old Norse sagas and ancient Egyptian royalty, as **brother-sister marriage**. This may have been the dominant form of mating in pre-human and primal society.

Evelyn Reed doubts that such a household form ever existed. She suggests that the first human society was the "maternal primal horde." Most primates are observed living as primal hordes or bands. Australopithecus, Homo erectus and Homo habilis may have lived this way 2 to 5 million years ago. Of course, this is all conjecture.[68]

At the **Punaluan, second stage**, in addition to age exclusion, brothers and sisters may not mate. This system, as with the first, is **matriarchal** in terms of certainty of descent on the mother's side only.

Among the Australian aborigines of the Mount Gambier area of the south, it was found what was considered to be the classic Punaluan form of household. An entire tribe divides into Kroki and Kumite, two large marriage groups.

Sexual intercourse is forbidden within each group; however, the women of one group are at birth the wives of husbands in the other group. Entire groups are married, not individuals. But most significant, there was **no exclusion on the basis of age difference**.

There may have been a **human primal horde** mating system 500,000 years ago. This mating system may have been carried forward from primate mating. The earliest humans probably formed "open" mating with mothers and females central to the horde.

As with baboons, **males at the perimeter provided security, food and other resources in exchange for mating privileges. Basically, not much has changed.**

Pairing family, or Clan-marriage, third stage is a form of arranged marriage between a man of one clan and a woman of another, in which all property reverts to the original clan. Even at this stage of human development, the pairing family was probably too unstable to permit the maintenance of an independent household. Early forms of trade and commerce may have initiated this family form.

Since **descent could only be verified through the mother**, it is likely that the mother held control of the clan and family structure in the communal household of the pairing family. In **pairing families the household structure was communal**.

All women belonged to the same clan while the men were of different clans. This may explain the supremacy of women in the primal household. The Iroquois of New York State may have best exemplified this type of family.

The "pairing" family may be the first true family. The earliest form being the matriarchal family, which was still part of the matriarchal clan, but not yet a father-family. When matriarchal families broke-up, the wife and children returned, with her belongings, to her clan; and the husband with his tools and possessions to his clan. This describes the Iroquois Federation family.

Patriarchal family, fourth stage includes the last two forms, the patriarchal and single mate families. These are true father-families belonging to the **patriarchal era**. The main difference between these two forms is that in the patriarchal family a **man may have multiple wives**. Both forms are patriarchal, with the father as the central figure, controlling the life and destiny of all his dependents.

Communal family-households, fifth stage, include the model from the Maoist era, 1960-1980. This experiment is significant as it involved one-quarter of the human race. The Maoist household is a uniquely **destructive attempt to reinvent tribal communes**, from the top-down. In some ways it is similar to the attempt by corporations to reinvent the primal household of single mother and child, from the top-down, by reducing household income.

Maoist households were a reflection of the social, political and economic outlook of revolutionary China. In the same way, the current corporate household reflects the outlook of the global corporation. The **goal of the commune-communal household is self-sufficiency**.

Debate continues over Maoist goals for China, but one vital objective was achieved. China is now a single cohesive people (mostly), compared to what had been a multitude of diverse tribes and warlords, early in the 1900's. China's "Great Leap Forward," while far from a glowing success, taught the Chinese people the elements of teamwork and "boot-strap" industrialization.

One cannot help but acknowledge that the failures of the past contribute to China's stature as the world's premier economic power in the 21st Century. **As the world's primary debt holder, China has become the first global landlord.** The goal of the great Kahn 800 years ago is achieved not with a bang, but with a whimper, and it took corporate greed for China to succeed.

Perhaps the most successful communal families are the Hutterite communities, as previously discussed. As with other successful communal societies, such as the Amish, Mennonites and Mormons, a **strong religious commitment provides the societal "glue"**. China, on the other hand, built a society based on political ideology and continues to be led by a Communist Government.

1) ***Cosmic Mother***:   Undoubtedly, the first people with conscious awareness noticed the sun, moon, stars and heavens. Standing upright with binocular vision, together with self-awareness, make the heavens part of human reality. They must have wondered about these, as we still do. The first mother using fire for warmth and to cook food, must have felt great satisfaction in "capturing the sun's fire."

Sitting by an open fire, I can easily imagine capturing part of the sun. Looking up at the heavens and living with Mother Nature's wondrous beauty, one can easily worship the heavens. After all, the warmth of the sun and the rains that grow the crops are all heaven-sent.

Much can be learned about early humans by studying burial sites. Often the only evidence of the first humans is from campfires and burial sites. Both campfires and especially burial sites document early culture. Neanderthal burial sites have been found with the pollen remains of flowers, suggesting the belief in an afterlife.

2) ***Reality and Myth***: The rule of queens preceded the rule of kings. Fertility of the household and tribe being paramount, motherhood and matriarchy controlled the magic and reality of reproductive success. Survival and reproductive success depend more on reproducing household life than on the actual work of securing household materials.

For this reason the mother-matriarch, was queen of her household, her tribe and the totality of society. This reality is dramatically recorded in "her-story" of the Amazons. They aided Troy in resisting the Greek invasions, and captured Athens early on. Amazon family life is described:

> No men were permitted to have sexual encounters or reside in Amazon country; but once a year, in order to prevent their race from dying-out, they visited the Gargareans, a neighboring tribe.
>
> The male children who were the result of these visits were killed, sent back to their fathers or exposed in the wilderness to fend for themselves; the females were kept and brought up by their mothers, and trained in agricultural pursuits, hunting, and the

art of war. In other versions when the Amazons went to war they would not kill all the men. Some they would take as slaves, and once or twice a year they would have sex with their slaves.[69]

The *Greek Myths* are valuable in providing links to the ancient transformation from matriarchy to patriarchy. This shift was gradual over a 1,500-year period, from 4,000 to 2,500 years ago. The suppression of matriarchy occurred in many small steps over a long period. That may explain why the Amazon nation tribe relocated from the Crimea to Turkey.

Climatic change at that time slowly forced the less advanced herder-hunter tribes of Northern Europe to seek refuge in the South of Europe. Robert Graves, in his *Greek Myths* considers that the decisive blow against matriarchal rule was struck by the fall of Troy, some 3,300 years ago.

It's likely that changes in the environment and climate affected the fertility of the land and the people. For thousands of years, perhaps 200,000 years, fertility and successful reproduction were credited to the Cosmic Mother, the Heavenly Mother Goddess, the Earth Mother Goddess and Her daughters on Earth.

Even now, our sense of the sacred develops at our mother's knee. We believe in what mom repeatedly teaches us, and it probably was always that way. The current resurgence of faith in Mary, Mother Mary, and Queen of Heaven has a clear connection to the matriarchal goddess, persisting since the beginning of human time.

At the age of one, I grew into a platinum-haired beauty, my Ma's pride and joy. Ma never let me forget that I was a gift from the Queen of Heaven. "Give thanks and pray to Mother Mary." That was Ma's mantra.

By the time I was in my teens I went over to Dad's way of thinking. Dad's view was purely practical. Yet, strangely his practical philosophy paralleled Ma's spiritual views closely. Dad firmly believed we come from the stars and return to the stars. He constantly talked about a "real" Cosmic Mother.

Dad's Cosmic Mother, Mother Nature, was literally a fact of nature. She constantly transformed the Cosmos, the universe, the Earth and us. As a student of thermodynamics, Dad maintained his certainty that energy is not created nor destroyed, but is perpetually transformed. There is no death, just transformation from one form of energy to another; and that's what housework is all about.

I became convinced that Dad was on to something. My studies over the decades affirm Dad's beliefs. And yet I still believe in Ma's complementary belief in the Queen of Heaven.

The point is that the fundamental premise of matriarchy is alive and well. Mother Nature provides fertility and reproductive success, since transforming all cosmic energy is what cosmic housekeeping is all about. And the goal of all housekeeping is reproductive success, and that amounts to transforming our energy into new offspring and producing new people. It's all cosmic housework.

3) *__Mother Nature__*: What the new patriarchy of Athens feared was the "heart's blood" of the Furies ... their menstrual blood. The reason has its roots in witchcraft, or nature worship (natural religion).

Household or hearth religion is traceable to the earliest of human societies. Archeological evidence suggests that at Çatal Hüyük the Nature Craft-Natural Religion was the core of human society at least 10,000 years ago. In some form, hearth-fertility worship, as the household religion, may be as old as humanity. In many ways fertility religion persists today.

Hearth religion involved the worship of the Great Goddess. It spread throughout the world up until 4,000 years ago. Graves suggested that the pre-Hellenic "Grakai," (Pelasgian, People of Pellas) were the people of the Grey Goddess. Originally they were called Canaans and arrived in Greece 5,400 years ago from the Middle East.

Characteristic of matriarchal, tribal and pre-patriarchal societies, Hearth Religion probably reached its zenith sometime between 4,000 and 3,500 years ago. After the establishment of Hellenic patriarchal society, Hearth Religion was forced underground as "mystery religions." The point is that mother-right is family-right.

Family Descent

The energy in human households, as with all cosmic energy, is in a constant state of transformation.

At the dawn of "modern" humans, household self-sufficiency was the rule set by nature. Both pre-human and human households consisted of mothers and children at the core, with males in a protective role outside the core. This primate "household" structure, at least ten-million years old, persists in the 21st Century. Elaine Morgan elaborates on this point in her book *Descent of Woman.*[70]

Goodall and deVore's work, filming chimpanzees and other primates in the wild, indicate that mother and child are extremely close (big surprise). Primates are organized with females at the center of the group, surrounded by young, including adult males up to the age of ten years.

Similar observations were reported with rhesus macaques. The females were primarily a source of food for the young. This may explain why young macaques spend so much time with females. The pre-human origin of the household is female primates serving as sources of food and protection for the young.

1) ***Pre-Human and Human Household:*** In *Descent of Woman,* Elaine Morgan suggests that the Pliocene period, five million years ago, is the likely origin of the female Australopithecus. It is that point in time when the human hominid line diverged from chimpanzees and bonobos.[71]

The rapidly drying jungle-arboreal Pliocene environment forced primates to seek refuge at the waters' edge. Out of their trees and jungle protection primates were easy prey for predators, especially the big cats. Some suggest that the big cats prodded primate to human evolution. Cats became competitors when early humans began hunting the same animals that cats hunted.

Heat and predators forced some of the primates into the water. As long as they could wade up to their necks some measure of safety was gained. Over many generations, of protection in the water, certain adaptive changes and mutations occurred. The changes transformed land and tree dwelling primates into marine primates.

Elaine Morgan mentions that gorillas in the wild are known to be inoffensive vegetarians who are gentle with females and the young. When threatened by outsiders, gorillas may be extremely aggressive. Chimpanzees in the wild are both aggressive and friendly, depending on the level of stress they encounter. From such beginnings a gorilla-chimpanzee-like hominid found refuge at the waters' edge.

At the water's edge (littoral) primates were faced with rapid change. Mutations were more likely to occur at the littoral if only because solar radiation has a greater effect than in the shelter of forests. The mutation and adaptation stress of the Pliocene environment included: heat, drought, solar radiation and animal competitors.

2) ***Selecting for Family Survival:*** Beneficial mutations, adaptations, and mating selection can occur in a few generations. It is well documented that genetic immunity to diseases such as: malaria, syphilis, black plague, small pox, yellow fever, typhoid and influenza developed over a period of a few hundred years.

Genetic immunity continues to develop and is likely to accelerate with innovative gene therapy. A case in point is the rapid development of immunity to various strains of viral influenza. Geneticists suggest that immunity is the result of viral code sharing. Viral and bacterial genetic code seems to be part of the human gene pool and the human family.

Similar human genetic code is found in viral and bacterial genes. Genome Project research suggests that life on planet Earth may have evolved from the first self-replicating organic molecules in the form of viral and bacterial life. Mitochondrial RNA genetic code for respiration, excretion, reproduction and other basic life functions is the same for all life on Earth.

Genome research suggests that as much as 50% of human genes, governing basic life functions, are the same as found in the oldest bacteria.

Transduction, the transfer of genetic code, continues to occur between virus, bacteria and all life on Earth. Disease infection is a type of transduction. Flu and cold virus genes are constantly transferred between virus, bacteria, animals and probably all forms of life.[72]

Five million years since humans diverged from older primates, a number of "humanizing" mutations occurred that helped to create the human family. The mutations summarized below are special for two reasons: first, they are unique to marine mammals; second, of all primates, they are found only in humans; (Elaine Morgan, *Descent of Woman*):

1. **Fat layer**—Adaptation to water developed a fat layer under the skin, more so in women than in men, providing padding, insulation, and radiation protection for mother and child. Body fat protects against radiation and temperature extremes; also providing a food source in hard times.

2. **Pendulous breasts**—are found only in marine mammals and are common to those land mammals that experienced a marine past. These include ruminants such as cows, goats, sheep, camel, buffalo, bison, hippopotamus, and elephants. Pendulous breasts provide a floating food supply for the young as well as floatation and balancing appendages for mother and child.

3. **Long hair**—provides an important "handle" for a child to grab while floating around the mother's shoulders. Long hair provides a radiation sunscreen. While other primates lack long hair, as opposed to fur, most marine mammals show some vestige of long hair.

4. **Toe-finger webs**—serve as swimming paddles. No other primate has the thin piece of skin between thumb and forefinger permitting a maximum separation of 90-degrees. All other primates can achieve 180-degree separation between thumb and forefinger.

5. **Skin-hair streamlining**—permits rapid water draining, body mobility and survival.

6. **Nose cartilage**—permits diving under water by sealing off the pharynx and lungs from water. Only marine mammals have this device, permitting rapid escape from attackers.

7. **Facial Frowning**—keeps reflected sunlight out of eyes; other primates lack this ability.
8. **Pregnancy thickened hair**— allows firm grasp by infants and protects from the sun.
9. **Heart beat slows under water**—slows oxidation use rate for longer time under water.
10. **Salt tears**—eliminate excess salt swallowed while swimming. No other primate sheds salt tears. Elephants, crocodiles, birds, humans, and animals with marine origins share this ability.
11. **Flat feet**—facilitate paddling and treading water.
12. **Steatopagus buttock**—provides a platform for infants; permits pivotal turning, twisting and balancing in an erect position, as well as fat-energy storage.
13. **Large body size**—is unique to marine animals; marine mammals tend to grow larger than land mammals. Humans are the largest primate.
14. **Forward-withdrawn vagina**—is positioned to avoid injury on rocky-sandy areas; the vaginal position is the result of a four-appendage human standing upright.
15. **Penis size**—in humans is larger than in other primates and is adapted to the forward-withdrawn vagina.
16. **Front-mounting coitus**—Humans are the only land mammals adapting to this sexual position.
17. **Speech**—is the only practical way to communicate in water.
18. **Children adapt easily to water**—of all primates, **only humans can swim from birth**. Toddlers have a natural inclination to be wary of the surf. When left alone at the water's edge young children are attracted to the water, yet are cautious.

These factors suggest that the human species evolved from a marine-adapted primate. If the human family needed to adapt once again to a marine environment, the genetic flexibility exists to do so once more. I have wondered why gill-slits for breathing underwater have never become an evolutionary option for humans and marine mammals.[73]

It should also be noted that the human family possesses body fluids, especially blood that closely resembles the composition of seawater. Normal seawater and the human blood network have similar ranges of acid-alkaline balance, pH 7.3 to 8.3.

The mineral salt content of seawater and human blood is also similar. The proportion of naturally occurring sodium bicarbonate (baking soda) is similar in both seawater and human blood. This is vital as high bicarbonate content permits increased levels of cell oxygen.

Acidic seawater and acidic blood reduce the oxygen-holding capacity of cells. Increasing the level of alkalinity with bicarbonate, limestone (calcium carbonate) and other alkaline salts increases the oxygen holding capacity of cells, while reducing acidifying oxidation wastes.

Body cells become cancerous when deprived of oxygen, the result of high cellular acidity. Cancer cells are normal cells that become anaerobic-acidic. Cancer cells die when oxygen-alkalinity levels are increased.

Some cancer therapies add baking soda mixed with maple syrup or honey to the body and blood system so as to increase cell oxygen levels, thereby killing only the anaerobic cancer cells. Oxygen is toxic only to anaerobic cancer cells. Cancer cells crave sugar and readily ingest maple syrup or honey, along with the toxic alkalinity of baking soda.

The human family is harmed by too much acidity. Cancer cells thrive on acidity, while normal cells thrive on balanced alkalinity. A healthy human family environment depends on normal acid-alkaline balance. An environment that becomes lethally hot and dry will become lethally acidic.

3) ***Self-sufficient and Dependent Families:*** Trade and barter between household groups probably cemented the trend toward human cooperation and civilization. As merchant trade became a primary mode of human interaction, "enterprise marriage" further provided a global network of human cooperation.

Enterprise marriage is a form of mating that cements tribes, clans, households and families for long-term enterprise and mutual benefit. Match-makers throughout the world still provide the services of matching couples and families for the purpose of mutual benefit or "enterprise marriage."

The reason for choosing the *Cinderella* theme in this book is precisely because that story dramatizes the changes affecting family, household, and housework over the last three centuries. Viewing the family and household as the foundation of human society, it is important to understand the shift from tribal cooperative self-sufficiency to aggressive competitiveness in the market economy.

Just as there are winners in "enterprise marriage," there are also losers, such as *Cinderella*. *Cinderella* dramatizes the transition from self-sufficiency to dependency and back again. The story of her subservience to her step-family is easy to understand.

Of all the lessons *Cinderella* can teach, the most important is that self-sufficiency extends from small groups to large groups via cooperative agreements. *Cinderella* rebuilt her humanity by finding people to work with, namely her godmother and the prince.

In tribal society there were no stepchildren at the banquet table of life. While there were feasts and famines, they were usually shared. The market system extracts the abundance of nature for a few and imposes the scarcity on the majority of families. In market society a few commandeer abundance, and distribute scarcity to the many.

4) ***Communal Households:*** Tribal societies, particularly "First Nation" Native Americans living east of the Mississippi, practiced communal gift-exchange as the primary method of building social ties. Even murder, death and injury settlements were arrived at communally.

Law and order among the Iroquois was a relatively simple and clear-cut practice, based entirely on communal gift exchange, (Frank Speck, *The Iroquois;*[74]

Injuries and killings within the Iroquois Federation could be compensated by a number of gifts. These might include payment from the offender in the form of children or slaves. Personal servitude for months or years by the offending person to the offended clan was also known.

Compensation among the Iroquois for any loss was in the form of tangible restoration. The current practice of "Restorative Justice" may be derived from the Iroquois Federation.

In her introduction to *Origin of the Family*, Eleanor Leacock pointed out that in the early phases of human society all work and property were collective. People consumed what they produced directly. Land was common community property. The people using them owned the household utensils and tools. In tribal society and farming communities, this lifestyle often persists.[75]

In terms of food supplied, women were usually the backbone of communal societies. They gathered most of the vegetable food and trapped much of the small game. Women often provided a major portion of the food in Iroquois society. This included the staples grown in garden plots such as maize, beans and squash (the three sisters).

Because of their vital role in the communal household, women usually held major decision making power. Among the Naskapi hunters of the Labrador Peninsula, women also held great power. The Naskapi housewife decided all undertakings, plans and journeys (*Origin of the Family*).

5) ***Women's Contribution:*** In mixed hunting-gathering societies, up to 80% of the diet consists of vegetable foods, usually gathered by women and children. Men primarily do the hunting, but put in as much time as the gatherers.

Both women and men spend roughly equal time in food production; however, women in tribal society usually contribute two to three times more food than the men. In communal and tribal society, women and children make a substantial contribution to the household larder.

There are three elements in communal Iroquois life: democracy, equality and matriarchy. Speck suggests the Iroquois Federation was the model for our own Bill of Rights, Declaration of Independence, and federation of thirteen original states.[76]

The point is that these values are essentially derived from the contribution of wives, mothers, and grandmothers. Men are usually the official chiefs, directors, managers, presidents, and leaders; but women are the gadflies and muses. Women suggest, cajole, persuade, reason and implore repeatedly, until the work is done right.

Women comprehend the "big picture." It's theorized that women have extra right-left hemisphere brain neuron connections. Such neuron links allow women to keep track of all family members and the internal-external issues that affect them. Men have the ability to focus and concentrate narrowly on the technology of the hunt, the job, the repair or a specific issue;[77]

The basic function of households and families is to do everything possible to promote the desired development, "reproductive success," of the people we love and care about. This is what "producing, re-producing, and re-creating" people is all about. The term "recreation" means re-creating people.

I suggest that the ultimate human value, "reproductive success," is rooted in the household-family. The "woman of the house" is now the "spouse of the house." **It is this five million-year heritage, coded in our genes and transmitted by women in their mitochondria RNA that allows humanity to care more about people than things.**

In the midst of the 21st Century Crisis, women continue to value and love family members above and beyond all other considerations. This ultimate human value begins with family-household nurturing by women.

The more we advance the people we care about, the more we are advancing ourselves. All leaders with women in their lives know this. Human success, society and survival is a direct result of the unacknowledged "hero in her-story," women. Woman's role in the global human tribe is to insure continued survival and reproductive success.

6) ***Social Dialectics of Cooperation:*** Human development is the result of an endless dialectic. The struggle stems from the ceaseless interaction between humanity and our environment. In terms of reproductive success there is a powerful dialectic between cooperation and competition. Human societies can be understood to the extent that cooperation and competition are known or deduced from archeological artifacts.

From the "primal horde household" of five million years ago to the "nuclear family" of today, cooperation within the household and family is the dominant form of socializing.

Cooperation is the primary method of production and reproduction within and between households and nations. Even during the "cold war" between East and West, there was more cooperation than competition. The proof is we have survived to tell the tail.

There were, and are now, sufficient agreements between nuclear powers to maintain an effective level of nuclear cooperation. This is not to say that terrorists won't cause disasters. These criminals have already killed thousands in terrorist attacks and impoverished millions.

Where does competition enter the human condition? Competition between males for "reproductive success" may be the primary source of conflict and success throughout the ages of humanity. There was always competition for mates. Hunter-gatherers competed for mates by supporting mates and offspring. Modern mating has become far more complex and abstract, but at its core it is basically unchanged.

Part of the package that comes with sexual reproduction is competition for mates. Some primal organisms are capable of **asexual** reproduction, usually when the environment offers an advantage to the more rapid, greater number and uniformity of offspring.

Sexual reproduction is more common than asexual modes. While sexual reproduction is slower and produces fewer individuals, sexual reproduction is better able to adapt to rapid environmental change compared to asexual reproduction.[78]

A rapid change in the environment, such as a disease epidemic, would result in greater survival rates in sexual populations, as sexual reproduction has the great advantage of a broad diversity of genetic information. The same epidemic could completely wipe out asexual populations. Sexual reproduction experiences less morbidity, but greater mortality. Asexual populations have more defects, greater morbidity, but live longer.

Within the 100,000 year struggle of "modern" *Gyna/Homo sapiens,* sexual reproduction has dominated human evolution. We might say that sexual reproduction is the single most significant determining factor influencing human conflict and cooperation. **At the root of sexual reproduction is the formation of households and families.**

The age of cloning has begun. Cloning is asexual reproduction. What effect cloning will have on the changing human family cannot be predicted. We do know that food production of turkeys, broiler chickens, eggs and other foods depend increasingly on cloning. Food crops are cloned to produce market uniformity. The marketplace does not want the variation of sexual reproduction.

7) ***Hutterite Households:*** A bright prospect emerges in human household evolution. That is the success of the communal household-family. Most noteworthy of these are the Hutterite Communes that have succeeded for almost 500 years, with so little change in its peaceful and cooperative lifestyle that it deserves some discussion; (John A. Hostetler, *Hutterite Life*).[79]

Hostetler described the Hutterites as the only one of three surviving Anabaptist groups to have abolished private property. They live in Christian communes. The other two are the Amish and Mennonites, originating from Austria-Moravia in 1528.

Since 1874 Hutterites set up hundreds of communes in the Northwestern U.S., Canada, Latin America, Europe and Japan. Land holdings, in at least one case exceed 7,000 acres (Alberta, Canada).[80]

From an original population of 400 less than 100 years ago there were over 15,000 Hutterites in 1964 living in about 100 communes. With a growth rate of over 4%, the Hutterites are probably the fastest growing people in the world.

Demographers have noted that Hutterite population growth doubles every 16 years. That suggests a population of perhaps 120,000 by 2012.

In many ways Hutterite communes resemble medieval hamlets. Their intellectual, emotional and psychological outlook resembles that of the medieval world. Hutterites succeeded in isolating themselves from the Renaissance and the Enlightenment. Their sense of curiosity, skepticism and competitiveness is more medieval than modern.

The communal dining hall is the center of the commune. Radiating from the dining hall are the long communal houses, divided into family units. There are separate buildings for welding, bathing, laundry, schoolhouses and kindergarten.

The government is democratic only for men, strictly a patriarchal arrangement. An elected preacher rules the commune aided by an assistant and five or six elected elders. Most work is shared communally. Every girl and boy work as apprentices and in group labor.

Hutterites are sufficiently progressive to utilize the latest technology and health care. Personal comfort and convenience is prohibited and considered subversive (stolzig, prideful). Radios, TV and consumer gadgetry is prohibited. Except for the preacher's bound sermons all other literature is prohibited. As they say, "The ungodly go each their own egotistical way of greed and profit. To such we should not be conformed."

Men and women may retire at 55 and 50 from active work and there is great respect for the aged. Not even the preacher is permitted to exclude manual work. When not working, their youth are in one of four schools: the public school (6-15 years), kindergarten, which they invented (2.5-5 years), the German school (6-15) and the Sunday school.

German is their sacred language. "The chief objective of training is to assure voluntary conformity to communal interests." Education for critical thinking is avoided and would be a threat to their religious community.

In spite of the emphasis on labor, woman's work seems to be less strenuous and more social then that of most American women. All work is organized in groups and each person only works at a task for one week and is shifted to another task. As far as marriage is concerned, the pattern is rigidly monogamous and highly puritanical. They say that the family function is biological and protective. The community provides all other functions. Birth control is therefore taboo.

There are many similarities between the Hutterites and early tribal societies, particularly in form and marriage. While first cousin marriage is prohibited more distant cousin marriages are quite common. Their style of religious communism has a historical counterpart in ancient Babylonian theocratic communal society and Hebrew sects such as the Essenes.

The Hutterites seem to have taken the strongest elements of tribal and technological societies in molding their long-running success: religious motivation; effective indoctrination; economic efficiency; and family as secondary to the totality of Hutterite society. The conflicts and contradictions of the human condition are minimized in communal societies, especially in the Hutterite Communes.

DISCLAIMER:

Up until the 1920's, only men had the vote in the U.S.A. Women had to struggle long and hard to get the vote. Recall also, that "colonial" America was a white, protestant, male society. For much of America's past, only white male property owners had the vote.

In no way do I advocate patriarchy, nor do I suggest a return to 1528 Moravia, nor any of the parochial beliefs and practices.

My point is solely to demonstrate that communal societies can be and are successful, under limited conditions.

Remember also, that communal societies can successfully shed the profit system, provide full employment in a peaceful contented society where human needs are fully met. Nothing more is implied or intended.

End Paper 4

Economic Judo

At a certain stage of human development and global trade, a quantitative change in the global balance of wealth brings about a qualitative change in the global economy and the household. Such changes occurred in the late 1940's, following World War II (WWII).

Specifically, I have in mind: 1) growing global power of the United States; 2) global corporate stimulus provided by the Soviet Union and the Cold War; 3) success of the Chinese Communist Revolution in 1949; and 4) decolonization of Southeast Asia, Africa and the Indian subcontinent. In terms of the current global economic crisis, the emerging star in the firmament of post-WWII is the Chinese Revolution.

The Soviet Union provided an early incubator for the Maoist Revolution in China. By 1960 the Eastern Bloc of nations in the Soviet orbit included China, the Soviet Union and Eastern Europe. Soviet influence extended into the Indian state of Kerala.

As a philosopher, poet and political planner, Mao Zedong looked far into the future. He planned far beyond the break with the Soviet Union in the early 1960's. His planning envisioned market globalization. China's plan for the future was built around the reality of global corporation greed and addiction to expansion.[81]

China planned to succeed in a world where market expansion, profit and cost-cutting ruled. China's development plans were built around a type of "economic judo." The "judo" harnessed the growing power of corporate expansion against itself. In exchange for cheap labor, the global corporations transferred much of their factories and technology to China.

The "economic judo" of market capitalism is symbolized in the design of the Chinese communist flag. The flag includes five gold stars on a red background. The main star represents the common program of the Communist Party. A second star represents workers; a third represents farmers, a fourth represents petty bourgeois (merchants and trades people), and the fifth star represents patriotic capitalists.[82]

The common program of the Communist Party (main star in the flag) includes the People's Liberation Army (PLA). This is significant since the PLA is the largest "investor" in the People's Republic of China. The army is the largest industrialist and financial entity in China.

The point is that China has long prepared for development and expansion in the global economy. The cost of China's development and growing global power is paid for by corporate addiction to global expansion. This is "economic judo" on a global scale. China's success is measured in trillions-of-dollars of global corporation indebtedness to China.

But the real power of "economic judo" is realized as global corporations increasingly control their national governments. Global **market** capitalism is now transformed into global **state** capitalism. China is rapidly transforming the world into fragmented nations deeply indebted to the Chinese Communist party.

Various global agreements such as the European Union, International Monetary Fund, World Bank, United Nations, World Health Organization, and the G-20 (Group of Twenty Finance Ministers and Central Bank Governors) are rapidly forcing central government planning on all nations.

During this global economic transformation, it appears that China leads the way in benefiting from the continuing global economic crisis. Some would say that this is China's long range plan for global "stewardship." Again, we need only "follow the money" to see how this works out.

It's a matter of viewpoint. U.S. corporations view China as a new market with one-and-a-half billion people. China views global corporations as part of a strategy to control the world economy. The debt crisis in Europe and the U.S.A. continues to weaken corporate capitalism.

Families throughout the world shape, and are shaped by the developing global economic crisis. Falling family income forces families to reduce purchases, further compounding the global crisis.

I suggest that **this first phase of the 21ˢᵗ Century Economic Crisis is largely fueled by reduced income and family inability to purchase homes, autos, healthcare as well as other goods and services.**

The recent revolutions in Tunisia, Egypt, Libya, Yemen, and now Syria, are cases in point. These revolutions were spear-headed by millions of unemployed people. And now **"Occupy Wall Street"** is rapidly becoming a world-wide movement. Are Wall Street and the super-rich so blind as to miss the direction that the global economic crisis is taking?

Bailouts of nations such as Greece, Ireland, Portugal, Spain and probably Italy further curtail the income and purchasing power of families that benefited from government subsidies. As I write this, Greece is being bailed out a second time, or is this the third time? I'm losing count.

In these nations, and most nations, the major sport is **tax evasion** … probably initiating the debt crisis in the first place. While not the sport of kings, tax evasion is the sport of the super-rich.

It is as if global corporations, in their short-sightedness, are hell-bent on self-destruction. As family income continues to decline, so does the purchase of goods and services. The result is a spiraling-down of the global economy as families are forced to pay for corporate fraud.

Global corporate greed helped China become the premier global manufacturer, exporter and debt holder. Of the total 4.2 Trillion dollar U.S. Treasury bond debt to the world, China holds 21%, Japan 20%, U.K 11% and Oil Exporters 5%. Those four nations account for 2.4 Trillion dollars, 57% of U.S. total world debt.[83]

In their effort to reduce production costs, increase profits, and penetrate the 1.5 billion person China market, corporations exported millions of jobs to China. This scenario is repeated in India and other low-labor cost regions. Often the "Made in U.S.A." label refers to Guam, the low-wage South Pacific Island … a U.S.A. possession since the end of WWII in 1945.

Just as your mortgage holder has a large measure of control over your home, family and household, so too does China, as the leading global debt holder, have a large measure of control over the U.S. and world economy. Ultimately, servicing this debt is at the expense of families and wage-workers throughout the world.

As this is written, Chinese workers are rebelling against low wages. Wages for Chinese workers has increased from $50 to $250 per month, in one year. This is still a fraction of what it would cost corporations in the USA. When the Chinese wage-worker demands $1000 a month, we may see jobs return to the USA.

While global households are the main victims in the global economic crisis, the fault lies not with China or any other nation. The threat to all families is from social unconsciousness, economic greed, political mendacity and short-sightedness. Mountains of corporate wealth accumulate, while the majority of families sink into the world of low-or-no-income.

When addressing the real power of Global Tyranny, it's the ability of corporations to extract and mine the energy and labor of households and families. The work performed by people is both housework and wage-work. This is the labor-power of families.

Capitalists were the first to organize large groups of workers and resources, in the same location, to produce large amounts of products. Utilizing human labor in this way extracts human energy to convert into labor-power. This process has been termed capitalist production. Handcrafts, work-shops and guilds were enlarged on a global scale by capitalist entrepreneurs.[84]

Early on, trading companies, colonial enterprises, and joint stock partnerships were formed to generate wealth for investors in the Jamestown and Plymouth colonies of North America. Dutch East Indies, East India and Hudson Bay companies were a few of the early enterprises with global reach. In the 1600's through 1800's, the "Gentlemen of London" were the contractors extracting labor from colonists, indentures, and slaves.

Merchants and traders globally advanced both civilization and slavery. Reproductive success and hormones are probably the driving forces that impel bands, clans, tribes, nations and corporations to dominate each other. Gradually, the death and destruction of military solutions become too costly for global corporate-states. This may explain how the army of China has become the most powerful economic force in China … and probably in the world.

The human dialectic is now dominated more by "Economic Judo," and less by military force. This is a positive step up in human "progress," in the same way that marriage is a step up from rape. It is "progress" in the same way that the "wafer and the wine" replaces cannibalism.

As people and the Earth are part of this cosmic energy dynamic, our part in the big cosmic energy picture may be genetically coded. So, imagine "Economic Judo" as a part of the grand cosmic energy dialectic, reduced to a human scale.

Since most investors cannot, or will not, envision a world of options outside their balance sheet, they are self-created economic lemmings that repeatedly lead our nation over the economic cliff. Allowing bankers to regulate the economy is akin to goats guarding the cabbage patch. The current economic study of U.S. self-destruction is detailed in Matt Taibbi's book, *Griftopia.*[85]

Regulation of finance and banking are relaxed to the point that corporations now govern, while government is bought and paid for by corporations. As it was in the beginning, is now, and is likely to continue, the family suffers the deprivation of corporate malicious intent.

GINI INCOME EQUALITY-INEQUALITY

Gini Income Equality-Inequality: Corporate cost-cutting exports jobs, resulting in falling family income and consumption. The extent of global cost-cutting, job "outsourcing-downsizing" results in 85% of U.S. families living as federally defined "low-income" families. If these conditions persist into 2012, low-income families will grow to 90% of the total, and the middle-class will disappear. I'm intentionally repetitious to hammer home this point.

An attempt at measuring the extent of income inequality is provided by the Gini coefficient. The Gini code measures the equality and inequality of income in many nations. The table below plots the relative equality-inequality of income, and is based on data from the United Nations and CIA-The World Factbook 2009.

Worldwide Gini income coefficients range from 0.23 for **Sweden, with the greatest income equality**, to 0.70 for **Namibia, with the highest income inequality**. The 2010 range of values for income equality-inequality is plotted below.[86]

Income Equality-Inequality in 2010 * Full Equality is 0.0 and Full Inequality is 1.0

Nation	0.2	0.3	0.4	0.5	0.6+
Sweden	0.23				
Scandinavia	.25-.29				
Germany*		.30-.34			
Japan		0.35-.39			
India		0.35-.39			
Indonesia		0.35-.39			
Egypt		0.35-.39			

Nation–cont.	0.2	0.3	0.4	0.5	0.6+
Russia			.40-.44		
Turkey			.40-.44		
U.S.			.45-.49		
China			.45-.49		
Mexico			.45-.49		
Switzerland				.50-.54	
Brazil				.55-.59	
Chile				.55-.59	
Columbia				.55-.59	
So. Africa/Namibia					.60+

*Germany, Holland, England, Canada, France, Spain, Italy, Australia, Austria, European Union and Cuba are all in the .30-.34 range.

The most equal income distribution is a society in which every person receives the same income. As a realistic measure of income equality, these data are extremely crude, but it is all we have at this time.[87]

In the above chart, Scandinavian nations achieve the most equal distribution of income and the lowest level of income inequality (.23 to .29). Not far behind are Cuba, England, and the European Union nations (.30 to .34). Japan, India, Indonesia, Switzerland and Egypt also exhibit relatively low-income inequality (.35 to .39).

Russia, U.S. and China show moderate inequality in the .40's. Brazil exhibits relatively high income inequality in the .50's. And South Africa shows the highest income inequality above 0.60.[88]

When discussing income equality-inequality, our concern focuses on low family income. The Gini data reflect gross generalities about family income. The Gini (UN 0.4 and CIA 0.45) estimates for the U.S. reflect 2007 data, prior to the economic crisis.

What effect the global economic meltdown has on the Gini is still to be determined. Since wealth is becoming more concentrated in the U.S., I suspect U.S. income inequality (Gini) will rise sharply by 2012 … unless there is a radical change.

*　*　*

The reality of global marketplace survival, at the expense of the family, has largely been material. But we should not be surprised to see the material extraction of human energy extend to our spiritual energy as well. The process begins, I suggest, with faith in human progress and technology.

The point is that mother-right is family-right ...
that too is part of housework.

REFERENCES

Brown, Judith, *Toward Anthropology of Women*, Monthly Review Press: NY & London, 1975, p. 163.

Carroll, Lewis, *Alice In Wonderland*, p. 157.
Through The Looking-Glass, p. 93.

Diner, Helen, *Mothers and Amazons,* Julian Press, wikipedia.org/wiki/Bertha_Diener; pp. 170-172.

Franklin, Benjamin, *Autobiography of Benjamin Franklin*, Collier & Son, Enterprise, NY, 1937. pp.160-162.

Graves, Robert, *The Greek Myths*, 2 vol, 1957, Baltimore, MD, Penguin; p. 172.

Hinds, Wm., 1902, *American Communities,* p. 32

Hostetler, John A., *Hutterite Life*, pp. 83-85.

Kaku, Michio, *Physics of the Future, by the year 2100*, Doubleday, New York, 2011, pp. 14-15.
Physics of the Impossible, Doubleday, New York, 2008, p. 19.

Katie, Byron, *Loving What Is*, Harmony Books, NY, 2001, pp. 124-125.

Leacock, E., Origin of Family, http://en.wikipedia.org/wiki/The_Origin_of_the_Family, pp. 149, 168, 180.

Minton, Michael and Jean Libman Bloch, 1983, *What Is a Wife Worth?* McGraw-Hill, NY, p. 71.

Morgan, E., *Descent of Woman,* Souvenir Press, 1972, wikipedia.org/wiki/Elaine_Morgan_(writer), pp. 173-174.

New York Times, Citations noted throughout the text.

Nordhoff, Charles, *The Communistic Societies of the United States*, 1875, pp. 32-33.

Oakley, Ann, *The Sociology of Housework*, pp. 35-35.

Perrault, Charles, *Cinderella,* first published in 1697, pp. 1, 36, 49, 81, 93, 107, and cited throughout the text.

Reed, Evelyn, *Woman's Evolution*, p. 33.
    wikipedia.org/wiki/Evelyn_Reed; pp. 168-169.
Roche, Joel, in his article "Confessions of a Househusband," p. 138.
Shlain, L., *Alphabet vs Goddess,* Viking, 1998,
    www.alphabetvsgoddess.com/bio.html,
    Sex, Time and Power, Penguin Books, 2003.
Speck, Frank, *The Iroquois,* wikipedia.org/wiki/Frank_Speck; p. 163
Wade, Nicholas, *Before the Dawn,* Penguin, pp. 130-131.
Wikipedia, Cited throughout the text.

CITATIONS INDEX

1. *Chronicle of Philanthropy*; content.usatoday.com/communities/kindness/post/2010/08/the-40-club-billionaires-pledge-at-least-half-of-fortunes-to-charity/1
2. www.newsdaily.com/stories/tre78k4gk-us-wealth-gap/
3. ("Secrets of the Bailout, Now Told," Bloomberg News and New York Times; www.nytimes.com/2011/12/04/business/secrets-of-the-bailout-now-revealed.html? _r=1&adxnnl=1&src=rechp&adxnnlx=1323003069-O+kMhlKSbvKQW+gTRqN1SQ
4. www.davemanuel.com/2009/09/10/median-household-income-in-the-united-states-falling-off-a-cliff/
5. wikipedia.org/wiki/Multiplier_%28economics%29
6. www.justice.gov/ust/eo/bapcpa/20100315/bci_data/median_income_table.htm.
7. www.census.gov/prod/1/pop/p25-1129.pdf.
8. wikipedia.org/wiki/Subprime_mortgage_crisis & wikipedia.org/wiki/Derivative_(finance).
9. www.archive.org/stream/cu31924002674665#page/n13/mode/2up.
10. wikipedia.org/wiki/Ann_Oakley.
11. Frequent Shopping Prolongs Life, www.sciencedaily.com/releases/2011/04/110406192437.htm, Science Daily (Apr. 9, 2011)
12. wikipedia.org/wiki/Second_Bill_of_Rights
13. www.constitution.org/mac/prince00.htm
14. wikipedia.org/wiki/Economy_of_ancient_Greece
15. www.law.cornell.edu/uniform/vol9.html#mardv
16. wikipedia.org/wiki/Underground_economy
17. www.nytimes.com/2010/07/31/business/31wyly.html?
18. marketplace.publicradio.org/display/web/2010/04/29/pm-rise-in-moonshine-microdistilleries
19. www.havocscope.com/ranking/

20. homedistiller.org/forum/viewtopic.php?f=9&t=5344

23. blogs.wsj.com/deals/2010/08/04/who-on-wall-street-hasnt-signed-billionaire-pledge/

24. David Leonhardt, November 6, 2009, *New York Times*; www.nytimes.com/2009/11/07/business/economy/07econ.html?_r=1&hp

25. www2.ed.gov/about/offices/list/ope/trio/incomelevels.html

26. www.justice.gov/ust/eo/bapcpa/20100315/bci_data/median_income_table.htm.

27. global-economy.suite101.com/article.cfm/millionaire_wealth_statistics_by_country

28. Bloomberg, Survey of high-net-worth U.S. households conducted by Spectrem Group, March 9, 2010 www.businessweek.com/news/2010-03-09/u-s-millionaires-ranks-rose-16-in-2009-study-says-update1-.html.

29. "World's Billionaires in 2010, Forbes, March 10, 2010," finance.yahoo.com/career-work/article/109029/worlds-billionaires-2010.

30. www.lcurve.org/index.html.

31. wikipedia.org/wiki/Nash_equilibrium

32. wikipedia.org/wiki/Monosodium_glutamate

33. wikipedia.org/wiki/Glutamic_acid

34. wikipedia.org/wiki/Nash_equilibrium

35. wikipedia.org/wiki/Second_Bill_of_Rights

36. historymatters.gmu.edu/d/5109

37. www.nytimes.com/2010/08/28/business/economy/28fed.html?_r=1&hp:

38. wikipedia.org/wiki/Group_of_20

39. wikipedia.org/wiki/Bank_for_International_Settlements

40. wikipedia.org/wiki/Derivatives_market

41. www.bcg.com/documents/file50074.pdf.

42. wikipedia.org/wiki/Global_assets_under_management

43. wikipedia.org/wiki/Subprime_mortgage_crisis

44. wikipedia.org/wiki/Mortgage_loan

45. www.nytimes.com/2010/08/27/business/27default.html.

46. www.thework.com/thework.asp#worksheet

47. wikipedia.org/wiki/Dasein
48. www.marxists.org/archive/marx/works/1861/us-civil-war/index. htm.
49. wikipedia.org/wiki/Multiplier_(economics)
50. www.tdaxp.com/archive/2007/05/02/review-of-before-the-dawn-by-nicholas-wade.html
    (books.google.com/books?id=nc4cAQAAMAAJ.**52. wikipedia. org/wiki/Betty_Friedan**
53. (Robert W. Smuts, *Women and Work in America)*, ann.sagepub.com/ content/327/1/153.extract.
54. www.bls.gov/oes/current/oes_nat.htm#00-0000:
55. illinoisiteam.com/blog/eo0915/.
56. libcom.org/library/power-women-subversion-community-della-costa-selma-james.
57. wikipedia.org/wiki/The_Origin_of_the_Family,_Private_Property_ and_the_State
58. www.infoplease.com/ipa/A0933935.html
59. www.justice.gov/ust/eo/bapcpa/20100315/bci_data/median_in-come_table.htm.
60. www.census.gov/hhes/www/cpstables/032010/rdcall/1_001.htm
61. www.forbes.com/wealth/forbes-400#p_40_s_arank_-1
62. wikipedia.org/wiki/Pemmican
63. wikipedia.org/wiki/Madame_Defarge

64. www.catalhoyuk.com/ & http://en.wikipedia.org/ wiki/%C3%87atalh%C3%B6y%C3%BCk.
65. wikipedia.org/wiki/%C3%87atalh%C3%B6y%C3%BCk.
66. wikipedia.org/wiki/ The Origin of the Family, Private Property and the State
67. wikipedia.org/wiki/Work_%28physics%29
68. (*Woman's Evolution*, wikipedia.org/wiki/Evelyn_Reed)
69. wikipedia.org/wiki/Amazons
70. wikipedia.org/wiki/Elaine_Morgan_(writer)
71. wikipedia.org/wiki/Pliocene

72. wikipedia.org/wiki/Transduction_%28genetics%29
73. wikipedia.org/wiki/Gill_slit.
74. wikipedia.org/wiki/Frank_Speck)
75. wikipedia.org/wiki/The_Origin_of_the_Family,_Private_Property_ and_the_State
76. (Frank Speck, *The Iroquois)*, wikipedia.org/wiki/Frank_Speck
77. wikipedia.org/wiki/Bicameralism_(psychology)
78. wikipedia.org/wiki/Reproduction
79. books.google.com/books?id=t1geOjQ6R0MC&printsec=frontcove r&source=gbs_navlinks_s#v=onepage&q=&f=false.
80. www.usi.edu/libarts/communal/
81. wikipedia.org/wiki/Mao_Zedong
82. flagspot.net/flags/cn.html.
83. www.guardian.co.uk/news/datablog/2010/mar/09/china-federal-deficit-us-america-debt
84. www.marxists.org/archive/marx/works/1867-c1ch13.htm.
85. *www.npr.org/templates/story/story.php?storyId=131106798*
86. wikipedia.org/wiki/Gini_coefficient
87. wikipedia.org/wiki/List_of_countries_by_income_equality
88. www.cia.gov/library/publications/the-world-factbook/ rankorder/2172rank.html

Index

CPSIA information can be obtained at www.ICGtesting.com
Printed in the USA
BVOW012232170512

290415BV00005B/6/P

9 781622 870028